CHAPTER 9 DEVELOPMENT OF PROBLEM-SOLVING SKILLS 451

PREFACE TO THE FIFTH EDITION

It is hard to believe, but it has been 30 years since the publication of the first edition of *Thought and Knowledge: An Introduction to Critical Thinking*. The world has changed in many ways over the last three decades. For the first edition, I wrote all of the text long hand (remember that?) and had it typed by a professional secretary who had a sleek new typewriter with a "tape" that allowed her to white out errors and a return key so she did not have to push the carriage return at the end of every line. I am guessing that most readers have no idea what any of this means because they never lived in a world with typewriters or heard of a "carriage return."

But, despite all of the changes in technology in the last 30 years (yes, there was a time when there was no Internet), the need to think critically has not changed. One might argue that it is even more important now that everyone has easy access to more information than they can possibly use and much of that information is biased in ways that can be difficult to detect. It is to the users of new and emerging technologies that I dedicate this book.

I have many wonderful colleagues, students, and reviewers to thank for their assistance with this edition. I thank Heather Butler, an extraordinary doctoral student who will be Dr. Butler by the time you are reading this. She has helped me question, research, and rethink much of what I know about critical thinking. I also thank Amanda Franco, a doctoral student at University of Minho in Portugal for carefully reading an early draft of this book and offering insightful recommendations. Special thanks to Dr. Heidi Riggio at California State University, Los Angeles, for her careful and creative work on the instructor's materials and student online exercises in this edition of *Thought and Knowledge* and in previous editions. This edition has a new publisher, Psychology Press, a division of the international publisher Taylor & Francis. The psychology editor Paul Dukes and the editor assigned for this book, Fred Coppersmith, have been supportive throughout the process of bringing this book to print. In addition, I have been fortunate to have suggestions from some of the top luminaries in the field of teaching critical thinking. Some of the reviewers have chosen to remain anonymous, so I thank them anonymously. Sincere thanks to the following reviewers:

Alan Bensley, Frostburg State University
Michael Bishop, Florida State University
Paul Carelli, University of North Florida
Mary Dolan, California State University San Bernardino
Dana S. Dunn, Moravian College
Frank Fair, Sam Houston State University
Garfield Gini-Newman, University of Toronto
Regan Gurung, University of Wisconsin Green Bay
Ken Keith, University of San Diego
Shari Kuchenbecker, Chapman University
Kenneth Manktelow, University of Wolverhampton
Rob McClary, USMC (ret.)
Joe Morrison, Queen's University Belfast
Lloyd Noppe, University of North Carolina Greensboro
Steven L. Schandler, Chapman University
Deborah Schweikert-Cattin, Regis University
Eric Stocks, University of Texas at Tyler

This edition benefited enormously from their insightful comments.

I also thank my dear family, who has been supportive of the very long periods of time I spent at my computer writing this edition, my husband, Sheldon Halpern, and my children Evan and Karen Halpern and Jaye Halpern-Duncan. Finally, there are the lights of my life—my incredible grandchildren, who have taught me much about the world, Amanda, Jason, and Belle.

It is my sincere hope that you will enjoy this book and come away with new skills and knowledge that will stay with you for life. Never stop questioning; never stop thinking. Our future depends on it.

CHAPTER 1

THINKING

AN INTRODUCTION

Contents

> Many people would sooner die than think. In fact they do.
> —Bertrand Russell (quoted in *Macmillan*, 1989)

Both of my grandmothers came from "the old country"—one from Poland and the other from Romania. I recall stories from my childhood about their dislike for each other, which was always kept as an unspoken but open secret because despite their mutual dislike, my maternal grandmother had a skill that was needed by my paternal grandmother. Because of this need, they had to at least feign liking each other. My maternal grandmother practiced the ancient art of cupping. Many people, including my grandmothers, believed that cupping cured a variety of illnesses. My maternal grandmother would light a match inside a small cup, then after burning off the oxygen in the cup, she would put out the match and place the hot cup on the back of the person seeking the cure. The cup would create a suction so that when it was removed, circles of red welts would appear on the skin where the cup had been placed. The theory behind this treatment was that when the cup was pulled off the body, it would suck out the illness. Did some people who sought this cure feel better afterwards? Anecdotal evidence suggests that they did, but were improvements caused by the sucking action of the cups or the belief that it would work? More importantly, why should we care if at least some people felt better after this treatment? These are all central questions for our discussion of critical thinking.

The Need for Critical Thinking Skills

Researchers have estimated the world's data storage capacity at 295 exabytes—enough information to fill a pile of CDs that would stretch beyond the moon. That vast pile of information is only getting vaster: It increases by a factor of 10 every five years.

—Lea Winerman (2012, p. 44)

We live in the information age. The pursuit of information has become so all-consuming that many people find that they are constantly multitasking—updating Facebook or other social media pages while in class, checking email while driving, and watching television while chatting with family members during dinner. With so much multitasking, many of us are on system overload, with the result that we do each task worse when doing them simultaneously than if we had concentrated on one at a time (Crenshaw, 2008).

The Internet is an integral part of most people's lives, with its wealth of information that exceeds anything we could have imagined even a decade ago. I cannot think of any topic that is so obscure that it cannot be found with just a few keystrokes from a nearby keyboard. The Internet has democratized knowledge. The "important stuff" is no longer kept in dusty library stacks that are available only to a privileged few. Massive quantities of information are available to anyone with a computer (or various other devices) and Internet access—which is almost everyone except those in the most remote regions of the world. But, the widespread availability of information has a down side. A racist-hate website may look like a reliable news source; bogus health information is sold as though it really was "doctor-recommended," and information about international conflicts can provide one-sided accounts that appear to be fair and unbiased. How can any of us know what to believe, and how can we use the massive amounts of information to make informed decisions?

The Twin Pillars of Knowing and Thinking

If we cannot think intelligently about the myriad of issues that confront us, then we are in danger of having all of the answers, but still not knowing what they mean. The twin abilities of knowing how to learn and knowing how to think clearly about the rapidly proliferating information that we must select from are the most important intellectual skills for the 21st century.

 Is there evidence that we need to learn how to think critically? Lots of it. In what may be the most horrifying tale ever told by the prolific science fiction writer, Isaac Asimov (1989), he reported on the true state of scientific understanding and knowledge by Americans. In a telephone survey conducted by the Public Opinion Laboratory at Northern Illinois University, Asimov noted that the researchers found over 20% of the more than 2,000 adults surveyed believe that the sun revolves around the earth. Why, asks Asimov, over 400 years since the scientific community agreed on the fundamental scientific fact that the earth revolves around the sun, are the vast majority of adults still unaware of a basic fact that is "taught" in grammar school science? More recent findings include the responses of 6% if

"Just go to www.criticalthinking.com" by Kirk Anderson. Used with permission.

Americans who say that the moon landing was staged (Griggs, 2009), and there is always the Flat Earth Society, dedicated to the proposition that well, you can guess the rest.

Over 2.5 million people have purchased the Power Balance Wristband, which claims to improve energy, flexibility, and balance (DiSalvo, 2011). More specifically, the Power Balance (2010) company claims that "optimal health and peak performance occur when your body maintains ionic balance (the exchange between negative and positive charges) and free flowing energy pathways (harmony) at the optimum frequency" (Energy Balance & Systemic Harmony Are the Keys, para. 1). These tiny silicon wristbands retail for $29.95 or more, and in 2010, the company sold over 2.5 million bracelets. Several famous athletes such as Shaquille O'Neal and David Beckham endorsed the product and CNBC even declared the wristband Sports Product of the Year in 2010 (DiSalvo, 2011). In 2010, after demands from the Australian government to produce evidence in support of their amazing claims, Power Balance LLC admitted that there was "no credible scientific evidence" to support their claims, and they offered a full refund to customers (Power Balance, 2010). This is just one example selected from a countless number in which millions of people spent billions of dollars on a worthless product.

The depressing list of findings and reports supports the conclusion that many adults do not have adequate thinking and learning skills. It is difficult to imagine any area where the ability to think clearly is not needed. Yet, few of us have ever received explicit instructions in how to improve the way we think. Traditionally, our schools have required students to learn, remember, make decisions, analyze arguments, and solve problems without ever teaching them how to do so. There has been a tacit assumption that adult students already know "how to think." Research has shown, however, this assumption is wrong. The situation is succinctly summed up by Bill Brock, formerly the Republican Party chairman and currently an international consultant, who, after reading a recent report on the low level of learning and thinking skills of college graduates, exclaimed, "It ought to terrify everybody" (quoted in Frammolino, 1993, p. A41).

What We Really Need to Know

> Proficiency in reading, writing, and arithmetic has traditionally been the entry-level threshold to the job market, but the new workplace requires more from its employees. Employees need to think critically, solve problems, innovate, collaborate, and communicate more effectively.
> —American Management Association, 2010, p. 1

What we need to know and be able to do as informed citizens has been changing at an increasingly rapid rate. The workforce is one critical place where we can witness the dizzying pace of change. There is an increased demand for a new type of worker—the "knowledge worker" or the "symbol analyst," a phrase that is used by the U.S. secretary of labor to describe someone who can carry out multistep operations, manipulate abstract and complex symbols and ideas, acquire new information efficiently, and remain flexible enough to recognize the need for continuing change and for new paradigms for life-long learning. Workers in almost every job category can expect to face novel problems in a workplace that is changing repeatedly. Familiar responses no longer work, and even newly acquired ones will not work for long.

Employers know what they want from their employees and what colleges should be teaching their future employees (Association of American Colleges & Universities, 2010). Their top choice is teach students to communicate effectively both orally and in writing, followed by "critical thinking and analytical reasoning skills." I would add here that no one can communicate clearly if their thinking is muddy, so these two top concerns are inextricably related. In fact, four of the top five learning outcomes that

employers want for their employees are subsumed under the general heading of critical thinking—applying knowledge in real-world settings, analyzing and solving problems, connecting choices to actions, and being able to
innovate and be creative. The Partnership for 21st Century Skills (2004), a
coalition of national organizations that advocate for the skills needed in a
global economy, makes it clear that "critical thinking and problem solving"
are essential for the citizens of today and for the future. Politicians of every
persuasion, blue ribbon panels, workers, and students all recognize the critical importance of critical thinking as the primary objective of education.

Consider this: Most people will finish their formal education between the
ages of 18 and 22. Today's young adults are expected to have the longest
average life span in the history of the world, with most living into their 70s
and many living into their 80s and 90s. We can only guess what life will be
like in the years 2075 or 2085 or beyond, years that many of you who are
reading this book will live through. One likely guess is that many of today's
young adults will be working at jobs that currently don't exist and dealing
with technologies that dwarf the imagination of present-day science fiction
writers. What do they need to learn during their first two decades of life
that will prepare them for their remaining 60+ years?

Thought and Knowledge

> Knowledge will forever govern ignorance: And people who mean to
> be their own Governours, must arm themselves with the power which
> knowledge gives.

—James Madison
(Texas Library Association
http://www.txla.org/groups/godort/kip-award.html)

One of the elementary schools that I attended as a child had the words
"Knowledge is Power" chiseled into a concrete block above its front door.
If I were asked to amend this maxim based on my experiences over the
many years since I last past through those doors, I would edit the concrete
block to read, "Thought and Knowledge are Power" because knowledge is
powerful only when it is applied appropriately, and thought is powerful
only when it can utilize a large and accurate base of knowledge.

This is a book about thought and knowledge and the relationship between
these two constructs. It is about thinking in ways that allow us to use previous knowledge to create new knowledge. Everything we know, and

[handwritten note:] •Knowledge is dynamic —we came our own meaning of it (we build on others K to create New K)

everything everyone else knows—that [...] as created by someone. When we learn E[...] arning about knowledge created by the gre[...] nilarly, other eminent inventions and insig[...], video games, toilet paper, $E = mc^2$, and the [...] present knowledge created by people. Knowl[...]at gets transferred from one person to another like pouring water from one glass to another. It is dynamic. Information becomes knowledge when we make our own meaning out of it. Of course, it is silly to think that we should all start from "scratch" and recreate the wheel or that each of us needs to re-invent our own version of algebra or knowledge in other fields that is readily available that others have created. We build on the knowledge created by others to create new knowledge.

We also create knowledge every time we learn a new concept. The newly acquired information is used to construct our own internal knowledge structures. ("Knowledge structures" is a technical term used by cognitive psychologists to describe all of the interrelated concepts that each of us has about different subjects.) Knowledge is a "state of understanding" that exists only in the mind of the individual knower (King, 1994, p. 16). We use our existing knowledge when we receive new information in order to make sense of the new information, thus the acquisition of knowledge is an active mental process. This idea was expressed more eloquently by Resnick (1985, p. 130) when she said: "Knowledge is no longer viewed as a reflection of what has been given from the outside; it is a personal construction in which the individual imposes meaning by relating bits of knowledge and experience to some organizing schemata."

A Working Definition of Critical Thinking

> Ultimately, it is not we who define thinking, it is thinking that defines us.
> —Carey, Foltz, & Allan (Newsweek, February 7, 1983)

Although many psychologists and others have proposed definitions for the term "critical thinking," these definitions tend to be similar with

Take a few minutes and think about your own definition of critical thinking. What would it include and what would it not include?

considerable overlap among the definitions. In a review of the critical thinking literature, Fischer and Spiker (2000) found that most definitions for the term "critical thinking" include reasoning/logic, judgment, meta-cognition, reflection, questioning, and mental processes. Jones and his colleagues (Jones, Dougherty, Fantaske, & Hoffman, 1995; Jones, Hoffman, Moore, Ratcliff, Tibbetts, & Click, 1995) obtained consensus from among 500 policy makers, employers, and educators who agree that critical thinking is a broad term that describes reasoning in an open-ended manner and with an unlimited number of solutions. It involves constructing a situation and supporting the reasoning that went into a conclusion.

We can think of critical thinking as good thinking, but that definition leaves us with the problem of recognizing what that is and differentiating good thinking from poor thinking. Here is a simple definition that captures the main concepts: *Critical thinking is the use of those cognitive skills or strategies that increase the probability of a desirable outcome. It is used to describe thinking that is purposeful, reasoned, and goal directed—the kind of thinking involved in solving problems, formulating inferences, calculating likelihoods, and making decisions, when the thinker is using skills that are thoughtful and effective for the particular context and type of thinking task.* Critical thinking is more than merely thinking about your own thinking or making judgments and solving problems—it is effortful and consciously controlled. Critical thinking uses evidence and reasons and strives to overcome individual biases. Decisions as to which outcomes should be desirable are embedded in a system of values and may differ from person-to-person, but the idea that critical thinking makes desirable outcomes more likely provides a way of defining critical thinking (Butler & Halpern, 2012; Moseley et al., 2005; Riggio & Halpern, 2006; Sternberg, Roediger, & Halpern, 2007).

One of my favorite definitions of critical thinking was published over 50 years ago (1960) and comes very close to a contemporary notion of critical thinking: "Critical thinking then is the process of evaluation or categorization in terms of some previously accepted standards . . . this seems to involve attitude plus knowledge of facts plus some thinking skills" (Russell, cited in d'Angelo, 1971, p. 6). In short, Russell's equation is:

Attitude + Knowledge + Thinking Skills = Critical Thinking

What's Critical about Critical Thinking?

The "critical" part of critical thinking denotes an evaluation component. Sometimes the word "critical" is used to convey something negative, as when we say, "She is a critical person." But, evaluation can and should be a constructive reflection of positive and negative attributes. When we think critically, we are evaluating the outcomes of our thought processes—how good a decision is or how well a problem has been solved. Critical thinking also involves evaluating the thinking process—the reasoning that went into the conclusion we've arrived at or the kinds of factors considered in making a decision. Daydreams, night dreams, and other sorts of thinking that are not engaged in for a specific purpose are not subsumed under the critical thinking category. Neither is the type of thinking that underlies our routine habits, which although goal-directed, involve very little conscious evaluation, such as getting up in the morning, brushing our teeth, or taking a usual route to school and work. These are examples of **nondirected or automatic thinking**. Other examples of *noncritical thinking* include the rote recall of information (e.g., listing state capitals) or the failure to consider evidence that might support a conclusion that you do not like.

In thinking about critical thinking, consider, for example, someone in need of money who decides to remedy this problem with a trip to the racetrack where he bets on a pretty filly named "Handsome Singer." There is some (small) chance that he will "win big" if his horse comes in, but this is not an example of critical thinking, even if he reflected on his actions and Handsome Singer was the first to cross the finish line. The most likely outcome is that he will lose the money he bet, surely an undesirable outcome. On the other hand, suppose that he invested his money in a "blue chip" stock instead of betting it on "Handsome Singer." There is some chance that he will lose his money with this strategy, but on average, in the long run, the likelihood of the desirable outcome of having more money is much higher with the stock investment than it is by betting at the race track. The investment is a rational or reasoned course of action, but it cannot guarantee a desirable outcome. The future is always unknown and there can never be guarantees about the future, even for the best of thinkers. A substantial increase in the likelihood of a desirable outcome is the best that critical thinking can promise, and it is the best hope for the future that anyone can offer.

The focus of this book is on the development and improvement of those skills that characterize clear, precise, purposeful thinking. It is a practical book, based primarily on applications of cognitive psychology to memory, reasoning, problem solving, creativity, language, and decision making. Despite the fact that some critics have claimed that critical thinking is just a "fad" that will surely go out of style, it has a very long history in psychology and education. John Dewey, the pioneering American educator identified "learning to think" as the primary purpose of education in 1933. Besides, it is difficult for me to consider that the need to think well is a "passing fancy" that will soon be out of style, much like Rubik's cube, "big hair," and bell bottom jeans.

Although psychology has been concerned with the way people think for much of its 100+ years of existence as an academic discipline, cognitive psychology, the branch of psychology that is concerned with thought and knowledge, has virtually dominated scientific psychology for the past 50 years. Cognitive psychologists are concerned with learning about the skills and strategies used in problem solving, reasoning, and decision making and the way these abilities relate to intelligence. All of this interest in human thinking processes has given birth to a new area of psychology that has come to be known as **cognitive process instruction**. Its goal is to utilize the knowledge we have accumulated about human thinking processes and mechanisms in ways that can help people improve how they think. For example, by examining correct and incorrect responses in a variety of situations, psychologists have found that at least some of the time, most people's spontaneous and intuitive approaches to solving problems are wrong. Furthermore, psychologists can often predict when an incorrect response will be made either because of the nature of the problem or because of common biases that a problem solver may bring to the problem. This knowledge is already being put to use to solve a host of applied problems that range from providing military personnel with map reading skills to designing "user-friendly" computer programs. Ariely (2009) has written extensively on what he calls "predictably irrational" behavior. The main theme of Ariely's writing is that psychologists can predict with a high level of accuracy the type of irrational thinking and behavior most people will engage in when they are faced with certain information and need to make a decision. By understanding how and when we are irrational, we can make better decisions, and by extension, we become better thinkers.

Changing How People Think: Should It Be Done?

We know that the average American, because of changes in the economy at home and abroad, will change work seven or eight times in a lifetime. . . . If that is true, it is clear that we need an agenda as a people for lifetime learning.

—U.S. President Bill Clinton ("Clinton's message," 1994, p. 6A)

The whole idea of influencing the way people think may seem scary. It suggests terms like "mind control" and "propaganda," or perhaps even a "Big Brother," like the one in Orwell's chilling novel *1984*, who knew what you were thinking. In reality, though, critical thinking is an antidote to the kind of mind control that worried Orwell. Learning the skills of clear thinking can help everyone recognize propaganda and thus not fall prey to it, analyze unstated assumptions in arguments, realize when there is deliberate deception, consider the credibility of an information source, and think a problem or a decision through in the best way possible.

When I discuss the topic of critical thinking with students and other people with whom I come in contact, I am sometimes told that there is no such thing as critical thinking because different viewpoints are "all a matter of opinion" and that everyone has a right to his or her own opinion. They argue that a "better way to think" does not exist. I certainly agree that we all have the "right" to our own opinion; however, some "opinions" are better than others. Everyone has the right to believe in phenomena such as astrology and extrasensory perception even if there is no sound evidence to support the existence of these phenomena. If someone wants to have an illness sucked from his body with warmed cups or buys a so-called Power bracelet that is purely bogus, why should anyone care? There is a great web site that answers this question. Aptly named *What's the Harm* (http://whatstheharm.net), it lists a large number of phony medical cures, supernatural and paranormal phenomena, pseudoscience, and more bogus claims than I could imagine and documents the harm that results when, for example, someone opts for a phony medical cure instead of one that is based on sound medical research. Cupping, the "medicine" practiced by my grandmother, is listed and along with it is a story of a man who was badly burned when the cupping procedure caught fire.

James Randi, a magician and escape artist who is best known for his work in debunking claims of psychics and others has a certified $1 million fund that will be given to anyone who can legitimately demonstrate paranormal ability under test conditions. There is a long list of applicants including psychics, clairvoyants, friends of the dead, someone who claimed she could make people urinate using the power of her mind, and even stranger claims. The $1 Million Paranormal Challenge is still unclaimed (James Randi Educational Foundation, 2013). All beliefs are *not* equally good.

There are countless examples of the need for critical thinking. In every political campaign, candidates tell voters that they are opposed to waste, fraud, pollution, crime, and overpaid bureaucrats. These speeches are inevitably followed with loud cheering and applause. (Pay attention to this when you watch the next political convention—regardless of the party.) What's wrong with these speeches? The candidates never really say anything. I've never heard any candidate claim to be *for* waste, fraud, pollution, crime, or overpaid bureaucrats. Voters should ask them to be more explicit about their goals, how they would accomplish them, and where the money would come from to finance political plans.

Here's another example, presented to a large sample of 13-year-olds: "An army bus holds 36 soldiers. If 1,128 soldiers are being bused to their training site, how many busses are needed?" (Chance, 1986, p. 26). Most of the students tested had no trouble carrying out the computations. The problem came in using the answer in a meaningful way. Many rounded the answer they received to the nearest whole number and concluded that 31 busses were needed. Others gave a decimal answer (31.33) or showed the remainder from their long division. The problem was not one of basic computational skills, but of thinking about the kind of answer that the problem required and using a strategy that was different from one that was taught in school, namely rounding "up" to the next highest whole number rather than rounding to the nearest whole number. Perhaps, simple examples like this one provide the most convincing answer to the question of whether critical thinking should be taught. The most precious commodity of any country is thinking, educated people. We must make this the goal of education.

Commercialization of Schools as a Threat to Critical Thinking

> According to the research literature, critical thinking is best cultivated in a school environment that encourages students to ask questions, to think about their thought processes, and thus to develop habits of mind that enable them to transfer the critical thinking skills they learn in class to other, unrelated, situations.
> —Alex Molnar, Faith Boninger, & Joseph Fogarty (2011, p. i)

Not surprisingly, many cash-strapped school districts have turned to commercial sponsors to pay expenses. As an often unacknowledged part of this "deal," commercial sponsors buy the right to promote their products to the children and adolescents in the schools they sponsor. The sponsor's interest is to promote the product that they sell. They do not want the children to learn to identify and critically evaluate the sponsor's point of view or to generate solutions that would make the children less likely to buy the sponsor's products (Molnar, Boninger, & Fogarty, 2011). I recall a situation in which a beer company paid part of the construction costs for a much-needed new building on a university campus. In return, the large auditorium in that building was named for the beer company. Many years ago (not at my current college), I taught classes in that auditorium. As part of a standard course in introduction to psychology, we would study the harmful consequences of alcoholism, and we did this is in a large room named for a beer company!

In a recent report on the way commercialization of schools has negatively affected critical thinking, the authors (Molnar, Boninger, & Fogerty, 2011) noted the importance of asking questions such as: "What additional information would you want?" "Are the assertions credible?" "What are two solutions for a given problem?" These and other similar questions are presented in multiple places throughout this book, but do students learn to ask these questions?

Empirical Evidence That Thinking Can Be Improved

Everyone agrees that students *learn* in college, but whether they learn to *think* is more controversial.
—Wilbert J. McKeachie (1992, p. 3)

If you have been thinking critically about the idea of improving how you think, then you've probably begun to wonder if there is any evidence that thinking can be improved. Although there has been some debate about whether it is possible to produce long lasting enhancements in the ability to think effectively, we now have a considerable body of evidence that thinking skills courses and thinking skills instruction that is embedded in other courses can have positive effects that are transferable to many situations. Numerous qualitatively different forms of outcome evaluations for thinking courses provide substantial evidence for the conclusion that it is possible to use education to improve the ability to think critically, especially when instruction is specifically designed to encourage the transfer of these skills to different situations and different domains of knowledge. In fact, it is difficult to identify any aspect of critical thinking that could not be taught and learned. We learn mathematics in the belief that mathematical skills can be used in real-world contexts where they are needed; similarly, we learn writing and speaking skills in the belief that learners will use these skills when they write or speak in any context. When students take courses designed to improve their ability to work with numbers, write, or speak, most students show improvements. There is no reason why we should believe that instruction in critical thinking would not show the same positive effects as when teaching mathematical, writing, or speaking skills. Here is a sampling of some positive outcomes:

(1) In a large-scale review of the critical thinking literature, the Thinking Skills Review Group (a group of professionals in Great Britain that conducted an extensive review of critical thinking, 2004, p 4) concluded that "The majority of studies report positive impact on pupils' attainment across a range of noncurricular measures (such as reasoning or problem-solving). No studies report negative impact on such measures." Even more importantly, they found evidence that pupils can apply or translate this learning to other contexts.

(2) A formal evaluation of a nationwide thinking skills program in Venezuela showed that students who had participated in classes designed for instruction in thinking skills showed greater gains in orally presented arguments and in answering open-ended essay questions than a comparable control group (Herrnstein, Nickerson, de Sanchez, & Swets, 1986). Although this is an older study, it is particularly notable because the researchers used an experimental design that allowed them to conclude that it was the instruction and not some extraneous factor that caused students in the experimental group to improve in their ability to think critically. Students were assigned at random either to receive the thinking skills instruction or some other "control" instruction. Additionally, the oral arguments and writing samples were graded blind; that is, the graders did not know if the students they were assessing had received the thinking skills instruction or were in the control group. The results showed that the targeted thinking skills were transferred and used appropriately with novel topics. Also, they showed greater gains than the control group students on tests of general aptitude (sometimes called intelligence tests), problem solving, decision making, reasoning, creative thinking, and language. This experiment provides strong support for the conclusion that improvements in thinking are possible when instruction is designed for this purpose.

(3) Van Gelder (2001) taught college students how to recognize the various components of an argument, including ways of determining how good any argument is and including ones that you make yourself. After one semester of training, he found that students made large gains on a multiple-choice test of critical thinking and a written test that was loosely based on the Graduate Record Examination's Writing Assessment (a commonly used test for entrance to graduate schools). He concluded that teaching students how to recognize the structure and strength of arguments "appears to dramatically accelerate improvement in critical thinking when compared with the 'indirect" strategy' (i.e., just being at university)" (p. 546).

Other studies support the idea that critical thinking is learned best when the skills are explicitly taught. In a study with high school students at low-performing schools, Marin and Halpern (2010) compared the critical thinking skills of students taught with explicit methods (labeling the skills, teaching ways to analyze arguments, recognize when correlations are being used to make causal claims, confirmation bias and stereotypes, and how to make sound decisions) to those of students who were taught these skills implicitly as part of the course materials. Critical thinking gains were assessed with the Halpern Critical Thinking Assessment, which uses both open-ended and multiple-choice responses. The results showed a clear benefit for explicit instruction in critical thinking.

(4) Researchers in the Netherlands examined the effect of critical thinking instruction on training and transfer in complex decision making. One group of students received the instruction while working with realistic scenarios that required complex decisions, and the other group used the same scenarios, but did not receive the training (Helsdingen, van den Bosch, van Gog, & van Merrienboer, 2010). The researchers concluded that "The results of this study warrant the implementation of critical thinking instruction . . . for decision makers that have to operate in complex and highly interactive dynamic environments" (p. 537).

(5) Using a skills approach, Facione (1991; Facione, Facione, & Giancarlo, 2000) found that college students who received coursework in critical thinking scored significantly higher on a multiple-choice test of thinking skills than comparable students who had not taken such a course. Other studies have also documented improvements on multiple-choice tests of critical thinking. For example, Lehman, Lempert, and Nisbett (1988) found that graduate-level college students improved significantly on a critical

thinking test that included short scenarios about realistic situations. They concluded that training with general "rules" of thinking is generalized to other contexts.

(6) Strong support for beneficial outcomes from critical thinking instruction comes from a collection of studies by Nisbett and his colleagues (Nisbett, 1993). For example, in one study, Nisbett and his coauthors phoned students at their homes after the coursework was completed, under the guise of conducting a survey. They found that students spontaneously applied the thinking skills that they had been taught in school when they encountered novel problems, even when the school-related context cues were absent (Fong, Krantz, & Nisbett, 1986). In a different study, inductive reasoning tasks were taught to college students using realistic scenarios from many different domains. Students were able to use these skills on a later test. The authors concluded that critical thinking is "a skill" and that "it is transferable" (Jepson, Krantz, & Nisbett, 1993, p. 82). Nisbett's (1993) edited book contains 16 chapters that show that rules of logic, statistics, causal deduction, and cost-benefit analysis can be taught in ways that will generalize to a variety of settings. A similar conclusion about the positive effects of courses designed to promote critical thinking was reached in another independent review of the literature (Chance, 1986; Bruer, 1993).

(7) Additional support for the conclusion that improvements in critical thinking transfer across settings was reported by Kosonen and Winne (1995), who studied the transfer of critical thinking skills to a novel domain in a study that used college, secondary school, and middle-school students as participants. Like Nisbett, they found that when students learned general rules about reasoning and practiced these skills with everyday "ill-structured" problems, the thinking skills transferred to new contexts and different domains. Appleton-Knapp, Bjork, and Wickens (2005, p. 266) reported similar results. They found that variation in how information is encoded results in "more multi-faceted memory representations, which enhanced recall." Thus, it seems that critical thinking skills are learned best and are most likely to transfer to novel situations when they are taught using a variety of different examples. Principles derived from empirical studies like these (and others) that show the successful transfer of critical thinking skills can serve as a model for instructional design. Many important principles from cognitive psychology are applied in this text to encourage effective learning that lasts.

All of the diverse findings (and many others that are not reviewed here because the relevant research literature is huge) point to the same conclusion: students can learn to think more critically when they receive instruction that is designed for this purpose.

Is Critical Thinking a Byproduct of a Good Education?

> Freshmen who enter higher education at the 50th percentile would reach a level equivalent to the 57th percentile of an incoming freshman class by the end of their sophomore year. Three semesters of college education thus have a barely noticeable impact on students' skills in critical thinking, complex reasoning, and writing.
>
> —Richard Arum and Josipa Roksa (2011, p. 35)

The evidence is clear: We can get good gains in critical thinking when teachers deliberately teach for critical thinking. But, what if teachers don't? Do students become better thinkers as a routine part of getting a good education? In fact, most do not. Arum and Roksa (2011) make this point in their condemnation of what happens in many college classes. They followed 2,300 students at 24 universities over four years. They concluded that more than one third showed no improvement in critical thinking. Critical thinking does not automatically result as a byproduct of standard instruction in a content area. Critical thinking instruction needs to focus overtly and self-consciously on the improvement of thinking, and the learning experience needs to include multiple examples across domains in order to maximize transfer.

Transfer of Training

> Why Johnny can't read was one of the central questions raised about American education in the 1970s. Why Johnny can't think replaced it in the 1980s.
>
> —A. L. Brown and J. C. Campione (1990, p. 108)

All of these studies that attest to the effectiveness of critical thinking instruction are studies of the generalizability or transfer of critical thinking skills. The real goal of any instruction to improve thinking is **transfer of training**. What I mean by transfer is the use of critical thinking skills in a wide variety of contexts. The whole enterprise of learning how to improve thinking is of little value if these skills are only used in the classroom or only on problems that are very similar to those presented in class. Ideally, critical thinking skills should be used to recognize and resist unrealistic campaign promises, circular reasoning, faulty probability estimates, weak arguments by analogy, or language designed to mislead whenever and wherever it is encountered. Critical thinkers should be better able to solve or offer reasonable solutions to real world problems, whether it is the problem of nuclear war or how to set up a new computer. These skills should also be long lasting and useful for the many decades of critical thinking that most of us will face. Admittedly, these are lofty goals, but they are important ones. The best way to promote the kind of transfer I am advocating is with the conscious and deliberate use of the skills that are learned in a wide variety of contexts.

Psychologists know that learning is enhanced when study time includes at least one test of the material being learned (Roediger & Karpicke, 2006), but more recent work shows that transfer is also enhanced when learners are tested during learning (Rohrer, Taylor, & Sholar, 2010). It seems that by recalling information, the strength of the memory increases and the information to be learned is then more available when it is needed in novel situations. It is important to work through a variety of different types of materials where critical thinking skills are needed to get the most of critical thinking instruction. For that reason, there is a variety of different types of problems presented about different topics in the ancillary materials that accompany this book. By working through these problems, you will increase the likelihood that you will recall and use the thinking skills that are presented in the text and in real life when you really need them. Be sure to be on the lookout for other instances when these thinking skills are needed, and be sure to use them!

Learning to Think Critically: A Four-Part Model

The model that I have proposed for critical thinking instruction consists of four parts (Butler & Halpern, 2011; Halpern, 1998):

1. Explicitly learn the skills of critical thinking.
2. Develop the disposition for effortful thinking and learning.
3. Direct learning activities in ways that increase the probability of transcontextual transfer (structure training).
4. Make metacognitive monitoring explicit and overt.

Let's consider each of these parts.

A Skills Approach to Critical Thinking

As you work your way through the chapters in this book, you will come across many different thinking skills, with each chapter containing those skills that are especially useful in thinking about the chapter topic. For example, the thinking skills used in understanding likelihood and uncertainty are presented in that chapter. You may be wondering what a "thinking skill" is. Some examples should help. Here is a list of some generic skills that are important in many situations.

A critical thinker will:

- recognize semantic slanting and guilt by association
- seek out contradictory evidence
- use the metacognitive knowledge that allows novices to monitor their own performance and to decide when additional help is needed
- make risk: benefit assessments
- generate a reasoned method for selecting between several possible courses of actions
- give reasons for choices as well as varying the style and amount of detail in explanations depending on who is receiving the information
- recall relevant information when it is needed
- use skills for learning new techniques efficiently and relate new knowledge to information that was previously learned
- use numerical information including the ability to think probabilistically and express thoughts numerically
- understand basic research principles
- demonstrate an advanced ability to read and write complex prose
- present a coherent and persuasive argument on a controversial, contemporary topic
- use matrices and other diagrams for communication
- synthesize information from a variety of sources
- determine credibility and use this information in formulating and communicating decisions.

Critical thinking instruction is predicated on two assumptions: (a) there are clearly identifiable and definable thinking skills that students can be taught to recognize and apply appropriately, and (b) if recognized and applied, the students will be more effective thinkers. Thus, one part of the model for learning to become a better thinker is learning how to use the skills of critical thinking and how to recognize when a particular skill (or set of skills) is needed.

The Disposition for Effortful Thinking and Learning

> All man's dignity lies in thought.
>
> —Blaise Pascal (1670, p. 83)

No one can become a better thinker just by reading a book or even by just learning a set of thinking skills that would be useful if they were used. An essential component of critical thinking is developing the attitude or disposition of a critical thinker. Good thinkers are motivated and willing to exert the conscious effort needed to work in a planful manner, to check for accuracy, to gather information, and to persist when the solution is not obvious or requires several steps.

In an empirical test of the relationship between a disposition to think critically and actual performance on a test of critical thinking, Butler (2012) found that adults who reported that they were more likely to engage in the effortful process of thinking (e.g., less likely to rely on gut decisions or to prefer one example to a well-conducted study and more likely to research products before buying) had higher scores on a critical thinking assessment and actually engaged in fewer negative behaviors that were indicative of poor thinking (e.g., rented a movie but had to return it without watching it, bought new clothes but never wore them, got locked out of the house) than those who were less inclined to think critically.

Many errors occur not because people can't think critically, but because they do not. One of the major differences between good and poor thinkers, and correspondingly between good and poor students, is their attitude. A critical thinker will exhibit the following dispositions or attitudes:

Willingness to Plan

> If everybody thought before they spoke, the silence would be deafening.
>
> —George Barzan

I have watched thousands of students (literally) take exams. There are always some students who begin to write as soon as the exam hits their desk. They just plow ahead and begin writing before they begin thinking. Not surprisingly, the results are a disoriented jumble that often bears little relation to the questions being asked. When asked a question in class, they will often answer with the first idea that comes to mind. These students need to learn to check their impulsivity and plan their response. They should be outlining or diagramming the structure of a response before they begin to write. Planning, the invisible first step in critical thinking, is essential. Planning seems to be an important component for changing many behaviors, especially health-related behaviors such as healthy eating and avoiding drug and alcohol abuse (Wiedemann, Lippke, Reuter, Ziegelmann, & Schwarzer, 2011). Regardless of the content, it is useful to plan how you will think and act. Plans are prescriptive descriptions about what to do and they prevent habitual responses that may not work. With repeated practice, anyone can develop the **habit of planning**.

Self-regulation is a popular concept in the psychological research literature. It is a complex term that has multiple components, which includes using feedback, monitoring comprehension, assessing progress towards a goal, and making judgments about how well something is learned (Bednall & Kehoe, 2011). There is voluminous literature showing that self-regulation is important in learning. It is now clear that critical thinkers are self-regulated learners (Phan, 2010). Researchers taught college students how to use self-regulatory behaviors, and they found that when compared with control groups, students who learned how to self regulate performed better on a test that required detecting and explaining thinking fallacies (Bednall & Kehoe, 2011).

Flexibility

In a classic old book, Rokeach (1960) talks about rigidity and dogmatism as the characteristics of a "closed mind." A person with a closed mind responds negatively to new ideas by stating, "That's the way I've always done it." Another common retort that shows the unwillingness to consider new ideas is the well-worn phrase, "If it ain't broke, don't fix it." This sort of close-minded response cuts off consideration of new ideas. By contrast, an attitude of flexibility is marked by a willingness to consider new options, try things a new way, and reconsider old problems. Cognitive flexibility is the ability to change how we think about something—to see things from another person's point of view, consider multiple options, think of several ways to respond, and seek information that may not be readily available (Dennis & Wal, 2010). An open-minded person is willing to suspend judgment, gather more information, and attempt to clarify difficult issues. This does not mean that all opinions are equally good or that judgment should take a back-seat to openness. It does not mean accepting every nonsense opinion that is offered. It does mean, though, that a critical thinker is willing to think in new ways, review evidence, and stick with a task until all reasonable options have been considered.

Persistence

> You may be disappointed if you fail, but you are doomed if you don't try.
> —Beverly Sills (quoted in James Rogan, *Bits & Pieces*, 1993, p. 7)

There are many factors that influence academic and career success, but persistence may be the most important one (Andersson & Bergman, 2011). It is the willingness and ability to keep at a task. It is key factor in successful problem solving. Closely related to persistence is the willingness to start or engage in a thoughtful task. Some people look at a seemingly difficult task and opt not to even begin the thinking process. They are defeated at the start. Good thinking is hard work that requires diligent persistence. It can make you as tired as any physical labor, but can be much more rewarding. In a comparison of students who were unsuccessful in mathematics with those who were successful, researchers found that much of the difference in success rates was directly attributable to differences in attitudes. The unsuccessful students believed that if a problem could not be solved in less than 10 minutes, then they would not be able to solve it. By contrast, the successful students persisted in working on difficult problems (Schoenfeld, 1985).

Willingness to Self-Correct, Admit Errors, and Change Your Mind when the Evidence Changes

> In science it often happens that scientists say, "You know that's a really good argument; my position is mistaken," and then they would actually change their minds and you never hear that old view from them again. They really do it. It doesn't happen as often as it should, because scientists are human and change is sometimes painful.
> —Carl Sagan

We all make mistakes. In fact, creative thoughts and actions would not be possible if we were unwilling to make mistakes, at least some of the time. Instead of becoming defensive about errors, good thinkers can acknowledge them and learn from them. Unfortunately, there is wide spread tendency to justify our mistakes—our faulty beliefs, our bad decisions. In a delightful book, Tavris and Aronson (2007) review multiple political and private mistakes. A main deterrent to admitting mistakes is **self-justification**. Self-justification is extremely strong because it keeps our image of ourselves intact. For example, is it important to think of yourself as an informed and intelligent citizen? For many of us, this is an important component of our self-image. Suppose that you believed that there really were "weapons of mass destruction in Iraq" at the time when the President of the United States was urging its allies to protect themselves and the future of their countries by invading Iraq. Later, the overwhelming evidence shows that there were no weapons of mass destruction. What now? Many people chose to ignore the evidence and maintain their original belief. It is not hard to see why. By maintaining, even strengthening the original belief, believers can continue to see themselves and to convince others that they were not wrong about something so important. Self-justification, which is making excuses for a belief or behavior, is a very strong human tendency and can be found everywhere—it is not just for politicians. Tavris and Aronson present many examples—husbands and wives each justifying a belief or action even when there is good evidence that the belief or action was wrong, defendants on trial for a variety of crimes, supervisors and the people they supervise, and so on. The disposition to be self-critical (evaluative) and consider when a mistake is a learnable moment and not a time for the auto-pilot of self-justification is a hallmark of critical thinkers.

It is interesting to note that the general public usually does not like it when a public figure changes his or her mind, especially when the change is away from a conclusion that was popular. However, if a person is open to a fair evaluation of new information, sometimes that information will lead to a different conclusion. It would be foolish to hold to an old conclusion or belief when it is no longer warranted. The ability to change one's conclusion when new or better information becomes known is not "waffling" or some other negative term that is used to describe someone whose views change as readily as the shifting direction of the wind. What is needed is a new term that has positive connotations to be used for critical thinkers who are willing to change conclusions when sound evidence warrants a change. Unfortunately, this is one attitude of critical thinking that is still all too rare.

Politics is filled with instances where one side took advantage of a change in the position of an opposing candidate. In a news article that lists numerous people throughout history who have changed their positive on core issues, including various candidates for the presidency of the United States (both Democrats and Republicans), the author (Schulman, 2007, para. 8) asks,

But are all flip-flops really so objectionable? Isn't it equally fair to argue that a willingness to shift, often abruptly and fundamentally, in response to changing circumstances is a venerable tradition in American governance? Indeed, the willingness to compromise is a crucial ingredient of serious leadership. The nation's most respected presidents, from the founding generation to modern times, have proudly and, in some cases, defiantly flip-flopped on important issues.

Being Mindful

In order to develop basic thinking skills, it is necessary to direct your attention to the processes and products of your own thoughts. Langer (2000) defines **mindfulness** as "the simple act of drawing novel distinctions" (p. 220). It is the opposite of the "automatic pilot" that we use for routine tasks like setting the dinner table, getting to school or work every day, or watching television in the evening. According to Langer, learning requires a mindful engagement with the task and materials. She told a humorous personal story about a case of mindlessness that makes this point well (Langer, 1989). When shopping one day, the clerk told her that she had not signed the back of the credit card she was using. Langer signed the card, and then handed it back to the clerk. The clerk then processed the sale and had Langer sign the credit slip. Then, dutifully, as she had no doubt been instructed, the clerk checked the signature on the back of the newly signed credit card with the signature on the credit slip. She never realized that she had just seen Langer sign both! As long as we respond in a mindless or routinized way, problems worth solving will never be recognized, and creative solutions will be missed.

Consensus-Seeking

Committee and group organizational structures are most often the norm in the world of work. Critical thinkers need to be predisposed to seek ways in which consensus among group members can be achieved. They maintain an awareness of the social realities that need to be overcome so that thoughts can become actions. Consensus-seekers need high-level communication skills, but they also need to find ways to compromise and to achieve agreement. Without this disposition and related interpersonal skills, even the most brilliant thinkers will find that they cannot convert thoughts to actions.

Consensus-seeking does NOT mean caving in to majority opinion, and it does not mean forcing others to agree with you. It is a disposition that

allows individuals to accept what is good or true about an alternative position as a way of gaining support for one's own position. In the chapter
on decision making, I talk about "group think," which is the pressure for
conformity in group decision making. Consensus-seeking is a different
concept—it refers to an openness in thinking that allows members of a
group to agree on some aspects of a solution and disagree on others—but
the goal is to allow other people and yourself to express doubts while working toward a solution that can be achieved.

Transfer of Training

In becoming a better thinker, it is important to have a large repertoire of
critical thinking skills and to be willing to engage in the effortful process
of using them. The third component of this model involves recognizing
when critical thinking is needed so that you can select the most appropriate skills for the situation. This is the Achilles' heel of transfer. The problem
in learning thinking skills that are needed in multiple contexts is that there
are no obvious cues in the context to trigger the recall of the thinking skill.
Critical thinkers need to create the recall cues from the structural aspects
of the problem or argument so that when the structural aspects are present,
they can serve as cues for retrieval.

When critical thinking skills are learned so that they transfer appropriately
and spontaneously, critical thinkers can focus on the structure so the underlying characteristics become salient instead of the domain specific surface characteristics. An example should help here because the idea of
transferring skills to novel areas is highly abstract.

Suppose that you understand the way contrast effects can influence one's
judgment. For example, if you are offered several part-time jobs that pay
$10 an hour, $13.50 an hour will seem like more money than if you had
been offered several part-time jobs that pay $14 an hour. Even if you know
that contrast effects can influence judgments, will you be able to recognize
the power of contrast effects on your judgment in a totally different situation, such as when your friend begins a story about his "brush with the law"
by telling you about all of the people from your old high school class who
are now in jail? His "brush with the law" will seem much less serious when
it is told after stories about people you know who committed serious crimes
than it would if he had told it after stories about people who have not committed any crimes. In this example, your hypothetical friend is making his
own crime seem less bad by contrasting it with more serious ones. How can

you recognize that the same principle of contrast is affecting your judgment in both situations (judgments about pay per hour and seriousness of a crime)? If you can recognize that the same principle is at work, you could use the same critical thinking skills to prevent the effect of contrast from influencing how you think. In other words, how can you learn to apply your knowledge about contrast effects in different sorts of situations?

There is an old saying in psychology that "the head remembers what it does." It is important to direct your own learning so that the skills of critical thinking are learned in a way that will facilitate their recall in novel situations. It is what learners do that determines what gets learned. Here are some examples of thinking tasks that are designed to help with the transfer of critical thinking skills. They require readers to perform certain tasks or answer carefully crafted questions that draw attention to structural aspects of the problem or argument:

- Draw a diagram or other graphic display that organizes the information.
- List additional information you would want before answering a question.
- Explain why a particular multiple-choice alternative was selected. Which is second best? Why?
- State the problem in at least two ways.
- Identify which information is most important. Which information is least important? Why?
- Categorize the findings in a meaningful way.
- List two solutions for problems.
- Identify what is wrong with an assertion that was made in the question.
- Present two reasons that support the conclusion and two reasons that do not support the conclusion.
- Identify the type of persuasive technique being used.
- Present two actions you would take to improve the design of a study that was described.

Tasks like these require learners to focus on structural aspects of the problems so that the learner can identify and use an appropriate critical thinking skill.

intelligence? The answer to this important question depends upon how intelligence is defined.

> Before you read further, stop for a minute to think about your own definition of intelligence. If a program of instruction can help learners think better, have they become more intelligent?

The Nature of Intelligence

> IQ tests measure only a small set of the thinking abilities that people need.
>
> —Keith E. Stanovich (2009, p. 3)

Intelligence is one of the most controversial topics in psychology. It is a basic topic in thinking because intelligence is the "stuff" of which thought is made. It is difficult to imagine a context in which intelligence is not manifested or needed. The term intelligence is used commonly in everyday language. Most people believe that they are at least about average or above average in intelligence (Brim, 1966). (Despite Garrison Keillor's assurances to the contrary, you should realize that this is mathematically absurd because most people cannot be above average.)

Psychologists continue to debate exactly what the term "intelligence" *should* mean. Here is a good working definition that was offered by Gottfredson (1997b):

> [Intelligence] . . . involves the ability to reason, plan, solve problems, think abstractly, comprehend complex ideas, learn quickly and learn from experience. It is not merely book learning, a narrow academic skill, or test-taking smarts. Rather it reflects a broader and deeper capability for comprehending our surroundings—'catching on', 'making sense' of things, or 'figuring out' what to do. (p. 13)

Intelligence is measured with tests that have been standardized on large groups of people. Most people are familiar with the concept of IQ, which stands for "intelligence quotient" (because it was originally formulated for children by dividing their mental age by their physical age). I agree with critics who claim that no single score can reflect the complexity of human intelligence, no measure is free from cultural bias, and there is a potential to misuse these scores, but it is also true that IQ scores can do a reasonable job at predicting grades in school, success at work, and other variables related to success in life (Nisbett et al., 2012). As many writers have noted, IQ tests measure only a subset of the thinking skills that people need to be successful in life. In his book on what intelligence tests miss, Stanovich (2009, p. 3) wrote "IQ tests are good measures of how well a person can hold beliefs in short-term memory and manipulate those beliefs, but they do not assess at all whether a person has the tendency to form beliefs rationally when presented with evidence." What we really want for our politicians, lawyers, doctors, and everyone else is to gauge their ability to think critically, which is largely absent from intelligence tests.

In other words, what *should* we mean when we refer to intelligence? This question leads to another and even more important question: Who is the appropriate authority to decide what it means to be intelligent? (The importance of thinking about definitions is a critical thinking skill that is presented in more detail in "Chapter 3: The Relationship between Thought and Language.") When Sternberg (1982) asked people to list the characteristics of an intelligent person, the following answers were frequently given: "reasons logically and well," "reads widely," "keeps an open mind," and "reads with high comprehension." Most people share these intuitive everyday notions of intelligence, which are consistent with the definition of critical thinking. Thus, for most people, intelligent thinking is very similar to the idea of critical thinking.

If people can learn to think better, and there are many types of evidence that show that they can, then by everyday definitions, they can learn to be intelligent. The idea that intelligence can be taught is not new. The notion of intelligence as learning and thinking was articulated early in the last century by the famous Russian psychologist, Lev Vygotsky (1978). He offered an alternative to the static view of human learning and intelligence as a "fixed quantity" that could be observed and assessed in laboratory settings. According to Vygotsky, intelligence is best indexed by the way in which people learn, especially when they receive feedback about their learning, rather than in the level of learning they have achieved at some point in time. This emphasis is not surprising in light of Vygotsky's work with disadvantaged populations in the aftermath of the Russian Revolutionary war, where many children never had the opportunity to develop their intelligence because of the severe privations of war. These same children often learned new skills and knowledge very quickly when they were given the opportunity to learn, demonstrating a level of intelligence that could not have been predicted by any standardized measure that might have been used to test them. Thus, it was their ability to learn from their experiences that Vygotsky used to define and measure intelligence, not a score on a test or similar other measure.

The Measurement of Intelligence

Rational thinking can be surprisingly dissociated from intelligence.
—Keith Stanovich (2009, p. 39)

As you can imagine, the measurement of intelligence has proven to be a difficult task. The underlying idea is that intelligence exists, and since it exists, it exists in some quantity (in each individual), and since it exists in some quantity, it can be measured. The only difficulty with this line of reasoning is: "How?"

There is an obvious need to be able to quantify or measure intelligence. Historically, intelligence tests were designed for a very practical reason. In the early part of the 20th century, the French government realized the need to know which children should receive regular classroom instruction and which should receive remedial or accelerated instruction. Binet and Simon were given the job of designing a test that could be used to place children in the appropriate educational setting. Modern day intelligence tests are still used for this purpose. The test designed in France by Binet and Simon has been revised many times. One popular revision was undertaken by Lewis Terman, a psychologist at Stanford University. Terman's revision of the earlier intelligence test is commonly referred to as the Stanford–Binet. Another popular battery of intelligence tests was written by David Wechsler. He authored two separate tests, the Wechsler Intelligence Scale for Children (WISC) and Wechsler Adult Intelligence Scale (WAIS) designed for adults over 15 years of age. The newest version of the WAIS is designated as "WAIS-IV." It yields four subscores of intelligence and an overall IQ score. The four subscores, which are usually called scales, include (a) a Verbal Comprehension Score comprised of scores on verbal subtests (e.g., similarities, vocabulary, information, and comprehension; (b) a Working Memory Score (remembering digits, arithmetic, and letter–number sequences); (c) a Perceptual Reasoning Score (making block designs, matrix reasoning, visual puzzles, picture completion, and figure weights); and (d) a Processing Speed Score (symbols search, coding, and cancellation) (Pearson Assessment, 2008).

"Which 3 of these pieces go together to make this puzzle?"

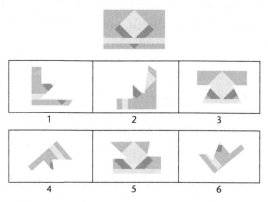

"Which one of these goes here to balance the scale?"

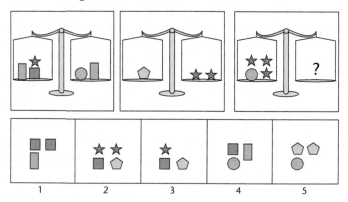

"When I say go, draw a line through each *medium blue* square and *light blue* triangle."

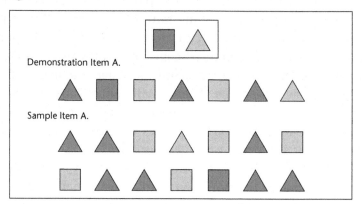

Figure 1.2 Wechsler Adult Intelligence Scale, Fourth Edition (WAIS-IV). Copyright © 2008 NCS Pearson, Inc. Reproduced with permission. All rights reserved. "Wechsler Adult Intelligence Scale" and "WAIS" are trademarks, in the United States and/or other countries, of Pearson Education, Inc. or its affiliates(s).

Sample items from three of the subtests that are new to the latest edition of the WAIS are shown in Figure 1.2.

As you can see from these items, intelligence is measured with a variety of questions. If you are hiring someone for a complex job or selecting students for admissions to a high-level educational program, you will want people who are intelligent. But, as measured with traditional tests, intelligence will be indexed as the ability to remember long lists of numbers, define words, and put puzzles together. These are important measures, but for many people, the ability to think about complex issues means that using the skills of critical thinking (for example, making strong conclusions from evidence, avoiding or minimizing common biases, and not being misled by commonly misused techniques for persuasion) is a better way to define intelligence. Critical thinking ability is not assessed with standard measures of intelligence. It is possible to obtain a high score on an intelligence test and then turn to astrology or palm reading when making decisions. Neither of these "ways of knowing" (astrology or palm reading) has any scientific basis or are better in selecting a good outcome than the proverbial "dart-throwing monkey" (a favorite phrase used by Kahneman, a Nobel Prize winner, when he wants to make the point that a random process is as good as the one being considered).

The notion of intelligence that is embedded in standardized tests is that intelligence is a fixed quantity, although recent research clearly shows the critical importance of environmental influences on intelligence. Because this text is concerned with thinking and helping you to learn how to improve your thinking, it seems reasonable to return to the question posed at the beginning of this section: "Will learning to be a critical thinker make you more intelligent?" For those psychologists who view intelligence as a fixed quantity that can be measured with test items that depend, in part, on the opportunities that are afforded to individuals (e.g., the rich have more and better educational opportunities than the poor, so on average they would be expected to score higher on intelligence tests), then their answer will be "no." However, along with an increasing number of psychologists, I believe that the static notion of intelligence is wrong and damaging. If any individual can learn to be a better thinker and subsequently can use newly acquired thinking skills across a wide variety of contexts, then I believe that, by definition, that person has learned to be more intelligent. There will always be some people who are more intelligent than others. There are individual differences and limits on how well each of us can think and reason, and certainly intelligence is also determined, in part, by genetics. However, we all have some amount of undeveloped potential; everyone can make substantial gains in his or her intellectual abilities. Even though we cannot all be geniuses, we can all learn to think more intelligently.

Many contemporary psychologists agree that intelligence is comprised of skills that can be enhanced with training. Stanovich (2009) has argued that intelligence tests do not test for rational thinking. For example, physicians who score high on standard intelligence tests may use shallow processing and choose less effective medical treatments, "smart" people may fail to assess risks, and parents may be misled by unsubstantiated claims that vaccines cause autism. He advocates for a test of critical thinking skills when assessing and conceptualizing what it means to be intelligent. (He uses the term "rational thought.") Thus, although there is a positive relationship between critical thinking and intelligence test scores, the relationship is not strong. So, will becoming a critical thinker make you smarter? No, if intelligence is measured with standardized IQ test, but yes, if we want to know how well someone thinks in everyday situations.

Becoming a Better Thinker: The Quick and Easy Way

> A sucker is born every minute.
> —P. T. Barnum (cited in Bartlett, 1980, p. 460)

As I raced through the supermarket after work one day, I was surprised to see a candy bar called "Think!" Just what I needed, a candy bar with "mind enhancing ingredients." And to think (oops, pardon the pun) that I was working hard to learn better thinking skills when all I had to do was eat a candy bar. This "food for thought" can be found on a web page that claims to advertise "natural products and more." Apparently, I am not the only one to wonder about "Think!" candy bars. The Center for Science in the Public Interest, a nonprofit organization, investigated this candy bar (Science in the Public Interest, 2000). They contacted the candy bar company for evidence to back up the claim that the ingredients in Think! can help you "stay sharp." Here's the company's response: " 'We're not claiming that it helps you think,' insists Garret Jennings, the inventor of Think!, the 'Food for Thought' bar. . . . But, if somebody feels great after a Think! Bar,' asks Jennings, 'who cares if that is just a placebo effect?'" (p. 12).

I hope that your response to the question posed at the end of the last paragraph is, "I do." A placebo is used as a control or comparison whenever drugs are tested—it is the condition that contains no active drugs—you may know it as a "sugar pill." Sometimes just the belief that we are taking a "drug" that will improve the ability to think can lead us to believe that we really are thinking better, even when we are not. But then, I guess this thinking-candy is targeted at consumers who are not good thinkers in the first place. Of course, it is possible that there are some ingredients that could enhance the ability to think. The question for thoughtful consumers is "What is the evidence that this product does what the manufacturer claims?" According to Science in the Public Interest, the answer is "none."

Unfortunately, there are no quick and easy programs that will make you a better thinker, despite some unscrupulous claims that you can think better instantly, without really trying. A trip through most so-called "health food stores" will reveal a wide variety of products and pseudo-medicines that claim or suggest that they can improve your memory, enhance your thinking, or do whatever else is desirable (e.g., make you thin, sexy, strong, and smart); there is usually little or no valid evidence that any of these products can bring about their promised effects.

Two Types of Thinking—Fast and Slow

> Bush told me, "I am a gut player, not a textbook player."
> —Bob Woodward (quoted in Love, 2010, para. 19)

Daniel Kahneman, the cognitive psychologist famous for his groundbreaking work in how people think and decide, has popularized the idea that there are two broad types of thinking, System 1 and System 2. System 1 is what is commonly thought of as intuition. It is automatic, effortless, and when it is good, it most likely associated with expertise. The quote about the way George Bush, a former president of the United States, described his thinking as from the "gut" is an example of System 1 thinking. By contrast, System 2 thinking is slow, effortful, and deliberate, and thus close in its definition to critical thinking, when it is done well.

System 1 Thinking

> Intuition is not subliminal perception; it is subtle perception and learning—knowing without knowing that you know.
> —Michael Shermer (2003, para. 11)

To understand the distinction between System 1 and System 2 thinking, try this simple exercise:

1. A bat and a ball cost $1.10

    i. The bat costs $1.00 more than the ball.

    ii. How much does the ball cost? (Kahneman, 2011, p. 44)

OK raise your hand if you said $.10—obvious and intuitive answer. If you answered $.10, the answer came to you in flash. It is as though you did not have to think at all. Unfortunately, you also came up with the wrong answer if you said $.10. With this answer, the bat is $1 and the ball is $.10, which makes the bat $.90 more than the ball. Of course, you could use simple algebra:

Bat + Ball = $1.10

and

Bat = Ball + $1.00

Now substitute the definition of Bat (it equals Ball + .10) into the first equation and you get

Ball + $1.00 + Ball = $1.10

2 Ball = $1.10—$1.00

2 Ball = $.10

Ball = $.05

If you gave the incorrect, but intuitive answer, you are in good company. More than half of the students at Harvard, MIT, and Princeton gave this answer, and more than 80% of the students at less selective universities did as well (Frederick, 2005). The Cognitive Reflection Test is a three-question test that assesses the extent to which people tend to give intuitive answers to simple problems. One of the three questions is the bat and ball question. The other two questions are

2. If it takes 5 machines 5 minutes to make 5 widgets, how long would it take 100 machines to make 100 widgets? ___ minutes

3. In a lake, there is a patch of lily pads. Every day, the patch doubles in size. It if take 48 days for the patch to cover the entire lake, how long would it take for the patch to cover half the lake? ____ days

How did you do? Did you answer 100 minutes for the second question? Buzz— as you probably guessed by now, that is the wrong answer. The correct answer is five minutes. The third problem appeared in all earlier versions of this book and was originally attributed to Fixx (1978, p. 50). The only way to solve this problem is to work backwards. Can you solve it with this hint? If the lake is covered on the 48th day and the area covered by the lilies doubles every day, how much of the lake is covered on the 47th day? The answer is half. Thus, by working backwards, the problem is easy to solve.

Respondents who gave the intuitive, fast, and in this case, wrong responses, were less likely to delay rewards (for example, they were more likely to prefer getting $5 now than $7 next week), thus suggesting that people who rely more on intuitive and quick thinking differ in other important ways.

Intuition

It's no secret that when researchers have pitted intuition against statistical prediction, the formula usually wins. Statistical prediction is fallible. But for predicting future behavior, human intuition—even professional intuition—is even more fallible.

—David Myers (2010, p. 376)

We love stories about human intuition. I remember spending an evening with a friend, who suddenly said that she was thinking about a third person whom we both knew well. This third friend was "very pregnant," a strange description for someone who has already gone past the projected due date that was given to her by her obstetrician. Wouldn't it be weird if this overdue friend was having her baby just when we thought about her? Well, actually no, although it might seem that way.

The intuitions of experts differ from everyday intuitions in important ways—most importantly, they are more likely to be useful if (1) the area of expertise is one that is governed by regularities and (2) the expert had repeated experience with immediate feedback in that area. It seems that these two criteria can explain why "professional intuition is sometimes marvelous and sometimes flawed" (Kahneman & Klein, 2009). Consider chess players. Expert chess players actually organize the information on a chess board into meaningful units in just fractions of a second (de Groot, 1946, 1965), and expert Scrabble players can recall more information on Scrabble boards, with those players with the longest history of playing out-performing experts who played fewer years (Halpern & Wai, 2007). In other words, experts developed a quick knowledge in these domains that have regular rules that can be learned over time. Or, consider this example (Klein, Calderwood, & Clinton-Cirocco, 1986). An experienced firefighter led several firefighters into the kitchen in a burning building. It was very quiet in the burning building, but something was not right—he did not know what it was, but he ordered everyone out of the building immediately. The building soon blew up. This experienced firefighter had a "sixth sense" about the danger. But another way of understanding his intuition that something very bad was about to happen is to think about the situation as recognition. Perhaps his feet were too warm—maybe this registered consciously and maybe it did not, but the fire was under the kitchen floor and the pattern of sensations on his body differed from the ones he felt when the fire was in an adjacent room. It is much like the superior recognizing abilities of the expert chess or Scrabble player. This intuition was the result of many years of practice with feedback (knowledge of results) regarding fires. It is not a magical gift that is possessed by a few lucky individuals. Years of practice can pay off with superior abilities to recognize situations, but only if the expert has received immediate feedback about earlier decisions and has been able to use that feedback in ways that make him a "true" expert in a field where there are regularities such as firefighting.

By contrast, the intuitions of experts where the domain is highly irregular or they do not get immediate feedback for their decisions are not any better than those of a novice. Kahneman reviews evidence showing that the professionals who select stocks for investment are no better at this task than novices because the field is so irregular they cannot learn what makes some stocks increase in value and others decrease. Interestingly, regardless of the quality of the intuitions, many people are highly confident in their ability to make rapid decisions that are correct. Kahneman tells about an early job that he had in the Israeli army selecting recruits who would undergo leadership training. Kahneman devised a task in which groups of eight men had to work together to lift an enormous pole over a high wall. He observed who took charge, who gave up, and who devised a plan that worked and persuaded others to carry it out. Confidently, he selected those who were most likely to become leaders and recommended them for additional training. One big problem—this test, which seemed to be so good to him (and sounds good to me), really did not work; there was no relationship between how the recruits performed on this task and their later abilities as leaders, yet Kahneman was highly confident in his expertise in this area. What was missing? He did not get immediate feedback on how well the selected future leaders performed in real leadership tasks, so he never developed the skill in knowing when and why a particular selection was right or wrong.

Intuitions are like visual illusions in some ways. They can sometimes help us understand the world, but they are often distorting and very difficult to ignore.

The two tables tops in Figure 1.3 appear to be very different in their size and shape, but if you cut out a piece of paper to fit over one table top, you would find that it also fit perfectly over the other table top. This is a common visual illusion. Thinking illusions, such as the belief that our intuitions are most often correct, are similar to visual illusions. With effort, we can learn that our intuitions are often wrong and we can use that knowledge to be wary of our own intuitions and those of others. Additionally, we can learn when intuitions are more likely to be correct—when they are done by an expert who has had repeated experience with feedback in her field of expertise.

In deciding when to trust the intuitions (or fast thinking) of an expert, ask these three questions: How much experience does the expert have that is directly relevant to the task? Is it a task where there are regular outcomes

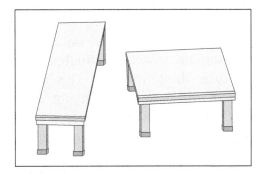

Figure 1.3 "Illustration of two tables," from the book *Mind Sights: Original Visual Illusions, Ambiguities, and Other Anomalies* by Roger N. Shepard. Copyright © 1990 by Roger N. Shepard. Reprinted by permission of Henry Holt and Company, LLC.

can be learned from experience? Is the "expert" in a field where there is immediate feedback about the quality of the decisions that were made?

System 2 Thinking

> Both self-control and cognitive effort are forms of mental work.
> —Daniel Kahneman (2011, p. 41)

Critical thinking is System 2 thinking. It is slow, deliberate, and effortful. It is also the engine that drives System 1 thinking, because the fast recognition processes of System 1 were originally learned in a deliberate and effortful way. If System 1 can be thought of as intuition, then System 2 can be thought of as critical thinking. It involves weighing evidence, evaluating risk, calculating probabilities, judging credibility, and similar activities that are the hallmark of good thinking. Thinking can be rational and people can learn to engage in rational thinking. We can learn from our mistakes, and by keeping track of them, make them less likely to occur in the future.

If you are familiar with Malcolm Gladwell, the popular writer for The New Yorker magazine and author of many books, you probably know about his notion of "Blink." According to Gladwell, it is sort of intuitive thinking that happens rapidly—in the time it takes to blink. In his book by this name, he tells many stories about the way professionals arrived at good decisions without going through the hard work and time-consuming effort to consider all available and relevant information. Indeed, there are many good stories where the rapid cognitive processes of System 1 thinking do a good job. But it is important to keep in mind that these stories tend to be about experts who spent many thousands of hours doing the hard work of System 2 thinking before they got good at making fast, intuitive decisions. Holt (2011) summed up the relationship between System 1 and System 2 thinking this way: "If you've had 10,000 hours of training in a predictable, rapid-feedback environment—chess, firefighting, anesthesiology—then blink. In all other cases, think" (para.23). This is good advice. You will learn the skills associated with System 2 thinking throughout this book, and after you put in the hard work of developing expertise, then you can be more confident of your intuitions.

Bounded Rationality

> We do understand today many of the mechanisms of human rational choice. We do know how the information processing system called Man, faced with complexity beyond his ken, uses his information pro-

cessing capacities to seek out alternatives, to calculate consequences, to resolve uncertainties, and thereby—sometimes, not always—to find ways of action that are sufficient unto the day, that satisfice.

—Herbert A. Simon (Nobel Memorial Lecture, 1978, p. 368)

In 1978, Herbert Simon was recognized with a Nobel Prize for understanding the boundaries of human thinking, especially when people are confronted with complex and changing environments. Simon coined the term "bounded rationality," which is a label for the idea that people are not completely rational; there are limits or boundaries on our ability to think rationally. We are limited by the fact that we can never have complete knowledge of the consequences of our decisions because the consequences will occur sometime in the future, and the future can never be known with certainty. We can never generate a complete list of alternative decisions, and very often, the amount of information we need to consider when making decisions is more that we can keep in mind at one time. Most of the time, people are **satisficers**, which means that they make "good enough" decisions. I return to Simon's notion of satisficing later in this book when I discuss decision making.

Fast and Frugal Thinking

Relying too heavily on intuition has its perils. Cogent medical judgments meld first impressions with deliberate analysis.

—Jerome Groopman (2007, p. 9)

Although Kahneman has been described as "the most important social scientist of his generation" (Goldstein, 2011), there are critics of his work. Gigerenzer, (2007; Gigerenzer, Hoffrage, & Goldstein, 2008) a German psychologist, takes a more positive view of rapid System 1-type thinking, stating that many of our "thinking shortcuts" are smart and lead to good decisions. According to Gigerenzer, thinking shortcuts are "fast and frugal," where frugal means that they do not require extensive mental work, and they are effective when time and information are limited. Here is one of Gigerenzer's favorite examples to demonstrate the (sometimes) superiority of fast and frugal thinking:

Which city has a higher larger population: San Diego or San Antonio? (Goldstein & Gigerenzer, 2002, p. 76)

If you live in the United States, you probably know something about the relative size of these two cities and will use that knowledge to answer that San Diego has a larger population. But, what if you live in Germany, and you have little or no knowledge about the relative size of these two cities. Guess what, you are more likely to answer correctly than are Americans who are more likely to know something about the comparative size of these two cities. Approximately two-thirds of people in the United States correctly answered that San Diego has a larger population than San Antonio. If you live outside the United States, it is likely that you have heard something about San Diego, maybe its world famous zoo or beautiful beaches, but never heard of San Antonio. You would quickly reason that a city you heard of is probably larger than one that you never heard of, and in this example, you would be correct. In fact, in one study, 100% of the respondents from Germany answered this question correctly (Goldstein & Gigerenzer, 2002). Gigerenzer uses examples like this one as evidence that intuitive fast thinking can be better than slow thinking.

But critics of the idea that fast thinking is better thinking have been vocal. For example, Groopman (2007) wrote a book describing how good doctors think, especially when they make diagnoses. He began his book with a story about a woman who had suffered with irritable bowel syndrome for many years, and, despite numerous doctor visits, her condition continued to get worse. After seeing somewhere between 15 and 30 different physicians, she found one that did not make a fast and frugal diagnosis—he did not rely on his first hunch or intuition. Instead, he painstakingly considered a wide variety of possible causes for her illness—recognizing that rare illnesses do occur. Instead of treating her for irritable bowel syndrome, he reassessed her illness history and came up with a new diagnosis that led to different treatments and ultimately to getting better. This is just one of many examples in which the fast and intuitive processes in thinking were wrong.

So, what can we conclude from all of the examples of fast and slow thinking? Fast thinking is more likely to be good thinking when done by an expert in the field where intuitions were born from thousands of hours of more careful thinking and with feedback. Sometimes we can rely on thinking short-cuts, but most often, we will need to put in the hard work of thinking before we should trust our intuitions or those of others.

Emotions Color our Thinking

What I want to believe based on emotions and what I should believe based on evidence does not always coincide.

—Michael Shermer (2009, para. 3)

A key idea from the field of classical economics is that people are rational, which means that they think in ways that maximize outcomes. But, as Simon, Kahneman, and others have shown, people are far from rational. For example, suppose that you are playing the Ultimatum Game. It is a simple game. There are two players. One of the players is given some money and told to divide it between herself and a second player. If the second player accepts the split, each side keeps what they have, but if the second player rejects the split, neither side gets to keep any money. Ready to play?

> Game 1. I am given $50 and I decided to give you $25. Is this OK with you?
>
> Almost everyone agrees to a 50–50 split.
>
> Game 2. I am given $50 and I decide to give you $2. Is this OK with you?
>
> Probably not. It is likely that you would decide to get no money at all rather than accept the $2 offered.

Now this is not a rational choice because it means that you will get no money at all instead of the $2 I offered you, but it is a likely one because people want a fair division, and when the division strays too far from fair, people reject the choice. It will probably not surprise readers to learn that there is considerable support for the idea that emotions are important influences on how and what we think. In support of this idea, psychologists used brain imaging techniques (functional magnetic resonance imaging, fMRI) that can detect which areas of the brain are active when people perform different tasks (Sanfrey, Rilling, Aronson, Nystron, & Cohen 2003). They found that participants who rejected an offer while playing the Ultimatum Game showed high levels of activity in brain areas that are related to emotion and cognition. These images correlated with participants' reports that they felt angry when the other player offered them an unfair amount of money. The authors conclude that "models of decision making cannot afford to ignore emotion as a vital and dynamic component of our decisions and choices in the real world" (p. 1,758).

Unconscious Influences on How We Think

> At long last, we have scientific guidance regarding that great question of social lubrication: Should you ask someone to meet for a drink or a cup of coffee.
>
> —Lawrence Williams and John Bargh (2008, p. 606)

We are often unaware of the multiples influences on how we think, feel, and behave. Something in the environment can trigger a stream of thought without our being aware of the trigger. Bargh and his colleagues (Bargh, 2008; Bargh & Williams, 2006) referred to the unconscious influences as the "automaticity of everyday life." They happen automatically without any conscious intent or awareness. Here are some examples.

In one study (Bargh, 2007), students showed up in a laboratory waiting room ready to participate in an experiment. When the researcher showed up, he had his hands full with books, clip boards, and a cup of coffee. He asked the participants to hold the coffee while he opened the door to the laboratory. Half of the participants held a hot cup of coffee; the other half held a cup of ice coffee. The participants who held the hot coffee rated a third person as "warmer" than those who held the ice coffee. None of the participants believed the coffee could have influenced the way they rated a third person, but it did. Many did not even recall if the coffee they held was hot or cold, but it affected the way the thought about a person whom they just met.

Along similar lines, when people lifted a heavy clipboard as opposed to a light one, they were more likely to evaluate a job candidate as "better over-all" and as having "more serious interest in the position," suggesting that the additional weight of the clip board unconsciously triggered ideas of being weighty and serious (Ackerman, Nocera, & Bargh, 2010). In addition, when participants sat on a hard chair as opposed to those who sat on a soft chair, they were more likely to make judgments about a hypothetical employee that reflected "strictness, rigidity, and stability" (p. 1,714). It seems clear that the way we think about people and objects in the world is influenced in ways that we are not only unaware of, but seem hard to believe.

We cannot know about all of the influences on our behavior, but we can develop an awareness of our environment that can help. If for example, you notice that you have positive feelings about a store that always plays upbeat positive music, you can consider the possibility that it is the music that is creating or contributing to how you feel about this store.

Thinking about Thinking

You are today where your thoughts have brought you; you will be to-morrow where your thoughts take you.

—James Lane Allen

There are many different ways to conceptualize the thinking process. From the perspective of a neuropsychologist or biologist, thinking is the activation of groups of neurons. Other researchers study the medium of thought, the conscious and unconscious use of symbols, images, and words. Another approach is to conceptualize thinking as the flow and transformation of information through a series of stages. But, can our brain reveal its own mysteries? Can we use our brain to think about how we use our brain to think?

Thinking as a Biological Process

The brain exists in order to construct representations of the world.
—Philip Johnson-Laird (quoted in Restak, 1988, p. 235)

Researchers from many fields have spent their lifetimes trying to understand what people do when they think. Brain researchers are interested in understanding how the brain and other parts of the nervous system work. Every time you have a thought, feel an emotion, or receive information through your senses, your nervous system is involved. If you could examine your own brain, you would no doubt be surprised to find that it looks like a giant mushy walnut with the consistency of a soft-boiled egg. There is nothing in its appearance to even suggest that it is the foundation of human thought.

The capacity of the human brain is awesome. "If each of the brain's 10 to 15 billion neurons is capable of only two states, on or off, the capacity of the brain would be 2^{10} billionth power. To write out this number at the rate of one digit per second would take ninety years" (The Chronicle of Higher Education, 1987, p. A2). Even if these figures are off by a few billion or so, and more recent estimates put the number of neurons as somewhere between 86 billion and 100 billion, it is clear that we each have some undeveloped potential. The human brain has remained essentially unchanged since the dawn of modern history, yet during that time humans have used this amazing mass to develop advanced technologies that include the ability to visit distant planets and have more than doubled the average expected life span. What has changed is "the information that is going into the brain and the processing it receives" (Machado, cited in Walsh, 1981, p. 640.) It is the ability to learn and to think that has changed the world.

Everything that we are or ever will be can, at least on one level, be attributed to patterns of neurons that communicate via chemical messengers. The connections among neurons change as a function of experience (and genetically coded information). Experience is the major architect of the brain. Consider, for example, a study in which adolescent girls played the popular computer game called "Tetris" for 1.5 hours a week for three months (Haier, Karama, Leyba, & Jung, 2009). In Tetris, different shapes appear to fall across the computer screen. The player learns to rotate each piece so that it completes a row at the bottom of the screen. Neuroimaging of the girls' brains before and after training showed increased cortical thickness relative to control participants (who did not play Tetris) that were associated with Tetris training. These large changes in the structure of the brain resulted from a relatively small manipulation. We can change our brains by selecting different sorts of experiences. Every time you learn something new, you have changed your brain. If you have learned anything new since you started reading this book, you are already a changed person—I have "messed with" your brain. I hope you will agree that I left it better than it was before you started reading.

Thinking as Imagery and Silent Speech

> Thinking is the talking of the soul with itself.
>
> —Author unknown; found in a fortune cookie

Psychologists at the beginning of the 20th century believed that thinking was composed of mental images. Later, other psychologists hypothesized that thinking was simply a form of "silent speech," much like talking to yourself without vocalization. In order to test these hypotheses, psychologists would ask subjects to describe what they did when responding to certain questions. Let's try some examples. As you answer each question posed below, try to be aware of what you did as you "thought about it."

1. How many windows are in your living room?
2. What does your mother look like?
3. What letter comes after N in the alphabet?
4. Name a word that rhymes with "shoe."
5. How much is 2 + 3?
6. Can you define "critical thinking?"

As you answered these questions, were you aware of the use of images and/or words? Most people find that when they are asked to describe some concrete object, like the number of windows in their living room or their mother, they are aware of picture-like images. In fact, it seems almost impossible to answer these questions without generating an internal

THE FAMILY CIRCUS   By Bil Keane

"Thinking is when the picture is in your head
with the sound turned off."

The Family Circus by Bil Keane. Used with permission by King Features.

representation or utilizing **imagery** in some way. Can you describe your mother or anyone else without creating an image? Questions like 3 or 4, which involve the order of letters in the alphabet and the sounds of words, usually require an individual to recite the items silently. (Did you sing "l-m-n-o-p" to yourself in order to answer Question 3?) When answering questions like 5 and 6, people are often unable to say how they arrived at an answer. (By the way, if your answer to Question 6 was "no," you should go back and reread the beginning sections in this chapter.) Most people feel that the answers just seemed to "pop into their heads" without their being conscious of the "medium" or "stuff" of thought.

Sometimes, thinking can be improved if we "work at" generating an image or using speech-like thought. Albert Einstein often credited his ability to solve difficult problems to his extensive use of imagery. The most famous use of imagery was recorded by the chemist Kekulé. He knew that if he could understand the structure of a benzene molecule he would have hit on one of the most important discoveries in organic chemistry. Kekulé knew that most chemical molecules are long strands of atoms, and that the structure of a benzene molecule had to be different. In order to solve this problem, Kekulé practiced generating visual images that might help him to find the right one. His hard work was rewarded when the historic answer came to him this way: "Again the atoms were gamboling before my eyes . . . My mental eye . . . could now distinguish larger structures . . . all twining and twisting in a snakelike motion. But look! What was that! One of the snakes had seized hold of its own tail, and the form whirled mockingly before my eyes. As if by a sudden flash of lightning I awoke" (Kekulé, quoted in Rothenberg, 1979, pp. 395–396; I note here that some experts are not convinced that this is a true story).

Words also serve to direct and stimulate thought. Although it may be obvious that thoughts are usually communicated with language, it is also true that language helps to generate thoughts. The generative role of language can be seen in an experiment by Glucksberg and Weisberg (1966). They used a classic problem in the psychology literature that was originally devised by Duncker (1945). In this problem, subjects are required to attach a candle to a wall so that it could be lit. They are given a candle, a box of matches, and some thumbtacks. Stop now and think how you would go about solving this problem if you were given only these materials. Do not go on until you've thought about it.

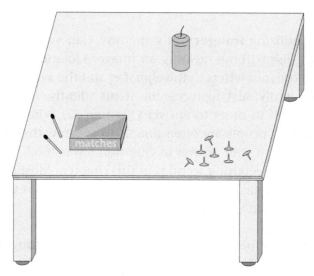

Figure 1.4 Using only the materials show in this figure, how would you attach the candle to the wall so that it can be burned?

The best solution is to dump the matches from their box, tack the box to the wall and set the candle in the box. Most subjects have difficulty with this task because they fail to think of the box as part of the solution—they see it only as a "box of matches." Glucksberg and Weisberg had people solve this problem under one of two conditions. The items were either labeled ("box," "tacks," "candle," and "matches") or they were not labeled. Subjects in the labeled condition solved the problem in about one minute, while those in the unlabeled condition took an average of nine minutes. The labels directed attention to the relevant items and changed how the subjects in the first group solved this problem. (I return to this problem in Chapter 9, where I discuss problems in problem solving.)

Let's consider a different example of the way language directs thought. There is a popular riddle that goes something like this:

> A young boy and his father went for a Sunday drive. A drunken driver swerved in front of their car, killing the father on impact. The young boy was rushed to the nearest hospital where the chief of neurosurgery was summoned to perform an operation. Upon seeing the boy, the chief of neurosurgery cried out, "I can't operate on him, he's my son!" How is this possible?

When I've posed this riddle to students, they have sometimes replied: "The chief of neurosurgery is the boy's stepfather"; "The real father didn't die"; or "It's impossible." Have you guessed the correct answer? The answer is that the chief of neurosurgery is the boy's mother. The reason for the difficulty is that in our society, when we hear terms like "chief of neurosurgery" we tend to consider only males. The words we use can determine the kinds of thoughts we think. (This concept is developed more fully in Chapter 3.)

Critical Thinking: Hollywood Style

Unfortunately, critical thinking sometimes has a pejorative connotation. This is especially true in common media depictions of the good thinker as someone who is cold and calculating. The quintessential example of stereotype is the pointy-eared Mr. Spock of Star Trek fame. As you probably know, Mr. Spock is a fictitious character from the popular television series and movies about space travel in the distant future. Spock, as he is most commonly called, is only half-human, a fact that is revealed by his pointy-ears.

The other half of his bi-species heritage is Vulcan, a species of being whose thinking is totally rational. In fact, he is so reasoned, that he is unable to understand the mushy and sentimental emotions that seem to plague mere humans—emotions like love and hate, which have no rational counterpart. The media depiction of this popular fictitious character presents the message that rational thought is cold and incompatible with human feelings.

Other times, the media depicts the "good thinker" or good student as the "nerd." The good thinker is rarely the attractive beauty queen or the athletic stud. More typically, this character is ridiculed for wearing thick glasses (often held together with masking tape), wiping at or sniffing with chronic rhinitis, and expressing a predilection for plaid clothing. This negative message about good thinking is a common theme in movies made for the huge teen market. In many ways, the idea that thinking reflectively or following a reasoned plan of action instead of an emotional one is made to appear "uncool." The impulsive and dashing bubbleheads who are portrayed as the heroes in this genre of immensely profitable movies are as ludicrous a stereotype as the nerdy good thinker. Perhaps if the movies showed the lives of these stereotyped teens a few years later, when the impulsive bubblehead is working at a low-paying job (or in jail) and the nerdy thinker is doing interesting work for a better salary, critical thinking would suddenly look very "cool." As long as these stereotyped movie images make money, it will be difficult to correct these negative stereotypes and make critical thinking a desirable goal.

The negative image of thinking is not just restricted to teen movies. After every televised presidential debate, a small army of "spin masters" come on the air to tell the American public what the candidates just said. Their task is to put a positive "spin" on their preferred candidate (e.g., He provided a clear vision for America . . . blah, blah, blah) and a negative spin on the opponent (e.g., He was perspiring and did not smile enough . . . blah, blah, blah). In one retelling of what the candidates just said, a prominent spin master faulted the opposition candidate for providing too much information and for hesitating before answering complex questions! It seems to be the expected format that candidates will provide quotable snippets that are completely unrelated to reasoned responses about immensely important issues (e.g., I knew John Kennedy and you're no John Kennedy; Read my lips!) and short answers that reduce complex issues to one liners. The general public often responds negatively when candidates give thoughtful, intelligent responses to complex questions, perhaps because we have been conditioned to associate this sort of response with the "loser" image that Hollywood and the other media seem to enjoy.

Critical thinking has been unfairly portrayed as cold and unemotional. The desirable goal of a problem or decision is often based on values, feelings, and predilections. In addition, one frequently recommended skill in improving an outcome is to try to "see" the issue from the perspective of other individuals. Empathy, imagination, and value setting are all part of critical thinking.

Becoming a Better Thinker: A Skills Approach

Critical thinking skills are those strategies for finding ways to reach a goal. Of course, dividing the thinking process, which is fluid and continuous, into discrete skills is artificial, but it is necessary to break the massive topic of critical thinking into manageable pieces. Although I have divided the topic of critical thinking into several chapters, each of which focuses on a different type of problem (e.g., reasoning, analyzing arguments, testing hypotheses, making decisions, and estimating likelihoods), these problems are not easily separable in real life. You will often need to estimate likelihoods when making a decision or generate possible solutions in a reasoning task. The division is necessary for teaching and learning and is not meant to imply that critical thinking can be cut into neat packages.

The development of critical thinking skills requires specific instruction, practice in a variety of contexts, feedback, and time to develop. I hope that working your way through this book will be mostly enjoyable and well worth all of the effort. An important part of learning is applying the skills of critical thinking to the many different examples that appear throughout the book. To become a critical thinker, you will need to practice, practice, practice. As the old joke goes, it is the only way to get to Carnegie Hall. So, please get comfortable, prepare for some interesting work, and enjoy this book.

Chapter Summary

- The rapidly accelerating pace of change and widespread availability of a glut of information has made the ability to think critically more important than at any other time in history.

- Critical thinking can be defined as the use of those cognitive skills or strategies that increase the probability of a desirable outcome. It is used to describe thinking that is purposeful, reasoned, and goal directed.

- There is considerable empirical evidence from a variety of sources that cognitive skills can be learned from instruction specifically designed to teach these skills and that these skills transfer to real-world settings when they are practiced in multiple contexts.

- Developing a critical thinking attitude and disposition is at least as important as developing the skills of critical thinking. The skills are useless if they are not used. The attitude of a critical thinker must be cultivated and valued.

- The attitude or disposition for critical thinking includes the willingness to plan, flexibility, persistence, the willingness to acknowledge one's errors and change your mind when the evidence supports a change in position, being mindful, and consensus-seeking.

- Metacognition refers to people's knowledge of their own thought processes. We often have little conscious awareness of how we think. Self-monitoring your own thought processes is one way to improve how you think.

- It is useful to consider thinking as having two components—a fast or intuitive component known as System 1 and a slower, more deliberate component known as System 2. Critical thinking is System 2 thinking.

- Although many people believe in their powers of intuition, intuitive thinking is more likely to be good thinking when done by an expert who has had repeated experience with feedback in her field of expertise.

- There are limits or boundaries on how rational people can be. Because we can never have complete information or know the outcome of our decisions with certainty, people are satisficers, which means that in most circumstances, they make "good enough" decisions.

- Emotions interact with how we think and can lead us to make decisions that are not purely rational. We are thinking and feeling beings; the emotional aspects of thinking cannot be ignored.

- What and how we think are influenced by multiple environmental cues that we are not aware of and that most of us find hard to believe are affecting the judgments we make.

- People report that thinking sometimes seems to rely on visual imagery and sentence-like propositions. There are individual differences and task differences in the use of these modes of thought.

- Remember, you are what (and how) you think! Have fun with this book.

Terms to Know

You should be able to define the following terms and concepts. A good way to review and check your comprehension is to cover up the definition, try to define each term, and then uncover the definition and compare your answer with the brief one that is provided. (Your answer is expected to be more complete that the one presented in this review.) The goal is not to memorize the terms; instead, you should be sure that your definition captures the meaning of the term. Be sure to cover the definition because it is easy to believe you know it when the answer is in front of you, but hard to fool yourself when you have to generate your own answer. If you find that you're having difficulty with any term, be sure to reread the section in which it is discussed.

Critical Thinking. The use of those cognitive skills or strategies that increase the probability of a desirable outcome. It is purposeful, reasonable, and goal directed. Also known as directed thinking. Compare with nondirected thinking.

Nondirected Thinking. Daydreams, night dreams, and rote memorization. Compare with directed (or critical) thinking.

Transfer of Training. The spontaneous use of skills that are learned in one context in a different context.

Habit of Planning. The repeated use of plans until the process becomes automatic.

Self-regulation. Using feedback, monitoring comprehension, and assessing progress toward a goal.

Self-justification. Making excuses for a belief or a behavior instead of considering the possibility that the belief or behavior may be wrong.

Metacognition. Our knowledge about our memory and thought process. Colloquially, what we know about what we know.

Intelligence. The ability to reason, plan, solve problems, and think abstractly.

System 1 Thinking. Type of thinking that is fast and effortless. It is sometimes thought of an intuition.

System 2 Thinking. Type of thinking that is slow and effortful. It informs System 1 thinking. Critical thinking is System 2 thinking.

Imagery. The use of an internal picture-like representation while thinking.

Critical Thinking Attitude. The willingness to plan, be flexible in one's thinking, be persistent, to self-correct, maintain mindful attention to the thought process, and seek consensus. It is not possible to be a critical thinker without this sort of attitude.

CHAPTER 2

THINKING STARTS HERE
MEMORY AS THE MEDIATOR OF COGNITIVE PROCESSES

Contents

In 1984, James Curtis Williams was convicted of a horrific crime that included the rape and shooting of a 27-year-old woman outside a Dallas bar and the theft of her car. The victim identified him as her assailant. In addition, three men testified that they saw two Black men with her car, and the three of them identified Williams as one of the men. In 2010, the Dallas police accepted Williams' request for DNA testing using the biological evidence that had been collected at the time of the crime. The DNA matched that of another man who was currently incarcerated for other crimes. Williams was declared innocent after spending over 25 years behind bars. There are many similar cases on the website of the Innocence Project, where the authors explain that misidentification is the greatest single cause of wrongful convictions. "Research shows that the human mind is not like a tape recorder; we neither record events exactly as we see them, nor recall them like a tape that has been rewound. Instead, witness memory is like any other evidence at a crime scene; it must be preserved carefully and retrieved methodically, or it can be contaminated" (Innocence Project, Understanding the Causes). We can be certain that we are remembering with great accuracy and be very wrong.

Try to imagine what life would be like if you had no memory. For most of us, this is a frightening thought. A loss of memory is a kind of death. If we had no memory for our past, the people we are would no longer exist, even if our bodies continued to function. Our memories are our most valuable possession. I do not know anyone who would sell the memories he or she has accumulated over a lifetime, no matter how much money was offered. Life without memory is unfathomable.

All intelligent systems (e.g., humans, computers, dogs, cockroaches) have the ability to learn and remember. These abilities play a crucial role in all of our lives. Most importantly, they are inevitable consequences of living. Because the ability to think clearly depends, in large part, on how well we can utilize past experiences, memory is a central topic in developing thinking skills. **Thinking** is often defined as the manipulation or alteration of an internal representation. People use information in memory and, in the process, the way the information is represented in memory is changed. Thinking is a cognitive process—what and how we think depends on what we know—the contents of our memories. In this chapter, we consider current views of how memory works, why forgetting occurs, when memory can be misleading, and ways to improve memory.

All thinking skills are inextricably tied to the ability to remember. Consider, for example, the perception of risk. Psychologists have found that hazards that are unusually memorable, such as a recent disaster or a sensationalized depiction in a film or televised newscast (e.g., stories about teenagers who kill their parents and knife-wielding wives who mutilate their husbands) distort people's perception of risk. Most people rate dramatic causes of death such as earthquake or shark attack to be many times more likely than they actually are, while less memorable causes of death are routinely underestimated (Lichtenstein et al., 1978).

The distortion in perceived risk is due to the sorts of events that people can think of when they make judgments about risk. People fear adverse events that are most readily available in memory. Consider, for example, the horrific attacks in the United States on 9/11/2001. For days, videos of airplanes flying into the World Trade Center in New York were played and replayed on television, web sites, and social media. The shocking images have been seared into the memories of many people who were old enough at the time to have seen them repeatedly. In the aftermath of 9/11, many people, especially in the United States, but in many other countries as well, decided that it was safer to drive than to fly. But, in fact, driving is far more lethal than flying, even when we include deaths from terrorist attacks. It is estimated that the additional auto traffic following 9/11 caused 2,170 more deaths on the road (Blalock, Kadiyali, & Simon, 2005). People tend to fear the wrong things. I do not mean to minimize the horrors of terrorist attacks, but we need to remember that terrorism is a psychological phenomenon designed to create fear and change how people live their lives. In fact, people are far more likely to die in a car accident, but most people do not have an appropriate fear of car accidents, because when they think about driving, they recall their many accident-free car trips. The ease with which we recall something is a critical determinant of how we think about it, but with conscious thought (and some data comparisons from a reliable source), we can get better at assessing risks.

Another example of the centrality of memory to the thinking process can be seen in decision making by juries. The jury process is at the heart of the legal system in many countries.

For countries that have a jury system, it is one of the most cherished rights as citizens. A group of strangers is cloistered in a small room for the sole purpose of evaluating evidence pertaining to the guilt or innocence of an accused. The synthesis, analysis, and weighing of evidence that is often contradictory is a complex cognitive process, which like all cognitive processes, depends on what is remembered as well as how jurors think about the information they remember (Bornstein & Green, 2011). If you were the attorney in a trial, you would want to make sure that the jurors (or judges) remembered the information that was favorable to your side because they cannot consider information in their deliberations if they cannot remember it. Attorneys who want to be sure that their information is recalled are often advised to show photos of their witnesses during the closing arguments so that jurors can remember who said what during the trial (Wilcox, n.d.). In addition, trial lawyers repeat key points throughout the trial to help jurors and judges remember them. (You will find that I repeat key points throughout this text for the same reason.) The critical importance of memory cannot be understated, whether it is in the context of a physician making a diagnosis, a voter deciding how to cast a vote, or a student preparing for an exam.

Memory: The Acquisition, Retention, and Retrieval of Knowledge

It's a poor sort of memory that only works backward.
—Lewis Carroll (1871)

The relationship among learning, retaining, and recalling involves the passage of time. Let's clarify this with an example. When you finish reading this section of the book, you should be able to answer a question like: "What is the relationship between learning, retaining, and recalling?" If you write the correct answer on an exam, your professor will infer that sometime before the exam you learned the relevant material, you retained it (kept it in memory), and you were able to recall it (retrieve it from memory) when it was needed. Learning and memory are not observable behaviors. They must be inferred from the activity of recall, such as writing the correct answer on a test.

If I asked you what notable athletic event occurred in London in 2012, and you answered correctly, then I would infer that you learned, retained, and recalled that London was the site of the 2012 Olympic Games. If you are unable to answer this question, then either: (a) you never learned the fact in question; or (b) you learned it, but forgot it; or (c) you could recall it in some other situation, maybe with some recall cues.

The relationship between learning and memory is a temporal one (time-based) that is depicted on the time line in Figure 2.1.

Something happens at Time 1 that we call learning or the acquisition of information. Following Time 1 is an interval, which can be as short as a few thousandths of a second or as long as a lifetime. Retention of information during this time interval is attributed to memory, but indexed by retrieval. At Time 2, the individual exhibits some behavior, like correctly answering an exam question that allows us to infer that the material was both learned and remembered.

Memories are Stored in Associative Networks

> Memory is deceptive because it is colored by today's events.
> —Albert Einstein (1879–1955)

Information is stored in long-term memory (other types of memory are discussed later in this chapter) in **associative networks**, which are spider-like organizations of information in which closely related topics are located near each other (e.g., woman-man; plane-train) and those that bear little

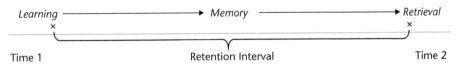

Figure 2.1 A time line depicting the relationship between learning, memory, and retrieval.

relationship to each other (e.g., woman-printer; plane-Lady Gaga) are farther away. Objects, emotions, and actions that frequently occur together become linked in memory so that when we retrieve information, one memory reminds us of a related concept, which reminds us of another, and so on. An example should help with this abstract concept.

Suppose I ask you to think about video games. Some of you have a great deal of knowledge about video games and can describe many different ones, the rules for playing them, and the differences between shooter games and strategy games. If you are knowledgeable about video games, you know about the type of strategic thinking needed to succeed in *World of Warcraft* or *Angry Birds*. It is likely that most readers are not scratching their heads and uttering, "huh?" at the mention of *World of Warcraft* or *Angry Birds*, two games that each claim tens of millions of players. If you are familiar with these games, you have an interconnected knowledge structure complete with the rules and strategies for playing them. If you know any *Angry Birds* addicts, you probably know that the goal is to destroy the green pigs who are stealing the birds' eggs. So, just by reading the words "angry birds," you are also activating your knowledge of related concepts, such as green pigs. If, on the other hand, you know little or nothing about these games, then you are no more likely to start thinking about green pigs than you are to think about the man in the moon when you read the words *Angry Birds*.

For a more mundane example, think about babies. You know that they often cry, wear diapers, drink breast milk or infant formula, and so on. These related concepts are all activated when you think about babies because they are associated in your memory. These associations affect how we think and act, often without our awareness. Here is an example of the associated nature of concepts in memory taken from Buonomano's (2011) book that explains how the brain works and why it sometimes works in flawed ways:

Answer the following three questions:

1. What continent is Kenya in?
2. What are the two opposing colors in the game of chess?
3. Name any animal.

Buonomano reports that approximately 20% of all people name a zebra in response to the third question and about 50% name an animal from Africa, yet very few people give these answers when they do not answer the first two questions immediately before answering the third. It seems that by thinking about Africa and then the colors black and white, zebra is more available in memory than when people are not asked these questions. Later in this book, I present several decision-making heuristics or rules of thumb that people use when faced with decisions. Many of these heuristics are based on the idea that memory is associative, and when one concept is activated, other concepts related to it are also activated at the same time, and it is these associations that often influence the way people make decisions or solve problems.

What We Believe about Memory is (Mostly) Wrong

> Thought and memory are closely related, for thought relies heavily on the experiences of life.
> —Donald Norman (1988, p. 115)

Table 2.1: Use the rating scale to indicate the truth about each of the statements about memory. Items excerpted from Simons and Chabris (2011).

	Strongly agree	Mostly agree	Mostly disagree	Strongly disagree	Don't know
Memory works like a camera, accurately recording the events we see and hear.					
People generally notice when something unexpected enters their field of view.					
Once you have a memory of an event, that memory does not change.					
The testimony of a confident eye witness is enough to convict someone of a crime.					

What do most people believe about memory? Simons and Chabris (2011) asked a representative sample of people in the United States several questions about how memory works and compared their responses to those of memory experts. Let's see how you do:

How did you do? If you responded like most people, you mostly or strongly agree with each of these four statements about memory. Memory experts, who study memory processes, disagree with all of these statements (except for 19 percent who "mostly agree" with the second statement). In fact, we can be quite confident about events that never occurred, and our memories change over time. Perhaps, most surprisingly, we often fail to even see strange and unexpected events happening right before our eyes.

Change Blindness Blindness

Would you notice if the person you were talking to suddenly changed into another person? Surely you would notice, wouldn't you? Yet, in a series of studies in which someone was giving directions to a stranger who was momentarily not visible when a large object passed between them and was then replaced with another person, 50% of the people giving directions never noticed the change in the person they were talking to (Simons & Levine, 1998). This experimental paradigm, which was first used to study change blindness, is shown in Figure 2.2.

Change blindness is so counterintuitive that few people are willing to believe that they would miss an unusual event that occurred "right before their eyes." The phenomenon of people rejecting (being blind to) the idea that they actually miss major events in their environment is called **change blindness blindness** (Scholl, Simons, & Levin, 2004). The best way to convince yourself that you would miss many major events in the environment is to try out a few of the demonstrations that are available on the Internet. I recommend the videos posted on the SimonLab web site, which is run by Daniel Simons at the University of Illinois, Champaign-Urbana (http://www.simonslab.com/index.html). After a few trials, you should be convinced that you can miss seemingly important and unusual events that occur right before your eyes.

Figure 2.2 In the first scene (a), the younger man is asking the older one for directions. As they are talking, a large object passes between them (b), and the younger man is replaced with a different person (c). The two people who gave directions are shown in the last scene (d). Like most people, this older man did not notice that the person to whom he was giving directions changed in the middle of their conversation. (Images from Simons and Levin, 1998, page 646. © 2011 Simons, Chabris. This is an open-access article distributed under the terms of the Creative Commons Attribution License, which permits unrestricted use, distribution, and reproduction in any medium, provided the original author and source are credited.)

Memory without Awareness

> Few judges are psychologists, or they would realize that nothing can be stricken out of a human consciousness after being one let in. Judges seem to be quite unaware that it is a hard task to put anything into the average mind and, once in, an impossible one to take it out.
>
> —Clarence Darrow (1932, p. 145)

One kind of memory that has fascinated many psychologists during the last decade is memory for information that we do not know we know. It is hard to understand how something that we do not know we know could be called memory, so an example should help. Suppose that I write a two-word phrase in such small type that you could not read it _{just suppose.} If I asked you to recall the phrase, you would say that you never saw it or it was so small you could not read it. What if I devised a task that demonstrated that, in fact, you did have some memory for that two-word phrase, even though you had no conscious knowledge of ever reading it. The memory test for unconscious memory could be a word fragment task, where you fill in the blanks to form a two-word phrase, for example, _ _ s _ s _ pp _ _ e. If you filled in the blanks to read "just suppose," and I found that none or very few people who had not been exposed to this two-word phrase in small print could fill in the blanks, then I would have evidence for memory without conscious knowledge. The words "just suppose" appeared earlier on this page, and even if you had no conscious memory that you just read these words, if you completed the blanks, it affected your memory without awareness. In fact, there is good evidence for just such a memory system. Because it is a memory that we cannot access by the usual methods of responding, it is called **implicit memory** (McCabe, Roediger, & Karpicke, 2011).

Can unconscious memories influence how we think? It seems that they can. For example, if you see the name of some unknown person but you have no conscious memory of seeing that name, you are more likely to judge that it is the name of a famous person when you encounter it at a later time than if you had not previously been exposed to the name (Seamon et al., 1995). It seems that stimuli that reside in a memory system that you have no conscious knowledge of "feel familiar" even though you do not know why. Memories "feel" different from new information, and we use these feelings about what we remember as a basis for judgments, without knowing that familiarity is causing us to make the judgments that we do.

You may be wondering about the relationship between critical thinking and unconscious memory. If we are not aware of our unconscious memories, how can we use this information to improve thinking? Although by definition we can never know about unconscious memories and the way they affect how we think and act, we can consider how recent memories and stereotypes could be affecting us. For example, you may believe that you are a rugged individualist, someone who is not easily swayed by the actions of others. Yet, when people follow others at a buffet line, they tend to take portions that mimic the serving taken by the person in front of them, and it is very likely that you would also (Wansink, 2012). It seems that in our day-to-day interactions, multiple encounters with words and people in our environment influence us in ways that most of us find hard to believe. Everyone can adopt a more mindful approach to decisions, judgments, and actions.

The Illusion of Truth

> Some stories are true that never happened.
>
> —Elie Weisel (Nobel laureate, b. 1928)

What would happen if I told you a lie, and you have no conscious memory that I told you this lie? Here's one possibility: Did you know that the president of your college was caught shoplifting at Sears? Sure, this is a lie, I do not know anything about the president of your college, in fact, I do not really know you, and you may never have attended college. Let's further suppose that you are a college student and that you forgot that I told you this lie, and sometime later you hear that there was a crime on campus and the president of your university is a possible suspect. It seems that the information linking the president and crime will "feel familiar," and even though you do not recall where you heard it before, you would be more likely to judge the statement that your president committed a crime as the truth than if I had not previously told you the lie that she was caught shoplifting at Sears. Can you see why this phenomenon is called the "**illusion of truth**?" Information that was encountered previously, even if at the time you knew it might be a lie, makes it more likely that you will believe the information when it is encountered a second time than if you had not been told the original lie (Moons, Mackle, & Garcia-Marques, 2009). In fact, repeatedly remembering something can have the same effect—with repeated remembering, people judge that memory to be more truthful (Ozubko & Fugelsang, 2011).

So what should I do if I want to influence how you evaluate information— if I want you to believe my lie? I could repeat the information that I want you to believe several times and then allow some time to pass so that you do not recall where you heard it. When you hear the information at some time in the future, it will seem familiar, so you will be more likely to assume it is true. (It would have a "familiar ring" to it.) Based on the illusion of truth, can you understand why rumors are effective, even when they are known to be lies? Have you ever heard the expression, "there is no such thing as bad publicity?" It seems that people often forget exactly what they heard, but when they encounter a person's name for a second (or more) time, the name seems familiar. We tend to interpret this feeling of familiarity in a way that gives it meaning.

As you might guess, politicians (or at least members of their staff) are well aware of the illusion of truth. Suppose that you were running for office and wanted voters to remember bad things about your opponent. Easy—you could repeat something your opponent said out of context or even distort what your opponent said in the belief that voters will forget where they heard it, but they will remember what they heard. Here are two real life examples. During the primary elections for U.S. President in 2012, the Republican candidate (Mitt Romney) ran an ad against the incumbent Democratic president, Barack Obama. According to reports in the New York Times (Shear, 2011) and CNN, this candidate repeatedly televised a portion of a speech by Obama in which Obama declared, "If we keep talking about the economy, we're going to lose." It is true that Obama said these words, but he was quoting from another Republican candidate's campaign. (The ad is available on YouTube.) Mr. Obama's allies attacked the ad as being deceitful and dishonest, but the reality is that more people will remember that Obama said these words than people who know (or remember) that he was actually quoting an opponent.

These tactics are used on all sides of virtually every political campaign. According to FactCheck.org, a nonpartisan project by a school of public policy, Obama ran an advertisement during the heated race for U.S. presidency in 2012 in which a grieving widower says that his wife "contracted cancer and died a short time after Mitt Romney closed the steel plant that employed him and left 'my family' without coverage" (2012). The independent analysis concluded that while Romney played a role in closing the plant and that people with health care often live longer than those without it, the link between Romney and the death of this woman is incredibly weak. The ad goes on to say that Romney was not concerned about "what he has done," which people remember as Romney was not concerned about the death of this woman. But even when the facts are made clear, what gets remembered is the original message rather than the fact that Romney was not responsible for her death and that we have no idea how he feels about it.

What can critical thinkers do to protect themselves from believing things that are not true, but come to feel that they are through repetition? Again, the best defense is a mindful scrutiny of questionable opinions. If in doubt, check it out. A little research can show who made any particular claim, whether it was in a reputable source, and whether there were motives to get you to believe something that is not true. Careful research and vigilance are the best protections.

Classical Conditioning

Another kind of memory without awareness is the result of classical conditioning. If you have taken an introductory class in psychology, then you probably learned about the pioneering work of Ivan Pavlov. He was able to get dogs to salivate to the sound of a bell by repeatedly pairing the sound of bell with the presentation of food. In human terms, that is like getting you to respond to the sound of a bell in much the same way that you would respond to the sight and smell of a thick, juicy steak sizzling on a grill. (If you are a vegetarian, then think of a juicy veggie burger or whatever the appropriate mount-watering meal is for you.) Classical conditioning can occur without conscious awareness, and clever propagandists have used this technique to influence how people think.

There is a striking example of the use of classical conditioning to influence thoughts and actions on display at the Museum of Tolerance in Los Angeles, California, which is a museum that is dedicated to documenting and explaining the origins and consequences of prejudice and intolerance. In one display, old movies that were shown in Nazi Germany depict the repeated pairing of revolting scenes of rats streaming out of sewers and running over garbage and other waste. Virtually everyone responds with disgust to these repulsive scenes. Exaggerated pictures of Jews were flashed onto the screen so that the long noses of the disgusting rats are superimposed over the exaggerated facial features of Jews. It does not take long before the facial features evoke feelings of disgust, which were learned through the repeated pairing of the repulsive rat scenes and the faces. For people who viewed these movies, the feeling of disgust can be elicited at some time later when similar facial features are encountered, without the viewer ever being aware of where or how this association was learned. This is a powerful and frightening example of the way memory without awareness can support a conscious program of prejudice and discrimination. As the learner (viewer of the films), you would attribute the feeling of disgust to some other reason or source, a fact that makes its effect so pernicious.

In one of the controversies that erupted during the presidential match between Al Gore and George W. Bush, two candidates for president of the

Figure 2.3 A reproduction of the television screen that was used during an anti-Gore commercial during the presidential campaign in 2000. (From http://political.adcritic.com)

United States in 2000, a controversial television advertisement criticized Gore's health plan as a plan that would be run by "bureaucrats." There is nothing unusual in this because name-calling is a common political technique used to persuade voters not to vote for the other candidate. What was unusual in this advertisement was that the word "RATS" was briefly flashed on the television screen as the announcer said the word "bureaucrats." This advertisement can be seen on the internet at a site that is maintained by "Political Ad Critic," (http://political.adcritic.com). The television screen is reproduced in Figure 2.3. In thinking about the effect of this advertisement, remember that the word "RATS" was flashed very quickly. I do not know what the intent of the advertising agency was, although I can guess at their intent. George W. Bush claimed that he had no knowledge of the advertisement.

Does flashing the word "RATS" on the television screen so quickly that no one would be consciously aware of it really have any effect on how viewers think and feel? A stimulus that is flashed too quickly to be recognized is called "subliminal," which means that it was not registered consciously. Two political psychologists investigated this question. Weinberger and Westen (2008) conducted several studies with subliminal stimuli. In one study, one of the following was flashed very quickly on a screen—RATS, STAR, ARAB, and XXX. It was immediately followed by a photo of an unknown man who was supposedly a politician. (The other stimuli were used as controls.) The participants then rated the politician along several dimensions including competence, honesty, positive feelings, and disgust, among other ratings. They found that when the word "RATS" was flashed before the photo was shown, the participants rated the politician more negatively than in the other conditions. Their conclusion, which was based on other studies as well, was that a negative subliminal message can make viewers feel more negative about a stimulus that follows it. It seems that without our awareness, negative affect can be activated from memory, and this negative affect spills over to other stimuli that appear near it in time. We do not know how long this effect lasts or whether it actually influences behavior like how people vote, but it is a powerful demonstration of how feelings can be activated without our conscious awareness.

Varieties of Memory

> The two offices of memory are collection and distribution.
> —Samuel Johnson (1759)

The goal of good remembering is to learn information that may be useful in the future and to learn it in a way that makes it likely to be recalled when it is needed. By gaining some insight into the way memory works, you should be able to use this knowledge to improve your ability to remember.

In the first chapter, I provided a working definition for "critical thinking" and earlier in this chapter for the more general term "thinking." A key idea is that thinking is the manipulation or transformation of some internal representation. Our internal representations are manipulated or transformed in symbolic ways, so that the knowledge we have can be used to solve problems and make decisions. Notice that I use the term "knowledge" whenever I refer to an internal representation. Information exists in the world. When we learn information—that is, incorporate it into our existing mental structures, and it becomes meaningful—it becomes knowledge. When we think, we use our knowledge to accomplish some goal. When we think in deliberate ways that increase the probability of obtaining that goal, we are engaging in critical thinking.

Memory is not a single process. It is a series of processes or systems, each of which has its own operating principles. In general, memory is divided into three parts. The first part is called sensory memory because it is closely tied to the sensory processes like seeing, hearing, and touching.

This memory system will not be considered here because there is little that we can do to improve sensory memory. The second part is called **working memory** because it represents the "place" and processes that are used when we think ("work on") information. The third part is **long-term memory** because it represents the retention (storage) of memories over longer periods of time. Memories that are more than 30 seconds old (not very long really) and those that last up to a lifetime are stored here.

Working Memory

A common theme among researchers who study memory is that memory has a limited capacity; that is, we cannot remember everything that we would like. Nor can we keep too many different "pieces" of information in an active form in memory so that we can use them all simultaneously. If I asked you to recite the alphabet backwards while solving calculus problems, you would object because there is simply not enough "space" or "effort" or whatever term you want to use to execute these two tasks simultaneously, although either one alone can be performed. The cognitive resources that are used to execute mental operations and to remember the outcomes of these processes are available only in a limited supply. The "place" where conscious thought occurs is called **working memory** because it is the hypothetical space where we perform the work of thinking. One goal of an efficient cognitive system is to make the work of thinking easier or, metaphorically, to reduce the amount of space or effort needed in working memory.

Based on what we know about how our memory works and what we are likely to forget, we make decisions about how to spend the limited resources of working memory. One of these decisions is to use external aids. For example, instead of trying to remember my shopping list, I write it down. I know that it is not worth the mental effort of committing this list to memory and that I cannot keep more than five to nine "pieces" of information (or perhaps even fewer—three or four according to some researchers; Cowan 2005) in my thoughts at the same time. We also categorize information to reduce the load on memory. I could remember to buy "stuff" for the dog (dog food, biscuits, flea powder) and "stuff" for the kids' lunches (sandwich makings, apples, lunch bags), etc. This strategy would reduce the number of items that I would have to recall and make forgetting less likely.

Another way we manage our memory is by making decisions about what information we need to use and how much mental effort to "spend" on a particular task. For example, suppose that you had to make a decision concerning a complex issue. You could decide to omit technical information that is difficult to understand, and therefore uses a great deal of working memory. Unfortunately, you could also reduce the mental workload by seeking simple explanations for complex issues such as crime (it's caused by unemployment), truancy (it's caused by bad parents), or economic down-turns that increased unemployment in some groups (it's caused by some minority group that is different from you). These simple purported causes for difficult problems help to reduce the amount of information that is used to reach a conclusion, but they are also a detriment to good thinking because complex problems do not have simple, single causes.

Long-Term Memory

Just as there are different processes in working memory, there are differences among the kinds of memories we store for a longer time. For example, memory operates differently when you learn a motor skill like skiing than it does when you study for a history test. Therefore, you would not use the same methods to learn to ski as you would to learn about an event in history. Similarly, what you do during the retention interval and at recall is different. The length of the retention interval also governs what and how you learn and recall. If you had to remember the date for the end of World War II for only five seconds, you would engage in different remembering activities during the retention interval than if you had to remember it for five months. What you already know about skiing or history is also an important determinant of the way in which you go about adding to that knowledge. Similarly, the complexity of the information and the context in which you learn and remember also play a role in the selection of the best strategies for learning and remembering. Intuitively, we all know about some of these differences, but an improved understanding of the operating principles of memory should help to use it more efficiently.

Perhaps another analogy would be useful at this point because the concept of memory systems is so abstract. Think about the many interrelated components in an automobile engine. If you understand that pumping too much gas into a stalled car can "flood" the engine, then you can avoid this problem. Similarly, if you understand that the battery can lose its charge if you run the heater, lights, and radio for a long time when the motor is off, you can also use this knowledge to avoid the problem of a dead battery. The many systems of memory also have operating rules, and if you acquire, retain, and recall information with these rules in mind, you should be a better driver of your own memory system.

Here are some of the distinctions that have been made to differentiate between memory systems: **Episodic memory** is the memory we have for events in which we can recall our own participation—when and where we learned them (Tulving, 2002). Examples of episodic memory include remembering where you spent your 17th birthday, recalling the plot from a movie you saw last week, and remembering the day you graduated from high school. This sort of memory is fairly easy to acquire because it seems to happen without much effort on your part. **Semantic memory** is the memory that we have for facts like the multiplication table and word meanings. You probably cannot remember where and when you learned that 7 x 9 = 63 or the definition of "chauvinist pig," but these are parts of your memory system. You probably can recall all of the trouble you had learning the multiplication tables. It is easy to talk about the knowledge contained in episodic and semantic memory. For this reason, these two systems are part of a larger grouping in memory that is called **declarative memory**.

Motor memory, as you might expect, pertains to remembering motor skills. Let's suppose that you are an excellent outfielder in baseball. You can get your glove to the place where the ball is going and throw it in the right direction within fractions of a second. This is certainly an impressive skill, but it is very difficult to verbalize exactly how you do it. You are able to call on your knowledge when it is needed, but can't exactly say what it is that you do. If you wanted to teach me to be a great outfielder (lots of luck), you could not just tell me what you do. It would be of little use for you to describe your activities, "I catch the ball instead of missing it, then throw it where it is most needed, instead of somewhere else." On the other hand, if you wanted to teach me the multiplication tables, you could do that in words.

Procedural memory, or remembering how to do something, shares some features with motor memory. The difference is that the procedure does not necessarily have to involve motor skills. For example, if you are as old as I am (unlikely), then you once learned how to use a slide rule. (For those of you who grew up in the age of cheap and efficient calculators, a slide rule is a device that looks like a ruler and can be used to perform mathematical calculations.) This is a kind of "knowing how" that is often differentiated from declarative tasks that involve "knowing that."

Another way of dividing memory depends on how hard you have to "work" in order to remember. This distinction is between automatic and effortful memory. How many movies have you seen in the last two months? Even avid movie-goers can almost always answer this question (Hasher & Zacks, 1984). Frequency information is one type of learning and remembering that occurs fairly automatically; that is, with little conscious awareness or practice (Balota, Pilotti, & Cortese, 2001). For this reason, it is often called **automatic memory**. By contrast, suppose that you need to remember a series of dates for a history exam. Unfortunately, this sort of information will require that you work at remembering—most probably you would repeat the dates until you could recite them without looking. This is an example of **effortful** memory. Some types of memory will require hard work, others will be easy, but with repeated practice and the acquisition of additional information, effortful processing will become more automatic. Perhaps one way of thinking about education is that it makes hard "things" easy. Experts in any area—history buffs, computer programmers, skilled athletes—have all done the hard work of learning and now make "it look so easy," so automatic.

Memory can also be categorized by the type of recall task that will be performed. If you have to recognize the correct response, you will need less effort at acquisition than if you actually have to generate the response with few cues. Students frequently tell me that they study differently when they are expecting a multiple-choice test (recognition) than an essay test (recall with few cues). When preparing for a test, students engage in **intentional learning** activities and do something to help them remember the material. Learning that occurs without deliberate effort is called **incidental**. For example, your memory for the plot of a television sitcom that you saw last night is incidental memory. I often hear from students who complain that they "can't do math" or "can't do science" or "can't write well." I think that what they really mean is that the learning of math (or science or writing—we all have different skills and abilities) is effortful. Of course, with hard work, they can. I think that if they understood that some kinds of learning are effortful and some are easy, then they would not be so quick to conclude that they "Can't do it," when in fact what they need to do is exert conscious effort and do the hard work of initial learning. Once they establish a solid base of knowledge, later learning is easier.

As you can see, there are many ways to categorize the multiple processes of memory. What you need to remember from this discussion is that you will have to consider what you need to remember and when and why you will need it, and what you already know about the topic when you engage in activities that promote remembering. But, whatever the nature of the memory task, a consistent theme throughout this book is that the knowledge we retain in that amazing organ that perches on top of our spines, directs the mental processes that we call thinking. A strong base of knowledge and good thinking skills operate together in the critical thinker. However, it is important to bear in mind that while an excellent memory may direct and influence thinking, a head full of good facts does not make someone a good thinker. One of the saddest sights is someone whose memory is an encyclopedic compendium of unintegrated factoids. Just as great thinking skills with a head that contains no knowledge is worthless, so is a head full of information without the thinking skills, unless you aspire to be a game-show contestant! Thought and knowledge—sounds to me like a great title for a book.

General Principles to Improve Learning and Remembering

Just as there are different varieties of memory, there are different strategies that can help us learn and remember better. In keeping with the time line presented earlier in this chapter, general principles are provided to help with learning, retaining information in memory, and retrieving the information when it is needed.

Acquisition

In 1935, *Time Magazine* featured the predictions of Ralph S. Willard, a Hollywood chemist who claimed to be able to freeze monkeys and resuscitate them. Willard suggested that this process could be used with prisoners because it was cheaper than jail, the unemployed, who could be kept frozen until the economy produced more jobs, and even the depressed, who could remain in the freezer until a cure was found. By the way, it is clear that "Willard was a humbug" who disappeared into science fiction history.

—S. B. Harris (1993, p. 55)

Unless you already knew this, you have just acquired new information. You can answer questions that you could not answer a few moments ago. You are a changed person, and you will never be the same again. The knowledge you have embedded in memory pertaining to *Time Magazine*, cryogenics (freezing people), and strange ideas from the 1930s is altered. So it is with all new information that causes you to change what you know and how you think.

The term "information explosion," which refers to the tremendous increase in the amount of information we have to deal with in contemporary society—information that has to be acquired, retained, and retrieved if we are to function in an increasingly complex world. The massive amounts of information now available are mind-boggling. There are tens of billions of photos on Facebook, the human genome project involves analyzing 3 billion base pairs, the giant retailer Walmart generates 2.5 petaytes of information about customer sales (more than 167 times the number of books in America's Library of Congress; Cukier, 2010), and even a simple search on an electronic database for information about memory can yield hundreds of thousands of articles. We are privy to staggering quantities of information. Increasingly, we need to know how to find the information we need in a world overloaded with information, decide what to eliminate, and judge which information is useful and good.

Strategies that Promote Learning

> There is no substitute for the serene pleasure that learning can bring.
> —Chizuko Izawa (1993, p. 43)

Although there are many different kinds of memory processes and contexts, several general rules have emerged that can promote the learning of new information. There is an old saying that goes something like this, "the head remembers what it does." (I really like this saying and use it a few times in this book—remembering that should help you remember this point.) Embarrassingly, I have to admit that I don't remember where I first heard it, but I do recall the message: What you do at acquisition (when you are learning something) is an important determinant of what you will remember. Simply put, if you engage in activities that promote learning, you will improve your memory.

Pay Attention

One of the primary determinants of what we know is what we attend to. Think back to the last time you were at a large, noisy party with people standing around in small groups talking to each other. Imagine that you're standing with two acquaintances discussing the weather. There are several small groups of people standing nearby who are also carrying on conversations. If someone near you, but not talking to you, mentions your name or something of interest (e.g., "Did you hear the latest news about Debbie and Stanley . . . ?"), this will attract your attention. If, however, the same person standing at the same distance from you, speaking in the same voice, is discussing tree blight, you probably would never notice, unless you have a special interest in tree blight. Think about what will happen to the conversation you've been having about the weather. If your answer is "Not much," you're correct. When you switched your attention to the more interesting conversation, you lost most of the meaning of the original conversation. If, at this point, the person who has been talking to you suddenly stops and asks, "What do you think about it?", you'd become embarrassed because you would have no knowledge of what she had been saying.

Most people can think of an episode where they've experienced this effect. It demonstrates several basic properties of attention.

1. If you do not pay attention, you will not acquire information. Let's consider the scenario a little more closely. When you were attending to the weather conversation, you knew very little or nothing about the other conversations around you. When you switched your attention to the more interesting conversation, you could not say what was happening in the weather conversation. Thus, attention will be a major factor in what gets remembered, because it determines what gets into the human information system.

2. There are limitations on your ability to process information. All of the conversations going on around you are not processed equally well.

3. There are individual differences in what is attended to. If you had no interest in "the latest news about Debbie and Stanley," but found the weather fascinating, then you would not have switched your attention and could have responded with more than a sheepish grin to the question, "What do you think about it?"

Many people complain that they forget the names of people soon after they've been introduced. It is likely that they never paid attention to the name at the time of introduction. If information is not acquired, then it can never be remembered. When meeting someone, it is a good idea to repeat the person's name aloud to be certain that you have heard it correctly and to be certain that you have paid attention. Saying the name, rather than just hearing it, is an important aid for remembering. If you cannot say the name soon after hearing it, you can be sure that you won't remember it sometime later. You need to develop the habit of monitoring your attention.

I tried to explain this principle to the manager at a sandwich shop where I frequently stop. Often the order is wrong, which costs money and hurts business. I suggested that he have the people taking the order repeat it back to the customer to ensure its accuracy and to help the order taker/sandwich maker remember the order as he or she works on it. The manager looked unimpressed with this sage advice. It is unfortunate because this simple generative task would significantly reduce the number of wrong orders and unhappy customers.

In case you're unimpressed with the rule that unless you attend to something you won't know it, let's try a demonstration. Most people will admit that they like money and have worked hard to earn it. In Figure 2.4 there are several drawings of a U.S. penny.

Only one is correct. If you're like most people, you will not be able to recognize the correct penny because you never attended to its details. Although you have dealt with pennies numerous times (if you are a resident of or visitor to the United States), you learned only enough of the details to tell it apart from other coins, which is all that you need to use coins. You

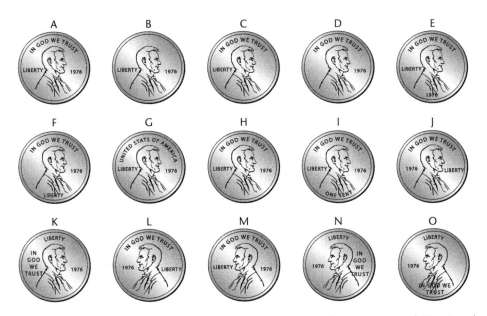

Figure 2.4 Fifteen drawings of a United States penny. Which one is correct? (Reprinted from *Cognitive Psychology*, vol. 11, Nickerson & Adams, "Long-term memory for a common object," Pages 287–307, Copyright (1979), with permission from Elsevier.)

probably never acquired a detailed memory of pennies. To find the "correct" answer, check it with a real penny, but be certain that you attend to all of the details carefully. The need to pay attention in school should be obvious. The skill of attending is an important predictor of the success that children have in school (Duncan et al., 2007). Think about how your mind sometimes seems to wander when reading textbooks or during lectures. Most students are not even aware when they are not paying attention. It should be obvious by now that in order to develop better memory skills, you will also have to develop attentional skills.

Monitor Meaning

Comprehension and memory are closely related concepts because memory is enhanced when the material is meaningful, and meaningful information is retained more easily than material that is low in meaning. If you are learning in a classroom setting, or from a textbook, or in some similar setting where the information is complex prose and you need to be able to recall it later, you need to monitor how much and what you are understanding. Stop at the end of each section, and state or write in your own words, without looking at the text, what you just read. This is important because it provides practice at remembering, but you still need to practice your remembering after some time has passed since reading the text. If you cannot meaningfully summarize each section just after reading it, then you will not be able to summarize it at some later date. You need to be aware of what you are learning, and take action if you have "lost it." This is a concrete way to check on your attention. If you finished a section in a text and have no idea what you just read, you need to go back and attend to the content. Additional suggestions for monitoring meaning are given later in this chapter in the section on metamemory and in the next chapter where questioning strategies are presented.

Stop now, cover this section of your book and say aloud or write out in two or three sentences what this section on memory is conveying. If you cannot paraphrase what you just read now, then you cannot recall it later.

* * *

Welcome back! How did you do? If you could not paraphrase what you just read, be sure to go back and reread, taking notes as needed, to keep the information in memory.

To demonstrate the powerful influence of meaning on memory, look at A, B, and C in Figure 2.5 for a few seconds, then cover the figures and reproduce them from memory. Try this now.

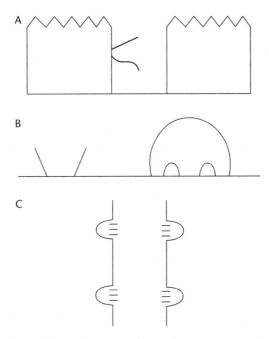

Figure 2.5 A demonstration of the effect of meaningfulness on memory. Look at these figures for a few seconds, then cover them and reproduce them from memory. (Figures A and B are adapted from Osgood, 1953. Figure C is adapted from Hanson, 1958).

You probably remembered some parts of the figures shown in Figure 2.5, but didn't remember them perfectly. Suppose I now tell you that Figure 2.5A is a soldier walking his dog behind a picket fence (Do you see the dog's tail and the end of the soldier's rifle?), and that Figure 2.5B is a washerwoman scrubbing the floor (Do you see her water bucket and the bottoms of her shoes?). If you recognized Figure 2.5C as a bear behind a tree, then you drew it more accurately than if it seemed more like abstract art. Making the figures meaningful will enhance how well they are remembered.

Your elementary school teachers recognized the role that meaning plays in memory when they told you to "read for meaning." We can add meaning to information by elaborating on it. For example, when you are learning something, try to relate it to something that you already know (Connor-Greene, 2000). In a clever demonstration of the principle that anything that improves comprehension will improve memory, psychologists (Bransford & Johnson, 1972) presented college students with the following passage to read. Read it for yourself and then see how much you can remember.

The procedure is actually quite simple. First you arrange things into different groups depending on their makeup. Of course, one pile may be sufficient depending on how much there is to do. If you have to go somewhere else due to lack of facilities that is the next step, otherwise you are pretty well set. It is important not to overdo any particular endeavor. That is, it is better to do too few things at once than too many. In the short run this may not seem important, but complications from doing too many can easily arise. A mistake can be expensive as well. The manipulation of the appropriate mechanisms should be self-explanatory, and we need not dwell on it here. At first the whole procedure will seem complicated. Soon, however, it will become just another facet of life. It is difficult to foresee any end to the necessity for this task in the immediate future, but then one never can tell. (p. 722)

You probably did not remember very much of this passage. I also doubt that you found it very understandable.

Read the passage again, this time keeping the title "Washing Clothes" in mind. It should seem much more memorable because the title provided a context or a framework for understanding the passage. When information is provided before a person reads a text or learns about a topic, the reader is better able to assimilate the incoming information. The **advance organizers**—the preliminary information—act as a guide or framework that helps the learner to anticipate information and to relate it to other topics. This is the rationale behind the outlines that appear at the beginning of each chapter in this book.

Distribute Learning

In plain English, this strategy means, "Don't cram." You will learn material in a way that is more resistant to forgetting if you space out the learning sessions. This seems to hold true whether you are learning a motor skill, like how to return the ball with a strong back hand in tennis, the derivation of chemistry formulas, or how to use a new piece of equipment. Spread out the study sessions for maximal benefit (Carpenter, Cepeda, Rohrer, Kang, & Pashler, 2012). If you can allocate only five hours to studying for an exam, spread it out over three or four days instead of spending the entire time at one sitting. Of course, study periods also need to be long enough to allow for integration of the information you're reading. The ideal study period depends on many factors, including the difficulty of the material, your own attentional capacities, and how much has to be learned. In fact, it seems that the more variability you use when learning, the better able you are to recall information in a wide variety of settings, so study for different lengths of time with different intervals between study sessions for the longest lasting memories.

Get Organized

"Clean up your room!" I don't think that there is a person alive who has not heard (or spoken) these words. The idea that "you'll never be able to find anything in this mess" may also apply to how you store information in memory. Although the similarity between memory and a messy room is obviously a gross oversimplification, organization does make it easier both to find a pair of socks that match and retrieve information from memory.

I would like to demonstrate this point with two lists of words. Read one list, at a rate of approximately one word per second, cover the list and write down as many of the words as you can remember, then repeat this process with the second list.

Girl, Heart, Robin, Purple, Finger, Flute, Blue, Organ, Man, Hawk, Green, Lung, Eagle, Child, Piano

Stop now, cover the above list, and write down as many words from this list as you can remember.

Now read the next list, cover it, and then write down as many of the words that you can remember from this list.

Green, Blue, Purple, Man, Girl, Child, Piano, Flute, Organ, Heart, Lung, Finger, Eagle, Hawk, Robin

Stop now, cover the above list and write down as many words from this list as you can remember.

Undoubtedly, you correctly recalled more words from the second list than from the first. You may not have realized that the lists were identical except for the order in which the words were presented. You might expect that you did better the second time because you already had a chance to practice the words once. This is true. The additional time spent studying the words can partially account for the improvement in recall. However, most of the improvement on the second list came from the organization provided by presenting words in categories. Research has shown that when lists of words are presented in categories, recall of material is two to three times better than when the same list of words is randomly presented (Bower & Clark, 1969). When words are presented in random order, as in the first list, recall is improved when subjects have enough time to generate their own categories.

You can apply this memory principle by organizing material that you need to learn. If you are learning a classification system for a biology course or the properties of metals for a course in science, study one group or category at a time. See how the groups relate and note similarities and differences within and between categories. Impose a structure or organization on the material to be learned.

Generate Multiple Cues for Retrieval

I've seen it happen many times. A good student, who works hard, finds that he cannot remember an answer on an exam, and then soon after turning in his paper, the answer seems to pop into his head. Or, similarly, as soon as he hears the answer, he realizes that he "knew" it, but couldn't remember it when it was needed. These are frustrating experiences that can have dire consequences if you cannot recall, for example, the CPR (cardio pulmonary resuscitation) you learned in high school or the emergency procedures for those times when you run low on air in the middle of a deep sea dive. Knowledge that you cannot recall when it is needed is called **inert knowledge.** Later, in the chapter on creative thinking, we will consider ways to help you think of new solutions for new problems. "Think of" is really the same as activating inert knowledge. Memory is central to all thinking. Psychologists know a great deal about remembering and forgetting, including some ways to make information that you "know" available when you need it. We know that what you do when you are learning something will have a strong effect on whether you are able to recall it when it is needed.

When you recall something, it is in response to some cue. For example, "name some strategies that promote recall." In this example, the terms "strategies to promote recall" are the cues for what is to be remembered. When you learn something, you need to learn it along with the cues that are likely to be present at recall. Ask questions about causes and consequences of the material you are learning. How does the newly acquired information relate to other concepts? What I am describing is the principle of **encoding specificity**, the idea that material is most likely to be recalled when you are presented with the same cues that were available when you learned it. Learning that encourages a "deep" or extensive knowledge will help to make the information spontaneously available in those situations when you need it (Gholson et al., 2009).

Overlearn

When can you stop studying? Well, if this question is applied to a specific example, like studying for a literature exam, then the best answer is when you can recall the material perfectly over several different sessions. Consider what happens when a child learns her multiplication tables. At some point, she gets through the entire pack of dreaded "flash cards" (remember them?) without an error. If she stopped learning there, you would find that the next time she went through the deck of flash cards, a few errors would "creep" in. She needs to overlearn, that is go through the pack of cards without errors many times, with sessions spaced out over time, to ensure accurate recall when these arithmetic facts are needed.

Be Aware of Noncognitive Factors

There are many factors that can affect your ability to learn that have little to do with cognition, but you do need to be able to recognize them so that you can find ways to minimize forgetting. Suppose that you are trying to learn something (anything) but are exhausted from lack of sleep or from excessive exercise (say, the marathon you just ran); your ability to attend, encode, and retain information will suffer. Your ability to learn can also be adversely affected by drugs (prescription and nonprescription varieties), an extremely anxious or depressed emotional state ("I'll never learn this, then I will flunk out, then everyone will know I am dumb, then I will have to sell hamburgers for the rest of my life," etc.), a lack of time for learning, a poor background in the subject area, and many more factors. Did you know that lack of sleep can be as detrimental to your ability to think and respond as being drunk? Sleep deprivation is a major cause of accidents. The scary part of sleep deprivation is that the sleep-deprived person has little knowledge of how poorly he or she is thinking. You will probably not allow friends to drive drunk, but think nothing of allowing them to drive when they are sleepy, a condition that can be just as dangerous. These are just a few of many possible behaviors that depress your ability to learn. I hate to sound like your mother, but take care of yourself, eat right, exercise, get enough sleep, and get help with physical and emotional problems. There is little point in working on the thinking skills that are presented throughout this book if you are going to be spending much of your life strung out on drugs, half-asleep, or too anxious to learn.

Retention

> The art of remembering is the art of thinking. . . . our conscious effort should not be so much to *impress* or *retain* (knowledge) as to *connect* it with something already there.
>
> —William James (1890)

The term "retention" is sometimes used synonymously with memory. Unfortunately, this term suggests that memory is like a vast storage tank or library where memories are stored and something like miniature pictures of events are retrieved when we need to recall an event. This notion of memory is wrong.

The Constructive Nature of Memory

As you already know, many of the popular notions people hold about memory are wrong. In a national study of what people in the United States remember about the terrorist attacks that occurred on 9/11/2001 (a topic which has been the subject of much research), researchers found that 10 years after the attacks, people were able to remember much of what happened on that day much better than they would be for neutral events, but their memories were not completely accurate (Chen, 2011). People believed that they would "never forget" and remained highly confident that they were accurately recalling events, but in fact there were many details that were forgotten or inaccurately recalled. The researchers found that they could not convince people that their memory was wrong. Several important facts about memory are demonstrated in this study: (a) memories are frequently inaccurate; (b) we tend to fill in missing information in memory with information that "fits" with our belief system or was acquired after the event occurred; and (c) although there is generally positive relationship between memory accuracy and confidence, we tend to be more confident about highly emotional events, and this is where the relationship between confidence and accuracy breaks down. People believe that their memory for emotional events is far more accurate than it really is. These are important points to remember about memory because we all rely on information stored in memory to make decisions and understand events, and we mostly believe that our own memory is highly accurate. However, this is not always the case, considering that memory is influenced by a set of factors:

Prior Knowledge

Your ability to learn and remember new material depends on what you already know. You certainly wouldn't take an advanced course in nuclear physics if you never had a basic course in physics. However, you probably never realized that prior knowledge, the information you already know, influences how you think and how you remember new information in almost any context. You can read a passage about a familiar topic more quickly than you can read a passage of (objectively) comparable difficulty regarding an unfamiliar topic because your prior knowledge about a known topic facilitates comprehension. Later in this book, I consider the differences between novices and experts in how they solve problems. The expert is better able to comprehend a problem and to remember important aspects of the problem because of prior knowledge of the field.

Stereotypes and Prejudice

> Stereotyping is a category based cognitive response to another person.
> —Susan Fiske (1993, p. 623)

A classic experimental demonstration of the idea that prior knowledge influences what people will remember was conducted by two psychologists, Snyder and Uranowitz (1978). Two groups of college students read the same story about a woman named Betty. The story contained information about her life. Among the information presented was the fact that she occasionally dated men. Up to this point, everything was the same for the students in both groups. After reading the story, one group of students was told that Betty had become a lesbian, while the other group of students was told that she was leading a heterosexual lifestyle. The question of interest was whether this would influence what they remembered about Betty's life story. One week later, all of the students returned to the laboratory to answer questions about the story they had read. They were asked many questions, but the critical question was:

In high school, Betty:

(a)   occasionally dated men

(b)   never went out with men

(c)   went steady

(d)   no information provided

Can you guess the results of this experiment? The group of students who were told that Betty is now a lesbian were much more likely to "remember" (b) as the correct answer than the group of students who were told that Betty is a heterosexual. The students who had been told that Betty is a lesbian believed that they remembered something that had not occurred. Their prejudices and beliefs about lesbians caused them to remember events that never transpired.

Our beliefs about lesbians, women, men, and other groups, especially racial and ethnic groups, exert strong influences on what we will remember about members of these groups. People may honestly believe that they are recalling something that, in fact, never occurred because their beliefs about what must have happened bias how they recall the events.

Experiments like the ones just described have important implications for understanding the nature of prejudice. Let's suppose that Betty was a real person whom you knew while growing up. There may be many things that you can remember about Betty. You now learn that she is a lesbian. Suppose further that you have a stereotype of lesbians as women who drive trucks, crush beer cans with one hand, and hate men. Because this stereotype contains very little truth about any hypothetical "average" lesbian, you would be forced either to change your stereotype or to change what you remember about Betty. It seems that it is our specific memories that change; not the more abstract memory information underlying our stereotypes. You might selectively remember information like the fact that she always liked to play basketball and forget other information about Betty that is inconsistent with your stereotype, like the fact that she also liked to cook and plant flowers. Allport (1954), in a classic book on prejudice wrote, "It is possible for a stereotype to grow in defiance of all evidence" (pp. 189–190). This is an important point that I want to reiterate. Our beliefs are not easily changed; instead, we tend to change our memory for what we saw and heard so that the memory is made consistent with the beliefs. Most often, memory is altered without conscious awareness that the information is being recalled in a way that does not match the event.

Inference and Distortion

Memory is malleable. Our memory depends on how we encoded or interpreted events, not the events themselves. What we remember changes over time (Schacter, Guerin, & St. Jacques, 2011). When our knowledge and experience change, our memories also change. There are additions made to memories so that we remember events that never occurred and deletions made so that we forget other events that did. Often, people cannot distinguish between their own thoughts and their perceptions. Have you ever wondered,

"Did she really say that or did I think she said that?" At your next high school or college reunion, get together with friends to remember old times. You may be surprised to find that the same events are remembered differently by each of you, and each will have memories that others don't have. Furthermore, each of several people who shared a common event and remembered it differently will be highly confident that his or her memory is highly accurate.

Real and False Memories

> People are, in general, highly susceptible to the creation of false memories; that is, people often accept as fact events that have never occurred but have merely been implied or hinted at.
>
> —Stephan Lewandowsky, Werner Stritzke, Klaus Oberauer, and Michael Morales (2009, p. 179).

An explosive controversy involving memory has shaken public confidence in many accounts of memories that were not recalled for long periods of time and then suddenly emerged, often during psychotherapy sessions. These memories usually involve traumatic events such as witnessing a murder or experiencing sexual or other physical abuse. Some psychologists believe that these memories are quite accurate and that they were not available for recall because they were repressed as a protective mechanism for the individual who could not deal with the trauma. Other psychologists believe that while some of these memories may be accurate accounts of real events, many are likely to be "false" memories for events that either did not occur or were very different from the way they were remembered (Loftus, 1993; Roediger & Bergman, 1998). Unfortunately, there is no objective way to discriminate between real memories and false ones. The false ones often "feel real," and the person doing the remembering is often very confident that the memory is accurate, even when other types of evidence show that it cannot be accurate. Try this demonstration:

Read the following list of words out loud, then when you are finished, cover the list and write down as many as you can remember.

Sour, Candy, Sugar, Bitter, Good, Taste, Nice, Honey, Soda, Chocolate, Heart, Cake, Pie, Tart

(Continued)

Now look over your list. How many of the words did you get correct? Did you remember reading the word "sweet?" Many people do, even though it is not on the list. Tests like this one show how people can be misled into remembering things that never happened (Roediger & McDermott, 1995). Many people are highly confident that they read the word sweet, when it was not on the list. Sweet is associated with the words on this list and it is activated in memory when it associated words are activated.

Lewandowsky et al. (2005, 2009) found that more Americans falsely remembered that there was evidence that Iraq had "weapons of mass destruction" during the Iraq War of 2003 than people from Australia or Germany. One interpretation of these data is that these beliefs allowed Americans to justify their country's actions in Iraq. The authors concluded that the best way to guard against false memories is to maintain a "healthy skepticism" so that people consider possible motives for actions.

Retrieval

What is your mother's maiden name? Unless you happened to be sitting here thinking about your mother's name, the name seemed to "pop" into your mind. The answer must have been stored in some way that allowed it to be retrieved with a simple question. In fact, it seems almost impossible not to remember your mother's maiden name, when you are asked this question. Now try this one: What are the names of the Seven Dwarfs in *Snow White and the Seven Dwarfs*? If you did not grow up in America or another Western culture, then you may have responded to this question with, "Huh?" Of course, you cannot remember something that you never learned. If you grew up in North America or another Western culture, then you probably saw the movie and read this fairy tale, and now you are having trouble with this question, even though you probably heard their names and read them several times. Forgetting can be a frustrating experience for everyone. How can we understand the retrieval process when it works so well sometimes and so poorly other times? (P.S. Are you ready to give up? Their names are Bashful, Sneezy, Sleepy, Grumpy, Happy, Doc, Dopey).

There is no memory without retrieval, but we need to be aware of the many ways that memories can be biased, and thus inaccurate. Certainly, successful retrieval of information is a goal for remembering, but a critical thinker will consider ways the memory could be biased.

Forgetting

> Happiness lies in good health and a bad memory.
> —Ingrid Bergman (quoted in Smith, 1992, p. A1)

One of the major theories of forgetting is that events interfere with each other in memory. This is called the **interference theory of forgetting**. Suppose that you are studying French and Spanish in college. You would probably find that you sometimes get them confused because what you learned about one language "interferes" with what you learned about the other. In general, the more similar two events are (or, in this case, languages), the more interference there will be. Knowing this, can you think of a way to reduce interference and improve memory? In the example just given, one way would be to take the courses in different semesters to minimize the interference, or at least one course early in the morning and the other in the evening. By keeping the French and Spanish courses as separate as possible, you can reduce some of the interference.

Thinking and Forgetting

By definition, we cannot recall what we have forgotten. Often, we will have partial information about the forgotten information, such as the frustrating, "I know that I know the answer, but I can't remember it now." Psychologists call this experience the "tip of the tongue" phenomenon because of the maddening way the information seems to be right on the tip of the tongue, but cannot quite be recalled. Other times, we simply do not know what we have forgotten. Researchers have found that most often people treat the absence of information as though it is evidence that there is none. Let me explain with an example. Should you marry your significant other? Suppose that you can think of ("thinking of" is the same as recalling) two reasons why you should and none why you should not. Because you cannot recall any reasons that run counter to this decision, you rely on what can be recalled to guide your decision. The problem, of course, is that we cannot know what we have forgotten. However, it is possible to spend some time and effort considering what sort of evidence might have been forgotten and overlooked. Did you forget to consider that she picks her nose and this really bothers you, or that he is a sloppy housekeeper, a trait that drives you "crazy?" The need to generate information so that it can be evaluated is discussed in several places throughout this book. For now, think of it as a forgetting problem that can be lessened, but not eliminated, with conscious effort to consider what might have been forgotten. Because we cannot recall any reasons why we may be making the wrong decision, people tend to be overconfident about the quality of their decisions. A second reason for the overconfidence that we have in our thinking and remembering processes is that we can only act on one decision (e.g., marry or not), and we can never know if another decision would have been better.

Recall Errors

It is clear that we store knowledge (or generate it) in highly organized ways. Sometimes, the errors we make can provide clues to how it is organized. Recall that long-term memories are stored in associative networks. Has your father or mother ever called you by your sibling's name? Most people respond "Yes." But, few people report that their father or mother called them by the name of the family dog. Intuitively, this would be insulting (unless they really love the dog) because it suggests some underlying facts about how your parent thinks about you. Similarly, if your boyfriend or girlfriend called you by the name of a former significant other, this is also perceived as insulting because it suggests that he or she was thinking about the former boyfriend or girlfriend or that information about you and the former love are stored together in memory.

I can think of several examples where these "slips of the tongue" have revealed some tell-tale signs about the way people store information in memory. In one embarrassing example, a university administrator kept mixing up the names of two African American deans. This painful mix-up showed how he had stored information about them in memory and tended to think about them as "African American deans" instead of some other grouping or as individuals.

Stop now, and answer the two questions in the following box. After you write in the answer for each question, rate how confident you are that your answer is correct. Use the numbers 1 to 7 to rate your confidence with 1 = not at all confident, 7 = completely confident, and 4 = middle level of confidence.

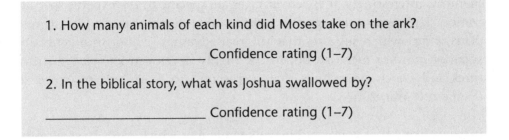

1. How many animals of each kind did Moses take on the ark?

_____ Confidence rating (1–7)

2. In the biblical story, what was Joshua swallowed by?

_____ Confidence rating (1–7)

Look over your confidence ratings and compare them with the ratings of other people to whom you asked these questions. If you responded like most people, you were very confident and very wrong. Did you respond with the "2" to the first question? If you did, you were wrong because Moses did not have an ark; you were thinking about Noah. What about the second question? Were you confident that the answer is a "whale?" If so, you were wrong again because it wasn't Joshua who was swallowed by a whale; it was Jonah. Demonstrations like this one show how memory works. When you read about animals on an ark, you activated your knowledge for the biblical ark story and never noticed that Moses was named in the question. The same thing happened with your knowledge of the biblical whale story. Reflect on what this shows us about human memory—the way it is organized and used and the way we can be completely confident and completely wrong. Try this demonstration with your family and friends and then explain to them what you have learned about remembering.

Chunking

As you can see, the strategies that we use to reduce the effort of thinking and remembering can lead to biases and errors. What is needed is an efficient way to reduce the demands on working memory that will not have a negative effect on what and how we think. Multiple studies of the ways that experts think have shown that one of the major differences between people with expertise in some field and those without the expertise is in the efficient way that the experts organize and recall information that is specific to their specialty. The experts are able to perceive large, meaningful patterns of information, which reflects the highly organized nature of the information in their memories. They also know how to search for answers to problems using information available in the environment and knowledge that they have stored in memory. Experts keep the goal clearly in mind, and regulate their thinking process. These highly compact memory "units" and efficient search strategies place fewer demands on working memory. Interestingly, these advantages are specific to the expert's specialization. They approach cognitive tasks in other domains much like the rest of us, a fact which suggests that the real advantage is not in a generally superior mind or memory, but in the highly developed knowledge structures and search procedures that correspond to one's area of expertise (Halpern & Wai, 2007).

It seems likely that good card players remember which cards have already been played because each hand is highly meaningful to them. For example, John Moss (1950, a pseudonym for the author of *How to Win at Poker*), describes a series of possible hands that a player can be dealt along with several possible cards that could be drawn. It would be easy for him or another poker shark to remember a "four of diamonds in the hole with a four of hearts, six of diamonds and ace of spades exposed." He could remember this as a single familiar hand, while a novice player would have to remember four separate cards. For the good players, this hand would represent a single chunk in memory. Reducing a large number of items to a single item to be remembered is called **chunking**. (No, it is not a brand of Chinese food.) It is a subtle and ubiquitous memory process that allows us to recall whole sentences instead of words and whole words instead of letters. As material becomes increasingly meaningful, we can reduce the number of items that need to be remembered. Master chess players and card players seem to have this memory advantage.

Look quickly at the row of letters and numbers presented below, and then cover them and try to remember as many as you can:

IB   MF   BI   TW   AJ   FK
816   44   93   62   51   69   41

If you had difficulty with this task, the reason may be that the information was not chunked or grouped into meaningful units. Suppose I reorganize the letters by changing the spacing but not their order. They now become IBM, FBI, TWA, JFK. You should have no difficulty remembering all of the letters now. The amount of information hasn't changed, but the cognitive demand has. It is much easier to recall information that it chunked into meaningful units. Consider the row of numbers. Suppose I tell you that this series, if regrouped, is the sequence 9^2, 8^2, 7^2, etc. Again, by relating the input to what's known to make it meaningful, a difficult memory task can be made trivial. The notion that meaning is important in memory will be raised again later in this chapter when we consider strategies for improving memory.

Metamemory

> If one has poor insights into the inner workings of their cognitive system, this should inhibit their performance on virtually all tasks, because it is hard to imagine a single cognitive task that does not require some level of metacognitive awareness for its successful completion.
>
> —Ceci and Ruiz (1993, p. 175)

The term **metamemory** refers to one's personal knowledge of his or her own memory system. It seems that much of the difference between good and poor learners can be attributed to metamemory. Bransford (1979) has summarized this:

[E]ffective learners know themselves, what they need to know and do in order to perform effectively; they are able to monitor their own levels of understanding and mastery. These active learners are therefore likely to ask questions of clarification and more efficiently plan their study activities. Such activities are quite different from passively accepting (yet momentarily actively processing) the particular information that a person or text presents" (p. 248).

This quote from Bransford brings up the important concept of active learning. Very little, if anything, can be learned passively. Good learners know when they understand the material and when they do not understand it; poor learners do not seem to notice the difference. Good learners know what they have to do to facilitate learning. These are the executive processes that keep the learner mindful of what and how much is being learned. For example, good learners may spontaneously link new information to information previously learned or think of possible applications for the new materials they are learning. As you read this paragraph, you may be applying this learning "device" by noting the similarity of this concept with one you learned in the section entitled organization, that imposing additional organization on material by activities like these will result in improved comprehension.

Nelson and Narens (1990) provided a list of tasks that are used in experimental settings to assess metamemory. This list can easily be adapted as a way to enhance metamemory. For example, before you begin a learning task, carefully assess the ease with which you expect to achieve the learning, called **ease of learning judgments**. If you are a senior in college who has majored in sociology, you might decide that the material presented in an introductory psychology text would be easy for you to learn. Alternatively, you could decide that a course in Asian philosophy would be relatively difficult to learn. The reason for making ease of learning judgments is that they require you think about the to-be-learned material, considering what you already know about the topic, your ability in the area, and the learning context. These reflections will prepare you to allocate the necessary time and mental resources to accomplish the task.

While you are learning, consider how well you know the material—that is, make judgments of how well you are learning—**quality of learning judgments**. If you can determine that it is not going well, then you can redirect your learning activities and seek help. After learning, think about how well you know and understand what has just been learned—**feelings of knowing judgments**. Finally, when you are using the material in a response, make **degree of confidence judgments** about your answers. Recent research has shown that when people monitor the types of information they are to learn, metamemory is improved (McCabe & Soderstron, 2011). Taken together, these four tasks will provide an ongoing monitor of learning and memory, and they can help with the selection of control procedures such allocating more time and effort, trying another study mode, and stopping the learning session.

These four metamemory tasks are summarized in Table 2.2.

Mnemonics

In an episode of the popular children's television show, *Sesame Street*, Bert and Ernie, two lovable muppets, discussed an intriguing memory phenomenon. Bert noticed that Ernie had tied a piece of string around his finger to help him remember something. In fact, Ernie tied string around each of his eight fingers (apparently muppets have eight fingers) to be really sure that he did not forget. After some prompting from Bert, Ernie recalled that the string was supposed to help him remember he should buy more string, as they had run out of string.

Although this story is humorous, it illustrates some fundamental assumptions and problems encountered by humans (and muppets) in dealing with their memory. The wide range of activities from tying a string around one's finger to the more elaborate procedures presented later are called **mnemonic devices**. They are techniques for organizing and elaborating

Table 2.2: Self-reflective tasks that can serve as a guide for monitoring the process of remembering.

When	What	How
Before Learning	Ease of Learning Judgments	Look over the material that is to be learned and judge the ease with which you will learn it. Consider what you already know about the topic, the reason why you are learning it, and your own abilities.
While Learning	Quality of Learning Judgments	As you learn, monitor how well you are understanding the information or performing a motor skill. Can you summarize in your own words what is being learned? Are you generating multiple cues and using techniques that foster deep learning?
After Learning	Feeling of Knowing Judgments	When the learning task is completed, reflect on how well you learned the material. Have you overlearned for maximal retention and used distributed practice? Will you be able to recall the material sometime in the future?
At Recall	Degree of Confidence Judgments	When you are recalling the information, consider how confident you are in your recall.

information so that it can be more easily remembered. Many students use mnemonic devices to prepare for exams and some of the techniques are so common that we usually don't think of them as mnemonics.

During the summers when I was in college, I worked as a waitress at a resort in the Catskill Mountains of New York. The resort had a nightclub with the usual array of singers, dancers, jugglers, and animal acts. (The kitchen help were not allowed to attend the nightclub, so, of course, we would sneak in as often as we could.) One particular act that amazed me was a memory act by Harry Lorayne. He went around the audience recalling people's names. His memory seemed limitless. I was also surprised at how much the audience enjoyed his performance and that an amazing memory would qualify as a nightclub act. After all, no one ever asked me to demonstrate the amazing powers of critical thinking as a nightclub act! (Perhaps there is a reader who books nightclub acts, who is just looking for this sort of late-night

CRANKSHAFT By Tom Batiuk & Chuck Ayers

Crankshaft © 2010 Mediagraphics, Inc. Dist. by North America Syndicate. Used with permission.

crowd-pleasing entertainment.) Harry Lorayne later wrote two books on this topic (Lorayne, 1975; Lorayne & Lucas, 1974). The mnemonic principles he used are presented here along with several others.

Most mnemonics are based on a few simple memory principles. They all force you to pay attention to the items to be remembered, and they provide either an organizational scheme or a meaningful context for unrelated items. The user is often required to organize the material and to use the mnemonic as an efficient retrieval cue. The use of mnemonics also requires metacognitive monitoring—keeping track of what you know. They are intentional strategies, ones that you can use when you decide that you want to remember something. Thus, from what you have already learned about memory earlier in this chapter, you can see that mnemonics are not mere theatrical tricks. They work because they represent applications of basic principles of memory.

We all employ memory aids every day. The most common aids are **external memory aids**, such as the sticky notes that are popular, entries in a PDA (personal digital assistant), timers to remind us to turn off the stove, and shopping lists. Mnemonics that are designed to help us retrieve information from memory are called **internal memory aids**. In this chapter, I present four basic types of internal memory aids. Each will be discussed in turn followed by some guidelines for selecting the appropriate mnemonic for the type of material to be learned.

Pegwords and Images

The following demonstration was presented by Norman (1976, p. 134). I have used it as a class demonstration many times, and students are always surprised at how well it works. The use of this mnemonic depends on first learning **pegwords**, which serve as "hooks" for information that is learned later. In this case, the pegwords are in the form of a simple poem to learn. Spend a minute or two learning this poem:

One is a bun,

Two is a shoe,

Three is a tree,

Four is a door,

Five is a hive,

Six are sticks,

Seven is heaven,

Eight is a gate,

Nine is a line, and

Ten is a hen.

Do you have this memorized? If not, go over the poem again.

Now, I am going to present a list of words to be remembered. You have to form an image or association between the listed items and the items in the poem you just learned. For example, the first item on the list is ashtray. Imagine an ashtray with a bun in it, since the bun was the first item in the poem. You could imagine something like a large hamburger bun sitting in a dirty ashtray. Read the items on the list one at a time, allowing enough time to form an image.

1. ashtray
2. firewood
3. picture
4. cigarette
5. table
6. matchbook
7. glass
8. lamp
9. shoe
10. phonograph

Now, cover the list of words and answer the following questions:

> What is number eight?
> What number is cigarette?

If your experience was like the one Norman described or the ones my students report, then you have been surprised to find that the answers were easily available. In this case you learned a list of rhyming pegwords and then used imagery to relate the words to be learned to the pegwords. Research has shown that images are best when they are interacting (e.g., the bun is in the ashtray and not just next to it) and when they are vivid and detailed (the bun that I was imaging was a hamburger bun with sesame seeds on it and the ashtray was glass). The deliberate use of both verbal and imagery modes of thought was introduced in the first chapter. We will use this strategy again in the chapters on creativity and problem solving. Of course, you are probably thinking, "Why not just write the list down on paper?" If paper and pencil are allowable and available, this is certainly the best and cheapest mnemonic that you can find, but often we need to commit lists to memory. If you are an anatomy student, you have to learn long lists of the names of nerves, bones, and other organs. Chemists need to learn complex formulas, and it would not instill confidence in me if I found that my surgeon kept a written list of body parts above the operating table (but, it might not be a bad idea). College students who were taught a pegword system for topics such as recalling the 10 highest mountains in the world showed better recall on both immediate and delayed tests (Carney & Levin, 2011). There are many real-life instances when we need to learn long lists of material in as efficient a way as possible.

Images can also be used alone (without pegwords). They are especially advantageous when you want to remember names and faces. This is the technique that Lorayne (1975) used. Change the names you want to remember to a concrete noun; pick out a distinctive feature of the face and image, the two as interacting. He suggested that you pay special attention to cheeks, lips, facial lines, forehead, nose, eyebrows, and eyes. For example, if you meet Ms. Silverstein and you notice that she has wide-set eyes, you could image a silver beer mug (stein) between her eyes. Mr. Dinter could be changed to dinner and an entire dinner could be imaged on his large forehead. Try this at the next party you attend. You'll find it fun, and you may surprise yourself with your new abilities.

A pegword mnemonic system has been developed especially for learning a second language (Atkinson, 1975). Suppose you are learning French and are faced with the following three vocabulary words with their English translations to learn:

French	English
homme	man
étoile	star
légume	vegetable

Students begin by generating their own pegwords. The pegword should sound like the foreign vocabulary word. Thus, for the word homme, I would generate "home," for etoile, I would use "a towel," and for legume, I would use "lagoon."

The second step makes use of imagery by linking an image of the pegword with the correct translation of the foreign word. I visualize a man entering a large home, a towel with a star painted on it, and vegetables floating in a lagoon. (It is best when the items are interacting.) When the foreign words homme, etoile, and legume are encountered, students would then automatically recall the images and retrieve the correct translations.

Atkinson claims that as facility with the foreign language develops, the need to remember the images diminishes and students can extract the intended meaning without the use of imagery. Students who are taught to use this method consistently recall more correct English translations (72% compared with 46%) than students who use the usual rote rehearsal method of repeating the words until they "stick." Furthermore, this method seems to work best when students generate their own pegwords and images. The need for active participation in learning and the pay off from the effortful work of learning are general rules for improving memory. This is a mnemonic that is well worth using if you are studying a foreign language.

How many different passwords do you have to remember for different accounts on the internet? More importantly, how many times have you forgotten a password and wasted time trying to find it? Here is a good mnemonic for passwords using imagery. In a study of using imagery to generate good passwords (not easily detected—usually have a combination of upper and lower case letters, numbers, and nonalphanumeric characters) and then recall them, participants were taught how to change an image into a password, so a photo of your friends might be used for a social media site and become "Fri3nds!" (Nelson & Vu, 2010). With a little effort (all mnemonics require effort), you can use this mnemonic for your own passwords.

Rhymes

We also use rhymes to help us remember. For example, there are few people who haven't heard:

I before E, except after C

or

Thirty days hath September, April, June, and November.

Answer this question quickly. What letter comes after N? Most people find that they need to sing that portion of the alphabet (l, m, n, o, p) to answer this question. Like rhymes, the rhythm established in songs help to deter forgetting.

Rhymes are useful when order is important because mistakes in order will usually destroy the rhyme. Notice that the first pegword poem I presented relied on pegwords, images, and rhymes (one is a bun, etc.). This is an especially easy mnemonic to use, probably because several mnemonic devices are employed in the same poem to guard against forgetting.

Method of Places

Before I describe how "places" works as a mnemonic device, I would like you to remember my back-to-school shopping list. Read the list through slowly once, then see how many items you can recall.

Pencils, Ruler, Notebook, Marking Pens, Compass, Tape, Paper, Scissors, Sharpener, Thumb Drive, Tablet, Glue

How many items on this list did you remember?

Here is how the **method of places** (or method of loci) could improve your recall for this list. Pick a familiar route, like the one from your house to school. Now imagine each of the items on this list placed somewhere along this route. The pencils could be very tall and form a fence around your front lawn, the ruler could be sitting across your car, the notebook could be the Stop sign at your corner, etc. Try this now with the back-to-school shopping list just presented. Once the images are formed, you should be able to remember every item by "mentally walking through" your route and noticing the items you've imagined along the way.

Research with the elderly has shown that they can perform as well as much younger college students when they are taught and use this mnemonic. This is important because America is an aging society, and many elderly fear a loss of memory. If you are elderly, or if you know someone who is, many of the simple mnemonics presented in this chapter such as the method of places and use of visual imagery can be used as an aid to memory and thus, postpone or reduce cognitive aging effects. It is also particularly useful to assist the elderly with the use of external memory aids such as medication boxes that have an alarm to signal the time for the medication, calendars, and timers. External aids have the advantage of helping those with failing (or poor) memory recall the tasks that are important.

First Letters

First Letter Mnemonics

They are probably most commonly used in preparing for tests. To use this technique, take the first letter of each term to be learned, insert vowels and other letters if necessary, and make a word. When you need to remember the list, you recall the word you formed and then use each letter as a retrieval cue for each item on the list. Many of us learned to remember the names of the Great Lakes as HOMES (Huron, Ontario, Michigan, Erie, and Superior). If you never learned this before, you will never forget it again.

In a recent study, college students in an accounting course were taught first letter mnemonics "as a useful tool for explaining the elements of accounting equations, the notion of debits and credit, and the principles of the basic accounting cycle" (Laing, 2010, p. 355). Here is an example from that study. The mnemonic was **PALER**, which stood for Proprietorship, Assets, Liabilities, Expenses, and Revenues. Students who learned this mnemonic did significantly better on a test of accounting principles that those who were not given this mnemonic. Student comments confirmed the test results—many students found that this mnemonic "helped them figure out what went where."

The first letter mnemonic organizes unrelated terms into a single word. You already know how important good organization is for memory. I can remember using this technique when I was a college student. The class had been told to be prepared to answer a long essay question that was to be written during an in-class exam. There were six points that I wanted to make in the essay, and I wanted to be sure that I included all of them in order. I took the first letter of each of the points, made up a word using these letters and used this word to help me remember all of the points for the exam. (It worked well.)

Mnemonic Principles

Mnemonic devices can be powerful aids for memory. They are also paradoxical because it seems that to remember better, you need to remember more. The first letter mnemonic requires that you remember the new word you created with the first letters as well as each of the words. The pegword systems require that you learn a pegword system, and the rhymes present you with a song or poem to be learned. Acquiring a good memory means working at it, but it is work that pays off in life-long dividends. There are hundreds of studies that demonstrate that the deliberate use of mnemonics improves recall (Worthen & Hunt, 2011).

There is probably no field that requires more rote memory, in addition to other sorts of remembering, than medicine. There are thousands of mnemonics to help students in the medical fields recall the names of anatomical parts and their connections. Here is one that I learned in biology class many years ago: "On Old Olympus Towering Tops, A Finn And German Viewed Some Hops": Some readers will recognize this mnemonic as a way to recall the 12 cranial nerves in order: Olfactory, Optic, Occulomotor, Trochlear, Trigeminal, Abducens, Facial, Auditory [or Vestibulocochlear], Glossopharyngeal, Vagus, Accessory [or Spinal root of the accessory], Hypoglossal.

Let's try to develop a mnemonic that could help you to remember the types of mnemonics. First, let's review what they are: pegwords and images, rhymes, method of places, and (first) letters. Although you could use the method of places and image each of these terms along a route, or associate them with a pegword, or make up a poem, my choice for a list like this one is the first letter mnemonic. Start by listing the first letter of each term: P, R, MP, L. You can modify the first letter technique by using each letter to begin a word in a sentence, since incorporating these letters in a single word may be difficult. Try it. The sentence one of my students came up with is "Pretty Round Men, Please Listen." Use imagery also to aid recall. Imagine a nice-looking round (fat) man with a kind face and very big ears (for listening). Make your images detailed and vivid. (Can you see his round tummy and elephant-size ears?) If you are asked to recall the mnemonic devices, you can list each one, and by remembering the name of each, all of the information you've learned about them should also be easily retrieved.

External Memory Aids

External memory aids, which are sometimes called "cognitive prostheses," are also valuable in helping with the multitude of remembering tasks that we all encounter. If you have to remember to do something, a kind of remembering called **prospective memory** because it is memory for a future event, why not set an alarm, post a note, tie a string on your finger, or leave something in an obvious and unavoidable place (e.g., leave a lunchbox in front of the door so that you do not forget to take it).

Some people have acquired specialized and specific external memory aids. I was impressed with such a system when I was attending a ballet at the grand Bolshoi Theatre in Moscow. Like many cities with very cold weather, it is customary to check your coat when you arrive at the theatre. In addition, many people also check bags, boots, and large hats. The workers at the wardrobe have to be able to dispense hundreds of possessions very quickly when the ballet is over. In addition, the checkers also rent binoculars and need to remember who rented the binoculars so as to be certain that the binoculars are returned. I found that the checkers had devised a simple external mnemonic system. The coat hooks are numbered (into the hundreds at each station). When someone checks a bag with the coat, the checker uses a number that ends in 4 (14, 24, 34, etc.). Then, when the claim ticket is presented at the end of the show, a 4 in the last digit means that the checker should look below for a package. If a person rents binoculars, then a chalk line is marked above the coat hook number. Then if a coat is retrieved and there is a chalk mark above the number, the checker knows that binoculars are to be returned. This simple system, which has probably developed over many years, helps to get a large number of people out of the wardrobe area and reduces the time spent in line. This last point is critical to Russians who often have to wait in long lines. If only such a system could be used to reduce the other lines as well.

Remembering Events

Most often we need to remember events rather than lists or related concepts. Much of the work done in the area of event memory has been conducted by psychologists trying to assist victims and witnesses of crime with recall of the criminal activity. We can borrow the mnemonic techniques that they use to improve memory.

The Cognitive Interview

"Information is the lifeblood of a criminal investigation" (Stewart, 1985). One way to improve the quantity and quality of what gets remembered is with the use of a memory aid for events known as the **cognitive interview** (Fisher, 1995). The cognitive interview is based on principles derived from cognitive psychology about how information is organized and the types of retrieval cues that can work to prime recall. It seems that the unflappable Sergeant Friday from the old television show "Dragnet" was wrong when he asked for "just the facts, ma'am." The accuracy and completeness of recall is improved by elaboration, especially about objects and activities that occurred near the crime in time or space. Geiselman and Fisher (1985) have found that recall for events can be enhanced by using the following strategies:

1. Start by recalling ordinary events that occurred before the target event (i.e., the crime). Visualize the circumstances. Think about the layout of the room, weather, traffic flow, or any other aspect of the scene. Think about your mood at the time.

2. Be as complete as possible in your recall. Don't edit your report or exclude something because you think that it might not be important.

3. Recall the event in both forward and backward order, or start from the middle and recall both forward and backward in time from some central incident.

4. Change your perspective. Try to recall the event as though you were some other person such as a spectator (real or imaginary) or you were the perpetrator of a crime.

If you are trying to remember the physical appearance of someone, does someone else whom you know come to mind? Why? In what ways are they similar? If you cannot recall a name, recite the alphabet to see if a particular letter can "jog" your memory. Sometimes partial information like the number of syllables in a name can be recalled. If numbers are involved (e.g., a

license plate), try to recall the number of digits or some physical characteristic of the digits like their size or color.

The techniques of the cognitive interview can be used anytime you need
to remember an event. Suppose you cannot remember where you left your
car keys. This can be a very frustrating type of forgetting. In this case, you
would try to retrace your steps and try to recall the last time you used
them. Recent research has shown that both young and older adults had
better recall for people and actions with the cognitive interview than a
control group (Holliday et al., 2012).

Biases in Memory

> Memory is a complicated thing, a relative to truth, but not its twin.
> —Barbara Kingsolver (p. 48)

Unfortunately, our memories are subject to certain biases. All items stored
in memory are not equally likely to be recalled, and when memory errors
occur, they are not random. Because all thinking relies on memory, it is
important to recognize the ways in which memory can be biased.

Confirmation Bias

> Virtually all violent regimes fan the flames of extreme confirmation
> bias in their citizens, especially their youth, by presenting them with
> only one point of view and assiduously insulating them from all others.
> —Scott O. Lilienfeld, Rachel Ammirati, and Kristin Landfield
> (2009, p. 391)

The bias to seek out and prefer information that is consistent with our beliefs is very strong (Jonas, Schulz-Hardt, Frey, & Thalen, 2001). It occurs
when people make decisions, solve problems, estimate likelihoods, decide
whom to trust, and how to invest money. I return to this idea several times
throughout this book because the confirmation bias is ubiquitous—it can
be found virtually everywhere. Lilienfeld (2010) urges that we become
constantly vigilant for its influences on memory. He quotes from the famed
astronomer Carl Sagan and his wife and coauthor Ann Druyan who note
that "science is like a little voice in our heads that says, 'You might be mistaken. You've been wrong before.'" No one is immune from confirmation

bias. The best safeguard is to recognize how often it occurs and to remain vigilant to guards against its insidious effects.

Vivid, Dramatic, Personal, and Familiar

We also know that there is a recall advantage to information that is well known, familiar, prominent (generally important or personal), recent, vivid, and dramatic. People tend to be very confident about their memory for emotional events, but these memories are often inaccurate (Phelps & Sharot, 2008). In addition, general knowledge about events is sometimes mistaken as memory for a specific event because people cannot tell the difference between events as they were experienced and events that they constructed from general knowledge (Jacoby, Kelley, & Dywan, 1989). These biases in memory have profound effects on how people think.

Long-Term Accuracy is Sometimes Excellent

> Memory is a heterogeneous, mottled system that both improves and declines over time, is both accurate and distortion prone.
>
> —Matthew Hugh Erdelyi (2010, p. 631)

Before you despair completely, you will be happy to know that memory can also be fairly good, especially if you practice the rules for good learning, retention, and retrieval that were presented earlier in this chapter. If you were wondering, "Why bother learning this, if I will soon forget it and not even know that I forgot," there are several good reasons to keep studying. It seems that memory for information learned in a cognitive psychology class was still fairly good for main concepts and important ideas, even 12 years after learning, although memory for many of the names of the theorists tended to be forgotten in about three years (Conway, Cohen, & Stanhope, 1991) and memory for high school math was almost perfect decades later for students who continued learning and took math in college (Bahrick & Hall, 1991). The original level of learning is important in determining how well something will be remembered over time, with higher levels of learning associated with better long-term memory. Similarly, memory for the neighborhood where adults grew up was also marked with a short period of forgetting followed by good memory (for what was not forgotten) for 40 or more years (Schmidt, Peeck, Paas, & van Breukelen, 2000). As in the other studies, good remembering was associated with overlearning and spacing of learning episodes. Thus, the more you learn, the better you remember information related to the topic of your learning, with broad principles and concepts generally well remembered for a lifetime.

You can take advantage of these operating principles of memory in two ways. First, you could use them to improve memory by considering information that you want to remember by overlearning and spacing learning sessions over time. In addition, make the material to-be-learned familiar and prominent, generate encoding cues, use organizational strategies, and elaborate by connecting the new information to knowledge you have already acquired. Perhaps, even more importantly, you can be aware of the ways your memory is likely to be biased and engage in deliberate attempts to debias your recollections.

Chapter Summary

- Memory was described as the mediator of cognitive processes because all of our thoughts depend upon the ability to use what we have stored in memory.

- Long-term memories are stored in associative networks, so remembering something automatically makes it more likely to remember related concepts.

- Most people believe that memory is like a video camera that records and replays an accurate version of what happened, but in fact, memory is often inaccurate, even when people are highly confident that they are remembering accurately. We often miss even unusual events that occur "right before our eyes," and we often believe information that seems familiar even when it is not true.

- The "illusion of truth" refers to the memory phenomenon in which we forget the source and sometimes even the content of a message, but when we encounter the name of a person who was part of the forgotten message, the "feeling of familiarity" is interpreted as "the new message must be true." This occurs without conscious awareness, so all we can do is be aware of the possibility that it is happening and be less willing to believe rumors or innuendos.

- There are many different varieties of memory. What and how you learn and remember will depend on the type of information to-be-remembered, what you already know, the length of the retention interval, and noncognitive factors like health and motivation.

- Working memory is the term used for the "place" in which we consciously think. It has a seriously limited capacity that we can control by deciding which information to attend to and how much effort a particular task is worth. When learning is difficult, we need to reduce the load on working memory. This can be done by writing information on paper, making it more automatic, or attending to the information to-be-learned.

- By engaging in the hard work of effortful learning, you can make whatever is being learned easier and more automatic, so there is a real pay-off in effort for those who are willing to work at their learning.

- There are many learning strategies that reflect the fact that all learning is not the same. Good learners will know what they have to do to learn and remember, and they will do it.

- Memory can be improved with appropriate retrieval cues and good organization. Generation of to-be-remembered information (with minimal or varied cues) spaced over time will result in enhanced recall relative to passive or massed rehearsal.

- Mnemonics improve recall because they utilize the basic memory principles of attention, organization, meaningfulness, and chunking. The mnemonics presented were pegwords and images, rhymes, method of places, and first letters.

- Memory for events can be improved with the cognitive interview technique, which uses elaboration at recall to improve memory.

- Although difficult to believe, even those memories in which we are very confident can be completely wrong. This is difficult for most people to accept because our phenomenological sense is that our own memories are "true."

- Our memories are biased in predictable ways. Examine your own recall for the possible influence of biases related to stereotypes, general knowledge, positive reflections on oneself, or for information characteristics such as being well known, familiar, prominent, recent, vivid, and/or dramatic.

The following skills to enhance your memory were presented in this chapter. Review each skill and be sure that you understand how and when to use each one.

- monitoring your attention
- developing an awareness of the influence of stereotypes and other beliefs on what we remember

- making abstract information meaningful as an aid to comprehension and recall
- using advance organizers to anticipate new information and to prepare for reading
- organizing information so that it can be recalled more easily
- overlearning because you know that it will increase the probability and accuracy of recall
- recognizing that although you may be very confident that you are recalling an event accurately, there is also a high probability that your memory is not as accurate as it feels
- generating retrieval cues at both acquisition and retrieval
- practicing recall for information that you are intentionally trying to learn
- monitoring how well you are learning
- using external memory aids
- employing pegwords and images, rhymes, places, and first letters as internal memory aids
- applying cognitive interview techniques
- developing an awareness of biases in memory so that you can consider the way your own beliefs, attitudes, and background knowledge could be influencing what and how you remember.

Terms to Know

You should be able to define or describe the following terms and concepts. If you find that you're having difficulty with any term, be sure to reread the section in which it is discussed.

Thinking. The manipulation or transformation of some internal representation.

Associative Networks. Spider-like organizations of information in which closely related topics are located near each other and those that bear little relationship to each other are farther away.

Change Blindness Blindness. People do not believe that they do not "see" (are blind to) major events that occur "right before their eyes."

Implicit Memory. Memory about which we have little conscious knowledge.

Illusion of Truth. When a message is forgotten and the name of a person (or an event) that was in the forgotten message is encountered at some time in the future, this person (or event) feels familiar. People look for reasons why it would feel familiar and decide that the new message must be true.

Working Memory. The "place" where knowledge is consciously manipulated or transformed. Thinking is constrained because working memory has a limited capacity.

Episodic Memory. Memory for events in which we can remember our own participation.

Semantic Memory. Memory for facts like word meanings and the multiplication tables.

Declarative Memory. Knowledge that can be verbalized easily.

Motor Memory. Memory for the performance of motor skills like swimming or riding a bicycle.

Procedural Memory. Memory for accomplishing some task such as using a slide rule or operating equipment.

Automatic Memory. Remembering that seems effortless such as the memory for the frequency of events.

Effortful Memory. Remembering that requires the deliberate and conscious use of strategies such as memory for a series of dates.

Intentional Learning. Used to describe learning efforts and activities that are engaged in when a learner is deliberately trying to learn something so that is can be recalled later.

Incidental Learning. When learning occurs without any deliberate effort, such as learning the plot of a television show or the habits of family members.

Acquisition. Used to describe learning. Also known as encoding, or putting information into memory.

Retention Interval. The time interval between the acquisition of new information (learning) and its retrieval.

Retrieval. The act of recalling or remembering information that had been previously acquired (learned).

Advance Organizers. Outlines or other summaries that are used before learning to assist with the process of acquisition

Inert Knowledge. Knowledge that isn't recalled when it is needed.

Encoding Specificity. The cues that are available at learning (or encoding) will be useful if they are also available at retrieval.

Interference Theory of Forgetting. A theory of how we forget that attributes forgetting to "interference" or displacement of the to-be-remembered items by other material that has been previously or subsequently learned.

Chunking. A memory process in which a number of related items are stored and retrieved as a unit in order to facilitate memory.

Metamemory. A person's knowledge about his or her own memory system; for example, knowing that you have to repeat a series of digits in order to maintain them in memory.

Ease of Learning Judgments. Individual estimates of how easy or difficult it will be to learn a skill or information. This type of judgment is made before the learning process.

Quality of Learning Judgments. Individual estimates of how well material is being learned. This type of judgment is made during the learning process.

Feelings of Knowing Judgments. Individual estimates of how well something is known. This type of judgment is made after the learning process.

Degree of Confidence. Individual estimates of whether a particular response is correct. This type of judgment is made at the time of retrieval.

Mnemonic Devices. Memory aids or techniques that are utilized to improve memory

External Memory Aids. The deliberate use of lists, timers, calendars, and similar devices to remind an individual to do something.

Prospective Memory. Remembering to do something at some time in the future.

Internal Memory Aids. Mnemonic devices or memory aids that rely on plans or strategies to make retrieval easier and more likely.

Pegwords. A mnemonic device or memory aid in which a previously learned list of words or rhymes serve as associates or "hooks" for the to-be-remembered items.

Method of Places. (Also known as method of loci) A mnemonic device or memory aid in which a familiar route is selected and the to-be-remembered items are imaged at intervals along the route. At recall, the individual "mentally traverses" the route to retrieve the items.

First Letter Mnemonics. A mnemonic device or memory aid in which the first letters of each word to be learned are combined into a single word.

Cognitive Interview. A technique for recalling events that uses principles of cognitive psychology to guide the retrieval process.

CHAPTER 3

THE RELATIONSHIP BETWEEN THOUGHT AND LANGUAGE

Contents

There is an old story about three umpires that goes something like this:

Three umpires were unwinding at a local pub after a very tough day. All three had endured abusive shouts like, "Kill the Umpire" and had numerous offers for new pairs of eyeglasses. After a few mugs of brew, they began discussing how they decide to call balls and strikes. The first umpire, Jim, explained that it was really quite simple. "I simply call them as I see them."

Donnie, the second umpire, disagreed when he said, "I see them as I call them."

Neil, the third umpire, emphatically shook his head in disagreement with the other two. "You're both wrong," he said, slurring his words somewhat. "They don't even exist until I call them."

Neil had a good point. Whether a ball whizzing past home plate is a ball or strike depends on what the umpire labels it. The words he uses both interpret and define reality.

Thought and Language

The development of mind, thought, and language is simply a nexus in which it is impossible to separate one from the other.
—Michael Studdert-Kennedy (quoted in Restak, 1988, p. 231)

How do you express your thoughts in words and sentences? How influenced are you by your particular language? You will have difficulty answering these questions because you use both so automatically and because you have no conscious awareness of the way your thoughts give rise to the words you use to express them. In fact, if you try to monitor your speaking process, you'll find yourself stuttering and interfering with the fluid speech that you normally create so easily. It is as though speech emerges automatically and preformed. Conscious attention directed at the process tends to interfere with it.

Psycholinguistics

> Communication is primarily an exercise in thinking.
> —Russell Pitt and Jack Leavenworth (1968, p. viii)

Psycholinguistics is the field of psychology concerned with how we acquire and use language. Language is a complex cognitive activity that all normal humans perform with apparent skill and ease. As speakers, we select the words we want to use and produce them in a (mostly) grammatically correct form. As listeners, we use the information in another's utterance to share the expressed thoughts. What do we know about the way speakers and listeners share thoughts through the medium of language?

Underlying Representation and Surface Structure

> Language appears to be simply the clothing of naked thought.
> —James E. Miller (1972, p. 43)

The comprehension of language is a process in which the message is used to construct a representation of the information referred to in the message. The sequence of sounds that we produce must correspond to our intended meaning if we are to communicate successfully. The "sender" and the "receiver" also must share a common knowledge of word meanings and grammar. Because language is always incomplete, the receiver must rely on prior knowledge, context, and other cues to comprehension to construct a correct representation.

Psychologists who are concerned with the way people use and understand language divide language into two structures or types of representations. The **underlying representation** of language refers to the meaning component of language—it is the thought you want to convey. **Surface structure** refers to the sounds of the verbal expression that you use or its written form on paper, a computer monitor, or some other writing surface. Look carefully at Figure 3.1 which depicts this process.

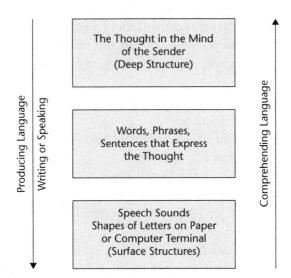

Figure 3.1 The problem of comprehension. The sender has a thought that she wants to communicate to a receiver. The thought (deep structure) is private and known only to the sender. It is transformed by speech sounds or the shapes of letters (surface structure), which are used by the receiver to reconstruct the meaning expressed by the sender's words.

As you can see, the thought in the mind of the "sender" is the underlying or deep structure. The thought is private and known only to the sender. The problem in producing language is deriving surface structure from the underlying representation in the sender's mind, while the problem in comprehending language is getting from the surface structure back to the speaker's (or writer's) underlying representation. Language is integral in these processes because it is the medium with which thoughts and emotions are most often expressed and interpreted (although other media such as dance, mime, and visual art are sometimes used to express thoughts and emotions).

A communication is "successful" when the underlying representation constructed by the receiver matches the underlying representation of the sender. The receiver's representation of the meaning is constructed over time because using language is a sequential process with words uttered or read one after the other. All strategies for improving comprehension involve ways of building representations so that they will most nearly match the one intended by the sender. It is the representation of knowledge about the world, the "architecture of the cognitive system," that mediates comprehension.

When language is ambiguous, the surface structure can have more than one meaning or underlying representation. Real newspaper headlines are written to be as short as possible, and in the writing, there are sometimes hilarious examples of ambiguity. Here are some examples (from fun-with-words.com):

Kids Make Nutritious Snacks
Grandmother of Eight Makes Hole in One
Milk Drinkers Are Turning to Powder
Drunk Gets Nine Months in Violin Case
Lack of Brains Hinders Research
2 Sisters Reunited After 18 Years at Checkout Counter

The reason that these headlines are so funny is that we start "down the garden path" assuming one meaning, which is then changed on us or we can think of more than one meaning at a time and one of the meanings is, well, less meaningful.

Implications and Inference

Communication depends as much on information that is implied as it does on the words that are explicitly stated. Comprehension of meaningful material will always require the listener or reader to make inferences by going beyond the words uttered. Consider this very simple three-sentence story:

Matt inherited a great deal of money.
Bertha loves diamonds and furs.
Bertha married Matt.

Although very little factual information was provided, it is a meaningful story. Readers infer that Bertha married Matt for his money and that she will use his money to buy diamonds and furs, although this interpretation may not be correct. All communication requires the receiver to fill in gaps between given bits of information to understand the intended meaning. Much of the meaning people convey goes beyond the meaning of the words they utter.

The Role of Inference in Advertisements

One of our defects as a nation is a tendency to use what have been called weasel words. When a weasel sucks eggs the meat is sucked out

of the egg. If you use a weasel word after another there is nothing left of the other.
—Theodore Roosevelt (1916 presidential speech, former president of the United States, from dictionary.com)

When you produce speech, the intended meaning is implied or suggested by the words you use, the context in which it is embedded, and verbal and nonverbal expressions. It is possible to say one thing while communicating something quite different. This technique is often used by advertisers who want to persuade you to buy their products, yet have legal restrictions on the kinds of statements they can make. If they get you to infer meaning from the advertisement, they are protected from making false claims. Here are some examples (modified just enough to keep me out of legal trouble):

Consuming fiber is an important part of a weight loss system.
FiberBars are the only fiber bar that tastes better than the box it comes in. Try one today!

The narrator never says that eating fiber will cause weight loss. Fiber is an important part of a weight loss system, but so are protein and exercise. "An important part of" is a common **weasel phrase** that is used so that the receiver of the communication infers something that is not said because it is not true. Weasel phrases convey the idea that something specific has been said, when it fact the words used are general and ambiguous. The image for a weasel phrase is that of an empty egg—something that appears to be solid and useful, but in fact is empty and devoid of content. Here's another example:

What should you do during those dreaded moments when you feel a cold starting? You could do nothing or take ColdAway.

The inference is that taking ColdAway will somehow make your cold go away. Of course, nothing like that is actually said—it is inferred because we automatically make meaning from communications and fill in the blanks in ways that make sense.

Carefully selected words in advertisements are used to create an inference that something is true when it is not. Airlines and other businesses often boast:

"Nobody beats our fares."

The air lines (or at least those who write their advertisements) expect that readers will infer that this means that they have the lowest fares. Of course, they never state that they have the lowest fares because that would be false. Nobody beats their fares because nearly all of the fares are the same. They could have said, "Our fares are the same as our competitors." But, if they said it that way, it would not mislead readers into believing that they have the lowest fares, and consumers would correctly conclude that it does not matter which airline they book with if cost is the sole determining factor. Always consider the distinction between the linguistic content of the message and the inference you draw from it.

When you start reading and listening critically to advertisements, you may be surprised to find appalling attempts to create impressions that can change beliefs. It is fun to start looking carefully at what advertisements actually say and what we infer. It is instructive to read the advertisements for supposed weight loss products (e.g., cellulite creams, sauna suits, herbal wraps, fat-burning vitamins, magic formula pills). Even the ubiquitous "before and after" photos are designed to create the inference that you will lose "30 or more pounds in two weeks" while eating anything you want and without "tedious" exercise.

The ubiquitous "studies show" is lampooned in the following cartoon.

Cognitive psychologists know that people remember the implied meaning of a message, and not the actual statements that were made. If you have already read the chapter on the development of memory skills, this should not be surprising to you. Meaningful information is more easily remembered than nonmeaningful information. We rarely remember statements

Non Sequitur by Wiley Miller. Used with permission by Universal Press Syndicate.

verbatim. Thus, our memory of events depends on the interpretations we give them when they occur.

Rules for Clear Communication

> "When I use a word," Humpty Dumpty said, in a rather scornful tone, "it means just what I choose it to mean—neither more nor less."
> "The question is," said Alice, "whether you can make words mean so many different things."
> "The question is," said Humpty Dumpty, "which is to be master—that's all."
> —Lewis Carroll (Through the Looking Glass, 1872, p. 190)

To communicate effectively, you need to know a great many things in addition to the thought being communicated and the words being used as the vehicle for the communication: What is the purpose of the communication? What are your listener's characteristics—what is your listener's age and social status? How much does the listener know or want to know about the topic? The answers to all of these questions shape the nature of communications. We implicitly change the way we speak or write, depending on how we answer these questions, and we make these changes without realizing the extent to which the listener shapes our use of language. Communication is governed by rules that we all obey, although you may never have consciously considered them.

Rule 1: Tell listeners what you believe they want to know

Consider how you would answer a simple question like, "Where do you live?" If I met you in Europe and asked you this question, you would probably respond with the name of your country, for example, "In the United States." If I asked you this question in New York, you would respond with the name of a state, "In Pennsylvania." If I asked you the same question on your college campus, you might respond, "In the dorms." If I asked you this question while we were in the dorms, you might respond, "In Wing D, Room 331." And, if I asked you this question in your dorm room, you would probably reply by giving the name of your hometown. The same question could be asked each time, yet you would give a different answer that depended on the context in which the question is asked and what you thought I wanted to know. The level of information you choose to convey depends on the purpose of the communication.

Rule 2: Don't tell listeners what they already know

In the first chapter, I began by introducing the topic of thinking and the need for the development of critical thinking skills. You probably did not think that this was unusual. Suppose I started every chapter in this book the same way. You would not only think that this was unusual, you may also question my mental status.

When you present information to an audience, you balance the amount of new information that you present with the old or already known information. If you present too much new information at once, listeners will be lost and will not be able to extract the intended meaning; if you present too much old or known information, listeners will be bored. The relative proportion of old information to new information is known as the **given/ new distinction**.

The ratio of given or known information to new information is a determinant of the difficulty of a communication. If a passage (spoken or written) contains too much new material for a listener or reader, it will be difficult to comprehend. No one would take an advanced course in biochemistry without first obtaining the requisite background in biology and chemistry. The educational process, if successful, fosters the transformation of new information into the students' systems of known information. This simple fact is often overlooked and communication fails. Have you ever had the experience of listening to a physician explain the cause or treatment of a health problem and been lost after the first sentence or two? Few physicians are skilled at understanding what their patients are likely to know about medicine, so they often use unfamiliar terms and assume that their patients have better medical knowledge than they actually do. The result is miscommunication, which can have disastrous consequences.

Rule 3: Vary the style of your communication, depending upon the knowledge, age, and status of the listeners

Suppose you are an expert computer programmer given the task of describing the operations of a computer center to a group of visitors. You would vary the way you convey the necessary information for each of the following: a group of politicians; a group of children from an elementary school; your history professor; a close friend; or an expert programmer from another university.

Your communication would be more or less technical depending on what you believe your listener knows about the topic. You might tell the politicians about the high costs of maintaining a computer center; the elementary school children might simply be told about the general use of computers; you might explain to your history professor how computers can be used in research; your close friend might be told that you feel you're being underpaid; and the visiting programmer might be told about the capacity of the computers and the steps you have taken to prevent the spread of computer viruses.

The readability of text or ease with which spoken language is understood depends, in large part, on the match between the text and the reader. The reason so many of us find income tax and legal documents so difficult is that they are written by and for accountants and lawyers—people with highly differentiated underlying representations of the topics referred to in these documents. The rest of us have to make many more inferences and more memory searches to understand the concepts because our underlying representations of these concepts are relatively sparse. This is why whenever we are engaged in communication, it is important to consider the characteristics of the reader or listener. This is a more formal way of saying that the beliefs, knowledge, and expectations of the intended audience for a communication should determine how much detail goes into a communication and which words are used. The difficulty of a text does not reside in the text itself, but in the reader-text interaction.

The idea that what people understand depends on what they already know was beautifully made in a book written for young readers. It is a tale about a fish who gets to learn about the world above the sea as it is explained to him by a friendly frog (Lionni, 2005). When the frog tells of humans who walk upright, we see the fish's mental image of walking fish. The story goes on to show how each description of the dry world would be interpreted by a learner who only knew of the water world. No matter how accurate the description, the fish's understanding was strictly limited by his own life experiences and knowledge of the world. A depiction of what the fish thought a cow would look like is shown in Figure 3.2

Rule 4: Tell the truth

When we communicate with each other, it is assumed that the information being conveyed is truthful. This is an imperative for meaningful communication. Of course, sometimes people lie. How do you process information when

Figure 3.2 Lionni's *Fish is Fish*. When a friendly frog tells a fish about cows, the fish envisions a cow that looks a lot like the fish. The reality that we each construct for ourselves is based on what we know about the world, and when our knowledge is limited, so is our perception of reality. (From *Fish is Fish* by Leo Lionni, copyright © 1970 by Leo Lionni. Copyright renewed 1998 by Leo Lionni. Used by permission of Alfred A. Knopf, an imprint of Random House Children's Books, a division of Random House, Inc. Any third party use of this material, outside of this publication, is prohibited. Interested parties must apply directly to Random House, Inc. for permission.)

you believe that the speaker may be lying? All components of the communication are scrutinized. In general, the communication process breaks down when the listener suspects that the speaker is violating this rule. This loss of communication is eloquently described by Chang (1993) in her description of life during Mao's reign over communist China, a time when no one dared to speak the truth: "The whole nation slid into doublespeak. Words became divorced from reality, responsibility, and people's real thoughts. Lies were told with ease because words had lost their meaning" (p. 298).

Rule 5: Use a simple straightforward style

Mark Twain said this best when he said, "Eschew surplusage." Information is transmitted best when simple and precise language is used. Some people think that the use of multisyllabic words and intricate sentence structures is a sign of intelligence. This is not true. It is a far more difficult task to express complex thoughts in simple language than to express simple thoughts in complex language. The transformation of our private thoughts into easily understood language is the benchmark of human cognition. Sloppy thinking can never be made good even with the most flowery language.

Rule 6: Use context and manner to clarify meaning

Meaning depends not only on the words that we use, but also on the context and the manner we use to convey it. Have you ever had the experience of having someone say, "I'll be happy to do that for you" in a manner that clearly showed that she was most unhappy?

Context is a critical aid for comprehension. "The food is on the table" can be an invitation to eat or a simple descriptive statement, depending on the context. Context is also used to decide which of two possible meanings is the intended meaning of an ambiguous sentence.

Ekman (1992) speaks of "lying truthfully," that is, literally telling the truth while leaving the listener with the opposite impression. For example, he tells about a man who had been unfaithful to his wife for years without getting caught. He had, on several occasions, taken money from her purse to buy flowers for other women. Each time he did this, she noticed the missing money and innocently commented to him: "I could have sworn I had an extra $50 in my purse; I must have lost it." Finally, one day she suspects that her partner has been unfaithful to her because she finds matches from a local hotel in his coat when she takes it to the cleaner. When she confronts him about this, he "honestly lies," by retorting: "Right. I've been having a torrid affair during my lunch breaks; and do you remember those times you thought you had lost money? Well, you didn't. I've been stealing your money to buy my noon-time lovers gifts. And, let me see, what other ignominies have I omitted?" This man just made a complete confession, yet the intent was to mislead his wife by casting it in irony. Intonation matters!

Here's another example: suppose you are asked to write a letter of recommendation for someone you do not want to recommend. Of course you could just decline the request, but what if you really wanted the person who did the asking to get a job somewhere else. You could write, "I cannot tell you how happy I am to write this letter of recommendation for Ama Zlotsky." The impression is that you are happy to recommend her, but the actual words say something quite different.

Figure 3.3 is a visual demonstration of the effect of context on what we see. You'll find that you have no difficulty reading any of the words in Figure 3.3. Now look carefully at the letters that make up the words. The "H" in "the" is the same form as the "A" in "cat," yet you may not have noticed this unless I pointed it out to you. Similarly, the way we perceive the other "inky" letters depends on the rest of the letters that make up the word context. Context provides strong cues that guide the way we construct knowledge about the nature of the world.

Analogy and Metaphor

> Midway between the unintelligible and the commonplace, it is metaphor which most produces knowledge.
>
> —Aristotle (Rhetoric III, 1410b)

One exception to the rule that the words used to convey a message should correspond to their intended meaning is the use of analogy and metaphor. (The English grammatical distinction between analogy, metaphor, and simile is not being considered here because it is irrelevant in this context.) If I tell you that "Myrtle is a hard-headed woman," the literal translation is not the one intended. In this case, the receiver must use his knowledge about the referent topic (hard surfaces) and "map" the relevant knowledge

Figure 3.3 Examples of the ways context influences meaning. Notice, for example, that the "D" in "RED" is identical to the "B" in "DEBT." (Adapted from Rumelhart, D.E., McClelland, J.L., and the PDP Research Group. [1986]. Parallel distributed processing. Cambridge, MA: The MIT Press, p. 8.)

onto his knowledge of Myrtle. Although you certainly have never met Myrtle, and you may never have heard the expression "a hard-headed woman," you can probably tell me that she is a stubborn, strong-willed person. You came to this understanding by taking your knowledge of hard surfaces, selecting characteristics of hard surfaces that might be relevant to a description of a person, and transferring that knowledge to what you already know about Myrtle.

Using Analogies as an Aid to Understanding

Analogies are pervasive in human thought. Whenever we are faced with a novel situation, we seek to understand it by reference to a known familiar one. When we think by analogy, we map the underlying structure of a known topic onto the target or unknown topic. This mental process is known as "structure mapping" (Wolff & Genter, 2011). Structure mapping assumes network-like representations of concepts in memory in which underlying structural relationships and surface attributes (physical characteristics) are coded along with each concept. For example, when we read that an atom is like a miniature solar system, the implication is that the solar system and the atom have similar relationships between their component parts—smaller bodies revolving around a larger one in fixed path patterns. Other aspects, such as surface similarity (e.g., the sun is hot and large and contains burning gases) are not implied. Analogies can be a useful tool in the comprehension and recall of scientific passages (Guerra-Ramos, 2011; Halpern, Hansen, & Riefer, 1990). Other examples that have been used to teach scientific concepts to elementary school students are (a) the function of enzymes is like a lock and key; (b) the heart is like a system of buckets and pumps; and (c) the circulatory system is like a railway. When students read technical passages that contained appropriate analogies to familiar topics, they scored higher on tests of comprehension and recall than a control group of students who read the same passage without the analogy.

All analogies and metaphors state that two concepts are alike in some way. Good analogies have similar underlying structures even when the topics are highly dissimilar. They maintain much of their underlying structure in the transfer from base (known) to target (unknown) domains, while surface features are of minimal importance. Poor analogies are ones in which only surface or superficial characteristics are similar. If I said that Myrtle is like milk because they both start with the letter *m*, I would be using a very poor analogy. Whenever you encounter an analogy, you need to consider the nature of the similarity relationship. Are the two concepts similar in their underlying structure so that relevant information about one concept can be used to understand the other concept, or is the similarity trivial?

Using Analogies as Problem-Solving Aids. What do you do when you are faced with a problem that has no obvious solution? I address this question in more detail in the chapter on problem solving, but one strategy that is appropriate to consider here is the use of a solution that is borrowed from a problem with a similar structure, often from a very different domain of knowledge. The conditions under which people do and do not recognize and use analogous solutions for problems from very distant domains of knowledge has been the subject of much research (e.g., Bearman, Ball, & Ormerod, 2007). In order for this strategy to "work," the problem solver must recognize that the essential characteristics of the two problems are similar, despite the fact that the topics may be very different.

Consider, for example, the problem of bonding (gluing) two surfaces during dental surgery. All bonding substances require a dry surface for bonding, and the mouth is a wet environment. How can this problem be solved? The use of the small towels or "teeth driers" does not work well during oral surgery, which can involve profusive bleeding and the production of much saliva. Some creative dental surgeon looked for similar problems in other domains. He or she (I don't know the identity of this unsung critical thinker) studied the way barnacles attach themselves to piers and other surfaces in the ocean. The adaptive barnacle displaces the water (sort of moves it aside) from the small area to which it (she or he?) is attaching. This displacement of fluids has been modified for use in dentistry. If you are like most people, you will agree that any discovery that makes dental surgery quicker and more successful is a welcome advance. In this example, the problem solver considered the similarities in the two problems of bonding in wet environments and then adapted a solution from one domain (barnacles in the ocean) to a very different one (dental bonding). In this way, an analogy was used to solve a problem.

Dunbar (2001) investigated the use of analogies in real-life settings where experts in a field solve real problems, not the artificial ones that cognitive psychologists create. He found very different results. Real experts involved in solving problems that are important to them use analogies that share "deep structural features" (p. 126). Scientists generate anywhere from between 3 to 15 analogies in a one-hour laboratory meeting, with the majority coming from the domain in which they are working. Dunbar concluded that analogies focusing on relational features are frequently used to help solve problems. More recent research found that novices can and do use analogies, and, like experts, they use them to solve problems and to illustrate a situation (Bearman et al., 2007). It seems that research done in laboratory settings underestimated the extent to which people use analogies as part of their everyday thinking.

Using Analogies to Persuade

> Analogies prove nothing, but they make us feel right at home.
> —Sigmund Freud (quoted in Rothy, 2009, p. 12)

In the classic movie, *Dead Poets Society*, the unlikely hero, Robin Williams, who plays a high school teacher of English, asks his class of young men, "What is the purpose of language?" After a short period of silence, a student yells out the obvious answer, "to communicate." Of course, this is not the correct answer in the movie. The hero-English-teacher-character responds that the purpose of language is to "woo women." An important point is made in this fictional exchange between student and teacher. The purpose of language is to persuade—to change how and what people think. We use language to persuade others to like or date us (as expressed in this movie), to alter or maintain political beliefs (e.g., capitalism is good), or to convince someone to make a purchase (e.g., a particular brand of jeans).

We frequently use analogies to persuade someone that X is analogous to Y, therefore what is true for X is also true for Y. A good example of this sort of "reasoning by analogy" was presented by Bransford, Arbitman-Smith, Stein, and Vye (1985). They described a legal trial in the book, *Till Death Us Do Part* (Bugliosi, 1978). Much of the evidence presented at the trial was circumstantial. The attorney for the defense argued that the evidence was like a chain, and like a chain, it was only as strong as its weakest link. He went on to argue that there were several weak links in the evidence; therefore, the jurors should not convict the accused. The prosecutor also used an analogy to make his point. He argued that the evidence was like a rope made of many independent strands. Several strands can be weak and break, and you will still have a strong rope. Similarly, even though some of the evidence was weak, there was still enough strong evidence to convict the accused. (The prosecutor won the case.)

Information found on a website for "persuasive litigators" reminds them that it is not easy for a judge or jury to forget or ignore an analogy "that seems to perfectly boil down the case" (Broda-Bahm, 2010, para. 1). The authors of this website offer this example, "A smoke detector that stops working due to a simple short circuit is like a life preserver that keeps you afloat until it gets wet." Now suppose that you are on a jury deciding about the culpability of a company that made a smoke detector and that detector did not work properly because of a short circuit. Does this analogy make it more likely that you would award a larger amount of money to someone who was injured because of a faulty smoke detector? Of course, that is the intent of the analogy. The legal advisors who recommend the use of analogies wisely add that like all legal persuasion, and I would add all communication, the success of an analogy depends on how you use it.

Some analogies are just plain bad—sometimes hilariously funny. I have an unattributed email that claims to contain the winners of a high school contest for the "worst analogy." I don't know if there ever was such a contest, or if these are winning entries, but they are certainly worthy of that dubious honor. Here are two attributed to "unknown": "Her vocabulary was as bad as, like, whatever" and "The red brick wall was the color of a brick-red Crayola crayon."

Politics seem to be a breeding ground for analogies. Rick Santorum, who campaigned to become the republican candidate for U.S. president in 2012, explained why voters who did not support him in the primary elections would vote for him for president: "I always tell the story about girls coming into the dance hall, walking past us and taking a turn with some other better-looking guys, and then at the end of the evening there's old steady Eddie, who's not flashy, but he's the guy you know you want to take home to Mom and Dad" (2011). Along similar lines, consider the term "RINO," which stands for Republican in Name Only. It is used to denigrate republican candidates that are more middle-of-the road (another analogy) in their politics. A commentator mused that "RINO has become an epithet of ideological enforcement, spit out in much the same way Mao cursed 'running dog capitalists'" (Goldberg, 2011).

Analogies are useful thinking strategies in many different contexts. The deliberate use of analogies as an aid to solving problems and enhancing creativity is discussed in greater detail in later chapters.

Words and their Meanings

Eight years after resigning as president, Richard Nixon denied *lying* but acknowledged that he, like other politicians, had *dissembled*.
—Paul Ekman (1992, p. 25)

Is alcoholism an illness or is it the lack of will power by weak people who could stop drinking if they really wanted to? Is drunkenness a crime that requires punishment or a mental health condition that needs treatment? I have frequently been asked questions like these, especially by students who are worried about or disgusted with a loved one who has a drinking problem. There are many important aspects to this question. First, the answer to the question of whether alcoholism is an illness depends on how the term "illness" is defined, and more importantly, who gets to do the defining. Second, it is possible that alcoholism would fit a definition of illness and be controllable by the individual. The way this question is posed reveals many unstated assumptions by the person asking the question regarding the nature of illness and alcoholism. The ramifications of the way we classify alcoholism are important. If we decide that it is a disease, then it is destigmatized and treatment could be paid for medical insurance plans. If it is a criminal offense, then alcoholics can expect to "do" jail time, or at least fall under the criminal justice system. Medical insurance does not cover crimes. The answer to this vexing question has varied over different geographical locations and throughout history.

Words often have both cognitive and emotional meanings. If I name my brand of cookies "Mother's Cookies," then presumably I am activating some of the emotional attachment you feel towards your mother when you think about my cookies. Furthermore, if I believe that most people will have positive emotions towards their own mothers (at least when mentioned in the context of cookies), then "Mother's Cookies" would be a good name for my cookies. Of course, you probably know that most store-bought cookies are baked in huge factories by people who may or may not be mothers. I suppose most people like to think that a mother-like figure or perhaps a group of playful elves are baking something tasty for them. The popularity of these marketing strategies suggests that it is good business to arouse positive emotional reactions toward a product.

Here's a deliberate attempt to affect how people think about a military action by the words used to describe it. In 2011, several countries sent

FRAZZ   **BY JEF MALLETT**

Frazz by Jef Mallett. Used with permission by Universal Press Syndicate.

military troops to Libya, but no one was willing to use the term "war." When asked, "Are we at war in Libya or not?" a spokesman for the U.S. President replied, "It's not a war; it's a frontloaded combat mission that's obviously going to recede into a coalition" (quoted in Catapano, 2011, paras. 13–14).

Definitions and the Control of Thought

> Need Press? Repeat: "green," "sex," "secret" "fat."
> —Joanne Kaufman (June 30, 2008)

An amazing event occurred in 1973—millions of mentally ill people were suddenly cured! Well, not exactly. What happened was that the American Psychiatric Association removed "homosexuality" from its list of official mental disorders, with the result that the millions of homosexuals were no longer considered mentally ill. The American Psychiatric Association maintains the powerful position of deciding which categories of human behavior and emotion should be defined as mental illnesses by listing them in the official "handbook" of mental disorders, the *Diagnostic and Statistical Manual* (*DSM*; American Psychiatric Association, 2013). This determines whether an individual will receive medical funding for treatment, whether a judge will decide to commit an individual to a mental facility or to a prison, and whether people label themselves and others as "normal." There is a raging debate over proposed changes that appear in the 5th edition of the DSM. One proposal is that the diagnosis of autism be replaced with a range of disorders, which would relabel some disorders as a type of autism (American Psychiatric Association, 2012). Psychologists, psychiatrists, support groups, insurance companies, and many others are lining up to support or protest the changes. Labels are powerful.

Who decides what a word means? Consider the defense used by Italian Prime Minister Silvio Berlusconi in 2009. The story is somewhat complicated, but essentially concerned whether senior politicians can be exempt from prosecution. The lawyers for one of the billionaire politicians argued that "He is no longer first among equals, but ought to be considered first above equals. . . . The law is equal for everyone, but not always in its application" (quoted in *The New York Times*, October 12, 2009). This pronouncement soon became known as the "Animal Farm Defense" because of its similarity to the motto in George Orwell's novel, "All animals are equal, but some are more equal than others." I don't know about you, but this defense makes me want to scratch my head and say, "huh!"

Terms that are heavily laden with emotional impact often elicit strong images. If you have already read the chapter on memory, then you recall (I hope) that imagery helps to maintain a concept in memory, a factor that is related to its ability to elicit strong emotions. This fact is well known by propagandists who want to convince the masses to act in extreme ways. In Mein Kampf, Adolph Hitler used expressions like "racial brew," "purity of the blood," "poisoning of the blood," and "bastardization" in his successful attempt to convince millions of people to participate in the killing of millions of other people who differed from them in their religious beliefs. Hitler even offered the "final solution," which means that he found a way to solve a problem: his solution was to massacre an entire religious group. It is interesting to note that the Nazis studied American advertising in the 1920s to develop their persuasive techniques. If you are thinking that no contemporary person would fall prey to such blatant tactics designed to increase racism, you have not read the papers lately.

Stop now and consider the way in which you would define the term "crime," if you had the power to write the definitions.

* * *

(Did you really stop and try to define what you think the word "crime" should mean?) Don't go on until you try this simple exercise.

According to Peck, there was a famous inmate in a federal jail, a gangster named Louis Lepke. In the cell next to his was a young conscientious objector from Iowa, named Lowell Naeve. Mr. Naeve tried to explain what a conscientious objector was to Mr. Lepke. Lepke replied incredulously, "You mean they put you in here for *not* killing?" (quoted in Peck, 1986, p. 146). Lepke then laughed and laughed. Did your definition of crime include the crime of refusing to go to war? Is Mr. Naeve a criminal?

Definitions are not static "truths." Meanings change over time as a function of technological development, changing social mores, and a drift in the way words are used. However, it is not true that a word can mean anything that anyone wants it to. There is an advertisement in a large city newspaper for a plastic surgeon who "specializes in nose reduction, breast enlargement and reduction, liposuction, baggy eyes, weak chins, face lifts, and saddlebag thighs." Putting aside the obnoxious idea that every body part needs "fixing," this surgeon claims to be able to do it all. How, then, can he claim to be a "specialist?" The word is being misused to convey the idea that he has great depth of knowledge and experience in *all* aspects of plastic surgery. If he can perform many types of plastic surgery, he is a generalist. By definition, he cannot specialize in everything.

The Power of Labels and Categories

As I sat with friends drinking coffee at my kitchen table, someone yelled, "Kill it, kill it!" as a very large bug darted across the floor. "Yuk, it's a cockroach." But on further inspection, we found that it was not a cockroach, but a "cute little cricket." A friend scooped up the cricket in a paper cup and gently released it outdoors while my daughter ran after it trying to feed it lettuce and grass. Why was it disgusting and in need of immediate extermination when we believed it to be one type of bug—a cockroach—and cute and in need of saving when it turned out to be another—a cricket?

The process of categorization is essential in understanding the world and guiding our responses. When we see a bug, or a baby, or an old person, or a professor, we use our knowledge about the categories to which they belong to make inferences about how they are likely to act. We know that a baby will share some essential features with all babies. It will sometimes cry for reasons that we cannot understand; it will need to have its diaper changed; it will slobber and coo. Of course, every baby is unique, but, fortunately, we can use our knowledge of category membership to know something about every baby. This is fortunate because it reduces the load on memory and allows us to understand and predict what will happen when interacting with any baby. The process of categorization is an example of **cognitive economy**, which means that it is a process that reduces the mental workload and makes thinking less effortful. Instead of having to learn a set of new expectations for every stimulus with which we come in contact, we can use category membership to reduce the uncertainty in the situation.

Although categories are necessary in dealing with the large variety of objects in the world, they also can be the cause of serious errors. Not all members of a category are the same, and often a stimulus is miscategorized. Stereotypes result from several cognitive and noncognitive processes, but one clear reason that they persist is due to the effect of categorical thinking. Think about a racial or religious group that is different from your own. Describe the members of that group. You will find that general terms emerge that clearly do not apply to all group members, and may not even apply to any group members.

Prototypical Thinking

At the local baseball game, the final score was 8–9, yet no man on either team ever crossed home plate.

How is this possible?

You should be able to solve this riddle fairly easily because it has the same structure and answer as a riddle that I posed in the first chapter. I repeat it here to make a point. We tend to think in terms of **prototypes** or best

Non Sequitur by Wiley Miller. Used with permission by Universal Press Syndicate.

examples of a category. Give up? The game was played in an all-women league. For those of you who could not solve this problem, it is probably because you automatically think of males when you think of baseball players, just as in the first chapter, many people did not think of a woman when the physician was described as a neurosurgeon. If you had heard the neurosurgeon puzzle before, did you recognize that the same principle was affecting your thinking when I changed the riddle so that it pertained to baseball players? Of course, you know that women play baseball, but this does not readily "come to mind."

Although I have never met you, I already know a great deal about what and how you think. Let me demonstrate this with an exercise devised by Decyk (1994). For each of the following categories, give a good example. In fact, give the first example that comes to mind:

1. a bird
2. a color
3. a triangle (a picture is okay)
4. a motor vehicle
5. a sentence
6. a hero
7. a heroic action
8. a game
9. a philosopher
10. a writer

Are you finished? Here is a list of your most likely answers: 1. for a bird, you probably named a robin or sparrow, or possibly an eagle; 2. for a color, you most likely said red or blue; 3. for your triangle, you either drew or named an equilateral triangle; 4. for a motor vehicle, you probably listed a car; 5. for an example of a sentence, you probably wrote a short declarative sentence (e.g., The girl ran home.); 6. the hero you named is most likely one of the following males—Superman, Batman, or possibly a fireman; 7. the heroic action you named probably involved a single act by a male, such as a rescue by a fireman; 8. most likely you listed Monopoly as an example of a game, or some other board game; 9. for a philosopher, you probably named Socrates or Aristotle; 10. and finally, for a writer, you probably named Stephen King, but if you named someone else, it is very probably a White male author.

What is the point of this demonstration? People tend to think in terms of **prototypes** or "best examples" of a category. Our prototypes vary from culture to culture, but they are relatively standard within a culture. If you live in Australia, you might name a "kiwi" as an example of a bird, a response that would be very unusual for Americans or Chinese. Thinking in terms of prototypes biases how and what we think. When we think about members of a category, only the most typical exemplars (examples of a category) readily come to mind. Consider the implications of the finding that most people name only living White males as an example of a writer. It means that we carry a standardized "picture" or "definition" of those characteristics that writers share and these characteristics are restricted with regard to time, race, and sex. Of course, different answers would be expected from people from countries other than the United States or, possibly, other cultural groups within the same country. Most Russians would probably name Puskin, or less probably, Tolstoy or Chekhov, if they were asked to give an example of a writer. But, regardless of what the particular prototype is, the reliance on the most typical member of a category limits thinking. Few people will name an older person or a child or a dog when asked to think of a hero, yet old people and children and even dogs (e.g., Lassie) can and do perform heroic acts. The most commonly named philosophers are dead, Greek males. With prototypes like this, few people will "think of" philosophy as a popular, contemporary profession that is open to all ages and races.

Language: Tool or Master of Thought?

> Learn a new language and get a new soul.
>
> —Czech proverb

We use language not only to convey our thoughts, but also to mold and shape them. Language and thought are inextricably related concepts that exert mutual influences on each other. Some psychologists believe that language, at least in part, influences thought. Examples of this concept were presented earlier in this chapter in the section on labeling and the way labels affect how we think. The hypothesis that the language we use affects how we think is called the **Sapir-Whorf hypothesis of linguistic relativity**, or more informally, the Sapir-Whorf hypothesis (Sapir, 1960; Whorf, 1956).

"How do I know what I mean until I see what I say?" (Miller, 1972, p. 43). In a humorous way, this question examines the relationship between thought and language. Although it seems clear to most people that our thoughts influence the language that we use, it is sometimes more difficult to understand the reciprocal nature of the relationship. Anthropologists and psychologists have studied whether people who speak different languages also think differently. Perhaps you have had the experience of translating a passage from one language to another and had difficulty conveying exactly the same meaning. Jokes are a good example of this. Ethnic jokes that are told in their native language frequently lose their humor when they are told in translation. Could this indicate that ways of thinking, as reflected in language, differ across cultures?

In 1984, George Orwell's classic book, written in 1949, the author wrote about a repressive society that was able to control the thoughts of its citizenry by redefining some words and removing others from the language. By gaining control of the language, this futuristic society dictated which thoughts were possible and which were not. The Orwellian example is an extreme interpretation of the Sapir-Whorf hypothesis that language absolutely determines thought. It is an alluring idea that language has power over the mind (Deutscher, 2010). According to this view, if a term does not exist within a language, speakers do not have the corresponding thought. It is the idea that your mother tongue restricts what you think. Do you believe that if the word "love" didn't exist in our language, then people wouldn't be able to feel the emotion represented by the word? Cross-cultural research that has examined the way different languages influence thought has not supported the strong version of the Sapir-Whorf hypothesis (Rosch, 1977). Contemporary psychologists have concluded that "Whorf was half right" (Regier & Kay, 2009, p. 439): language influences but does not determine thinking. As an example of this, consider the following terms carefully and decide if each elicits a different thought: senior citizen; old man; golden-ager. Did each term connote a different thought? Did you think about a different type of person with each word? Most people agree that they did. (See Figure 3.4.).

The Direction and Misdirection of Thought

> All words are pegs to hang ideas on.
> —Henry Ward Beecher (1812–1887)
> *Proverbs from Plymouth Pulpit* (cited in Drysdale, 1887, p. 33)

| Senior Citizen | Old Man | Golden-Ager |

Figure 3.4 The words we use influence how we think. Compare the different thoughts that are evoked by the terms "senior citizen," "old man," and "golden-ager."

Given that language will influence what we think, it is only a short leap to suggest that language can be used in deliberate ways to shape thinking so that it conforms to a particular ideology or point of view. It also seems likely that if we understand how language is used to direct how we think, then an awareness of the ways in which this occurs should help us to resist the automatic type of thinking that goes along with an uncritical approach to communication.

Emotional Language and Name Calling

> Slurs are uniquely and stubbornly resistant to attempts to neutralize their power to hurt or offend.
>
> —Ernie Lepore (2010, para. 3)

As described in the earlier section on labeling, the same event can be described in several different ways. Yet, the words we use to describe an event are not interchangeable in the meaning they convey. Language that is highly emotional has a different effect on readers and listeners than more mundane ways of conveying the intended meaning. This is the weaker version of the Sapir-Whorf hypothesis—while language may not *determine* thought, it directs, and sometimes misdirects, it. Consider the heated debate between those for and against abortion. The faction opposed to abortion realized that it is better to be for something than against something and therefore decided to call their stance "pro-life" rather than "anti-choice." On the other side, those who favored abortion certainly didn't want to be called "anti-life" and decided to label their stance "pro-choice." They hoped that people would think differently about a position that is "pro-choice" than they would about one that is "anti-life." Of course, the position has not changed—only its label or name has changed, but presumably the way the position is labeled influences how people think about it. One "pro-lifer" told a colleague that the best way to win a debate on this topic is to use frequently the words "kill" and "baby" in the same sentence (Kahane, 1992). The juxtaposition of these two words is sure to bring about an emotional response.

Another example of the deliberate choice of words to create a carefully planned impression concerns the "rewriting" of history. All history texts (indeed, everything) were written by someone with a particular point of view. Recently, the word "aggression" was taken out of Japanese history books that described World War II invasions. Do the same descriptions of an act seem "better" in some sense when they are not modified by the word "aggressive?" The contemporary Japanese historians who asked for this deletion apparently think so. Similarly, Russian historians are now using harsher terms to describe Stalin's role when he was the leader of the former Soviet Union. They now know and are free to say that Stalin slaughtered millions of innocent Russians whose "crime" was to disagree with his policies. Such people were officially labeled "enemies of the state," a label that was meant to instill fear in the individual who received such a label and to convey to everyone else that disagreement with Stalin's official policies would be considered an act of treason.

The lesson is clear: when you want to influence how people think, choose your words carefully. You also need to be aware of the ways in which other people attempt to manipulate your thoughts by the labels they use. The deliberate use of words designed to create a particular attitude or foster certain beliefs is called **semantic slanting**. The meaning or semantics is slanted so that the listener's thoughts will be directed in some way. It is fairly easy to find examples of this around election time when issues and groups label themselves with favorable terms and others with negative terms (name calling). Be wary of attempts to influence your thinking through the use of positive and negative labels, especially on the important issues that concern social and political policies. I received a political solicitation that may be among the most blatantly slanted in the choice of words that it used. The outside of the envelope read, "The bloated, blathering bottom-feeders of big government hope that you'll never uncover *these* secrets." For some reason, I didn't expect to find reasoned and impartial information inside the envelope. Would you?

Ambiguity, Vagueness, and Equivocation

The thinking process can also be misled when words are imprecise or misused. Words are **ambiguous** when they can have multiple meanings depending on context, and the appropriate meaning is unclear in a given context. Although ambiguous words have multiple meanings, vague words have imprecise meanings. **Vagueness** refers to a lack of precision in a communication. Consider the "clarification" provided by Justice Brennan of the U.S. Supreme Court when he provided a working definition that would assist those in the legal process of determining the sort of punishment that is cruel and unusual. As you probably know, punishment that is cruel and unusual is prohibited by the U.S. Constitution. But, we have little guidance for determining what makes a punishment cruel and unusual. He offered, "a punishment is cruel and unusual . . . if it does not comport with human dignity." Such a definition will not help a judge or jury decide whether a particular punishment is cruel and unusual. Justice Brennan's comments are much too vague to be useful. It is not any easier to determine which actions do not comport with human dignity than it is to decide if they are cruel and unusual. A communication is vague if it does not specify enough details for its intended purpose.

There is legislation in California that requires that warning notices be posted in all places where the public may come in contact with cancer causing chemicals. The sign designed for gas stations is shown in Figure 3.5.

As you can see, the signs are too vague to be of value. There is no information about the level of risk, or the likelihood of developing cancer, or how

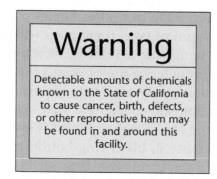

Figure 3.5 An example of vagueness. California law requires that warning signs be posted in all places where consumers come in contact with cancer-causing chemicals. Signs like this one are being used at all gas stations. The information they convey is too vague to be meaningful.

long you would have to be exposed to these chemicals to reach some level of risk. There is no way to use this information to make a meaningful decision about whether the risk is so high the area should be avoided. This is a clear example of a deliberately unclear communication. The gasoline companies were opposed to this law and have registered their complaint by posting the required signs but not providing the public with interpretable information.

Vagueness is sometimes a socially polite way of handling an unpleasant situation. If you ask someone about her divorce you may get a vague response like, "We were incompatible" rather than a more precise, but less acceptable, "The stinking rat cheated every chance he could get."

Equivocation occurs when the meaning of a word is changed in the course of the same discussion, and thus is different from ambiguity or vagueness. Consider the following "line of reasoning": (Reasoning will be considered more fully in the next chapter.)

1. Man is the only rational animal.
2. No woman is a man.
3. Therefore, no woman is rational. (Damer, 1987)

The meaning of the word "man" changed from the first to the second sentence. In the first sentence, "man" stood for all of humanity—both female and male. In the second sentence, it was used as a sex specific term, with females conveniently omitted.

There is a classic comedy sketch by Abbott and Costello called "Who's on First?" In this sketch, Abbott names the players on a baseball team. The name of the player on first base is "Who." Costello repeatedly asks the name of the player on first base. Abbott responds, "Who is on first base." You can imagine how they go back and forth asking, "Who is on first base?" and getting the response that "Who is on first base."

Etymology and Reification

These two terms both concern word meanings. **Etymology** is the study of word origins. It is often interesting to learn how language evolved and developed. However, it is wrong to conclude that a word has a particular meaning or nuance based on the word from which it was derived. Consider, for example, the use of the word "gay" to refer to homosexual men. The word is commonly used today to denote pride and other positive attributes of male homosexuals. The origin of the word was quite different. The word "gay" was derived from a definition meaning "wanton and licentious." It would be wrong to conclude that gays are therefore wanton and licentious. Language is a living entity and word definitions evolve and change. Returning to a word's origins to find its contemporary meaning is like studying the writings of Karl Marx to understand how modern communism is practiced in Cuba.

Reification is a more difficult concept to explain. Reification occurs when something abstract is given a name and then treated as though it were a concrete object. Consider the idea of "mother nature." You have probably heard the saying that you cannot fool mother nature. We tend to treat the idea of a human force of nature as though it had a physical reality when it is an abstract concept. There is no "mother nature" or "father nature" for that matter. Perhaps the most obvious case of reification involves the concept of intelligence, where intelligence tests yield "IQ" scores that are said to measure it, and then IQ is used as though it were the physical embodiment of intelligence.

Bureaucratese and Euphemism

Two language barriers to comprehension are bureaucratese and euphemism. **Bureaucratese** is the use of formal, stilted language that is unfamiliar to people who lack special training. The same information can be expressed better with simpler terms. Bureaucratese is different from the use of precise technical terms that may be needed in specialized disciplines; in bureaucratese, the style and language hinders our understanding instead of aiding it. The legal profession is often guilty of bureaucratese. I once read a legal document that began with the term "Witnesseth." Of course, I questioned what meaning was being conveyed with the use of this term, which is standard on many legal forms. The answer was, "very little." It could have been deleted altogether or replaced with "Notice" or "Read this document," both of which would have been more meaningful than the obscure "Witnesseth." Ditto for other obscure terms like "party of the first part" and "party of second part," not to mention the archaic Latinisms that riddle the law (e.g., "ex parte" and "corpus delecti").

Euphemism is the substitution of a desirable term for a less desirable or offensive one. Although there is nothing inherently wrong with polite conversation, the result is often a loss of communication. Euphemism is common in hospital and medical facilities where bodily functions need to be discussed. Hospital personnel may ask a patient if he has "voided his bladder." Many patients do not realize that this refers to urination. In fact, it has been shown that a majority of patients do not understand the language that is commonly used in their interactions with medical staff. Many patients do not understand words like "malignant," "benign," "terminal," and "generic." You can imagine a solemn physician telling a patient that she is "terminal," with the patient then brightly inquiring when she will get better. It is easy to see how the use of euphemisms can lead to misunderstandings.

Euphemisms abound in advertisements of all sorts. Do "bathroom tissue" and "feminine hygiene products" seem more desirable and glamorous than toilet paper and menstrual pads? Euphemisms often obscure the intended meaning. Although polite speech is a necessary rule of society, euphemistic terms that are not commonly used interfere with the communication of ideas and thus should be avoided.

Euphemisms are designed to change the effect or emotion that we feel when we confront topics that we may find repugnant. The idea is that feelings will be less negative if a phenomenon is given a more acceptable name. For example, many people have complained that "beauty pageants," like the "Miss America Pageant," are demeaning to its participants whose value is determined by their appearance—much like a horse or cow at an auction. Officials and sponsors of these pageants disagree. They argue that these pageants are opportunities for the contestants to demonstrate their talents and to win money and other prizes that can be used to finance an education or to launch a career. Those who believe that such displays are demeaning reply that the bathing suit competition, in which women march around in skimpy bathing suits and high-heeled shoes, should not be a requirement for scholarship money for a college education. In recognition of the fact that a contestant's appearance when clad in scanty clothing probably is unrelated to her talent, academic potential, or scholarship, the officials of the Miss America Pageant decided to remedy this situation. They renamed the competition. Women still parade in scanty swimsuits and high heels, but now it is called "health and fitness in a swimsuit" (Leive, 1994). This is a strange euphemism for the portion of the competition that leads the contestants to resort to starvation diets and plastic surgery—neither of which promotes health and fitness.

Probably the biggest perpetuators of euphemisms are politicians. In response to public protests over tax increases, we now have "revenue enhancement" bills, and sex education classes are often called "family education." One of my favorite examples is in the change of a class title that was offered in a junior high school. Based on the idea that boys as well as girls need to know about cooking, nutrition, and similar topics, a teacher offered a course called, "home economics for boys." It had zero enrollment. She then got wise and retitled the course, "bachelor living." So many boys wanted to take the class with this new name, there was a waiting list. With very little effort, you should be able to find other examples where the change of a label changed how people think.

The Perils of Polite Speech

> Politeness taxes mental resources and creates confusion as to what is truly meant.
>
> —Jean-Francoise Bonnefon, Aidan Feeney, and Wim De Neys (2011)

The popular writer Malcolm Gladwell (2008) tells about a fatal plane crash that was caused when the second pilot used overly polite language to tell the first pilot that there was a dangerous amount of ice on the wing of their airplane. Politeness can obscure the true meaning, tax the limits of working memory, and in high-stakes conditions, cause a disaster (Bonnefon, Feeney, & De Neys, 2011, p 322). Consider this hypothetical exchange between two workers:

First worker says: "If the water level is low, the machine stops."

Second worker replies: "If the oil level is low, the machine stops."

When the stakes are high, it is important to communicate clearly—more important than leaving the meaning harder to interpret with the use of polite statements.

Framing with Leading Questions and Negation

Framing occurs when a question is asked is a way that suggests what the correct response should be. The reader is "led" into assuming a particular perspective or point of view.

Consider the following problem:

> Imagine that the U.S. is preparing for the outbreak of an unusual disease, which is expected to kill 600 people. Two alternative programs to combat the disease have been proposed. Assume that the exact scientific estimate of the consequences of the programs are as follows:
>
> > If Program A is adopted, 200 people will be saved.
> > If Program B is adopted, there is 1/3 probability that 600 people will be saved, and 2/3 probability that no people will be saved.
> > Which of the two programs would you favor? (Tversky & Kahneman, 1981, p. 453)

Now consider the same problem, and select between the following two programs:

> > If Program C is adopted, 400 people will die.
> > If Program D is adopted there is 1/3 probability that nobody will die, and 2/3 probability that 600 people will die.
> > Which of these two programs would you favor?

When this problem was presented to college students, 72% of those given the first set of choices selected Program A, while 78% of those given the second set of choices selected Program D. Look closely at the choices. Program A and C are effectively identical—they differ only in that A is described in terms of the numbers of lives saved, while C is described in terms of the number who will die. Program B and D are also identical, differing only in the language used to describe the outcomes. It seems that most people are **risk adverse**, which means that they prefer options that do not involve loss. When an alternative makes a potential loss prominent (e.g., focuses on the number that die), people will reject that alternative. It is clear that when an option is stated in terms of a loss, it is judged more negatively than a mathematically identical statement about gains. This is an important result, showing that human judgments and preferences can be readily manipulated by changes in the way questions are asked or framed. If I tell you that a new medical treatment has a 50% success rate you will be more likely to endorse its use than if I tell you that it has a 50% failure rate. The only difference is whether the information was presented in a positive (success rate) frame or a negative (failure rate) frame (Halpern & Blackman, 1985; Halpern, Blackman, & Salzman, 1989).

Framing can be used to influence thinking in many different contexts, so its effects can be powerful. If you understand how they work, you can use framing to your advantage and recognize when others are using it to their advantage. Suppose you are interviewing for a job and you have gotten to the "sticky" issue of negotiating salary. If you said to the prospective employer that you really wanted $50,000 a year, but you are willing to take $45,000, the employer begins to see this offer as a gain of $5000. Similarly, if the prospective employer were to say that she was ready to offer $40,000 but is willing to go as high as $45,000 (after all you studied critical thinking and should be worth more salary), then you would have the "feeling" of having gained $5000.

Salespeople know that leading questions can be good for business. If I am showing you some household items, a good sales technique is to ask, "How many will you take?" The assumption here is that the sale is made, and it is only a matter of how many you will buy, not whether you will buy. Similarly, a car salesperson who is ready to "close the deal" will ask, "What color do you want?" This question makes it clear that you have already decided that you will buy the car and the only decision left is that of color.

Advertisers and merchants like to price their wares in uneven amounts, like $19.99 and $24.95. Have you ever wondered why they don't simplify matters and price garments to the nearest dollar so that $19.99 would become $20.00 and $24.95 would become $25.00? The frame or perspective being induced here is one of considering the price as "less than $20.00." Of course, the one-cent difference is negligible, but it does seem to change how people think about the price.

Listeners can also be framed or misled with **negation**. Suppose you read that a prominent politician is not a drunk. Suppose further that this is absolutely true; she is not a drunk. Most people would infer that there was some question about her sobriety and the truth of the assertion. The pragmatic function of negation is to deny something that is plausible (Carroll, 1986). Thus, listeners will infer the plausibility of that which was denied. President Richard Nixon hadn't considered this psycholinguistic principle when he uttered the now famous words in response to his Watergate debacle, "I am not a crook." Most people took this to mean that it is plausible that he is a crook. Thus, the denial of some act often has the paradoxical result that people now believe it is more likely to be true than they would have if no denial had been made.

Contrast and Context

Are you making a good salary? How is your health? Is the new love in your life intelligent and kind? Do you approve of the current president? The way you are likely to answer all of these questions depends on what you are comparing them to and the context in which the comparison is being made. Contrast and context provide meaning to cognitive activities like judging and evaluating. In a classic study, Parducci (1968) asked subjects to decide how bad it is to "pocket the tip which the previous customers left for the waitress." Half the subjects were asked to judge this event along with the following mild infractions: stealing a loaf of bread from a store when you are starving; playing poker on Sunday; cheating at solitaire. The other half of the subjects were asked to judge the same event (pocketing the tip which the previous customers left for the waitress) along with the following infractions: spreading rumors that an acquaintance is a sexual pervert; putting your deformed child in the circus; murdering your mother without justification or provocation.

Taking a waitress' tip was judged to be a more serious offense when it was presented along with milder infractions than when it was presented among a list of serious infractions. The event (pocketing a tip) was exactly the same in each case, and the wording was identical. Changes in the context in which it was presented created changes in the way it was evaluated. Context is an important determinant of the meaning we assign to events. This principle is used quite well in the letter that is reprinted from a delightful book by Cialdini (1993) and shown in Figure 3.6.

Dear Mother and Dad:

Since I left for college I have been remiss in writing and I am sorry for my thoughtlessness in not having written before. I will bring you up to date now, but before you read on, please sit down. You are not to read any further unless you are sitting down, okay?

Well, then, I am getting along pretty well now. The skull fracture and the concussion I got when I jumped out the window of my dormitory when it caught on fire shortly after my arrival here is pretty well healed now. I only spent two weeks in the hospital and now I can see almost normally and only get those sick headaches once a day. Fortunately, the fire in the dormitory, and my jump, was witnessed by an attendant at the gas station near the dorm, and he was the one who called the Fire Department and the ambulance. He also visited me in the hospital and since I had nowhere to live because of the burntout dormitory, he was kind enough to invite me to share his apartment with him. It's really a basement room, but it's kind of cute. He is a very fine boy and we have fallen deeply in love and are planning to get married. We haven't got the exact date yet, but it will be before my pregnancy begins to show.

Yes, Mother and Dad, I am pregnant. I know how much you are looking forward to being grandparents and I know you will welcome the baby and give it the same love and devotion and tender care you gave me when I was a child. The reason for the delay in our marriage is that my boyfriend has a minor infection which prevents us from passing our premarital blood tests and I carelessly caught it from him. I know that you will welcome him into our family with open arms. He is kind and, although not well educated, he is ambitious. Although he is of a different race and religion than ours, I know your often expressed tolerance will not permit you to be bothered by that.

Now that I have brought you up to date, I want to tell you that there was no dormitory fire, I did not have a concussion or skull fracture, I was not in the hospital, I am not pregnant, I am not engaged, I am not infected, and there is no boyfriend. However, I am getting a "D" in American History, and an "F" in Chemistry and I want you to see those marks in their proper perspective.

Your loving daughter,

Sharon

Figure 3.6 This fictitious letter is a good example of the use of context to influence judgments of "how bad" different events are perceived. From Cialdini, R.B. (1993). Influence: Science and Practice (3rd edition). HarperCollins: NY.

Contrast can be used effectively in a wide range of situations. For example, Zimbardo and Leippe (1991) offer this advice when you want to borrow money from a friend or parent. They suggest that you first ask for a large sum that you are fairly certain will be refused. (Hey, can you loan me $75?) Follow this by asking for the smaller sum that you really need. (No, well, how about $25?) They found that you are more likely to receive the smaller amount when it follows a large request than when it is requested without the larger request being made first. Zimbardo and Leippe reported that charitable contributions are also more likely when the requestor asks for any amount—"even a penny will help." When solicitors for charities request "even a penny," people are more likely to give larger sums of money to the charity than to charitable appeals that do not emphasize that "even small amounts will help."

Anchoring

When we have little basis for making a meaningful decision, we often rely on whatever information is available, even when we know it is probably worthless. For example, compare these two questions (from Mussweiler & Strack, 2000; values listed have been changed to reflect current pricing):

Is the average price of a new car higher or lower than $45,000?

Is the average price of a new car higher or lower than $14,000?

You probably answered lower to the first question and higher to the second. Now, suppose I ask you to estimate the price of the average new car. If you had only been asked the first question, you are likely to give a higher estimate than if you had only been asked the second question. The price asked served as an **anchor**—a figure that you used as a beginning point or comparison for making your estimate. Anchors influence our thinking, but they operate without conscious awareness unless we are vigilant for them. Suppose you are judging something important like the severity of a crime. Think how you might respond to "Should the defendant serve life in jail without the possibility of parole?" compared to "Should the defendant be sentenced to three years on probation and community service?" Without knowing anything else, like the nature of the crime, can you see that most people would use these examples of sentences as anchors and tend to suggest much more severe sentences if they are asked the first sentence than if they are asked the second?

Anchors create reference points that are misleading, and sometimes, irrelevant to a decision. There are many experimental and real-world examples of the way anchors influence how we think. For example, an investor might see a stock drop in price from $20 to $14 (Lee, 2011). If he focuses on the $20 price, he is likely to conclude that the stock is undervalued at

$14, when it fact, the $20 price may have been overvalued. The correct way to think about the stock price is to estimate what it is likely to be worth "going forward."

Have you ever wondered why solicitations for charities or political organizations have check boxes that you are supposed to check to indicate the amount of your contribution? Almost always, the highest values are listed first. The next time you receive a solicitation, look at the reply card. It is likely to read something like: ___ $1000 ___ $500 ___ $200 ___ $100

The implied message is clear—start by thinking about giving us $1000. The high start rate should anchor your contributions so that they will be closer to $1000 than they would have been without these suggested levels of "giving."

Here's a compelling example of the power of anchors. To start, write down the last two digits of your social security number. Now suppose that I ask you how much you are willing to pay for a bottle of rare wine or a wireless keyboard. Guess what? According to Ariely (2003), a psychologist at Massachusetts Institute of Technology, the number that you just wrote down influences how much you are willing to pay. Graduate students who participated in this study were willing to pay more money if they had high social security numbers (which could range from 00 to 99) than those with lower social security numbers, even though these students were reminded that the last two digits of a social security number are assigned at random. Yet, once they were written down, they created an anchor or starting point for deciding how much to pay for things where their market value is difficult to predict.

Barometers of Thought

Public opinion polls are often used to provide information to policy makers who want to sample from a population of interest to infer how the population will react to some action like a tax cut or a military response in a troubled place in the world. Suppose they you want to know how average American citizens will think about a controversial issue. It is impossible to provide a straight-forward answer to the question, "What do Americans think?" Not only is there the obvious problem that Americans are quite diverse in their thinking, there is also the problem of assessing what any individual thinks. The kind of answers that people give to opinion questions depends on the way the questions are asked. Politicians and their supporters conduct "push polls" that are designed to lead respondents to respond in certain ways (Schwartz, 2007).

Consider these questions (Herbers, 1982):

> "Suppose the budgets of your state and local governments have to be curtailed, which of these parts would you limit most severely?"

When one choice was "public welfare programs" 39% of the respondents selected it for cutting.

When one choice was "aid to the needy" only 8% of the respondents selected it for cutting.

The difference is in how this choice was framed. What do you associate with "public welfare programs" and what do you associate with "aid to the needy?" Can you see how easily our thoughts can be influenced by the way a situation is framed?

It is fairly easy to deliberately slant the results of an opinion poll by carefully selecting wording that will favor one position or another. In fact, it may not be possible to find any wording that would be unbiased. Try this one for yourself:

> Are you in favor of a national program that ensures good quality, affordable day care for infants and young children whose parents work outside of the home?
> YES   NO   NO OPINION

> Are you in favor of programs that are paid for with your tax dollars that place infants and young children in child care institutions for 9 to 10 hours each day?
> YES   NO   NO OPINION

This is another example of how easy it can be to present data to Congress and other decision-making bodies that either support or refute the idea that most Americans are in favor of or opposed to a program of national day care. Before you interpret the results from any poll or respond to one, consider very carefully the way in which the questions were posed. What sort of background information was given and what words were used? Try to create different frames when you are presented with opinion polls or similar types of information. If a different frame leads you to think about the topic in a different way, then try to find a neutral way to ask yourself about the topic. We can become aware of framing effects and we can find ways to minimize their effects.

Comprehension: The Reason for Language

Language is the first medium of the rational mind.
—Geraldine Ferguson (1981, p. 120)

A student once told me that despite the fact that she really wanted to understand the material in her textbook, she found that the information went "in one eye and out the other." In other words, it "didn't stick" or seem to involve her brain at all. Although her "eyes" read every word, she was unable to understand or remember the material. We can sympathize with her since we have all had this experience at one time or another. Comprehension failures often result from the language used to express an idea and not from the difficulty of the idea itself. Good teachers know how to communicate complex ideas so that they can be easily understood, while poor teachers could talk or write for days without conveying the ideas to their students.

Strategies for Comprehension

What can you do to enhance your ability to comprehend? There are many comprehension strategies or skills designed to help make information that is presented in natural (everyday) language more understandable. These strategies aid in discovering, retaining, and utilizing the information in speech and written prose. They all involve ways of building a meaningful representation that matches the one used by the "sender" (i.e., speaker or writer).

The process of comprehension may be best described with an analogy. Imagine that a friend has a large jungle gym (child's climbing toy) in his back yard, and that he is giving it to you as a present. Because it is too large to transfer in its assembled state, you need to take it apart to move it to your home. Once you get it home, you need to reassemble it. To do so, you have to identify which part is the base and then add component parts to it. When it is reassembled, it should look the same as it did in your friend's yard.

The same is true of comprehension. If your friend has a complex knowledge structure in his head (think back to associative networks as explained in the memory chapter), he would transfer the information to you via language. You would have to identify the main ideas (or base) in order to build your own mental representation. You would also have to understand the relationships between the parts of the information so that you can graft them onto the main ideas in the correct way. Comprehension is attained when your knowledge structure "looks the same as" the one your friend has in his head. In other words, you would both have the same underlying representation for the transferred information. All comprehension strategies are activities that aid in the transfer of underlying structures. They provide guides for identifying main ideas and determining the relevance of various components of the message. They assist the comprehender in discovering the underlying relationships between the constituent parts of the message.

What do you do when you comprehend a passage? Most people respond that they have no idea what they do to aid their understanding, yet they can say what they do when they study. Remember, any cognitive activity that aids comprehension will also aid memory, so any effective comprehension strategy is also a memory strategy.

Re-representation

In understanding complex phenomena—anything ranging from planetary motions to our beliefs about racial and ethnic groups—we rely on mental models. These models are connected knowledge structures that help us to make sense out of our experiences. They guide what we see, how we interpret events, and how we remember them. For example, if I believe that boys are more aggressive than girls, then I may interpret a scuffle on the playground between two boys as being more aggressive than the same scuffle if it had involved two girls. In addition, I may remember details that are consistent with this interpretation (e.g., torn clothing) even when they did not occur. It seems that we are often more likely to alter our memory for events in ways that are consistent with our mental models than we are to alter the models. Our goal is to maintain models or beliefs about the world that are as accurate as possible, but it seems that we are better at preserving faulty mental models than we are at altering them to reflect true experiences.

Questioning and Explaining

Good thinkers are good questioners.

—Alison King (1994, p. 18)

The best-known technique for studying from text is based on the process of asking good questions about the material being read and then demonstrating comprehension by answering the questions. Psychologists have found that when college students respond to questions during a lecture (as compared to a control group that is given statements about the correct answer), they have better memory for the information and are better able to transfer what they learned (Campbell & Mayer, 2009). When students generate and answer their own questions about a text, their comprehension and recall improves (e.g., Wilson & Smetana, 2011).

Recent research has shown that repeated testing, particularly when the test requires the generation of information, enhances learning. This practice produces gains in understanding and memory when the tests are aligned with important content (Karpicke & Roediger, 2007; Roediger, Agarwal, McDaniel, & McDermott, 2011). According to standard "memory trace" theories of how people remember, the act of remembering strengthens some memory traces and weakens, or perhaps fails to strengthen, others, a fact that should influence how we test students. There are complex mathematical models and functions that describe the course of remembering (or forgetting) over time (Anderson et al., 2004; Oberauer & Lewandowsky, 2011). The single most important variable in promoting long-term retention and transfer is "practice at retrieval"—students need to generate responses, with minimal retrieval cues, repeatedly over time. For example, one of the headings for this section of text is "strategies for comprehension." A good question that you should be able to answer when you finish this section is, "What are some strategies for comprehension, and how do they work?" If you can't answer this question with the book closed when you finish this section, then you do not know the information presented. A good question for this subsection on "questioning and explaining" is, "How are questioning and explaining used to improve comprehension?"

King (1989, 1992; King, Staffieri, & Adelgais, 1998) conducted a series of studies that clearly demonstrate the value of **reciprocal peer questioning**, a technique in which learners learn to pose thoughtful questions that they then take turns answering. She concluded that the ability to ask thoughtful questions is a skill that needs to be learned because most people tend to ask "low level" simple recall questions (e.g., What is the date of . . . Who did . . .) and not those that require a meaningful analysis of complex information if they are not trained in the formulation of thoughtful questions. King has devised a series of **generic questions**, which can be used with modifications in almost any context. Look at the generic questions that are presented in Table 3.1.

Table 3.1: A list of generic questions provided by King (1994). These question stems can be used in almost any context. Research has shown that comprehension and memory are improved when students learn to ask and answer thoughtful questions based on these stems. More importantly, students use these generic questions in novel contexts, showing that transfer of critical thinking skills occurs when students understand that transfer is the goal of activities that improve thinking.

Generic Questions	Specific Thinking Skills Induced
What is a new example of . . . ?	Application
How could . . . be used to . . . ?	Application
What would happen if . . . ?	Prediction/hypothesizing
What are the implications of . . . ?	Analysis/inference
What are the strengths and weaknesses of . . . ?	Analysis/inference
What is . . . analogous to?	Identification and creation of analogies and metaphors
What do we already know about . . . ?	Activation of prior knowledge
How does . . . affect . . . ?	Activation of relationship (cause–effect)
How does . . . tie in with what we learned before?	Activation of prior knowledge
Explain why . . .	Analysis
Explain how . . .	Analysis
What is the meaning of . . . ?	Analysis
Why is . . . important?	Analysis of significance
What is the difference between . . . and . . . ?	Comparison–contrast
How are . . . and . . . similar?	Comparison–contrast
How does . . . apply to everyday life?	Application to the real world
What is the counterargument for . . . ?	Rebuttal argument

Generic Questions	Specific Thinking Skills Induced
What is the best . . . and why?	Evaluation and provision of evidence
What are some possible solutions to the problem of . . . ?	Synthesis of ideas
Compare . . . and . . . with regard to . . .	Comparison–contrast
What do you think causes . . . ? Why?	Analysis of relationship (cause–effect)
Do you agree or disagree with this statement: . . . ?	Evaluation and provision of evidence
What evidence is there to support your answer?	
How do you think . . . would see the issue of . . . ?	Taking other perspectives

When learners completed these questions using information from a lecture or text, they showed better recall and comprehension than control groups who were instructed to study independently, engage in group discussions, generate summaries, or ask questions without training in how to ask good questions (King, 1992, 1994). More importantly, King found that when students become proficient at using higher-level questioning, they spontaneously ask these questions in a variety of other learning situations. These studies provide further support for the conclusion that I presented in the first chapter: critical thinking skills transfer to novel contexts when instruction emphasizes the need to practice and use these skills in many contexts. Thus, there are very strong indications that you can improve your comprehension and memory by using the generic questions that appear in Table 3.1. Here are some examples applied to the information in this chapter:

How does context affect judgment?

Compare underlying structure with surface structure with regard to their role in the process of communication.

Explain how analogies can be useful in enhancing comprehension.

How does anchoring apply to everyday life?

What is the difference between ambiguity and vagueness?

What is the meaning of the term "generic questions?"

Can you answer these questions?

Concept Maps

An oft-repeated theme in this book is to utilize both verbal and spatial-like strategies as thinking aids. **Concept Maps**, sometimes called graphic organizers, are spatial arrays that require learners to attend explicitly to the underlying structure in a passage. They can provide a picture of a learner's knowledge structures and show the way in which new information is incorporated into information that is already known. Mayer (1987) calls the deliberate use of graphic organizers "structure training techniques" because they force the learner to focus on the structure of a text. Recent reviews found that drawing concept maps is a more effective method for facilitating recall than creating lists or outlines (Nesbit & Adesope, 2006). Concept maps can reflect what a learner is learning by starting with a simple map and then elaborating on it over time as learning occurs. There are several varieties of concept maps, but all of them use spatial representations to make efficient use of the information in a text.

Linear Arrays

Sometimes, the best way to understand a topic is to represent the information in a **linear array**. This is useful when the information presented is fairly linear or straight-line-like in its structure. An example of this would be a very simple "line" of events occurring one after the other: The girl hit the boy. He started to cry. The teacher heard the boy's cry. She ran into the room. She punished the girl. The girl was sent to the principal's office. Etc. This rather boring story is a straightforward sequence of events that followed each other in a strict temporal ordering. A simple linear representation would adequately capture all of the relevant information.

| girl hit boy

| boy cried

| teacher arrived

| teacher punished girl

| girl to principal's office

↓ etc.

Another example when a modified linear array would be a good choice of representation is in representing any parts or processes that are aligned linearly in the physical world. Vaughan (1984) taught medical students how to utilize graphic organizers when learning from medical texts. The digestive system is aligned in a fairly linear manner beginning with the mouth and ending with the rectum. Students who read about the digestive system

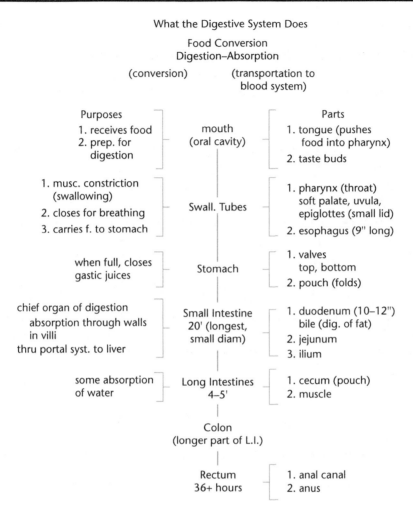

What the Digestive System Does

Food Conversion
Digestion–Absorption

(conversion)   (transportation to
blood system)

Purposes   Parts
1. receives food   mouth   1. tongue (pushes
2. prep. for   (oral cavity)   food into pharynx)
   digestion   2. taste buds

1. musc. constriction   1. pharynx (throat)
   (swallowing)   soft palate, uvula,
2. closes for breathing   Swall. Tubes   epiglottes (small lid)
3. carries f. to stomach   2. esophagus (9" long)

                                         1. valves
when full, closes   Stomach   top, bottom
gastic juices   2. pouch (folds)

chief organ of digestion Small Intestine 1. duodenum (10–12")
absorption through walls 20' (longest,   bile (dig. of fat)
in villi   small diam)   2. jejunum
thru portal syst. to liver   3. ilium

some absorption   Long Intestines 1. cecum (pouch)
of water   4–5'   2. muscle

                         Colon
                         (longer part of L.I.)

                         Rectum   1. anal canal
                         36+ hours   2. anus

Figure 3.7 Modified linear array depicting the purposes and parts of the digestive system. A linear array is a good spatial arrangement for this information because, like the array, the digestive system is linear. Adapted from Vaughan (1984).

listed the parts of the digestive system in linear order and noted along with each part its purposes in the digestive process and its components. The resulting linear array is shown in Figure 3.7. Vaughan reported that the medical students who learned to use graphic organizers like this one showed significant improvement in their comprehension of medical school texts.

Time lines that are commonly used in history are helpful in providing a visual picture of and appreciation for time spans and the co-occurrence of events. When the distance between events is proportional to the time between their occurrence, a much more accurate understanding of the importance of time as the key underlying dimension of history is possible than with any verbal description.

Hierarchies

Most of the information we deal with is considerably more complex than simple linear chains. An alternative structural form for information is that of **hierarchies** or tree structures in which information is organized around class inclusion rules. Class inclusion rules are those rules in which something is a part of or a type of something else. Examples of class inclusion rule are the classification of toes as part of the foot and roses as a type of flower. Information of this sort can usually be categorized into levels with higher levels dividing into lower levels according to some rule. Biological classification systems are a good example of hierarchically organized information. Bower (1970) studied organizational factors in memory using hierarchically arranged information about minerals. Figure 3.8 depicts this hierarchy. Bower found that when subjects organized information this way, they had significantly better recall than a group of control subjects. He also found that when a "node" or branch of the hierarchy was forgotten, subjects failed to recall the entire portion of the "tree" that was below it. I'll be returning to these results later in this book in the chapter on problem solving because hierarchies or tree diagrams are sometimes used as problem-solving aids.

Networks

The relationships between ideas in a communication are not usually based on simple class inclusion rules. Concepts can be related to each other in

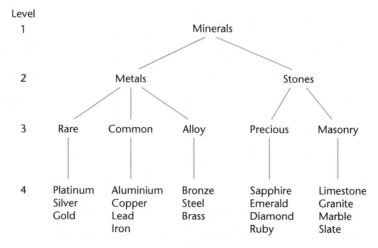

Figure 3.8 Hierarchy of minerals. An example of a hierarchical graphic organizer. Hierarchies are particularly useful when the information is organized according to class inclusion rules. Adapted from Bower (1970).

numerous other ways, and it is the depiction of the correct relationship between concepts that is central to all graphic organizing techniques. **Networks** are graphic organizers in which several different types of relationships are made explicit. Much of the work in this area has been conducted by Dansereau and his colleagues. He developed a training manual and program for counselors in substance abuse programs where concept maps (he calls them guide maps) are used to create treatment plans and to assess progress in the program (Dees & Dansereau, 2000). He found that these maps promote organized thinking in the messy real world of drug treatment.

When students learn the technique of networking, they are taught to focus on and identify six different types of relationships or links between concepts (Holley et al., 1979; Dansersau, 1995). Two of these relationships are the *class inclusion* rules of hierarchies: X is a part of Y (e.g., France is a part of Europe), and X is a *type of* Y (e.g., mangoes are a type of fruit). The third relationship is called a *leads to link*. This type of relationship occurs whenever X leads to Y (e.g., stealing leads to jail). The other three relationships or links are *analogy*, X is like Y (e.g., a paw is like an arm); *characteristic*, X is a characteristic or feature of Y (e.g., brilliance is a characteristic of diamonds); and *evidence*, X is evidence that Y occurred (e.g., antibodies are evidence of infection). These six relationships are described more fully in Table 3.2.

The relationships are then depicted in a network-like array with all of the relationships labeled. There are many studies showing the benefits of using concept maps to improve recall and critical thinking about complex topics (Wilgis & McConnell, 2008).

An example of a completed network is shown in Figure 3.9. The network shows the relationships between concepts in a nursing text on wounds. Look carefully at this figure. "Types of wounds" and the "process of healing" are *parts* of the discussion of wounds. "Open," "closed," "accidental," and "intentional" are *types* of wounds. In the process of healing, the "lag phase" *leads to* the "fibroplasia phase" which *leads to* the contraction phase. "Soft, pink, and friable" is a *characteristic of* tissue continuity. The other two types of relationships, analogy and evidence, are not used in this network.

Identification and use of these six types of relationships or links and their combination in a unified network requires considerable practice. This is an effortful strategy, which, like some of the mnemonic techniques, pays off once it is well learned. Holley et al. (1979) found that when subjects were well trained in this technique, they performed significantly better on subsequent tests than control students who did not learn this technique, with the biggest improvement for students with low grade point averages. It seems that the students who were doing very well in school were already attending to the relationships between concepts. Then it was the poorer students who benefited most from explicit instruction and practice in identifying, labeling, and diagramming the relationships between concepts.

Table 3.2

Type	Example	Structure	Key Words
Part of link	hand | p finger	*Hierarchy*—the lower node is part of the higher node	is a part of is a segment of is a portion of
Type of/ example of link	school | t private	*Hierarchy*—the lower node is an example of the higher node	is a type of is in the category is an example of is a kind of three procedures are
Leads to link	practice | l perfection	*Chain*—the object of the higher node leads to or results in the lower node	leads to results in causes is a tool of produces
Analogy link	school _a_ factory	*Cluster*—the content of one node is analogous to the other node	is similar to is analogous to is like corresponds to
Characteristic link	sky _c_ blue	*Cluster*—the content of one node is analogous to the other node	has is characterized by feature is property is trait is aspect is attribute is
Evidence link	broken _e_ x-ray arm	*Cluster*—the content of one node is evidence for the other node	indicated is illustrated by supports documents is proof of confirms

Note. This table is adapted from Holley et al. (1979). Notice how the "key words" suggest the type of link that is being described.

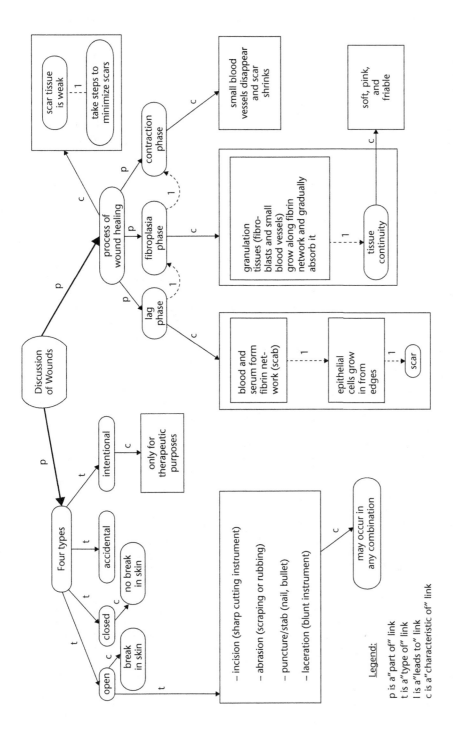

Figure 3.9 Example of a network of a chapter from a nursing text on wounds. The use of linking relationships forces the learner to consider the way concepts are related. (Reprinted from *Contemporary Educational Psychology*, vol. 4, Holley et al., "Evaluation of a hierarchical mapping technique as an aid to prose processing," pp. 227–237, Copyright [1979], with permission from Elsevier.)

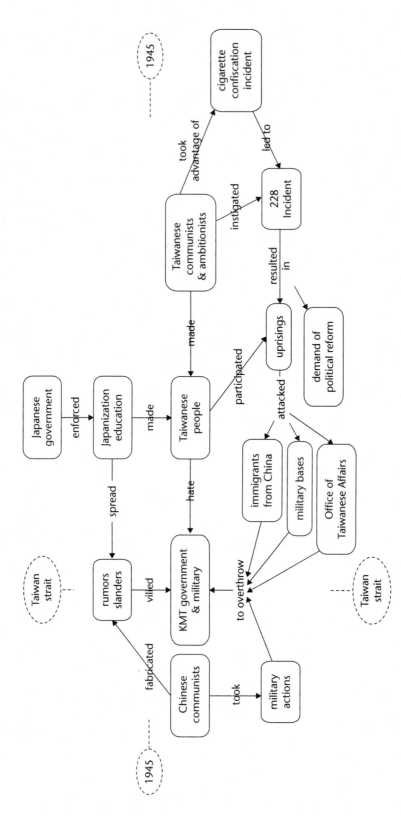

Figure 3.10 A comprehensive map showing the historical events known as the 228 Incident. From Tzeng, J. (2010). Designs of concept maps and their impacts on readers' performance in memory and reasoning while reading. *Journal of Research in Reading*, 33(2), 128–147. doi:10.1111/j.1467-9817.2009.01404.x (With permission from Wiley.)

Concept maps can be used in any field, and the named links can be altered to fit the topic being learned. For example, the concept map on the previous page shows information about the 228 Incident that followed Japan's return of Taiwan to the Chinese government in the aftermath of World War II. In a study of concept maps with high school students in Taiwan, Tzeng (2010) allowed students to progressively elaborate concepts maps about this topic as they learned more about the topic. She found that these maps helped students achieve deep learning. A comprehensive map of this historical event is shown in Figure 3.10.

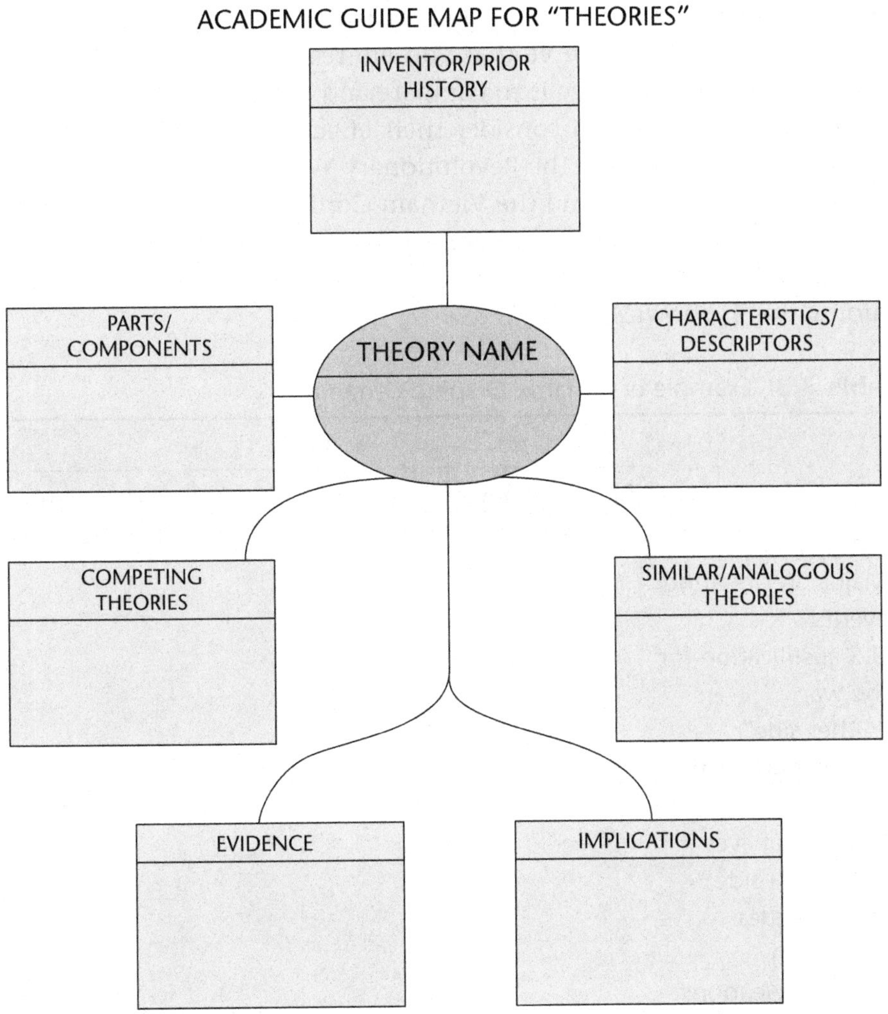

ACADEMIC GUIDE MAP FOR "THEORIES"

Figure 3.11 A generic fill-in-the-blank concept map that can be used to understand any theory in any domain of knowledge. When you fill in the various "boxes"—for example, giving evidence for the theory—you will be developing a "deep" knowledge of the theory. (Adapted from Dansereau, 2001).

Look carefully at the generic "fill-in-the-blank" concept map on page 163 that can be used to understand any theory, shown in Figure 3.11 (Dansereau, 2001). If you take this generic map for understanding theories to any class where theories are being taught, you can think of yourself as being "armed" with an information aid. As you fill in the boxes and circles, you will be developing an enhanced understanding of the theory you are learning.

Matrices

When the material to be comprehended involves comparisons of several topics along a number of dimensions, a **matrix** is the representation of choice. Suppose, for example that you are reading a passage about wars. The purpose of the passage is to compare and contrast various antecedent conditions of war and to consider their effect. Suppose further that the wars being considered are the Revolutionary War, World War I, World War II, The Korean Conflict, and the Vietnam Conflict. In order to understand the nature of these wars, you need to organize the information so that commonalities and distinctions will emerge. A suggested matrix for this information is shown in Table 3.3.

Table 3.3: Example of a Matrix Graphic Organizer

	War				
	Revolutionary War	**World War I**	**World War II**	**Korean Conflict**	**Vietnam Conflict**
Major precipitating events					
U.S. justification for the war					
"Other side" justification for the war					
Number of lives lost—each side					
Major battles					
Resolution					
Types of weapons					
Relationship to later war, if any					

Note. Matrices are particularly good spatial arrays when the information involves several different topics (e.g., wars) that are being compared on several dimensions (e.g., characteristics of war).

By filling in the empty cells in Table 3.3, selected categories of information can readily be compared, and similarities and differences can easily be spotted. A coherent "pattern" of information about these wars can then be extracted. The framework can be applied to other wars involving other countries to determine, for example, if there are universal commonalities for all wars. Similarly, matrices can be useful when a judgment has to be made about products or courses of action that differ along multiple dimensions. If you are familiar with the way in which the magazine *Consumer Reports* provides information about products to consumers, you will recognize that this is the technique that they use. For example, if you want to buy a refrigerator, you will find that Consumer Reports rates several different brands and models of refrigerators along many dimensions. The models would be listed in the left-hand column and the dimensions across the top, such as cost to operate, ease of opening the door, how well it maintains a set temperature, storage space built into the door, and the other features that differ between refrigerators. The ratings in each cell are pictorial (colored circles) that help to convert a large amount of information to a format that is comprehensible in a single glance. A similar technique was used by the RAND Corporation (1992, p. 7) in their analysis of three different plans for financing health insurance. Look at this matrix, which is presented in Figure 3.12.

As you can see, the RAND Corporation listed five desirable goals for any health care plan. These are listed under "goal." The three health care plans

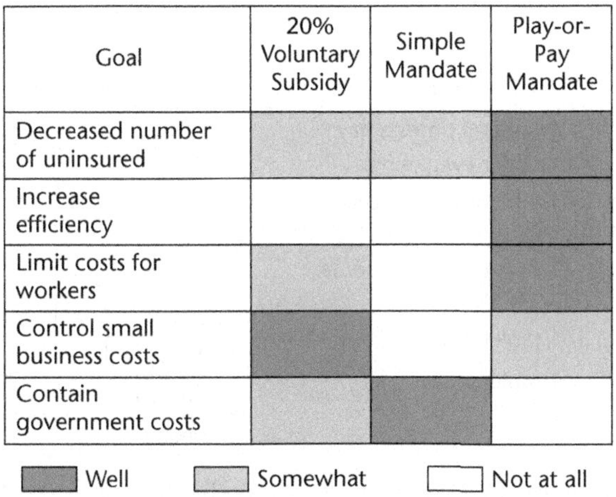

Goal	20% Voluntary Subsidy	Simple Mandate	Play-or-Pay Mandate
Decreased number of uninsured			
Increase efficiency			
Limit costs for workers			
Control small business costs			
Contain government costs			

█ Well   ▒ Somewhat   ☐ Not at all

Figure 3.12 A shaded matrix that compares three possible health care plans compared on five "goals." The use of shading with a matrix allows for an easier comparison between the plans. Adapted from RAND (1992). Health care and the uninsured: Who will pay? *RAND Research Review*, XVI, pp. 6–8.

they compared are a 20% voluntary subsidy, a simple mandate or law that would require employers to provide health insurance, and a play-or-pay plan that would allow employers to shop for the best plan for their employees. The degree of shading in a square is an indication of how well the particular plan satisfies a goal. Which plan seems the best given their evaluation and the way they presented the data? It is easy to see that the third option meets three goals very well, one goal somewhat, and one goal not at all. Thus, it would seem that the third plan is the best over-all, but this conclusion is only warranted if all of the goals are equal in importance. If the containment of government costs is much more important than any of the others, then the third plan is not a good one because it does not satisfy this goal. The relative importance of each goal depends on individual judgment that, ideally, is informed by knowledge of the issues.

Matrices can also be used to organize information so that it can be used more easily. Day, Rodin, and Stoltzfus (1990) investigated the effect of changing the representation of information on the ease with which it is used. A medication schedule that was given to a (real) patient is shown in Figure 3.13. The list format shown on the left side of Figure 3.13 is the way that the physician presented the medication schedule to the patient. The matrix format shown on the right provides the same information, but is clearly easier to use. Not surprisingly, Day, Rodin, and Stoltzfus found that both young and old subjects were more accurate in their understanding of and memory for the medication schedule when it was provided in a matrix format. It is clear that

LIST FORMAT	
Inderal	- 1 tablet 3 times a day
Lanoxin	- 1 tablet every a.m.
Cafafate	- 1 tablet before meals and at bedtime
Zantac	- 1 tablet every 12 hours (twice a day)
Quinaglute	- 1 tablet 4 times a day
Coumadin	- 1 tablet a day

MATRIX FORMAT

	Breakfast	Lunch	Dinner	Bedtime
Inderal	✓	✓	✓	
Lanoxin	✓			
Cafafate	✓	✓	✓	✓
Zantac		✓		✓
Quinaglute	✓	✓	✓	✓
Coumadin				✓

Figure 3.13 Two representations of medication schedules for an elderly patient. The list on the left is the format that was given to the patient. The matrix on the right was devised by Day, Rodin, and Stoltzfus (1990). Adapted from Day, R.S., Rodin, G.C., and Stoltzfus, E.R. (1990). Alternative representations for medication instructions: Effects on young and old adults. Paper presented at the 3rd Cognitive Aging Conference, Atlanta, GA.

some representations will facilitate the use of information and others will hinder it. One goal is to understand which representation matches the underlying structure of the information being conveyed.

Spatial Representation of Thought

In the chapter on memory, I presented the idea that our minds are a network of meaningful concepts with closely related concepts represented as being close in space. Near ideas are clustered and more distant ones are farther apart. New visual representations of words are now possible that take advantage of the network of thinking. For example, instead of looking up words in a standard dictionary, we can now look up word networks using interactive programs that can be found on the Internet. For example, *Visuwords* is an online graphical dictionary that can be found at http://www.visuwords.com/.

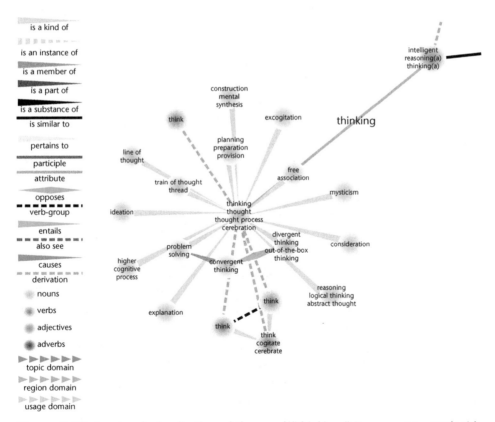

Figure 3.14 A network visualization of the word "thinking." It was constructed with the Visuwords online graphical dictionary, which can be found at http://www.visuwords.com/.

You can try it for yourself—just type in any word and it will prepare a word net. The visualization of the word "thinking" is shown below in Figure 3.14 along with the labels used to create the linkages.

General Guidelines and Principles

In a study of "at risk students" (those identified as being at risk of failing and not completing their education), Pogrow (1992) concluded that these students have academic difficulties because "they do not understand 'understanding'" (p. 90). What he means by this is that these students do not know what they need to do to ensure that information is acquired in a way that is meaningful and resistant to forgetting. Many ideas about learning and knowing are foreign to them such as: complex information will contain multiple interacting concepts; learners need to understand how concepts relate to one another; difficult material has to be questioned, explained, drawn, and discussed; and comprehension needs to be continually monitored. There is ample empirical evidence that more of these "at risk" students could complete their education if they were taught how to improve their comprehension.

All of the strategies for comprehension require learners to monitor their understanding of the information. They are all active cognitive strategies that facilitate the construction of meaningful representations. The graphic organizers offer ways to transform text into explicit spatial representations that display relationships between concepts. They all make abstract concepts more concrete. Like all good cognitive strategies, they require the learner to relate new information to prior knowledge in a way that makes remembering most efficient. Like many of the other thinking skills presented in this book, they require effort and must be practiced in order to be useful. It is not enough to read about them. They have to be used in a variety of situations to ensure transfer.

Although most of this chapter has been concerned with the process of comprehension, that is going from surface structure to underlying structure, many of the principles can be used in language production or going from underlying structure to surface structure. The task of writing involves transforming your internalized meaning into words. Many people have difficulty with writing because they find that this is a difficult translation. Kellogg (1990) compared the quality of persuasive papers written by college students who either prepared an outline before they began their papers (a linear display) or used a clustering technique in which associated ideas were first generated from memory and then connected with lines that showed how the ideas were related. He found that the students who were required to outline before they wrote improved in their organization and writing style (writing is a mostly linear activity), and the students who used clustering produced a larger number of ideas than those who used outlines. I will return to these results in the chapter on creativity, where I discuss the generation of ideas.

Graphic organizers, like clustering of ideas or creating flow charts or matrices, can be terrific aids in the writing process. Suppose you were to write an essay about Acquired Immune Deficiency Syndrome (AIDS). You could begin the planning process by considering the kinds of links employed in networking (type of, part of, leads to, evidence for, characteristics of, and analogy). What "types of" people are most and least at risk? What is the "evidence for" AIDS (laboratory tests, symptoms)? What are the "characteristics of" at-risk groups or risky activities? Some people have called for quarantine, which is "analogous to" the way the way society has responded to other dread diseases. Once you have considered the information you want to present, the relationship between the facts can be depicted in a network. The network offers a nonlinear alternative to outlines when planning the writing process. Thus, by "running comprehension strategies backward," they can be used to produce language (spoken or written) instead of their more usual role in comprehending language.

Chapter Summary

- Psycholinguistics is the branch of psychology that is concerned with understanding how people produce and comprehend language.

- Psychologists view language as comprising two components or levels: a meaning component (underlying representation) and a speech sound component (surface structure). The problem of comprehension is moving from a thought by the sender (underlying structure) through language and then reconstruction of the thought by the receiver.

- Language is ambiguous when a single surface structure has two or more possible underlying representations.

- Language and thought exert mutual influences on each other with our thoughts determining the language we use and, in turn, the language we use reshaping our thoughts.

- Six rules of communication were presented. Every time we attempt to communicate with others, we utilize these rules to determine what information we will convey and how to express the information.

- Language comprehension requires that the listener make many inferences. The kinds of inferences we make depend on context, manner, and the words selected to convey the message. Our understanding can be misled by communications that cause faulty inferences, such as advertisements and political opinion polls.

- There are many ways that words can be used to mislead the listener deliberately. The deliberate use of emotional and nonemotional words is designed to influence how you think about a topic.

- Emotional words often elicit strong mental images. Because images are highly resistant to forgetting, they are readily available when the topic is mentioned.

- Prototypes, or the most typical member of a category, are usually thought of first when we think about an example of a category. These prototypes bias what we think. This bias can be overcome with deliberate practice at generating examples that are not typical.

- A value that is easily available in memory can unconsciously serve as an anchor or starting point that we use to estimate quantities or cost. We need to think consciously of many different possible values that could serve as anchors as a way of reducing the effect of anchors.

- Strategies to improve the comprehension of text were described. They all require learners to attend to the structure of the information and to make the relationships between concepts explicit. Multiple representations—both visual spatial displays and verbal strategies—are used as aids to comprehension.

- The following skills to understand the way language influences thought were presented in this chapter. Review each skill and be sure that you understand how and when to use each one:

  o Defending against the inappropriate use of emotional language, labeling, name calling, ambiguity, vagueness, and arguments by etymology;

o   Developing the ability to detect misuse of definitions, reification, euphemism, and bureaucratese;

o   Thinking about the reason for a communication, the background knowledge of the listener, and the context when deciding what and how to communicate;

o   Understanding the use of framing with leading questions and negation;

o   Using analogies appropriately, which includes examining the nature of the similarity and its relationship to the conclusion;

o   Deliberately giving a variety of examples when thinking about members of a category so that you are not thinking about category members in terms of a prototype (e.g., thinking about many ways to be successful, not just the most common examples like making a high salary);

o   Recognizing the emotional components of some words and the way word choices can affect how you think and feel;

o   Recognizing when an anchor may be biasing your judgments about a quantity or cost and deliberately trying other values that could be alternative anchors;

o   Employing questioning and explaining as a skill for text comprehension;

o   Practicing at retrieval of information so that remembering becomes more accurate and easier with spaced practice;

o   Selecting and using graphic organizers (linear arrays, hierarchies, networks, matrices, flow charts).

Terms to Know

You should be able to define or describe the following terms and concepts. If you find that you're having difficulty with any term, be sure to reread the section in which it is discussed.

Psycholinguistics. The branch of psychology that is concerned with the acquisition, production, comprehension, and usage of language.

Underlying Representation. The meaning component of language. It is the thought that you want to convey with an utterance. Compare with surface structure.

Surface Structure. The sounds of an utterance or the outward appearance of a language expression. Compare with underlying representation.

Weasel Phrase. A phrase that is used to infer something that is not true by suggesting that something specific has been said, when it fact the words are ambiguous.

Given/New Distinction. The ratio of known (given) information to new information in a communication. It is a primary determinant of the difficulty of a communication.

Cognitive Economy. Any process that reduces the mental workload and makes thinking or remembering less effortful.

Prototypical Thinking. Using the most typical member in a category as a guide to making inferences about other members of that category.

Prototype. The best or most typical example of a category. For example, dog is the prototype for the category "animal."

Sapir-Whorf Hypothesis of Linguistic Relativity. The hypothesis that language, at least in part, determines or influences thought.

Semantic Slanting. The deliberate use of words designed to create a particular attitude or foster certain beliefs.

Ambiguous. An utterance is ambiguous when it can have more than one meaning or underlying representation.

Vagueness. A lack of precision in a communication. A communication is vague if it does not specify enough details for its intended purpose.

Equivocation. A change in the meaning of a word in the course of the same discussion.

Etymology. Reference to the origin of a word in order to determine its meaning.

Reification. Occurs when an abstract concept is given a name and then treated as though it were a concrete object.

Bureaucratese. The use of formal, stilted language that is often unfamiliar to people who lack special training.

Euphemism. The substitution of a desirable term for a less desirable or offensive one.

Framing. Occurs when a question is asked is a way that suggests what the correct response should be. The reader is "led" into assuming a particular perspective or point of view.

Risk Adverse. A general preference for options that do not involve possible loss over options that involve possible gain, even when the expected value is higher for the option that describes a loss.

Negation. The use of denial to imply that a fact is plausible.

Anchor. The unconscious use of a value that is easily accessible in memory as a "starting point" for making a judgment about a quantity or cost.

Reciprocal Peer Questioning. A technique in which learners pose thoughtful questions, which they take turns answering.

Generic Questions. Question "stems" that can be modified and applied to many different topics.

Concept Maps (sometimes called graphic organizers). The use of spatial displays to organize information.

Linear Arrays. A graphic organizer in which information is presented in a list format.

Hierarchies. A type of graphic organizer that uses a tree structure. Most useful when information is organized according to class inclusion rules.

Networks. Graphic organizers in which several different types of relationships between concepts are depicted.

Matrix. A rectangular array that is useful when the information presented involves comparisons along several dimensions.

CHAPTER 4

REASONING

DRAWING DEDUCTIVELY VALID CONCLUSIONS

Contents

As far as Joan's opponent was concerned, the debate wasn't going well. It was clear from the sea of nodding heads and sounds of "uh huh" and "yeah" that Joan was scoring points and convincing the audience, whereas he seemed to be losing support every time he spoke. He wasn't surprised; he had been warned. Joan had studied reasoning and now knew how to make people believe anything. Soon she would have everyone convinced that the war was justified and what was wrong was right. The way she's going, she could probably make people believe that day is night. It certainly wasn't fair, but what can you expect from someone who studied reasoning?

This fictional vignette was taken from a real life incident. I was present at a debate where one debater accused the other of cheating by using reasoning. At the time, I thought that this was pretty funny because I had come to think of reasoning as an important critical thinking skill—the sort of skill that you would use to make valid conclusions when dealing with information that is complex and emotional. To the losing side of this debate, it was a trick. Trick, skill, or strategy, reasoning is the best way to decide whom and what to believe.

Logical and Psychological

The trick, of course, is to reason well. It isn't easy and it isn't automatic.
—Howard Kahane (1980, p. 3)

Reasoning is often taken to be the hallmark of the human species. Colloquially, reasoning tells us "what follows what." When we reason, we use our knowledge about one or more related statements that we can reasonably believe are true to determine if another statement, the conclusion, is true. A **conclusion** is an inferential belief that is derived from other statements.

The ability to reason well is a critical thinking skill that is crucial in science, mathematics, law, forecasting, diagnosing, and just about every other context you can imagine. In fact, I cannot think of an academic or "real world" context in which the ability to reason well is not of great importance.

Many definitions of the term "critical thinking" identify reasoning as central to the concept as seen in the definition that was derived from three rounds of rankings by school administrators in the United States. The procedure they used to derive their preferred definition of critical thinking is called the Delphi technique, which refers to a method for achieving agreement among experts in some field. In this case, definitions were circulated among all participants three times. They agreed that "critical thinking is . . . cohesive, logical reasoning patterns" (Stahl & Stahl, 1991, p. 84).

Pragmatism and Logic

When we reason logically, we are following a set of rules that specify how we "ought to" derive conclusions. **Logic** is the branch of philosophy that explicitly states the rules for deriving valid conclusions. The laws of logic provide the standard against which we assess the quality of someone's reasoning. According to logic, a conclusion is **valid** if it necessarily follows from some statements that are accepted as facts. The factual statements are called **premises**. Conclusions that are not in accord with the rules of logic are **illogical**. Although we maintain that the ability for rational, logical thought is unique to humans, all too often we reach invalid or illogical conclusions. This fact has led Hunt (1982, p. 121) to award "A flunking grade in logic for the world's only logical animal."

Psychologists who study reasoning have been concerned with how people process information in reasoning tasks. The fact is that, in our everyday thinking, the psychological processes quite often are not logical. Although there is a very large amount of research literature on why people have trouble when using deductive reasoning, I think the problem was explained well in a classic paper on the relation between logic and thinking. Henle (1962) noted that everyday thought does not generally follow the formal rules of logic because people use their own imperfect rules. If we were not logical, at least some of the time, we wouldn't be able to understand each other, "follow one another's thinking, reach common decisions, and work together" (Henle, 1962 p. 374). To demonstrate this point, stop now and work on one of the problems Henle posed to her subjects in one of her studies:

A group of women were discussing their household problems. Mrs. Shivers broke the ice by saying: "I'm so glad we're talking about these problems. It's so important to talk about things that are in our minds. We spend so much of our time in the kitchen that, of course, household problems are in our minds. So it is important to talk about them" (p. 370). (Does it follow that it is important to talk about them? Give your reasoning.)

Do not go on until you decide if it is valid to conclude that Mrs. Shivers is correct when she says that it is important to talk about household problems. Why did you answer as you did?

In standard form, this paragraph becomes:

Premise 1. It is important to talk about things that are on our mind.
Premise 2. Household problems are on our mind.

Therefore (conclusion): It is important to talk about household problems.

When Henle posed this problem to graduate students, she found that some students arrived at the wrong answer (as defined by the rules of logic), whereas others arrived at the right answer for the wrong reasons. Consider the following answer given by one of her subjects: "No. It is not important to talk about things that are in our minds unless they worry us, which is not the case" (p. 370). Where did this student go wrong? Instead of deciding if the conclusion followed logically from the earlier statements, she added her own opinions about what sorts of things it is important to talk about. Thus, while the answer is incorrect as evaluated by the standard rules of logic, it is correct by the student's own rules. Consider this answer: "Yes. It could be very important for the individual doing the talking and possibly to some of those listening, because it is important for people to "get a load off their chest," but not for any other reason, unless in the process one or the other learns something new and of value" (p. 370). This time, the participant gave the correct answer, but for the wrong reasons. This participant, like the first one, added her own beliefs to the problem instead of deriving her conclusions solely on the basis of the information presented. Henle has termed this error in reasoning the **failure to accept the logical task**.

It seems that in everyday use of reasoning, we do not determine if a conclusion is valid solely on the basis of the statements we are given. Instead, we alter the statements we are given according to our beliefs and then decide if a conclusion follows from the altered statements. We function under a kind of **personal logic** in which we use our personal beliefs about the world to formulate conclusions about related issues.

When Logic and Belief Collide

> When logic and belief collide . . . people often respond on the basis of their prior knowledge, giving rise to a "belief-bias" effect.
> —Edward J. N. Stupple, Linden J. Ball, Jonathan St. B. T. Evans, and Emily Kamal-Smith (2011, p. 931)

According to the rules of deductive reasoning, the task is to determine if a conclusion "follows from" the statements or premises that are presented. It should not matter if the premises are true or false. It also should not matter if the topic of the reasoning problem is an abstract category labeled with letters or nonsense words or a real-life category about which you have extensive knowledge. But, psychologists know that the topic does matter when people reason deductively. The difference between reasoning that takes personal beliefs into account and reasoning with premises that refer to abstract categories (such as reasoning about all things that belong to category 'A') may reflect the differences between System 1 and System 2 thinking (Bonnefon, Eid, Vautier, & Jmel, 2008). Recall from the first chapter that System 1 thinking is faster and more intuitive, whereas System 2 thinking is slower and more deliberate and rule-bound. People rely on both types of thinking, but for deductive reasoning to be considered "correct," the reasoning must adhere to the rules for reasoning, and for most people, deductive reasoning will require effortful and deliberate thinking (characteristic of System 2 thinking). This concept will become easier to understand as you work your way through this chapter.

Scientists have argued that the ability to reason logically from false premises (or premises that may be false) is an important ability for mathematicians, lawyers, scientists, and other professions where the premises are often counterintuitive or arbitrary (Markovits & Kirtue-Forgues, 2011). For example, scientists may have to reason about unfamiliar planets where there is no gravity or about viruses that do not follow the usual rules of what we know about viruses. The legal system relies on many definitions of what constitutes different types of crimes. Consider the difference between larceny and embezzlement. The difference hinges on whether the perpetrator of the crime ever had possession of the stolen property before the crime was committed. By definition, if you had possession of someone else's property and then converted it to yourself, the crime is embezzlement. Given these definitions, you would reason deductively to determine if a particular crime "follows from" the definition for larceny or embezzlement. Your personal beliefs are irrelevant to determining how to classify a crime. The ability to reason logically with abstract premises or conclusions that conflict with personal beliefs is difficult, but there is considerable evidence that with instruction and practice people can improve their performance (Markovits & Kirtue-Forgues, 2011).

© King Features Syndicate, Courtesy KFS, INC.

Hägar the Horrible by Dik Browne. Used with permission by King Features.

In real life, people have *a **pragmatic** reason for reasoning*, and sometimes the laws of logic are at odds with the setting, consequences, and commonly agreed upon reasons and rules for deriving conclusions. In real life, we add our own beliefs and knowledge to the facts we are given when we determine if a conclusion is supported by the premises. In most everyday settings, this is a pragmatic or practical approach to reasoning problems.

Inductive and Deductive Reasoning

> Actual thinking has its own logic; it is orderly, reasonable, reflective.
> —John Dewey (1933, p. 75)

A distinction is often made between inductive and deductive reasoning. (See the Thinking as Hypothesis Testing chapter for a related discussion of this topic.) In **inductive reasoning**, observations are collected that support or suggest a conclusion. It is a way of projecting information from known examples to the unknown (Heit, 2000). For example, if every person you have ever seen has only one head, you would use this evidence to support the conclusion (or suggest the hypothesis) that everyone in the world has only one head. Of course, you cannot be absolutely certain of this fact. It is always possible that someone you have never met has two heads. If you met just one person with two heads, your conclusion must be wrong. Thus, with inductive reasoning you can never *prove* that your conclusion or hypothesis is correct, but you can disprove it. With inductive reasoning, if the premises are true, the conclusion is **probably** true.

In **deductive reasoning**, we begin with statements known or believed to be true, like "everyone has only one head," and then conclude or infer that La Tisha, a woman you have never met, will have only one head. This conclusion follows logically from the earlier statement. If we know that it is true that everyone has only one head, then it **MUST be true** that any specific person will have only one head. Similarly, if I show you a rectangle that is 2' by 3', then the area of the rectangle must be 6 square feet. Deductive reasoning is sometimes described as reasoning "down" from beliefs about the nature of the world to particular instances. Rips (1988) argues that deduction is a general purpose mechanism for cognitive tasks: deduction "enables us to answer questions from information stored in memory, to plan actions according to goals, and to solve certain kinds of puzzles" (p. 117).

The notion of "reasoning up" from observations and "reasoning down" from hypotheses is schematically shown in Figure 4.1.

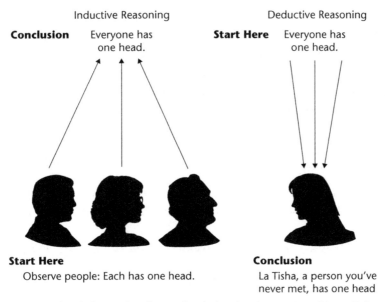

Figure 4.1 A pictorial distinction between deductive (reasoning "down" from premises) and inductive reasoning (reasoning "up" from examples). In most real-world settings, we use both types of reasoning recursively.

Although it is common to make a distinction between inductive and deductive reasoning, the distinction may not be a particularly useful description of how people reason in real life. In everyday contexts, we switch from inductive to deductive reasoning in the course of thinking. Our hypotheses and beliefs guide the observations we make, while our observations, in turn, modify our hypotheses and beliefs. Often, this process will involve a continuous interplay of inductive and deductive reasoning. Thinking in real-world contexts almost always involves the use of multiple thinking skills.

Linear Ordering

Reasoning is simply a matter of getting your facts straight.
—B. F. Anderson (1980, p. 62)

Joel is stronger than Bill, but not as strong as Richard. Richard is stronger than Joel, but not as strong as Donald. Who is strongest and who is second strongest?

Although I am sure that you've never met Joel, Donald, Richard, and Bill, I am also sure you could answer this question. The premises or statements in this problem give information about the orderly relationship among the terms; hence it is called a **linear ordering** or **linear syllogism**. Like the all deductive reasoning problems, the premises are used to derive valid conclusions—conclusions that must be true if the premises are true. In linear ordering problems, we are concerned with orderly relationships in which the relationships between the terms can be arranged in a straight-line array.

Linear Diagrams

How did you solve the problem about Joel, Donald, Richard, and Bill? Most people work line-by-line, ordering the people as specified in each line:

"Joel is stronger than Bill but not as strong as Richard" becomes

"Richard is stronger than Joel, but not as strong as Donald" adds Donald to the previous representation:

Thus, it is easy to "see" that Donald is strongest and Richard is second strongest. Research with linear syllogisms has shown that people rely, at least in part, on spatial imagery or some sort of spatial representation to answer the question.

Work through the following linear syllogisms:

1. Pat is not taller than Jim.
    Jim is shorter than Tiffany.
    Who is tallest? Pat, Jim, Tiffany, or don't know.

2. Les is worse than Moshe.
    Harold is worse than Moshe.
    Who is worst? Les, Moshe, Harold, or don't know.

3. Stuart doesn't run faster than Louis.
    Louis doesn't run slower than Dena.
    Who is slowest? Stuart, Lois, Dena, or don't know.

As you worked through these problems, did some seem more difficult to you than others? Problem 1 contains the negation term "not," which adds to the complexity of the problem. In addition, information is given in terms of both taller and shorter, which makes this a difficult problem. The correct answer is Tiffany. (Pat could be the same height or shorter than Jim.) You can represent this relationship graphically as:

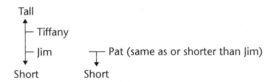

Although the second problem contains all congruent comparison terms (worse, worse, worst), some people find it tricky since we do not know if Les or Harold is worst. In addition, research has shown that it is more difficult to comprehend terms like "worse" than it is to use terms like "better" because it denotes that all three are bad, while "better" is a more neutral term—it does not imply that they are all good. (The correct answer is "don't know.") The third problem contains negative terms as well as incongruent comparison terms (faster, slower, slowest). From the information given, we cannot determine who is slowest.

As you worked through these problems, you should have discovered some of the following psychological principles of linear orderings:

1. Orderings are easiest to solve when comparison terms are congruent (e.g., short, shorter, shortest).

2. Solutions will be facilitated if the second term in the first premise is the first term in the second premise (A is better than B; B is better than C).

3. Negations make the problem more difficult (e.g., A is not hairier that B).

4. When you are faced with a difficult linear syllogism, draw a linear array, so that the relationships between the terms can be inspected visually.

5. Comparison terms that limit the meaning of a sentence, like worse and dumber, are more difficult to process than more general and neutral terms like better and smarter—these terms do not imply that they are all good or smart. The adjectives that connote a bias (e.g., worse, dumber) are called **marked adjectives**, while the neutral adjectives are called **unmarked adjectives**.

These summary remarks can be used as an aid for clear communication of linearly ordered information. When you want someone to understand a linear ordering, use congruent terms, make the second term in the first premise the first term in the second premise, and avoid negations and marked adjectives. These few rules for communicating linear information show a basic cognitive principle: negative information (no, not) is more difficult to process than positive information, in part because it seems to place additional demands on working memory. There are many times when negation is critical in understanding a concept, so you *cannot totally avoid* the use of negatives (including its use in this sentence). Here is an example from Goodwin and Johnson-Laird (2010, p. 253): "The concept of a 'ball' in baseball is defined as: a pitch at which the batter does *not* swing *and* which does *not* pass through the strike zone." Diagrams are a good way of testing the validity of conclusions in deductive reasoning because they reduce the demands on working memory (you do not need to keep all of the relationships in memory when you put them on paper). Diagrams make relationship among the terms obvious and visible.

Confusing Truth and Validity

Knowing is only part of being educated, thinking and reasoning with what we know completes it.

—Leona Schauble & Robert Glaser (1990, p. 9)

Logically, the rules for deciding if a conclusion is valid are the same no matter what terms we use. In the first example in this section, I could provide the premise that Donald is stronger than Richard, or I could substitute any name that I wanted (Igor is stronger than Yu-Chin or any letter or symbol, C is stronger than A). The truth is not important in these examples, because the premises are treated as though they were true. This probably bothered some of you. Suppose I said,

> Your sister is uglier than the wicked witch in the Wizard of Oz.
> You are uglier than your sister.
> Therefore, you are uglier than the wicked witch in the Wizard of Oz.

You would probably protest this conclusion. You may not even have a sister, but given the premises, the conclusion is valid. Test it for yourself. However, that does not make it true. A considerable portion of the next chapter will address the issue of determining the truth or believability of the premises. So far, we have only considered the question of validity: whether a conclusion must be true if the premises are true. People very often have trouble separating truth from validity. This is particularly difficult when the conclusion runs counter to cherished beliefs or strong emotion.

Although the rules of logic dictate that content is irrelevant to the conclusions we formulate, in most real-life situations, content does influence how we choose valid conclusions. It is possible to construct deductive reasoning problems so that the beliefs most people maintain conflict with logical conclusions. **Belief bias** or **confirmation bias** occurs when an individual's beliefs interfere with her or his selection of the logical conclusion. This effect has been demonstrated many times, and it is so pervasive that it interferes with good thinking in almost every context (Nickerson, 1998). Confirmation bias is discussed in several chapters because its effects are so widespread. We all seem to have difficulty in thinking critically when the reasoned conclusion is one that we do not believe to be true.

It should come as no surprise to you that human reasoning becomes illogical when we are discussing emotional issues. This is true for people in every strata of society, even for Justices of the United States Supreme Court. When Justice William O. Douglas was new to the Supreme Court, Chief Justice Charles Evans Hughes gave him these words of advice, "You must remember one thing. At the constitutional level where we work, ninety percent of any decision is emotional. The rational part of us supplies the reasons for supporting our predilections" (Hunt, 1982, p. 129). Unfortunately, appellate legal proceedings are sometimes exercises in politics, with decisions changing as frequently as the political climate. Legal "reasoning" has sometimes served as a framework to persuade others that a conclusion is valid. If you understand how to formulate valid inferences, you will be able to withstand and recognize its misuse by those who would use it to their advantage.

"If, Then" Statements

> Reason, of course, is weak, when measured against its never-ending task.
>
> Weak, indeed, compared with the follies and passions of mankind, which, we must admit, almost entirely control our human destinies, in great things and small.
>
> —Albert Einstein (1879–1955)

"If, then" statements, like the other examples of reasoning presented in this chapter, use premises that are known or assumed to be true to determine if a valid conclusion follows. "If, then" statements are concerned with **contingency relationships**—some events are dependent or contingent on the occurrence of others. If the first part of the contingency relationship is true, then the second part must also be true. "If, then" statements are sometimes called **conditional logic** or **propositional logic**. Work through the four following "if, then" statements. Decide if the third statement is a valid conclusion.

1. If she is rich, she wears diamonds.
   She is rich.
   Therefore, she wears diamonds.
   Valid or Invalid?

2. If she is rich, she wears diamonds.
   She is not wearing diamonds.
   Therefore, she is not rich.
   Valid or Invalid?

3. If she is rich, she wears diamonds.
   She is wearing diamonds.
   Therefore, she is rich.
   Valid or Invalid?

4. If she is rich, she wears diamonds.
   She is not rich.
   Therefore, she is not wearing diamonds.
   Valid or Invalid?

In each of these problems, the first premise begins with the word "if"; the "then" is not explicitly stated, but can be inferred ("then she wears diamonds"). The first part of this premise (If she is rich) is called the **antecedent**; the second part (she wears diamonds) is called the **consequent**.

Tree Diagrams

Like the other types of deductive reasoning problems, conditional statements can be represented with a spatial display. **Tree diagrams**, diagrams in which the critical information is represented along "branches"—like a tree— are used in several chapters in this book and can be used to determine validity with "if, then" deductive reasoning problems. Tree diagrams are very handy representational forms in many situations and are well worth the trouble of learning to use. We will use tree diagrams in the chapter on understanding likelihood, the chapter on problem solving, and the chapter on creativity.

Tree diagrams are easy to begin. Every tree diagram begins with a "start" point. A start point is a dot on the paper that you label "start." Everyone finds the first step easy.

- Start

The dots are more formally called **nodes**, and branches (lines) come out from nodes. The branches represent everything that can happen when you are at that node. In "if, then" problems, there are two states that are possible from the start node. In this example, either she is rich or she is not rich. There are two possibilities, so there will be two branches coming from the start node. The antecedent is the first event on the "tree," with a second branch representing the consequent. The validity of the conclusion can be determined by examining the branches. Let's try this with the first problem.

"If she is rich" becomes

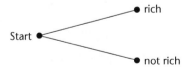

"She wears diamonds" is added as a second set of branches by showing that the "rich" node is always followed by "diamonds," but the "not rich" node may or may not be followed by "diamonds." We put both possibilities on the branches leading from "not rich" because we are not given any information about the relationship between being "not rich" and "wearing diamonds."

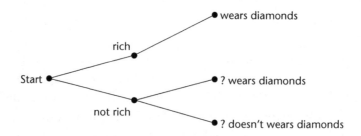

When we are told that "She is rich," circle the branch or branches that have this label and move along the branches from the "rich" node and conclude that she "wears diamonds." There is only one node in this diagram that represents the possibility that she is rich, and this node has only one branch attached from it—the branch that lead to "wears diamonds." Once you locate the "rich" node, the only possible consequent is "wears diamonds." Thus, the conclusion to problem number 1 is valid. The technical term for this problem is **affirming the antecedent**. In this case, the second premise affirms or indicates the antecedent is true; therefore, its consequent is true.

Problem 2 also contains a valid conclusion. The tree diagram is exactly the same as in the first problem because the same "if, then" statements are made. In determining the validity of the conclusion, we begin with "She is not wearing diamonds," which is represented at only one node, so we trace this back to the "not rich" node. Because the second premise indicates that the consequent is not true, this sort of problem is technically called **denying the consequent**.

Many people are willing to conclude that problem 3 is also valid when, in fact, it is not. Although it must be assumed to be true that if she is rich, she wears diamonds, it is also possible that poor people wear diamonds. I have found that intelligent college students (and yes, many of their professors also) have difficulty with this problem. Because the second premise states that the consequent has occurred, this sort of problem is called **affirming the consequent**. It is fallacious (i.e., wrong) to believe that because the consequent is true, the antecedent must also be true. "If," in these reasoning problems, doesn't mean "if and only if," which is how many people interpret it. Of course, she may be rich, it may even be more likely that she is rich, but we cannot conclude that she is rich just because she is wearing diamonds. You can see this on the tree diagram. There are two different nodes labeled "wears diamonds," one connected to the "rich" node and one connected to the "not rich" node. We cannot determine which must be true because either is possible.

The fallacy of affirming the consequent is one type of deductive reasoning error called **illicit conversion.** Illicit conversions, in "if, then" statements occur when people believe that "If A, then B" also means "If B, then A."

Problem 4 is also invalid, although it is tempting to conclude (especially if you are letting personal beliefs or previous knowledge interfere with your deductive reasoning) that if she is not rich, she is not wearing diamonds. Can you guess the technical term for this sort of problem? It is called **denying the antecedent** because premise 2 states that the antecedent is false. Again, by starting at the "not rich" node, you can see that it is connected to both "wears diamonds" and "does not wear diamonds," so either is possible.

A summary of these four kinds of reasoning, with examples of each, is shown in Table 4.1.

Table 4.1: Four Kinds of Reasoning with "If, Then" Statements

	Antecedent	**Consequent**
Affirming	Affirming the Antecedent Valid Reasoning Example: If I am dieting, then I will lose weight. I am dieting.	Affirming the Consequent Invalid Reasoning Example: If Harry went to the supermarket, then the refrigerator is full. The refrigerator is full.
	Therefore, I will lose weight.	Therefore, Harry went to the supermarket.
Denying	Denying the Antecedent Invalid Reasoning Example: If it is raining, then my hair is wet. It is not raining.	Denying the Consequent Valid Reasoning Example: If Judy and Bruce are in love, then they are planning to marry. They are not planning to marry.
	Therefore, my hair is not wet.	Therefore, Judy and Bruce are not in love.

Several popular advertisements take advantage of people's tendencies to make invalid inferences from "if, then" statements. There is a commercial for yogurt that goes something like this:

Some very old people from a remote section of the former Soviet Union are shown. We are told that people in this remote region live to be 110 years old. We are also told that they eat a great deal of yogurt. The conclusion that the advertisers want people to make is that eating yogurt will make you live 110 years.

Implicitly, we are being told that if we eat yogurt, then we will live to be 110 years old. Of course, it is possible to live to be 110 without ever tasting yogurt, and we have no reason to believe that yogurt added years to their lives. There is no basis for making the causal inference that eating yogurt can *cause* anyone to live a long time. These remote Russians engage in strenuous physical labor most of their lives and do not come into contact with many outsiders who carry potentially contagious diseases. Either of these facts, or countless others, including heredity, could account for their longevity. (It is also possible that the longevity claim is subject to question.) The advertisers are obviously hoping that the viewers will fall prey to the fallacy of affirming the consequent and say to themselves, "If I eat yogurt, I will live to a very old age."

"If, Then" Reasoning in Everyday Contexts

> In questions of science, the authority of a thousand is not worth the humble reasoning of a single individual.
> —Galileo Galilei (The Quoteaholic, http://www.quoteaholic.com.)

"If, then" statements, like linear orderings, appear implicitly in standard prose. Of course, we seldom find them neatly labeled "premise and conclusion." Yet, they are often the basis for many common arguments. The fallacies of denying the antecedent and affirming the consequent in everyday contexts are quite common.

There is an acrimonious debate over the issue of providing junior and senior high school students with contraceptive information. The pro side argues that if students are given this information, then they will act responsibly when engaging in intercourse. Formally, this becomes: If students receive contraceptive information, then they will engage in "protected" intercourse. The con side argues that students should not engage in intercourse (whether protected or not); therefore, they should not receive contraceptive information. This is an example of the fallacy of denying the antecedent. It does not follow that if they are not given contraceptive information, then they will not engage in intercourse.

Here is another example, virtually verbatim, from a news report. The specific details are not important because examples of this sort probably can be gleaned from the news on any day of the week. Viewers were told that if the president of the United States handled a tense situation with a potentially hostile country well, then a tense international situation would be resolved without escalation of hostilities. The situation was resolved well (hostilities did not escalate), so the commentator concluded that the president handled the tense situation well. Of course, it is possible that the information in the "if, then" statement is really not true, and even if the president did a good job, the situation could get worse. When we reason deductively with the laws of logic, we assume that the propositions are true, so let's put aside the very real possibility that we should not assume it to be true and apply the principles of "if, then" reasoning.

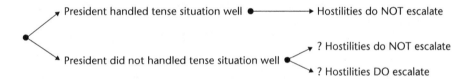

When the situation is drawn out in a decision tree, it is easy to see that it could have been resolved well, even if the president had not handled the tense situation well. A point that has been made repeatedly throughout this chapter is that people often do not reason according to the laws of formal logic without instruction in reasoning. This is an example where using the laws of logic would help us understand the situation better.

In everyday (practical) reasoning, we use information that is not stated in the premises in order to decide if the conclusion follows from the premises. One sort of knowledge we rely on is our knowledge about the content of the premises. The following two sentences demonstrate this point (Braine, 1978, p. 19):

If Hitler had had the atomic bomb in 1940, he would have won the war.

and

If Hitler had had one more plane in 1940, he would have won the war.

Although logic dictates that people should be able to reason identically with both of these premises and should avoid the fallacies of affirming the consequent and denying the antecedent, in fact most people find it easier to reason correctly with the first premise than the second. As with all of the forms of deductive reasoning that will be covered in this chapter, the content of the premises and our own belief biases influence the way we determine what sorts of conclusions we are willing to accept as valid. According to the rules of formal logic, we should be able to reason in ways that are independent of content. We should all arrive at identical, logically correct conclusions, no matter what the content is. Of course, humans are not perfect logic machines, and there are important individual differences in the sorts of models people use to solve reasoning problems (Bucciarelli & Johnson-Laird, 1999). We do and should determine if the premises are true before deciding if a conclusion follows. (This point will be emphasized in the following chapter.)

Confirmation Bias

> Once people form a hypothesis, they tend to confirm rather than refute it: they search for information to support it, interpret ambiguous information as consistent with it, and minimize inconsistent evidence.
> —Barbara O'Brien (2009, p. 328)

Confirmation bias, the predilection to seek and utilize information that supports or confirms your hypotheses or premises, can be seen in this classic problem (Johnson-Laird & Wason, 1970):

> Four cards are lying face up on a table in front of you. Every card has a letter on one side and a number on the other. Your task is to decide if the following rule is true, "If a card has a vowel on one side, then it has an even number on the other side." Which card or cards do you need to turn over in order to find out whether the rule is true or false? You may turn over only the minimum number necessary to determine if this rule is true. Please stop now and examine the cards below to determine which ones you would want to turn over. Don't go on until you have decided which cards you would want to turn over.

Few people select the correct cards in this problem, which has become known as the **four-card selection task**. It is a widely studied task that is popular in the literature of cognitive psychology. Most people respond "A only" or "A and 4." The correct answer is "A and 7." Can you figure out why? The best way to solve this reasoning problem is to draw a tree diagram that corresponds to the statement, "If a card has a vowel on one side, then it has an even number on the other side." It should look like this:

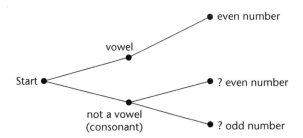

If A does not have an even number on the other side, the rule is false. Similarly, if 7 has a vowel on the other side, the rule is false. What about D and 4? D is a consonant. It does not matter if there is an even or odd number on the back because the rule says nothing about consonants. Because 4 is an even number, it does not matter if there is a vowel or consonant on the back. The reason that this is such a difficult problem is that people interpret the rule to also mean "If a card does not have a vowel on one side, then it does not have an even number on the other side" or, without negatives, "If a card has a consonant on one side, then it has an odd number on the other side." These alternate interpretations are incorrect. Do you recognize the error as denying the antecedent? This is a robust (strong) effect. It is an extremely difficult task because of the crucial role of disconfirmation. People fail to appreciate the importance of a falsification strategy. That is, we need to think of ways to show that a hypothesis may be false, instead of looking for evidence that would show that a hypothesis may be correct. This is exacerbated with the incorrect assumption that the converse of the rule is also true. The only correct way to solve this problem is to select only cards that can falsify the rule.

Part of the difficulty people have with this task may be related to the abstract nature of the problem. After all, there is very little we do in our everyday life that relates vowels and even numbers. Try out a more realistic and less abstract version of this task (adapted from Johnson-Laird, Legrenzi, & Legrenzi, 1972):

In order to understand this task, you may need some background information (depending on your age). Many years ago, the United States Post Office had two different postage rates known as first-class and second-class mail. You could pay full postage, which was 5 cents, if you sealed your letter (first class), or you could pay a reduced, 3-cent rate, if you merely folded the flaps closed and did not seal them (second class). (First class mail had priority for delivery over second-class mail.) Suppose you are a postal employee watching letters as they move across a conveyor belt. (I actually had a job like this when I worked for the postal service while in college.) The rule to be verified or disconfirmed is: "If a letter is sealed, then it has a 5 cent stamp on it." Four letters are shown in Figure 4.2. Which ones would you have to turn over to decide if the rule is true?

Stop now and work on this problem. Do not go on until you have decided which letters (at a minimum) you would have to turn over to test this rule. Did you notice that this is the same task that was posed earlier? The correct answer is the first sealed envelope and the last envelope (the one with the 3-cent stamp). This is an easier problem than the more abstract one because people find it easier to understand that a letter that is not sealed could also have a 5-cent stamp on it than it is to understand that if the letter is not a vowel it could also have an even number on the back. Your tree diagram should look like this:

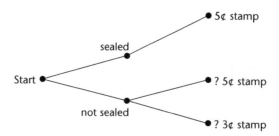

Johnson-Laird and Wason (1977) found that when the problem is presented in this realistic manner, 22 out of 24 subjects were able to solve the

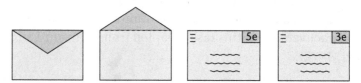

Figure 4.2 Which of these letters would you turn over to decide if the following rule is true: "If a letter is sealed, then it has a 5-cent stamp on it." (Adapted from Johnson-Laird, Legrenzi, & Legrenzi, 1972.)

problem. They concluded that our everyday experiences are relevant in determining how we reason.

These results (and many others) show that most people can reason with "if, then" statements when the topic is familiar to them. But, when the topic is unfamiliar, most people make the same type of error. In fact, the bias to confirm information that we believe to be true is so pervasive that confirmation bias comes up repeatedly throughout this book.

Permission and Obligation Schemata

Many researchers have tried to understand why so many people have difficulty with the four-card selection task (I also find it very confusing), but have little difficulty when it is rephrased in the stamped letter example. These are identical problems from the perspective of logic—the rules for reasoning are the same in the two problems.

Cheng and Holyoak (1985) explored the basic differences in how people think about these two problems. They postulated that when people use "if, then" reasoning for pragmatic purposes, they usually involve either the permission to do something, called **permission schema** (if something is true, then you have permission to do something else) or they involve an obligation or contractual arrangement, called **obligation schema** (if something is true, then you have an obligation to do something else). In real life, these are the two most common situations in which people use "if, then" reasoning. Instead of using the rules of formal logic, people tend to develop abstract general rules that work well in specific situations and help them to achieve their goals. Cheng and Holyoak found that the permission and obligation schemata operate across domains. In other words, it does not matter if the topic concerns stamped letters, an agreement to perform a job, or permission to borrow the car. Here is an example of each:

> *If a passenger has been immunized against cholera, then he may enter the country. (permission schema)*
> *If you pay me $100,000, then I'll transfer ownership of this house to you. (obligation schema)*

When "if, then" statements involve permission or obligation, then people make few reasoning errors. Furthermore, when most people understand the rules of permission and obligation, the content of the statement does not matter—people apply the rules appropriately across domains. Cheng and Holyoak (1985) also found that when they included a rationale for the rule, most of the people they asked to solve this problem had no difficulty with it. In the sealed envelope problem, they added the following rationale for the rule, "The country's postal regulation requires that if a letter is sealed, then it must carry a 20-cent stamp" (p. 400). Thus, a rule that was extremely difficult to apply when it was presented in an abstract form was easily used by most people when it was used in a familiar context with an explanation.

"If, and Only if"

Certain contexts seem to require that we understand them in a way that is inconsistent with the laws of logic. Suppose you are told: "If you mow the lawn, I'll give you five dollars" (Taplin & Staudenmeyer, 1973, p. 542). This statement invites the interpretation, "If you do not mow the lawn, I will not give you five dollars." In the everyday inference we make from language, this is a valid conclusion, although it is erroneous from the perspective of formal logic. In understanding statements of the "If p, then q" variety, the conclusions that we are willing to accept as valid depend very much on what p and q are. In this lawn-mowing example, the intended meaning is "if, and only if you mow the lawn, then I'll give you five dollars." In dealing with real world "if, then" statements, you need to decide whether the intended message is "if p, then q" or "if, and only if p, then q." The important point of this example is that context is irrelevant to the laws of logic, which are the same whether you are talking about pay for mowing a lawn or turning over a card to check an abstract rule. It is not surprising that people vary their thinking depending on context because context is important in real-life settings.

Chained Conditionals

We can make things just a little more complicated (just what you were hoping for), by building on "if, then" statements and making them into longer chains. A **chained conditional** occurs when two "if, then" statements are linked so that the consequent of one statement is also the antecedent of the other statement. With a chained conditional, the two premises are interdependent—they depend upon each other. In skeleton form, or fill-in-the-blank form, this becomes:

If A, then B. If B, then C.

As before, it does not matter what we use to fill in for A, B, and C if we are reasoning according to the laws of logic. For example, "If Jodi wants to be a physicist, then she will study calculus. If she is studying calculus, then she has a final exam on Wednesday." With this conditional chain, we can conclude that she has a final exam on Wednesday if we learn that she wants to be a physicist.

Do not be tempted to assume that every time you have three terms, you have a chained conditional. Consider this example.

If she wants to be a physicist, then she will study calculus.
If she wants to be a physicist, then she will have an exam on Wednesday.

These are two conditional statements, but they do not have the chained structure because the consequent of one statement is not the antecedent of the other statement.

"If, Then" Reasoning in Legal Contexts

Consider the sad saga of an American star who was accused of killing his ex-wife and her friend. The specifics of this American tragedy are not relevant because there are always similar crimes in which the key to the defense or prosecution hinges on "if, then" reasoning. In this particular case, the suspect had an excellent alibi from 11 p.m. and later on the night of the killing. In other words,

If the murder occurred any time from 11 p.m. or later, the defendant is innocent.

The prosecutor attempted to show that the murder occurred prior to 11 p.m. Suppose that she was successful in convincing the jury that the murder occurred at 10:30. What can we conclude about the guilt or innocence of the defendant?

To make it easier for you, I have drawn the tree diagram that corresponds to this real-life situation.

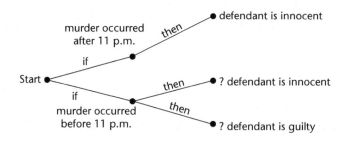

I hope that you determined that if the murder occurred at 10:30, we do not know if the defendant is guilty or innocent. Unless there is other evidence that "proves beyond a reasonable doubt" that the defendant committed these grisly murders, then the jury must acquit him. They cannot convict a man because of the error of denying the antecedent. If anyone tries to tell you that this critical thinking stuff is a "bunch of bunk" (or some more colorful phrase), then give him this example in which misunderstanding could lead to a wrongful conviction. Whom would you want on a jury that decides your guilt or innocence—people who think critically or those who rush to a hasty decision and are easily misled with persuasive techniques?

"If, Then" Reasoning as Therapy for Children with Attention Deficit Disorder

> The mental links created by if-then plans support goal attainment on the basis of psychological processes that relate to both the anticipated situation (if-part) and the goal-directed response (then-part). As forming an if-then plan implies the selection of a future situation, the mental representation of this situation becomes highly activated, and therefore more easily accessible.
> —Caterina Gawrilow, Peter M. Gollwitzer, and Gabriele Oettingen
> (2011, pp. 618–619)

"If, then" reasoning is the basis for a treatment that is used with children who have Attention Deficit Hyperactivity Disorder (ADHD; Gawrilow, Gollwitzer, & Oettingen, 2011). As the name of the disorder implies, children with this disorder are inattentive and hyperactive. One way of helping children "stay on task" is to provide them with the cognitive tools that can help them self-regulate their behavior. Children with ADHD are taught "if, then" planning in the format of "If situation X is encountered, then I will perform Y." Research has shown that "if, then plans" are beneficial for children with ADHD. Researchers believe that this is an effective strategy because it creates a mental representation that can be recalled automatically, thus making fewer demands on working memory.

Combinatorial Reasoning

> We recognize the gravity of the challenge to get our students to think, to think critically, and even to think scientifically. Certainly it is abundantly clear to me that science education fails if it doesn't tackle the matter of thinking.
>
> —A. Hugh Munby (1982, p. 8)

One approach to enhancing reasoning skills is based on a model of intelligence that was proposed by the Swiss psychologist Jean Piaget. Piaget was primarily concerned with the way people acquire knowledge and the way cognitive processes change throughout childhood and early adulthood. According to Piaget, there are four broad developmental periods (each broken into stages). As people move from infancy into adolescence, their cognitive abilities mature in qualitatively distinct stages culminating with the ability to think in orderly, abstract ways. It seems that Piaget underestimated the age at which most people would master this task. In a study of the age at which most people are able to use combinatorial reasoning (without instruction), graduate students with an average age of 36 outperformed undergraduates with an average age of 24, showing that these abilities continue to develop long after adolescence (Mwamwenda, 1999). It seems that most people would benefit from a short review of combinatorial reasoning. Piaget's examples of abstract thought involve thinking skills that are needed to understand scientific concepts. One of the scientific reasoning skills that Piaget believed to be important is **combinatorial reasoning**, which is the use of systematic and orderly steps when making combinations so that all possible combinations are formed. Here is a classic task that involves this skill:

Mixing colorless chemicals: This task involves mixing chemicals until a yellow color is obtained. Suppose that you were given four bottles of odorless, colorless liquids. They appear to be identical except for being labeled 1, 2, 3, and 4. You are also given a fifth beaker labeled X, which is the "activating solution." The activating solution is always needed to obtain the yellow color, which results from a chemical reaction. How would you go about finding which of the chemicals in combination will yield the yellow color?

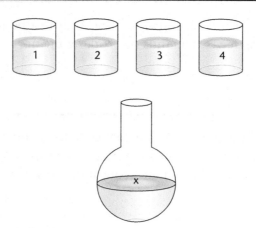

Figure 4.3 Mixing colorless liquids.

Some rules: The amount of each chemical is not important, nor is the order in which you combine them. It may help you in working on this problem to visualize the materials as presented in Figure 4.3.

Stop now and think about how you would approach this problem. Do not go on until you have written down all of the tests you would perform.

How did you approach this problem? Did you realize that you needed an organized plan or did you begin by randomly mixing the liquids? The best approach to this task is a very methodical one. It must include mixing each liquid separately with the activating solution (1+X, 2+X, 3+X, 4+X), then carefully mixing two liquids at a time with X (1+2+X, 1+3+X, 1+4+X, 2+3+X, 2+4+X, 3+4+X), then three at a time with X (1+2+3+X, 1+2+4+X, 1+3+4+, 2+3+4+X), then all four at once (1+2+3+4+X), being careful to observe which combinations would yield the yellow color. Look over the way the chemicals were combined in a systematic manner so that no combinations would be missed or duplicated. This technique of systematic combinations will be needed to perform the reasoning tasks in the next section.

Syllogistic Reasoning

Nothing intelligible ever puzzles me.
Logic puzzles me.

—Lewis Carroll (1832–1898)

Syllogistic reasoning is a form of reasoning that involves deciding whether a conclusion can properly be inferred from two or more statements. One type of syllogistic reasoning is categorical reasoning. **Categorical reasoning** involves **quantifiers**—terms like "all," "some," "none," and "no"—which indicate how many items belong in specified categories.

A **syllogism** usually consists of two statements that are called **premises** and a third statement called the conclusion. In categorical syllogisms, quantifiers are used in the premises and conclusion. The task is to determine if the conclusion follows logically from the premises.

The premises and conclusion of a syllogism are classified according to **mood**. (The word "mood" has a special meaning in this context that is unrelated to its more usual meaning about how someone feels.) There are four different moods, or combinations of positive and negative statements with the terms "all" or "some." The four moods are:

Mood	Abstract Example	Concrete Example
Universal Affirmative	All A are B.	All students are smart.
Particular Affirmative	Some A are B.	Some video games are fun.
Universal Negative	No A are B.	No smurfs are pink.
Particular Negative	Some A are not B.	Some democrats are not liberals.

As you can see from this table, a statement is universal if it contains the terms "all" or "no"; it is particular if it contains the term "some"; it is negative if it contains "no" or "not"; and it is affirmative if it is not negative. Thus, it should be easy to classify the mood of any statement by identifying the key terms.

Work through the following syllogism and decide if the conclusion is valid (V) or invalid (I). To be valid, the conclusion must *always* be true given its premises. In other words, when you decide that a syllogism is valid, you are saying "if the premises are true, then conclusion must be true." In other words, "Does the conclusion 'follow from' the premises?" *If you can think of one way that the conclusion could be false when the premises are true, then it is invalid.*

Premise #1:   All people on welfare are poor.
Premise #2:   Some poor people are dishonest.
Conclusion: Some people on welfare are dishonest. Valid or Invalid?

According to the rules of logic, it should not matter if the syllogisms are presented in abstract terms of A's and B's (e.g., Some A are not B), nonsense terms like zev and creb (All zev are creb), or meaningful terms like lawyers and cool (No lawyers are cool). The logical rules for deciding if a conclusion can be validly inferred from the premises remain the same. We are really saying "All _____ are _____." It should make no difference how we fill in the blanks; any letters, nonsense or meaningful words, or even fancy pictures should be handled in the same way. However, from a psychological perspective, there are important content differences, and people have difficulty using the rules of syllogistic reasoning when the conclusion is not one that they believe to be true, even if logically it follows from the premises. One way to avoid the problem of having one's biases affect how we reason with quantifiers is to use circle diagrams which, like linear diagrams and tree diagrams, alleviate the limitations of short term memory and make relationships obvious and visible.

How did you go about deciding if the conclusion was valid? There are two different types of strategies that can be used with syllogisms to determine if a conclusion follows from its premises. If you've been reading the chapters in order, then you know that a common approach to improving thinking is the deliberate use of both spatial and verbal strategies. The same two approaches apply here. First, I present a spatial method for testing conclusions, and then I provide verbal rules that can also be used. Either method will "work," but you will probably find that you prefer one method over the other. I have been teaching this material to college students for many years and have found that individual students have very strong preferences for either circle diagrams or verbal rules.

Circle Diagrams for Determining Validity

One way of determining if a conclusion is valid is with the use of circle diagrams that depict the relationships among the three terms (A, B, C, or whatever we used to fill in the blanks). The degree to which the circles overlap depicts the inclusion or exclusion of the categories.

There are several different methods of drawing diagrams to depict the relationships between the terms in a syllogism. One of these methods is known as Venn Diagrams, named for a 19th century English mathematician and logician who first introduced them. These are the same diagrams that you probably used in mathematics classes if you ever studied set theory. (This was a very popular way to teach the "new math" before it was abandoned and replaced with the "old math.") A second method of diagramming relationships is known as Euler Diagrams. According to popular lore, this method was devised by Leonard Euler, an 18th century Swiss mathematician who was given the task of teaching the laws of syllogistic reasoning to a German princess. Because the princess was having difficulty understanding the task, Euler created a simple procedure that could be used to understand the relationships between the terms and to check on the validity of inferences. A third method is called the ballantine method because of its use of three overlapping circles. In all of these methods, circles are used to indicate category membership. The differences between these methods are not important here, and the general strategy of checking conclusions with circle drawings will be referred to as **circle diagrams**. If you have learned a different method of circle diagrams in another context (e.g., a class on set theory or a logic class), then continue to use that method as long as it works well for you.

Look very carefully at Figure 4.4 on page 204.

The four moods that statements in syllogisms can have are listed in the left-hand column of Figure 4.4. Next to each statement are circle diagrams that are correct depictions of the relationships in the statement. One circle represents everything that is A, and a second circle represents everything that is B. For the purposes of deductive reasoning, it does not matter what A and B are. In the example in Figure 4.4, A is used to stand for angels and B is used to stand for bald, but it could be anything. I could just as easily have used A to stand for college students and B to stand for punk rockers.

Look at the way the circles are combined so that they form a "picture" of what is being said in words. Let's start in the middle of the figure, with "Universal Negative," the easiest example. When we say, "No A are B," this means that nothing that is in category A is also in category B. This is depicted by drawing a circle labeled A and one labeled B that do not touch or overlap in any way. There is only one way to draw this relationship. Notice that when we say, "No A are B," we are also saying that "No B are A." Can you see that from the circle diagram? Every time you have a universal negative, the relationship will be "pictured" with two circles that do not overlap—one for things that are A and one for things that are B.

Consider now Universal Affirmative, "All A are B." Again we use two circles—one labeled A and one labeled B. And again, we want to draw the

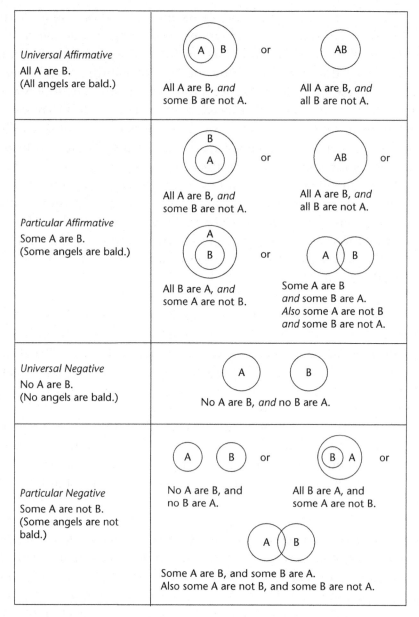

Figure 4.4 Circle diagrams depicting correct interpretations of the premises used in syllogisms. Note that "all" can have two correct interpretations, "some" can have four correct interpretations, "no" has one correct interpretation, and "some not" can have three correct interpretations.

two circles so that they represent the relationship in which everything that is A is B. As you can see in Figure 4.4, there are two different ways of depicting this relationship because there are two possible correct ways of understanding what it means. By drawing the A circle inside the B circle, we are depicting the case where "All A are B," but there are some B that are not A (some bald people are not angels). The second drawing shows the case where "All A are B," and "All B are A" (all bald people are angels). Either of these two interpretations could be true when we are told that "All A are B."

Do not be discouraged if this seems difficult to you. It will soon be easier as it becomes more meaningful and you work your way through the examples. Look at the other two possibilities in Figure 4.4. There are three possible ways to depict Particular Negative (Some A are not B) and four possible ways to depict Particular Affirmative (Some A are B). Now look at all of the moods and notice the different ways that two circles can be combined. There are five different possible ways to combine two circles, and each combination represents a different meaning.

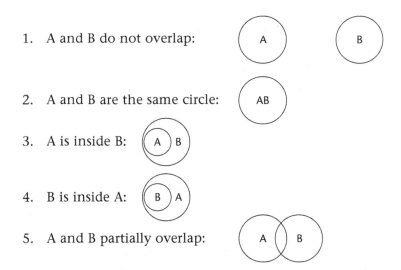

1. A and B do not overlap:

2. A and B are the same circle:

3. A is inside B:

4. B is inside A:

5. A and B partially overlap:

Let's draw circle diagrams to depict the relationships in the syllogism about poor people. The first two sentences are the premises. Write out each premise and next to each premise, draw the appropriate circle diagrams. For example, the first premise states, "All people on welfare are poor." In skeletal form, it is "All A are B" with A standing for "people on welfare" and B standing for "poor." You should recognize this as Universal Affirmative. Go to Figure 4.4, look across from Universal Affirmative, and you will see that there are two possible ways to draw circles that correspond to this premise. Repeat this with the second premise: Some poor people are dishonest. You already decided that A = people on welfare, and B = poor. The new term, dishonest, can be represented by C. The second premise then becomes: Some B are C. This is an example of Particular Affirmative. Look across from Particular Affirmative on Figure 4.4 and you will see that there are four possible ways to draw circles to represent this relationship. The only difference is that for Premise 2, we are using the letters B and C to stand for the categories. Thus, the first two premises will look like this:

A = people on welfare; B = poor; C = dishonest.
Premise 1: All people on welfare are poor.
(All A are B.)

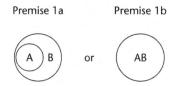

Premise 2: Some poor people are dishonest.
(Some B are C.)

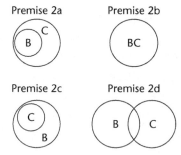

To determine if the conclusion is valid, we systematically combine each of the figures in the first premise with each of the figures in the second premise. If we find one combination that would not correspond to the conclusion, then we can stop and decide that the conclusion is invalid. If we make all possible combinations of figures from Premise 1 and figures from Premise 2, and they are all consistent with the conclusion, then the conclusion in valid. In other words, if all combinations of Premise 1 with Premise 2 support the conclusion, then the conclusion is valid. The first few times you work on these, it may seem laborious, but you will soon "see" the answers and find ways to short cut the process of working through all the combinations.

Here is the conclusion:
Some poor people on welfare are dishonest.
(Some A are C.)

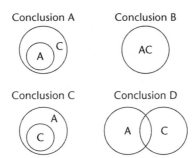

Premise 1 has two possible drawings and Premise 2 has four possible drawings. You can see that I labeled the two Premise 1 drawings 1a and 1b and the four Premise 2 drawings 2a, 2b, 2c, and 2d. To work systematically, you need to use the combinatorial reasoning rules that were presented in the last section. Start with 1a and combine it with 2a, then 1a and 2b, 1a and 2c, 1a and 2d. Then repeat the pattern by combining 1b with 2a, then 1b with 2b, then 1b with 2c, and finally 1b with 2d. Of course, you hope that you won't have to go through this entire procedure because you can stop as soon as you find one combination that violates the conclusion that "Some A are C." Work along with me.

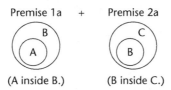

When I combine these two depictions, I will get a figure with A inside B inside C:

This combination shows a result that is consistent with the conclusion that "Some A are C." Go on!

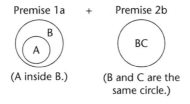

When I combine 1b and 2b, I get a depiction where A is inside the B/C circle.

This is consistent with the conclusion that "Some A are C." Go on!

Premise 1a + Premise 2c

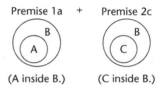

(A inside B.)   (C inside B.)

This gets a little tricky here, because there are several different ways to combine 1a and 2c and we have to try all of them until we run out of combinations or find one that is not consistent with the conclusion. Here we draw all ways that A can be inside B and C can be inside B.

A and C are the same circle inside B.

This is still consistent with "Some A are C." Go on!
A and C partially overlap inside B.

This is still consistent with "Some A are C." Go on!
A and C are two circles inside B.

This does not agree with the conclusion that "Some A are C." Stop here! As soon as you draw one combination of the premises in which the conclusion is invalid, you can decide that it is invalid. I know that this seems like a lot of work (because it is), but after you work a few problems, you can spot the combinations that will make a conclusion invalid, so you will not need to try every possible combination. Until then, work systematically through all combinations. A list of steps for checking the validity of conclusions with circle diagrams is shown in Table 4.2. Stop now and look over the steps.

Verbal Rules for Determining Validity

It is a peculiar thing about circle diagrams: Some people love working on them and others seem to hate them. The problem in working with them is trying all possible combinations of representations for both premises. People who prefer to think spatially seem to "see" the combinations with apparent ease, while those who prefer verbal modes of representation seem to have more difficulty. For those of you who have difficulty combining premises into circle relationships, take heart because there are verbal rules for determining if the conclusion of a syllogism is valid. These rules will work just as well as circle diagrams. There are seven rules that can be used to determine the validity of a conclusion. In order to use these rules, there are two additional terms that you need to learn.

Table 4.2: Steps for Determining the Validity of Conclusions Using Circle Diagrams

---

1. Write out each premise and the conclusion of the syllogism.

2. Next to each statement, draw all correct diagrams using the diagrams shown in Figure 4.1.

3. Systematically combine all diagrams for Premise 1 with all diagrams for Premise 2. Try Premise la (the first diagram for Premise 1) with Premise 2a (the first diagram for Premise 2). Continue combining Premise la with all Premise 2 diagrams, then go on and combine all Premise lb with all Premise 2 diagrams. Continue in this manner (Premise lc with all Premise 2 diagrams, then Premise ld with all Premise 2 diagrams) until

4. You find one diagram in which the conclusion is invalid or

5. You have tried all combinations of Premise 1 and Premise 2 diagrams.

Note. Sometimes there will be more than one way to combine diagrams form the two premises. Be sure to try all combinations.

When trying out all combinations, remember that there are five possible ways to combine two circles: (a) A inside B, (b) B inside A, (c) A and B overlapping partially, (d) A and B with no overlap (two separate circles), and (e) A and B represented by one circle (A and B are the same circle).

There are three categories named in syllogisms—the A, B, and C, or whatever category names we substitute for them in more concrete examples. One of these categories is called the **middle term**. To determine which term is the middle term, go to the conclusion. There are two categories in the conclusion; one is the subject of the sentence, the other is in the predicate. The category that is *not* mentioned in the conclusion is the middle term. It is called the middle term because it links the other two terms in the premises. Look back at syllogism we just solved with circle diagrams. The conclusion is "Some people on welfare are dishonest." "People on welfare" is the subject of this sentence, and "dishonest" is in the predicate. The middle term is "poor." The middle term is in both premises, but it is not in the conclusion.

The second term that you need to know is **distributed**. A term is distributed if the statement applies to every item in the category. Consider the four types of category relationships shown in Table 4.3. Next to each one I have indicated which terms are distributed and which terms are undistributed. As you will see in Table 4.3, categories that are modified by "all," "no," and "not" are distributed.

Look carefully at the statement "All A are B." B is undistributed in this statement because there may be some B that are not A, so the statement is not about every B. On the other hand, consider "No A are B." In this case, B is distributed because when we say "No A are B," we are also saying "No B are A." Thus, in the second case, the statement is about all B.

For a conclusion to be valid, the syllogism must pass all of the rules in Table 4.4. If it fails on any one of them, then it is invalid.

Table 4.3: Distributed and Undistributed Terms in the Four Modes of Syllogisms

All A are B.	A is distributed. (A is modified by "all.")B is undistributed. (B is undistributed because there may be some B that are not A.)
Some A are B.	Both A and B are undistributed.
No A are B.	Both A and B are distributed. (Both A and B are modified by "no.") (This is the same as saying that "No B are A.")
Some A are not B.	A is undistributed.B is distributed. (B is modified by "not.")

Table 4.4: Rules for Determining Validity of Conclusions When Reasoning with Quantifiers

1. If the conclusion is negative, one premise must be negative, and conversely, if one premise is negative, the conclusion must be negative.

2. The middle term must be distributed in at least one premise.

3. Any term that is distributed in the conclusion must be distributed in at least one premise.

4. If both premises are particular, there are no valid conclusions.

5. If one premise is particular, the conclusion must be particular.

6. At least one premise must be affirmative. (There are no valid conclusions with two negative premises.)

7. No syllogism with a particular conclusion can have two universal premises.

Let's apply these rules to the syllogism we have already solved with circle diagrams.

Syllogism: A = people on welfare; B = poor; C = dishonest

All people on welfare are poor. (All A are B.)
Some poor people are dishonest. (Some B are C.)
Some people on welfare are dishonest. (Some A are C.)

The middle term for this syllogism is B. It is the one mentioned in both premises and is missing from the conclusion. The first rule starts "if the conclusion is negative." Because the conclusion is positive, we can immediately go on to the second rule. The second rule states that the middle term must be distributed in at least one premise. Let's check this. The middle term is B (poor people). Is it modified by "all" or "not" in either premise? It is not distributed in either premise, so we can stop here. This conclusion is invalid. But, of course, you already knew that because you discovered that it was invalid when you completed the circle diagrams.

Reasoning with False Premises

Some syllogistic conclusions are not believable, even if they are valid, and it seems that these types of syllogisms are the most difficult to solve. Consider for example:

All computer programmers spend more than 30 hours a week on their computer.
You spend more than 30 hours a week on your computer.
Therefore, you are a computer programmer.

It seems that if you really are a computer programmer, you are more likely to conclude that this syllogism is valid than if you are not a computer programmer. There seems to be three processes involved in understanding what happens when the conclusion of a syllogism collides with it personal beliefs (Ball, Phillips, Wade, & Quayle, 2006; Stupple, Ball, Evans, & Kamal-Smith, 2011). The three kinds of processing are (a) using deductive logic; (b) relying on personal beliefs, and (c) responding to their interaction, which in this case means that people are more likely to reason with their personal beliefs when the conclusion is invalid. There are also individual differences in how people respond, with some people quickly responding based on their personal beliefs and others taking longer to respond as they work through the steps to determine if a syllogism is valid. As explained earlier in this chapter, the more deliberate and rule-based approach has been called System 2 thinking, and the quicker approach that is based on personal beliefs has been called System 1 thinking. This distinction is made in numerous places throughout this book.

Syllogisms in Everyday Contexts

Human reasoning deviates in many ways from the norm provided by standard deductive logic.
—Henrik Singmann and Karl Christoph Klauer (2011, p. 247)

Somewhere during the last section, you may have said to yourself, "Why bother!" It may seem that syllogisms are artificial stimuli created solely to make work for students and teachers. If you did have this thought, you were questioning the **ecological validity** of syllogisms. Ecological validity concerns the real world validity or applications of a concept outside of the laboratory or classroom. In other words, do people use syllogistic reasoning in real-world contexts? When the premises are not meaningful or useful (e.g., "some lawyers are rich"), it is easy to see why so many people believe that learning the skills of deductive reasoning is also not meaningful or useful. Many people have argued that it is irrelevant to how we think in our everyday lives (Evans & Elqayam, 2011) and that "few problems of consequence in our lives have deductive or even any meaningful kind of 'correct' solution" (Sternberg, 2011, p. 270). I think it is more accurate to

Reasoning **213**

Calvin and Hobbes   by Bill Watterson

© 1988 Universal Press Syndicate. Reprinted with permission. All rights reserved.

Calvin and Hobbes by Bill Watterson. Used with permission by Universal Press Syndicate.

conclude that they are of some, but limited, usefulness. There are many areas where they are important, such as making a diagnosis or solving a mathematical problem or deciding if a particular legal conclusion is valid given an existing law. There are many more situations in which the correct conclusion depends on probabilities and whether a particular source of information is credible. Anyone solving mathematical proofs or other problems that are in the form of syllogisms will need to know how to determine deductive validity.

Syllogistic reasoning and the other types of reasoning like linear ordering and "if, then" statements are sometimes considered as a subset of problem solving. Often, when solving a problem, we begin with statements that we believe or know to be true (the premises) and then decide which conclusions we can logically infer from them. Syllogisms also appear implicitly in normal English prose. Of course, in natural context, the premises and conclusions are not labeled, but the underlying structure is much the same. They are especially easy to spot in legal and political arguments and thus often appear on standardized tests for college, graduate, and law school admissions.

Here is an example of syllogistic reasoning that may seem more like the kind of syllogism you would find in everyday contexts: The death sentence should be declared unconstitutional. It is the cruelest form of punishment that is possible, and it is also very unusual. The constitution specifically protects us against cruel and unusual punishment.

Can you conclude from these statements that the death sentence is unconstitutional? Try to formulate these sentences into standard syllogism form (two premises and a conclusion). Use circle diagrams or the seven rules to check on the validity of the conclusion. Stop now and work on this natural language syllogism.

Your syllogism should be similar to this:

Premise 1:	The death sentence is cruel and unusual punishment.
Premise 2:	<u>Cruel and unusual punishment is unconstitutional.</u>
Conclusion:	The death sentence is unconstitutional.

If we put this in terms of A, B, and C, this roughly corresponds to:

A = the death sentence
B = cruel and unusual punishment
C = unconstitutional

This then becomes

All A are B.
<u>All B are C.</u>
All A are C.

In its abstract form, this becomes a syllogism that can be tested with either circle diagrams or verbal rules that will determine if the conclusion validly follows from the premises. The point here is that syllogisms are often contained in everyday arguments. Medical providers are often faced with problems that take this form: Everyone with disease X will have results from the lab test Y. Some people with results from the lab test Y will not have disease X. Although this does not "look like" some combination of "all," "some, "no," and "some not," can you see how it is the same sort of problem with different terms to represent these relationships? Often, we do not recognize syllogisms because they are not neatly labeled by premise and conclusion, but if you get in the habit of looking for them, you may be surprised how frequently they can be found.

Here is a political example: Tim Russert was a popular American journalist who reported regularly on the televised news program *Meet the Press*. In an interview with former U.S. President George W. Bush, Russert questioned

Bush's military service. Russert told Bush that several different news reporters found that there was no evidence that Bush had reported to military duty during the time when Bush claimed that he had. Here is Bush's response to this allegation:

> Bush replied, 'Yeah, they're just wrong. There may be no evidence, but I did report. Otherwise, I wouldn't have been honorably discharged.' That's the Bush syllogism: The evidence says one thing; the conclusion says another; therefore, the evidence is false. (William Saletan, Slate, Feb. 2004)

Here is Bush's response as a quantitative syllogism:

Everyone who has been honorably discharged from the military served in the military.
George W. Bush was honorably discharged from the military
Therefore: George W. Bush served in the military.
The missing quantifiers are: A = Everyone honorably discharged, B = served in the military, C = Bush, which becomes
All A are B.
All C are A.
Therefore: All C are B. (Think of Bush as All of Bush)
Alternatively, you could think of this exchange as "if, then" reasoning. It would become
If someone was honorably discharged from the military, then that person served in the military.
Bush was honorably discharged from the military.

Both of these deductive forms of reasoning make Bush's response valid. Of course, it is possible that the premises are false, but if the task is to determine whether the conclusion follows validly from the premises that are stated, then Bush is logically correct.

Circle Diagrams can Capture Complex Relationships

There are many reasons to learn how to use circle diagrams as an aid to thinking. A well drawn set of circle diagrams can convey complicated information in a single figure. Figure 4.5 shows the percentage of Americans who believe in evolution (14%), creationism (44%) and a mix of the two in which God created the world through evolution (36%). Notice that these

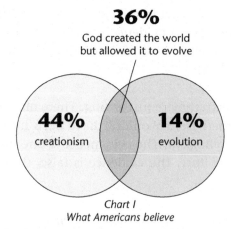

Chart I
What Americans believe

Figure 4.5 The beliefs of Americans about evolution shown in circle diagrams. From "Darwin's Rottweiler" by Lisa Miller, *Newsweek*, September 25, 2009, p. 53.

numbers do not add up to 100%, most probably because the missing 6% did not fit into any of these categories, perhaps responding that they do not know or they refuse to answer.

Missing Quantifiers

> If there is any equality now, it has been our struggle that put it there. Because they said "all" and meant "some." All means all.
> —Beah Richards (in Beilensen & Jackson, Eds., 1992, p. 22)

When syllogisms are found in everyday use, the quantifiers are often missing. Sometimes this absence is done deliberately in the hope that you will infer one particular quantifier (e.g., assume "all" instead of the more truthful "some.") Here is an example of categorical reasoning used in a presidential campaign. A presidential candidate (in the U.S. primaries) was questioned about his extramarital affairs. He responded this way: I have not been perfect in my private life, but we have had other great presidents who were also not perfect in their private lives.

Let's convert this to a categorical syllogism:

Premise 1:	I am not perfect (in my private life).
Premise 2:	Some great presidents were not perfect (in their private lives).
Conclusion:	I will be a great president. (implied)

In its abstract form this becomes

A = I (the speaker)
B = people who are not perfect
C = great presidents

or

All A are B.
Some C are B.
All A are (will be) C.

The conclusion he wanted listeners to draw is that he would also be a great president. Check the validity of this conclusion either with circle diagrams or the seven rules. Is the implied conclusion valid? Note also his choice of words to describe his extramarital affairs (not perfect).

In everyday language, the quantifiers may be different from those used here. "Every" and "each" may be used as substitutes for "all," and "many" and "few" may be used as substitutes for "some." It is a simple matter to change them to the quantifiers used here and then check the conclusion for its validity.

Here is an example (with some editing) that I recognized in a recent conversation. "People who go to rock concerts smoke dope. Jaye went to a rock concert. Therefore, Jaye smokes dope." The validity of this everyday syllogism depends on whether the speaker believes that "All people who go to rock concerts smoke dope" or "Some people who go to rock concerts smoke dope." In understanding statements like these, it is important that you specify which missing quantifier is intended. If "some" is intended, then you quickly point out that it is not valid to conclude that Jaye was among those who smoke dope. If "all" is intended, then you can question whether it is the appropriate quantifier.

Changing Attitudes with Syllogisms

The basic organization of two premises and a conclusion is frequently used to change attitudes. When used in this fashion, the first premise is a belief premise, the second premise is an evaluation of that belief or a reaction to the belief premise, and the conclusion is the attitude (Shaver, 1981). The basic structure is like this:

Belief premise
Evaluation premise
Attitude conclusion

Consider how this works in the following example (Shaver, 1981):

Preventing war saves lives.
Saving lives is good.
Therefore, preventing war is good.
Over time, attitude syllogisms become linked so that the conclusion from one syllogism is used as the evaluation premise of another:

Defense spending prevents war.
Preventing war is good.
Therefore, defense spending is good.

In these syllogisms, the middle term (remember what this means?) becomes the reason for the conclusion. In general, the greater the number of syllogisms with the same conclusion that we believe are true, the greater the support for the conclusion. If I wanted you to conclude that defense spending is good, I'd also tell you that

Defense spending creates jobs.
Creating jobs is good.
Therefore, defense spending is good.

The quantifiers are implicit in these syllogisms, but the underlying organization is the same. It is a matter of determining whether a conclusion follows from the premises. Of course, like all deductive reasoning problems, it may be valid, but still not be true. We consider how to decide what is probably true and what is probably not true. Deductive reasoning is only one type of reasoning.

Common Errors in Syllogistic Reasoning

Some syllogisms are more difficult to solve than others. An analysis of the erroneous conclusions that people make has revealed that the errors fall into distinct types or categories. One category of errors that we will consider here is illicit conversions.

JUMP START By Robb Armstrong

Jump Start by Robb Armstrong. Used with permission by Universal Press Syndicate.

Illicit Conversions

No, this term has nothing to do with people who make you change religions when you do not want to. It has to do with changing the meaning of a premise. When most people read statements like, "All A are B," the representation they form in their mind is one in which it is also true that "All B are A" (Chapman & Chapman, 1959). As you should realize by now, "All A are B" is not the same as "All B are A." Transforming a premise into a nonequivalent form is a type of error known as an **illicit conversion**. An example of an illicit conversion in "if, then" reasoning is the erroneous assumption that "If A, then B" is the same as "If B, then A" In real world terms, knowing that "all republicans voted for this bill" is not the same as saying that everyone who voted for this bill was republican. These are not equivalent statements. Another common illicit conversion is the belief that "Some A are not B" also implies that "Some B are not A." The second statement is not equivalent to the first.

Probabilistic Reasoning

In everyday reasoning, we do not view premises as "truths" that will necessarily require certain conclusions; instead, we think of premises as statements that either support or fail to support certain conclusions. Probabilistic reasoning occurs when we use the information we have to decide that a conclusion is probably true or probably not true. In everyday reasoning, we rely on notions of probability to assess the likelihood of a conclusion being true. Although probability is discussed in Chapter 6, it is also a reasoning skill that we need to consider in this context.

Suppose you learn that people who have untreated diabetes are frequently thirsty, urinate often, and experience sudden weight loss. You notice that you have these symptoms. Does it necessarily follow that you have diabetes? No, of course not, but these symptoms do make a diagnosis of diabetes more likely. In everyday contexts, much of our reasoning is probabilistic.

Consider this example presented by Polya (1957, p. 186):

> If we are approaching land, we see birds.
>> Now we see birds.
>> Therefore, it becomes more credible that we are approaching land.

In a shorthand format, this becomes:

> If A, then B.
>> B is true.
>> Therefore, A is more probable than it was before we knew that B is true.

Much of our everyday reasoning is of this sort, and while A is not guaranteed with probabilistic reasoning, it does become more probable after we've told the second premise. When viewed from the perspective of "if, then" reasoning, we would be committing the fallacy of affirming the consequent. However, in real life, we need to consider many variables and goals. Although seeing birds does not guarantee that land is near, I would be happy if I saw birds while I was drifting and lost at sea. Probabilistic reasoning is often a good strategy or "rule of thumb," especially since few things are known with absolute certainty in our probabilistic world. From the standpoint of formal logic, it is invalid to conclude that land is near. As long as you understand the nature of probabilities and the distinction between probabilistic and valid (must be true if the premises are true) reasoning, considering probabilities is a useful way of understanding and predicting events. When we reason in everyday contexts, we consider the strength and likelihood of the evidence that supports a conclusion and often decide if a conclusion is probable or improbable, not just merely valid or invalid. This point is explained more fully in Chapter 7 on understanding probabilities.

As much of our reasoning is dependent on the rules of probability, McGuire (1981) has coined the term **probabilogical** to describe the joint effects of these disciplines on the way we think. Accordingly, we place greater faith in conclusions when we believe that the premises are highly probable than when we believe that the premises are unlikely.

Bounded Rationality

> Nothing has an uglier look to us than reason, when it is not on our side.
> —George Saville (n.d.)

Does the fact that people often do not use the laws of logic when they reason mean that we, mere mortals, are illogical or irrational (not reasoned)? Many psychologists object to the idea that most people are illogical. As you have seen, people reason differently depending on the context and seem to be able to use the rules of reasoning better when the valid conclusion is one that we believe to be true than when it is not. In the real world, the content of our reasoning *does* matter, so perhaps it is not surprising that we find it difficult to reason from false or questionable premises. It seems that people are rational, but with some limitations. The term **bounded rationality** is used to describe this state of affairs (Gigerenzer & Goldstein, 1996; Simon, 1956). We usually need to reach conclusions and make decisions with incomplete information and under time limits, and we rarely have "true premises." For example, we know if we are asking permission or making an obligation and the very different implications of "if, then" statements under these situations.

Reasoning in Everyday Contexts

> Reasoning is the only ability that makes it possible for humans to rule the earth and ruin it.
> —Michael Scriven (1976, p. 2)

Syllogisms, linear orderings, disjunctions, and "if, then" statements are commonly found in everyday conversation. Of course, they are embedded in discourse and not labeled by premise or conclusion. They are sometimes used in ways that seem either to be deliberately misleading, or at least to capitalize on the common reasoning errors that most people make.

If you pay careful attention to bumper stickers, you'll probably be surprised to find that many are simple reasoning problems. Consider the bumper sticker I saw on a pick-up truck:

> Off-road users
>
> Are not abusers

The off-road users that this bumper sticker refers to are dirt bike riders who enjoy racing through open land (unpaved areas). Many people are concerned that this sport is destroying our natural resources by tearing up the vegetation. This bumper sticker is designed to present the opposing view. Notice how this is accomplished. The term "all" is implied in the first premise, when in fact "some" is true. You should recognize this as a syllogism with missing quantifiers.

Another popular bumper sticker that relies on missing quantifiers to make the point is:

> If guns are outlawed,
>
> Only outlaws will have guns.

This is a standard "if, then" statement. The implied conclusion is "do not outlaw guns."

Suppose someone responded to this bumper sticker by suggesting that if guns are outlawed, approximately 80% of the crimes of violence and 90% of the petty crimes that are committed with a gun would probably be committed with a less dangerous weapon. How does an argument like this refute the "if, then" statement and its implied conclusion on the bumper sticker?

Reasoning with Diagrams

Although it seems like a lot of work to get used to thinking with diagrams, they are useful in many situations where you have to check relationships and conceptualize. The following discussion is loosely based on a discussion by Rubinstein and Pfeiffer (1980) that I have applied to the events surrounding the Los Angeles riots that occurred in 1992.

In 1992, following an unpopular verdict in which Los Angeles police officers were acquitted of the crime of beating a suspect, an event that was captured on video, a massive, bloody riot occurred. In the painful trials that followed, the prosecution attempted to show that a particular defendant was at the scene of the riot. One piece of evidence was a footprint that was at the site. The strategy for the defense was to show that many people could have left that particular foot print, while the prosecution tried to show that few people other than the defendant could have left the foot print. Look at these two diagrams.

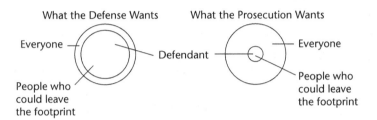

An expert from the Nike shoe company was called to testify that the print was left by a Nike sneaker. The prosecution then showed that the defendant owned a pair of Nikes in the same size as the footprint. This shrinks the size of the circle, so that few people besides the defendant would fit those particular shoes.

By contrast, the defense tried to widen the circle by showing that many people in that neighborhood wear Nike sneakers and that it was a popular shoe size. Each side, in turn, tried to widen and then narrow the circle in an attempt to persuade the jury that the defendant and few others could have left that footprint or many people could have left that footprint.

Similar strategies are used implicitly in many trials. Here is a quote from an article that appeared in the *Los Angeles Times* (Timnick, October 18, 1989). It is a description of a trial for an accused child molester: "Telling an attentive jury in Los Angeles Superior Court that the totality of evidence 'draws the ring around R.B. and P.B. closer and tighter, to the extent that you should find them guilty.'" Here the idea of drawing smaller and smaller circles was used explicitly in the prosecution's arguments. Once you get used to using diagrams as a thinking aid, you will find that you will use them often.

Reasoning Gone Wrong

I hope that you are developing an appreciation for the critical importance of good thinking. If you are not yet convinced, then I expect that this section will be a "chilly awakening." In later chapters, I will continue to develop the theme that there are many people who want to persuade you to believe that something is true—for a variety of reasons.

Motivated Reasoning

> Reason is supposed to be the highest achievement of the human mind, and the route to knowledge and wise decisions. But as psychologists have been documenting since the 1960s, humans are really, really bad at reasoning. It's not just that we follow our emotions so often, in contexts from voting to ethics. No, even when we intend to deploy the full force of our rational faculties, we are often as ineffectual as eunuchs at an orgy.
>
> —Sharon Begley (2010, para. 2)

A popular science writer explained that the reason why so many people have trouble reasoning logically is that their real task is not to decide if a conclusion is valid (Begley, 2012). Instead, they are really trying to prove that the conclusion they believe to be true is valid. In other words, "People mistakenly assume that their thinking is done by their head; it is actually done by the heart which first dictates the conclusion, then commands the head to provide the reasoning that will defend it" (de Mellow, n.d.) As Begley (2010, para. 2) described the situation: "Women are bad drivers, Saddam plotted 9/11, Obama was not born in America, and Iraq had weapons of mass destruction: to believe any of these requires suspending some of our critical thinking faculties and succumbing instead to the kind of irrationality that drives the logically minded crazy." In order to reason deductively, you must put aside prior beliefs and determine what would logically follow if the premises were true.

Often the purpose of a seemingly reasoned communication will be to sell you something—a product, a philosophy, a political candidate or point of view, or even a new view of history. Groups that are attempting to rewrite history are called revisionists. Your only defense against the onslaught of "sales" pitches is critical thinking. I heard a revisionist speaker (someone who believes that we need to revise what we know about history) who was attempting to convince a group of young adults that slavery in the United States was "not really so bad." The presentation had all the outward appearances of a standard reasoning problem. First, listeners were asked if they agreed that people do not harm valuable property. Most nodded in agreement. Then they were told that slaves were valuable property; therefore, most slave owners took good care of their slaves. The speaker went on to say that "most slaves enjoyed being taken care of," so slavery was not as bad as we had been led to believe. The scary part of this scene was that there were many listeners who seemed to be considering this ludicrous idea or could not figure out what was wrong with it. Can you?

I hope that you are outraged at this attempt to rewrite a disgraceful part of U.S. history and to use what seems like reasoning to do it. It is true that most people do not harm valuable property, but there are massive amounts of historical evidence that slaves were often subject to the most brutal and dehumanizing conditions. The speaker left out far too many relevant facts to make his conclusion logical. There was a seductiveness to the speaker's "logic," but it was patently wrong. There is no substitute for critical thinking.

Chapter Summary

- Deductive reasoning is the use of premises or statements that we accept as true to derive valid conclusions.

- People do not approach reasoning problems according to the laws of formal logic. Instead of determining whether a conclusion logically follows from the premises as they are stated, there is a tendency to alter the premises according to one's own beliefs and then decide whether a conclusion follows from the altered statements.

- In linear orderings, we use premises to establish conclusions about ordered relationships. A good strategy for solving linear orderings is to use a spatial representation with the items arranged in an ordered manner.

- It is common to confuse truth with validity. Validity refers to the form of an argument and is unrelated to content. If a conclusion necessarily follows from the premises, then it is valid. The topics of truth and believability of premises are addressed in the next chapter.

- Personal beliefs often bias our ability to determine validity, such that conclusions we believe to be true are more likely to be judged valid than conclusion we do not believe to be true.

- In "if, then" statements a conditional relationship is established. The premises that are given in this format are used to determine valid conclusions.

- "If" is frequently interpreted as "if and only if" in "if, then" statements. Although this conversion is an error according to the rules of formal logic, sometimes it is justified by the context in which it is embedded.

- Confirmation bias is the predilection or tendency to seek and utilize information that supports or confirms the hypothesis or premise that is being considered. The "four-card selection task" is a demonstration of this robust bias.

- "If, then" reasoning is used to help children with Attention Deficit Hyperactivity Disorder regulate their behavior.

- Quantitative syllogisms indicate which terms belong in the categories that are specified. Statements in syllogisms can take one of four different moods: universal affirmative, particular affirmative, universal negative, and particular negative.

- When syllogisms involve meaningful terms and categories, people often use their knowledge of the categories and their beliefs about the topics to determine which conclusions are valid instead of reasoning from the form of the syllogism.

- Circle diagrams are useful aids for understanding relationships and checking inferences in syllogisms. The extent to which circles overlap depicts category inclusion and exclusion. An alternative to circle diagrams that many people prefer is to check conclusions for validity using the verbal rules of syllogisms.

- The greatest difficulty in using circle diagrams is being certain that all combinations of the two premises have been represented.

- Illicit conversions are common errors in syllogisms. The most frequent illicit conversion is to interpret "All A are B" as also meaning that "All B are A."

- Diagrams are useful reasoning tools in many situations. The logic of circle diagrams is frequently used in legal settings and other settings in which evidence is considered.

The following skills to determine whether a conclusion is valid were presented in this chapter. Review each skill and be sure that you understand how and when to use each one.

- discriminating between deductive and inductive reasoning
- identifying premises and conclusions
- using quantifiers in reasoning
- solving categorical syllogisms with circle diagrams
- solving categorical syllogisms with verbal rules
- understanding the difference between truth and validity
- recognizing when syllogisms are being used to change attitudes
- using linear diagrams to solve linear syllogisms
- watching for marked adjectives
- using the principles of linear orderings as an aid to clear communication
- reasoning with "if, then" statements
- using tree diagrams with "if, then" statements
- avoiding the fallacies of confirming the consequent and denying the antecedent
- examining reasoning in everyday contexts for missing quantifiers

Terms to Know

Check your understanding of the concepts presented in this chapter by reviewing their definitions. If you find that you're having difficulty with any term, be sure to reread the section in which it is discussed.

Reasoning. Has two forms: deductive and inductive. When reasoning deductively, we use our knowledge of two or more premises to infer if a conclusion is valid. When reasoning inductively, we collect observations and formulate hypotheses based on these observations. With deductive reasoning with valid syllogisms, the conclusion MUST be true if the premises are true. By contrast, with inductive reasoning, the conclusion is PROBABLY true if the premises are true.

Conclusion. An inferential belief that is derived from other statements.

Logic. A branch of philosophy that explicitly states the rules for deriving valid conclusions.

Valid. A conclusion is valid if it must be true if the premises are true. It "follows from" the premises.

Premises. Statements that allow the inference of logical conclusions.

Illogical. Conclusions in deductive reasoning tasks that are not in accord with the rules of logic.

Failure to Accept the Logical Task. In everyday reasoning, we alter the statements we are given according to our personal beliefs and then decide if a conclusion follows from the altered statements. We reject the logical task of deciding if a conclusion follows from the statements as they are given.

Personal Logic. The informal rules that people use to determine validity.

Pragmatic. Anything that is practical. In this context, the consideration of context and purpose when engaging in real world reasoning tasks.

Inductive Reasoning. Observations are collected that suggest or lead to the formulation of a conclusion or hypothesis.

Deductive Reasoning. Use of stated premises to formulate conclusions that can logically be inferred from them.

Linear Ordering. (Also known as linear syllogism) Reasoning that involves the inference of orderly relationships along a single dimension (e.g., size, position) between terms.

Linear Syllogism. See linear ordering.

Marked Adjectives. Adjectives that connote bias when they appear in a question (e.g., poor, dumb, or small). When asked "How poor is he," it is presumed that the response will be toward the poor extreme and not towards the rich extreme.

Unmarked Adjectives. Adjectives that are neutral in that they don't connote a particular direction when they appear in a question (e.g., big, smart, tall). When asked "How big is he?", the response could be a larger or a small number. Compare with marked adjective.

Belief Bias. Also known as **Confirmation bias.** The interference of one's personal beliefs with the ability to reason logically.

"If, Then" Statements. Statements of a contingency relationship such that if the antecedent is true, then the consequent must be true.

Contingency Relationships. Relationships that are expressed with "if, then" statements. The consequent is contingent or dependent on the antecedent.

Conditional Logic. Also known as propositional logic. Logical statements that are expressed in an "if, then" format.

Antecedent. In "if, then" statements, it is the information given in the "if" clause appealing to your reason.

Consequent. In "if, then" statements, it is the information given in the "then" clause.

Tree Diagrams. Diagrams in which the critical information is represented along the branches of a "tree."

Affirming the Antecedent. In "if, then" reasoning, the second premise asserts that the "if" part is true.

Denying the Consequent. In "if, then" reasoning, the second premise asserts that the "then" part is false.

Affirming the Consequent. In "if, then" reasoning, the second premise asserts that the "then" part is true.

Denying the Antecedent. In "if, then" reasoning, the second premise asserts that the "if" part is false.

Illicit Conversion. Illicit conversions in "if, then" statements occur when people believe that "If A, then B" also means "If B, then A."

Double Negation. The denial of a negative statement.

Four-Card Selection Task. A task that is often used to demonstrate confirmation biases. Subjects are required to indicate which of four cards they need to turn over in order to verify a rule about the contents of each side of the card. Overwhelmingly, subjects only select cards that will confirm the hypothesis that they are considering instead of seeking information that would disconfirm their hypothesis.

Permission Schema. Informal rules that people use when reasoning with "if, then" statements that pragmatically give permission.

Obligation Schema. Informal rules that people use when reasoning with "if, then" statements that pragmatically create an obligation.

Chained Conditional. Two "if, then" statements linked so that the consequent of one statement is also the antecedent of the other statement.

Combinatorial Reasoning. The use of systematic and orderly steps when making combinations so that all possible combinations are formed.

Syllogistic Reasoning. A form of reasoning that involves deciding whether a conclusion can be properly inferred from two or more statements that contain quantifiers.

Quantifiers. Terms like "all," "some," "none," and "no" that are used in syllogisms to indicate category membership.

Categorical Reasoning. A type of syllogistic reasoning in which the quantifiers "some," "all," "no," and "none" are used to indicate category membership.

Syllogism. Two or more premises that are used to derive a valid conclusion or conclusions.

Mood. Used to classify the premises and conclusions of a categorical syllogism. There are four moods that are dependent on the quantifiers used in the statements. The four moods are: universal affirmative (all A are B); particular affirmative (some A are B); universal negative (no A are B); and particular negative (some A are not B).

Universal Affirmative. The mood of statements in a categorical syllogism with the format "All A are B."

Particular Affirmative. The mood of statements in a categorical syllogism with the format "Some A are B."

Universal Negative. The mood of statements in a categorical syllogism with the format "No A are B."

Particular Negative. The mood of statements in a categorical syllogism with the format "Some A are not B."

Circle Diagrams. A spatial strategy for determining the validity of a conclusion in a categorical syllogism. Circles are used to represent category membership.

Middle Term. In a categorical syllogism, it is the term that is omitted from the conclusion and is mentioned in both premises.

Distributed. In a categorical syllogism, a term is distributed when it is modified by "all," "no," or "not."

Ecological Validity. Concerns the real world validity or applications of a concept outside of the laboratory.

Illicit Conversions. Transformations of the premises in a syllogism into non-equivalent forms (e.g., converting "All A are B" into "All B are A").

Probabilogical. Term coined to label the joint influences of probability and logic on the way we think.

Bounded Rationality. People are rational, within limits. People do not behave like logic machines, but use thinking shortcuts to save time.

CHAPTER 5

ANALYZING ARGUMENTS

Contents

Eat all Day and Still Lose Weight

Trade your old body for a new one now through an amazing scientific breakthrough. Doctors and medical technicians have made it possible for people like you and me to lose weight quickly and permanently. Tested at university labs, retested at clinics and major hospitals and acclaimed by doctors all over the world, finally there is something that helps you lose weight. If years of stubborn fat build up have been your problem, NOW AT LAST THERE IS A WAY TO ELIMINATE FAT, A WAY TO LOSE WEIGHT FAST AND EASILY. We call it XXXXXXX because it totally attacks excess fat and fluids that have plagued most people for years. . . . Everyday you will feel stronger and full of pep and energy as the excess weight you have carried for so long is carved off your body. . . . DON'T LET THIS GOLDEN OPPORTUNITY AND CHANCE OF A LIFETIME PASS YOU BY. Just fill out the coupon below and let it be the ticket to a slimmer you. So, what are you waiting for?

I hope that you were not looking for a coupon for this marvelous weight loss product. The paragraph above was taken (virtually) verbatim from a full-page advertisement in a popular fashion magazine. The only change that I made was to omit the name of this "miracle" diet. The name has a chemical sound to it. It's multisyllabic and ends with a number. The name sounds like a chemical formula. I had trouble selecting which advertisement I wanted to use here because there were so many that made numerous unsupported claims. Advertisements like this one can be found in most magazines and newspapers. I'll refer back to this advertisement later in this chapter when I talk about analyzing arguments and recognizing fallacies. Hold onto your money until you've read this chapter.

The Anatomy of an Argument

Neither a closed mind nor an empty one is likely to produce much that would qualify as effective reasoning.

—Ray Nickerson (1986, p. 1)

The technical meaning of the word "**argument**" is different from its everyday meaning. We say two people "are having an argument" when they disagree about something in a heated or emotional way. More technically, an argument consists of one or more statements that are used to provide support for a **conclusion**. The statements that provide the support for a conclusion are called the **reasons** or **premises** of the argument. The reasons or premises are presented in order to persuade the reader or listener that the conclusion is true or probably true. Let's consider an example. Suppose that I want to convince you to stay in college until graduation. Here are some reasons (premises) that I could give. You can think of this as an addition problem with each premise summing to the conclusion.

Premise #1:	College graduates earn more money than college dropouts or people who have never attended college.
+ Premise #2:	College graduates report that they are more satisfied with their lives than people who have not graduated from college.
+ Premise #3:	College graduates are healthier and live longer than people who have not graduated from college.
+ Premise #4:	College graduates have jobs that are more interesting and more responsible than people who have not graduated from college
Conclusion:	You should graduate from college.

Arguments are sometimes called "the giving of reasons." Harman (1986) calls this process "a change in view" because the objective is to change an "old view" or belief into a "new view" or belief with reasoning.

Reasoning

Old View   →   New View
or Belief   or Belief

Every argument will have one or more premises (or reasons) and one or more conclusions. Usually, there will be several premises for one conclusion, but other combinations (one premise for several conclusions and several premises for several conclusions) are possible. **If you cannot identify at least one premise *and* at least one conclusion, then it is not an argument**. Of course, in everyday, natural-language arguments, the premises and conclusions are not labeled. They are usually embedded in extended prose. The extended prose could be a paragraph, a section or chapter of a book, or even an entire book or semester-long class.

Here are some examples of prose that are *not* arguments:

- I like my critical thinking course better than my chemistry course. (No reasons are given for this preference.)
- We drove up to the mountains, went skiing, and then drove home. (This is just a descriptive list of activities linked together. There are no reasons or conclusions.)
- Buy your burgers at Burgerland. (No reasons given, but reasons are often inferred from context in statements like this one.)
- We saw the Martians land. (This is a simple description.)
- Never trust anyone over 30. (This is an opinion without reasons.)
- Is dinner ready? (Simple question.)

It may seem that it should be fairly simple to determine whether a statement or set of statements contain an argument, but in everyday language most arguments are incomplete. Sometimes the premises aren't stated, but are inferred, and other times the conclusion is unstated. Sometimes arguments are deliberately disguised so that it may appear that the speakers are not supporting some conclusion, when they really are.

Premises

The premises are the reasons that support a conclusion. They are the "why" part of an argument. In everyday language, they can appear anywhere among a set of statements. Sometimes, the conclusion will be stated first followed by its premises. (Here is what I believe and the reasons for this belief are . . . .) Other times the conclusion may be presented last or embedded in the middle of a paragraph or other text with premises both before and after it. Premises are not always easy to recognize. There are certain key words, called **premise indicators** or **premise markers** that often signal that what comes after them is a premise. Although premise indicators are not *always* followed by a premise, they often are, and for this reason, it is a good idea to check for these key words when identifying premises. These terms often indicate that what follows is a reason.

Premise Indicators

because
for
since (when it means because and not the passage of time)
if

given that (or being that)
as shown by
as indicated by
the reasons are
it may be inferred (or deduced) from
the evidence consists of
in the first place (suggests that a list of premises will follow)
secondly
seeing that
assuming that
it follows from
whereas

Here are some simple examples of the use of premise indicators:

- You should graduate from college **because** you will earn more money with a college degree.

- The need for the United States to send troops to Central America **is indicated by** the buildup of armed rebels in countries neighboring those with civil wars.

- **Seeing that** the current policy of supplying organ transplants is benefiting the rich, a new program is needed.

Premises can be "matters of fact" or "matters of opinion" or both. Consider, for example, the following sentences:

- All teenagers should be taught safe sex practices because of the risk of AIDS and other sexually transmitted diseases. (The reason is a matter of fact.)

- All teenagers should be taught how to knit because this will provide them with an enjoyable hobby. (The reason is a matter of opinion.)

Conclusions

The conclusion is the purpose or the "what" of the argument. It is the belief or point of view that is supported or defended with the premises. Both the premises and the conclusion are important, and both are essential components of any argument.

It is usually easier to identify the conclusion of an argument than the other components. For this reason, it is a good idea to start with the conclusion when you are analyzing arguments. There are **conclusion indicators** or **conclusion markers** that indicate that what follows is probably a conclusion. As with premise indicators, they do not guarantee that a conclusion follows them.

Conclusion Indicators

> therefore
> hence
> so
> thus
> consequently
> then
> shows that (we can see that)
> accordingly
> it follows that
> we may infer (conclude) (deduce) that
> in summary
> as a result
> for all these reasons
> it is clear that

Here are some simple examples of the use of conclusion indicators:

- Based on all of the reasons just stated, we **can conclude that** the flow of illegal drugs must be stopped.

- **In summary**, postal rates must be increased because we can no longer afford to run the postal system with a deficit.

- We have had very little rain this season. **Consequently**, water will have to be rationed.

Has my use of the word "simple" to describe these examples made you feel uneasy? Have you begun to expect that things will soon get more complex? If so, you are right. Natural language is complex and so are natural-language arguments. (A natural language is a language that has evolved over time for the purpose of communication between people. Artificial languages are those languages that were created for special purposes, such as computer languages.) Although all arguments *must* contain at least one argument and one conclusion, most arguments consist of additional components. Three additional components will be presented here. They are assumptions, qualifiers, and counterarguments.

Assumptions

> With enough assumptions, any policy can be justified.
>
> —Tim Brennan (January 12, 2001, from *A Guide to Understanding how Washington Really Works*)

An **assumption** is a statement for which no proof or evidence is offered. Although assumptions can be either stated or unstated (implied), they are most often unstated. Assumptions are important components in arguments, and they are the most often forgotten part because they are often omitted. The reader or listener will usually have to supply the missing assumptions.

The arguments that are used to build the main argument are called **subarguments**. The main argument in an extended passage and is called the **main point**. The kinds of arguments that are often found in books, book chapters, and sometimes sections of chapters proceed in stages with subarguments linked to provide support for a main point.

Here is an example of an unstated assumption, taken from a catalogue that sells copper bracelets. I have altered it only slightly for this context.

> For hundreds of years people have worn copper bracelets to relieve pain from arthritis. This folklore belief has persisted and copper bracelets continue to be popular. These bracelets promote close contact between the copper and your wrist.

The writers of this advertisement expect that readers will assume that copper can help alleviate the pain of arthritis and that the "medical" effect is enhanced by the close contact with the wrist. Notice that this is never stated—it can't be because there is no evidence that shows that copper has any effect on arthritis. However, this advertisement for copper bracelets is clearly written to suggest that it works. (Many people believe that it does.) Furthermore, there is a suggested assumption that the popularity of copper bracelets is due to its medical effects. Maybe they have just become fashionable, or cheaper, or better advertised, or perhaps there are just more people with arthritis who are willing to believe anything that promises to relieve their pain. We'll discuss the need to consider missing information and alternative conclusions in a later section of this chapter.

Qualifiers

A **qualifier** is a constraint or restriction on the conclusion. It states the conditions under which the conclusion is supported. An example might be helpful:

> It is important that we have some indicators of what and how much students are learning in college. For this reason, a national college-level testing program is needed. However, if the national assessment is not related to the subjects taught in the college curriculum, then it will not be a valid measure of college-level learning.

Let's dissect this paragraph into its component parts:

> *The conclusion is*: A national college-level testing program is needed.
> *A premise is:* It is important that we have some indicators of what and how much students are learning in college. (This is the reason that supports the conclusion. It tells us why we should believe that the conclusion is true.)
> *An unstated assumption is:* A national college-level testing program is a good way to indicate what students are learning.
> *A qualifier (or limiting condition) is:* The conclusion is valid only when the assessment is related to what is the curriculum.

As you can see from this example, a qualifier states the conditions under which the conclusion is valid. It sets limits or constraints on the conclusion.

Counterarguments

> Critical thinking requires a sense of the complexity of human issues.
> —Alan Sears and Jim Parsons (1991, p. 64)

Sometimes, an extended argument will state reasons that support a particular conclusion and reasons that refute the same conclusion. The set of statements that refute a particular conclusion is called a **counterargument**. Let's extend the previous argument so that it now also contains a counterargument.

> It is important that we have some indicators of what and how much students are learning in college. For this reason, a national college-level testing program is needed. However, if the national assessment is not related to the subjects taught in the college curriculum, then it will

not be a valid measure of college-level learning. Of course, the results of a national assessment of college students could be misused in a way that would keep good students from entering graduate or professional school.

I hope that you are paying careful attention to the way the additions are altering the argument. As presented above, the conclusion, premise, assumption, and qualifier remain the same. The counterargument presents a reason for *not* having a national college-level test. The reason presented (results could be misused) is counter to the conclusion that we should have a national test—that is why these statements are called counterarguments. Even with the addition of the counterargument, the conclusion remains unchanged. The argument was written in a way that suggests that the counterargument is weaker than the main argument. The point being made is that despite the counterargument, we should still have a national test of college students—the conclusion is the same.

Does this particular example make you uneasy? Can you think of other premises that might support a different conclusion? If so, you have already begun to anticipate the content of the section on how to evaluate arguments.

Diagramming the Structure of an Argument

> Argument is a central feature of the resolution of scientific controversies.
> —Driver, Newton, and Osborne (2000, p. 287)

Arguments are a related series of statements that are made in an attempt to get the reader or listener to believe that the conclusion is true. In order to analyze or dissect an argument, we need to know not only its component parts, but also how the parts are related to each other. Arguments are made up of parts that are synthesized or put together when an argument is made, and parts that can be disassembled as one way to understand them. The parts that make up an argument are premise(s), conclusion(s), assumption(s), qualifier(s), and counterargument(s). The only restriction on arguments is that each must have at least one premise and one conclusion. Beyond this, a large variety of arrangements is possible. A good way to understand the relationships between the parts of a prose passage is to draw a diagram. Diagrams are used in every chapter of this book because they require the drawer to be specific about the relationships being depicted and to think about underlying relationships. Drawing a diagram is a good general thinking strategy.

Let's consider the simplest argument with only one premise and one conclusion.

1	2
[Be sure to get plenty of aerobic exercise] because	[aerobic exercise will help you build a strong cardiovascular system.]

This argument is made up of two statements. I have indicated them by putting brackets around each and numbering them "1" and "2." A **statement** is a phrase or sentence for which it makes sense to ask, "Is this true or false?" The answer to this question is not relevant here; that is, it doesn't matter if the statement really is true or false, only whether it makes sense to ask if the phrase is true or false. For example, the following are NOT statements: Rinse the spaghetti. Who lives here? Is that house for sale? Wow! Commands, questions, and exclamations are not statements because it makes no sense to ask if they have a "truth value," that is, it makes no sense to ask if they are true or false.

Look again at the simple argument in the paragraph above. Identify which of the two statements is the conclusion and which is the premise.

Conclusion: [Get plenty of aerobic exercise]. Remember, the conclusion is the statement that indicates what you should believe or what you should do. (I started with the conclusion because this is often the easiest part of the argument to identify.)

Premise: [Aerobic exercise will build a strong cardiovascular system.] This is the "why" part of the argument that gives a reason for believing the conclusion.

A diagram of this relationship shows that the conclusion is supported by the premise:

[1] [Get plenty of aerobic exercise]—the conclusion
↑
[2] [Aerobic exercise will help you build a strong cardiovascular system]—the premise

As you can see, the statement that is the conclusion [1] is at the top of the diagram and the premise [2] is holding it up. This is shown with the arrow that points from the premise to the conclusion.

Now let's consider an argument in which two different premises support one conclusion. Again, I have bracketed each statement and numbered each:

1	2	3
[Be sure to get plenty of aerobic exercise] because	[aerobic exercise will help you build a strong cardiovascular system] and	[it will lower your resting heart rate].

> *[1] Conclusion*: Get plenty of exercise.
>
> *[2] Premise:* Aerobic exercise will build a strong cardiovascular system.
>
> *[3] Premise:* Aerobic exercise will lower your resting heart rate.

A diagram of this argument will look like this:

```
        [1]
     ↗      ↖
  [2]          [3]
```

In this diagram, we have two premises supporting one conclusion. Both of the arrows point to the same conclusion. This is called a **convergent structure** because both premises converge onto the same conclusion; that is, they are both reasons why you should get plenty of aerobic exercise. Longer arguments will often contain several premises that support a conclusion.

Let's consider an example in which there are three premises and two conclusions.

1	2
[Taylor was late for school] because	[she over-slept] and

3	4	5
[she had to stop for gas.]	[Taylor doesn't care much about school]; therefore	[she is often late.]

In the chapter on deductive reasoning, I talked about skeleton structures—sort of fill-in-the-blank structures where it doesn't matter what gets filled in. The skeleton is the "bare bones" of an argument, the place where you hang your statements. Let's reduce this argument to its skeleton:

[1] because [2] and [3]. [4] therefore [5].

This is a good way to think about premise and conclusion indicators. Any statement that follows *because* will probably be a premise ([2] and [3]), and any statement that follows *therefore* will probably be a conclusion ([5]).

Can you see how [2] and [3] are premises for [1], and [4] is a premise for [5]?

A diagram of this argument will look like this:

```
        [1]                    [5]
      ↗     ↖                   ↑
  [2]          [3]             [4]
```

This is an example of two separate arguments in the same paragraph.

Guidelines for Diagramming Arguments

In understanding complex arguments, it is wise to identify the conclusions, premises, assumptions, qualifiers, and counterarguments, and then diagram the structure of their relationship. It is often useful to turn the argument into its skeleton form so that relationships can be seen more clearly. The major difficulty in using this procedure is that complex arguments have complex structures. Sometimes there is more than one possible interpretation and, correspondingly, more than one possible diagram. Sometimes the difficulty lies in deciding if a statement is really part of a subargument or part of the main argument. In longer text, you will often have to restate premises, conclusions, counterarguments, assumptions, and qualifiers in your own words. This process can involve reducing whole chapters of books to single statements. While this can be difficult, it is an excellent strategy for comprehension. Often the process of diagramming will reveal what is wrong or right about a certain argument. If more than one diagram of an argument is possible, then you can consider each separately. Does one diagram provide stronger support for the conclusion? Is one diagram a "truer" representation of the statements being made?

Using Argument Structure when Writing and Speaking

In your own writing and speaking, you often need to persuade an audience that your conclusions are correct. Before you write or make an oral presentation, be sure that you can answer the following questions:

1. What is your conclusion? In other words, what is the point (or points) you want to make? Arguments are made, or constructed, from their parts, and there is no argument if there is no conclusion. Although this question is first on the list, do not start with the conclusion that you want or believe to be true and then find reasons to support it. Look at reasons and evidence that address a particular issue in as unbiased a way as possible to determine what conclusion is best supported. The idea of taking a position on a controversial issue and then finding support for that position is a close-minded approach to thinking. If an issue is controversial, then there should be support for both sides (or more than two sides), and critical thinkers should be able to cite support for multiple positions and decide on the best conclusion by weighing all of the available evidence.

2. What are the reasons that support your conclusion? How strong are they?

3. What assumptions are you making? Are they reasonable assumptions? Should they be explicitly stated?

4. What are the conditions under which the conclusion might not be true? In other words, are qualifiers needed?

5. What are the counterarguments? Why should a reader or listener *not* believe in your conclusion? What alternative conclusions have you actively considered?

6. What's missing? Are other conclusions possible given the reasons? Are there other reasons? Other counterarguments? Other assumptions? This step requires that you look beyond the information that you are using to consider what else might be important.

Actively Open-Minded Thinking

People display myside bias: they evaluate evidence, generate evidence, and test hypotheses in a manner biased towards their own opinions. . . . People also display a one-sided bias: they prefer arguments that are one-sided rather than arguments that reflect many different perspectives.

—Keith E. Stanovich and Richard F. West (2008, p. 130)

Another reason why you should learn how to analyze arguments concerns what Seech (1993) calls "points of logical vulnerability." There are some topics about which we have trouble being objective. For example, I know that it would be difficult for me to be objective about the Ku Klux Klan. This is an emotional topic for me, and I would have great difficulty concluding anything positive about this group. If I used argument analysis, especially by reducing an argument to its skeleton and then diagramming its structure, then I could assess the strength of the support for a conclusion more fairly than I could without this sort of analysis. Of course, I could still decide that any belief or action that they are advocating is wrong.

There is a theme that reoccurs in almost every chapter in this text—the pervasiveness of the confirmation bias—the bias to look for and prefer information that confirms prior beliefs (O'Brien, 2009). Some authors call it "my-side bias" as a way of emphasizing the strong general tendency to prefer evidence that supports what they believe to be true (Stanovich & West, 2008). It is a very strong influence on the way many, perhaps all, of us think and feel, and for the most part, we are unaware of its effects. Information that supports conclusions that we believe to be true just seems better than information that does not. Furthermore, the bias to prefer information that is consistent with our preexisting biases does not vary as a function of intelligence (Stanovich & West, 2008). In a study of the relationship between intelligence and critical thinking, people who scored high on standardized tests designed to assess intelligence were as likely to show a bias for explanations they preferred as those who scored lower on the intelligence test.

Think about some topic about which you have strong feelings—it could be gun control, censorship, school vouchers, innate differences between the sexes, the United Nations, the death penalty, same-sex marriage, or anything else where the conclusion (what to do or believe) is clear to you. Now suppose that you come across strong evidence that supports a different conclusion than the one you prefer—let's say it makes a strong case for allowing open access to guns and you favor strict control of gun access or you are given data that show that the death penalty increases the crime rate and you favor the death penalty. How would you respond? I suppose that you would want to know more—how the data were collected, what the data actually showed—but assume for now that there are strong data that support a conclusion you totally oppose. Now what? Baron (1993) used the term "actively open-minded" to describe people who can change a cherished belief when given good reasons to do so. It turns out that actively and honestly processing information that runs counter to prior beliefs is very difficult, but there are people who can remain open-minded enough to evaluate an argument objectively, independent of their prior beliefs (Baron, 1995; Stanovich & West, 1997). It is not impossible to be fair-minded, but it is difficult.

Historical Evidence

How do you know that World War II really happened and that it is not just a made up story to serve as the background for Hollywood war movies? When I asked this question in class one day, a student told me that he knew that World War II really happened because his grandfather was there—his grandfather fought in the war, and it was as horrible as we have read in our history books. Based on the information we had, it was easy to conclude that the student's grandfather was a credible source of information for this topic. In addition, he had war injuries to support his story. The question may seem strange, but there are groups of people who claim that stories about World War II are exaggerated (or lies) and that there was no mass extermination of the Jews in Europe. Similarly, there are groups that claim that slavery in the United States was not so bad (as mentioned in the last chapter). In fact, there may be groups that deny everything we know about history and science. How can we honestly assess these claims? It seems that all "fringe" groups that advocate a point of view that is not well supported use similar methods in constructing their arguments.

How can we analyze historical arguments? In an outstanding analysis of the arguments used by "Holocaust Deniers' (people who claim that the Holocaust never happened or that it has been exaggerated), Shermer (1997, p. 212) wrote that these groups

(a)   concentrate on any weakness in their opponents' argument instead of providing strong evidence to support their own argument;

(b)   exploit errors in the opposing argument—by focusing on a mistake made by someone who supports an opposing view, they can suggest that all or most of the evidence is wrong;

(c)   take quotes out of context so that the meaning is altered;

(d)   recast honest debates between scholars to make them seem as though the honest scholars disagree about fundamental issues, when in fact they may disagree only about tertiary issues; and

(e)   focus on what is not known rather than what is known.

Historical arguments are correctly evaluated with the same methods that are used in anthropology, botany, geology, and every other field. Converging evidence (remember converging arguments from the earlier section?) shows that demographic data, historical records, eye witness accounts, physical evidence, etc. all support the conclusion that the holocaust deniers twist and distort evidence and argument to advance a racist agenda. A basic understanding of arguments—reasons, evidence, conclusions, counterarguments, etc.—can protect you from falling prey to fringe groups who are trying to advance a political agenda (often a racist agenda) that is not supported by data.

Evaluating the Strength of an Argument

> Advertising persuades people to buy things they don't need with money they ain't got.
>
> —Will Rogers (1879–1935)

All arguments are not equally good or equally bad. Think about how your belief about an issue can be swayed or reinforced as each speaker in a debate presents the reasons and conclusions supporting or refuting a position. In this section, we consider how to evaluate the strength of an argument.

Arguments are evaluated by how well they meet three criteria. The first criterion concerns the acceptability and consistency of the premises. The second criterion concerns the relationship between the premises and the conclusion. Do the premises support the conclusion? Does the conclusion follow from them? The third criterion concerns the unseen part of the argument. What's missing that would change your conclusion? Let's consider each of these criteria in turn.

Acceptable and Consistent Premises

> No man can think clearly when his fists are clenched.
> —George Jean Nathan (quoted in Byrne, 1988, p. 390).

The premises are the "why" part of an argument. The premises must be **acceptable**. A premise is acceptable when it is true or when we can reasonably believe that it is true. Let's consider what this means. If I say that the sun is hot, this is an acceptable premise. I have never touched the sun, but many experts in the field have said that the sun is hot. Much of what we believe to be true comes from experts' statements and personal and common or shared knowledge. Similarly, I have no direct, first-hand knowledge of bacteria, but it is reasonable to believe that they exist. Acceptable premises are commonly acknowledged "truths" of science. I believe that California is larger than New Jersey although I have never measured them. You could probably give a long list of "facts" that are commonly believed to be true. These are examples of acceptable premises.

Premises that are false are unacceptable. Examples of false premises include: men can give birth to babies, whales can fly, all mammals are dogs, and Spanish is the primary language of Canada. I do not want to get into the philosophical considerations of how we can ever know "truth." Personal or common knowledge and expert testimony will be the guide for determining acceptability.

Unfortunately, acceptability is not an either/or proposition in which a premise is either acceptable or it is not. Sometimes, part of the job of analyzing an argument involves determining how acceptable a premise is. This may require research on your part. Suppose that you are listening to an argument about the safety of a nuclear facility near your home. The corporation that wants to build the facility argues that it is safe; therefore, you have nothing to worry about. One way to decide about the acceptability of this premise is to spend some time in the library reading about the kinds of accidents that have occurred in the past, the kinds of safety precautions that are used, and whether there were important benefits in communities that have such facilities. You will also need to consider the statements of experts in this area.

In a good argument, the premises are also **consistent**. When several premises are presented to support a conclusion, they must not contradict each other. For example, an argument in which one premise states that we have to reduce unemployment in order to improve the economy and another premise states that we have to increase unemployment in order to improve the economy is an argument that contains inconsistent premises. Sometimes, when premises are inconsistent, it is possible to eliminate one of them because it is weak or faulty. If you can eliminate the inconsistency between the premises, you will be able to judge more clearly the strength of the argument.

Credibility

> Trustworthiness refers to the willingness of a source to provide accurate, reliable information, with trustworthy sources influencing readers' beliefs, attitudes, and expectations more so than untrustworthy ones.
>
> —Jesse R. Sparks and David N. Rapp (2011, p. 230)

What makes an expert credible? In deciding whom and what to believe, you need to consider the source of the information. Ask yourself the following questions about an expert who is presenting the reasons for a belief:

1. Is the "expert" a recognized authority in the *same field* in which she is providing testimony?

2. Is the expert an *independent* party in this issue? If the expert who says the nuclear facility is safe was hired by the corporation that owns the laboratory, then her testimony is suspect. The testimony is not necessarily dishonest or wrong, but you should be wary because a motive for personal gain maybe involved.

3. What are the expert's *credentials*? Did she write several journal articles on the subject, which were then published in respected journals, or is her expertise documented with a single night school course in the topic? Is the expert current in the field?

4. Does the expert have *specific and first-hand knowledge* of the issue? She could conclude that nuclear facilities are generally safe, but have no direct knowledge of the one being proposed. Did she check the plans for safety features?

5. What *methods of analysis* were used by the expert? Are there standard safety assessments for nuclear facilities? Were these used?

It is interesting to note that a similar list of variables was found in a study of what makes jurors believe experts. Legal researchers found that the most important factors in the way jurors' assessed credibility were the expert's qualifications, reasoning, familiarity with the particular case, and impartiality (Shuman & Champagne, 1998).

Reread the advertisement presented at the beginning of this chapter that states that we can "eat all day and still lose weight." Who are the doctors and universities that support this claim? (No names are given. You should immediately begin to question the credibility of this information.) Was their expertise in weight loss? What are their credentials? Are they independent or will they make money if you buy this product? What were the methods of analysis that were used to document the statement that it will make you feel stronger and full of pep? (None were mentioned.) Are the claims made in this advertisement credible?

Decisions about the acceptability of premises will often depend on how you evaluate the source of the information. When you have two experts who disagree, which is frequently the case, you need to understand the nature of the disagreement and their relative expertise. Are they disagreeing on research findings or the interpretation of those findings? Try to zero in on the specific points on which they disagree so that you can scrutinize these points.

Carlson (1995) distinguished between experts with regard to matters of reality and matters of value. When the topic concerns "reality" (e.g., Do people who live near nuclear facilities plants suffer from more illnesses than people who do not live near them?), then the expert can provide evidence, such as the results of studies, that support her conclusion. When the topic concerns values, the identification and role of the expert is more difficult. For example, should euthanasia be allowed? This sort of question involves issues such as whether anyone has the right to terminate his own life, and experimental data will not be useful in formulating a conclusion in this situation. A chemist might be a credible expert for questions concerning chemical warfare, but who is a credible expert for questions of euthanasia? Are the opinions of medical personnel, clergy, or ordinary citizens equally good in making these decisions? There are few guidelines for selecting credible experts in matters of value. Fischhoff (1993) is an expert on expertise. As he wisely notes, by definition, experts know more about some topic than most of us. However, expert knowledge is always incomplete and people can legitimately disagree about a wide range of topics, such as which risks are worth taking.

The Credibility Crisis

The rapid, phenomenal expansion of information on the Internet has created a credibility crisis. Almost anyone can provide information on almost any topic on the Internet, and it is easily accessible with a few clicks of a mouse. Users must know how to decide if the source of the information is credible. Some sites have "seals of approval" from credible groups like the American Association for the Advancement of Science, but others are so junky that reading from them might be closer to a crime than a legitimate educational experience. Sometimes, the site looks great—spiffy graphics and science-sounding names, but after a few screens are read, advertisements pop up to sell you something or an obviously biased message is shown.

When evaluating information from a web site, look for the following (suggestions from Tate & Alexander, 1996):

(a) The authority—Who is sponsoring the site? What are the authors' qualifications?

(b) Accuracy—Where did the information come from? Are the data clearly labeled?

(c) Objectivity—Is the site a public service or is it just a fancy "sales-pitch?"

d) Currency—When was the site last revised? Is the information still relevant?

e) Coverage—Is the information complete?

Premises that Support the Conclusion

Consider the following argument:

> It is important that we elect a prime minister from the New Democratic Party (a political party in Canada) because the rain in Spain falls mainly on the plain.

I hope that your response to this was, "huh?" The premise or reason why we should support a candidate from the New Democratic Party had nothing to do with it. The rain in Spain is unrelated to political elections in Canada. In technical terms, the premise does not support the conclusion.

In determining the relevance or relatedness between the premises and the conclusion(s), I like to use an analogy to a table. The conclusion is the top of the table and the premises are the legs. When the premises are unrelated to the conclusion, they are off somewhere in another room and cannot support the table. It is easy to detect instances in which the premises are totally unrelated to the conclusion. Other examples are more difficult as relatedness is a matter of degree. Premises can be more or less related to the conclusion.

Determining the relatedness between the premises and the conclusion can be tricky. This is exactly the sort of determination that judges are required to make all of the time. Consider a rape case in which the defense wants to show that the woman agreed to sexual intercourse. Is her previous sexual behavior related to this issue? Most of the time, the courts have ruled that a woman's past sexual history is unrelated to whether she was coerced at the time in question, but under special circumstances, such evidence may be admissible because the judge decides that it may be related to a particular case.

The premises not only have to be related to the conclusion, they also have to be strong enough to support the conclusion. Some authors call this condition **adequate grounds**. When premises provide good support for the conclusion, we say that there are adequate grounds for believing that the conclusion is true or likely to be true.

Let's return to the table analogy. Think of the conclusion as a solid wooden table top. A solid wooden table top will topple over if we try to support it with a few toothpicks. The only way to support it is to use one or more strong legs or many weaker legs that, when used together, will form a strong base of support. These possibilities are depicted in Figure 5.1.

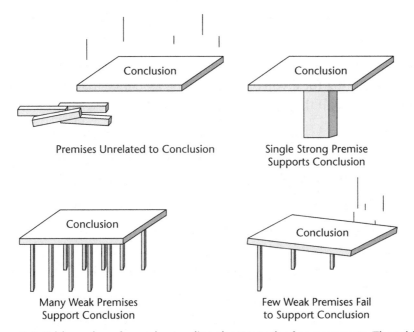

Figure 5.1 Table analogy for understanding the strength of an argument. The tabletop is the conclusion and the legs are the premises. Strong arguments have a firm base of support.

Let's consider some examples of strength of support.

1   2

1. [Marion and Engelbert have filed   [they plan to get a divorce].
   for divorce]. Therefore,

As before, I have bracketed and numbered the statements.

In skeleton form, this is [1] therefore [2].

I hope that you can see that statement [1] is a reason for statement, and [2] is the conclusion. Since we have one reason and one conclusion, this is an argument.

The unstated assumption that they are married will be omitted from the diagram because it is not relevant to the point being made; but if it were included, it would point to [1].

Graphically, this becomes:

[2]
↑   } strong
[1]

I have rated the strength of support for the conclusion as strong because I believe that filing for divorce is very strong evidence that they plan to get divorced (although there are other possibilities which is why it is not absolutely certain).

1   2

2. [Marion and Engelbert had eggs   [they plan to get a divorce].
   for breakfast]. Therefore,

In skeleton form, this is still [1] therefore [2].

Because the premise is unrelated to the conclusion, it provides no support for the conclusion.

In this example, the reason provides no support for the conclusion. We have no reason to believe that they plan to get a divorce.

              1   **2**

3. [Marion and Engelbert had a fight [they plan to get a divorce].
   this morning.] Therefore,

The skeleton structure is still [1] therefore [2].

In this example, the premise is related to the conclusion, but the support is weak.

        1   **2**   **3**

4. [Marion and   [they fight everyday].   [Engelbert is moving
   Engelbert had a fight   out of their apartment
   this morning]. In fact,   and plans to move in
                                                with his mother].

        4   **5**

[Marion made an   [they plan to get a
appointment with a   divorce].
divorce attorney].
Therefore,

This example contains five statements. Statement [5] is the conclusion. The other four statements are premises for the conclusion. Let's consider each premise and decide how well it supports the conclusion.

> *[5]:* Marion and Engelbert plan to get a divorce. This is the conclusion.
> *[1]:* Marion and Engelbert had a fight this morning. (weak)
> *[2]:* They fight every day. (weak)
> *[3]:* Engelbert is moving out to live with his mother. (moderate)
> *[4]:* Marion made an appointment with a divorce attorney. (strong)

In this example, there are multiple premises to support the conclusion. Taken together, they provide strong support.

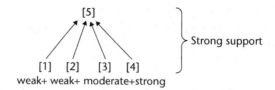

Look at the list of premises. With only the first one, the support for the conclusion was very weak. The addition of the second made the support somewhat stronger because there were now two separate weak premises, which are stronger together than one weak premise. As additional premises were added, support for the conclusion increased. This is an example of a convergent argument structure in which multiple premises point to (converge on) the same conclusion. Additional premises, even weak ones, increase the strength of the argument. Using the table analogy, ask yourself if the table top has a sound base of support or is it shaky and easy to topple over.

You may have been looking for rules or guidelines to determine the strength of support. There really are no firm rules, only guidelines. How you judge the strength of an argument depends on many personal factors, including what you already know about the topic, your personal values, and how you make judgments. Some psychologists and others have advocated for teaching children and adults about values, which would include teaching them to view complex issues from multiple perspectives—a technique that is frequently used in critical thinking instruction, although we do not usually think of this as "teaching values." Thinking, at its heart, is still a very personal activity. Although there are many skills that you can learn that will improve how you think, we are in no danger of turning all thinking into a rigid set of steps that will make us all think the same.

Here is a good example where thoughtful people disagree. How important is a candidate's personal life in determining whether the candidate should be elected? Is it an indication that the candidate will not be honest if you know that he cheats on his spouse? Some people believe that anyone who cheats in marriage will be dishonest in other situations; others believe that the two are unrelated. Public reaction to the sexual relationship between Monica Lewinsky, a White House intern, and former U.S. President Bill Clinton showed that there were many different opinions about the relevance of this relationship to Clinton's job as president. Similarly, in Russian elections, not long ago, the leading candidate was known to have a problem with alcohol. How important would this be in your decision of whether to vote for this candidate? In answering this question, you would also want to know about the other candidates running for office and the extent of the alcohol problem, but ultimately, many people disagree over issues such as these.

Missing Components

> They will try to tell you to prove you are right; I tell you to prove you are wrong.
>
> —Louis Pasteur (1822–1895)

Most arguments are written to persuade the reader or listener that a conclusion is true or probably true. Good examples of this can be found in advertisements and political rhetoric. A big problem in attempts to persuade is missing and distorted claims. In other words, it is the missing parts of most arguments that are often the most important parts. In order to evaluate the quality of an argument, you need to consider what has been left out.

When evaluating an argument, consider each component separately and think about ways the statements could have been distorted and what has been omitted. Let's analyze a more complicated argument with an example that is paraphrased from a newspaper editorial written by a resident of Douglas, Arizona (Skippar, 2012) in response to an article that advocated the legal use of marijuana for medical conditions. This editorial appeared in the *Douglas Dispatch* on May 9, 2012.

In this commentary, the author argues against the legal use of marijuana for medical conditions. I have excerpted sections from the original article. Consider the conclusion, the support for the conclusions, the strength of the evidence, the counterarguments, and any missing components.

I am opposed to [name of person] receiving a permit to grow medical marijuana in our neighborhood. She just doesn't have all the facts. I have enclosed articles from the *Denver Post* and other sources stating there is criminal activity surrounding medical marijuana growing and dispensary facilities in Denver and elsewhere. While crime in general may not go up appreciably, criminals are going after medical marijuana facilities because, quite frankly, they are easy targets. The criminals have just changed their venue. Marijuana is easy to sell illegally on the street for as much as $300 to $600 an ounce, which makes it the perfect thing to steal. According to law enforcement officials, the other advantage to crooks is many thefts involving medical marijuana are never reported by the victims.

If a medical marijuana cultivation site were permitted in our rural neighborhood, it would be like putting up a neon sign inviting trouble into our neighborhood from both sides of the border. We are only four miles from the Mexican border. The County Sheriff's Department has told us that with current staffing limitations, they don't know how well they could respond to all the potential problems they anticipate we could see if medical marijuana is permitted in our rural community. I guarantee you, our concerns are legitimate. We would be at risk. "No pot plant here," neighbor.

One of the best ways to think about what's missing is to change your point of view so that you now become an advocate for the "other side." In this case, try to view the argument from the perspective of someone who does not agree with the conclusion that is being advocated. What premises are missing or additional information is needed that would support an opposite conclusion? First, what is the conclusion? That is easy—we should not allow the legal sale of marijuana in this neighborhood. What data support the conclusion? There is the idea that crime will increase, but this point is muddied by the admitted fact that "Crime in general may not go up appreciably." The author argues that criminals will target medical marijuana facilities because they are easy targets and the criminals can sell the stolen marijuana for "as much as $300 to $600 an ounce." So far, seems good, but when you consider the issues from the perspective of what is not given as information, you often will arrive at a different conclusion.

What is missing from this argument? What about medical benefits that come from the medical use of marijuana such as relieving the intense nausea caused by chemotherapy? The author omitted all counterarguments about the benefits of allowing people to use marijuana for medical reasons. Is the analogy to putting up a neon sign inviting trouble a good one? Pharmacies have all sorts of drugs that can be sold illegally. Should they also be banned for similar reasons? What is being assumed by the reference to Mexico? Are the data provided accurate and unbiased? Does marijuana really sell for that much money? Did crime increase in other cities that allowed the use of medical marijuana? Overall how strong is this argument? Reasonable people will disagree on the importance of different types of data and what type of data are relevant; but in argument analysis, the focus is on the quality of the reasons and counter reasons, which moves the discussion away from appeals to emotions. We will not all think the same by using argument analysis, but we will think better.

Sound Arguments

A good argument is technically called a **sound argument**. An argument is sound when it meets the following criteria:

1. The premises are acceptable and consistent. (You may have to eliminate some premises so that the others are consistent.)
2. The premises are relevant to the conclusion and provide sufficient support for the conclusion.
3. Missing components have been considered and are judged to be consistent with the conclusion.

Satisfying each of these criteria is a matter of degree. Premises are usually acceptable on some continuum from unacceptable to totally acceptable. The nature of support that they provide for the conclusion also lies on some continuum from no support to complete support. Similarly, the missing components, especially counterarguments, may weaken the argument anywhere from completely to not at all. Because all of these assessments have to be combined to decide if an argument is sound, we usually think of soundness as ranging from unsound to completely sound. An argument is unsound if its premises are false, or if they are unrelated to the conclusion, or if a critical counterargument is missing. An argument is completely sound if the premises are acceptable and related to the conclusion in a way that guarantees the acceptability of the conclusion. Most real-life arguments fall somewhere between these two extremes. For this reason, conclusions are often preceded with probability terms like, "it is likely that" or "we can probably conclude that." Here are some examples of different degrees of soundness:

Completely Sound Argument (premises are acceptable and related to the conclusion in a way that guarantees the conclusion):

All mothers are women who have (or had) children. Suzi is a woman who has a son. Therefore, Suzi is a mother.

Unsound arguments (either the premises are unacceptable or they are unrelated to the conclusion):

All fathers have given birth to a child. Norbert has a son. Therefore Norbert has given birth to a child. (premise is unacceptable)

Non Sequitur by Wiley Miller. Used with permission by Universal Press Syndicate.

Norbert has a son; therefore, Norbert also has a daughter. (premise is unrelated to the conclusion)

Don't confuse the truth or acceptability of a conclusion with the soundness of an argument. A conclusion can be objectively true, even when the argument is unsound. The conclusion could be true for reasons that have nothing to do with the information stated in the argument. Here is an example of a conclusion that is objectively true embedded in an unsound argument.

The structure of the family has been changing rapidly, with more single parents now heading their own households. Consequently, the divorce rate has begun to level off and decline slightly.

The conclusion about the divorce rate is true (according to demographers), but the argument is unsound because the premise does not support the conclusion.

Complex issues rarely have one correct conclusion. More often, many conclusions are possible, and the task of analyzing an argument involves deciding which of two or more conclusions has the greater strength or support.

How to Analyze an Argument

1. The first step is to read or listen to the passage to determine if it contains an argument. Are there at least one premise and at least one conclusion? If not, no further analysis is needed.

2. Identify all the stated and unstated component parts: premises, conclusions, assumptions, qualifiers, and counterarguments.

3. Check the premises for acceptability and consistency. If all of the premises are unacceptable, stop there because the argument is unsound. If only some of the premises are unacceptable, eliminate them, and continue with the acceptable premises. If the premises are inconsistent with each other, decide if you can justifiably eliminate one or more. An argument cannot be sound if the premises are inconsistent or contradict each other, but you may be able to eliminate the contradiction.

4. Diagram the argument. Consider the strength of the support that each premise provides for the conclusion. Rate the strength of support as nonexistent, weak, medium, or strong. Look over the number of supporting premises. A large number of supporting premises can provide strong support for the conclusion in a convergent structure, even when separately each only provides weak support.

5. Consider the strength of counterarguments, assumptions, and qualifiers (stated or omitted) and omitted premises. Do they undermine the support provided by the premises or strengthen or weaken it?

6. Finally, come to a global determination of the soundness of the argument. Is it unsound, completely sound, or somewhere in between? If it is somewhere in between, is it weak, medium, or strong?

You may be thinking that analyzing arguments is a lot of work. You are absolutely right. Diagramming and evaluating complex arguments can be as demanding as a long proof in mathematics or comprehending a complex novel. I realize that few people will formally diagram an argument in real life; however, it is a powerful and useful tool for comprehending complex arguments. Practice with diagramming arguments will aid in the analysis of other arguments even when, for time or other reasons, actual diagramming is not feasible. It will help you distinguish between the components of an argument and make judgments about its strength. When the issue is important and complex, making a diagram of its structure can be well worth the time and effort required.

A Template for Writing Sound Arguments

The importance of being able to write a sound argument is recognized as a critical thinking task that is essential for success in college and in professional careers. Several different standardized examinations are requiring test-takers to write an argument as a means of assessing critical thinking and writing skills. At the present time, written arguments are required for everyone who takes the Graduate Record Examination, the selection test used for entry to most graduate schools in the United States, as well as the examination used for selection for entry into business schools. Here is a template for writing sound arguments.

The template is designed to help you organize your thinking on complex issues and be able to explain evidence on two or more sides of an issue, such as the evidence for and against evolutionary hypotheses of mate selection or for and against the idea that parents are important influences on their children. In completing this template, you will have to gather and assess evidence to determine the best conclusion or conclusions and not start with what you believe is true. You will need to consider both supporting and disconfirming evidence—an exercise that can help you avoid the confirmation bias. Here is an applied example:

Making Arguments Template

Example 1: Does violence on television have a negative influence on children's behavior?

1. State your conclusion. (Although you may begin your formal writing here, be sure that the conclusion follows from your reasons.) As you work, this is the last part that is filled in, not the first.

2. Give three reasons (or some other number) that support your conclusion.

   a.

   b.

   c.

3. Rate each reason as weak, moderate, strong, or very strong.

   Rating for a:

   Rating for b:

   Rating for c:

4. Give three counterarguments (or some other number) that weaken your conclusion. Rate how much each counterargument weakens the conclusion: little, moderate, much, or very much.

a.

Rating for a:

b.

Rating for b:

c.

Rating for c:

5. List any qualifiers (limitations on the reasons for or against—for example some evidence may be restricted to early childhood).

6. List any assumptions.

7. Are your reasons and counterarguments directly related to your conclusion?

8. What is the overall strength of your argument: weak, moderate, strong, or very strong?

Now that you have completed this worksheet, rate the overall strength of your argument.

Once the template is completed, the writing will be the easy part because you already know what you want to say and have listed your reasons and considered the strength of your argument. (If you are planning on taking any of the standardized admissions examinations that now require that you write an argument, this exercise should greatly improve your score.)

Reasoning and Rationalizing

People are irrational, short-sighted, destructive, ethnocentric, emotional, and easily misled by demagogues.

—Philip E. Tetlock (1994, p. 3)

When you evaluate arguments, you are also evaluating your own knowledge about the subject matter. There may be other counterarguments that are quite strong but that are unknown to you. Similarly, your ratings of the strength of the components may be biased in ways that support a conclusion that you favor. Nickerson (1986) makes an important distinction between reasoning and **rationalizing**. When we rationalize, we attend to information that favors a preferred conclusion. We may selectively gather information that supports a preferred conclusion or rate counterarguments as weak because they detract from a preferred conclusion. Rationalizing also influences the nature of the missing components that we supply to an existing argument. When we add to an argument, the information that we supply is information that is readily recalled. If you have already read the chapter on memory, then you are well aware of the many ways that memory can be biased. Rationalizing is usually not a deliberate process to distort the analysis of arguments, which makes it difficult to recognize and guard against. It is easier to recognize rationalizing when someone else is doing it. Perhaps the best you can do is realize that rationalization does occur and to try to be especially vigilant for rationalizing when you prefer a conclusion.

Just telling people that we tend to judge information that we favor as stronger than information that we oppose does not work to correct this bias. Is it any wonder why it is so difficult to get people to assess controversial issues in a fair-minded manner? Because we are not aware that we judge reasons in a way that supports what we believe to be true, it is very difficult to change the way we evaluate information. One successful attempt was accomplished by Koriat, Lichtenstein, and Fischhoff (1980). They required students to list reasons that support a conclusion and reasons that run counter to a conclusion (counterarguments) and to rate the strength of each. This should be familiar because they are the steps used in analyzing arguments. They found that students became more accurate in their assessments after this training in "giving reasons." These results have been replicated in more recent studies in which the bias for information that confirms a prior belief was reduced by requiring people to provide reasons that did not support the preferred conclusion (Lenski, 2001; Flannelly & Flannelly, 2000). The authors of one of the studies summarized their research: "critical thinking skills of students should be fostered so the students come to appreciate the importance of weighting both positive and negative evidence" (Flannelly & Flannelly, 2000). These sorts of experimental results show that the giving and assessing of reasons can have beneficial results that improve the thinking process.

You can practice the giving of supporting and contradicting evidence and reasons for any controversial topic. Consider, for example, capital punishment. By filling in all four cells below and providing reasons for and against capital punishment, you will have to think about both sides of this controversial issue. It should help you to defend against my-side bias.

	Reasons that support the conclusion	Reasons that run counter to the conclusion
A. We should have capital punishment.	Reason 1: Strength of Reason 1: Reason 2: Strength of Reason 2:	Reason 1: Strength of Reason 1: Reason 2: Strength of Reason 2:
B. We should NOT have capital punishment.	Reason 1: Strength of Reason 1: Reason 2: Strength of Reason 2:	Reason 1: Strength of Reason 1: Reason 2: Strength of Reason 2:

How People Reach Different Conclusions from the Same Evidence

> The problem may be less what politicians are actually saying, but rather how their words are heard and interpreted.
> —Martin McKee and David Stuckler (para. 5, 2010)

The dramatic increase in the number of people diagnosed with diabetes is creating a health crisis of huge proportions. How do we understand the cause of diabetes, and what actions should we take (collectively) to stem the tide of increasing numbers? The idea that people prefer reasons and explanations that are consistent with their prior beliefs—confirmation bias—appears in many chapters in this book because of its strong and ubiquitous effect on how we think. In a study of the way confirmation bias operates, researchers (McKee & Stuckler, 2010) presented people with political affiliations ranging from liberal to conservative with information about diabetes. There were four conditions: (a) control condition in which no information about the cause of diabetes was presented; (b) a condition that discussed its genetic basis; (c) a condition that discussed the way individual life choices affect diabetes; and (d) a condition that discussed how social variables can affect diabetes. The authors found that people with more socially oriented political beliefs (i.e., Democrats) were more likely to believe that social determinants were important in causing the rise in diabetes, regardless of which version they read, and they were more likely to endorse restrictions on junk food as a way of reducing the diabetes problem than those with more individually oriented political beliefs (i.e., Republicans). In other words, the participants in this study used their preexisting biases to interpret new information and derived conclusions that were consistent with their preexisting political beliefs.

Persuasion and Propaganda

> By the skillful and sustained use of propaganda, one can make people see even heaven as hell, or an extremely wretched life as paradise.
> —Adolf Hitler (1889–1945)

Whenever you are confronted with an argument, keep in mind that the material you are reading or hearing has been written to persuade you to do something or to believe something. Much of the communication that you receive is concerned with getting you to act or think in a certain way. Pratkanis and Aronson (1992) define **propaganda** as "mass suggestion or influence through the manipulation of symbols and the psychology of the individual" (p. 9). This broad definition is applicable to a great variety of situations. Propaganda, like beauty, is often in the eye of the beholder. It does not require that the information be false or misleading, but it does at least imply less concern for truth or rigorous argument than the sort of arguments found in scholarly journals or presented by independent parties. It may distort the truth or alter evidence. Frequently, the information provided is charged with appeals to emotion rather than reason, and counterarguments are omitted or presented in a way that diminishes their effectiveness.

Arguments were most frequently used to persuade Nazis and others that millions of people should be slaughtered, but there were other propaganda techniques that Goebbels used, including visual images and threats of violence, for anyone who did not agree. Although other techniques are considered in more detail later in this chapter and in other chapters, I note here the particularly blatant ploy of showing pictures of Jews that were alternated with pictures of rats and roaches, so that viewers would come to associate certain facial features that are common in many Jews with disgusting rodents and bugs. This example was provided in Chapter 2 as a type of learning known as classical conditioning. These same sorts of techniques have been used to promote other types of equally horrific genocide. The propaganda used to justify slavery and lynchings in the United States, the slaughter of Cambodians in Asia, and the purges by Mao Tse-Tung in China and Stalin in the former Soviet Union show that propaganda has been used all over the world to encourage prejudice and killing. For examples, how did millions of Chinese, in the last century, believe that Mao was their "loving father" when he was responsible for the death of millions of Chinese? Why didn't they stop to consider if the reasons they were given to support this Chinese holocaust (i.e., the Cultural Revolution) were not acceptable? Do you understand Hitler's now infamous quote, "What luck for rulers that men do not think" (quoted in Byrne, 1988, p. 359)?

The Psychology of Reasons

> Just because you are intelligent or have great knowledge does not mean you can think critically. A profound genius may have the most irrational of beliefs or the most unreasonable of opinions. Critical thinking is about how we use our intelligence and knowledge to reach objective and rationale viewpoints.
>
> —Greg R. Haskins (2006, p. 2)

Warren Buffet is one of the richest men in the world. Forbes magazine listed his wealth in 2012 at $44 billion, so it is not surprising that people turn to him for advice about how to make money. Here is a sampling of his advice on how to get very, very rich. His first comment is a theme that you have read before, if you are reading the chapters in this book in order (Zweig, 2008; paras. 5–6): "I tell the students who come visit me that if you have more than 120 or 130 I.Q. points, you can afford to give the rest away. You do not need extraordinary intelligence to succeed as an investor. You need a philosophy and the ability to think independently." He then goes to say: "You should be able to write down on a yellow sheet of paper, 'I'm buying General Motors at $22, and GM has [566] million shares for a total market value of $13 billion, and GM is worth a lot more than $13 billion because _____." And if you can't finish that sentence, then you don't buy the stock. (Note that Buffett mentioned GM for illustrative purposes only.) So, his wisdom is that you don't need extraordinary intelligence, but you do need to have good reasons for your investment choices. In other words, you need to support your conclusion with good evidence—you need to know how to make a good argument.

You probably think that irrelevant reasons for a conclusion would have no effect on how people evaluate a conclusion. It seems that this should be true because irrelevant reasons are, well, irrelevant. But, psychologically, irrelevant reasons often influence what we believe and how we act even though logically, they should not. A study of consumer decisions showed that irrelevant reasons in support of a product tend to weaken support for the product (Simonson, Nowlis, & Simonson, 1993). For example, suppose that you are a runner who is looking for good running shoes. As a salesperson, I tell you that Adibok brand is well known for their aerobic shoes, but they also make good running shoes. The fact that they are well known for their aerobic shoes should be irrelevant to the selection of running shoes, but it seems to work against this hypothetical brand. Consumers assume that if Adibok is good at making aerobic shoes, then it is less good at making running shoes. Thus, an irrelevant reason in support of this brand is psychologically converted into a reason against this brand.

Explaining as Knowing

"How do you know what you know?" (Kuhn, 2001). It seems that most people make judgments about their own knowledge by thinking about how well they can explain a phenomenon. For example, in studies of how jurors decide on the guilt or innocence of a defendant, researchers found that jurors weave a story about what might have happened at the scene of a crime and then decide how good that story is. This mode of knowing is often labeled "explaining." Another way of knowing is to examine the strength of the evidence that supports or refutes a particular conclusion—this is known as argument analysis. Most people use "explanations" as the primary way of justifying claims (Rassin, Eerland, & Kuijpers, 2010). Consider this example:

Which is the stronger argument?

A. Why do teenagers start smoking? Smith says it's because they see ads that make smoking look attractive. A good-looking guy in neat clothes with a cigarette in his mouth is someone you would like to be like.

B. Why do teenagers start smoking? Jones says it's because they see ads that make smoking look attractive. When cigarette ads were banned from TV, smoking went down. (Kuhn, 2001, p. 4)

Answer A provides an explanation that links smoking and teens in a way that most people think "makes sense." Answer B provides data, albeit limited, that links smoking and advertisements. The alternative that provides evidence for the relationship is stronger than the one that merely explains, even though many people prefer the explanation. There are many plausible explanations that could be generated, and without evidence (i.e., data) there is no good way to choose between them. Far too many people are very confident in their knowledge of something and very wrong. Think about your own understanding. How do you know about the nature of the world? This is not meant to be an idle navel-gazing question. If you can develop the disposition to look for evidence instead of relying on an explanation that "just seems right," you will make large gains in critical thinking.

It is important to understand that people are quite confident in their knowledge because it makes sense to them, but "making sense" is a poor measure of the quality of your knowing. Sometimes, it is difficult to understand why data should be preferable to explanation. Consider these two examples: (1) During World War II, many Germans refused to believe that the German army burned an entire village in Poland as they were retreating from the Soviet front. They refused to believe it because the massacre did not make sense. Why should the German troops slaughter innocent people in Poland? In fact, historical records (eye witness accounts, physical evidence, written accounts, etc.) clearly show that this is what happened—the village was destroyed by frustrated German troops who were seeking revenge for their humiliating loss. The evidence is more compelling than the "make sense" explanation. It is important that we learn to value evidence when formulating conclusions. The use of data is a critical part of critical thinking.

The preference for explanations over evidence is just one of many ways that thinking can "go wrong." In the next section, we consider other common ways that thinking can go astray. Unsound reasoning techniques used for the purpose of persuasion are called fallacies. As you go through the list of fallacies presented in the next section, you can classify each as violating one or more of the criteria for sound arguments—(a) the premises are unacceptable, (b) the premises are unrelated to the conclusion or (c) are inconsistent, (d) the expert is not credible, or (e) important information is missing.

It is impossible to list every fallacy that has been employed to change how people think. The list would be too long to be useful, with only subtle differences between several of the techniques. Accordingly, only the most common and representative techniques are discussed. If you understand how fallacies work in general, you'll be better prepared to recognize and defend against them. Toulmin, Rieke, and Janik (1979) call the ability to recognize fallacies "a kind of sensitivity training" because they train the reader to be sensitive to common tricks of persuasion.

Twenty-One Common Fallacies

1. Association Effects

One of the oldest principles in psychology is the notion that if two events occur close together in time and/or space, the mind will form an association between them. Thereafter, when one occurs, the other is expected to occur. This principle has become widely used in the political arena, especially to create **guilt by association**. Suppose you read in the newspaper that a violent mass murderer endorsed a presidential candidate. This endorsement would be detrimental to the candidate, even if she did not desire it and did nothing to promote it.

A classic example of the propagandistic use of association came from a political speech (so many great examples in political speeches) in which a United States Congressman attacked the record of a gubernatorial candidate by stating that this candidate would not fight for the concerns of people who live in cities because he grew up "in a chicken shack on Duck Run" (quoted in Pickrell, 2010). The underlying argument was that this candidate was associated with rural areas (with negative imagery about rural areas) and therefore he would not care about the cities in his state. He may or may not care about the cities in his state, but is it reasonable to conclude that he would not *because* he grew up in a rural area? Are there any behaviors or statements that this candidate made that would support that conclusion? In this example, the answer is no. (Note also the use of the emotion laden phrase "chicken shack.") Whenever you see examples of associations with no justifiable connection like this one, be wary of the rest of the message. It is likely to contain an appeal to your emotions rather than to your cognition.

Just as one can have guilt by association, it is also possible to have **virtue by association**. In this instance, the names or label attached to the person are "good" ones. Perhaps this is why certain political offices tend to run in families. People expected the Kennedy brothers to be similar as politicians because of their obvious association with each other or that the Bush children will be similar to their father, former president George Bush,

Sr. This expectation is being passed onto the children and other relatives of political figures, many of whom are now involved in or considering political careers. Would you vote for or against an unknown Kennedy or Bush or some other politician simply because he or she is from the same family as a former politician?

A wary recipient of messages that rely on association will ask about the nature of the association. If a candidate is a leader of the Ku Klux Klan, then associating the doctrine of the Klan with this individual is reasonable. If, on the other hand, a friend of the candidate's mother is a member of the Klan, the association is ludicrous.

Why would a supporter of a U.S. President (Obama) suggest that he stop using a nicotine gum that helps him stop smoking and go back to the real thing (Horwitz, 2008)? Can you guess the answer? Consider the demographics of smokers in America. Americans who earn between $24,000 and $36,000 a year are twice as likely to smoke cigarettes as those who earn more than $90,000 a year. According to Horwitz (2008, para. 5): "Bottom line: small-towners in the Rust Belt and Appalachia don't cling to guns and religion so much as they do cigarettes." By smoking in public, any candidate would be signaling that he is similar to this group of people and the similarity should help him at the polls and in general approval ratings. What do you think? Would a political candidate become more popular among voters who smoke if he also smoked publicly?

2. Arguments against the Person

Arguments against the person is the formal term for name calling or, in its Latin form, argumentum ad hominem. This form of persuasion or propaganda attacks the people who support a cause, and not the cause itself. From the standpoint of argument analysis, the personal attack is irrelevant to the conclusion. For example, the Nazis believed that the theory of relativity was wrong because its discoverer was a Jew named Albert Einstein. They never considered the evidence for or against the theory, just the religion of its originator. It is basically another form of the association effect. In this case, the association that is being made is between an idea and a person. The underlying principle is that if you don't like the person who supports an idea, then you should also oppose the idea itself because the idea and the person are associated.

Suppose you were serving on a jury that had to decide which of two witnesses was telling the truth. Would you be swayed if one attorney told you to disregard one man's testimony because he had been divorced twice? Presumably not, because the man's marital status is irrelevant to the issue. Suppose you were told that one of the men had two previous convictions for lying to a jury. Would this argument against the person be relevant? I would think so. In this case, the information provided about the witness is relevant to the question of whether he is lying. Consider the strength and relevance of the argument and the purpose for which it is used, and don't be misled by irrelevant attacks on the supporters or detractors of any position.

3. Appeals to Pity

> Logical reasoning is set adrift on a sea of emotions.
>
> —Hans Bluedorn (2008, para. 4)

An **appeal to pity** is easy to spot. Appeals to pity are often found in legal pleadings. A defendant's poor background or turbulent home life will often be brought up during a trial. These appeals to pity have nothing to do with the question of whether a defendant is guilty or innocent, although they may be persuasive appeals for leniency in sentencing if the defendant is found guilty. Sometimes, students use appeals to pity when attempting to persuade a teacher to raise a low grade. The grade is assigned on the quality of the work that is done, but students sometimes argue that if they work hard (or some other sad reason), the work should be graded higher than comparable work by someone who did not work as hard.

4. Popularity and Testimonials

The **popularity** technique (also known as the "bandwagon") relies on the need for conformity for its persuasive power. It is persuasive because it explains that everyone supports a position or buys a certain product. It is expected that the recipients of the message will adopt the belief or buy the product in order to feel as if she or he belongs to the groups mentioned. Implicitly, the message is, "if everyone is doing it, it must be right."

A variation of the popularity technique is **testimonials**. Respected politicians or movie stars endorse a belief or product. It is believed that people will want to be similar to the people they respect, so they will choose to

Calvin and Hobbes   by Bill Watterson

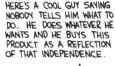

Calvin and Hobbes by Bill Watterson. Used with permission by Universal Press Syndicate.

use the same deodorant or foot powder or support the same causes. The recipients of testimonials are expected to infer a conclusion from the information stated. It is expected that they will reason along these lines: Christie Brinkley is a gorgeous model with very few wrinkles. She uses the advertised beauty product. If I use this beauty product, like Christie Brinkley, I will have very few wrinkles. Of course, this conclusion does not follow from the first two sentences, but many people believe that it does or, at least implicitly, that it might. This fallacy is worsened when the testimonial is not even in the area in which the personality has expertise. Christie Brinkley also endorses a national newspaper. As far as I know, this is an area in which she has no expertise. She is not a credible expert in the area of journalistic quality. Yet, advertisements like these do sell products.

Sometimes, however, the popularity technique and testimonials can be valid persuasive techniques. If, for example, all of the members of an unbiased expert panel established to study the effects of a drug decide that it is unsafe, I would consider this information relevant to the question of the drug's safety because it passes the test of credibility. Similarly, if a leading educator endorses a reading text, this might properly have an impact on your evaluation of the text. Both of these examples presume that the "experts" have no personal motives for their endorsements—that is, they're not being paid for saying these things, and their expertise is relevant to the position or product that they're supporting. In this case, they are credible sources of information.

5. False Dichotomy

> Don't give him two sides to a question to worry him.
> Give him one;
> better yet, give him none!
>
> —Ray Bradbury (Farenheit 451, 1950)

There are very few political or social decisions that have simple answers or that can be solved with simple choices. Yet, simple slogans are the **prototype** or most common and representative form of persuasive techniques. **False dichotomy** is sometimes called simplification or the **Black or White Fallacy** because readers are asked to decide between two positions, without allowing other alternatives or "gray areas" that would combine aspects of both choices.

The following question appeared in a questionnaire that was sent by an assemblyman to his constituents ("Assemblyman Montjoy Needs Your Views," 2001):

Would you prefer that government cut spending or increase taxes?

Does this question bother you? It should. The answers to our fiscal problems are not this simple. You should ask where and how the cuts would be made and how and how much taxes would be increased. Perhaps "cuts" could be combined with small or temporary increases in taxes. Can you guess which answer the Assemblyman prefers? Given this choice, I believe that most people would prefer to "cut spending," yet, for many, an entirely different response would result from a question that was worded differently.

It does seem that people engage in black or white thinking when they think about political issues. Bill O'Reilly (2006), a political commentator for Fox television, which is generally acknowledged as having a conservative bias, claims that there are two kinds of Americans: people like him, who love and cherish traditional values, and "secular progressives." Dividing Americans into two types—good ones like me and bad ones who want to change America for the worse—is a good example of a false dichotomy. People vary along multiple dimensions and cannot be classified into one of two categories.

When you are faced with a false dichotomy or the simplification of a complex issue, do not ask yourself if the ideas are good or bad. Ask instead what is good about the ideas and what is bad about them. Consider other alternatives and combinations of ideas. Remember that one of the steps in analyzing arguments calls for supplying missing components—omitted premises, assumptions, qualifiers, and counterarguments.

6. Appeals to Pride or Snobbery

> Speech was given to man to disguise his thoughts.
> —Talleyrand (1754–1838; quoted in Macmillan, 1989, p. 544)

An **appeal to pride or snobbery** usually involves praise or flattery. A blatant and humorous example can be found in an advertisement that was mailed to me at home. (Notice that it begins with my name, a sure attention-getting technique.)

> Dear Dr. Halpern,
>
> You may just be the solution.
>
> Here is the problem: How do you find the right subscribers for an extraordinary magazine that is about to be published—BUT, a magazine that isn't for everyone? A magazine that is, in fact, for only a handful of bright, literate people, people who still in this world of instant communication love to sit down with a good book.

I would love to believe that the publishers know me personally and have written a magazine just for the kind of person I would like to be. The truth is, this letter went to tens of thousands of people whose names were bought as part of various mailing lists. Clearly, they are attempting to persuade me to purchase their magazine by appealing to my pride or snobbery. In its skeletal form, that message says that if there is a group that I want to belong to (in this case, bright, literate people, but it could be any group), then I should buy X (in this case a magazine).

7. Card Stacking or Suppressed Information

Card stacking or suppressed information operates as a persuasive technique by omitting information that supports the unfavored view. An automobile company recently compared the car they were advertising on television with a competitor. The advertisers stressed that their car got better mileage and cost less. What about the variables they omitted? Which car needed fewer repairs, had the more comfortable seating, or accelerated better? What about other makes of cars? When considering persuasive information, be sure to consider what has not been stated along with the stated claims. This is another example of the need to consider the missing components in an argument.

8. Circular Reasoning

In **circular reasoning**, the premise is simply a restatement of the conclusion. If you were to diagram the structure of this sort of argument, you would get a circle because the support for the conclusion is a restatement of the conclusion. Here is an example of circular reasoning:

We need to raise the speed limit because the current legal speed is too slow.

In this example, the reason given (current speed is too slow) is just another way of saying that we need to raise the speed limit. It does not support the conclusion. The conclusion would be supported with premises such as the assertion that there has been no change in the number or severity of automobile accidents with a lower speed limit or some similar statement that supports this conclusion.

9. Irrelevant Reasons

Arguments that utilize irrelevant reasons are fairly common. The Latin word for this sort of fallacy is *non sequitur,* which literally translates to "it doesn't follow." In other words, the reason or premise is unrelated to the conclusion. Of course, you recognize the importance of having relevant premises as one of the criteria for sound arguments. (If you do not, go back over the section of evaluating the quality of an argument.)

One example that comes to mind is a statement that a faculty member made at a curriculum committee meeting in which we were discussing whether we should require every student to take classes in a foreign language. The faculty member in favor of this proposal made this statement: "We should require every student to study a foreign language because it is important that we provide our students with a quality education." Look carefully at the conclusion and the premise. Is the premise related to the conclusion? Everyone on the curriculum committee believed that all students should receive a quality education, but the issue was whether all students should be required to study a foreign language. There were no reasons given as to why studying a foreign language should be a required part of a quality education. The conclusion did not follow from the reason that was given.

10. Slippery Slope or Continuum

The **slippery slope** fallacy is best described by an example. One of the arguments against court-ordered desegregation of the schools was that if we allow the court to determine which public schools our children will attend, the court will also tell us whom we have to allow into our churches, whom we have to invite into our homes, and even whom we should marry. In this example, the action (court-ordered desegregation) lies on a continuum with the court ordering of whom we should marry at an extreme end. The argument being made is that if we allow the court to have jurisdiction over events at one end of the continuum, then it will take over the other events on the continuum. For this reason, this fallacy is called either slippery slope (once you start sliding down a slope you can't stop) or the fallacy of **continuum**.

Most life events can be placed along a continuum. It does not necessarily follow that actions concerning some part of the continuum will also apply to other portions of the continuum. Let's consider a second example. There are many arguments being made for and against same-sex marriages. One of the arguments against it is that if we allow same-sex couples to marry, we will then allow groups of people to marry, and then people can marry their animals, and so on. This sort of thinking does not take into account the fact that processes can be stopped, and it does not make a qualitative distinction between two people marrying, groups of people marrying, or marrying an animal. A more colorful name for this fallacy is "the camel's nose in the tent." It is based on the idea that if we let a camel stick its nose in the tent on a cold night, the rest of the camel will soon follow and you will have large smelly camel in your tent.

11. Straw Person

A **straw person** is weak and easy to knock down. With a straw person argument, a very weak form of an opponent's argument is set up and then knocked down. It occurs when an opponent to a particular conclusion distorts the argument in support of the conclusion and substitutes one that is much weaker. For example, in a discussion about whether students should be evaluating their professors, one opponent to this idea offered this straw person argument: "You say that students' evaluations of their professors should be included in decisions about which professors we should be promoting. Well, I certainly don't think that the decision as to which professors get promoted should be made by students." Notice how the original argument that "student evaluations should be included in the decision-making process" was changed to "students should not be deciding which professors get promoted." The original argument was for student evaluations to be *part of* the criteria used in the decision-making process. This is not the same as having students actually make the decisions. In its changed form, the argument is easier to knock down, just like a straw person.

12. Part–Whole Fallacies

Part–whole fallacies are flip sides of the same error. A part–whole fallacy is made whenever a speaker or writer assumes that whatever is true of the whole is also true of all of its parts, and whatever is true of the parts is also true of the whole. Consider some outstanding, prestigious university. (Are you thinking about your own school?) As a whole, the student body is highly intelligent, but it would be wrong to believe that every student who attends that university is therefore highly intelligent.

13. Appeals to Ignorance

The peculiar thing about **appeals to ignorance** is that they can often be used to support two or more totally different conclusions. This should be a clue to you that the reasoning involved is fallacious. In appeals to ignorance, the premise involves something we don't know. Our ignorance is being used to argue that since there is no evidence to support a conclusion, the conclusion must be wrong. Our ignorance of a topic can also be used to support a conclusion by stating that since there is no evidence that contradicts it, the conclusion must be right. I have heard both sides argue this way in a debate on the existence of God. Believers have argued that since no one can prove that God doesn't exist, He therefore must exist. Nonbelievers have argued that since no one can prove that God exists, He therefore doesn't exist. The absence of evidence doesn't support any conclusion. The absence of evidence for one conclusion is not evidence for another conclusion.

14. Weak and Inappropriate Analogies

The topic of analogies was presented in the chapter "The Relationship between Thought and Language." It also appears later in the book in the chapters on problem solving and creativity. Analogies are a basic thinking skill. We use analogies whenever we encounter something new and try to understand it by reference to something we already know. Although analogies can be extremely useful aids to comprehension, they can also be misused. Two objects or events are analogous when they share certain properties. When we argue with analogies, we conclude that what is true of one object or event is true of the other.

15. Appeals to Authority

Despite the fact that most people *say* they take TV or Internet reports with a grain of salt, few actually do. There's something deeply compelling about hearing a claim from an authoritative source; we all have a voice in the back of our heads that wants the new claim to be true, and this desire gets confirmed by the belief that the story wouldn't have made it all the way to the TV news without having been pretty well substantiated. What are you going to do?

—Brian Dunning (2011, para. 5)

I already introduced this fallacy in an informal way earlier in this chapter when I discussed expert credibility. Much of what we know and believe is based on what we learn from authorities. The fallacy of **appeals to authority** occurs when the authority we use to support the premises in an argument is the wrong authority. If I wanted to sell you a stereo, it would be valid if I quoted from an article on stereos written by a professor of acoustics (who is an independent authority). It would be a fallacious appeal if I told you that Kobe Bryant (a basketball star) called it the best stereo system he had ever seen. Thus, the fallacy is not in appealing to an authority on a topic, but to appealing to someone who is not a credible authority.

16. Incomplete Comparisons

"More doctors agree that Dopeys can give you the fastest pain relief." Advertisements like this one are so common, that it is almost impossible to open a magazine without seeing one. Two different comparisons are made in this statement and both are incomplete. Whenever you see comparative terms, ask yourself "more than what?", "fastest compared to what?" **Incomplete comparisons** are missing the other half of the equation.

17. Knowing the Unknowable

Sometimes we are given information that is impossible to know. This is the fallacy of **knowing the unknowable**. Suppose you read in the newspapers that we need to increase the size of the police force because the number of unreported rapes has increased dramatically. A little alarm should go off when you read this: How can anyone know about the number of unreported rapes? I don't doubt that many rapes are not reported to the police or that this is an important issue. What is at question is the increase or decrease in the number when the actual number is unknowable.

18. False Cause

The fallacy of **false cause** is discussed more completely in the chapter "Thinking as Hypothesis Testing", but it is also important to discuss in the context of reasoning fallacies. The fallacy of false cause occurs whenever someone argues that because two events occur together, or one follows the other closely in time, that one caused the other to occur. For example, consider the finding that as the number of churches increases in a city, so does the number of prostitutes. It would be false to conclude that churches cause an increase in prostitution or that prostitutes cause more churches to be built. In fact, as the size of a city increases so does the number of churches and the number of prostitutes, as well as the number of schools, dry cleaners, volunteer agencies, and so on. Neither of them caused any of the others. They all resulted from a third factor—in this case, an increase in population. Of course, it is possible that one variable *did* cause the other to occur, but more than co-occurrence is needed to justify a causal claim.

19. Put Downs

Only a fool would endorse this candidate! No patriotic American would disagree! You'd have to be stupid to believe that! These are all examples of **put downs** (also known as belittling the opposition). An opposing viewpoint is belittled so that agreeing with it would put you in the class of people who are fools, or unpatriotic, or stupid. This technique is not so much a reasoning fallacy as it is an emotional appeal or dare.

20. Appeals to Tradition

"That's the way we've always done it." Anyone who has tried to change a policy has heard this sentence or its variant, "If it ain't broke, don't fix it." In **appeals to tradition,** the unstated assumption is that what exists is best. It may be true that current policy is better than some suggested change, but it also may not be true. There is nothing inherent in the fact that "that's the way we've always done it" that makes it a good or best way to accomplish an objective. One of the attitudes of a critical thinker that was presented in the first chapter is flexibility. Appeals to tradition deny the possibility that a different way may be an improvement.

21. False Charge of Fallacy

That's a fallacy! It seems that after some people learn to recognize fallacious reasoning, they then label everything that anyone says as a fallacy (Levi, 1991). Not every statement is a fallacy. The idea of critical thinking is to develop an amiable skepticism, not a cynical view that everything and everyone is false. It is important to know when to accept some statements as acceptable as it is to know when and what to question.

Distinguishing between Opinion, Reasoned Judgment, and Fact

Compare the following three statements.

Lady Gaga is a great singer.
Lady Gaga is a great singer because she can sing a wider variety of songs than any other contemporary artist.
Lady Gaga is a great singer with several different songs at the top of the chart and albums that have gone platinum.

In the first example, I have expressed an **opinion**. It is a simple assertion of a preference. I like it; I think it is best. No reasons were given to support the evaluation. Opinion reflects how an individual or group has assessed a position or product—e.g., "Vote for Max Lake; he's the best man for the job!"

The second example also expresses a preference, but in this example, the preference is supported a reason. I like X because Y. This is an example of **reasoned judgment**. Other examples of reasoned judgment are provided throughout the chapter.

The third statement concerns factual claims. **Facts** have a verifiable truth value—e.g., Gravel-Os breakfast cereal has 100% of the recommended daily requirement of iron. Although I cannot personally check the truth-value of these facts, a credible authority (e.g., the Food and Drug Administration) has verified these claims for me. Often, the distinction between fact, opinion, and reasoned judgment is a fine one. If we say that Gravel-Os is a good cereal because it has 100% of the recommended daily requirement of iron, this is a reasoned judgment based, in part, on the unstated assumption that it is good to eat cereals that contain 100% of the recommended daily requirement of iron. The distinction becomes even more difficult when you recall that opinions can serve as the premises (reasons) in an argument. Thus, when I say that Gravel-Os is a good cereal because I like its nutty taste, I have a reason to support my conclusion. If I were to add that Gravel-Os is a good cereal because I like its nutty taste and it supplies all of my iron needs for the day, the strength of my argument is increased.

"Pure" facts that are untainted by opinion are often hard to find. Take, for example, your daily newspaper. Although news reporters are obligated to provide readers with facts, their opinions certainly color what they report and how they report it. Compare the way two different newspapers cover the same story. One newspaper could make it the headline on page one, thus making it important news that will be read by many, whereas the other could place it in an inside section in smaller print, thus making sure that fewer people will read the story. Look at the words used to convey the same story.

Most news media (news magazines, newspapers, television news) are biased toward providing information that "sells." The news media often treat complex issues in a very simplistic manner with a heavy emphasis on controversies because they are more interesting than agreements. The usual rules of scientific evidence and reasoning often are abandoned in the news media where deadlines determine the news you get and interest value can drive content. The distinction between fact and opinion is becoming increasingly difficult to discern. How much of reality television is real? The fuzzy distinction between the real and unreal gets even more difficult now that "virtual reality" computer programs are available and rival "real reality." It is a brave, new world that we are entering—one that makes critical thinking more necessary than ever.

It has been said that there is never just one war fought. Each side has its own version, and rarely do they agree. Unfortunately, there is always fighting somewhere around the world so that you can verify this statement for yourself. It is not unusual for each side to claim that the other fired first, or for both sides to claim victory in a battle. Obviously, in the absence of verifiable truth, there is no way to know which, if either, side is presenting the facts. As before, the best way to assess the quality of the information provided is to consider the credibility of the reporter. I would prefer a report from an independent third party with first-hand and direct knowledge and appropriate credentials to a report from spokespersons from either of the sides involved in a dispute. It is now possible to get news from multiple sources, including Al Jazeera (an Arabic language news program that is broadcast in multiple languages, including English), BBC (British Broadcast Corporation), and many more. It is useful to see how they cover the same news story.

Evaluating Information on the Internet

A website hosted by the Mankato Area Chamber & Convention Bureau extolled the many attractions in this beautiful city in Minnesota, including whale watching on the Minnesota River (n.d.). Surprised? You should be because the web site was originally created by a professor at Mankato State University to highlight the importance of critically evaluation information found on the Internet. (I assume you figured out that there are no whales on the river in Minnesota.) We are far too trusting of the information we find while searching legitimate-looking web sites. There are many guides for evaluating information, whether it is on the Internet or in a book (even this one). Bell (2012) suggests that every reader ask these questions:

1. Does the author state the goals for the publication? (Is it meant to persuade, advocate, inform, or sell something?)

2. Is the author biased? (Is there only one point of view? Does the author acknowledge bias? Are there facts and arguments for all sides of controversial topics? Is the language meant to arouse emotions?)

3. Is the author's affiliation reflected in the information? (Does the argument support the mission of the affiliation? Are there benefits to the organization if people agree with the arguments presented?)

4. Is the information valid and well-researched? (Are opinions disguised as facts? Are conclusions supported with evidence? Are the assumptions reasonable?)

Visual Arguments

He who controls images controls everything.
—Robert Townsend (quoted in Beilensen & Jackson,
Eds., 1992, p. 15)

We are living in an increasingly visual society where we get more of our information from visual displays than from words. Television is a major source of information and entertainment for many people. The average television viewer will see approximately two million commercials by age 65 (Mitroff & Herr, 2007). The message in each is mostly the same—whatever your problem is (e.g., rough elbows, teeth that do not dazzle with sparkling whiteness, being overweight), you can buy a product that will solve it. Much of the persuasive message in television commercials is conveyed through the pictures that we see, often with the accompanying dialogue being of secondary importance. Images are also important in magazines, newspapers, video games, the Internet, and on billboards.

The effects of visual images are more difficult to gauge because they are often subtle. Consider a sample of cigarette advertisements. Smoking is linked to beauty, glamour, youth, health, and popularity. A popular theme in visual cigarette advertisements is horses and the "great" outdoors. We are shown beautiful, happy people smoking and enjoying the good life. The horses suggest ruggedness and an unrestrained independence—just the sort of person who won't be swayed with facts that link smoking with many diseases. Careful market research pinpoints specific markets for cigarette smokers and designs images to appeal to market segments, for example, young women, with no more than a high school education, who wear jeans, and work at blue collar jobs. The images in these ads are very different from those targeted at more educated women, who are shown reading and talking while they smoke.

Visual images can be powerful determinants of public opinion and policy. I cannot forget the pictures of starving children in Somalia, which eloquently spoke of the dire need to send U.S. troops to assist with this disaster or the image of a dead U.S. serviceman being dragged through the dusty streets of Somalia. Which image moved the United States to promptly leave Somalia? What if the images had been different? Suppose that instead of the dead peacekeeper being dragged through the street, the media had shown pictures of Somalians receiving food and clean water—people who were alive because of the peacekeepers? The images we are shown have profound effects on how we think and feel.

Figure 5.2 shows some old propagandist images that were popular in Russia in the early and mid-20th century. Note the image of the fat, rich capitalist. His pig-like face and bloated body are deliberately unattractive, and his sea of gold depicts his solitary concern with material wealth. Look also at the Soviet Army recruiter with the outstretched, pointing finger, urging Russians to volunteer. Compare him to the military recruiting posters that were popular in the United States during the same time period, a time when people in the United States knew that "Uncle Sam wants you."

Figure 5.2 Images of persuasion. The piglike man surrounded with his gold was designed to represent the capitalist. It was a common image during the years when Soviet Communists needed to keep the idea that "capitalism is bad" alive. By contrast, the Soviet recruiter has his arms open to welcome all to the great cause. He bears an uncanny similarity in pose and nonverbal gestures to the American recruiting poster where we were told that "Uncle Sam Wants You" ("Warning! Our Homes Are in Danger Now!" poster, General Motors Corporation, 1942, National Archives, Powers of Persuasion.)

Often an image can speak more persuasively for a point of view than even the most eloquent prose. The images in Figure 5.3 were all advertisements. You do not need to be able to read the words to understand the message. There is the gruesome death from cigarettes advertisement, the seductive child, the dangerous looking dark man, and two old favorites—doctors recommending cigarettes and the hard working wife who takes "pep" for vitamins. Cognitive psychologists know that we have very good picture memory—a fact that is exploited in these advertisements. Oftentimes we do not scrutinize the images that bombard us with the same care that we use for verbal arguments. Pay attention to the images you encounter throughout the day and consider how each is influencing what and how

Figure 5.3 Visual images can make arguments. You don't need to be able to read the language to recognize the gruesome face of death due to cigarettes. Other images show the use of stereotypes to sell something—the sexualization of children to sell products, doctors to sell cigarettes, "dark" men who are dangerous, and the oldie, but goodie image of the happy wife who takes "Pep" vitamins. (Anti-smoking advertisement appears courtesy of the Department of Health, the Government of the Hong Kong Special Administrative Region.)

you think. These images are often used as nonverbal communication that reinforces stereotypes, and they are so ubiquitous that we often take them for granted. Look at and think about the images you see. Are some groups usually depicted in menial jobs on television or in advertisements? Who is used to display high fashion and who is depicted in warnings about criminal activity? It is only when you become consciously aware of the images you are viewing that you can think critically about the visual arguments you are receiving.

How to Change Beliefs

We are constantly surrounded by individuals and groups who want to change what we think and how we act. Nearly every social interaction involves persuasion. Advertising agencies want us to buy whatever product they are selling; political candidates want our votes; the beef council wants us to eat more beef. The list is endless. Some of these beliefs and actions are beneficial, but others are not. One of the best ways to understand the dynamics of changing beliefs is to consider the issues from the perspective of someone who wants to change the beliefs of someone else. You can use this knowledge to change beliefs or to resist change. The following list is loosely adapted from a summary of the attitude change literature.

1. Provide a credible source for the information you are presenting. The source of information should be a person or agency with the necessary expertise in the field and who is independent with respect to the issue. Additional requirements for assessing the credibility of an information source are provided in this chapter.

2. Anticipate counterarguments, raise them, and provide counterexamples. This is a good technique when debating an issue before an audience. It can leave the opposition with few points to make. As you know, counterarguments weaken the support for a conclusion. This technique allows you to weaken the counterarguments.

3. Do not appear one-sided, especially when the audience may be predisposed to the opposite side. The willingness to use qualifiers and to consider counterarguments make your position appear more credible.

4. Be direct. Tell your audience what to believe. By explicitly stating the conclusion, you eliminate the possibility that the audience will arrive at a different conclusion or not "see" the support for the conclusion that you are advocating.

5. Encourage discussion and public commitment. These variables have not been discussed in this chapter, although they appear in other places in the book. The discussion allows the audience to generate reasons and to "own" them or view them as reasons that they provided. Public commitment is a powerful motivator. If someone signs a document or speaks in favor of a position, a host of psychological mechanisms are brought into play. It is a kind of a promise to believe or act in a certain way. A restaurant owner in Los Angeles has borrowed the technique of commitment. A big problem for many restaurants is the large number of people who make reservations and then neither show up for the reservation nor call to cancel it. In the past, when customers called to make reservations, they were told, "Please call if you have to cancel the reservations." Now, the person who takes the reservation asks, "Will you please call if you have to cancel the reservations?" The customer needs to make a commitment to call—and the simple act of committing seems to make a difference. The number of customers who do not cancel their reservations when they are not keeping them is greatly reduced. What a difference two words can make.

6. Repeat the conclusion and the reasons that support the conclusion several times. People prefer positions that are familiar to them. You can make the same points in several different ways. Repetition is a useful aid in recall. Thus, reasons that are easily remembered (i.e., more available in memory) are more readily used to assess the strength of an argument. (The potent effects of repeated exposure are presented in the chapter on decision making.)

7. Provide as many reasons to support the conclusion as is feasible. As you already know, one way to increase the strength of an argument is by increasing the number of reasons that support it.

8. The message should be easy to comprehend. People are negatively affected by messages they find incomprehensible.

9. You could use any of the 21 common fallacies presented in this chapter. But be wary, they are examples of unsound reasoning. If you want to persuade someone, your reasoning should be sound. Shoddy reasoning is detectable, and if detected, it could (and should) destroy your credibility.

10. Use vivid images that will be difficult to forget and be sure that they make your point.

Chapter Summary

- An argument is an attempt to convince the reader (or listener) that a particular conclusion is true based on the reasons presented.

- All arguments must have at least one conclusion and one premise (reason). Arguments may also have assumptions, qualifiers, and counterarguments.

- Arguments have structures that can be identified and diagrammed.

- Sound (good) arguments meet three criteria: the premises are acceptable and consistent; the premises provide support for the conclusion by being relevant to the conclusion and are sufficiently strong; and missing components of the argument (e.g., assumptions, counterarguments, qualifiers, premises, and rival conclusions) have been considered.

- When analyzing the strength of an argument, the amount of support each premise supplies to the conclusion is weighed along with the negative effects of counterarguments. Missing components are made explicit and are considered along with the stated components.

- It is often necessary to assess the credibility of a source of information when deciding on the acceptability of a premise. There are important differences between experts for issues of fact and experts for issues of value.

- People like to believe that their beliefs and actions are "reasoned"; however, most people are not sensitive to poor or weak reasoning. Unfortunately, there is a general preference for explanations that "make sense" over conclusions that are justified by available data. Critical thinkers need to understand the importance of data and value data-based conclusions.

- There is a widespread bias to assign greater importance to reasons that support a conclusion that we favor (my-side bias) than to reasons that run counter to a conclusion that we favor. This bias can be reduced by listing reasons and counterarguments and consciously deciding how strongly they support or run counter to a conclusion.

- A critical part of the analysis of arguments is the consideration of missing parts and misleading statements.

- Arguments of all sorts have been used to justify genocide and other versions of "ethnic cleansing." The techniques presented here could prevent future horrors if people are willing to invest the time and hard work in analyzing arguments.

- Twenty-one common techniques of propaganda were presented. Most can be categorized as types of unsound reasoning in which emotional appeals are often substituted for reasons.

- A distinction was made between the terms "opinion," "reasoned judgment," and "fact." An opinion is an unsupported statement of preference. Reasoned judgment is a belief that is based on the consideration of premises that support that belief. Facts have a verifiable true value. It is often difficult to discern the difference between these terms in real-life settings.

- Visual images are used to persuade. Strong images that are difficult to forget can support or refute a conclusion. They usually appeal to emotions and often use stereotypes to support the implied conclusion.

- The beliefs of others can be changed with sound and unsound reasoning. Beware of attempts to manipulate your beliefs with shoddy reasoning techniques.

The following skills for analyzing arguments were presented in this chapter. If you are unsure about how to use any of these skills, be sure to reread the section in which it is discussed.

- identifying arguments
- diagramming the structure of an argument
- evaluating premises for their acceptability
- examining the credibility of an information source
- determining the consistency, relevance to the conclusion, and adequacy in the way premises support a conclusion
- remembering to consider missing components by assuming a different perspective
- assessing the overall strength of an argument
- recognizing, labeling, and explaining what is wrong with each of the 21 fallacies that were presented
- recognizing differences between opinion, reasoned judgment, and fact
- understanding how visual arguments can be effective
- judging your own arguments for their strength.

Terms to Know

Check your understanding of the concepts presented in this chapter by reviewing their definitions. If you find that you are having difficulty with any term, be sure to reread the section where it is discussed.

Argument. An argument consists of one or more statements that are used to provide support for a conclusion.

Conclusion. The belief or statement that the writer or speaker is advocating. It is what the speaker wants you to do or believe.

Reasons. The bases for believing that a conclusion is true or probably true. Note: This word may be singular or plural as there may be one or more reasons for a conclusion. When we reason (singular only), we are following rules for determining whether an argument is sound.

Premises. The formal term for the statements that support a conclusion.

Premise Indicators. Key words that often (but not always) signal that the statement or statements that follow them are premises.

Conclusion Indicators. Key words that often (but not always) signal that the statement or statements that follow them are conclusions.

Assumptions. In an argument, an assumption is a statement for which no proof or evidence is offered. They may be stated or implied.

Subarguments. Arguments that are used to build the main argument in an extended passage.

Main Point. The principal argument in an extended passage.

Qualifier. A constraint or restriction on the conclusion.

Counterargument. Statements that refute or weaken a particular conclusion.

Statement. A phrase or sentence for which it makes sense to ask the question, "Is it true or false?" Questions, commands, and exclamations are *not* statements.

Convergent Structures. A type of argument in which two or more premises support the same conclusion.

Chained (or Linked) Structures. Argument types in which the conclusion of one subargument becomes the premise of a second argument.

Acceptable. A standard for assessing the quality of a premise. A premise is acceptable when it is true or when we can reasonably believe that it is true.

Consistent. A standard for assessing the quality of an argument. When the premises that support a conclusion are not contradictory, they are consistent.

Adequate Grounds. A standard for assessing the quality of an argument. Occurs when the premises provide good support for a conclusion.

Sound Argument. Meets three criteria: 1. Acceptable and consistent premises; 2. Premises are relevant and provide sufficient support for the conclusion; 3. Missing components are considered and evaluated.

Rationalizing. A biased analysis of an argument so that a preferred conclusion will be judged as acceptable or a nonpreferred conclusion will be judged as unacceptable. The process of rationalizing is usually not conscious.

Propaganda. Information presented by proselytizers of a doctrine or belief. It may distort the truth, alter evidence, and appeal to emotions. The objective is to get the reader or listener to endorse the belief.

Fallacies. Unsound reasoning techniques that are used to change how people think.

Guilt by Association. The fallacy of associating a position or person with an undesirable position or person in order to create a negative impression.

Virtue by Association. The fallacy of associating a position or person with a desirable position or person in order to create a favorable impression. Compare with guilt by association.

Arguments Against the Person. A form of propaganda that attacks the people who support a cause and not the cause itself.

Appeals to Pity. A fallacy that asks for your compassion instead of appealing to your reason.

Popularity. A fallacy in which the only reason for the conclusion is that it is endorsed by "everyone."

Testimonials. An appeal in which the sole support for a conclusion is someone's unsupported opinion.

False Dichotomy. An argument in which two possible conclusions or courses of action are presented when there are multiple other possibilities. (Also known as Black or White Fallacy.)

Card Stacking. A fallacy that omits important information that might support an unfavored view.

Appeals to Pride or Snobbery. The use of praise or flattery to get its recipient to agree with a position.

Circular Reasoning. An argument structure in which the premise is a restatement of the conclusion. If diagrammed, it would be a circle.

Slippery Slope. Counterargument for a conclusion in which the premise consists of the idea that because certain events lie along some continuum, it is not possible to take an action without affecting all the events on the continuum.

Continuum. Fallacy of the Continuum is the same as Slippery Slope.

Straw Person. A type of fallacy in which an opponent to a conclusion distorts the argument that supports the conclusion by substituting a weaker argument.

Appeals to Ignorance. An argument in which the premise involves something that is unknown.

Knowing the Unknowable. Fallacy in which numbers are provided for events that cannot be quantified.

False Cause. Fallacy in which one event is said to have caused the other because they occur together.

Put Downs. Belittling an opposing point of view so that it would be difficult for a listener to agree with it.

Appeals to Tradition. A fallacy that utilizes the reason that what already exists is best.

CHAPTER 6

THINKING AS HYPOTHESIS TESTING

Contents

Suppose that the following is true: You are seriously addicted to heroin and you have two choices of treatment programs.

Program #1: This program is run by former heroin addicts. Your therapist will be a recovered addict who is the same age as you. The literature about this program states that among those who stay with the program for at least one year, the success rate is very high (80%). One of the biggest advantages of this program is that your therapist knows what it's like to be seriously addicted and can offer you insights from his own recovery.

Program #2: The therapists in this program have studied the psychology and biology of heroin addiction. The success rate that they provide is much lower than that provided for Program #1 (30%), but the percentage of successes is based on everyone who enters treatment, not just those who are still using the program after one year. Your therapist has never been addicted to heroin, but has studied various treatment options.

This is an important decision for you. Which do you choose?

Understanding Hypothesis Testing

> Research is an intellectual approach to an unsolved problem, and its function is to seek the truth.
>
> —Paul D. Leedy (1981, p. 7)

Much of our thinking is like the scientific method of **hypothesis testing**. A **hypothesis** is usually a belief about a relationship between two or more variables. In order to understand the world around us, we accumulate observations, formulate beliefs or hypotheses (singular is hypothesis), and then observe if our hypotheses are confirmed or disconfirmed. Thus, hypothesis testing is one way of finding out about the "way the world works." Formulating hypotheses and making systematic observations that could confirm or disconfirm them is the same method that scientists use when they want to understand events in their academic domain. Thus, when thinking is done in this manner, it has much in common with the experimental methods used by scientists.

Explanation, Prediction, and Control

> Government policies—from teaching methods in schools to prison sentencing to taxation—would also benefit from more use of controlled experiments.
>
> —Timo Hannay (2012, p. 26)

There is a basic need to understand events in life. How many times have you asked yourself questions like, "Why did my good friends get divorced when they seemed perfect for each other?" or "How can we understand why the son of the U.S. Surgeon General, the chief doctor in the United States, is addicted to illegal drugs?" When we try to answer questions like these, we often function as an "intuitive scientist." Like the scientist, we have our own theories, which are explanations about the causes of social and physical events. It is important to be able to explain why people react in certain ways (e.g., He's a bigot. She's tired and cranky after work.), to predict the results of our actions (e.g., If I don't study, I'll fail. If I wear designer clothes, people will think I'm cool.), and to control some of the events in our environment (e.g., In order to get a good job in business, I'll have to do well in my accounting course.).

The goal of hypothesis testing is to make accurate predictions about the portion of the world we are dealing with (Holland, Holyoak, Nisbett, & Thagard, 1993). In order to survive and function with maximum efficiency, we must reduce the uncertainty in our environment. One way to reduce uncertainty is to observe sequences of events with the goal of determining *predictive* relationships. Children, for example, may learn that an adult will appear whenever they cry; your dog may learn that when he stands near the kitchen door, you will let him out; and teenagers may learn that their parents will become angry when they come home late. These are important predictive relationships because they reduce the uncertainty in the environment and allow us to exercise some control over our lives. The process that we use in determining these relationships is the same one that is used when medical researchers discover that cancer patients will go into remission following chemotherapy or that longevity is associated with certain life styles. Because the processes are the same, some of the technical concepts in scientific methods are applicable to practical everyday thought.

Inductive and Deductive Methods

> Inductive reasoning is a major aspect of cognitive development and plays an important role in both the development of a system of logical thought processes and in the acquisition of new information.
> —James Pellegrino and Susan Goldman (1984, p. 143)

Sometimes a distinction is made between inductive and deductive methods of hypothesis testing (see the chapter on reasoning skills). In the **inductive method**, you observe events and then devise a hypothesis about the events you observed. For example, you might notice that Armaund, a retired man whom you know, likes to watch wrestling on television. Then you note that Minnie and Sue Ann, who are retired older-adults, also like to watch wrestling on television. On the basis of these observations, you would hypothesize (invent a hypothesis or explanation) that older people like to watch wrestling. In this way, you would work from your observations to your hypothesis. The inductive method is sometimes described as "going from the specific to the general." In a classic book entitled *Induction* (Holland et al., 1986), the authors argue that the inductive process is the primary way in which we learn about the nature of the world. As explained in Chapter 5, with inductive reasoning, if your premises are true and the reasoning is valid, then you can decide that the conclusion is probably correct. So, for example, if you are a juror, you can decide "beyond a reasonable doubt" that the defendant is guilty, or using the example just given, that older people like to watch wrestling. By contrast, with deductive methods, if the premises are true and the syllogism is valid, then the conclusion must be true.

Although a distinction is usually made between inductive and deductive reasoning, in real life they are just different phases of the hypothesis-testing method. Often people observe events, formulate hypotheses, observe events again, reformulate hypotheses, and collect even more observations. The question of whether the observations or the hypothesis comes first is moot because our hypotheses determine what we choose to observe, and our observations determine what our hypotheses will be. It is like the perennial question of which came first, the chicken or the egg. Each process is dependent on the other for its existence. In this way, observing and hypothesizing recycle, with the observations changing the hypotheses and the hypotheses changing what gets observed.

If you are a Sherlock Holmes fan, you will recognize this process as one that was developed into a fine art by this fictional detective. He would astutely note clues about potential suspects. For example, Sherlock Holmes could remember that the butler had a small mustard-yellow stain on his pants when it is well known that you don't serve mustard with wild goose, which was the main course at dinner that evening. He would use such clues to devise hypotheses like, "the butler must have been in the field where wild mustard plants grow." The master sleuth would then check for other clues that would be consistent or inconsistent with this hypothesis. He might check the butler's boots for traces of the red clay soil that surrounds the field in question. After a circuitous route of hypotheses and observations, Sherlock Holmes would announce, "The butler did it." When called on to explain how he reached his conclusion, he would utter his most famous reply, "It's elementary, my dear Watson."

Many of our beliefs about the world were obtained with the use of inductive and deductive methods, much like the great Sherlock Holmes. We use the principles of inductive and deductive reasoning to generate and evaluate beliefs. Holmes was invariably right in the conclusions he drew. Unfortunately, it is only in the realm of fiction that mistakes are never made because conclusions that result from inductive reasoning can never be known with absolute certainty. Let's examine the components of the hypothesis testing process to see where mistakes can occur.

Operational Definitions

> Scientific reasoning and everyday reasoning both require evidence-based justification of beliefs, or the coordination of theory and evidence.
> —Deanna Kuhn (1993, p. 74)

An **operational definition** tells us how to recognize and measure a concept. For example, if you believe that successful women are paid high salaries, then you will have to define "successful" and "high salary" in ways that will allow you to identify who is successful and who receives a high salary. If you have already read the chapter "The Relationship between Thought and Language" (Chapter 3), then you should recognize the need for operational definitions as being the same as the problem of vagueness. You would need to provide some statement like, "Successful individuals are respected by their peers and are famous in their field of work." You will find that it is frequently difficult to provide good operational definitions for terms. I can think of several people who are not at all famous, but who are successful by their own and other definitions. If you used the operational definition that requires fame as a component of success, then you would conclude that homemakers, skilled crafts people, teachers, nurses, and others could not be "successful" based on this definition. Thus, this would seem to be an unsatisfactory operational definition. Suppose, for purposes of illustration, that this is our operational definition to classify people into "successful" and "unsuccessful" categories.

How would you operationally define "paid a high salary?" Suppose you decided on "earns at least $2,000 per week." Once these terms are operationally defined, you could go around finding out whether successful and unsuccessful women differ in how much they are paid. Operational definitions are important. Whenever you hear people talking about "our irresponsible youth," "knee-jerk liberals," "bleeding hearts," "red-necks," "reactionaries," "fascists," or "feminists," ask them to define their terms operationally. You may find that the impact of their argument is diminished when they are required to be precise about their terms.

Many arguments hinge on operational definitions. For example, consider the debate over whether homosexuality is a mental disorder. The issue turns on the answer to operational definitions. What defines a "mental disorder?" Who gets to decide how "mental disorder" should be defined? Does homosexuality possess the defining characteristics of a mental disorder? The vitriolic arguments about whether abortion is murder can be transformed into calmer arguments over what is the appropriate definition of murder, and again the more important question of who is the right authority to define what constitutes murder. Thus, with critical thinking, explosive divisions over issues like abortion will not be resolved, but they will be changed in their character as people consider what is really being argued about. Although most people tend to think that topics like the need for operational definitions are only relevant when discussing research, in fact, these topics are useful everyday thinking skills. Consider this example from a computerized learning game (Halpern et al., 2012): Imagine how you would respond to "My roommate and I got into an argument yesterday over who was more influential on hip hop: James Brown or Stevie Wonder." You might respond, "You know, you could have resolved the argument by using what scientists call an operational definition." When you use operational definitions, you avoid the problems of ambiguity and vagueness. Try, for example, to write operational definitions for the following terms: love, prejudice, motivation, good grades, sickness, athletic, beautiful, and maturity.

Independent and Dependent Variables

> Psychologists have been making the case for the 'nothing special' view of scientific thinking for many years.
>
> —David Klahr and Herbert Simon (2001, p. 76)

A **variable** is any measurable characteristic that can take on more than one value. Examples of variables are gender (female and male), height, political affiliation (Republican, Democrat, Communist, etc.), handedness (right, left, ambidextrous), and attitudes towards traditional sex roles (could range from extremely negative to extremely positive). When we test hypotheses, we begin by choosing the variables of interest.

In the opening scenario of this chapter, you were asked to determine which of the two programs would more likely help you kick your heroin habit. In this example, there are two variables—type of treatment, which is the **independent variable**, or the one that is under your control (Program #1 and Program #2) and recovery, which is the **dependent variable** or the one that you believe will change as a result of the different treatments—you will either (a) recover from the addiction, or (b) you will not recover from it. You want to select the program that is more likely to help you to recover. In the jargon of hypothesis testing, you want to know which level of the independent variable will have a beneficial effect on the dependent variable.

The next step in the hypothesis-testing process is to define the variables operationally. Suppose we decide to define "recovery" as staying drug-free for at least two years and "not recovering" as staying drug-free for less than two years, which would include never being drug-free. It is important to think critically about operational definitions for your variables. If they are not stated in precise terms, the conclusions you draw from your study may be wrong.

Measurement Sensitivity

When we measure something, we systematically assign a number to it for the purposes of quantification. Someone who is taller than you are is assigned a higher number of inches of height than you are. If not, the concept of height would be meaningless.

When we think as scientists and collect information in order to understand the world, we need to consider how we measure our variables. For example, suppose you believe that love is like a fever, and that people in love have fever-like symptoms. To find out if this is true, you could conduct an experiment, taking temperatures from people who are in love and comparing your results to the temperatures of people who are not in love. How will you measure temperature? Suppose that you decide to use temperature headbands that register body temperature with a band placed on the forehead. Suppose further that these bands measure temperature to the nearest degree (e.g., 98°, 99°, 100°, etc.). If being in love does raise your body temperature, but only raises it one-half of a degree, you might never know this if you used headband thermometers. Headband thermometers just wouldn't be sensitive enough to register the small increment in body temperature. You would incorrectly conclude that love doesn't raise body temperatures, when in fact it may have. As far as I know, this experiment has never been done, but it is illustrative of the need for sensitive measurement in this and similar situations.

Populations and Samples

> People make innumerable decisions daily about other people that affect their lives and careers. These decisions are inevitably fraught with errors of judgment that reflect ignorance, personal biases, or stereotypes. . . .
> —W. Grant Dahlstrom (1993, p. 393)

In deciding which heroin treatment program to enter, or for that matter, which college to attend or which job to accept, you are making a bet about the future, which necessarily involves uncertainty. Hypothesis testing principles are used to reduce uncertainty. We cannot eliminate uncertainty, but we can use the principles of hypothesis testing to help us make the best choice. In the example at the beginning of the chapter, you would have to examine and evaluate information about the success rate of both programs. You would then use this information to make your decision.

The group that we want to know about is called a **population**. Since we obviously cannot study every heroin addict to determine which program has more successes, we need to study a subset of this population. A subset of a population is called a **sample**. In this example, all of the people who entered each of the programs constitute the sample.

Biased and Unbiased Samples

> Self-selected samples are not much more informative than a list of correct predictions by a psychic.
> —John Allen Paulos (2001, p. 152)

We want our sample to be representative of our population. To be representative, the addicts in our sample would need to be both female and male, from all socioeconomic levels, all intellectual levels, rural and urban areas, and so on, assuming that heroin addicts come from all of these demographic groups. We need **representative samples** so that we can generalize our results and decide, on average, that one program is more successful than the other. **Generalization** refers to using the results obtained with a sample to infer that similar results would be obtained from the population if everyone in the population had been measured. Generalizations are valid only if the sample is representative of the population.

What happens when the sample is not representative of the population? Suppose that one program is very expensive and one is county-run to serve the poor. These are examples of **biased samples**. Because they are not representative or unbiased, you could not use these samples to draw conclusions about the population of all heroin addicts. Far too often, mistakes occur because a sample was biased. One of the biggest fiascoes in sampling history probably occurred in 1936 when the *Literary Digest* mailed over 10 million straw ballots to people's homes in order to predict the winner of the presidential election that was to be held that year. The results from this large sample were clear-cut: The next president would be Alf Landon. What, you don't remember learning about U.S. President Landon? I am sure that you do not because Franklin Delano Roosevelt was elected president of the United States that year. What went wrong? The problem was in how the *Literary Digest* sampled voters. They mailed ballots to subscribers to their literary magazine, to people listed in the phone book, and to automobile owners. Remember, this was 1936, and only the affluent belonged to the select group of people who subscribed to literary magazines, or had phones, or owned automobiles. They failed to sample the large number of poorer voters, many of whom voted for Roosevelt, not Landon. Because of biased sampling, they could not generalize their results to the voting patterns of the population. Even though they sampled a large number of voters, the results were wrong because they sampled in a biased way.

It is often not easy to recognize the profound effect that biased sampling can have on the information that we receive. For example, phone-in polls are very popular, probably because someone makes money from the phone calls. Suppose that a phone-in poll shows that 75% of the people who responded to a question about same-sex marriage were opposed to it. What can we conclude from this poll? Absolutely nothing! Polls of this sort are called "SLOPs," which stands for **S**elected **L**istener **O**pinion **P**olls and also describes their worth. Only people with extreme views on a topic will take the time and expense to call in their opinions. Even though these polls are usually preceded with warnings like "this is a nonscientific survey," the announcer then goes on to present meaningless results as though they could be used to gauge public opinion.

Another pitfall in sampling is the possibility of **confounding**. Confounds confuse the interpretation of results because their influence is not easily separated from the influence of the independent variable. Suppose that patients in the two hypothetical heroin treatment programs differ systematically in more than one way—that is, Program #1 provides peer counseling and the addicts in this program are very wealthy, while addicts in Program #2 get a different type of treatment and they are very poor—we cannot determine if any differences in recovery rate are due to the type of treatment or income levels of the patients. Because you cannot separate the effect of type of treatment and income, you could not use these results to decide which treatment is more successful.

Usually, scientists use **convenience samples**. They study a group of people who are readily available. The most frequently used subjects in psychology experiments are college students and rats. The extent to which you can generalize from these samples depends on the research question. If you want to understand how the human visual system works, college students should be useful as subjects, especially if you want to know about young, healthy eyes. If, on the other hand, you want to understand sex-role stereotyping or attitudes toward subsidized health insurance for the elderly, college students would not be a representative sample. In this case, you could only generalize the results you obtained to college students.

There has been much debate over the issue of establishing a voucher system as a means of paying for K–12 education, especially in my home state of California. As you may know, some people believe that education would improve if parents received vouchers in an amount that is equal to what the state pays to educate a child in the public schools. The parents could then use this voucher to select any school that they deemed best for their children. This is a complex issue as proponents argue that the competition would improve all schools, and opponents argue that wealthy parents would supplement the voucher and send their children to private schools, while the poor parents would have to use the vouchers at cheaper and inferior schools. I do not want to debate the issue of vouchers here, but I do want to repeat an advertisement that was continually seen during the pre-election period. It went something like this:

The public schools in California are doing a poor job at educating our children. Did you know that the California high school students score much lower than high school students from Mississippi on the college entrance examinations?

There are many ways the thinking in this advertisement could be criticized (including the obvious slur on the state of Mississippi), but for the purpose of this discussion, consider only the nature of the samples that are being compared. Only students who are planning on attending college take the college entrance examinations. A much greater proportion of high school students in California take these examinations than those in Mississippi. Although I do not know what the actual figures are, suppose that the top 40% of California high school graduates take these exams, but only the top 10% of Mississippi high school graduates take these exams. Can you see why you would expect Mississippi students to score higher because of the bias in sampling? There are other reasons why we might expect these results, which do not relate directly to the quality of education. California has many recent immigrants, which means many students whose English is not as good as that of native English speakers. This fact would also lower state-wide averages. Again, this is a sampling problem because comparable groups that differ only on the variable of interest (state in which education was obtained) are not being made. Of course, it is possible that students in Mississippi are getting a better education than those in California, but we cannot conclude this from these data.

Sample Size

> Given a thimbleful of facts, we rush to make generalizations as large as a tub.
>
> —Gordon Allport (1954, p. 8)

The number of subjects you include in your sample is called the **sample size**. Suppose that treatment Program #1 had six patients/participants and Program #2 had 10 patients/participants. Both of these numbers are too small to determine the success rate of the treatments. When scientists conduct experiments, they often use large numbers of subjects because the larger the sample size, the more confident they can be in generalizing the findings to the population. This principle is called the **law of large numbers**, and it is an important statistical law. If, for some reason, they cannot use a large number of subjects, they may need to be more cautious or conservative in the conclusions that they derive from their research. Although a discussion of the number of subjects needed in an experiment is beyond the scope of this book, it is important to keep in mind that for most everyday purposes, we cannot generalize about a population by observing how only a few people respond.

Suppose this happened to you:

> After months of deliberation over a new car purchase, you finally decided to buy the fuel-efficient Ford Focus. You found that both *Consumer Reports* and *Road and Track* magazines gave the Focus a good rating. It is priced within your budget, and you like its "sharp" appearance. On your way out the door to close the deal, you run into a close friend and tell her about your intended purchase. "A Focus!" she shrieks. "My brother-in-law bought one and it's a tin can. It's constantly breaking down on the freeway. He's had it towed so often that the rear tires need replacing."

What do you do?

Most people would have a difficult time completing the purchase because they are insufficiently sensitive to sample size issues. The national magazines presumably tested many cars before they determined their rating. Your friend's brother-in-law is a single subject. You should place greater confidence in results obtained with large samples than in results obtained with small samples (assuming that the "experiments" were equally good). Yet, many people find the testimonial of a single person, especially if it is someone they know, more persuasive than information gathered from a large sample, especially when there is preference for the results obtained from the small sample.

We tend to ignore the importance of having an adequately large sample size when we function as intuitive scientists. This is why testimonials are so very powerful in persuading people what to do and believe. However, testimonials are based on the experiences of only one person, and often that person is usually being paid to say that some product or purchase is good. I would like to dismiss testimonials and similar sorts of "evidence" as hog wash that no one would fall for, but I know differently. A family member spent over $300 in calls to psychics when struggling with decisions regarding her critically ill husband. This was money that she did not have for advice that was, at best, harmless, and, at worst, caused her to ignore the recommendations of the hospital staff. I later was told that psy-chics are not permitted to predict that anyone will die, so they gave her false hope, which made the death even more difficult to bear. I am telling you this true personal anecdote because I hope that it will be effective in causing you to think about the sort of evidence that you would need to spend hundreds of dollars for advice by a paid stranger who has no creden-tials or training in psychology or science.

Variability

> But all evolutionary biologists know that variation itself is nature's only irreducible essence. Variation is the hard reality, not a set of im-perfect measures for a central tendency. Means and medians are the abstractions.
>
> —Stephen Jay Gould (1985, para. 14)

The term **variability** is used to denote the fact that all people are not the same. Suppose that you know someone who "drank a six-pack" twice a day and lived to be 100 years old. Does this mean that the hype about the nega-tive effects of alcohol on health is wrong? Of course not! The effect of al-cohol on health was determined by numerous separate investigators using large numbers of subjects. Not everyone responds in the same way, or maintains the same opinion, or has the same abilities. It is important to remember the role of variability in understanding results. Our studies can tell us, with some probability, what is generally true, but there will be indi-viduals who do not conform to the usual pattern. There are people who drink heavily and live to a ripe old age, but this does not mean that the studies that show that heavy drinking causes many terminal illnesses are wrong. It just means that people are different.

There are many examples where people generalize inappropriately from small samples. In a tragic example, the teenage son of a prominent politi-cian in the United States committed suicide after taking a commonly pre-scribed acne medication. The family was absolutely convinced that the suicide was a result of depression caused by the drug, and they began an active campaign to get the drug taken off the market. In their view, their son had been a normal teen until he took the medication, and soon after taking the medication, he committed suicide. Large-scale studies did not support their belief that teens taking this drug were more likely to be de-pressed or commit suicide than similar teens not taking this drug.

However, for the family of this teen, their own tragic experience was far more convincing than data collected on thousands of teens.

People's willingness to believe that results obtained from a small sample can be generalized to the entire population is called the **law of small numbers** (Tversky & Kahneman, 1974). In fact, we should be more confident when predicting to or from large samples than small samples. In an experimental investigation of this phenomenon (Quattrone & Jones, 1980), college students demonstrated their belief that if one member of a group made a particular decision, then the other members of that group would make the same decision. This result was especially strong when the college students were observing the decisions of students from other colleges. Thus, it is easy to see how a belief in the law of small numbers can maintain prejudices and stereotypes. We tend to believe that the actions of a single group member are indicative of the actions of the entire group. Have you ever heard someone say, "_____'s (fill in your group) are all alike."? An acquaintance once told me that all Jamaicans are sneaky thieves. She came to this conclusion after having one bad experience with a person from Jamaica. Expressions like this one are manifestations of the law of small numbers. Can you see how the law of small numbers can also explain the origin of many prejudices like racism? A single memorable event involving a member of a group with which we have little contact can color our beliefs about the other members of that group. Generally, when you collect observations about people and events, it is important to collect a large number of observations before you reach a conclusion.

There is one exception to the general principle that we need large samples in order to make valid generalizations about a population. The one exception occurs when everyone in the population is exactly the same. If, for example, everyone in the population of interest responded exactly the same way to any question (e.g., Do you approve of the death penalty?) or any treatment (e.g., had no "heart attacks" when treated with a single aspirin), then sample size would no longer be an issue. Of course, all people are not the same. You may be thinking that this was a fairly dumb statement because everyone knows that people are different. Unfortunately, research has shown that most of us tend to underestimate the variability of groups with which we are unfamiliar.

Minorities who are members of any group often report that the leader or other group members will turn to them and ask, "What do African Americans (or women, or Hispanics, or Asians, or whatever the minority is) think about this issue?" It is as though the rest of the group believes that the few minority members of their group can speak for the minority group as a whole. This is a manifestation of the belief that groups other than the ones to which we belong are much more homogeneous (less variable) than the groups to which we belong. The ability to make accurate predictions depends, in part, on the ability to make accurate assessments of variability. It is important to keep the concept of variability in mind whenever you are testing hypotheses, either formally in a research setting, or informally as you try to determine relationships in everyday life.

Science versus Science Fiction

Science is a method for understanding; it is a way of "knowing" about the world. Data (or evidence) are at the heart of the scientific method but not just "any old" data or evidence—data or evidence that were collected under controlled conditions, data that can be openly scrutinized, and data that can be replicated. Consider, for example, the hypothesis that there are psychics who can accurately predict future events. What sort of data or evidence would convince you that at least some people have psychic powers?

Amazing and Not True

I have been told by believers in psychics that they have good data—a psychic made amazingly true predictions about their lives. Testimonials by one or even several people are offered as evidence that psychics exist. Believers claim that they "know" psychics have true powers because they "saw it with their own eyes." (If you have already read the chapter on memory, then you know that eye witness testimony can be highly inaccurate, an important fact, but not the main point in this discussion.) I like to remind them that they also saw Mr. Ed, the talking horse who had his own television show and a talking pig in the children's classic move *Babe*, just to name two examples; do they believe that there are horses and pigs that can talk?

I like to begin my college classes in critical thinking by demonstrating my own amazing psychic powers. Each semester, before the start of the first class, I check my class roster and then look up some of the students in the university records. The records include date of birth and sometimes information about siblings (if they are also students), so I can determine the astrological sign and some family information for the students enrolled in my class. I then amaze students by asking a series of questions that lead up to my ability to name students I have never met and tell them their astrological sign and some family information. (Let's see—I am getting the feeling that you are a Taurus. Your name—don't tell me—it's something like Jean or Jane, no wait, it's Jackie, isn't it? I also see a family picture with a younger sister in it. Is that correct? And her name is Latisha, right? And so on.) It is really an easy trick; yet, students wonder how I was able to know so much about people I have never met. The fact that I could tell students their name, astrological sign, and other information might look like evidence in support of psychic phenomena, and without appropriate controls, it is a very easy trick.

Cold Reading

There are many people who claim to be psychics or clairvoyants—some even claim to be able to speak with the dead. I think we can all understand the pain of grieving relatives who really want to believe that they can talk to the dead. Televised shows have sometimes shown a portion of the séance or session with the dead. Typically, viewers will see only a few minutes of a session that may last for several hours—usually a portion where the psychic made a successful prediction like, "the person you are trying to contact—is it a parent?" What we do not see is the many instances where questions like this one are incorrect. As explained earlier, James Randi has offered a $1,000,000 challenge to anyone who, "under proper observing conditions," can show evidence of "paranormal, supernatural, or occult power." The Australian Skeptics Society also offers a cash prize of $100,000 for any proven demonstration of psychic powers. No one has collected either of these two prizes. Ray Hyman, a psychologist who studies ways to debunk psychics, explains how they "read" your mind, "speak with the dead," and other similar shows. The technique is called "cold reading." The psychic relies on body language and basic statistical information (e.g., common boys' names that start with a known letter). He offers these 13 points for amazing your own friends with cold reading (Hyman, 1977):

1. Look confident—act as though you believe in what you are doing.

2. Use polls, surveys, and statistical abstracts—predict attitudes from a person's educational level and religion.

3. Stage the reading—make no excessive claims; be modest.

4. Gain the subject's cooperation—make the subject try to find truth in what you say.

5. Use a gimmick—crystal balls and palm reading are good.

6. Have a list of stock phrases available—there are fortune telling and other manuals that have lots of good ones.

7. Use your eyes—observe clothing, jewelry, speech—, these can be good hints.

8. Fish—get the subject to tell about him or herself.

9. Listen—subjects want to talk about themselves.

10. Be dramatic—ham it up for effect.

11. Pretend to know more than you are saying—subject will assume you do.

12. Flatter the subject—people love flattery.

13. Always tell the subject what she or he wants to hear.

Hyman also suggests some "stock Spiels" that make a plausible case for your ability to "read" people. For example, here is one suggestion.

> Does it accurately reflect your personality? Some of your aspirations tend to be pretty unrealistic. At times you are extroverted, affable, and sociable, while at other times you are introverted, wary, and reserved. You have found it unwise to be too frank in revealing yourself to others. You pride yourself on being an independent thinker and do not accept others' opinions without satisfactory proof. You prefer a certain amount of change and variety and become dissatisfied when hemmed in by restrictions and limitations. At times you have serious doubts as to whether you have made the right decision or done the right thing. Disciplined and controlled on the outside, you tend to be worrisome and insecure on the inside.

People who talk to the dead, read palms or tea leaves (pattern of tea leaves left in a cup after you drink from it), and have visited beings from other planets use similar methods when providing evidence of their unusual abilities. Remember, just because it looks like someone has made a rabbit appear from the inside of a hat does NOT mean that is what really happened. Magic tricks and science fiction can be great fun, but they are not substitutes for critical thinking. If there is only one goal that I could have for readers of this book, it is that you come to value data and evidence for the purpose of making sound decisions. It may be the most critical part of critical thinking.

Determining Cause

- Do you believe that children who are neglected become teenage delinquents?
- Does jogging relieve depression?
- Will a diet that is low in fat increase longevity?
- Do clothes make the man?
- Will strong spiritual beliefs give you peace of mind?
- Does critical thinking instruction improve how you think outside the classroom?

All of these questions concern a causal relationship in which one variable (e.g., neglect) is believed to cause another variable (e.g., delinquency). What sort of information do we need to determine the truth of causal relationships?

Isolation and Control of Variables

Stop and think for a minute about the way you would go about deciding if neglecting children causes them to become delinquent when they are teenagers. You could decide to conduct a long-term study in which you would divide children into groups—telling some of their parents to cater to their every need, others to neglect them occasionally, and still others to neglect their children totally. You could require everyone to remain in their groups, catering to or neglecting their children as instructed until the children reach their teen years, at which time you could count up the number of children in each group who became delinquents. Remember, of course, that you would have to define operationally the term "delinquent." This would be a good, although totally unrealistic, way to decide if neglect causes delinquency. It is a good way because this method would allow you to control how much neglect each child received and to isolate the cause of delinquency, as this would be the only systematic difference among the people in each group. It is unrealistic to the point of being ludicrous, because very few people would comply with your request to cater to or neglect their children. Furthermore, it would also be unethical to ask people to engage in potentially harmful behaviors.

In some experimental settings, it is possible to isolate and control the variables that interest you. If you wanted to know if grading students for course work will make college students work harder and therefore learn more, you could randomly assign college students to different grading conditions. Half the students could be graded as pass or fail (no letter grades), while the other students would receive traditional letter grades (A, B, C, D, or F). At the end of the semester, all students would take the same final exam. If the average final exam scores of the students who received grades were statistically significantly higher than of the students in the pass/fail condition, we could conclude that grades do result in greater learning. (See the chapter on probability for a discussion of significant differences.)

Can you see why it is so important to be able to assign students at random to either the graded or pass/fail conditions instead of just letting them pick the type of grading they want? It is possible that the students who would pick the pass/fail grading are less motivated or less intelligent than the students who would prefer to get grades or vice versa. If the students could pick their own grading condition, we would not know if the differences we found were due to the differences in grading practices, due to differences in motivation or intelligence, or due to some other variable that differs systematically as a function of which grading condition the students select. If we cannot use random assignment, then we usually cannot make any causal claims.

Let's return to the question of whether child neglect causes delinquency. Given the constraint that you cannot tell parents to neglect their children, how would you go about deciding if child neglect causes delinquency? You could decide to find a group of parents and ask each about the amount of care he or she gives to each child. Suppose you found that, in general, the more that children are neglected, the more likely they are to become teenage delinquents. Because you lost control over your variables by not assigning parents to catering and neglecting groups, it is not possible, on the basis of this experiment alone, to conclude that neglect causes delinquency. It is possible that parents who neglect their children differ from caring parents in other ways. Parents who tend to neglect their children may also encourage drug use, or engage in other life style activities that contribute to the development of teenage delinquency. A point that is made in several places in this book is that just because two variables occur together (in this example, neglect and delinquency), it does not necessarily mean that one *caused* the other to occur.

Three-Stage Experimental Designs

When researchers want to be able to make strong causal claims, they use a three-stage experimental design. An experimental design is a plan for how observations will be made.

1. The first stage involves creating different groups that are going to be studied. In the example about the effect of pass/fail grading on how much is learned, the two groups would be those who receive a letter grade and those who receive a grade of either "pass" or "fail." It is important that the two groups differ systematically only on this dimension. You would not want all the students in the letter grade group to take classes taught by Professor Longwinded while those in the pass/fail group take classes taught by Professor Mumbles. One professor may be a better teacher, and students may learn more in one condition than the other because of this confounding variable. One way to avoid this confound is to assign half of the students in each class to each grading condition with the assignment of students to either group done at random. Strong causal claims will involve equating the groups at the outset of the experiment. *The random assignment of subjects to groups is essential in discovering cause and effect.*

2. The second stage involves the application of the "experimental treatment." If we were conducting a drug study, one group would receive the drug, and the other group would not receive the drug. Usually, the "nondrug" group would receive a placebo, which would look and/ or taste like the drug, but would be chemically inert. The reason for using a placebo is to avoid any effects of subjects' beliefs or expectancies. We know that placebos can have positive effects on a variety of symptoms (Bishop, Jacobson, Shaw, & Kaptchuk, 2012.) The topic of expectancies and the way they can bias results is discussed later in this chapter.

3. Evaluation is the final phase. Measurements are taken and two (or more) groups are compared on some outcome measure. In the grading example, final examination scores for students in the letter grade group would be compared to the scores of students in the pass/fail group. If students in the graded group performed significantly better than the students in the other group, then we would have strong support for the claim that one grading method *caused* students to study harder and learn more than the other.

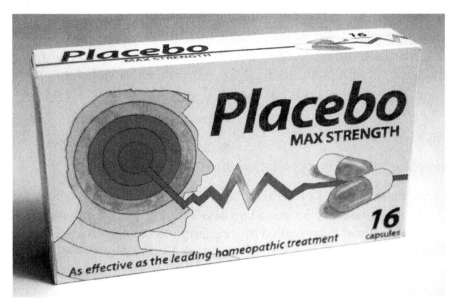

Figure 6.1 A real advertisement for a placebo, including its sole ingredient which is sugar and the (puzzling) additional fact that it is "not for human consumption." (http://www.etsy.com/listing/99763771/placebo-max-strength, with permission by Darren Cullen)

Of course, we are not always able to equate groups at the outset and randomly assign subjects to groups, but when we can, results can be used to make stronger causal claims than in less controlled conditions.

Consider this hypothetical example:

> Researchers at Snooty University have studied the causes of divorce. They found that 33% of recently divorced couples reported that they had serious disagreements over money during the two-year period that preceded the divorce. The researchers concluded that disagreements over money are a major reason why couples get divorced. They go on to suggest that couples should learn to handle money disagreements as a way of reducing the divorce rate.

What, if anything, is wrong with this "line of reasoning"? Plenty. First, we have no data from a comparison group that did not divorce (i.e., no control group). Maybe 33% of all families disagree about money; maybe the number is even higher in families that stay together. Second, there is no reason to believe that disagreements over money *caused* or even contributed to divorce. Maybe couples in the process of breaking-up disagree more about everything. Third, there is the problem of retrospective review, a topic that is discussed in the next section. Studies like this one are found everywhere from radio talk shows, to news reports, to scientific journals, and to people's casual examinations of life. If you rely on the principles of hypothesis testing to interpret findings like this one, you are less likely to be bamboozled.

Using the Principles of Isolation and Control

In an earlier chapter, I presented Piaget's notion that people who have attained the highest level of cognitive development can reason about hypothetical situations. Piaget called the highest level of cognitive development the Formal Stage of thought. He developed several different tasks that could be used to identify people who could think at this level. If you already read Chapter 4, then you will recall the "combinatorial reasoning" task devised by Piaget. It required a planful and orderly procedure for combining objects. Another one of Piaget's tasks involved using the principles of isolation and control that are integral to hypothesis testing. Try this task.

Bending Rods: This task is to determine which of several variables affects the flexibility of rods. Imagine that you are given a long vertical bar with 12 rods hanging from it. Each rod is made of brass, copper, or steel. The rods come in two lengths and two thicknesses. Your task is to find which of the variables (material, length, or thickness) influence how much the rods will bend. You can test this by pressing down on each rod to see how much it bends. You may perform as many comparisons as you like until you can explain what factors are important in determining flexibility. It may help you to visualize the set up as presented in Figure 6.2.

What do you need to do to prove that length, or diameter, or the material the rods are constructed from or some combination of these variables is important in determining flexibility? Stop now and write out your answer to this problem. Do not go on until you have finished this problem.

Bending Rods: How did you go about exploring the effect of length, diameter, and material on rod flexibility? In order to solve this problem, you had to consider the possible factors that contribute to rod flexibility and then systematically hold constant all of the variables except one. This is a basic concept in experimental methods. If you wanted to know if material

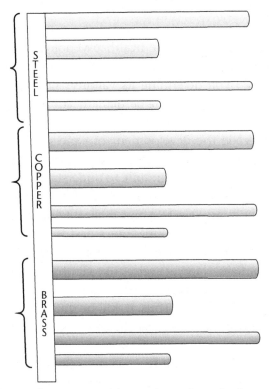

Figure 6.2 Bending rods. How would you determine whether material, length, or thickness affects rod flexibility?

was an important factor, which rods would you test? You would bend a brass rod, a copper rod, and a steel rod of the same length and diameter. This would hold constant the length and diameter variables while testing the material variable. Some possible tests of this would be to compare flexibility between the short and wide brass, copper, and steel rods. Similarly, if you wanted to find out if length is important, you would bend a short and a long rod of the same diameter that was constructed with the same material. An example of this would be to compare the short and wide copper rod with the long and wide copper rod.

How would you decide if diameter influences rod flexibility? By now it should be clear that you would compare two rods of the same material and length and different diameters. You could test this by bending a short and wide steel rod with a short and thin steel rod. Thus, you should be able to recognize that the same principles used in hypothesis testing were needed in this task and be able to apply them correctly in order to solve this seemingly unrelated problem.

Prospective and Retrospective Research

Consider a medical example: Some health psychologists believe that certain stressful experiences can cause people to develop cancer. If this were your hypothesis, how would you determine its validity? One way would be to ask cancer patients if they had anything particularly stressful happen to them just before they were diagnosed as having cancer. If the stress caused the cancer, it would have to precede the development of cancer. When experiments are conducted in this manner, they are called **retrospective experiments**. Retrospective experiments look back in time to understand causes for later events. There are many problems with this sort of research. As discussed in the memory chapter, memories are selective and malleable. It is possible that knowledge of one's cancer will change how one's past is remembered. Moderately stressful events like receiving a poor grade in a college course may be remembered as being traumatic. Happier events, like getting a raise, may be forgotten. It is even possible that the early stages of the cancer were causing stress instead of the stress causing the cancer. Thus, it will be difficult to determine if stress causes cancer from retrospective research.

A better method for understanding causative relationships is **prospective research**. In prospective research, you identify possible causative factors when they occur and then look forward in time to see if the hypothesized result occurs. In a prospective study, you would have many people record stressful life events when they occur (e.g., death of a spouse, imprisonment, loss of a job) and then see which people develop cancer. If the people who experience more stressful events are more likely to develop cancer, this result would provide support for your hypothesis.

Most of the research we conduct as intuitive scientists is retrospective. We often seek explanations for events after they have occurred. How many times have you tried to understand why a seemingly angelic child committed a serious crime, or why a star rookie seems to be losing his touch, or why the underdog in a political race won? Our retrospective attempts at explanations are biased by selective memories and lack of systematic observations. (See the section on hindsight in the decision-making skills chapter for a related discussion.)

Correlation and Cause

> The process by which children turn experience into knowledge is exactly the same, point for point, as the process by which those whom we call scientists make scientific knowledge.
>
> —John Holt (1964, p. 93)

What you are about to read is absolutely true: As the weight of children increases, so does the number of items that they are likely to get correct on standardized tests of intelligence. In other words, heavier children answer more questions correctly than lighter ones. Before you start stuffing mashed potatoes into your children in an attempt to make them smarter, stop and think about what this means. Does it mean that gaining weight will make children smarter? Certainly not! Children get heavier as they get older, and older children answer more questions correctly than younger ones.

In this example, the variables weight and number of questions answered correctly are related. An increase in one variable is associated with an increase in the other variable—as weight increases the number of questions answered correctly concomitantly increases. **Correlated variables** are two or more variables that are related. If you've already read the previous chapter on analyzing arguments, then you should recognize this concept as the Fallacy of False Cause.

People frequently confuse correlation with causation. Consider the following example: Wally and Bob were arguing about the inheritance of intelligence. Wally thought about everyone he knew and concluded that since smart parents tend to have smart children, and dumb parents tend to have dumb children, intelligence is therefore an inherited characteristic. Bob disagreed with Wally's line of reasoning, although he concurred with the facts that Wally presented. He agreed that if the parents score high on intelligence tests, then their children will also tend to score high, and if the parents score low on intelligence tests, then their children will also tend to score low. When two measures are related in this way, that is they tend to rise and fall together, they have a **positive correlation**. Although parents' intelligence and their children's intelligence are positively correlated, we cannot infer that parents caused their children (through inheritance or any other means) to be intelligent. It is possible that children affect the intelligence of their parents, or that both are being affected by a third variable that has not been considered. It is possible that diet, economic class, or other life style variables determine intelligence levels, and since parents and children eat similar diets and have the same economic class, they tend to be similar in intelligence. In understanding the relationship between two correlated variables, it is possible that variable A caused the changes in variable B (A→B), or that variable B caused the changes in variable A (B→A), or that both A and B caused changes in each other (A→B and B→A), or that both were caused by a third variable C (C→A and C→B). Of course, it also possible that you found two variables that are related just by chance, and if you repeated the study, they would not be correlated.

Let's consider a different example. Many people have taken up jogging in the belief that it will help them to lose weight. The two variables in this example are exercise and weight. I have heard people argue that because there are no fat athletes (except perhaps sumo wrestlers), exercise must cause people to be thin. I hope that you can think critically about this claim. It does seem to be true that exercise and weight are correlated. People who tend to exercise a great deal also tend to be thin. This sort of correlation, in which the tendency to be high on one variable (exercise) is associated with the tendency to be low on the other variable (weight) is called a **negative correlation**. Let's think about the relationship between exercise and weight. There are several possibilities: (1) It is possible that exercise causes people to be thin; or (2) It is possible that people who are thin tend to exercise more because it is more enjoyable to engage in exercise when you are thin; or (3) It is possible that a third variable, like concern for one's health, or some inherited trait, is responsible for both the tendency to exercise and the tendency to be thin. Perhaps there are inherited body types that naturally stay thin and also are graced with strong muscles that are well suited for exercise.

If you wanted to test the hypothesis that exercise causes people to lose weight, then you would use the three design stages described earlier. If the subjects who were assigned at random to the exercise group were thinner after the treatment period than those in a no-exercise condition, then you could make a strong causal claim for the benefits of exercise in controlling weight.

Actually, the question of causation is usually complex. It is probably more accurate to use the word "influence" instead of cause because there is usually more than a single variable that affects another variable. Recent

Dilbert by Scott Adams. Used with permission by Universal Press Syndicate.

research has found that when states decriminalize the use of marijuana, traffic fatalities are reduced (Anderson & Rees, 2011). How can that happen? According to the researchers, alcohol use decreases when marijuana is legally available, and it is the decrease in alcohol consumption that reduces traffic fatalities. In this example, Variable A, decriminalizing marijuana, caused a change in a third variable, alcohol consumption, and it was the third variable that influenced Variable B, the reduction in traffic fatalities.

Illusory Correlation

An amusing anecdote of attributing cause to events that occur together was presented by Munson (1976):

> A farmer was traveling with his wife on a train when he saw a man across the aisle take something out of a bag and begin eating it. "Say, Mister," he asked, "What's that thing you're eating?"
>
> "It's a banana," the man said, "Here, try one."
>
> The farmer took it, peeled it, and just as he swallowed the first bite, the train roared into a tunnel. "Don't eat any, Maude," he yelled to his wife. "It'll make you go blind!" (p. 277)

Do blondes really have more fun? A popular advertisement for hair dye would like you to believe that having blonde hair will cause you to have more fun. Many people believe that they see many blondes having fun; therefore, blondes have more fun than brunettes and redheads. The problem with this sort of observation is that there are many blondes who are not having "more fun" (a term badly in need of an operational definition) than brunettes, but because they are at home or in other places where you are unlikely to see them, they don't get considered. The term **illusory correlation** refers to the erroneous belief that two variables are related when, in fact, they are not. Professionals and nonprofessionals alike maintain beliefs about relationships in the world. These beliefs guide the kinds of observations we make and how we determine if a relationship exists between two variables.

Validity

The **validity** of a measure is usually defined as the extent to which it measures what you want it to measure. If I wanted to measure intelligence and measured the length of your big toe, this would obviously be invalid. Other examples of validity are less obvious. A popular radio commercial touting the benefits of soup points out that tomato soup has more Vitamin A than eggs. This is true, but it is not a valid measure of the goodness of tomato soup. Eggs are not a good source of Vitamin A. Thus, the wrong comparisons were made, and the measure does not support the notion that soup is an excellent food. If you have already read the previous chapter "Analyzing Arguments," then you should realize that the claim that tomato soup has more Vitamin A than eggs does not support the conclusion that "soup is good food." It may well be true that soup is an excellent source of vitamins, but claims like this one do not support that conclusion.

Convergent Validity

When several different measures all converge onto the same conclusion, the measures are said to have **convergent validity**. If, for example, you wanted to measure charisma—the psychological trait that is something more than charm that people as diverse as Beyoncé, Justin Bieber, and Jennifer Lopez are said to possess—you would need convergent validity for your measure. People who scored high on your charisma test should also be the ones who are selected for leadership positions and have other personality traits that are usually associated with charisma. If the class wallflower scored high on your test of charisma, you would need to rethink the validity of your test.

Intuitive scientists also need to be mindful of the need for convergent validity. Before you decide that your classmate, Willa Mae, is shy because she hesitates to talk to you, you need to determine if she acts shy with other people in other places. If she frequently speaks up in class, you would not want to conclude that she is a shy person because this inconsistency in her behavior would signal a lack of convergent validity. The idea of convergent validity is very similar to the topic of convergent argument structures that was presented in the previous chapter. If you have already read the chapter "Analyzing Arguments", then you should recall that the strength of an argument is increased when many premises support (or converge on) a conclusion. This is exactly the same situation as when several sources of evidence support the same hypothesis. The language used in these two chapters is different (support for a conclusion versus support for a hypothesis), but the underlying ideas are the same: the more reasons or evidence we can provide for believing that something is true, the greater the confidence we can have in our belief.

Illusory Validity

> Everyone complains of his memory and no one complains of his judgment.
>
> —François La Rochefoucauld (1613–1680)

Both professionals and nonprofessionals place great confidence in their conclusions about most life events, even when their confidence is objectively unwarranted. Overconfidence in judgments is called **illusory validity**. In an experimental investigation of this phenomenon, Oskamp (1965) found that as clinicians were given more information about patients, they became more confident in the judgments they made about patients. What is interesting about this result is they were not more accurate in judgment, only more confident that they were right. Why do people place confidence in fallible judgments? There are several reasons why we persist in maintaining confidence in our judgments. A primary factor is the selective nature of memory. Consider this personal vignette: As a child, I would watch Philadelphia Phillies baseball games on television with my father. As each batter would step up to home plate, my father would excitedly yell, "He's going to hit a home run, I just know it!" Of course, he was usually wrong. (Phillies fans had to be tough in the 60s.) On the rare occasions when a Phillies batter actually did hit a home run, my father would talk about it for weeks. "Yep, I knew as soon as he stepped up to home plate that he would hit a home run. I can always tell just by looking at the batter." In this instance, and countless others, we selectively remember our successful judgments and forget our unsuccessful ones. This tends to bolster confidence in the judgments we make.

A second reason for the illusion of validity is the failure to seek or consider disconfirming evidence. (See the chapter on decision making for an additional discussion of this phenomenon.) This is the primary reason why people tend to believe that variables are correlated when they are not. Suppose that you have the job of personnel officer in a large corporation. Over a period of a year, you hire 100 new employees for your corporation. How would you go about deciding if you're making good (valid) hiring decisions? Most people would check on the performance of the 100 new employees. Suppose that you did this and found that 92% of the new employees were performing their jobs in a competent, professional manner. Would this bolster your confidence in your judgments? If you answered yes to this question, you forgot to consider disconfirming evidence. What about the people you didn't hire? Have most of them gone on to become Vice Presidents at

General Motors? If you found that 100% of the people you did not hire are superior employees at your competitor's corporation, you would have to revise your confidence in your judgmental ability.

Part of the reason that we fail to utilize disconfirming evidence is that it is often not available. Personnel officers do not have information about the employees they did not hire. Similarly, we do not know much about the person we chose not to date, or the course we did not take, or the house we did not buy. Thus, on the basis of partial information, we may conclude that our judgments are better than they objectively are.

In a scathing review of the Rorschach test, commonly known as the inkblot test because subjects are asked to tell what they see in amorphous, symmetrical blots of ink, Dawes (1994) concluded that it is not a valid measure of mental functioning. A recent review of the Rorschach arrived at the same conclusion (Wood, Nezworski, Lilienfeld, & Garbm, 2008). That is, there is no evidence that it is useful in diagnosing or treating mental disorders (although it is possible to determine if someone gives unusual answers). **This means that the Rorschach has no validity.** Despite these empirical results, Dawes reports that some psychotherapists respond to this fact with, "Yes, I know that it has no validity, but I find it useful." Do you see why this is a ridiculous statement? If it has no validity, then it cannot be useful. If therapists believe that it is useful, they are fooling themselves and demonstrating the phenomenon of illusory validity. It may seem useful because they interpret the responses in ways that they believe make sense, but its only real value is as a clear demonstration of the biases that we maintain.

Why do some psychologists continue to use projective tests when many reviews of the literature show that these tests are not valid? Most psychologists genuinely want to do a good job, and many believe that the tests are valid despite the lack of data to support that conclusion. They believe these tests are valid because they "feel or look right"—the results confirm what they believe to be true. Few people will cast aside their own sense of what is true for a mass of cold and impersonal data collected by and from people they don't know. In general, the scientific method is not valued when it conflicts with our personal belief system. Humans are ill-equipped to use data from large samples, perhaps because the only information that was available to us for most of the history of humankind came from personal experience or the second-hand personal experience of those we know. It is important that we use critical thinking skills for conclusions that we like and do not like.

Reliability

> Both law and science must weigh the reliability of evidence, the trustworthiness of experts, and the probability that something is true beyond a reasonable doubt.
>
> —K. C. Cole (1995, June 29, p. B2)

The **reliability** of a measure is the consistency with which it measures what it is supposed to measure. If you used a rubber ruler that could stretch or shrink to measure the top of your desk, you would probably get a different number each time you measured it. Of course, we want our measurements to be reliable.

Researchers in the social and physical sciences devote a great deal of time to the issue of reliable measurement. We say that an intelligence test, for example, is reliable when the same person obtains scores that are in the same general range whenever she takes the test. Few of us even consider reliability when we function as intuitive scientists. When we decide if a professor or student is prejudiced, we often rely on one or two samples of behavior without considering if the individual is being assessed reliably.

Thinking about Errors

> To a scientist a theory is something to be tested. He seeks not to defend his beliefs, but to improve them. He is, above everything else, an expert at changing his mind.
>
> —Wendell Johnson, p. 39 (1946)

When we try to understand relationships by devising and testing hypotheses, we will sometimes be wrong. This idea is expanded on more fully in the next chapter, which concerns understanding probabilities. For now, consider this possibility: Suppose that you drive into work every day with a friend. Every morning you stop at a drive-through window and buy coffee. You decide that, instead of hassling every morning with who will pay ("I'll get it—No, no let me"), he will flip a coin. When the outcome is heads, he will pay; when the outcome is tails, you will pay. Sounds fair enough, but on nine of the last ten days, the coin landed with tails up. Do you think that your friend is cheating?

The truth is that your friend is either cheating or he is not cheating. Unfortunately, you don't know which is true. Nevertheless, you need to make a decision. You will decide either that he is cheating or he is not cheating. Thus, there are four possibilities: (1) He is cheating, and you correctly decide that he is cheating; (2) He is not cheating, and you correctly decide that he is not cheating; (3) He is cheating, and you incorrectly decide that he is not cheating; and (4) He is not cheating, and you incorrectly decide that he is cheating. With these four possibilities, there are two ways that you can be right and two ways that you can be wrong. These four combinations are shown in Table 6.1.

As you can see from Table 6.1, there are two different ways that we can make errors in any hypothesis-testing situation. These two different errors are not equally "bad." It is far worse to decide that your friend is cheating when he is not (especially if you accuse him of cheating) than it is to decide that he is not cheating when he is. Thus, you would want stronger evidence to decide that he is cheating than you would want to decide that he is not cheating. In other words, you need to consider the relative "badness" of different errors when testing hypotheses.

If you take a course in statistics or experimental design, you'll find that the idea of error "badness" is handled by requiring different levels of confidence for different decisions. The need to consider different types of errors is found in many contexts. A basic principle of our legal system is that we have to be very certain that someone has committed a crime (beyond a reasonable doubt) before we can convict her. By contrast, we do not have

Table 6.1: Four possible outcomes for the "Who Buys the Coffee" Example

	You Decide	
The truth is	**He is cheating**	**He is not cheating**
He is cheating.	He is cheating, and you decide that he is cheating. Correct Decision!	He is cheating, and you decide that he is not cheating. An Error!
He is not cheating.	He is not cheating, and you decide that he is cheating. A Serious Error!	He is not cheating, and you decide that he is not cheating. Correct Decision!

Note. The error associated with deciding that he is cheating is more serious than the error associated with deciding that he is not cheating. Because of the difference in the severity of the errors, you will want to be more certain when deciding that he is cheating than when deciding that he is not cheating.

to be convinced beyond a reasonable doubt that she is innocent because wrongly deciding that someone is innocent is considered a less severe error than wrongly deciding that someone is guilty. Similarly, when you are testing hypotheses informally, you also need to be aware of the severity of different types of errors. Before you decide, for example, that no matter how hard you study, you'll never pass some course or that the medicine you are taking is or is not making you better, you need to consider the consequences of right and wrong decisions. Some decisions require that you should be more certain about being correct than others.

Experience is an Expensive Teacher

Perhaps one of our greatest strengths is our ability to explain. In one study, participants were confronted with the following puzzle: "If a pilot falls from a plane without a parachute, then the pilot dies. This pilot didn't die. Why not?" A perfectly valid deduction would be that the pilot must not have fallen out of the plane without his parachute, but many participants relied instead on inductive reasoning to answer the question. They came up with creative explanations, like "The plane was on the ground and he didn't fall far," "The pilot fell into deep snow or a deep cushion," and, Johnson-Laird's favorite, "The pilot was already dead." Humans are extraordinarily good at this kind of reasoning—we can explain just about anything.

—Philip Johnson-Laird (2011, para.7)

Suppose that your friend shares her "secret" for curing a cold—she rubs her stomach with garlic and the symptoms of the cold go away. You are dubious, but she persists, "I know it works. I've tried it, and I have seen it work with my own eyes." I am certain that there are many people who would respond to this testimonial by rubbing garlic over their stomach, just as there are many people who willingly swallow capsules filled with ground rhinoceros penis to increase their sexual potency, megavitamins to feel less tired, and ginseng root for whatever ails them. You may even join the ranks of those who tout these solutions because sometimes your cold will get better after rubbing yourself with garlic—sometimes a desired effect follows some action (like taking capsules of ground rhinoceros penis). But, did the action cause the effect that followed it? This question can only be answered using the principles of hypothesis testing. Personal experience cannot provide the answer.

Dawes (1994) corrected the famous expression that we attribute to Benjamin Franklin. It seems that Franklin did not say that "experience is the best teacher," instead he said "experience is a dear teacher," with the word "dear" meaning expensive or costly. Sometimes, we are able to use systematic feedback about what works and what does not work so that we can use our experience to improve at some task, but it is also possible to do the same thing over and over without learning from experience. We are far better off using information that is generated by many people to determine causal relationships than to rely on personal experience with all of its biases and costs.

Anecdotes

> The recent medical controversy over whether vaccinations cause autism reveals a habit of human cognition—thinking anecdotally comes naturally, whereas thinking scientifically does not.
> —Michael Shermer (July 25, 2008, para. 1)

I have a dear friend who is 80 years old and in great health. Guess what—he smoked a pack of cigarettes just about every day for the last 60 years! Yes, this is a true story. Can I conclude that cigarette smoking is (a) good for your health, (b) good for the health of some people, or (c) none of the above? The answer is (drum roll please) none of the above. The problem is that the image of my friend is so vivid and personal to me that it is tempting to let it override the massive research literature and conclusions of just about every credible medical society that smoking is a major cause of cancer, heart disease, and premature death. An isolated anecdote can be found to support almost any point of view, and even though you may already know this, it is very hard to discredit anecdotal evidence (Cox & Cox, 2001).

Maybe using smoking as an example of anecdotal thinking is unfair because of the wide spread antismoking campaigns. So, how about wheatgrass? (You can fill in your own examples here.) You probably know someone who swears about the positive health benefits of wheatgrass. It is easy to find testimonials from people who claim that they were sick and then got better after drinking a juice made from this type of grass. The National Council Against Health Fraud (www.ncahf.org) counters claims that it can "detox" your body and takes the clear position that there is no evidence that it is beneficial. (You can check them out—they are a credible medical authority.)

Several years ago, it was my great honor to present testimony to the United States House of Representatives Committee on Science about using principles from the science of learning as part of educational reform. On the way into the hearing room, a helpful legislative aide coached me about how to provide effective testimony to the Committee on Science. More than once she warned me not to present too many numbers because the Committee Members tended to get bored and confused by data. She advised that a good story works best. I could not believe that I should tell anecdotes in an attempt to persuade the United States House of Representatives Committee on Science that educational methods supported by research findings were more likely to provide beneficial outcomes than those that are not. Wouldn't such an approach be insulting to the highest elected officials in the United States who are the national guardians of science? I now know the answer to what I had intended to be a rhetorical question. Unfortunately, public policies are often made by anecdotes. We like stories—they make abstract concepts come alive and provide flesh and bones to colorless data. Astute readers will realize that I began this paragraph with an anecdote. A single vivid example can often outweigh a huge body of data collected from a random sample of a population, whereas anecdotes are self-selected, based on a sample size of 1, subject to all of the biases of memory, and likely to be atypical because they would not be told if they represented an expected outcome. It can take some practice, but it is possible to overcome the tendency to prefer anecdotes to the conclusions from carefully controlled research. It is an important critical thinking skill.

The need to develop the habit of thinking like a scientist can be seen in this eloquent quote from Bloom (2012):

> Consider science. Plainly, scientists are human and possess the standard slate of biases and prejudices and mindbugs. This is what skeptics emphasize when they say that science is "just another means of knowing" or "just like religion." But science also includes procedures—such as replicable experiments and open debate—that cultivate the capacity for human reason. Scientists can reject common wisdom, they can be persuaded by data and argument to change their minds. It is through these procedures that we have discovered extraordinary facts about the world.

Self-Fulfilling Prophecies

> Science is not simply a collection of facts; it is a discipline of thinking about rational solutions to problems after establishing the basic facts derived from observations. It is hypothesizing from what is known to what might be, and then attempting to test the hypotheses.
>
> —Rosalyn S. Yalow (quoted in Smith, 1998, p. 42)

In a classic set of experiments, Robert Rosenthal, a well known psychologist, and his colleagues (Rosenthal & Fode, 1963) had their students train rats to run through mazes as part of a standard course in experimental psychology. Half of the students were told that they had rats that had been specially bred to be smart at learning their way through mazes, while the other half of the students were told that they had rats that had been specially bred to be dumb at this task. As you probably expected, the students with the bright rats had them out-performing the dull rats in a short period of time. These results are especially interesting because there were no real differences between the two groups of rats. Rosenthal and Fode lied about the rats being specially bred. All of the rats were the usual laboratory variety. They had been assigned at random to either group. If there were no real differences between the groups of rats, how do we explain the fact that students who believed they had been given bright rats had them learn the maze faster than the other group?

The term "**self-fulfilling prophecies**" has been coined as a label for the tendency to act in ways that will lead us to find what we expected to find. I do not know what the students did to make the rats learn faster in the "bright" group or slower in the "dull" group. Perhaps the bright group was given extra handling or more food in the goal box. (When rats learn to run through mazes, they are rewarded with food when they reach the goal box.) Maybe the students given the "dull" rats dropped them harshly into the maze or were not as accurate in the records that they kept. Whatever they did, they somehow influenced their experimental results so that the results were in accord with their expectations.

If self-fulfilling prophecies can influence how rats run through mazes, what sort of an effect will it have on everyday thinking and behavior? Earlier in this chapter, illusory correlations were discussed as the tendency to believe that events that you are observing are really correlated because you believe that they should be. Psychologists are becoming increasingly aware of the ways that personal convictions direct our selection and interpretation of facts. When you function as an intuitive scientist, it is important to keep in mind the ways we influence the results we obtain.

One way to eliminate the effects of self-fulfilling prophecies is with **double blind procedures**. Let's consider a medical example. There are probably 100 home remedies for the common cold. How should we decide which, if any, actually relieve cold symptoms? Probably, somewhere, sometime, someone gave you chicken soup when you had a cold. Undoubtedly, you got better. Almost everyone who gets a cold gets better. The question is, "Did the chicken soup make you better?" This is a difficult question to answer because if you believe that chicken soup makes you better, you may rate the severity of your symptoms as less severe even when there was no real change. This is just another example of self-fulfilling prophecies. The only way to test this hypothesis is to give some people chicken soup and others something that looks and tastes like chicken soup and then have each group rate the severity of their cold symptoms. In this example, all of the subjects are unaware or blind to the nature of the treatment they are receiving. It is important that the experimenters also be unaware of which subjects received the "real" chicken soup so that they do not inadvertently give subtle clues to the subjects. Experiments in which neither the subjects nor the experimenters know who is receiving the treatment are called double blind experiments.

Although the chicken soup example may seem a little far-fetched, the need for double blind procedures is critical in deciding whether any drug or treatment is working. Formal laboratory research on drugs that may be effective against AIDS or cancer always uses double blind procedures. Most people, however, do not apply these same standards when making personal decisions, such as which type of psychotherapy is effective or whether massive doses of a vitamin or advice from a palm reader will improve some aspect of their life. Before you decide to see a therapist who claims to be able to improve your diabetes by manipulating your spine or to engage in screaming therapy to improve your self-confidence, look carefully for double blind studies that support the use of the proposed therapy.

Occult Beliefs and the Paranormal

"Media distortions, social uncertainty, and deficiencies of human reasoning seem to be at the basis of occult beliefs."
—Barry Singer and Victor Benassi (1981, p. 49)

Do you believe that houses can be haunted, or that the position of the stars and planets can affect people's lives, or that extraterrestrial beings invaded the earth, or perhaps that witches are real and not just a Halloween fantasy (Lyons, 2005)? If you answered "yes" to any of these, you are not alone. Although a recent Gallup Poll showed that the proportion of the general population in the United States, Canada, and Great Britain who believe in these paranormal phenomena is well below a majority, there is a sizeable number of believers for each of these paranormal (outside of normal) phenomena. One possible explanation for these beliefs is the increase in the number of television shows about these topics, some of which have an almost "news-like" appearance to them, that carry the message that beings from outer space are living among us or that other paranormal phenomena (e.g., ghosts) are real. Often these shows are narrated by people who appear to be honest and sincere. Few people remember the difference between actors and scientists when the actors provide a good imitation of something that looks like science.

How can we understand these beliefs when there is **no good evidence** that they have any basis in fact (Shermer, 1997; Stanovich & West, 2008)? In our attempt to make sense out of events in the world, we all seek to impose a meaningful explanation, especially for unusual events. Have you thought about a friend whom you have not seen in many years and then received a phone call from him? Did you ever change your usual route home from school or work and then learn that there was a tragic accident that you probably would have been in if you had not changed your route? What about stories of people who recover from a deadly disease after they use imagery as a means of healing? We are all fascinated by these unusual events and try to understand them. Support for paranormal experiences comes from anecdotes. Can you understand how small sample sizes (usually a single example), retrospective review (in hindsight we seek explanations that are available in memory), illusory correlations, self-fulfilling prophecies, difficulty in understanding probabilities, and other cognitive biases contribute to the popularity of paranormal beliefs? It is a fact that there is no positive evidence whatsoever for the existence of any psychic abilities. Remember—no one has collected the million-dollar prize offered by the James Randi Foundation or other similar foundations for credible evidence of psychic or other paranormal phenomena. There are many anecdotes, but there has never been a statistically significant finding of psychic power that has been duplicated in another independent laboratory. "Anecdotes do not make a science" (Shermer, Benjamin, & Randi, 2011). They are, however, powerful in directing what we believe to be true.

There are many real mysteries in the world and much that we do not understand. It is possible that someone has found a strange herbal cure for cancer, or that the lines on the palms of our hand or pattern of tea leaves in our tea cups are indicators of important life events, but if these are "real" phenomena, then they will hold up under the bright lights of double-blind, controlled laboratory testing. We can all laugh at the predictions made by various "psychics," such as the prediction that Fidel Castro would move to Beverly Hills after his government was overthrown and the many predictions about Princess Diana that included almost everything imaginable except her tragic death (Emery, 2001). We need to become much more skeptical when a friend tells us that crystals have healing powers or vitamin E can be used to revive those who have recently died. This topic is also addressed in the next chapter where I discuss how to reason with probabilities.

Conspiracy Theories

A **conspiracy theory** is an explanation for something that is based on the idea that there is a secret group that was responsible for that event. Common examples of conspiracy theories are that president Kennedy's assassination was the result of a covert military operation and that the rapid spread of AIDS was caused by a secret plot of a powerful (and homophobic) group. According to Barkun (2006), conspiracy theories share four characteristics: they (a) challenge the predominant theories, (b) rely on secret knowledge and flimsy evidence, (c) do not entertain doubt or permit rebuttals, and (d) divide the world into black or white categories of good and evil. In the United States, the assassination of President Kennedy was momentous. It is hard to think that something so important was caused by just one or a few people. Similarly, the spread of AIDS has decimated many groups of people. As humans, we search for reasons to understand events, and momentous events seem to require weighty reasons.

Although not quite the same, it is useful to think about the vast array of so-called "cures" for horrible diseases that are touted on the Internet and in other outlets as similar to conspiracy theories. In these cases, the "conspiracy" is some group of physicians or some government agency who is keeping knowledge of the cure from the people who need it. Imagine finding the cure for such heart breaking disorders as autism, and diseases such as cancer and Alzheimer's. Many people believe that they have. The proponents of these cures claim to have evidence that the medical establishment (note the negative language that suggests an impersonal corporation) will not pay attention to, and of course, the ones claiming to have cures are the "good guys" and anyone who disagrees with them are the "bad guys." They often argue that the group that is suppressing news of the cure is doing so for financial gain—arguing that doctors who specialize in cancer, for example, would go broke if the rest of us knew about the secret cure. A quick search on Google will reveal many such claims (maybe as many as 100 "cures" for autism), and it is not surprising that desperate families fall for these phony cures. Infomercials, which are commercials that look a lot like regular programming, show miraculous recoveries. If there were a cure for any of these diseases, you would read about it on the front page of every reputable newspaper and medical journal, and not learn about it from someone who is selling the cure on late-night television or a web site that no reputable organization (e.g., reputable organizations have credentials similar to those found in the National Autism Association and National Cancer Association) endorses.

A colleague (Larry Alferink at Illinois State University) suggested several flags for skepticism when reading about these miracle cures, including a high degree of self-promotion (buy my vitamins, DVDs, books, etc.), and vague references to "peer-reviewed journals" that turn out not to have the rigorous review process that highly regarded medical journals have, and a vague reference to published research that cannot be verified. As one medical commentator noted (Burton, 2009, para. 6): "To support his fringe opinion, Dr. [name deleted] has used what I refer to as a cut-and-paste technique; he takes isolated observations out of context to generate a theory not proven or justified by the findings."

Thinking as an Intuitive Scientist

> Most people seem to believe that there is a difference between scientific thinking and everyday thinking. . . . But, the fact is, these same scientific thinking skills can be used to improve the chances of success in virtually any endeavor.
>
> —George (Pinky) Nelson (1998, April 29, p. A14)

One theme throughout this chapter is that everyday thinking has much in common with the research methods used by scientists when they investigate phenomena in their academic domains. Many of the pitfalls and problems that plague scientific investigations are also common in everyday thought. If you understand and avoid some of these problems, you will be a better consumer of research and a better intuitive scientist.

When you are evaluating the research claims of others or when you are asserting your own claims, there are several questions to keep in mind:

1. What was the nature of the sample? Was it large enough? Was it biased?

2. Are the variables operationally defined? What do the terms mean?

3. Were the measurements sensitive, valid, and reliable? Were the appropriate comparisons made to support the claims?

4. Were extraneous variables controlled? What are other plausible explanations for the results?

5. Do the conclusions follow from the observations?

6. Are correlations being used to support causative arguments?

7. Is disconfirming evidence being considered?

8. How could the experimenter's expectancies be biasing the result?

Let's apply these guidelines to the choice of treatment programs that was presented at the opening of this chapter. The scenario presented you, as a heroin addict with two choices of treatment programs. The first program is run by former heroin addicts and the second is run by therapists. First, what is the evidence for success rates? Although Program #1 cites a much higher success rate than Program #2, these numbers cannot be used to compare the two programs because Program #1 gives the success for those who stayed with the program at least one year, and we have no information about how many dropped out before achieving the one-year mark. Thus, the success rate for Program #1 is not a valid measure of success. We also have no information about how likely someone is to maintain recovery without treatment. In other words, there is no control group against which to measure the efficacy of treatment. Unfortunately, there is no information about the sample size because we are not told how many patients entered each program. If this were a real decision, then you would ask for this information. So far, there is little to go on.

I have found that most people like the idea that the therapist is a recovered addict who "has been there himself." The problem with this sort of qualification is that his anecdotes about "what worked for him" may be totally worthless.

Dawes (1994) is highly critical of the sort of reasoning that leads people to believe that a former addict is a good choice for a counselor. As Dawes noted, the thinking that goes into this evaluation is something like this:

> The therapist was an addict.
>
> He did X and recovered.
>
> If I do X, then I will also recover.

I hope that you can see that this is very weak evidence. If you have already read the chapter on reasoning, then you will recognize this as a categorical syllogism—one that is invalid. You have a single individual (sample size of one), all the biases of memory, no independent verification that X is useful, the problem of illusory correlation, and more. Of course, this individual could be an excellent therapist, but with the information that you are given, there is no reason to expect it. On the other hand, the therapist who has studied the psychology and biology of addiction should know about different treatment options, theories of addiction, and most importantly, the success rates for a variety of different types of treatments based on results from large samples of addicts. This is an important point. Try posing the question that I used at the opening of this chapter to friends and relatives. You will probably find the bias toward selecting the recovered addict as a therapist.

If you scrutinize your own conclusions and those of others with the principles of hypothesis testing in mind, you should be able to defend yourself against invalid claims and improve your own ability to draw sound conclusions from observations.

Chapter Summary

- Much of our everyday thinking is like the scientific method of hypothesis testing. We formulate beliefs about the world and collect observations to decide if our beliefs are correct.

- In the inductive method, we devise hypotheses from our observations. In the deductive method, we collect observations that confirm or disconfirm our hypotheses. Most thinking involves an interplay of these two processes so that we devise hypotheses from experience, make observations, and then, on the basis of our observations, redefine our hypotheses.

- Operational definitions are precise statements that allow the identification and measurement of variables.

- Independent variables are used to predict or explain dependent variables. When we formulate hypotheses, we want to know about the effect of the independent variable on the dependent variable(s).

- When we draw conclusions from observations, it is important to utilize an adequately large sample size because people are variable in the way they respond. Most people are too willing to generalize results obtained from small samples.

- In order to generalize about a population, the sample needs to be representative of the population. You need to ask if the sample you are using is biased in any way before making generalizations.

- In determining if one variable (e.g., smoking) causes another variable (e.g., lung cancer) to occur, it is important to be able to isolate and control the causal variables. Strong causal claims require the three-stage experimental design that was described in this chapter.

- In every day contexts, we often use retrospective techniques to understand what caused an event to occur. This is not a good technique because our memories tend to be selective and malleable and because we have no objective systematic observations of the cause. Prospective techniques that record events when they occur and then see if the hypothesized result follows are better methods for determining cause–effect relationships.

- Variables that are related so that changes in one variable are associated with changes in the other variable are called correlated variables. Correlations can be positive, as in the relationship between height and weight (taller people tend to weigh more; shorter people tend to weigh less), or negative, as in the relationship between exercise and weight (people who exercise a great deal tend to be thin, and those who exercise little tend to be heavy).

- A common error is to infer a causative relationship from correlated variables. It is possible that variable A caused variable B, or that variable B caused variable A, or that A and B influenced each other, or that a third variable caused them both.

- The belief that two variables are correlated when they are not (illusory correlation) is another type of error that is common in human judgment.

- It is important that you use measurements that are sensitive, valid, and reliable or the conclusions you draw may be incorrect. Few people consider the importance of measurement issues when they draw everyday conclusions about the nature of the world.

- Although many of our judgments lack validity, people report great confidence in them. This is called illusory validity.

- Inadvertently, we may act in ways that will lead us to confirm or disconfirm hypotheses according to our expectations. These are called self-fulfilling prophecies.

The following skills to determine whether a conclusion is valid were presented in this chapter. Review each skill and be sure that you understand how and when to use each one.

The skills involved when thinking as an intuitive scientist include:

- recognizing the need for and using operational definitions
- explaining the need to isolate and control variables in order to make strong causal claims
- checking for adequate sample size and unbiased sampling when a generalization is made
- describing the relationship between any two variables as positive, negative, or unrelated
- recognizing the limits of correlational reasoning
- seeking converging validity to increase your confidence in a decision
- checking for and understanding the need for control groups
- being aware of the bias in most estimates of variability
- considering the relative "badness" of different sorts of errors
- determining how self-fulfilling prophecies could be responsible for experimental results or everyday observations
- knowing when causal claims can and cannot be made.

Terms to Know

Check your understanding of the concepts presented in this chapter by reviewing their definitions. If you find that you're having difficulty with any term, be sure to reread the section in which it is discussed.

Hypothesis. A set of beliefs about the nature of the world, usually concerning the relationship between two or more variables.

Hypothesis Testing. The scientific method of collecting observations to confirm or disconfirm beliefs about the relationships between variables.

Inductive Method. A method of formulating hypotheses in which you observe events and then devise a hypothesis about the events you observed.

Deductive Method. A method of testing hypotheses in which you formulate a hypothesis that you believe to be true and then infer consequences from it. Systematic observations are then made to verify if your hypothesis is correct.

Operational Definition. An explicit set of procedures that tell the reader how to recognize and measure the concept in which you are interested.

(A) Variable. A quantifiable characteristic that can take on more than one value (e.g., height, gender, age, race).

Independent Variable. The variable that is selected (or manipulated) by the experimenter who is testing a hypothesis to see if changes in the independent variable will result in changes in the dependent variable. For example, if you want to know if people are more readily persuaded by threats or rational appeals, you could present either a threatening message or a rational appeal to two groups of people (the message type is the independent variable) and then determine how much their attitudes toward the topic have changed (the dependent variable).

Dependent Variable. The variable that is measured in an experiment to determine if its value depends on the independent variable. Compare with independent variable.

Population. For statistical and hypothesis testing purposes, a population is the entire group of people (or animals or entities) in which one is interested and to which one wishes to generalize.

Sample. A subset of a population that is studied in order to make inferences about the population.

Representative Sample. A sample that is similar to the population in important characteristics, such as the proportion of males and females, socioeconomic status, and age.

Generalization. Using the results obtained in a sample to infer that similar results would have been obtained from the population if everyone in the population had been measured. (When used in the context of problem solving, it is a strategy in which the problem is considered as an example of a larger class of problems.)

Biased Sample. A sample that is not representative of the population from which it was drawn.

Confounding. When experimental groups differ in more than one way, it is not possible to separate the effects due to each variable. For example, if you found that teenage girls scored higher on a test of verbal ability than preteen boys, you wouldn't know if the results were due to sex differences or age differences between the two groups.

Convenience Samples. The use of a group of people who are readily available as participants in an experiment. Such samples may be biased in that they may not be representative of the population from which they were drawn.

Sample Size. The number of people selected for a study.

Subject. A person, animal, or entity who serves as a participant in an experiment.

Variability. Term to denote the fact that people (and animals) differ in the way they respond to experimental stimuli.

Random Sample. A sample in which everyone in a population has an equal chance of being selected.

Law of Small Numbers. The willingness to believe that results obtained from a few subjects can be generalized to the entire population.

Retrospective Research. After an event has occurred, the experimenter looks backward in time to determine its cause.

Prospective Research. A method of conducting research in which possible causative factors of an event are identified before the event occurs. Experimenters then determine if the hypothesized event occurs.

Correlated Variables. Two or more variables that are related. See positive correlation and negative correlation.

Positive Correlation. Two or more variables that are related so that increases in one variable occur concomitantly with increases in the other variable, and decreases in one variable occur with decreases in the other.

Negative Correlation. Two or more variables that are related such that increases in one variable are associated with decreases in the other variable.

Illusory Correlation. The belief that two variables are correlated, when in fact they are uncorrelated.

Validity. The extent to which a measure (e.g., a test) is measuring what you want it to.

Convergent Validity. The use of several different measures or techniques that all suggest the same conclusion.

Illusory Validity. The belief that a measure is valid (measures what you want it to) when, in fact, it is not. This belief causes people to be overconfident in their judgments.

Reliability. The consistency of a measure (e.g., a test) on repeated occasions.

Double-Blind Procedures. An experimental paradigm in which neither the subjects nor the person collecting data know the treatment group to which the subject has been assigned.

Self-Fulfilling Prophecy. The tendency to act in ways that influence experimental results so that we obtain results that are consistent with our expectations.

Conspiracy Theory. An explanation for something that is based on the idea that there is a secret group that is responsible for that event.

CHAPTER 7

LIKELIHOOD AND UNCERTAINTY
UNDERSTANDING PROBABILITIES

Contents

The jury was facing a difficult decision in the case of *People vs. Collins* (cited in Arkes & Hammond, 1986). The robbery victim could not identify his assailant. All he could recall was that the robber was a woman with a blonde ponytail who, after the robbery, rode off in a yellow convertible driven by a Black man with a moustache and a beard. The suspect fit this description, but could the jury be certain "beyond a reasonable doubt" that the woman who was on trial was the robber? She was blonde and often wore her hair in a ponytail. Her codefendant "friend" was a Black man with a moustache, beard, and yellow convertible. If you were the attorney for the defense, you would stress the fact that the victim could not identify this woman as the robber. What strategy would you use if you were the attorney for the prosecution?

The prosecutor produced an expert in probability theory who testified that the probability of these conditions "co-occurring (being blonde *plus* having a ponytail *plus* having a Black male friend *plus* his owning a yellow convertible and so on, when these characteristics are independent) was 1 in 12 million. The expert testified that this combination of characteristics was so unusual that the jury could be certain "beyond a reasonable doubt" that she was the robber.

The jury returned a verdict of "guilty."

Probabilistic Nature of the World

The theory of probabilities is nothing but common sense confirmed by calculation.

—Pierre Simon La Place (1951, p. 196)

The legal system recognizes that we can never have absolute certainty in legal matters. Instead, we operate with various degrees of uncertainty. In the United States, juries are instructed to decide that someone is guilty of a crime when they are certain "beyond a reasonable doubt." This standard was adopted because there is always some small amount of doubt that the accused may be innocent. Jurors are instructed to operate under a different level of doubt when they are deciding about guilt or innocence in a civil case. In civil cases, they are told to deliver a verdict of guilty when the "preponderance of evidence" supports this decision. Thus, jurors are instructed to operate under two different levels of uncertainty depending on whether the case before them is criminal or civil. They need to be more certain when deciding that an accused party is guilty in a criminal case than in a civil case.

Probability is the study of likelihood and uncertainty. It plays a critical role in all professions and in most everyday decisions. All medical diagnoses and treatment decisions are inherently probabilistic, as are decisions made in business, college admissions, advertising, and research. Probability is the cornerstone of science; the laws of probability guide the interpretation of all research findings. Many of our leisure activities also rely on the principles of probability, most notably horse racing and card games. Every time you decide to take an umbrella, invest in the stock market, buy an insurance policy, or bet on a long shot in the Kentucky Derby, you are making a probability judgment. Other than the proverbial death and taxes, there is very little in life that is known with certainty. Because we live in a probabilistic world, critical thinking will require an understanding of probability.

There is good evidence that training in the use of probability will improve your ability to utilize probability values in an appropriate manner. In an investigation of the use of statistical thinking in everyday reasoning tasks, researchers concluded that, "This study indicated clearly that statistical training can enhance the use of statistical rules in reasoning about everyday life and can do so completely outside the context of training" (Fong, Krantz, & Nisbett, 1986, p. 280). In other words, although the thinking skills presented in this chapter will require the use of basic arithmetic and probably some concentrated effort, it is likely that you will be a better thinker for having worked through the problems.

Likelihood and Uncertainty

If your facts are wrong but your logic is perfect, then your conclusions are inevitably false. Therefore, by making mistakes in your logic, you have at least a random chance of coming to a correct conclusion.
—Christie-Davies' Theorem (reference unknown, taken from a calendar)

If I flip a "fair" coin (i.e., one that is not biased, which means that either a head or tail is equally likely) into the air and ask you to guess the probability that it will land heads up, you would say that the probability of a head is 50% (or .50). This means that the coin is expected to land heads up half of the time. Although the word "probability" is used in several different ways, the definition of probability that is most useful in the present context is the number of ways a particular outcome (what we call a success) can occur divided by the number of possible outcomes (when each possible outcome is equally likely). It is a measure of how often we expect an event to occur **in the long run**. Success may seem like a strange word in this context, but you can think of it as the outcome in which you are interested. In this case, a success is getting the coin to land heads up. There is only one way for a coin to land heads ups, so the number of ways a success can occur in this example is one. What are all the possible outcomes of flipping a coin in the air? The coin can either land heads up or tails up. (I've never seen a coin land on its edge, nor have I ever seen a bird come along and carry it off while it's flipped in the air, so I am not considering these as possible outcomes.) Thus, there are two possible outcomes, each of which is as likely to happen as the other. To calculate the probability of getting a coin to land heads up, compute the number of ways a head can occur (1), divided by the number of possible outcomes (2), or 1/2, an answer you already knew. Because many people find it easier to think in percentages than in fractions, 1/2 is sometimes changed to 50%.

Let's try another example. How likely are you to roll a 5 in one roll of a die? As there is only one way for a 5 to occur, the numerator of the probability fraction is 1. A die is a 6-sided (cube) figure; thus there are 6 possible outcomes in one roll. If the die is not "loaded," that is when each side of the die is equally likely to land facing up, the probability of rolling a 5 is 1/6, or approximately 17%.

What is the probability of rolling an even number in one roll of a fair die? To find this probability, consider the number of ways a success can occur. You could roll a 2, 4, or 6, all possible even numbers. Thus, there are 3 ways a success can occur out of 6 equally likely outcomes, so the probability of rolling an even number is 3/6 = 1/2.

What is the probability of rolling a whole number less than 7? If someone asked me to bet on this happening, I would put up my house, my children, and my meager savings account to make this bet. In other words, I would bet that this *will* happen. Let's see why. The number of ways a whole number less than seven can occur in one roll of a die is 6 (1, 2, 3, 4, 5, or 6), and the number of possible outcomes is 6. Thus, the probability is 6/6, or 1. When a probability is equal to 1 (or 100%), it must happen; it is certain to occur.

What is the probability of rolling an 8 in one roll of a die? Again, I would put up everything I own, but this time I would bet against this occurrence. The number of ways an 8 can occur is 0. Thus, the probability of this occurring is 0; it cannot occur. This situation also reflects absolute certainty. Probabilities range from 0 (can never happen) to 1 (must happen). Probability values close to 0 or 1 represent events that are almost certain not to occur or almost certain to occur, while probabilities near .5 (50%) represent maximum uncertainty, because either outcome is equally likely, and thus there is no basis for predicting either one. This relationship is depicted in Figure 7.1.

Odds

It is often convenient to discuss probabilities in terms of odds. If a friend gives you 3-to-1 odds that his school's championship tiddly-winks team will beat your school's tiddly-winks team, this means that if 4 games

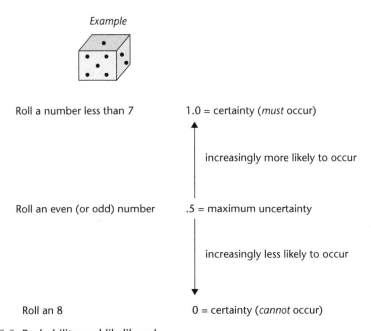

Figure 7.1 Probability and likelihood.

were played, he would expect his team to win 3 of them. Authorities on organized sports (announcers, sports page editors, and almost everyone else) usually express their degree of belief in the outcome of a sporting event in terms of odds. (Betting odds like those posted at racetracks and boxing matches refer to the amount of money that has been bet on each contender and, thus, have a slightly different meaning from the one described here.) To convert odds to a probability, add the two numbers that are given (e.g., 3:1 = 4), use the first number as the numerator and the sum as the denominator (3/4), and this is the equivalent probability.

The Laws of Chance

> Uncertainty is an essential and integral facet of all forms of life and is, in principle, unavoidable.
> —Gideon Keren and Karl Halvor Teigen (2001, p. 191)

The most important phrase in the last section was "in the long run." Except for those special cases when the probability of an outcome is either 0% or 100%, we cannot know with certainty what will happen. I cannot know when I roll a die whether I will roll a five, but, if I keep rolling a fair die for many, many trials, I do know that about 17% of the time I will roll a five. I cannot know which roll will produce a five, but I do know approximately how many rolls will land with a 5 showing if I keep rolling for a long time. This is an important point. When we speak of the **laws of chance** (or laws of probability), we are referring to the ability to predict the number or percentage of trials on which a particular outcome will occur. With a large number of trials, I can be very accurate about the number of times a particular outcome will occur, but I cannot know which trials will yield a particular outcome. This means that I can make good "long run" predictions and poor "short run" predictions.

Let's consider insurance as an applied example of this distinction. When you buy a life insurance policy (or any other type of insurance policy), you are making a bet with the insurance company. You agree to pay a certain amount of money to the insurance company each year. They agree to pay your beneficiary a certain amount of money when you die. There are many different types of life insurance policies available, but for the purposes of this chapter, we will consider the simplest. I will use some simple numbers to demonstrate the statistical point that I want to make— in real life, the actual costs and payoffs are different from those used in this example. Suppose that you are 30 years old and that you agree to pay the insurance company $1,000 per year. When you die, your beneficiary will receive $20,000. You are betting with the insurance company that you will die at a fairly young age (a bet that you hope to lose) so that you will have paid them only a small amount of money and your beneficiary will receive a larger amount of money. If you die before the age of 50, you win the bet. Ignoring complications like inflation and interest, you will have paid less than the $20,000 your beneficiary will receive if you die at a young age. The insurance company, on the other hand, will win the bet if you live to a ripe old age. If you die when you are 70 years old, you will have paid them $40,000 and your dearly beloved will receive only $20,000.

Insurance companies can make money because of the laws of chance. No one knows when you or anyone else will die, but insurance companies do know how many people aged 30 (the age at which you bought your policy) will die before they reach their 50th birthday. Thus, although no one can predict accurately the age at death for any single individual, we can use the laws of chance to predict how many people will live to be any particular age.

How We Explain Chance Events

> At the beginning of the 20th century the father of modern science fiction, Herbert George Wells, said in his writings on politics, "If we want to have an educated citizenship in a modern technological society, we need to teach them three things: reading, writing, and statistical thinking." At the beginning of the 21st century, how far have we gotten with this program? In our society, we teach most citizens reading and writing from the time they are children, but not statistical thinking.
>
> —Gerd Gigerenzer (2003, para. 1)

Most people can understand the laws of chance when they think about tossing a coin or rolling a pair of dice, but find it more difficult to recognize how chance operates in complicated real-world settings. Unusual events—the sort that make you say "imagine that"—are often reported in the news. Consider, for example, this newspaper headline: "Three Sisters Give Birth on the Same Day" (Snell, Peterson, Albert, & Grinstead 2001, pp. 23–25). According to an article in the March 14, 2001 edition of the *Point Stevens Journal*, Karralee Morgan, Marrianne Asay, and Jennifer Hone (real people—real names—no names have been changed to protect anyone) are sisters who all gave birth on March 11, 1998 (as reported in Chance Magazine). It is hard to hear this story and NOT ask, "What is the probability that three sisters would give birth on the same day?" As it turns out, this is a tricky question because there are several ways of interpreting what is being asked. Consider these two possible interpretations:

> What is the probability that these three sisters (Karralee, Marrianne, and Jennifer) will all give birth on March 11, 1998?

> What is the probability that somewhere in the United States (or anywhere in the world) there will be three sisters (any set of three sisters) who all give birth on the same day (any day of any one year)?

Before I give you the answers, think about what is being asked and decide which of these two interpretations is more likely to occur. Did you understand that the situation described in Question #2 is *much more likely* than the situation described in Question #1? According to calculations presented in a magazine that teaches about chance events (Chance Magazine, Spring 2001), the answer for #1 is about 1 in 50 million, but the answer for #2 is about 1 in 6,000. It seems likely that most people are thinking about Question #2 when they ask about the chance of three sisters giving birth on the same day, but it is easy to see why these are difficult concepts because the question is prompted by situation #1. If we want to know about any three sisters on any day in any one year (there are 365 different possible days, so there are more ways for this to happen), it is much more likely than if we mean a specific three sisters on a specific day.

Degrees of Belief

Probability is sometimes used to express the strength of a belief about the likelihood of an outcome. This is a second definition for the term probability. For example, if you interview for a job and believe that the interview went well, you might assess the probability that you will be offered the job as 80%. This probability value was not mathematically derived by calculating the number of ways a success could occur divided by the number of possible outcomes. Instead, it indicates your degree of belief that the job will be offered. It suggests a moderate to high likelihood. If someone else interviewed for the same job and believed that his chance of being offered the job was 50%, it would be obvious that he was less confident about getting the job than you were.

It's a Miracle (or Maybe Just Statistics)

> Given enough opportunities, outlier anomalies—even seeming miracles—will occasionally happen.
>
> —Michael Shermer (2008, para. 1)

It happens to all of us, admittedly not often, but it happens. Sometimes we are thinking of a friend, perhaps getting ready to call him when the phone rings, and it is he. Not exactly a miracle, but rare enough to make us think, "Now what is the probability of that happening?" But, even seeming miracles can be explained with probabilities. First, because of confirmation bias, the strong tendency to find evidence that confirms what we believe to be true and to ignore evidence that is contrary to our beliefs, we remember astonishing coincidences and not the vast array of every interactions in which we all engage. Shermer (2008) explained how we can explain something as weird as "death premonitions"—dreams in which someone we know has died or is about to die.

Shermer provides this rough analysis:

> The average person has about five dreams a night, or 1,825 dreams a year. If we remember only a tenth of our dreams, then we recall 182.5 dreams a year. There are 300 million Americans, who thus produce 54.7 billion remembered dreams a year. Sociologists tell us that each of us knows about 150 people fairly well, thus producing a network grid of 45 billion personal relationship connections. With an annual death rate of 2.4 million Americans, it is inevitable that some of those 54.7 billion remembered dreams will be about some of these 2.4 million deaths among the 300 million Americans and their 45 billion connections. In fact, it would be a *miracle* if some death premonitions did not come true. (para. 4)

I have not checked Shermer's math, but let's assume that it is correct. Most of us cannot "get our heads" around numbers in the millions or billions—we are far better at marveling at our personal experiences and the anecdotes of others whom we know. A common theme in this chapter is that the laws of probability are not intuitive, and even though we may prefer to rely on personal experiences, we will make better decisions if we can think probabilistically.

Factors Affecting Judgments about Likelihood and Uncertainty

> The odds against there being a bomb on a plane are a million to one, and against two bombs a million times a million to one. Next time you fly, cut the odds and take a bomb.
> —Benny Hill (quoted in Bryne, 1988, p. 349)

There is a large body of research literature documenting the fact that most people are biased in their assessment of probabilities. We fail to appreciate the nature of randomness and have strong misconceptions about likelihood and uncertainty (Hill, 2012). This is not a surprising finding given that we can only use probabilities to understand events "in the long run," and most of our everyday experiences are based on "short run" observations. For example, there is a large body of data that show that, on the average, people who smoke die at a younger age than those who do not (American Cancer Society, 2012). Most of us cannot discover this relationship on our own because we do not know the age of death for large numbers of people, but we may know one or two people who smoked two packs a day and lived into their 90s. This sort of personal experience would lead us to doubt the statistics that were collected from many people. Remember though, personal experience is *not* a good way to make many judgments about the world. Recall from the last chapter that experience is an expensive teacher, but not a good one.

The Search for Meaning

> To live, it seems is to explain, to justify, and to find coherence among diverse outcomes, characteristics, and causes.
> —Thomas Gilovich (1991, p. 22)

We seek causes for events that happen to us and to others, but most of us rarely consider the randomness of many events. We look for patterns and meaning, a quest that can often be helpful, but also can lead to beliefs that are groundless. For example, consider this true story: A student stopped in my office to talk with me. He told about an "amazing thing" that just happened to him. He was a student in a class of 15 students. Each student had to make an oral presentation, and the order in which they were to present was determined by drawing numbers from a box. "Guess who picked number 1?" he asked excitedly. I guessed that he did. "Exactly, and do you know the probability of that!" I did, it was 1/15 or approximately 7 percent. "Isn't that amazing? Out of 15 people in the class, I picked number 1. How can you explain that?" I attributed this not-so-amazing outcome to chance; after all, someone had to pick number 1. He was certain that it was a sign of something; maybe the "gods" had intervened or his karma had gone berserk (whatever that means). He was looking for a cause that could explain this event, and he never considered just plain "chance."

There seems to be a universal need to find meaning in the vast array of everyday events that confronts us, a trait that makes it difficult to recognize chance events. You may have heard about the controversy over the "Bible Code," which is the title of a book that describes how letters sampled at regular intervals (for example, every 50th letter) from the Bible had embedded in them the names of famous people and foretold events that would happen in the future (Drosnin, 1997). Statisticians howled with laughter (and scorn) at this book because chance alone would result in many words appearing in these letter strings. On the other hand, it is easy to understand how someone who does not understand concepts in probability might be persuaded by the seemingly amazing number of names and words that were embedded in long strings of letters.

The author of the *Bible Code* (Drosnin, 1997) challenged statisticians to use the same technique of letter sampling with "Moby Dick," a book which presumably would not have embedded special messages about the future into its letter sequences. A group of Australian computer scientists (McKay, Bar-Natan, & Kalia, 1999) took up the challenge and found "M. L. King" near the phrase "to be killed by them," "Kennedy" near the word "shoot," and many more famous names and meaningful phrases (including "Princess Di" and "Lincoln") in letter strings taken from Moby Dick, thus showing that mere chance would result in many meaningful names and phrases embedded in long strings of letters. In general, we tend to underestimate the importance of being able to think about probabilities. In an editorial on this topic, one columnist chided the American public for making fun of a politician's poor grammar because we should be far more concerned about our politicians' math skills, especially their poor understanding of probabilities (Cole, June 11, 2001). There are a many critical issues that depend on the ability to think with numbers—global warming, population growth, and the economy, to name a few.

Overconfidence

> Most people . . . tend to overestimate the degree to which we are responsible for our own successes.
>
> —Simon Gervais and Terrance Odean (2001, p. 1)

By definition, there is always some uncertainty in probabilistic events. Yet, research has shown that people tend to be more confident in their decisions about probabilistic events than they should be. Consider an example that Daniel Kahneman, a researcher in this area, likes to use. When he and his coauthors began working on a text on decision making, they were fairly confident that they would have it completed within a year, despite the fact that they knew that most books like the one they were writing take many years to complete. They believed that they would beat these "odds." In fact, it took them several years to complete the text.

In an experimental investigation of the **overconfidence phenomenon**, people were asked to provide answers with a specified degree of confidence to factual questions (Kahneman & Tversky, 1979). Try it with this question: "I feel 98 percent certain that the number of nuclear plants operating in the world in 1980 was more than _____ and less than _____." Fill in the blanks with numbers that reflect 98% confidence. The researchers investigating this effect found that nearly one-third of the time, the correct answer did not lie between the two values that reflected a 98% level of confidence. (The correct answer to this question is 189.) This result demonstrates that people are often highly confident when their high degree of confidence is unwarranted.

Have you ever bought a lottery ticket? Do you know what the odds are against your hitting the jackpot? The laws of probability dictate that you should expect to lose, yet countless numbers of people expect to win. In fact, a disturbing poll published in *Money* magazine revealed that almost as many people are planning for their retirement by buying lottery tickets (39%) as are investing in stocks (43%) (Wang, 1994).

Overconfidence about uncertain events is a problem even for experts in many fields where there is great uncertainty. In an analysis of political predictions (who is likely to win, for example), Silver (2011, para.3) wrote: "Experts have a poor understanding of uncertainty. Usually, this manifests itself in the form of overconfidence: experts underestimate the likelihood that their predictions might be wrong." Overconfidence can be disastrous for financial investors. In a study of individual investors, two economists found that most people fail to recognize the role that chance plays in the stock market, so they tend to attribute gains to their own expertise in picking stocks and losses to external forces that they could not control. The result is that overconfident investors trade their stocks far too often because they believe that they are making wise choices (Gervais & Odean, 2001). If they could recognize the effects of random fluctuations in the stock market instead of attributing the changes to their own trading behaviors, they would have traded less often and ended up in better financial shape.

Using Probability

Without giving it much thought, we utilize probabilities many times each day. Let's start with one of the few examples where probability values are made explicit. Many people begin each day by reading the weather forecast in the morning paper. What do you do when you read that the probability of rain is 80% today? Most people will head off to school or work toting an umbrella. What if it does not rain? Can we conclude that the forecaster was wrong? The forecast of an 80% probability of rain means that out of every 100 days when the weather conditions are like those on this particular day, there will be rain on 80 of them. Thus, a probability of rain is, like all probability values, based on what we would expect in the long run. Weather experts know that 80 out of 100 days will have rain, but the forecasters cannot know with absolute certainty which days it will rain.

Suppose that you are to be married on this hypothetical day, and a magnificent outdoor ceremony is planned. Suppose that an 80% probability of rain was forecast, and it did not rain. Would you believe that something other than chance was responsible for the good weather or that the absence of rain is a good (or bad) sign for your marriage? If you would interpret the good weather as a sign from the heavens or some other astral body, then you have demonstrated the point that was just made—we seek meaning in events, even events as seemingly uncontrollable as the weather, and we rarely consider plain old chance.

The number of instances in which we are given explicit probability values that have been computed for us is relatively small. One area where this practice is growing is in the use of medical information sheets that are designed to help patients understand the risks and benefits of taking a particular drug. The Food and Drug Administration requires that all oral contraceptive medications (birth control pills) be packaged with statistical information about the health risks associated with them. To arrive at an intelligent decision based on the information provided, potential oral contraceptive users must be able to understand the statistical summaries that are presented in the medical information sheets.

Consider the following: Suppose you read that the risk of developing heart disease is 10.5 times more likely for oral contraceptive users than for non-users. Most people will conclude from this information that taking oral contraceptives presents a substantial risk of heart disease. Suppose now that you are told that only 3.5 women out of 100,000 users will develop heart disease. You probably would interpret this sentence as meaning that there is little risk associated with oral contraceptive use. Consider the "flip side" of this information and think about how you would assess safety if you read that 99,996.5 women out of 100,000 users will *not* develop heart disease. Does it seem even safer? Another way of presenting the same information is to convert it to a percentage. There is only a .0035% chance that oral contraceptive users will develop heart disease. Most people would now consider the risk associated with oral contraceptive use to be minuscule.

Which of these statements is correct? They all are. The only way they differ is the way in which the statistical information is presented, and different ways of presenting the same statistical information lead to very different assessments of safety (Halpern, Blackman, & Salzman, 1989). It is important to keep this in mind when interpreting statistical information. There is a trend to provide consumers with statistical risk information so that they can make informed safety judgments about a diverse assortment of topics including how to treat a particular type of cancer and the safety of nuclear energy. Although the topic of risk is considered in more detail later in this chapter, keep in mind that the best way to convert risk probabilities to a meaningful value is to write out all of the mathematically equivalent values (i.e., X out of Y occurrences, number of times greater risk than a meaningful comparison event, number that will die, number that will not die). Graphic representations of relative risks can also be helpful when there are many values that need to be compared simultaneously. The use of spatial arrays is touted throughout this book (e.g., circle diagrams when interpreting syllogisms, graphic organizers to comprehend complex prose, tree diagrams for use in making sound decisions). One advantage that they confer in this situation is that they reduce the memory load in working memory and allow us to consider several different alternatives "at a glance."

Games of Chance

People love to play games. From Las Vegas to Atlantic City, and in all of the small towns in between, and in many other countries in the world, people spend countless hours and dollars, euros, and pounds playing games of chance, skill, and semi-skill. For many people, the only serious consideration they have ever given to probability is when playing games of chance.

Cards. Card playing is a ubiquitous pastime, with small children playing "Fish" and "Old Maid," while their older counterparts play Canasta, Bridge, Poker, Pinochle, Black Jack, Hearts, and too many others to mention. The uncertainty inherent in card games adds to the pleasure of playing (although the camaraderie and pretzels and beer also help).

Good card players, regardless of the game, understand and utilize the rules of probability. Let's apply the definitional formula for probability to card games. For example, how likely are you to draw an Ace of Spades from a deck of 52 cards? The probability of this happening is 1/52, or approximately 2%, because there is only one Ace of Spades and 52 possible outcomes. How likely are you to draw an ace of any suit from a full deck of cards? If you have been following the probability discussion so far, you will realize that the answer is 4/52, or approximately 8%, because there are 4 aces in a 52-card deck.

Although some professional card players claim to have worked out careful plans that will help them to change the odds of winning in their favor, it is not possible to "beat the house" for most card games, no matter how good a player one is. It is always difficult to tell the extent to which these stories of successful gamblers are hype. Professional gamblers often enjoy bragging about their winnings and conveniently forget about the times when they lost. Furthermore, most of the self-proclaimed expert gamblers are selling their "winning system." I hope that you recall from the chapters on reasoning and analyzing arguments that when an "expert" stands to gain from the sale of a product, the expert's opinion becomes suspect.

According to Gunther (1977), Vera Nettick (who is a real person) is a lucky lady. While playing a game of bridge, she was dealt a hand that contained all 13 diamonds. Breathlessly, she won a grand slam with the once-in-a-lifetime card hand. Any statistician will be quick to point out that every possible combination of cards will be dealt to somebody sooner or later. Thus, Vera Nettick's hand was no more unusual than any other card hand, although it certainly is more memorable. Can you guess how often such a hand would occur? Gunther (1977, p. 30) figured this out as follows:

> There are roughly 635 billion possible bridge hands. Of these, eight might be called 'perfect' hands, though some are more perfect than others. To begin with, there are four perfect no-trump hands. Such a hand would contain all four aces, all four kings, all four queens, and one of the four jacks. Any of these four hands would be unequivocally perfect, because no bid could top it. Slightly less perfect, in descending order, are hands containing all the spades, all the hearts, all the diamonds, and all the clubs. If there are eight of these perfect hands in a possible 635 billion, the statistical probability is that such a hand will be dealt one in every 79 billion tries, give or take a few.
>
> Now all we have to do is estimate how many games of bridge are played every year and how many hands are dealt in each game. Using fairly conservative estimates, it turns out that a perfect hand should be dealt to some lucky bridge player, somewhere in the United States, roughly once every three or four years.

Consider the two card hands shown in Figure 7.2 on page 353. Every possible combination of cards is equally likely when the cards are dealt at random. This topic is also discussed in the following chapter on decision making.

Roulette

Roulette is often thought of as an aristocratic game. It is strange that it has gained this reputation, because it is a game of pure chance. Unlike most card games, there is no skillful way to play roulette. As you probably know, roulette is played by spinning a small ball inside a circular array of numbered and colored pockets. Eighteen of the pockets are red; eighteen are black; and two are green. Players can make a variety of bets. One possible bet is that the ball will land in a red pocket. What is the probability of this event when the ball is equally likely to land in any pocket? There are 18 red pockets out of 38 pockets (possible outcomes); therefore, the probability of the ball landing in a red pocket is 18/38. Because this is a number less than .5, we know that it will land in a red pocket slightly less than half of the time. Thus, if you kept betting on red, you would lose slightly more often than you would win. Suppose now you bet on black pockets. Again, the probability would be 18/38; and again, if you continue

Figure 7.2 Which of these two card hands are you more likely to be dealt from a well-shuffled deck of cards?

to bet on black pockets, you will lose more often than you win. Of course, sometimes you will win, and at other times you will lose, but after many spins—in the long run, you will lose at roulette.

The odds or probability of winning at any casino game are always favorable to the "house," otherwise casinos could not stay in business. Actually, there is one person who has been able to "beat" the roulette odds. One of my heroes is Al Hibbs, a scientist who gained fame for his work at the Jet Propulsion Laboratory in Pasadena, California, where much of the work on the U.S. space program is done. When he was a student, he used his knowledge of probability to run his original stake of $125 up to $6,300 at the Pioneer Club in Reno. Here is how he did it: Hibbs knows that although every number in a roulette wheel should be equally likely to occur, all manufactured devices have imperfections. These imperfections make some numbers more likely to occur than others. Hibbs and a friend recorded the results of 100,000 spins of roulette wheel to find the numbers that occurred most often. Accordingly, they bet on these numbers. Unfortunately, none of us can duplicate his success, because the wheels are now taken apart and reassembled with different parts each day. Thus, while each wheel is still imperfect, the imperfections differ from day to day.

Computing Probabilities in Multiple Outcome Situations

> If the weather forecaster announced a 50% chance of rain on Saturday and a 50% chance of rain on Sunday, does that definitely mean that it will rain this weekend?
>
> —Gigerenzer (2003, para. 2)

We are often concerned with the probability of two or more events occurring, such as getting two heads in two flips of a coin or rolling a six at least once in two rolls of a die. These sorts of situations are called **multiple outcomes**.

Using Tree Diagrams

Although it is relatively easy to understand that the probability of getting a head on one flip of a fair coin is 1/2, it is somewhat more difficult to know intuitively the probability of getting four heads in four flips of a fair coin. Although an example of flipping a coin may seem artificial, it is a good way of showing how probabilities combine over many trials. Let's figure it out. (Follow along with me, even if you are math-phobic. The calculations and mathematical thinking are relatively easy, if you work along with the examples. Do *not* look at the next several figures and exclaim, "no way, I'll just skip it." It is important to be able to think with and about numbers.)

On the first flip, only one of two possible outcomes can occur; a head (H) or tail (T). What can happen if a coin is flipped twice? There are four possible outcomes: a head on the first flip and a head on the second (HH), a head on the first flip and a tail on the second (HT), a tail on the first flip and a head on the second (TH), and a tail on the first flip and a tail on the second (TT). Since there are four possible outcomes and only one way to get two heads, the probability of this event is 1/4 (again assuming that the coin is fair, that is, that getting a head is as likely as getting a tail). There is a general rule, the "and rule," for calculating this value in any situation. When you want to find the probability of one event *and* another event (a head on the first and second flip), you multiply their separate probabilities. By applying the "and rule," we find that the probability of obtaining two tails when a coin is flipped twice is equal to 1/2 x 1/2, which is 1/4. Intuitively, the probability of both events occurring should be less likely than either event alone, and it is.

A simple way to compute this probability is to represent all possible events with **tree diagrams**. Tree diagrams were used in the chapter on reasoning when we figured the validity of "if, then" statements. In this chapter, we will add probability values to the "branches" of the tree to determine the probability of different combinations of outcomes. Later in this book, I will return to tree diagrams once again as a way of generating creative solutions to problems.

On the first flip, either an H or T will land facing up. For a fair coin, the probability of a head is equal to the probability of a tail, which is equal to .5. Let's depict this as follows:

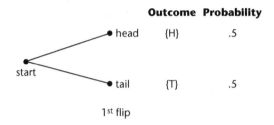

When you flip a second time, either an H on the first flip will be followed by an H or T, or a T on the first flip will be followed by an H or T. The probability of a head or tail on the second flip is still .5. Outcomes from a second flip are added as "branches" on a tree diagram.

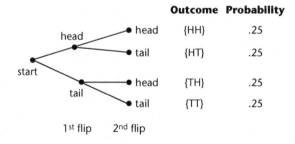

As you can see from this tree, there are four possible outcomes. You can use this tree to find out the probability of other events. What is the probability of getting exactly one H in two flips of a coin? Since there are two ways for this to occur, (HT) or (TH), the answer is 2/4 or 1/2. When you want to find the probability of two *or* more different outcomes, add the probability of each outcome. This is called the "or rule." Another way to ask the same questions is, "What is the probability of getting either a head followed by a tail (1/4) *or* a tail followed by a head (1/4)?" The correct procedure is to add these values, which equals 1/2. Intuitively, the probability of two or more events occurring should be higher (more likely) than the probability of any one of them occurring, and it is.

We can only use the "or rule" and the "and rule" when the events we are interested in are **independent**. Two events are independent when the occurrence of one of them does not influence the occurrence of the other. In this example, what you get on the first flip of a coin does not influence what you get on the second flip. In addition, the "or rule" requires that the outcomes be mutually exclusive, which means that if one occurs, the other cannot occur. In this example, the outcomes are mutually exclusive because we cannot obtain both a head and a tail on any single flip. If you are still wondering about the answer to the question posed in the opening of this paragraph about whether it will rain this weekend given a 50% probability of rain on Saturday and a 50% probability of rain on Sunday, you should be able to "see" that if you replaced the word "heads" with "rain" and the word "tails" with "no rain" in the figures above, you have the same problem. The probability of rain on Saturday and Sunday would be 25% (.50 X .50). The probability of rain on at least one of these days is 75% (.25 + .25 + .25).

Let's get away from the artificial example of coin flipping, and apply the same logic in a more useful context. I am sure that every student has, at some time or other, taken a multiple-choice test. (Some students like to call them multiple-guess tests.) Most of these tests have five alternative answers for each question. Only one of these is correct. Suppose also that the questions are so difficult that all you can do is guess randomly at the correct answer. What is the probability of guessing correctly on the first question? If you have no idea which alternative is the correct answer, then you are equally likely to choose any of the five alternatives, assuming that each alternative is equally likely to be correct. Because the sum of all possible alternatives must be 1.0, the probability of selecting each alternative, when they are equally likely, is .20. One alternative is correct, and four are incorrect, so the probability of selecting the correct alternative is .20. A tree diagram of this situation is shown here.

What is the probability of getting the first two multiple-choice questions correct by guessing? We will have to add a second branch to a tree that will soon be very crowded. To save space and to simplify the calculations, all of the incorrect alternatives can be represented by one branch labeled "incorrect." The probability of being incorrect on any single question is .8:

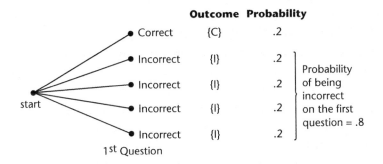

The probability of two correct questions by guessing is .2 x .2, which equals .04. That means that this would happen by chance only 4% of the time. Suppose we extend our example to three questions. I will not draw a tree, but you should be able to see by now that the probability is .2 x .2 x .2 = .008. This is so unusual that it would occur less than 1% of the time by chance. What would you conclude about someone who got all three of these questions correct? Most people (professors are people, too) would conclude that the student was not guessing, and that she really knew something. Of course, it is possible that the student was just lucky, but it is so unlikely that we would conclude that something other than luck was responsible for the outcome we obtained. Let me point out a curious side to this kind of reasoning. Consider the plight of Sara. She took a fifteen question multiple-choice test in which every question had five alternatives. Sara got all fifteen questions wrong. Can you determine the probability of this happening by chance? I won't draw the tree diagram to depict this situation, but it is easy to see that the probability of being wrong on one question is .80; therefore the probability of being wrong on all 15 questions is $(.80)^{15}$. This is .80 times itself 15 times, which equals .0352. Because this would happen by chance only 3.52% of the time, can Sara present the argument to her professor that something other than chance determined this unusual result? Of course, Sara can make this argument, but would you be willing to believe her if you were her professor? Suppose she argued that she must have known the correct answer to every question. How else could she have avoided selecting it in all fifteen consecutive questions? I don't know how many professors would buy her assertion that getting all 15 questions wrong demonstrates her knowledge, even though identical reasoning is used as proof of knowing correct answers when the probability of getting all the questions correct is about the same. (In this example, the probability of getting all 15 questions correct just by guessing is $(.20)^{15}$, which is a number far less than .0001.) Personally, if I were the professor, I would give Sara high marks for creativity and for her understanding of statistical principles. It is possible that Sara did know "something" about the topic, but that "something" was systematically wrong. I would also point out to her that it is possible that she was both unprepared and unlucky enough to guess wrong fifteen times. After all, unusual events do happen sometimes.

Conjunction Error—Applying the "And Rule"

The following problem was posed by Tversky and Kahneman (1983, p. 297):

> Linda is 31 years old, outspoken and very bright. She majored in philosophy. As a student, she was deeply concerned with issues of discrimination and social justice, and also participated in anti-nuclear demonstrations.
>
> For the following list of statements, estimate the probability that it is descriptive of Linda.
>
> A. Linda is a teacher in elementary school.
> B. Linda works in a bookstore and takes yoga classes.
> C. Linda is active in the feminist movement.
> D. Linda is a psychiatric social worker.
> E. Linda is a member of the League of Women voters.
> F. Linda is a bank teller.
> G. Linda is an insurance salesperson.
> H. Linda is a bank teller and is active in the feminist movement.

Stop now and estimate the probability for each statement.

* * *

The short paragraph about Linda was written to be representative of an active feminist, which is statement C. Thus, if we rely on common stereotypes of the "typical feminist," C would seem to be a likely description. Look at statements F (bank teller) and H (feminist *and* a bank teller). How did you rank these two sentences? Most people believe that H is more probably true than F. Can you see why F *must be* more likely than H when being a bank teller and being a feminist are independent of each other? There are some bank tellers who are not active in the feminist movement. When determining the probability of both of two events occurring, you multiply the probabilities of each one occurring (the "and rule"). Thus, the probability of two events *both* occurring must be less likely than the probability of one of these events occurring. In Tversky and Kahneman's study, 85% of the subjects judged statement H to be more probable than statement F. The error of believing that the occurrence of two events is more likely than the occurrence of one of them is called the **conjunction error**.

For those of you who think better with spatial arrays, let's represent this problem with circle diagrams, a form of representation that was used with syllogisms in the chapter on reasoning. Draw one circle to represent every bank teller in the world, and a second circle to represent every feminist. The two circles have to overlap somewhat because there are some bank tellers who are feminists. This area of overlap is shaded in Figure 7.3. As you can see in Figure 7.3, the shaded area that represents all people who are *both* bank tellers and feminists must be smaller than the circle that represents all bank tellers because there are bank tellers who are not feminists.

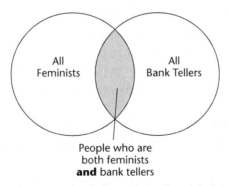

Figure 7.3 The two circles represent "All Feminists" and "All Bank Tellers." The intersection of these two circles shows those individuals who are both feminist and a bank tellers. Because there are feminists who are not bank tellers and bank tellers who are not feminists, the area of their overlap must be smaller than either set alone.

Now that you understand the conjunctive error, try the next question (also taken from Tversky & Kahneman, 1983, p. 308):

> A health survey was conducted in a sample of adult males in British Columbia, of all ages and occupations.
>
> Please give your best estimate of the following values:
>
> What percentage of the men surveyed have had one or more heart attacks? _____
>
> What percentage of the men surveyed both are over 55 years old and have had one or more heart attacks? _____
>
> Stop now and fill in the blanks above with your best estimate of these values.

Over 65% of the respondents believed that a higher percentage of the men would be both over 55 and have had a heart attack than the percentage of men who reported that they had a heart attack. Do you recognize this as another example of a conjunction error? The probability of two uncertain events both occurring cannot be greater than the probability of just one of them occurring.

There are some psychologists who object to all of the emphasis on the ways people make mistakes in their thinking (Gigerenzer, Todd, & the ABC Research Group, 2000; Gigerenzer, 2007). They argue that most of us think pretty well, given real-life circumstances, which include limited time to think through problems and limited information. Most of the time, we rely on heuristics, which are "rules of thumb" or shortcuts for thinking. Gigerenzer and his colleagues consider problems like the "Linda" problem to be "tricks." In this case, we are asked to make a decision about one person, when the probability data refer to the population of all bank tellers and all feminists. He argues that it is not irrational to use "typicality information" (e.g., the typical feminist has certain traits) when making a "best guess" about one person.

There has been much heated debate over the "Linda" problem, probably because so many of us get it wrong. Gigerenzer (2007, p. 97) argues that the word "and" is sometimes used to signify a chronology of events and when used this way, it conveys a different message. Consider this example:

Mark got angry *and* Mary left him. The implication is that Mary left him after and probably because he got angry.

Or this example:

Verona is in Italy and Valencia is in Spain.
This is identical in meaning to:
Valencia is in Spain and Verona is in Italy.

The underlying idea with these examples is that the word "and" does not always signal the conjunction of two events and that is why so many people get the "Linda" problem wrong. Others argue that regardless of the fact that "and" does not always signal conjunctions, it does in the "Linda" problem, and most people get it wrong. This is an area where psychologists disagree about what is rational or reasoned thinking, and it is likely to continue to be a hotly debated topic in the next several years. The point made by Gigerenzer and others who are more optimistic about the quality of human cognition is certainly valid. Many of the examples that show how poorly most of us think seem artificial or lack important information that we normally would consider. Like many of psychology's debates, each side seems to have part of the answer. Under some circumstances, people are easily misled and thinking goes wrong in predictable ways, but under other circumstances, people can think fairly well. The situation is like the proverbial glass that is both half-full and half-empty. Regardless of your personal opinion about this debate, it is true that with hard work, we can all learn to think better—a fact that should make both the optimists and pessimists very happy.

Cumulative Risks—Applying the "Or Rule"

It should be obvious that the probability of getting three questions correct by chance when there are five alternatives will be much smaller than the probability of getting just one question correct by chance, and the probability of getting at least one question correct by chance out of three questions will be higher than the probability of getting one question correct when there is only one question. The kinds of examples presented so far were deliberately simple. Let's see how this principle applies in real world-settings.

Most real-life risks involve repeated exposure to a risky situation. Consider driving. The probability of having an accident in one car ride is very low. But what happens to this probability when you take hundreds or thousands of car rides? According to the "or rule," this is the probability of an accident on the first *or* second *or*. . . . nth car ride. In an interesting study of how people understand the concept of cumulative risk, Shaklee (1987) gave subjects different probability values that supposedly corresponded to the yearly risk of a flood. The subjects then had to estimate the likelihood of a flood in one month, five years, 10 years, and 15 years. Only 74% of her subjects knew that the likelihood of a flood increased with intervals over one year. Among those who gave higher probability values for intervals over one year, most seriously underestimated the **cumulative probability**.

The message here should be clear: When you are determining risk, it is important to understand whether the value you are being given is per some unit of time (e.g., one year) and how cumulative risks increase with repeated exposure. It seems that many people do not understand the concept that cumulative risks are greater than one-time risks.

Expected Values

Which of the following bets would you take if you could only choose one of them?

1. The Big 12

It will cost you $1 to play. If you roll a pair of dice and get a 12, you will get your $1 back, plus another $24. If you roll any other number, you will lose your $1.

2. Lucky 7

It will cost you $1 to play (same cost as above). If you roll a "lucky 7" with a pair of dice, you will get your $1 back, plus another $6. If you roll any other number, you will lose your $1.

Stop now and select either 1 or 2.

Most people choose 1, reasoning that $24 if a 12 is rolled is four times more than they can win if a 7 is rolled, and the cost is the same for each bet. Let's see if this thinking is correct.

In order to decide which is the better bet, we need to consider the probability of winning and losing and the corresponding value of each. There is a formula that will take these variables into account and yield the

expected value (EV) for each gamble. An expected value is the amount of money you would expect to win on each bet if you continued playing over and over. Like all probability values, it depends on what would happen **in the long run**. The formula for computing an expected value (EV) is:

> EV = (probability of a win) x (value of a win) + (probability of a loss) x (value of a loss)

Let's consider the EV for Choice 1. We will begin by computing the probability of rolling a 12 with a pair of dice. This is shown in Figure 7.4.

There is only one way to roll a 12, and that is with a 6 on each die. The probability of this happening when the dice are fair is 1/6 x 1/6 = 1/36 = .028. (Because we are interested in finding the probability of a 6 on the first *and* the second die, we use the "and rule" and multiply.) Thus, we would expect to roll a 12 about 2.8% of the time. What is the probability of not rolling a 12? Because we are certain that you will either roll a 12 or not roll a 12 (this covers all possible events), you can subtract .028 from 1.00. The probability of not rolling a 12 is .972. (You could also arrive at this figure, with some small rounding differences, by calculating the probability of each of the 35 other possible outcomes—each will be 1/36—and adding them together.)

Using these probability values, the EV formula for Choice 1 becomes:

(Choice 1):

EV = (Probability of a 12) x (Value of a 12) +

(Probability of *not* getting a 12) x (Value of *not* getting a 12)

EV = [(.028) x ($24)] + [(.972) x (-$1)]

EV = $.672 -$.972

EV = -$.30 for (Choice 1)Let's review what happened in this formula. If you rolled a 12, you would win $24, which is the value associated with this win. If you rolled a number other than a 12, you would lose the $1 you paid to play this game, thus -$1 is the value associated with this loss. The probability of a win was multiplied by the value of a win. The probability of a loss was multiplied by the value of a loss. Then, these two products were added

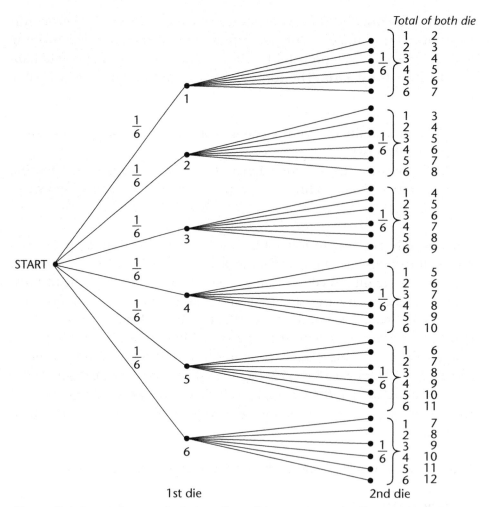

Total of both die

Figure 7.4 A tree diagram depicting all possible outcomes of rolling a pair of dice.

together. The EV of this bet, -$.30, means that in the long run, if you continue playing this game many times, you could expect to lose, on the average, $.30 for every game played. Of course, on any single game, you would either lose $1 or win $24, but after many, many games you would have lost an average of $.30 per game. If you played 1,000 games, making the same bet each time, you would be $300 poorer.

How does this compare with Choice 2? To calculate the EV of Choice 2, we will begin by computing the probability of rolling a 7. How many ways is it possible to roll a 7 with a pair of fair dice? You could get a 1 on one die and a 6 on the other; a 2 and a 5; a 3 and a 4; a 4 and a 3; a 5 and a 2; or a 6 and a 1. Thus, there are 6 possible ways to roll a 7 out of 36 possible outcomes. The probability of any one of these outcomes is 1/6 x 1/6, which equals 1/36. (This is the probability of rolling, for example, a one on the first die and a six on the second die.) Thus, to determine the probability of one number followed by a second number, you would apply the "and rule." Because you are now concerned with the probability of a 1 followed by a 6 *or* a 2 followed by a 5 *or* a 3 followed by a 4 *or* a 4 followed by a 3 *or* a 5 followed by a 2 *or* a 6 followed by a 1, you should recognize the second step as a case where the "or rule" is needed. Since there are six possible combinations, you would add 1/36 six times (which is, of course, the same as multiplying it by 6). Thus, the probability of rolling a 7 with a pair of dice is 6/36 (1/6 or .167). The probability of not rolling a 7 is 1—.167, which equals .833. Now we calculate the EV of Choice 2.

(Choice 2):

EV = (Probability of a 7) x (Value of a 7) +

(Probability of not getting a 7 x (Value of not getting a 7)

EV = [(.167) x ($6)] + [(.833) x (-$1)]

$\quad$ = ($1.002—.833)

$\quad$ = $.169, or approximately $.17 for (Choice 2)

This means that if you continued to gamble on Choice 2, you would win an average of $.17 for every game played. Thus, after 1,000 games, you could expect to be $170 richer. Of course, as in Choice 1, you would never actually win this amount on any single game; this is what would result if you continued playing many, many games. This is what would happen "in the long run."

Even though you might have originally thought otherwise, Choice 2 is the better choice because of the relatively high probability associated with rolling a 7. Seven has a high probability because there were six possible combinations that would add up to a 7.

There is a party game that is based on the principle that the more ways an event can occur, the more likely it is to occur. Suppose you get a random sample of 40 people together in a room. Estimate the probability that two of them share the same birthday. You may be surprised to learn that the probability is approximately .90. Can you figure out why it is so high?

There are many, many ways that 40 people can share the same birthday. To figure out the exact probability, you would take all combinations of 40 people, two at a time. Thus, we would have to start with the combination of person 1 with person 2, then person 1 with person 3, and so on until person 1 is matched with person 40; then we would begin again matching person 2 with person 3, 2 with 4, on until 2 is matched with 40. This whole process would have to be repeated until every one of the 40 people is matched with every other one. Because there are so many possible combinations of any two people sharing any birthday in the year, this "coincidence" is more probable than it may have seemed at first. The probability of two people sharing a common birthday is over .50 when there are 23 people and over .75 when there are 32 people (Loftus & Loftus, 1982). You can use this knowledge to make wagers at parties or at any gathering of people. It is a fairly good bet when the number of people is close to 40. Most people find it hard to believe that the probability is so high.

You can also use your knowledge of probability to improve your chances in other situations. Take, for example, Aaron and Jill, who have been arguing over who should take out the garbage. Their mother agrees to help them settle this matter by picking a number from 1 to 10. The one whose number comes closer to the one selected by their mother will win the dispute. Aaron goes first and picks "3." What number should Jill select to maximize her chances of winning? Stop now and decide what number she should select. The best number for Jill to pick is 4. If her mother were thinking of any number greater than 3, Jill would win with this strategy. Thus, she can change the probability of winning in what seems like a chance situation.

Subjective Probability

We usually do not deal directly with known or objective probabilities, such as the probability of rain on a given day or the probability of developing heart disease if oral contraceptives are taken. Yet, every day we make decisions using our best estimate of the likelihood of events. **Subjective probability** refers to personal estimates of the likelihood of events. This term is in distinction from **objective probability**, which is a mathematically determined statement of likelihood about known frequencies. Subjective probabilities are often wrong in two ways. First is the best guess or subjective estimate of the probability of an event. Consider Charlie, whose dating hopes are described below. More than anything in the world, he wants a kiss from the fair Louise. As you read below, he estimates the probability that she will agree to go on a date with him as .10 and the subsequent probability that she will kiss him as .95. He estimated these probabilities, and he could be way off.

A second way that subjective probabilities can be in error is in his estimate of how high is the "value" of this kiss. There is a large body of research literature on **affective forecasting**, which refers to our ability to predict (forecast) how we will feel (affect) about an event (Hoerger, Quirk, Lucas, & Carr, 2010). As you can probably guess, most people are not very good at accurately predicting how they will feel about something in the future. Alas, Charlie may have overestimated the power of his first kiss. Psychologists who have studied subjective probability have found that human judgments of probability are often fallible, yet we rely on them to guide our decisions in countless situations.

Base-Rate Neglect

Charlie is anxious to experience his first kiss. If he asks Louise to go to the movies with him, he is only 10% sure that she will accept his invitation, but if she does, he is 95% sure that she will kiss him goodnight. What are Charlie's chances for romance?

Initial or a priori probabilities are called the **base rate**. In this problem, the first hurdle that Charlie has to "get over" is getting Louise to go out with him. The probability of this occurring is 10%. It is important to think about this figure—the base rate. Ten percent is a fairly low value, so it is likely that she will not go out with him. He wants to know the probability of two uncertain events occurring—she both goes out with him *and* she kisses him. Before we start to solve this problem, think about the kind of answer you would expect. Will it be greater than 95%, between 95% and 10%, or less than 10%?

To solve this problem, we will use a tree diagram to depict the possible outcomes and the probability associated with each. Of course, it is not likely that Charlie or any other Romeo-wanna-be will actually compute the probability values or draw a tree diagram for determining the probability of this momentous event, but this example demonstrates how likelihoods combine. Maybe he will decide that the probability of a kiss from Louise is so small that he will opt for Brunhilda, who is both more likely to accept his offer of a date and succumb to his romantic charms. Besides, anyone who has actually estimated probability values for romance might also want to be more precise in his estimates of two or more events.

We will start with a tree diagram that first branches into "Louise accepts his date" and "Louise declines." A second branch will be drawn from the Louise accepts his date node indicating whether he gets kissed or not. Each branch should have the appropriate probability labels. Of course, if Louise declines his invitation, Charlie definitely will not get kissed. The branch from the "Louise declines" node is thus labeled 1.00 for "Charlie doesn't get kissed."

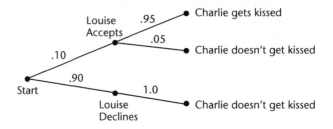

According to the *and* rule for finding the probability of two (or more) events, the probability that Louise will kiss Charlie goodnight is:

.10 × .95 = .095

Are you surprised to find that the objective probability is less than the low base rate of 10% and much less than the higher secondary or subsequent rate of 95%? Most people are. Hopefully, you recognized that any value greater than 10% would have been indicative of a conjunction error. Recall from the earlier section on conjunction errors that the probability of two uncertain events both occurring (Louise accepts *and* kisses Charlie) must be less than the probability of either event alone. Most people ignore (or underestimate) the low base rate and estimate their answer as closer to the higher secondary rate. In general, people tend to overestimate the probability of two or more uncertain events occurring. This type of error is known as **base-rate neglect**. Of course, in real life, estimates of probabilities for events like having a date accept your invitation and then the probability that she or he will kiss you are not very exact, so it may be a bit of a stretch to ask poor Charlie, in this example, to compute the combined probabilities of both of these events actually happening. Other situations in which probabilities are calculated from population values, like the "probability of getting malaria if you travel in a tropic country during a rainy summer" and the "probability of having a reaction to malaria medicine" may be a more realistic example where you might want to calculate joint probabilities. But, in either case, it is important to understand that if one event occurs rarely, the likelihood of that event plus another one will be even less than the rare one alone.

Gambler's Fallacy

The "Wheel of Fortune" is a popular game at fairs, casinos, amusement parks, and on television game shows. It consists of a large wheel, which can be spun. The wheel is divided into many numbered sections, much like a roulette wheel. A rubber marker indicates the winning number.

Suppose that your friend, Vanna, decides to approach the Wheel of Fortune in a scientific manner. She sits at the Wheel of Fortune and records when each number comes up as the winning number. Suppose Vanna has recorded the following series of winning numbers: 3, 6, 10, 19, 18, 4, 1, 7, 7, 5, 20, 17, 2, 14, 19, 13, 8, 11, 13, 16, 12, 15, 19, 3, 8. After examining these numbers very carefully, she proclaims that a 9 has not appeared in the last 25 spins; therefore, she plans to bet heavily on number 9, because it is now much more likely to occur. Would you agree with her that this is a good bet?

If you responded, "Yes," you have committed a very common error in understanding probability. The Wheel of Fortune has no memory for which numbers have previously appeared. If the wheel had been built so that each number is equally likely to win, then a 9 is equally likely on each spin, regardless of how frequently or infrequently it appeared in the past. People believe that chance processes like spinning a Wheel of Fortune should be self-correcting so that if an event has not occurred in a while it is now more likely to occur. This misconception is called **Gambler's Fallacy**. (Of course, if you recall the roulette example, there are some likely imperfections in the wheel which would make some numbers more likely than others, but if this were so, then the fact that 9 was not a recent outcome would mean that it is less likely to occur in a future spin—a prediction that is opposite from gambler's fallacy.)

Gambler's fallacy can be found in many settings. Consider a sports example. A "slumping" batter who has not had a hit in a long while is sometimes believed to be more likely to have a hit because he is "due" one. A sports enthusiast, who is a friend of mine, told me the following story about Don Sutton, a former pitcher for the Dodgers. One season, Sutton gave up a great many runs. He predicted that this "slump" would be followed by a "correction" so that he would end up the season at his usual average. Unfortunately, there is no correction for chance factors and, because he had such a poor start to the season, he ended the season below his usual average.

Often, people will continue to believe in Gambler's Fallacy even after it has been explained to them. Students have told me that while they can understand on an intellectual level why Gambler's Fallacy must be wrong, on an intuitive or "gut" level, it seems that it ought to be right. Understanding probability often requires that we go against our intuitive hunches because they are often wrong. Let's try another example.

Wayne and Marsha have four sons. Although they really do not want to have five children, both have always wanted a daughter. Should they plan to have another child, because they are now more likely to have a daughter, given that their first four children were boys? If you understand Gambler's Fallacy, you will recognize that a daughter is as likely as a son on the fifth try, just as it was on each of the first four. (Actually, because slightly more boys than girls are born, the probability of having a boy baby is slightly higher than the probability of having a girl baby.) Gambler's Fallacy also has a flip side, the belief that random events run in streaks. Consider the following two scenarios:

A. A basketball player has just *missed* 2 or 3 of the last shots in a row. She is about to shoot again.

B. A basketball player has just *made* 2 or 3 of the last shots in a row. She is about to shoot again.

Is she more likely to make the basket in A or B?

Gilovich (1991) asked questions like this one to knowledgeable basketball fans and found that 91% believed that the player was more likely to be successful in B than in A. In other words, they believed that players shoot in streaks. In order to determine whether there is any evidence to support the "belief in streaks," Gilovich analyzed data from the Philadelphia 76ers. He found that:

- if a player just made a shot, 51% of the next shots were successful;
- if a player just missed a shot, 54% of the next shots were successful;

- if a player made 2 shots in a row, 50% of the next shots were successful;

- if a player missed 2 shots in a row, 53% of the next shots were successful.

These data show no evidence that players shoot in streaks. Yet, interviews with the 76ers players themselves showed that they believe that they shot in streaks. It is very difficult to convince people that chance is exactly that—it doesn't self-correct or run in nonrandom streaks.

Making Probabilistic Decisions

Most of the important decisions that we make in life involve probabilities. Although decision making is discussed more fully in the next chapter, let's consider how tree diagrams can be an aid for decision making.

Edith is trying to decide on a college major. She attends a very selective university that has independent admissions for each of its majors. She is seriously thinking about becoming an accountant. She knows that the Accounting Department accepts 25% of the students who apply for that major. Of those accepted, 70% graduate, and 90% of those who graduate pass the national accounting examination and become accountants. She would like to know what her chances are of becoming an accountant if she pursues the accounting major.

To answer this question, draw a tree diagram with branches that represent the "path" for success in accounting.

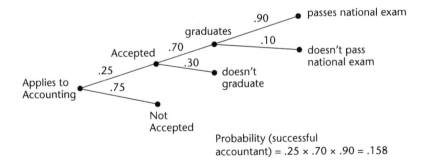

Probability (successful accountant) = .25 × .70 × .90 = .158

From the above diagram, you can see that the probability of becoming a successful accountant is equal to .25 x .70 x .90, which is .158. At this point, Edith might want to consider other options. For example, she could consider applying to both the accounting major and to the education major. She could recalculate her chances for success in one of these majors, both of these majors (if this is a possible option for her), and neither of these majors.

This example assumes that we have no additional information on which to base Edith's chances of success. Suppose instead that we know that Edith has excellent math skills. Shouldn't this sort of information change the probabilities involved and make it more likely that Edith be admitted, graduate, and succeed in a math-related occupation? Intuitively, the answer is "yes." Let's see how the problem changes by considering José's probability for success in the following example.

Combining Information to Make Predictions

José has always wanted to be an actor. Accordingly, he plans to sell his worldly possessions and head for a career in the "Big Apple" (the loving nickname for New York). Suppose that you and José both know that only about 4% of all aspiring actors ever "make it" professionally in New York. This value is the base rate; it is based on information that is known before we have any specific information about José. Stop and think about this figure—the base rate. It tells us that very few aspiring actors become professionals in this field. In other words, the chance of success is low. Suppose that you had no additional information about José. What value would you predict as his chance of success? If you said 4%, right on! In the absence of any other information, use the base rate.

José tells you not to worry, because 75% of those who are successful have curly hair and can sing and tell jokes well. Because he has curly hair and is a good singer and a hilarious comedian, he feels confident that he will soon be sending 8 x 10 glossy pictures of himself to his fan club members. This second value is called the secondary; it is the probability value that relates specific information about characteristics that are associated with José and with an outcome. We will use these two probability values to decide if José's optimism is warranted. Exactly how likely is he to succeed? Before you continue, make a probability estimate for his chance of success. Remember, probabilities range from 0 to 1, with 0 meaning he will definitely fail and have to return to Peoria, and 1 meaning he will definitely succeed on Broadway. Stop now and make a subjective probability judgment of his chance for success.

Can you think of a way of objectively finding his chance of success? In order to arrive at an objective probability, you will need to know another number, one that is often ignored—the percentage of those who fail and have the attributes that are associated with success (in this case, curly hair and the ability to sing, dance, and joke). Few people realize that they need to consider this value in assessing the probability of success. For ease of reference, I will call the attributes that are associated with success (curly hair and ability to sing and tell jokes) "curly hair," and the absence of these attributes, I will call "not curly hair." Suppose that 50% of those who fail have these attributes. Once again, tree diagrams can be used to determine probabilities in this context. Let's begin at a starting point and consider all possible outcomes. In this case, he will either succeed or fail, so we will label the first branches "succeed" and "fail." As before, we will put the probability of each event along the appropriate branch:

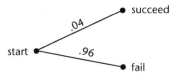

These two probabilities (.04 and .96) sum to 1.0 because they include all possibilities. One of these two possibilities must occur, so they will add up to 1.0 to indicate absolute certainty.

José knows that 75% of those who succeed have curly hair. In this example, what we are trying to find is the probability of a certain outcome (success) *given that* we already have information that is relevant to the probability of that outcome. Let's add a second branch to the tree diagram, branching off from the succeed node and the fail node. There are four different probabilities involved in this example: the probability of succeeding and having curly hair, the probability of succeeding and not having curly hair, the probability of failing and having curly hair, and the probability of failing and not having curly hair. These four possibilities are shown in the next tree diagram.

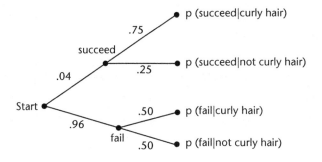

Because 75% (.75) of those who succeed have curly hair and 25% (.25) do not have this attribute, the sum of all probabilities from a tree node must sum to 1.0. Similarly, 50% of those who fail have curly hair, while 50% of those who fail do not possess this attribute. Because we are considering everyone who fails, these values must also sum to 1.0.

Once the tree diagram is drawn, it is a simple matter to compute José's objective probability of success. As before, multiply along each branch to find the probabilities. In this case, we would multiply the values along each branch of the tree diagram and compile the information in a chart:

P[Succeed & Curly Hair]	= .04 x .75 =	.03
P[Succeed & Not Curly Hair]	= .04 x .25 =	.01
P[Fail & Curly Hair]	= .96 x .50 =	.48
P[Fail & Not Curly Hair]	= .96 x .50 =	.48
		1.0000

To determine José's true chance of success, we need to divide the proportion of those who succeed and have curly hair (.03) by the total proportion who have curly hair (.48 + .03 = .51). We are trying to *predict* José's success based on the knowledge that he has curly hair and that some proportion of all people with curly hair are successful. Of all of those with curly hair (.51), what proportion of them succeed (.03)?

$$\frac{\text{Proportion who succeed \& curly hair}}{\text{Total proportion of people with curly hair}} = \frac{03}{.03 + .48} = .06$$

Thus, José's chances for success are 50% higher (6% versus 3%) than they are for any unknown, aspiring actor, but they are still very low. Knowing that he has certain attributes that are associated with success improved his probability of success above the base rate, but the improvement was very small.

You may find it easier to follow the logic of these calculations by putting the information in a table format.

	Succeed	Fail	Row Totals
Curly hair, etc.	0.03	0.48	0.51
No curly hair, etc.	0.01	0.48	0.49
Column Total	0.04	0.96	1.00

Are you surprised to find that his chance of success is so low given that the posterior or secondary probability value was so high (75%)? Most people are. The reason that José has such a slim chance of becoming an actor is because so few people, in general, succeed. The probability value José obtained was close to the a priori, or base rate, of success among all aspiring actors. Because so few actors, in general, succeed, José, and any other would-be thespian, has a low chance for success. In general, most people overestimate success when base rates are low and underestimate success when base rates are high. In the earlier example concerning Edith, we had only base-rate information to use in predicting success. By contrast, we had additional information about José that allowed us to improve upon the base rate when predicting his success, although because of the low rate of success for actors in general, the improvement was slight.

For those of you who prefer to think spatially or think in terms of frequencies instead of probabilities, think about a group of 100 people, 4 of whom are successful actors (4%) and 96 are not (96%). This group is shown in Figure 7.5. Four of the 100 "people" depicted are smiling—these represent the successful actors. If you had no other information to use to predict success for José, you would use this base rate information and give him a 4% probability for success.

Now let's consider the additional information. Three of the 4 of those who are shown smiling have curly hair (3/4 or 75%), whereas half (50%) of those who are not smiling have curly hair. This information is combined with the base-rate information. It is depicted in Figure 7.6 with the addition of curly hair to the successful and unsuccessful actors. Of the 4 smiling faces, 3 have curly hair (75%), and of the 96 frowning faces, 48 (50%) have curly hair.

By examining these figures, it should be easy to see that what we are doing mathematically is finding the proportion of smiling faces with curly hair relative to all of the faces with curly hair in order to use this information about José to predict his success. Graphically, this is 3 smiling faces with curly hair as a proportion (or fraction) of the 51 faces that have curly hair:

$3/51 = 0.06$

To review, when you are calculating the probability of an outcome, given that you have information that is relevant to its probability, you will:

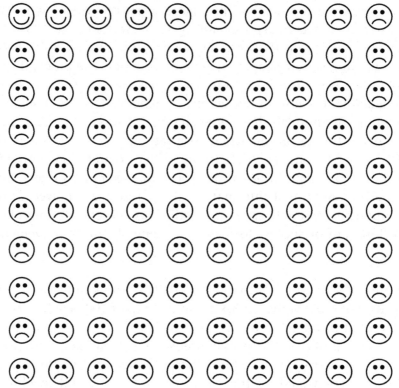

Figure 7.5 Pictorial representation of a 4% success rate. Note that 4% of the faces are smiling, which represents the base rate—4% of all aspiring actors succeed. If we had no personal information about José, his expected probability of success would be 4%.

1. Draw a complete tree diagram, with the base rate information (e.g., success or failure) as the first set of nodes. Use the secondary information to draw the second set of nodes.

2. Make a chart with all combinations of the base rate information and secondary information as the rows in the chart.

3. Multiply probabilities across each of the branches of the tree diagram and fill in each row of the chart with these values.

4. Form a ratio (fraction) with the probability value from the branch that you are interested in (e.g., success given that he has curly hair) as the numerator, and the sum of this value and the other branch that contains the same conditional statement (e.g., failure given that he has curly hair). In this example, 51 people had curly hair (3 were successful and 48 were not successful), so that is the denominator.

5. Check your answer. Does it make sense? Would you expect, as in this example, that the probability of success is higher than the base

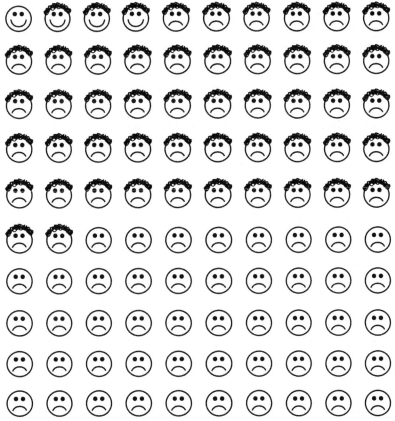

Figure 7.6 Pictorial representation of the relative proportion of successful and unsuccessful actors who have the same attributes of José. These are depicted by the addition of curly hair. When we use personalized information to make predictions, we form a fraction of the proportion of those who are successful and have the attribute (smiling and curly hair) over the total proportion of those who have the attribute (curly hair). In this case, 3 smiling faces with curly hair form the numerator and the 51 faces that have curly hair form the denominator.

rate because we know something about the individual that is associated with success? (If we knew that José had some trait that was associated with failure, we would predict that his chance of success would be less than the base rate, but with low base rates, it probably will not be much less.)

Let's try a more realistic example: There are many diseases that occur with low base rates in the population. Medical test results must be interpreted in light of the relevant base rates for each disease. Medicine, like most other disciplines, is a probabilistic science, yet few physicians receive training in understanding probabilities. Failure to utilize base-rate information can lead to improper diagnoses. Base rate neglect is a pervasive error in thinking about probabilistic outcomes. Consider Dreman's (1979) summary of a large body of research on this effect:

> The tendency to underestimate or altogether ignore past probabilities in making a decision is undoubtedly the most significant problem of intuitive predictions in fields as diverse as financial analysis, accounting, geography, engineering, and military intelligence. (cited in Dreman, D., 1998, p. 236)

Thinking with Frequencies

A common response to problems like the one with José is that the problem is too difficult. In fact, even though many physicians have to interpret laboratory tests where the information is similar to that in the José problem, many of the physicians admit that they do not understand how they can use probability information to make important decisions about the health of their patients. Many people find it easier to think about probabilities in situations like this one by imaging frequencies (Gigerenzer & Hoffrage, 1995; Lovett & Schunn, 1999). Here is a real-life example that was used by Gigerenzer and his colleagues who looked for ways to make computing probability information easier to understand. Everyone was given the same opening paragraph:

> To facilitate early detection of breast cancer, women are encouraged from a particular age on to participate at regular intervals in routine screening, even if they have no obvious symptoms. Imagine you conduct in a certain region such a breast cancer screening using mammography. For symptom-free women aged 40 to 50 who participate in screening using mammography, the following information is available for this region:

After reading this paragraph, half of the physicians in the study were given the probability format and half were given the frequency format. Here is the same information in two different formats (Gigerenzer & Hoffrage, 1995):

Probability format: The probability that one of these women has breast cancer is 1%. If a woman has breast cancer, the probability is 80% that she will have a positive mammography test. If a woman does not have breast cancer, the probability is 10% that she will still have a positive mammography test. Imagine a woman (aged 40 to 50, no symptoms) who has a positive mammography test. What is the probability that she actually has breast cancer?

_____? (fill in your answer)

Frequency Format: Ten out of every 1000 women have breast cancer. Of these 10 women with breast cancer, 8 will have a positive mammography test. Of the remaining 990 women without breast cancer, 99 will still have a positive mammography test. Imagine a sample of women (aged 40 to 50, no symptoms) who have positive mammography tests. How many of these women actually have breast cancer? ____ out of _____?

How did you go about answering these questions?

For the probability format:

Test / Cancer	Lab test shows cancer	Lab test does not show cancer	Row totals
Has cancer	.01 × .80 = .008	.01 × .20 = .002	.01
Does not have cancer	.99 × .10 = .099	.99 × .90 = .891	.99
Column Totals	.107	.893	1.00

Probability: has cancer given that/test shows

$$\text{"has cancer"} = \frac{.008}{.008 + .099} = 7.5\%$$

$$\textit{Frequency:} \ \frac{\text{number who have cancer and positive test}}{\text{number with positive test}} = \frac{8}{107} = 7.5\%$$

The researchers found that when this information was given in the probability format, only 10% of the physicians could reason correctly, but when the information was given in the frequency format, 46% reasoned correctly. The ability to combine probability information is an important thinking skill—decisions about treatment options depend on how people understand numbers. With practice, we can all think better with numbers.

The Problem of False Positives

People may not like or even understand what scientists say, especially when what they say is complex, counterintuitive or ambiguous.

—John Allen Paulos (2009, December 10, para. 1)

The public outcry against two recent recommendations from national health organizations shows the difficulty in understanding information about health risks. Scientists at the U.S. Preventive Services Task Force (USPSTF, 2009) have recommended against routine mammograms for women in their 40s who have no symptoms of cancer. A similar recommendation for men was issued by the same group in 2011; they recommended against a commonly used test (PSA, which stands for protein-specific antigen) that screened for prostate cancer. These recommendations are counterintuitive because most people reason that early screening increases the likelihood that cancer will be detected while in an early stage and early detection can save lives. How can responsible scientists make these recommendations?

The scientists determined that these early screening tests do more harm than good, but it will require some work to explain the reasoning behind this decision. I rely on the excellent article on the prostate screening controversy by Arkes and Gaissmaier (2012) for this explanation. First is a concept that comes up repeatedly in this book—anecdotes are powerful. The statistical analysis behind the USPSTK report does not have the same impact as learning that the brother-in-law of your karate teacher is alive today because he has a PSA test that identified prostate cancer. The limitations of anecdotes are repeated throughout this book.

To explain the reasoning behind NOT getting screened for cancer, Arkes and Gaissmaier (2012) ask you to imagine two large rooms each containing 1,000 men. The men in the Screened Room all had a PSA test, and those in the Not Screened Room did not. About eight men from each room will die from prostate cancer in the next 10 years (Djulbegovic et al., 2010). But how is that possible if many men claim that the PSA test saved their lives?

Now imagine three groups of men in the Screened Room.

Group 1: The PSA Test detected prostate cancer, which led to early treatment, and these men are alive today. The data are not clear as to whether or not their lives were really extended by early detection and treatment, but the men in this group believe their lives were saved by the PSA Test.

Group 2: The second group consists of approximately 20 men who had positive identifications of cancer from the PSA Test, and they received early treatment. But, for the men in this group, the cancers would not have done any harm (they had a slow growing type of cancer) if it had not been detected. Unfortunately many of these men have serious side effects from the treatment, including impotence and/or incontinence. They also had a small risk of dying from the treatment. They do not know that they would have been better off without the PSA Test because the treatments were unnecessary and harmful, so they erroneously believe that the test saved their lives.

Group 3: There are about 180 men in the Screened Room with **false positive** tests. This means that the test was wrong—it diagnosed prostate cancer when they did not have cancer. They underwent biopsies (with some small risk in addition to the pain and expense). Most of these men are relieved to find out that they really do not have cancer and few will be angry about the false positive test result.

With this thought experiment, we can understand why many men who were screened for prostate cancer believe that it is a good test. They do not know about the men in the Unscreened Room where the death rate from prostate cancer is identical to that for men who were screened. Of course, in real life, these rooms do not exist, and we do not have the information about screening presented in a way that is easy to understand. The real situation is actually even more negative when considering cancer screening. Let's assume that 6% of the population of all men actually has prostate cancer. This is a low base rate—which means that it occurs with a low probability. When the base rate is low (as seen in the example presented earlier with the low probability of becoming a successful actor), there will be many false positives (men who are diagnosed with cancer and do not have it) and false negatives (men with cancer who are not identified with the test). Unfortunately, many people have an emotional need for certainty, especially when dealing with health information (Gigerenzer, Gaissmaier, Kurz-Milcke, Schwartz, & Woloshin, 2007). Traditionally, doctor–patient relationships were based on trust, not statistics, but by understanding basic principles in likelihood and uncertainty, we can all make better choices and live better lives.

Nonregressive Judgments

Harris is a new student at Rah-Rah State University. The average grade point average (GPA) for all students at Rah-Rah is 2.8. Harris is new to this college and has not yet taken any exams. Although we have no information about Harris specifically, what would be your best guess that his grade point average will be?

Stop here and make your best guess for his grade point average.

After his first set of midterm exams, Harris has a midterm GPA of 3.8. Given this new information, what would you now predict for Harris' GPA at the end of the school year? Most people readily answer the first question with 2.8, the average GPA for all students at Rah-Rah. This is a correct answer, as in the absence of any specific information, the average for all students, the population at Rah-Rah, is the best estimate for anyone. Most people answer the second question with 3.8. Unfortunately, this is not the best answer. Although it is true that someone who scores high on midterms will also tend to score high on finals, the relationship is not a one-to-one or perfect relationship. In general, when someone scores extremely high on some scale, she or he will score closer to the average the second time. Thus, the best prediction for Harris' GPA at the end of the school year will be less than 3.8 and greater than 2.8. (The actual value can be mathematically determined, but the calculations are beyond the scope of this book.) This is a difficult concept to understand because most people find it to be counterintuitive.

It may be useful to think about a sports example. Consider your favorite athletes. Although they may have a truly exceptional performance one day, most often they will perform closer to average, but still above average on other days. After all, no one bowls all perfect games or bats 1,000. Sports enthusiasts will recognize this principle as the "sophomore slump." After an outstanding first year at a sport, the star will usually perform closer to average during her second year. This phenomenon is called **regression toward the mean**. (Mean is just another term for average—it is computed by adding up all the values you are interested in and dividing that sum by the number of values.)

Earlier in this chapter, I talked about the Laws of Chance. No one can predict accurately the height of any particular individual. But, in the long run, that is with many, many extremely tall fathers, most of their son's heights will show regression toward the mean. Thus, as before, we can make better predictions by knowing about the Laws of Chance, but we will not always be accurate. It is important to understand this concept whenever dealing with probabilistic events.

Kahneman and Tversky (1973) studied what can happen when regression toward the mean is not understood by professionals. Israeli flight instructors were told that they should praise their students when they successfully performed difficult flight patterns and maneuvers and that they should criticize exceptionally poor performance. Based on what you have just learned about regression toward the mean, what, in general, should happen after a pilot performs extremely well? Subsequent maneuvers should be closer to average, or less than exceptional, because the performance moved or regressed toward the mean (average). Conversely, what should you expect to happen following very poor performance? Again, subsequent maneuvers should tend to be more average, or in this case, they would improve, although they may still be less than average. The Israeli flight instructors did not understand regression toward the mean and erroneously concluded that praise led to poorer performance and criticism improved it.

Regression to the mean is ubiquitous, yet few people ever recognize it. Let's consider another example of regression to the mean. Suppose that you learn of a self-help group for people with children who seriously misbehave. (There really are such groups.) Most parents will enter these groups when their child's behavior is at its worst because most parents will seek help only when the behavior is extremely bad. After a few weeks in the program, many parents report an improvement in their child's behavior. Can we conclude that the program probably worked to help parents control their children's behavior? Think regression to the mean! If parents entered the program when the behavior is extremely bad, then no matter what they do, including nothing at all, the child's behavior will most likely regress toward the mean. In other words, if a child is extremely misbehaved, it is statistically true that the child will move toward the average on measures of behavior. We would not predict angelic or even average behavior, just some improvement or movement toward the mean. Because this is a statistical prediction, sometimes, we will be wrong, but on the average and in the long run, we will be right with this prediction. Thus, we cannot conclude anything about the effectiveness of this program unless we conduct a true experiment of the sort that was described in the last chapter. We might randomly assign children and families to these groups and to "no treatment control groups" and then determine if the children in the self-help group were significantly better behaved than those who received no treatment. We must be able to randomly assign families to groups before we can conclude that the self-help group was helpful in improving the child's behavior. Once you start looking for regression to the mean, you will be surprised how many events in life are best explained by "moving toward the average" and not to other causes.

Risk

> We pride ourselves on being the only species that understands the concept of risk, yet we have a confounding habit of worrying about mere possibilities while ignoring probabilities, building barricades against perceived dangers while leaving ourselves exposed to real ones.
>
> —Jeffrey Kluger (2006, para. 4)

If we examine data from thousands of communities around the United States or around the world, we will find that some communities have exceptionally high rates of some sorts of cancers, birth defects, brain tumors, unexplained deaths, and other maladies. How can we know if there are links between these high rates of illness and toxic substances, such as pesticides in the water, magnetic fields from electrical power lines, or chance?

The notion of frequency, or how often an event occurs, is inherent in the definition of probability. If an event is frequent, then its occurrence is highly probable. To determine the risk involved with a disastrous event, we need first to determine the frequency with which it occurs. Because most disastrous events are rare (e.g., plane crashes, leaks from nuclear plants) and, in some cases, take years before they are evident (e.g., cancers from environmental hazards), determining their frequency is a very difficult task. To understand how people make judgments involving risks, we need to understand how they determine the frequency of real-life risky events. Several researchers (e.g., Lichtenstein, Slovic, Fischoff, Layman, & Combs, 1978) have focused on the way people judge the frequency of lethal events. They studied these phenomena by asking college students and members of the League of Women Voters to decide which of two possible causes of death is more probable for several pairs of lethal events. To understand their experiment and their results, let's try a few examples. For the following pairs of items, indicate which is the more likely cause of death and then estimate how much more likely your choice is than the other event:

A. asthma	or	tornado
B. excess cold	or	syphilis
C. diabetes	or	suicide
D. heart disease	or	lung cancer
E. flood	or	homicide
F. syphilis	or	diabetes

G. asthma	or	botulism
H. poisoning by vitamins	or	lightning
I. tuberculosis	or	homicide
J. all accidents	or	stomach cancer

[Researchers found that while, in general, people were more accurate as the differences in the true frequencies of occurrence between the events increased, they made a large number of errors in estimating the relative frequencies of the events. Their subjects overestimated the frequencies of events that occurred very rarely and underestimated the frequencies of those events that occurred very often. In addition, lethal events that had received a great deal of publicity (e.g., airplane crashes, flood, homicide, tornado, botulism) were overestimated, while those that were undramatic, silent killers (e.g., diabetes, stroke, asthma, tuberculosis) were underestimated. It seems that publicized events were more easily brought to mind, and this biased their judgments of frequency. Hazards that are unusually memorable, such as a recent disaster or an event depicted in a sensationalized way on the news, like a major plane crash or botulism in undercooked hamburgers, distort our perceptions of risk. This was clear when a few incidents of shootings in high schools in the United States were immediately followed by anxious parents who took their children out of public high schools and enrolled them in private schools. Of course, the shooting death of high school students was extremely tragic, but these same parents would allow their children to drive when they were sleepy or never instructed them about ways to prevent sexually transmitted diseases, both of which are far more likely to occur than a school shooting. The more salient events were perceived to be the greater risk than the less publicized but more likely dangers of an automobile accident or sexually transmitted disease. In Chapter 2, I made the point that memory is an integral component of all thinking processes. What we remember is a major influence on how we think.

Assessing Risks

How do the experts make decisions that involve potentially disastrous outcomes? How can we, as informed citizens and voters, make less risky decisions? Questions like these are timely, but not easy to answer.

The goal of risk assessment is to find ways to avoid, reduce, or manage risks. Risk is associated with every aspect of life. For example, approximately 200 people are electrocuted each year in accidents involving home wiring or appliances, and 7,000 people die each year in U.S. homes as a result of falls (most of these people are over 65). Yet, few of us would interpret these risks as great enough either to forgo electricity or stop walking in our homes. Other risks are clearly too large to take. Few of us, for example, would decide to cross a busy freeway wearing a blindfold. And still other risks are largely unknown, such as the release of a new chemical into the environment or the development of a new technology. Wilson and Crouch (1987) suggested several ways of estimating risks that voters and consumers should consider when deciding if an action or a technology is safe enough.

- One method of risk assessment involves examining historical data. For example, to understand the risk of cancer due to exposure to medical x-rays, there are data that indicate that for a given dose per year (40 mrem), there is an expected number of cancers (1,100). This sort of risk information can be compared to other known risks so that consumers can decide if the benefits of medical x-rays outweigh the risks.

- The risk of a new technology for which there are no historical data can be computed when the occurrence of the events are independent by calculating the risk of separate components and multiplying along the branches of a decision tree. This method of calculating probabilities was presented in an earlier section of this chapter. A well-known example is the probability of a severe accident at a chemical plant.

- Risks can also be calculated by analogy. (The use of analogies as an aid to problem solving is discussed more fully in the following two chapters.) When animals are used to test drugs, the experimenter is really using an analogy to extrapolate the risk to humans.

Biases in Risk Assessment

Understanding the role of optimistic biases in consequential and emotional domains such as health, relationships, and investments requires studying judgments in circumstances in which passions are strong. . . . We found that people are optimistic in their predictions—they judge preferred outcomes to be more likely than nonpreferred outcomes.
—Cade Massey, Joseph P. Simmons, and David A. Armor
(2011, p. 279).

Psychologists and others who study the way people determine if something is "too risky" know that most of us fall prey to common biases when we assess the "murky psychometrical stew" (Paulos, 1994, p. 34) that constitutes the numerical information and misinformation that we need to interpret. Here are some common biases (Wandersman & Hallman, 1993):

1. When a risk is voluntary, it is perceived to be less risky than one that is not voluntary. For example, cosmetic surgery is often believed to be safer than a nonelective surgery. After all, patients choose to undergo cosmetic surgery, so they must rationalize that it is "safe enough."

2. Natural risks are believed to be less hazardous than artificial ones. For example, many people believe that naturally occurring toxins in our food are less dangerous than ones that are caused by pesticides or preservatives that are added.

3. Memorial events in which many people are harmed at once are perceived as riskier than more mundane and less vivid events. An example of this effect is the large number of people who are terrified of plane crashes, but give little thought to automobile safety.

It is clear that personal risk perceptions are not the same as scientific risk estimates. Experts in risk assessment perceive risks based on annual mortality so that the event that results in the greater number of deaths is judged to be the greater risk. Experts, for example, ranked motor vehicles as riskier than nuclear power (because more people are expected to die from motor vehicle accidents), whereas samples of college students and members of the League of Women Voters ranked nuclear power as the greater risk (because it is an example of a spectacular dreaded outcome).

Answers to the questions about the probability of lethal events with the true frequency of each event (rate per 100,000,000) are found on the next page. Check your answer and see if you made the common errors of overestimating events that are more memorable and likely to affect many people at one time (like a plane crash) and underestimating those risks over which we believe have some control (like driving an automobile).

More Likely	Rate	Less Likely	Rate
A. Asthma	920	Tornado	44
B. Syphilis	200	Excess Cold	163
C. Diabetes	19,00	Suicide	12,000
D. Heart Disease	36,000	Lung Cancer	37,000
E. Homicide	9,200	Flood	100
F. Diabetes	19,000	Syphilis	200
G. Asthma	900	Botulism	1
H. Lightning	52	Poisoning/ Vitamins	.5
I. Homicide	9,200	Tuberculosis	1,800
J. All Accidents	55,000	Stomach Cancer	46,600

Statistical Use and Abuse

> There are three kinds of lies: lies, damned lies, and statistics.
>
> —Disraeli (1804–1881)

When we want to find out something about a group of people, it is often impossible or inconvenient to ask everyone in the group. Suppose you want to know if people who donate blood to the Red Cross are, in general, kind and generous people. Because you cannot examine everyone who donates blood to determine how kind and considerate she or he is, you would examine a portion of the population, which is called a **sample**. A number calculated on a sample of people is called a **statistic**. ("Statistics" is also the branch of mathematics that utilizes probability theory to make decisions about populations.)

Statistics are found everywhere, from baseball earned run averages to the number of war casualties. Many people are rightfully suspicious of statistics. A small book by Huff (1954) humorously illustrates many of the possible pitfalls of statistics. The book is entitled *How to Lie With Statistics*. In it, he rhymes the following message: "Like the 'little dash of powder, little pot of paint,' statistics are making many an important fact look like what she ain't" (p. 9). But, the real message is that you will not be bamboozled with statistics if you understand them.

On the Average

What does it mean to say that the average American family has 2.1 children? This number was computed by finding a sample of American families, adding up the number of children they have, and dividing by the total number of families in the sample. This number could provide an accurate picture of American families, as most may have about two children, with some having more and others less, or it could be very misleading. It is possible that half of the families had no children and half had four or more children, thus misleading the reader into believing that most families had "about" two children, when in fact none did. This is like the man who had his head in the oven and feet in the freezer and reports that, on the average, he is quite comfortable. It is also possible that the sample used to calculate this statistic was not representative of the population—in this case, all American families. If the sample consisted of college students or residents in Manhattan, the number obtained would be too low. On the other hand, if the sample was taken in rural farm areas, the number obtained may be too high. When samples are not representative of the population, they are called **biased samples**. The statistics calculated on biased samples will not yield accurate information about the population.

Averages can also be misleading since there are three different kinds of averages. Consider Mrs. Wang's five children. The oldest is a successful corporate executive. She earns $500,000 a year. The second is a teacher who earns $25,000 a year. Child 3 is a waiter who earns $15,000 a year. The other two are starving artists, each earning $5,000 a year. If Mrs. Wang wants to brag about how well her children turned out, she could compute an arithmetic average, which is called the **mean**. The mean is what most people have in mind when they think about averages. It is the sum of all of the values divided by the total number of values. The mean income for Mrs. Wang's children is $550,000/5 = $110,000. Certainly, anyone who is told this figure would conclude that Mrs. Wang has very successful and wealthy children.

The reason that the mean income for Mrs. Wang's children was so high is because there is one extreme score that inflated this type of average. Averages are also called **measures of central tendency**. A second kind of measure of central tendency is the **median**. It is not affected by a few extreme scores. To compute the median, the values are lined up in ascending or descending order. The middle value is the median. For Mrs. Wang's children, this would be:

$5,000; $5,000; $15,000; $25,000; $500,000.

The middle value, or median, is the third value of $15,000. Thus, she could also claim that her children earn, on the average, $15,000. (When there is an even number of values, the median is equal to the mean of the middle two values.)

Mrs. Wang can honestly claim that her children earn, on the average, $110,000 or $15,000. The point of this discussion is that you should be wary of average figures. To understand them, you need to know whether the average is a mean or median as well as something about the variability of the data and the "shape" of the distribution (the way the numbers "stack up").

Precision

Suppose I tell you that a scientific survey was conducted on the length of workdays for office workers. Furthermore, this study found that the mean workday is 8.167 hours long. Does this sound impressive and scientific? What if I told you that most office workers work about 8 hours a day? Most of you would say, "I know that. Why did they bother?" The point is that we are often impressed with precise statistics, even when the precision is unwarranted. A more humorous example of over-precision comes from one of America's most famous authors, Mark Twain. He once reported that the Mississippi River was 100 million and 3 years old. It seems that three years earlier, he learned that it was 100 million years old.

Significant Differences

If you wanted to know the mean height of all women, you could select a sample of one hundred women, measure their height, and compute the mean. Suppose you took another sample of one hundred women and computed their mean height. Would you expect the means of these two samples to be exactly the same? No, of course not, since there could be expected to be small differences or fluctuations between these values. Each value was computed on different women, and each will yield a slightly different mean value.

If someone measured a sample of women who belong to sororities and found that their mean height is 5'5" and then measured women who do not belong to sororities and found their mean height to be 5'4 1/2", would you conclude that sorority sisters are taller than nonsorority women? I hope not, because small differences between groups can be expected to occur just by chance. There are statistical procedures to determine if a difference computed on two or more samples is likely to have happened by chance. If it is very unlikely to be a chance occurrence, it is called a **significant difference**.

The question of whether a change is meaningful also applies to populations as well. If your college enrollment went from 15,862 to 15,879, would the administrators be justified in concluding that the increase in enrollment is meaningful? The answer to this question depends on many other variables. If the enrollment figure has been edging up slowly every year for the last five years, then these figures may represent a slight, but steady, trend. On the other hand, the relatively small increase could be due to chance fluctuations and may not represent a meaningful trend. Because of chance factors, it could just as easily have gone down. Similarly, a change in the unemployment rate from 10.0% to 9.9% may be nothing more than random fluctuation, or it may be signaling the end of an economic quagmire. You can expect that Democrats and Republicans will interpret these figures differently depending on who is in office at the time.

Extrapolation

Extrapolation occurs when a value is estimated by extending some known values. If the number of psychology majors over the last five years

"Compare pornography today with pornography 100 years ago... Then extrapolate 100 years into the future... Now <u>that</u> stuff is going to be nasty."

From www.CartoonStock.com. Used with permission.

at Podunck University was approximately 150, 175, 200, 225, and 250, respectively, then most people would feel comfortable about the prediction that the number of psychology majors next year will be approximately 275.

Extrapolation can be wrong, and sometimes even ridiculous. For example, suppose we were to examine the drop in the size of American families between 1900 and 1950. By extrapolation, we would predict that the average family size will soon be zero, and then become a negative number. This is, of course, an inconceivable idea! This is like saying that if the times for the 100-meter dash keep decreasing, eventually someone will run it in zero seconds and then in negative time.

Chapter Summary

- Because few things are known with certainty, probability plays a crucial role in many aspects of our lives.

- Probability is defined as the number of ways a particular outcome (what we call a success) can occur divided by the number of possible outcomes (when all outcomes are equally likely). It is also used to indicate degrees of belief in the likelihood of events when the objective probabilities are unknown. People are often inaccurate when they estimate the likelihood of future events.

- In general, people tend to be more confident about uncertain events than the objective probability values allow. We underestimate the role of chance when thinking about many events and invent our own explanations for random outcomes.

- Mathematically equivalent changes in the way probability information is presented can lead to dramatic changes in the way it is interpreted.

- Tree diagrams can be used to compute probabilities when there are multiple events (e.g., two or more flips of a coin). When the events are independent, the probability of any combination of outcomes can be determined by multiplying the probability values along the tree "branches."

- Expected values can be computed that will take into account the probabilities and values associated with a loss and a win in betting situations. One real-life problem with expected values is that people often misjudge the value of an outcome (e.g., how much they will enjoy or dislike something).

- Subjective probabilities are our personal estimates of how likely events with unknown frequencies will occur. These values are distorted systematically when people believe that they have some control over probabilistic events.

- Most people fail to consider the cumulative nature of the likelihood of risky events.

- People judge events that are dramatic and more publicized to be more likely than events that are less dramatic or less well known. In general, people overestimate frequent events and underestimate infrequent ones.

- There is a tendency to ignore base-rate information, especially when making predictions that involve combining information.

- Few people realize that if a person scores extremely high or low on one measure, she or he will tend to score closer to average on the second measure. Regression to the mean is not an intuitive concept, but it is relevant in many settings.

- There are two measures of central tendency that are frequently used—the mean and median. Each is computed with a different mathematical formula.

- There are several systematic biases that operate when most people assess risks. These include downgrading the probability of voluntary risks and those over which we have some perceived control, and overestimating risks that are artificial, memorial, and unobservable.

- Many people erroneously believe that statistics that are expressed in precise numbers (e.g., many decimal places) are highly credible.

- Extrapolation occurs when a value is estimated by extending a trend from known values. Depending on what is being extrapolated and the quality of the data, our best bets for future outcomes can range from fairly accurate to wildly unbelievable.

The following skills for understanding likelihood and uncertainty were presented in this chapter. Review each skill and be sure that you understand how and when to use each one.

- computing expected values in situations with known probabilities
- recognizing when regression to the mean is operating and adjusting predictions to take this phenomenon into account
- using the "and rule" to avoid conjunction errors

- using the "or rule" to calculate cumulative probabilities

- recognizing and avoiding Gambler's Fallacy

- utilizing base rates when making predictions

- using tree diagrams as a decision-making aid in probabilistic situations

- adjusting risk assessments to account for the cumulative nature of probabilistic events

- understanding the differences between mean and median

- avoiding overconfidence in uncertain situations

- understanding the limits of extrapolation

- using probability judgments to improve decision making

- considering indicators like historical data, risks associated with different parts of a decision, and analogies when dealing with unknown risks.

Terms to Know

Check your understanding of the concepts presented in this chapter by reviewing their definitions. If you find that you are having difficulty with any term, be sure to reread the section where it is discussed.

Probability. The number of ways a particular event can occur divided by the number of possible outcomes (when all outcomes are equally likely and the events are independent). It is a measure of how often we expect an event to occur *in the long run*. Probability is also used to express degrees of belief in the likelihood of a future event when there is no objective information about its occurrence.

In the Long Run. Refers to the need for numerous trials in order to derive accurate estimates of the proportion of outcomes that will be a "success." The laws of probability apply to outcomes when there are many trials and not to the outcome on any single trial.

Odds. A mathematical method for indicating probability that is commonly used in sporting events.

Laws of Chance (or Probability). The ability to predict the number or percentage of trials on which a particular outcome will occur.

Overconfidence Phenomenon. The tendency for people to be more confident in their judgments of probability than the objective probability values allow.

Multiple Outcomes. Refers to the probability of an event occurring in two or more trials, such as getting two heads in two flips of a coin.

Tree Diagrams. Branching diagrams that may be used to compute probabilities by considering all possible outcomes in a sequence of events.

Independent Events. Two or more events are independent when the occurrence of one event does not affect the occurrence of the other events.

Conjunctive Error. Mistaken belief that the co-occurrence of two or more events is more likely than the occurrence of one of the events alone.

Cumulative Probabilities. The probability of an event occurring over many trials.

Expected Value. The amount of money you would expect to win in the long run in a betting situation. The mathematical formula for determining expected values is the probability of winning times the value of winning plus the probability of losing times the value of losing.

Subjective Probability. Personal estimates of the probability or likelihood of uncertain events.

Objective Probability. Mathematically determined statements about the likelihood of events with known frequencies.

Affective Forecasting. People tend to be poor at predicting (forecasting) how they will feel in the future if a particular event occurs.

Base Rate. Initial or *a priori* probability that an event will occur.

Base-Rate Neglect. Pervasive bias to ignore or underestimate the effect of initial probabilities (base rates) and to emphasize secondary probability values when deciding on the likelihood of an outcome.

Gambler's Fallacy. The mistaken belief that chance events are self-correcting. Many people erroneously believe that if a random event has not occurred recently, it becomes more likely.

Relative Frequency. How often an event occurs relative to the size of the population of events at the time of its occurrence.

False Positive. A false positive outcome occurs when a test incorrectly predicts an outcome, such as when a test erroneously identifies someone with a disease or other characteristic.

Regression Toward the Mean. In general, when someone scores extremely high or low on some measure, she or he will tend to score closer toward the mean (average) in a second measurement.

Sample. A subset of a population that is studied in order to make inferences about the population.

Statistic. A number that has been calculated to describe a sample. (In its plural form, it is the branch of mathematics that is concerned with probabilities and mathematical characteristics of distributions of numbers.)

Biased Sample. A sample that is not representative of the population from which it was drawn, so you cannot use information from that sample to make inferences about the population.

Measures of Central Tendency. Numbers calculated on samples or populations that give a single number summary of all of the values. Two measures of central tendency are the mean and median.

Mean. A measure of central tendency that is calculated by taking the sum of all the values divided by the total number of values. Also called the average.

Median. A measure of central tendency that is calculated by finding the middle value in a set of scores.

Sample Size. The number of people selected for a study. Samples need to be large enough (actual values are not given here) to make a valid inference about the population.

Significant Difference. A difference between two groups or observations that is so large that it probably did not occur by chance. Statistical tests are used to determine if a difference between samples is statistically significantly different.

Extrapolation. The estimation of a value from a trend suggested by known values.

CHAPTER 8

DECISION MAKING

IT IS A MATTER OF CHOICE

Contents

Six doctors in white hospital coats approach your bed. No one is smiling. The results of the biopsy are in. One doctor explains that the cells were irregular in shape; they appeared abnormal. It seems that the tumor was not clearly malignant, but not clearly normal either. They probably removed the entire tumor. It is hard to be certain about these things. You have some choices. You could leave the hospital this afternoon and forget about this unpleasant episode, except for semi-annual checkups. There is an above-average chance, however, that some abnormal cells remain and will spread and grow. On the other hand, you could choose to have the entire area surgically removed. While this would be major surgery, it would clearly reduce the risk of cancer.

How do you decide what to do? Your first response is probably to ask the doctors what they recommend. But if you do, it is likely that you will not receive a consensus of opinion. Often physicians disagree about the best way to treat a disease, especially when there are many options, as in the case of complicated diseases like cancer, kidney disease, or AIDS. It is possible that some will believe that the risk of cancer is small enough to warrant the wait-and-see decision (why rush to operate?); others will believe that immediate surgery is the best decision (better safe than sorry). Ultimately, the decision is yours.

Of course, not all decisions are a matter of life and death. We are constantly making minor decisions without much thought, such as what to wear, what to eat for breakfast, which pen to buy, and when to go to sleep. Everyone is faced with a lifetime of decisions, and some of them have major and far-reaching consequences. In this chapter, we are concerned with life's major decisions. Major decisions include medical decisions like the one at the beginning of this chapter, whether to marry, whom to marry, if and when to have children, what kind of occupation to choose, how to spend your hard-earned dollars, etc. These are all personal decisions that virtually every-one has to make. We also must decide on a host of political and business issues like whether to support off-shore drilling for oil, when to increase a company's inventory, which stock to invest in, how to negotiate a contract, which party to support during political upheaval, and how to increase prof-its. In this chapter, you will learn skills designed to help you make sound decisions. To accomplish this, we look at the way psychologists and others study decision making, examine common pitfalls and fallacies in the deci-sion-making process, consider the risks involved, and develop a general strategy or plan that you can use when faced with a major decision.

Decision making always involves making a choice between a set of possible alternatives. If you have read the previous chapters in this book, then you have already encountered several sections on how to make intelligent choices. In the chapter on analyzing arguments, for example, you consid-ered the way in which reasons support or refute a conclusion. When ana-lyzing arguments, you make many decisions about the relevance and accuracy of information and how well the reasons that are provided sup-port an action or a belief. In the chapters on hypothesis testing and using probabilistic information, you learned about drawing tree diagrams, col-lecting information, and computing likelihoods to make decisions. Because decision making is a central theme in critical thinking, different aspects of it are presented throughout this book.

Making Sound Decisions

Decisions *per se*, take place when a goal is specified, when information is gathered and judged, when values are used to choose the best solu-tion, and when detailed plans are made and valuated.

—Wales & Nardi (1984, p. 1)

The decision-making process is frequently stressful. Ask anyone you know who has recently made an important decision and you will most likely be told about sleepless nights, loss of appetite (or excessive eating), irritability, and generalized feelings of anxiety.

It may seem that one way to cope with the stress of decision making is to avoid making decisions whenever possible. Although avoidance is one way of handling stressful decisions, it is seldom a good way. You should be pleased to know that there is good evidence that people make better deci-sions after they receive instruction in critical thinking (Helsdingen, van den Bosch, van Gog, & Merrienboer, 2010). Every time you find yourself avoiding a decision, remember that, in most cases, avoiding a decision is, in fact, making one without any of the benefits of a carefully thought out consideration of the problem.

A Framework for Decision Making

> Results from past research have indicated that poor decisions with regard to drugs, alcohol, and other issues involving personal risks often stem from poor decision-making *strategies.*
>   —Kevin Knight and Donald F. Dansereau (1992, p. 1)

There is a common model or framework that can be used to organize our thinking about decision making. It will be extended in the following two chapters, which are concerned with solving problems and thinking creatively. The three topics that are discussed in these chapters—decision making, problem solving, and creative thinking—have a great deal of overlap in the way they are conceptualized. The term "decision making" is used when the task requires the decision-maker to select the best alternative from among several possibilities, and the term *problem solving* is used when the task requires the problem solver to generate alternatives. This sort of distinction is arbitrary, and in real life, it is often difficult to decide if the task requires the generation of alternatives or the selection of alternatives. A decision or solution is creative when it is both unusual and good or effective. Take the time to examine Figure 8.1 carefully. It contains the essential components of a framework for understanding and improving decision making, problem solving, and creative thinking.

In Figure 8.1, the process of making a decision is depicted as a series of boxes, each of which represents a different component, and several arrows that show the recursive nature of the process. These boxes are set in a large oval, which represents the context in which the decision is being made. The first stage in making a decision is the identification or realization that a decision is needed. This is followed by the generation of alternatives that would satisfy a goal or the desired outcome that is implied by the decision. Usually each alternative has pros and cons associated with it, or, in the language of decision making, costs and benefits. The task for the decision-maker is to choose the "best" alternative. The consideration of what is "best" requires an evaluation phase in which "best" often turns out to be multidimensional. Best for whom? Best by what criteria? Best in the immediate future or long-term?

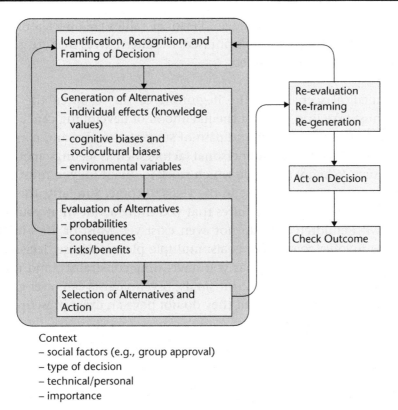

Figure 8.1 A multiprocess model of decision making. Each of the boxes represents a stage in the decision-making process. The arrows show that the process is recursive with frequent recycling through the stages (e.g., generating alternatives may be followed by reframing the decision). The rectangular boundary represents the effects of context.

Decisions also involve uncertainty because we cannot know in advance the consequences of our actions. Much of the difficulty when making decisions lies in judging which alternative is most likely to turn out best. Decisions usually are made with missing information and involve guesses and predictions about future events. Decision making is also a recursive or recycling process because the nature of the decision may change as more alternatives are generated and evaluated. The decision also requires an action, although it may not be an overt movement—you could decide whom or what to believe, or to do nothing at all. All of these processes occur in a context that influences what happens and rely heavily on the information you bring with you to the decision and the information that you obtain during the decision-making process. For example, you may make a different decision if you are being observed by your friends than if you were alone (context effect), and an expert in a field may reach a different decision than a novice (effect of prior knowledge). Personal values are also a strong influence on the way the decision is phrased, the alternatives that are generated, and the way they are evaluated.

In the medical scenario at the beginning of this chapter, the decision-maker must take into account the likelihood of developing cancer at some time in the future, the risks and pain of surgery, the pros and cons of various treatment regimens, and personal factors such as feelings about quality of life issues. When you decide which stock to invest in, you must consider what the economy will be like in the years to come. Similarly, the decision whether to have children requires that you think about what your life will be like with children who do not even exist yet. Most of life's important decisions involve competing goals: multiple players whose decisions will, in turn, affect the choices that you have; time constraints; and uncertain and changing contexts. Not surprisingly, psychologists can offer guidelines for making good decisions, but they do not have an exact prescription that will work for all decisions.

Good Decisions and Subjective Utility

> After critical thinking instruction, trainees considered more observations, identified more cause-and-effect relations, provided better arguments, and made better decisions according to subject matter experts.
> —Anne S. Helsdingen, Karel van den Bosch, Tamara van Gog,
> and Jeroen J. G. van Merrienboer (2010, p. 537)

Decision making is an active process. The decision-maker takes responsibility for her or his own future. After all, you are in the best position for determining how you want to spend your life and how you should make the business and professional decisions that will ultimately reflect on you. Good decision-makers are more likely to get the good jobs and make favorable decisions about their personal lives as well. Recall from the first chapter that *critical* thinking was defined as the use of those skills or strategies that increases the probability of a desirable outcome. But, the quality of a decision needs to be judged on the basis of what was known or should have been known at the time the decision was made; sometimes, good decisions will have undesirable outcomes and sometimes poor decisions will have good outcomes. Although many famous instances of good decisions (profitable investments, successful army maneuvers) and bad decisions (Watergate, the U.S. attempt to rescue American hostages in Iran) come to mind, it is important to realize that a decision should be judged to be good or bad before the outcome is known, not after the fact. You could decide to bet your life savings on a horse race (a bad decision) and "get lucky." Of course, good decisions will result in desirable outcomes much more frequently than poor decisions will.

Often, we will never know if the best decision was made. If you are a college senior who must decide between a lucrative career in accounting or a more personally rewarding career as a high school English teacher, you may never be sure if you picked the better option because you can only speculate about the career you did not select. Robert Frost, the famous American poet, captured this feeling in his poem about a traveler who comes to a fork in the road. The traveler can never know about "the road not taken."

Good decision-makers will have more desirable outcomes than poor decision-makers, but what makes an outcome desirable? This is a difficult question to answer because people have different values and different goals. In deciding on a career path, it seems obvious that decisions must reflect the individual predilections of each person making this decision, just as we would not all want to marry the same person or live the same life. Somehow, we need to weigh personal values, probabilities of success, costs, and benefits to determine which choice is the best balance of these and other difficult-to-quantify variables (Baron, 1997). The term **subjective utility** refers to the value of a particular choice to an individual. It is a personal assessment about a choice (subjective), which is one reason why decision making will never be an exact science like mathematics.

As I said previously, before a decision can be made, the individual must realize that a decision is needed and that there are several possible alternatives. Let's consider an example. Monica is taking several demanding college courses. She needs to supplement her income by working part-time and has family obligations as well. Her free time is virtually nonexistent. Monica needs to consider alternatives to her current life style. She must decide how to juggle all of these commitments. Monica has to realize that she can change her life. Too often, this first step is missed and inertia sets in. Simply stated, the problem is that Monica has too many responsibilities and this is making her feel anxious and stressed. The best solution will give her more time for herself while still allowing her to fulfill her responsibilities; the way she decides to balance these competing demands will depend on her personal value system (e.g., importance of spending time with her family versus the amount of money she "needs" to maintain a life style that she wants). As these are essentially conflicting goals, the best decision will probably involve a compromise that will only partially satisfy each goal. It is not likely that she will find a course of action that will allow her to fill her days with leisure activities while maintaining high grades, earning money, and caring for her family.

The objective criterion for a good decision is that it has high subjective utility for the person making the decision. Some possible good decisions for Monica include finding a higher paying job, reducing her expenses so she would need to work fewer hours, beginning a more efficient study program, taking a lighter course load, and visiting her family less frequently. You may be surprised to find that with a little effort, several possibilities occur to you that you might otherwise never have considered.

Devoted "Trekkies" (fans of the television and movie series called *Star Trek*) can recall many stories in which the plot involved particularly clever decision making. Consider, for example, the Trekkie-classic movie, *Star Trek II: The Wrath of Khan*. In the opening scene, an attractive pointy-eared Vulcan is facing a serious problem. A sister spaceship has wandered into enemy territory and has sent a distress signal. If she does not go in to save them, they will perish; if she does, she risks enemy attack. She nervously decides to follow them into enemy territory and is immediately apprised that her starship is under attack. We soon learn that this is a computer-simulated drill designed to test the decision-making skills of future Starfleet commanders and that only one person has made the correct decision in this drill. Of course, it is Captain James T. Kirk, the hero of this series. The question of interest is whether to attempt to save the sister ship by entering enemy territory and thus risk enemy attack. Captain Kirk did neither—he redesigned the computer problem so that he would have additional choices with more favorable outcomes. For him, the problem was "how to change contingencies in a mock drill." For others, the problem had been "how to save the sister starship without being attacked." Captain Kirk made a superior decision because he defined the problem in a unique way. His unusual and excellent alternative made this decision very creative, a topic that is discussed in a later chapter. Some may say that he cheated or "copped out" by redesigning the simulation, but perhaps, he would use his ability to define problems in a unique way if he were out in space and that is what makes him an outstanding Starfleet commander. The point being made here is that often there are alternative ways of formulating what the decision requires, and some formulations will result in more favorable outcomes than others. Different formulations will lead to different solutions.

Descriptive and Prescriptive Processes

> Whenever there is a simple error that most laymen fall for, there is always a slightly more sophisticated version of the same problem that experts fall for.
>
> —Amos Tversky (quoted in Gardner, 1985, p. 360)

Researchers who study decision making look at what people do when they are making a decision, often contrasting what people actually do with what they should do in order to maximize the probability of a good decision. This is the difference between a descriptive and a prescriptive account of the process. Any program that is designed to help people make better decisions will have to take into account what typically is right and wrong with most decisions (Descriptive Process), and then provide a systematic way of eliminating or reducing common errors while increasing those processes that underlie good decisions (Prescriptive Process). With so many processes involved and so many decisions that need to be made, it is easy to find ways that decision making goes wrong.

Baron (1990) analyzed all thinking into "search" and "inference" stages. The search occurs when we have to generate alternatives, and to a lesser extent, when we decide what constitutes a good decision. The inference relates to the kinds of judgments that are made and the way information is used. Thinking goes wrong when the search process misses some good alternatives or when the inference is incorrect (e.g., selecting an alternative that really will not solve the problem or will create other problems).

The alternatives that people generate are tied to the way memory is structured and accessed. An oft-repeated theme throughout this book is the pervasive influence of memory on all aspects of thinking. The sort of alternatives that are generated will depend on what we can recall in the particular situation. Decision making is also constrained by the amount of cognitive effort that is invested in the processes of generation and evaluation. We do not want to spend huge amounts of time and energy in making most decisions, so we rely on shortcuts that are likely to be useful, but sometimes lead to poor decisions. The idea is to be flexible so that the cognitive effort is proportional to the importance of the decision.

Pitfalls and Pratfalls in Decision Making

> Great moments in history all turned on someone's judgment as to what should be done and someone's decision to do it.
>
> —Hal R. Arkes and Kenneth Hammond (1986, pp. 211–212)

A pitfall is a danger or difficulty that is not easily avoided. If you have ever spent long afternoons at the beach, you have probably seen bratty kids creating pitfalls. They dig holes in the sand and cover them with newspaper so that unsuspecting sun lovers will fall into them. The word "pratfall" needs no formal definition for fans of comedians who are famous for their frequent pratfalls. The American Heritage dictionary defines a pratfall as "a fall on the buttocks." Put these terms together and you will realize that unless common pitfalls in decision making are avoided, the decision-maker will slip and fall on the part of the anatomy that is featured on blue jeans commercials. Let's examine some of the common fallacies or pitfalls in decision making.

Failure to Seek Disconfirming Evidence

> Some of the worst disasters nations have known are traceable to faulty judgments or distorted perceptions of their political leaders.
> —Arie W. Kruglanski (1992, p. 455)

Suppose you have a friend who is always working on crossword puzzles, anagrams, mazes, and other similar problems from puzzle books. He corners you one day with the following problem:

> I am going to give you a series of numbers. This series conforms to a simple rule. You have to figure out what the rule is. The way to do this is by coming up with your own series of numbers. I will tell you whether your own series conforms to this rule. You can give me as many series of numbers as necessary to discover the rule. When you believe that you know the rule, tell it to me and I will let you know if you are right.

Reluctantly you agree to participate. You are given the following number series:

2 4 6

Stop right now and think how you would go about generating other number series that conform to the same rule as this one.

This problem was actually presented to many subjects in an experiment conducted by Wason (1960, 1968). He found that most people had difficulty with this task. Suppose that you believe that the rule is "any continuous series of even numbers." To test this rule most subjects would try series like "14, 16, 18." The experimenter would respond that this series conforms to the rule. To be certain, most subjects would try again with another series, "182, 184, 186." Again, the experimenter would respond affirmatively. Confidently, the subject would announce the rule, "Any continuous even series of numbers." The experimenter then informs the subject that this is not the correct rule.

Typically, subjects will try again, this time thinking up a new rule that will describe the correct number series. Suppose, this time the subject decides to try out the rule "the middle number is halfway between the other two." Now the subject asks about the series "50, 100, 150." The experimenter answers that this series is correct. The subject tries again "1006, 1007, 1008" and is told that this also conforms to the rule. Even more confident this time, the subject announces that the correct rule is "the middle number is halfway between the other two." The experimenter tells him that this is not the correct rule.

Have you discovered the correct rule by now? It is "increasing whole numbers." After almost an hour of working on this problem, one of Wason's subjects came up with this rule: "The rule is that either the first number equals the second minus two, and the third is random but greater than the second, or the third number equals the second plus two, and the first is random but less than the second." You can imagine how this poor subject felt when he was told that this rule was incorrect.

Why is this problem so difficult? In all of the sample number series most of the ones people actually try, the number series conform to the rule they have in mind. There is an infinite number of possible number series that conform to the correct rule, "numbers in increasing order of magnitude." What subjects should have done is try out series that would disconfirm the rule they were trying out. For example, if you believed that the correct rule is "any continuous series of even numbers" you should try the series "1, 2, 4." If the experimenter tells you that you are correct, then you know that the rule "any continuous series of even numbers" must be wrong.

The tendency to seek information that agrees with the ideas we have is called confirmation bias. We have a bias or predilection to look for confirming information. It is among the most pervasive and pernicious biases in decision making. Other examples of the confirmation bias or failure to seek disconfirming evidence were discussed in the chapter on the development of reasoning skills. Examples can probably be found in every applied setting. For example, studies of military decision making have identified confirmation bias as a particular problem because it leads decision-makers to focus on a single hypothesis and then seek only information that confirms that hypothesis (Puvathingal & Hantula, 2012).

What can we infer from the bias to seek confirming evidence? Suppose someone confronts your best friend with "the opportunity of a lifetime." A dynamic saleswoman offers him the chance to invest in a new corporation that will manufacture and sell computers that are so small they will fit in your wallet. It sounds good, but he is unsure. Prudently, he decides to do some investigating. He checks out 10 computer companies that are listed on the New York Stock Exchange. He finds that IBM is a large profitable corporation. If he had only invested in IBM when it was just being formed, he would be a rich man today. He can already imagine himself lighting cigars with $10 bills. What advice would you give your friend?

Hopefully, you would point out to him that he only looked for evidence that supports the decision to invest in the corporation as only substantial corporations are listed on the stock exchange. He also needs to seek evidence that would disconfirm this decision. He should find out how many new computer corporations with big dreams have gone bankrupt and how many have not gone bankrupt in the last 10 years. He also should attempt to estimate the future market for wallet-sized computers.

The confirmation bias is a pitfall in decision making. A large-scale study of NASA scientists showed a strong confirmation bias (Mynatt, Doherty, & Tweney, 1978). (And yes, these are rocket scientists!) We all need to be trained to seek and examine data that are inconsistent with the ideas we are considering. There is good evidence that when people are required to consider counterevidence, they make better decisions (Koriat, Lichtenstein, & Fischhoff, 1980). In general, people spend resources (time, effort, money) looking for the wrong sort of information to inform their decisions— we need to deliberately seek information that would run counter to a preferred choice.

Can people learn to avoid, or at least reduce, the strong bias for information that supports a favored view? Lilienfeld, Ammirati, and Landfield (2009) believe that this is the most important question we can pose about decision making, and that if we can correct this cognitive error, human welfare will be enhanced. The research literature on this question is surprisingly scant, but Lilienfeld et al., (2009, p. 395) conclude that they are among the *meliroists*, "namely those who believe that human thinking often departs from rational standards and that such departures may be rectifiable by intervention efforts." Every time you recognize your own tendency toward confirmation bias and take deliberate steps to consider evidence that does not support your preferred conclusion, you are proving them right.

Overconfidence

Overconfidence is a decision-making pitfall that is related to the bias to seek confirming evidence. In general, most people do not see the need to improve the way they make decisions because they believe that they are already making excellent decisions. The unwarranted belief that we are usually correct is a major, real-life barrier to critical thinking. The tendency to be overconfident about the quality of our thinking is a theme that runs through several chapters in this book. Most people believe that they think well—it is other people whose thinking needs improvement. After all, if most people are very confident that they are making the correct decision, why should they exert the time and effort to learn and apply the skills of critical thinking?

Do you think that groups make better decisions than individuals do when they are working alone? In other words, are two (or more) heads better than one? Most people reason that when several people come together to make a decision, it will be better than any of the participants alone because collectively there is more knowledge in a group. Virtually all public policies and legal and corporate decisions are made by groups. But, it seems that a big disadvantage of groups is that the participants in groups are overconfident in their collective decisions and thus disregard information that might cause them to alter their decision (Minson & Mueller, 2012). Researchers found that dyads (groups of two people) tend to make decisions that are as good as larger groups, and obviously, there are lower costs associated with smaller groups. Most importantly, groups need to be made aware of their tendency toward overconfidence and learn to be open to additional information that might alter their decision.

Irving Janis (1972) did classic work on the overconfidence of groups. His analysis (some of which is presented later in this chapter) was based on numerous real-life examples and the concept of **group think** has been applied to decisions about the Bay of Pigs, Watergate, Pearl Harbor, the launch of the Challenger, and more recently, the belief by many people in the United States that Iraq had weapons of mass destruction. Group think refers to the "illusion of invulnerability, myopia, biased selective attention, and overconfidence" (Hastie, 2006). Group think results when groups do not welcome dissent and pressure its members to make unanimous decisions.

Availability Heuristic

A **heuristic** is any "rule of thumb" that we use to make decisions and solve problems. It does not always give us the right answer, but it is a helpful aid. (Definitions of these terms sometimes differ in mathematics.) Psychologists usually distinguish between heuristics and algorithms. An **algorithm** is a procedure that will always yield the correct answer if you follow it exactly. Let's try a simple example from mathematics to clarify these terms. Remember the procedures you learned in solving long division problems. Given a problem like $176\overline{)7019}$, you were first told to estimate about how often 176 would "go into" 7019, as it is unlikely that you ever learned the 176 tables. You might estimate it to be about 4 times. The problem thus far would look like this:

$$\overset{4}{176\overline{)7019}}$$

You would check out this estimate with the appropriate multiplication.

$$\begin{array}{r} 4 \\ 176\overline{)7019} \\ \underline{704} \end{array}$$

Oops, too large!

You would soon realize that 4 was too large and would probably try 3. This procedure is a heuristic. It is a guide or aid to help you find the correct answer, but it does not always work perfectly as seen in the above example. On the other hand, an algorithm always leads to the correct answer. If you want to find the area of a rectangle that is 3 feet long and 2 feet wide, you will always get the correct answer if you use the formula: length x width, or in this case, 3 feet x 2 feet = 6 square feet. The use of an appropriate algorithm is an example of cognitive economy, a topic that was introduced earlier in this book. We do not need to use mental effort and "reinvent" ways to find the area of a rectangle when there is a ready-to-use algorithm that we can call upon for the correct answer.

Availability is a commonly used heuristic. It is the belief that information that is easily available in memory occurs more frequently than information that is more difficult to recall. The term *availability heuristic* was coined by two prominent psychologists, Daniel Kahneman and Amos Tversky (1973; Tversky & Kahneman, 1974), who conducted numerous experiments on decision making and, in the process, provided a catalog of thinking errors. In order to understand the availability heuristic, consider the following questions:

1. Are there more words in the English language that begin with the letter "r" or have the "r" in the third position?

2. Would you expect the 2010 census to show that there are more librarians or farmers in the United States?

3. Are there more deaths due to homicide or due to diabetes-related diseases?

If you answer the first question like most people, you believe that there are more words that start with the letter "r" than there are words with "r" in the third position. In answering this question most people find that they can think of more words that start with "r" (rice, root, room, roam, religion, rhinoceros, rye) than have "r" in the third position (bird, torrid, horror, hero). In the jargon of psychology, words starting with the letter "r" are more available (in memory) than words with "r" in the third position. That is, they come to mind more easily. If you answered "words that start with 'r,'" you were wrong. According to Berger (1995), the English language contains many more words with "r" in the third position than in the first position. It is just more difficult to think of them because it is easier to retrieve words from memory by the first letter than by the third. Earlier in this chapter I talked about the pervasive influence of memory in every aspect of critical thinking. This is another example of the way in which the kinds of memories we retrieve can determine how decisions are made.

If you have already read the chapter on likelihood and uncertainty, then you already know that there has been a backlash against the idea that humans are poor thinkers. In recent years, there has been more emphasis on accuracy in everyday thinking than in errors in thinking. Gigerenzer and his colleagues (e.g., Gigerenzer & Goldstein, 2011) examined several thinking biases to show that under some conditions, thinking with heuristics is fairly accurate. For example, in a study where students in Turkey and

England were asked to forecast the results of English soccer matches, the students from Turkey, who knew very little about soccer in England, were as accurate as their English counterparts (Ayton, Onkal, & Reynolds, 2011). It seems that the Turkish students used the **recognition heuristic**— if they recognized the name of a team or the city it represented, they estimated that team would win more often than a team they never heard of or came from a town they never heard of. This heuristic worked well. The conclusion from this line of research is that accuracy in decision making depends on the way questions are asked, what is being compared, and a host of other variables. The goal of this book is to improve thinking, not to argue how good most of us are as thinkers—we can all always improve.

Your answer to the second question probably depends on whether you live in an urban or rural area. Most city dwellers believe that there are more librarians than farmers in the United States. After all, few city dwellers have ever met a farmer while they probably know, or at least know of, several librarians. Actually, there are many more farmers in the United States than there are librarians, a fact that was more likely to be answered correctly by readers from rural farm regions. This is another example of how the use of the availability heuristic can lead to the wrong decision.

Most residents of large cities probably believe incorrectly that there are more deaths due to homicide than to diabetes. The reason for this is not difficult to understand. Pick up any newspaper or watch television news on any day and there is likely to be a report of one or more homicides. Although you may know only a few people who have diabetes and may not know personally anyone who has been murdered, you have heard or read about many homicide victims, so there seems to be more of them. A study of people who watch many violent television shows found that these people believe that they are more likely to be a victim of a violent crime than those who do not watch these shows (Gerbner, Grass, Morgan, & Signorielli, 1980). Presumably they maintain this belief because examples of violent crimes are more readily available in their memory. This finding has important implications because it would be expected to affect how frequent viewers of televised violence vote on crime-related propositions and how they make decisions like buying a home burglary alarm, keeping a gun in the house, or going out at night.

The availability heuristic can be found in many applied settings. Its influence can best be understood with an example:

In a medical text written by Gifford-Jones (1977), the author discussed the difficult medical decision concerning whether women in their late thirties or early forties should have their ovaries removed when they are having a hysterectomy. Like all difficult decisions, there are costs and benefits associated with each alternative. In discussing how this decision is often made, Gifford-Jones (1977, pp. 174–175) wrote:

> I recall operating some time ago with a former professor of gynecology at Harvard. He was in a rather philosophical mood and was pondering the pros and cons of what to do with the ovaries. "Sometimes whether or not I remove the ovaries depends on what has happened to me in the last few weeks," he said. "If I've watched a patient die from cancer of the ovary, I often remove them. But if I've been free of this experience for a while, I'm more inclined to leave them in."

Availability has been carefully studied in the laboratory by research psychologists because it plays a role in the way decisions are made in a wide range of settings. Consider how students rate the quality of a particular course or instructor. In one study, students were asked to list either two ways in which a course could be improved (an easy task) or 10 ways (a difficult task; Fox, 2006). Because most students could not think of 10 ways to improve a course, which they assumed to be the norm, they decided that they liked the course much more than those students who were told to list 2 ways the course could be improved. The ease with which we can retrieve information from memory plays an important role in the decisions we make.

The availability heuristic was used during an election in 2010 in California, in which Carly Fiorina (a business executive) was challenging the long-time incumbent Senator Barbara Boxer. In her campaign advertisements, Fiorina asked voters what Boxer had done for them. In fact, few people are able to name any action that their Senator has taken, so when asked this question, most people could not recall anything and concluded that Boxer had not done much during her multiple Congressional terms. But, politics are messy, and Boxer ended up winning, most probably because of various alleged scandals pertaining to Fiorina.

Representativeness Heuristic

Suppose that a young man in a pinstriped suit, black shirt, and white tie comes up to you and asks if you would like to make some money by betting on whether a coin lands on "heads" or "tails." You look at him dubiously.

He explains that it is really quite simple. He will flip one coin six times. All you have to do is bet on the pattern of heads and tails that will result from six tosses of a coin. Although there are many sequences possible, you decide to concentrate on three of them. Using the letter "H" to represent heads and "T" to represent tails, on which of the following three outcomes would you bet?

H-T-H-T-T-H
H-H-H-T-T-T
H-T-H-T-H-T

If you responded like most other people, then you selected the first series of heads and tails, probably because it seemed more similar to a random or chance pattern of heads and tails. In fact, all three series are equally likely. Any series of heads and tails taken six at a time is as likely to occur as any other. The above example demonstrates the belief that an outcome of a random process should look like or be representative of randomness. Because our common sense notion of randomness is that of a process without a pattern, we tend to think that H-T-H-T-H-T is not as likely to occur from six tosses of a coin as a more random-looking series. This, however, is not true. (What some people find even more surprising is that H-H-H-H-H-H is as likely to occur as H-T-H-T-H-T.)

Of course, you are more likely to get approximately equal numbers of heads and tails after many coin flips than you are to get mostly or all heads or mostly or all tails because there are more possible patterns that yield these outcomes. For example, there is only one pattern of outcomes that will correspond to 6 heads (H-H-H-H-H-H), while there are many ways to get 3 heads and 3 tails in 6 flips of a coin (e.g., H-H-H-T-T-T; H-T-H-T-H-T; T-T-T-H-H-H; H-T-H-T-H-T; etc.). Each series or pattern of heads and tails is equally likely. This concept is also discussed in Chapter 7.

To clarify the **representativeness heuristic**, which is the belief that any member of a category should "look like" or have the traits associated with its category, let's try another example. Suppose you get a letter from an old friend from whom you have not heard in many years. He tells you that he is the proud father of six children—three girls and three boys. After trying to consider what life is like with six children, you then wonder about their birth order. Which of the following orders do you think is more likely (with "G" standing for girls and "B" standing for boy)?

B-B-B-G-G-G

or

B-G-G-B-G-B

If you have followed the discussion so far, you will realize that although the second series appears to be more representative of a random process, they are, in fact, equally likely.

Wishful Thinking (Pollyanna Principle)

People are excessively optimistic about marriage, work, sports, health, and life expectancy.

—Cade Massey, Joseph P. Simmons, and
David A. Armor (2011, p. 274).

Quite often, people will overestimate their chances for success or the likelihood of a desired outcome. Halpern and Irwin (1973) found that when participants in an experiment wanted an event to occur (they would win money), they believed that it was more likely to occur than when its occurrence would have been unfavorable (they would lose money). It seems that humans are an optimistic species. The tendency to believe that pleasant events are more likely than unpleasant ones is a manifestation of **wishful thinking**, the idea that if we want something to happen it will. This has also been called the Pollyanna Principle in honor of the protagonist of a 1913 novel who always found something to be happy about, no matter how bleak the situation.

Optimism is a potent human trait that often directs how we think and act. Seligman (1991) identified optimism as a critical element in political elections. It seems that candidates who are optimistic about the future are more likely to garner winning votes than those who are pessimistic. He found that in 9 out of 10 presidential elections in the United States, the candidate who gave the more optimistic speeches won the election. Optimism may be a wonderful human trait, but not when it distorts the decision-making process. Good decisions rely on realistic assessment of likelihood, not optimistic ones. Failure to consider seriously unpleasant outcomes can lead to disastrous consequences.

Entrapment

Suppose you were offered the opportunity to bid on a $1 bill. You and some friends can make bids, and the highest bidder will pay the amount bid and get $1 in return. The only hitch is that both the highest bidder and second highest bidder must pay the amount they bid, but only the highest bidder will receive the dollar in return. Suppose that you agree to play and that you continue to raise your bid until you have offered 80 cents. Now a friend bids $1. What do you do? You will probably decide to bid $1.05 for the $1 because you will certainly lose $.80 unless you continue to increase your bid. Shubik (1971) has found that people will continue to bid amounts over $1 to win the dollar bill in an attempt to keep their losses at a minimum in this game.

What has happened in this game is **entrapment**, a situation in which an individual has already invested money, time, or effort and decides to continue in this situation because of the initial investment. Entrapment is also called **sunk costs** because of the importance that we attach to the costs we have already "sunk" into a course of action. People commonly fall prey to sunk costs. Consider Fred's decision about his automobile. He has already replaced the muffler, brakes, and ignition system when he finds out that his car needs a new transmission. Because he has already invested so much money into his car, he feels "trapped" into replacing the transmission instead of buying a new car. Or consider another common example. Everyone has had the frustrating experience of calling on the phone for some information and being put on "hold." After listening to the irritating strains of "elevator music" for several minutes, you need to decide whether to hang up or continue waiting. Many people continue to wait because of the time they have already invested. Astute readers are probably wondering if entrapment also works in relationships. The answer is "yes." Can you think of a time when you or a friend decided to stay in a relationship because of the time already invested in that relationship?

Making decisions in light of previous investments requires that the individual consider *why* the investment has been so high either in terms of money or time, and whether, at this point in time, the car is worth the additional sum of money or the phone call is worth an additional 10 minutes on "hold." Examples of entrapment are commonly found in government budget hearings (Fischer & Johnson, 1986). One argument in favor of continuing to support the development of the MX missile is that the millions of dollars that have already been spent on it would be lost if we decided to discontinue the project. Sometimes, politicians and others will try to minimize the appearance that they have wasted money by continuing to fund projects that should be discontinued (Arkes, 1996). If more people were vigilant for sunk costs, we would save money and other valuable resources that could be put to better uses. In a study of how people respond in sunk-costs situations, researchers asked subjects open-ended questions about common decisions (Larrick, Morgan, & Nisbett, 1990). Consider this one:

> You and a friend just spent $7 each to see a movie. About a half hour into the movie, you both realize that it is "two thumbs down"—a really bad movie. What do you do? List some good reasons for staying until the end of the movie, then list some good reasons for leaving after a half hour.

Stop now and try this demonstration.

* * *

Look over your reasons. Of course, you just read about entrapment, so you are not a naive subject, but review the answers that you gave anyway. If you listed the fact that you spent $7 as a good reason for staying, you are demonstrating the fallacy of entrapment. If you listed as a good reason for leaving the fact that the movie is a waste of time, then you receive partial credit for recognizing the cost of staying. If you also listed the fact that you could be doing something better with your time, then you would get credit for recognizing that by staying you would also be losing out on doing some better activity. Let's go over the reasoning again because I have found that many students have difficulty with this concept:

You already spent the $7 for the movie. No matter what you decide to do at this point in time, the money is gone, and you are down by $7, so it should not be relevant to your decision. You lost $7, no matter what you decide to do. At a half-hour into the movie, you have a decision to make. If you stay, you will not only have to endure a bad movie, but you will also miss out on a more pleasurable activity that you could be doing. Thus, there is a dual cost to staying—seeing a bad movie and missing out on some better activity. Try out this example with some friends or family. Explain the fallacy of sunk costs to them.

Psychological Reactance

Our emotional states have a major impact on the kinds of decisions that we make (Puvathingal & Hantula, 2012). We select alternatives that seem "best" to us, and our determination of what is best is not always based on sound rational criteria. One example of the effect of emotional states on the kinds of decisions people make has been labeled **psychological reactance**, which is resistance arising from restrictions of freedom. Consider

Non Sequitur by Wiley Miller. Used with permission by Universal Press Syndicate.

this example: It has been a bitterly cold winter and you can hardly wait for a much deserved spring break. One of your close friends is planning on basking in the Fort Lauderdale sun. Another friend cannot wait to hit the slopes in Vail. Both friends have asked you to join them in their spring break revelry. As you consider the options, you begin to favor the bikini-clad vacation when your Florida-bound friend tells you that you *must* go to Florida with him. How does this loss of freedom affect your decision?

Logically, it would seem that being told that you must do what you want to do would have no effect on your decision, but many people do not react this way. Some people would react to this loss of freedom by deciding to go skiing instead. Whether you are dealing with your parents, an employer, or a foreign government, psychological reactance can interfere with the decision-making process by causing you to select a less desirable alternative.

Liking

It should seem obvious that people select alternatives that have been evaluated positively along some dimension. This point will be made more explicitly later in this chapter; however, it is important to consider here some of the factors that influence positive evaluations of an alternative when making a decision. In other words, what are some factors that determine liking?

Reciprocity

When assessing the costs and benefits of various alternatives, our subjective feelings about the alternatives play a large role in decision making. Simply put, we choose people and actions that we like. Reciprocity is one determinant of what and whom we like. We tend to like people who like us. In Cialdini's (1993) delightful book about myriad influences that affect our thoughts and actions, he tells about the "World's Greatest Car Salesman." The super salesman seems to differ from other more mundane sellers in several ways, but the most interesting is his strange habit of correspondence. Super salesman sends a card to each of his more than 13,000 former customers each month. Can you guess the message on this card? No, it is not a list of maintenance tips or repair coupons. In fact, every card every month contains the same message: "I like you." Twelve times a year, every former customer receives the same obviously impersonal message. It seems to work. When the time comes to decide where to purchase another car, these former customers are reminded of their "friend" who likes them. Reciprocity of liking apparently has a powerful effect on decision making in this context. Apparently this story has "gotten out" among car salespeople. When I was buying a new car, the salesman gave me a CD of his favorite music. The unspoken message was that I "owed" him for this gift and the only way to repay him was to buy the car he showed me.

The psychological literature is full of other examples of the influence of reciprocity on decisions. For example, you are much more likely to buy a product if I give you a free sample than if I do not. The next time you are in the supermarket when samples are being given away, watch how people respond to the covert pressure to buy the product they have just tasted. You will find that a surprisingly high number will buy the product. People seem to feel that they owe something in exchange for the "free" sample. Political favors are blatant examples of reciprocity-induced liking as are charitable requests that are accompanied by "gifts" like address labels, key rings, and stamped return envelopes.

Mere Exposure Effect

Suppose that you walked into a voting booth on a primary election day and were faced with the following choice:

County Solicitor (Choose One)

Myron Jones

John Adams

Victor Light

Unfortunately, you have not kept up with local politics, and are unfamiliar with the record of any of these candidates. Which candidate would you vote for? Studies indicate that you probably chose John Adams.

In an election in New Hampshire about 20 years ago, John Adams, an un-employed cab driver who did not campaign, won the Republican nomina-tion for the State's First Congressional District. Why did John Adams, a man who spent no money on his campaign and who never gave a speech, win his party's nomination? Psychologists believe that when voters were confronted with three names they did not recognize, they picked the one linked in history with a political figure. Hence, prior exposure creates a sense of familiarity, which in turn can enhance your liking for the stimu-lus, a phenomenon known as the **mere exposure effect**.

Political commercials often operate on this principle. They repeatedly hark, "Vote for Brandon Lee, He's the One!" Such commercials give absolutely no information about the candidate. They rely on the well-documented effect that familiarity will enhance liking. Based on this principle, repetition was commonly used in Nazi Germany and North Korean prison camps during World War II in an attempt to make their political ideologies more palat-able to the prisoners.

What should you do if you face unknown candidates' names in a voting booth? If you cannot vote intelligently for an office, skip that section and vote for the offices with which you are familiar. Intelligent voters ask them-selves, "What do I know about these candidates?" and do not fall prey to a familiar sounding name.

Emotional States

Like many cognitive psychologists, I often forget the critical role that emo-tions play in the thinking process. (Astute readers will probably recognize this as due to the availability heuristic.) Intuitively, we all know that emo-tions are important. For example, would you ask your boss for a raise if you knew that she just had a fight with her husband? Of course, your boss's relationship with her husband should be irrelevant to whether you get a raise, but a bad mood tends to spill over and affect unrelated decisions. So does a good mood. In an investigation of the way mood influences the way decisions are made, Bower et al. (1994) found that interviewees for a job were rated higher when the interviewers were given good news prior to the interview than when they were given bad news.

Do you want to know if you are at risk for a serious disease, such as Parkinson's or cancer? In a recent study (Howell & Sheppard, cited in Wargo, 2012), participants underwent a simulated annual physical examination. Half of the participants first wrote about a time when they exhibited positive traits and thus felt good about themselves; the other half did not receive the "positive affirmations." Participants who felt positive about themselves were more likely to opt for screening for a (hypothetical) serious illness. This is only one example of many of the benefits of positive affirmations, which have been found to improve achievement in school (Cohen, Garcia, Apfel, & Master, 2006) and to make people more open to political information that they originally opposed (Binning, Cohen, & Heitland, 2010).

It is easier to recognize the effect of emotions on the way we think than it is to correct for it. It is important that we all consider how our own moods may be affecting the quality of the decisions that we make, and we may also try to influence the mood of others who will be making decisions that affect us.

Unconscious Influences

> Legally irrelevant situational determinants—in this case merely taking a food break—may lead a judge to rule differently in cases with similar legal characteristics.
>
> —Shai Danziger, Jonathan Levav,
> and Liora Avnim-Pesso (2011, p. 6,892)

Judges are one group of people we count on for fair and reasoned decisions. We expect that legal decisions are based on facts, the laws, and reasoned judgment. But, like everyone else, judges are influenced by a host of variables about which they have no conscious knowledge. I am not referring to usual types of prejudices such as negative feelings toward the homeless or people with prior criminal records. Judges already know about prejudice, but like everyone else, it is easier to know about the negative effects of stereotypes than it is to fight against them. But, what about other types of influences? What about the effects of being tired and hungry? In a fascinating study, researchers found that approximately 65% of rulings are favorable to defendants at the start of a court session, but this percentage drops to close to 0% within a court session, then returns to 65% after a break that usually included a late morning snack or lunch (Danziger, Levav, & Avnim-Pesso, 2011). The researchers noted that they cannot determine whether it was the break, the food, or both that was responsible for the higher rates of decisions that were favorable to defendants, but this study clearly supports the literature showing that even experienced judges are subject to the same psychological biases that influence the rest of us, usually without our conscious awareness.

Few judges would believe that their decisions depend on the state of their stomachs or how rested they feel, but when they are confronted with the data, they could take steps to minimize these effects, such as taking multiple short breaks or consuming small snacks on a more frequent basis. The researchers assert that they expect similar results across a wide range of decision-making situations, including medical, financial, and admissions decisions, to name just a few. As the literature on unconscious influences on how we think, feel, and act grows (the first chapter has more examples), it underscores the need to take deliberate steps to make the unconscious conscious. The problem, of course, is that we cannot know about all of the possible unconscious influences, so we need to maintain a general mindfulness of the power of what we do not know, and we need to be humble about how rational we actually are.

What about other sorts of decisions—like financial ones? It seems that all sorts of decisions are influenced by factors that we do not realize. In one study, researchers varied the information people were given about the ratios of adult unmarried men to adult unmarried women in different cities (Griskevicius et al., 2012). When there was an excess of men, the men reported that they would save less money and would be more likely to borrow money for immediate expenses. Varying the ratios did not influence women's intentions to save or spend money. These results were replicated across several studies using different types of dependent measures. For example, when there was an excess of men, they reported that they would spend more on an engagement ring, a dinner entrée on a date, and on a Valentine's Day gift. Yet, the men were not aware that their responses varied according to the sex ratios they read about. The message is clear—decisions can be manipulated without our awareness or knowledge. We probably can never understand all of the influences on our decisions, but by carefully considering the type of decision we are making and using a system like the work sheet presented later in this chapter, we may be able to minimize the effect of unconscious influences.

Nudging a Decision

Decision makers do not make choices in a vacuum. They make them in an environment where many features, noticed and unnoticed, can influence their decisions. The person creates the environment . . . [He] is a choice architect.

—Richard H. Thaler and Cass R. Sunstein (2011)

A nudge is a gentle push in a direction that someone wants you to move. A **cognitive nudge** is much like a physical one—information is arranged in a way that makes it more likely that you will behave in a certain way. It is not like unconscious influences because the person is (usually) aware of that there is an attempt to influence an outcome, but it is subtle, and when done well, it can be effective. In their popular book, *Nudge: Improving Decisions about Health, Wealth, and Happiness*, Thaler and Sunstein (2008) provide multiple examples of the way seemingly small changes in the environment change the decisions that people make.

Consider the problem of keeping public restrooms clean. A clever airport maintenance worker at the Schiphol Airport in Amsterdam did just that and came up with the idea of etching a picture of a fly into men's urinals—to give them something to improve their aim. According to Krulwich (2009), this is actually an old idea and one that apparently works. "Spillage" rates at the airport have dropped 80 percent because there it seems that men like to aim at targets. This is an example of a "nudge."

If you find the idea of urinal behavior silly or even offensive, consider other more sober examples of the value of a nudge. Are you an organ donor? If you live in Austria, Belgium, France, or Poland, you almost certainly responded "yes." But if you live in Denmark, Netherlands, the United Kingdom, or Germany, you probably are not. How can we explain huge national differences in rates of organ donation? In countries with

Figure 8.2 An image of a fly etched in urinals is an example of a "nudge." Men engage in more "targeted" behaviors when there is a "fly" in the urinal. Photo "Aim at the Fly" by Thomas Quine (quinet), used courtesy of Flickr Creative Commons Licensing.

high rates of organ donations, citizens are organ donors unless they register not to be; whereas in countries with low rates of organ donors, citizens have to register if they want to donate their organs (Johnson & Goldstein, 2003). Most people decide to accept the status quo. In the United States, polls show that 85% approve of organ donation, but only 28% have signed a donor card, which would allow the donations of their organs (after their death). Researchers believe a simple change from the "opt-in" system that is currently in use in the United States to an "opt-out" system would result in a substantial number of lives saved with the use of donated organs. The rate of organ donors for several countries in the European Union is shown in Figure 8.3.

Financial decisions can also benefit from a nudge in the desired direction. International research from the United States, Chile, Mexico, and Sweden has shown that when employees are automatically enrolled in savings plans, including retirement plans, they are much more likely to save than when they have to "opt-in" to a savings plan (Beshears, Choi, Laibson, & Madrian, 2006). Along similar lines, the state of Washington was faced with a serious budget crisis and was going to have to close many state parks. What did they do to fund the parks so that they could remain open? You probably guessed that they changed a default. In this example, drivers

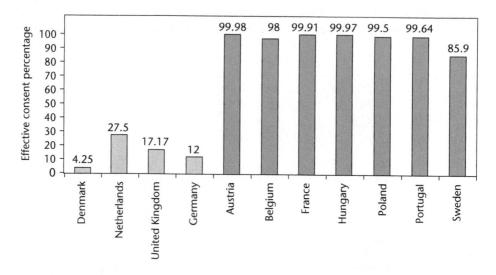

Effective consent rates, by country. Explicit consent (opt-in, light blue) and presumed consent (opt-out, dark blue).

Figure 8.3 Rates of organ donations for countries in the European Union. From Johnson & Goldstein (2003), *Science*. Reprinted with permission from AAAS.

had been given a choice to donate $5 for the parks when they renewed their license. Under the new plan, drivers would have to decide NOT to donate $5 when they renewed their license (Thaler & Sunstein 2011). Defaults offer the course of least resistance and it seems that is a path that most of us prefer. The research is clear—defaults matter. Seemingly small changes in the way choices are presented can have a huge effect on what people decide to do.

Evaluating Consequences

> Murphy's Law: Anything that can go wrong, will.
> Comment on Murphy's Law: Murphy was an optimist.

If you return to Figure 8.1, you will see that evaluation is done repeatedly as new alternatives are generated, the decision is phrased differently, and the consequences of alternatives are considered. Decision making always involves uncertainty because we are thinking about the way different actions will have some future effect. The decisions that we make have implications for the future, and the future inherently involves unknowns. For this reason, the principles involved in assessing likelihood and uncertainty that were presented in Chapter 7 are an integral part of the decision-making process.

Research on how people typically deal with uncertainty has shown that the usual response is to ignore it, which is probably why so many people accept default options. Although doing nothing may reduce the immediate complexity of a decision, it is often a maladaptive procedure that could lead to catastrophic results. It is possible to reduce the number of unknowns in any situation. This will almost always involve some work by the decision-maker, but if the decision is an important one, it will be time well spent. Let's consider a common example. Most of us will purchase several automobiles in our lifetimes. For a majority of Americans, this will represent the second largest expenditure that they will make, exceeded only by a home purchase. The quality of this decision can be improved with a little research. You can determine which automobile variables are important to you and gather relevant data about each car you are considering for possible purchase.

Almost any decision can be improved with a little research that would reduce the uncertainty. For example, if you are uncertain about the safety of genetically-altered foods, an afternoon at the library reading both pro and con materials, with benefits and cost information, respectively, should allow you to make a much more informed decision about this important issue.

Assessing Desirable and Undesirable Consequences

> We can understand judgment as the quality of analysis, reflection, and ultimately insight that informs the making of politically consequential framing decisions.
>
> —Jonathan Renshon (1992, p. 481–482)

The decision-maker must always be aware of the risks and benefits associated with taking or not taking a particular course of action. The way consequences are evaluated will depend on the context. For example, the consequences of *not* taking an umbrella will be greater if you are heading off for a business meeting where showing up dry is important than if you are taking the dog for a walk and then returning home.

If you live in an apartment near a college campus, you are well aware of the "joys" associated with apartment hunting. Rental units are often in short supply in college communities and are priced in a range that strains the typical student's budget. Students may find themselves considering an apartment that lacks the amenities they were hoping for at a price that is really above their income. The risk associated with turning the apartment down is that they might not find another apartment within walking distance to the college campus. The risks associated with renting the apartment must also be considered. What if they find that they really cannot afford to keep up the monthly rental payments? The decision-maker has to decide which risk is greater and the likelihood of each occurring. Obviously, both risks need to be assessed very carefully and additional alternatives considered. Perhaps a cheaper apartment can be found in another section of town with good public transportation to campus, or perhaps a roommate can be found to share the rent.

A poignant example of failure to assess risks adequately can be found in an analysis of the United States' military actions just prior to the attack on Pearl Harbor. Admiral Kimmel, Commander-in-Chief of Naval Operations in the Pacific, had received several warnings from Washington that a Japanese attack in the Southwest was possible. He decided to downplay the probability of an attack on Pearl Harbor because he believed that other naval sites were more likely targets. Quite by accident, and almost an hour before the attack, two army privates spotted on a radar screen large numbers of unidentified aircraft flying towards Pearl Harbor. Realizing that these could be Japanese bomber planes, they reported the presence of the unidentified aircraft to the Army's radar center.

Let's consider the plight of the officer on duty at the radar center. The United States was not at war with Japan. He had never received the recent warning that a Japanese attack was imminent. He had to decide whether the unidentified objects on the radar screen belonged to the United States or Japan. There were costs and risks associated with either choice. If he had erroneously decided that they were Japanese planes, he would have been responsible for recalling personal "leaves" for large numbers of servicemen and women and creating havoc and panic on the military base. There were also large financial costs involved in preparing for anti-aircraft maneuvers. Because he assessed the possibility of a Japanese attack to be low, he told the two privates to forget about the objects detected by radar. He decided that they were probably the Army B-17s that were expected to arrive some time that day. With the unfortunate benefit of hindsight, it is clear that he failed to assess adequately the risks associated with each decision. The result was the worst naval disaster in United States history with over 2,000 lives lost. Even though he believed that an attack was unlikely (wishful thinking), he should have realized that the risks were too great to justify his decision. Decisions made under extreme risks need careful scrutiny and not an off-hand dismissal. In this case, the risks associated with deciding that the planes belonged to the United States were many times less than those associated with the decision that they were Japanese bombers.

Research has shown that the Pearl Harbor scenario is not unusual. Whenever extreme risk is associated with a course of action, there is a tendency to minimize the unfavorable consequences (Janis & Mann, 1977). This is sometimes called **biased discounting**—the bias or predilection to discount or reduce perceived risk or its probability. It often operates along with wishful thinking, which causes the decision-maker to assess the probability of a desirable outcome too high, the failure to seek disconfirming evidence, which is the tendency to ignore evidence that would not support your favored hypothesis, and overconfidence in the quality of the decision that was made. These tendencies, taken together, allowed the radar officer to bolster his decision to ignore the unidentified objects by rationalizing either that even if they were Japanese bomber planes, they probably would not do much damage, or it was extremely unlikely that they were Japanese aircraft. A more recent example in which the failure to consider the consequences of certain decision alternatives can be seen in an analysis of the Gulf War that involved the United States, Iraq, and Kuwait. The researcher who conducted the Gulf War analysis found many similarities to the decisions that were made at Pearl Harbor (Renshon, 1992).

When making decisions, many people prefer risks associated from not acting to the risks associated with taking action. The bias or preference for inaction is known as **omission bias** (Baron, 1994). Consider the decision to vaccinate your child against some dread disease. Many parents will decide NOT to vaccinate their children even when the risk of serious illness or death from the vaccine is extremely small and the risk of getting a serious disease or dying is many times higher if the child is not vaccinated. Many people prefer the harm done by inaction (not getting a flu vaccine, for example) to possible harm from action (e.g., getting a flu vaccine), even when the likelihood of a negative effect is less with an action than with inaction (daCosta DiBonaventura & Chapman, 2008).

Elimination by Aspects

Let's return to the earlier problem of deciding which automobile to buy. With so many automobiles on the market, where do you begin? Most people begin a decision-making processes of this sort with a strategy known as **elimination by aspects**, although few people know it by this name (Tversky, 1972). An individual who is concerned about unemployment in the U.S. car industry would begin by eliminating cars that are not manufactured in the United States. In this instance, the aspect under consideration is the place in which the automobile is manufactured. At this point, most people will decide which features (or aspects) of automobiles are important to them. Suppose that you are on a limited budget so that cost is an important feature to you. You would probably determine the cost of various models of Fords, Chevrolets, and other U.S. autos. Models that cost more than your price ceiling would be eliminated.

Let's suppose further that frequency of repair is another important variable. Of course, no one can tell you how frequently the car you choose will need repair, but you can reduce some of the uncertainty associated with this variable by finding out how often other models similar to the ones you are considering have needed repair in the past. This information is available in consumer periodicals in every library. If some of the models that you are still considering are judged as "worse than average" on the frequency of repairs, then presumably these would be eliminated from further consideration. The elimination by aspects strategy would be recycled repeatedly until the decision-maker is left with a few possible models from which to choose. Typically, small and seemingly insignificant differences will come into play to complete the process—for example, "I'm tired of shopping," or "Let's just take this one," or "The dealer will include at no extra cost furry dice to hang from the rear view mirror if I buy this model," or "I can drive this one home today." The use of small and relatively inconsequential factors to close the decision is an example of mindlessness, a topic that was discussed earlier in this book. Most consumers are not aware that something as "small" as free fuzzy dice tilts the balance of what had been a prudent process.

The method of elimination by aspects can be used in many contexts. Political candidates, for example, can be thought of as choices that vary along several criteria. If you decide that the issues that are important to you include a strong military defense, reduction of taxes, and school prayer, then you could rank each of these candidates along these aspects and eliminate the candidates who do not share your views. You would have to determine which of these aspects is most important if you find that none of the candidates shares all of your views about these important issues. Elimination by aspects is "fast and frugal" reasoning (Gigenzer, Todd, & the ABC Research Group, 1999; Gigenzer & Goldstein, 1996). It is one of several "short-cuts" in reasoning where the decision-maker does not carefully weigh a large amount of data, but relies instead on a quicker (and some would say "dirtier") method of reaching a decision. It is much faster than the worksheet method that is presented below, and it works well when there are time constraints or when the decision does not warrant the extensive work of a worksheet.

Preparing a Worksheet

> The time is ripe for a major national and international effort to include thinking and decision making in school curricula.
> —Jonathan Baron and Rex V. Brown (1991, p. 6)

We have clear evidence that decision making biases do not go away just by telling people not to make them, but decision making can be improved with effective training programs (e.g., Kylesten & Nahlinder, 2011). Researchers have found that the best way to make an important decision involves the preparation and utilization of a decision worksheet. The purpose of a worksheet is to optimize decision making. Psychologists who study **optimization** compare the actual decision made by a person to a theoretical "ideal" decision to see how similar they are. Proponents of the worksheet procedure believe that it will yield optimal (best) decisions. Although there are several variations on the exact format that a worksheet can take, they are similar in their essential aspects. Worksheets require framing the decision in a clear and concise way, listing many possible alternatives that would achieve a desired goal, listing the relevant considerations that will be affected by the decision, determining the relative importance of each consideration, and mathematically calculating a decision. The end product of the worksheet procedure is a single numerical summary of each possible solution or alternative. In theory, the alternative with the highest number of points emerges as the best decision, but more usually, the careful consideration of alternatives and their probabilities and value to the decision-maker leads to a decision before the entire process is completed because it helps to clarify values and keeps the decision-maker focused on the task.

Most important problems are multifaceted, with several different ways of framing the decision and many alternatives to choose from, each with unique advantages and disadvantages. One of the benefits of a pencil and paper decision-making procedure is that it permits us to deal with more variables than our immediate processing ability would allow. If you have already read the chapter on utilizing memory, you will recall (I hope) that working memory is limited in the number of pieces of information it can deal with at one time. A worksheet can be especially useful when the decision involves a large number of variables with complex relationships.

Let's consider the worksheet procedure with a realistic example for most college students: "What will I do after graduation?" A hypothetical student, Evan, has several post-graduation opportunities. He is contemplating the following: (1) a job in a large fashionable department store where he will train to be a buyer; (2) a teaching position in an inner-city school, probably a 5th or 6th grade class; (3) a graduate school degree in business administration; (4) a law school degree; and (5) a year off to "bum around" Europe. A decision-making worksheet will be very important in helping him choose the best alternative. Notice that I did not say "correct" alternative because there are many possible good alternatives for real life, complex decisions.

Framing the Decision

> It is critical to be cognizant of the frame of a decision and to consider alternative perspectives.
>
> —Mark D. Rogerson, Michael C. Gottlieb, Mitchell N. Handelsman,
> Samuel Knapp, and Jeffrey Younggren (2011, p. 617)

The first step in making a sound decision is the realization that a decision needs to be made. A decision-making worksheet begins with a succinct statement of the problem that will also help to narrow it. Thus, the problem for Evan becomes "What will I do after graduation that will lead to a successful career?" If Evan words his decision this way, he has already decided that his decision will involve long-range goals and not immediate ones. It is important to be clear about this distinction because most often, long-range goals will involve a different decision than short-range ones. Thus, the options of attending graduate or law school are really statements about working in business or as a lawyer and not decisions about school per se.

The importance of this first step cannot be overemphasized. The entire decision-making process depends on the way the problem is defined. If Evan had posed the problem as "How can I best earn a good living?", he would find that the process would focus on monetary considerations. Similarly, the process would change if he posed the problem as, "Should I go to graduate school?" Research with business managers has shown that the ability to redefine business problems is an important characteristic of good decision making in management (Merron, Fisher, & Torbert, 1987). The way the decision is framed will determine the alternatives that are generated and the way they are evaluated. This is an important point. If you are worried about world hunger, you could frame the decision about what to do about it several ways: How can we produce enough food to feed all the people in the world? How can we adjust the world population so that it does not exceed the food supply? How can we move food from wealthy countries to poor ones? How can we develop nonfood alternatives that are nutritious? Each of these decisions will suggest different alternatives.

Similarly, be mindful of the way others have framed decisions for you. The media may adhere to all guidelines of fairness and still present decisions in ways that limit broader considerations. For example, I served as a juror on a complex trial where the attorney for the defense framed the question for the jury as "Why should you believe the alleged victim?" By contrast, the attorney for the prosecution framed the question for the jury as "Is there sufficient evidence that the defendant committed the alleged crime?" Each of these "decision frames" led to the consideration of different types of evidence. The jury had to be aware of the differences in framing and attempt to see the decision about guilt or innocence from several different perspectives as they conducted their deliberations.

A worksheet procedure can have many important applications for social problems. Consider the contemporary problem of violence, which is filled with numerous decision points. It seems that it should be possible to teach aggressive children and adults to reframe their problems in ways that suggest nonviolent alternatives. For example, instead of asking, "How can I get even with a classmate?", the child could be trained to ask, "How can I improve a bad situation?" Perhaps a thoughtful, creative reader will devise an educational program that teaches children, and perhaps even politicians, to reframe decisions so that nonaggressive alternatives are generated.

Generating the Alternatives

The next step is to write out in separate columns across the top of the worksheet all possible alternatives that could solve the problem. You will need a large sheet of ruled paper or a computerized spread sheet because it would make no sense to cut the worksheet process short because you ran out of space on your paper. It is important that you do not evaluate the alternatives at this stage; however, this is not the place for fiction either. If you are tone deaf, this is not the time to fantasize about a career in the opera. Allow room for two columns under each alterative that will be used later for calculations. Research on decision making by physicians found that one of the most common errors was "premature closure," the tendency to stop thinking about alternative diagnoses as soon as a likely diagnosis was found (Norman & Eva, 2010). Remember, you cannot select an alternative that you never considered.

Thus far, Evan's worksheet would look something like this:

Table 8.1: What Will I Do After College That Will Lead to a Successful Career?

Alternatives	Dept. Store Buyer	Teacher— Inner-City School	Graduate School— Business	Law School	"Bum in Europe" for a Year

Evan notices while drawing up his worksheet that these alternatives are not all mutually exclusive. There is no reason why he cannot decide to travel around Europe for a year and then select a career goal; besides, a vacation in Europe is not a long-range plan, and the decision currently being made is for life career goals. He decides at this point to erase the fifth alternative because it seems to require a separate decision from the other four. He also remembers at this point that his father always hoped that Evan would want to run the family-owned lumber business after his graduation from college. Although this is not an appealing idea to Evan, he substitutes it as an additional choice because the rules for this step of the process do not allow for evaluation.

Listing the Considerations

The decision Evan makes will have multiple effects. His feelings about making a personal contribution to society, his income and his future life style, his parents' and friends' opinions of him, the quality of his workday, and many other variables are at stake. If Evan were married and had children, the impact of each decision on his spouse and children would also need to be considered. At this point, Evan should cover the alternatives and list on the left-hand side of his worksheet the considerations or variables that will be affected by his decision. The worksheet would now look like this. (See Table 8.2.)

Table 8.2: What Will I Do After College That Will Lead to a Successful Career?

Alternatives	Dept. Store Buyer	Teacher—Inner-City School	Graduate School—Business	Law School	Run Family Lumber Business
Considerations Desire to Help Society Income Parents' Opinions Friends' Opinions Interest in the Work					

Before proceeding, Evan should now put the worksheet away and mull over the way the decision was framed and the alternatives and the considerations that he listed. Often people find that in the course of worksheet preparation, they think of new alternatives and discover which considerations are important to them. It is also a good idea to ask other people you trust if they can think of additional alternatives and considerations. Considerations and alternatives that are not listed on the worksheet will not be considered, so it is extremely important to list all the relevant alternatives and considerations. Do not cut this part of the decision-making process short. It is important.

Be sure, however, that you do not let other people make the decision for you. Suppose that Evan's friend suggests that Evan seriously pursue his interest in music and become a jazz musician. In addition, Evan thinks up several additional considerations, which he lists on his worksheet. He also decides that as he is planning for his future, he should realistically consider his chances for success at each alternative. (See Table 8.3.)

Table 8.3: What Will I Do After College That Will Lead to a Successful Career?

Alternatives	Dept. Store Buyer	Teacher— Inner-City School	Graduate School— Business	Law School	Run Family Lumber Business	Jazz Musician
Considerations Desire to Help Society Income Parents' Opinions Friends' Opinions Interest in the Work Prestige of Occupation Employment Security Amount of Vacation and Free Time Likelihood of Success						

Listing all relevant considerations is an important part of the worksheet process. Janis and Mann (1977) believe that poor decisions often result from failures to think through all of the relevant considerations. They suggest that considerations be listed under four categories—gains and losses for self, gains and losses for significant others, self-approval and disapproval, and social approval and disapproval to avoid overlooking important considerations.

Weighing the Considerations

> Balancing the pros and the cons is certainly among the most intuitive approaches that one might take to decision making. It was already at the core of Benjamin Franklin's 'moral algebra' (explained in his famous 1772 letter to Joseph Priestley) and it has certainly not fallen from grace since then.
>
> —Jean-François Bonnefon, Didier Dubois,
> Hélène Fargier, and Sylvie Leblois (2008, p. 71)

It is almost always true that the considerations are not equally important to the decision-maker and therefore need to be weighed accordingly. A five-point scale in which 1 = of slight importance, 5 = of great importance, and the numbers 2, 3, 4 reflect gradations of importance between these end points can be used to quantify the relative importance of each consideration. Weighing considerations is a personal matter. It is likely that each of us would assign weights somewhat differently. If Evan felt that his desire to help society was moderately important to him, he would rate it a "3." Similarly, if he believed that income was more than moderately important to him, but less than "of great importance" he would rate it a "4." The appropriate weights are placed alongside each consideration.

After assigning numbers (the weights) to each consideration, you should stop to survey the weights. If Evan rated "friend's opinions" with a larger number than "parents' opinions," this reflects how he feels about their relative opinions. This is a good way to clarify which considerations are most important to you. It is a good way to consider your own values. It is not unusual to find that the process ends here because the decision-maker realizes which alternatives are important and does not need to complete the process.

Weighing the Alternatives

Now is the time to think carefully about each alternative and determine how well each satisfies the considerations listed. The alternatives will be weighed using the numbers –2, –1, 0, +1, and +2. A positive number indicates that it is favorable or "pro" the consideration, with +2 indicating that it is highly favorable, and +1 indicating that it is somewhat favorable. A negative number will be used if an alternative is incompatible with or "con" a consideration, with –2 indicating that it is highly incompatible, and –1 indicating that it is somewhat incompatible. Zero will be used when an alternative is neither favorable nor unfavorable to a consideration.

We will use Evan's worksheet to demonstrate how to weigh alternatives. First, Evan has to contemplate how becoming a department store buyer will satisfy his desire to help society. Certainly it will not hurt society, but it probably will not help it either. Evan believes that while it may create additional jobs in related industries (fashion, sewing, etc.), this is not really what he had in mind when he thought about helping society; therefore, he rates it a zero on this consideration. This number is placed under "Department Store Buyer" in the left hand column on the first row. Subsequent ratings will be placed directly below this number. If he does eventually become a buyer for a large department store, he probably will earn a satisfactory income. He certainly will not be rich, but it will be enough money to allow him to live comfortably; therefore, he gives it a +1. Both his parents and friends will consider it to be a moderately good job, so he rates it a +1 on both these considerations. He believes that it should be very interesting work and rates it a +2 on "interest in the work." It should be a moderately prestigious occupation and thus rates a +1 in this category. Unfortunately, it probably will not offer much employment security because department store sales are tied to the economy, which seems to fluctuate erratically; he therefore rates it –1 on "employment security." A department store buyer is required to work a 40-hour or more work week with only a few weeks a year for vacation; he thus rates it a –2 on vacation and free time. He notes that he is moderately likely to succeed as a department store buyer, so he rates it +1 on this consideration.

It is usually necessary to gather more information at this stage of the decision-making process. Evan may need to check various income web sites to find out what the median salary is for school teachers. He also might seek the advice of his college advisor to determine if he has the math skills needed to succeed in business administration. We know that the way alternatives are evaluated is influenced by feelings, which in this case, is perfectly rational because the choice is a personal one, and Evan's feelings about the alternatives should be part of the decision-making process.

Table 8.4: What Will I Do After College That Will Lead to a Successful Career?

Alternatives		Dept. Store Buyer	Teacher—Inner-City School	Graduate School—Business	Law School	Run Family Lumber Business	Jazz Musician
Considerations							
Desire to Help Society	(3)	0	+2	0	+1	0	0
Income	(4)	+1	−1	+2	+2	0	−1
Parents' Opinions	(2)	+1	0	+1	+2	+2	−1
Friends' Opinions	(3)	+1	+2	0	+1	−1	+2
Interest in the Work	(5)	+2	+2	+1	0	−1	+1
Prestige of Occupation	(1)	+1	−1	+2	+2	−2	+1
Employment Security	(3)	−1	−2	0	+1	+2	−2
Amount of Vacation and Free Time	(2)	−2	+2	−2	−2	+1	+2
Likelihood of Success	(5)	+1	+1	−1	−1	+2	−2

Each alternative is rated in a similar manner by thinking how well it satisfies the objectives of each consideration. When he completed weighing the alternatives, Evan's worksheet looked like this. (See Table 8.4.)

Calculating a Decision

If you have carefully followed the worksheet procedure this far, you have realized that it requires numerous decisions before even coming close to yielding the one you want to make. By now, Evan has decided what type of decision he is making (long-range), has listed all the alternatives and all the considerations that he believes to be necessary, and has decided how important each consideration is to him and how well each alternative satisfies the objectives of each consideration.

There are three different strategies for calculating a decision at this point. They are overall assessment, dimensional comparison, and the "2/3 Ideal Rule." Each utilizes a different criterion for selecting the best decision from a worksheet.

Overall Assessment

An **overall assessment** of the various weights is obtained by determining how well each alternative satisfies the considerations taken as a whole or overall. This is calculated by multiplying the weight previously assigned for each consideration by the value assigned to how well an alternative satisfies that consideration. For example, Evan has rated his desire to help society a "3" and the department store buyer alternative a "0" on this consideration. The first cell of the worksheet is 3 x 0 = 0. This result, 0, is placed in the right-hand column under "department store buyer." Continuing down to the next consideration, we see that Evan rated income as "4" and the department store buyer alternative "+1" on income. Because 4 x 1 = 4, he would place a "4" in the right hand-column below department store buyer and next to "income." This procedure is repeated for each alternative. The right hand-column for each alternative is then added yielding a total score for each alternative. This procedure is demonstrated in Table 8.5.

Perusal of the worksheet will now show that based on an overall assessment, the alternative with the highest total score is "Teacher—Inner-City School." You will also notice that the alternative to become a department store buyer obtained a fairly high score that was close to a winning alternative. Thus far, it seems that Evan should seriously be thinking about a career as a teacher, although his close second is department store buyer.

Table 8.5: What Will I Do After College That Will Lead to a Successful Career?

Alternatives		Dept. Store Buyer		Teacher—Inner-City School		Graduate School—Business		Law School		Run Family Lumber Business		Jazz Musician	
Considerations													
Desire to Help Society	(3)	0	0	+2	6	0	0	+1	3	0	0	0	0
Income	(4)	+1	4	−1	−4	+2	8	+2	8	0	0	−1	−4
Parents' Opinions	(2)	+1	2	0	0	+1	2	+2	4	+2	4	−1	−2
Friends' Opinions	(3)	+1	3	+2	6	0	0	+1	3	−1	−3	+2	6
Interest in the Work	(5)	+2	10	+2	10	+1	5	0	0	−1	−5	+1	5
Prestige of Occupation	(1)	+1	1	−1	−1	+2	2	+2	2	−2	−2	+1	1
Employment Security	(3)	−1	−3	−2	−6	0	0	1	3	+2		−2	−6
Amount of Vacation and Free Time	(2)	−2	−4	+2	4	−2	−4	−2	−4	+1	2	+2	+4
Likelihood of Success	(5)	+1	$\frac{5}{18}$	+1	$\frac{5}{20}$	−1	$\frac{-5}{8}$	−1	$\frac{-5}{14}$	+1	$\frac{2}{12}$	−2	$\frac{-10}{-6}$

Dimensional Comparison

In a **dimensional comparison** strategy, each consideration (the "dimensions") is examined to find which alternative has the highest score. For example, if "Desire to help society" is examined, you will see that "Teacher—Inner-City School" had the highest rating among all the other alternatives; therefore, it would "win" on this consideration and get one point. Looking at "Income," you will see that both "Graduate School—Business" and "Law School" were assigned +2 on this dimension. In the event of ties, each of the winning tied alternative is awarded one point. If each consideration is examined in a similar manner, the following number of considerations won for each alternative will result:

Number of Considerations Won					
Department Store Buyer	Teacher, Inner-City School	Graduate, Business School	Law School	Run Family Lumber Business	Jazz Musician
1	4	2	3	3	2

As seen above, the alternative "Teacher, Inner-City School" scored highest among the alternatives on four considerations. Thus, the results of the dimensional comparison strategy agree with the overall assessment results. Notice that both "Law School" and "Run Family Lumber Business" won three considerations each, yet scored fairly low on the overall assessment. Several prominent researchers believe that this is the best method for making decisions and that weighting each consideration is unnecessary (Gigerenzer, 2008). The method of weighting considerations is time consuming and many people will not go to that much work for decisions that are not critically important. For most people, the longer methods shown here, with various weighting, would only be used for life's most important decisions (perhaps to choose between different treatments for cancer or to decide whether to make life-changing decisions). Even if you never or rarely use the longer method of weighting, it is good to know that you can come back and use this method if you ever need or want to.

2/3 Ideal Rule

The "**2/3 Ideal Rule**" was suggested by Carkhuff (1973). It requires the decision-maker to calculate an overall assessment total for a perfect or ideal alternative. If an ideal alternative were added to Evan's worksheet, it would rate +2 on each consideration since it would be highly favorable to each consideration. A total overall score for an ideal alternative can be arrived at by adding all of the consideration weights and multiplying the total by 2 as seen below:

$$3 + 4 + 2 + 3 + 5 + 1 + 3 + 2 + 5 = 28$$

$$28 \times 2 = 56$$

The reasoning behind the "2/3 Ideal Rule" is that a best alternative may not be good enough if it fails to measure up to 2/3 of an ideal solution. Thus, according to this rule, a minimally acceptable alternative would score an overall 37.5 (2/3 x 56 = 37.5). If you turn back to the completed worksheet, you will see that the highest total was for the teacher alternative and it rated, by the overall assessment method, a 20 (considerably less than the 37.5 required by this rule). Evan has several choices at this point. He can disregard the "2/3 Ideal Rule" (which is likely if he is pleased with the decision to become a teacher), or he can expand and recycle the process by generating additional considerations and alternatives until he reaches a consensus with all three calculating procedures.

The "2/3 Ideal Rule" is based on the idea that some alternatives are "good enough," while others are not. Searching for alternatives that are good enough is called **satisficing** (Schwartz, Ben-Haim, & Dasco, 2011; Simon, 1956), which was described in an earlier chapter. It refers to terminating the decision-making process when an alternative that is "good enough" to satisfy most of the important considerations is found. The decision-making process cannot go on forever, so at some point, the decision-maker will have to decide that one alternative is "good enough." The problem really is *when* to terminate the process, and there are no simple answers to this question. Important decisions like the one considered in this example should be given the time and effort they deserve. Often, better decisions are possible if the decision-maker would invest more time and effort into generating alternatives and listing considerations.

The Problem with Numbers

One problem in using worksheet procedures to make decisions is the reliance on subjective estimates—estimates of the probability of success, estimates of the importance of consideration, and estimates of the extent to which an alternative is favorable or unfavorable for a consideration. Although a large table of numbers can look very scientific, the end result is only as good as the numbers that go into the calculations. Sometimes, small differences in how you assess probabilities or values can change the outcome. Most people can only give a rough evaluation of how strong a cost or benefit is for a decision and find it difficult to assign numerical values (Bonnefon, Dubois, Fargier, & Leblois, 2008). So, it is important that you think about the worksheet procedure as an aid or "decision making helper," not an absolute determinant of what you do. It should help you to clarify your values, force you to think systematically about multiple variables, and aid in the generation of additional possible alternatives. Ideally, the decision will become clear as you work on the worksheet, so that it is more of a process for making a decision than an absolute determinant of what you decide.

Dilemmas in Decision Making

The decision-maker will often encounter dilemmas in calculating a decision. It is not unusual for two or more alternatives to have exactly the same high score or for one alternative to obtain the highest total with the overall assessment and a different one with the dimensional comparison. This stalemate can always be remedied by generating additional considerations and repeating the process until an alternative emerges as best. It is also possible to combine two or more alternatives. For example, Evan could become a buyer in a department store and volunteer to tutor children on weekends. This would allow him to realize his desire to help society while maintaining the benefits of the buyer alternative. Sometimes the decision-maker will abandon the worksheet before it is completed because the process helped to clarify the issues and led directly to a decision without the calculations.

Certainly, the worksheet procedure requires a great deal of work, as its name implies. You might be wondering if there is any evidence to suggest that it is worth the extra effort—that it actually leads to better decisions. Yes, there is. Mann (1972) randomly selected 30 high school seniors (15 females and 15 males) from a college preparatory program to participate in an experimental investigation of the worksheet procedure. He taught them how to prepare a worksheet that would help them make decisions about college. The procedure he used was similar to the one presented here, but not identical to it. He also employed a "control group" of 20 students who were not taught the worksheet procedure. Mann contacted the students approximately six weeks after they notified the colleges about their decision concerning which college they planned to attend. The group that had received worksheet training (the experimental group) had less post-decision stress and anxiety and was happier about the decisions they made than the control group. Mann also reported that they had considered possible unfavorable consequences of their decision more carefully than the control group. Thus, if something does go wrong, they will more likely be prepared for it than those in the group without worksheet training.

One of the benefits of the worksheet procedure is that it allows people to feel more confident about difficult decisions and better prepared for decision-making situations because they are required to evaluate alternatives in a systematic manner.

Post-Decision Commitment and Evaluation

> To begin with it was only tentatively that I put forward the views that I have developed . . . but in the course of time they have gained such a hold upon me that I can no longer think in any other way."
> —Sigmund Freud (1856–1939)

The decision-making process does not end with the decision. Once a course of action has been selected, the decision-maker must make detailed plans to carry it out and needs to remain committed to the decision. However, if a major change occurs in the evaluation of the consideration, then the process should be repeated. For example, if Evan were unexpectedly offered a lucrative contract to become a jazz musician, he would be wise to reconsider this alternative. Success at this alternative would now seem much more likely and a large income would be assured. Decision making is not a static process. Our major life decisions will have to be reconsidered whenever a major variable changes.

Cognitive Dissonance

> Because smoking is a health-damaging behavior, smokers must use dissonance-reducing strategies . . . in order to maintain their behavior.
> —Julia Kneer, Sabine Glock, and Diana Rieger, (2012, p. 81).

Most of the time, people are pleased with their decisions. This finding has been of considerable interest to research psychologists. Leon Festinger (1964), a famous research psychologist, proposed his theory of **cognitive dissonance** to explain this phenomenon. It is based on the idea that people like their beliefs, attitudes, and actions to be consistent, and when they are not consistent, an unpleasant internal state arises—dissonance.

Dissonance needs to be reduced. If you believe that it is wrong to smoke marijuana and you attend a party where you smoke marijuana, you will feel uncomfortable because your actions and beliefs are not in agreement. They are not consistent with each other. In order to reduce the discomfort of cognitive dissonance, which is an unpleasant internal state, you will generally change your beliefs and conclude that you did the right thing.

The theory of cognitive dissonance only applies when a conscious decision has been made. If you were coerced in some way, there would be no dissonance. Suppose that you were required to write an essay on some topic that you are opposed to, like the inferiority of a racial or ethnic group, or why drugs should be available to elementary school children. If you were coerced into doing this, there would be no need to change your attitudes to keep them consistent with this behavior. However, if you voluntarily decided to write such an essay, then cognitive dissonance theory would predict a change in your attitude toward the position you took in the essay. This is a major theory in social psychology that explains why people are usually satisfied with the decisions they make. It is easy to see how it contributes to the unwarranted confidence that most people have in their decisions.

Foot-in-the-Door

Cognitive dissonance can be used to understand a common persuasive technique known as the **foot-in-the-door**. The phrase comes from common parlance among door-to-door salespeople who claimed that they could make a sale if only they could get a "foot-in-the-door"—get the perspective customer to allow the salespeople to make their sales pitch. Research on the use of this technique shows that if people agree to a small request—like signing a petition in favor of safe driving—later, they are more likely to agree to a larger request—like donating money to a safe driving campaign (Cialdini, Trost, & Newsom, 1995). People are more willing to agree to an inconvenient or costly request when it follows a smaller or less costly request that is consistent with the larger one. It seems that many people reason that they must really care about the issue or topic because they already showed their support with a smaller action.

Perspective Taking

Perspective-taking is an essential part of interacting with the world: we need to be able to see things from others' perspectives in order to understand them and interact with them. . . . Indeed, so poorly trained

are we at actually taking someone else's point of view that when we are explicitly requested to do so, we still proceed from an egocentric place.
—Maria Konnikova (2011, paras. 8–9)

Often, the decisions that we make involve other people, and often those other people want different outcomes than we do and have different values from our own. Any time you enter into a negotiation or politicians from different parties attempt to pass legislation, the two parties have different interests. It is helpful to "see" the issue from the other side's perspective. This skill could go a long way toward reducing violence and hostilities and allowing what Fisher, Ury, and Patton (2011) call "Getting to yes." Also, successful negotiations depend on getting the other side to make decisions that you want. Several studies have documented the advantages of taking the perspective of the other side when at the bargaining table: "perspective taking increased individuals' ability to discover hidden agreements and to both create and claim resources" that led to better decisions (Galinsky, Maddux, Gilin, & White, 2008). The best way to get to that position is to understand what is important to the other side—it may be money, but it could also be time, prestige, or something that has sentimental value.

Hindsight and Forethought

Hindsight can sometimes see the past clearly—with 20/20 vision.
—9/11 Commission, 2004, cited in Bernstein, Erdfelder, Meltzoff, Peria, & Loftus, 2011, p. 3,788)

The term **hindsight** was discussed in earlier chapters. After a decision has been made and the relevant events occur, well meaning friends will often tell you they could have predicted the consequences of your decision. If you have ever been divorced (or have exchanged confidences with someone who has), there were probably several acquaintances who claimed to have known all along that, "he (or she) was no good for you." Events appear different with the benefit of hindsight. Forethought is the opposite of hindsight. There should be fewer unfortunate consequences if decisions are carefully thought out before they are made.

In experimental investigations of hindsight, most participants erroneously believed that they could have predicted the consequences of historical and personal decisions before they occurred. In our earlier analysis of the Pearl Harbor disaster, it seemed obvious that the only possible decision was to assume that the aircraft belonged to the Japanese. It should be remembered that we analyzed the disaster with the full knowledge of the ensuing events. Hindsight occurs only when poor or wrong decisions have been made. It is seldom that good decisions are analyzed after the fact. Forethought and hindsight are qualitatively different. At the time of the decision (fore-thought) there is doubt and deliberation, but following the unfavorable consequences of the decision (hindsight) there is often a great sense of certainty that the future should have been predicted more accurately.

Hindsight is of little value in the decision-making process. It distorts our memory for events that occurred at the time of the decision so that the actual consequence seems to have been a "forgone conclusion." Thus, it may be difficult to learn from our mistakes. Retrospective (after the fact) review, on the other hand, can be a valuable aid in improving future deci-sions. Unlike hindsight, it does not involve a faulty reconstruction of the information available at the time of the decision so that the consequence appears obvious.

Chapter Summary

- Decision making is an active process that begins with a clear defini-tion of the decision and a set of alternative solutions from which to choose.

- One way to improve on the way in which decisions are made is to frame the decision in several ways. Additional alternatives can emerge by changing the focus of what is being decided on.

- Few people ever receive formal instruction in thinking skills, and even trained professionals commit common decision-making falla-cies. Research has shown that with training, people make better decisions.

- A common error in decision making is the failure to seek discon-firming evidence. Confirmation bias is a persistent problem when people make decisions.

- One problem with group decision making is that groups tend to be overconfident in collective decisions, which causes them to disre-gard information that suggests that other decisions may be better.

- People often rely on heuristics or "rules of thumb" to help them make decisions. The availability heuristic or reliance on events that are readily recalled is a common decision-making heuristic. When time is limited or the decision does not merit a large investment of time or effort, there are many heuristics (thinking shortcuts) that often work quite well.

- Because of the widespread but erroneous belief that the laws of chance are self-correcting, many people believe that "random-looking" sequences of outcomes are more probable outcomes of a random process than orderly sequences of outcomes.

- Unwarranted optimism can also lead to poor decisions because it prevents realistic assessment of both desirable and undesirable consequences of a decision.

- People often fall prey to entrapment. They find it difficult to reverse their decision after having invested large amounts of time or money.

- Decisions are often biased by emotional states like psychological reactance (the resistance to a loss of freedom), mood, and liking induced by reciprocity and familiarity.

- There are unconscious influences on how we decide. The best we can do to guard against their influence is to be mindful and consider how other influences may be affecting the decisions people make.

- The way a situation is crafted can "nudge" people to make certain decisions. Across a wide variety of topics, most people select the default option instead of taking action.

- Risky decisions require special care. There is often a tendency to downplay the likelihood of a disastrous outcome.

- When the alternatives vary along several dimensions, decisions are sometimes made by eliminating alternatives until only one or two choices remain.

- Important decisions can be optimized by preparing a worksheet in which alternatives and considerations are listed and weighed in a table format.

- People are most often satisfied with the decisions that they make, possibly because cognitive dissonance works to maintain consistency between actions and beliefs, and because they cannot think of any reason why they might be wrong. Thus, we reason that if we decided on a course of action, it must have been the best one.

- After the consequences of a decision have occurred, there is a great sense of certainty that the consequences should have been obvious. Hindsight is a ubiquitous phenomenon that distorts how we perceive the information that was available before the decision was made.

- There is an important distinction between a good decision that is based on the information that is available when the decision is being made and its outcomes. Sometimes, good decisions will have undesirable outcomes because of the inherent uncertainty in most important decisions.

The following skills for making decisions were presented in this chapter. Review each skill and be sure that you understand how and when to use each one:

- listing alternatives and considering the cost and benefits of each
- reframing the decision so as to consider different types of alternatives
- recognizing the need to seek disconfirming evidence and deliberately seeking disconfirming evidence
- understanding the way that information that is readily recalled or information that appears representative of a random process can influence how decisions are made
- considering how overly optimistic assessments bias the selection of alternatives
- recognizing arguments that are based on entrapment and considering why the costs have been high
- being mindful of the way liking and other emotional states can affect the evaluation of alternatives
- evaluating positive assessments of alternatives that are based on reciprocity or familiarity
- seeking information to reduce uncertainty when making risky decisions
- preparing a decision-making worksheet for important decisions
- understanding the distinction between the quality of a decision and its outcome
- understanding the way emotional states like reactance and anger can affect the way we evaluate alternatives and behaving in ways that minimize their effects
- recognizing that hindsight analysis of a decision is usually biased and of limited value.

Terms to Know

Check your understanding of the concepts presented in this chapter by reviewing their definitions. If you find that you are having difficulty with any term, be sure to reread the section in which it is discussed.

Subjective Utility. The value of a choice to an individual who is a making a decision.

Overconfidence. An unwarranted confidence in the quality of decisions that are being made.

Group Think. The illusion of being invulnerable as part of a group; this illusion results from the pressures for unanimous decisions and the need to squash dissent to maintain group solidarity.

Heuristic. A general "rule of thumb" or strategy that we use to solve problems and make decisions. Although it does not always produce a correct answer, it is usually a helpful aid. Compare with algorithm.

Algorithm. A problem-solving or decision-making procedure that will always yield the solution to a particular problem if it is followed exactly. Compare with heuristic.

Availability Heuristic. A decision-making "rule of thumb" that is used when estimates of frequency or probability are made based on the ease with which instances come to mind; for example, many college students believe that there are more professors in America than farmers because they can think of more professors whom they know than farmers.

Recognition Heuristic. When the level of knowledge is low, people decide that towns, teams, or people whose names they recognize are more likely to have positive outcomes than ones they have never heard of.

Representativeness Heuristic. A decision-making "rule of thumb" in which the determination of a sample's likelihood is made by noting its similarity to a random process. If it "looks like" a random process, it is judged to be more probable than if it appears orderly or patterned.

Wishful Thinking. People tend to overestimate their chances of success or the likelihood of a desirable outcome.

Entrapment. A situation in which an individual has already invested much money, time, or effort and, therefore, decides to continue in this situation because of the money, time, or effort that has already been invested.

Sunk Cost. Thinking error that occurs when people make decisions based on their prior investments instead of the value of additional resources (e.g., you already spent time or money on something—that investment is gone). Decisions should be based on future costs (e.g., is it worth more time or money?).

Psychological Reactance. Resistance arising from restrictions of freedom. Some people will select a less preferred alternative if they are told that they must select the preferred alternative.

Mere Exposure Effect. Very often, repeated exposure to a stimulus will enhance your liking for it.

Mindlessness. Making decisions with little or no conscious effort.

Cognitive Nudge. When information is arranged in a way that makes some decisions more likely than others.

Biased Discounting. Predilection to discount or reduce the magnitude or probability of risk.

Elimination by Aspects. A decision-making strategy in which choices are sequentially eliminated if they fail to meet one or more considerations.

Optimization. Making the best possible decision in any situation.

Overall Assessment. A method of calculating a decision from a worksheet. The alternative with the highest worksheet total would be selected. Compare with dimensional comparison and "2/3 Ideal Rule."

Dimensional Comparison. A method for calculating a decision from a worksheet. The alternative that has "won" the greatest number of considerations would be selected. Compare with overall assessment and "2/3 Ideal Rule."

"2/3 Ideal Rule." A method for calculating a decision from a worksheet. Only alternatives whose worksheet totals are at least 2/3 as large as the ideal choice would be chosen. Compare with dimensional comparison and overall assessment.

Satisficing. Terminating the decision-making process when an alternative that is "good enough" to satisfy most of the important considerations is found.

Cognitive Dissonance. A theory based on the notion that people want their beliefs, attitudes, and actions to be consistent. When they are not consistent, an unpleasant internal state arises—dissonance—which needs to be reduced. We reduce dissonance by changing our beliefs and attitudes so that they are in accord with our actions.

Foot-in-the-Door. A two-stage persuasive technique. People are more likely to comply with a large request if they first comply with a smaller but related request.

Perspective Taking. "Seeing" what the other side desires and understanding what is important to the other side when negotiating.

Hindsight. Reevaluation of a decision after it has been made and its consequences have occurred, with the belief that the consequences should have been known before the decision was made.

CHAPTER 9

DEVELOPMENT OF PROBLEM-SOLVING SKILLS

Contents

> The Monty Hall Problem was inspired by the game show *Let's Make a Deal*. It is your lucky day, and you are called on stage (probably wearing a silly costume, after all this is television) to play a game. In this game, there are three closed doors. A goat is behind two of the doors (not a great prize) and a new car is behind one door. You pick a door. At this point all doors are equally likely to be hiding the car. To make the game even more exciting, the game show host (who knows which door is hiding the car) opens one of the doors that you did not pick. You hear "Bahhhh," which is supposed to be the sound that goats make, and see (and smell) a goat. Now you have another choice. You may either stay with the door you originally picked or change to the other door that is still closed. Do you stay with your original choice or switch doors?

This is a difficult problem, which is probably why it is so popular. If you are thinking as most people do, it should not matter whether you stay with the door you selected or switch because each door had a 1/3 chance of hiding the car. This was true when you first selected a door, but the probabilities changed after that selection. Once you pick a door, the probability is 1/3 that the car is behind the one you selected and 2/3 that it is behind the doors you did not select. When a goat is revealed behind a door you did not select, the probability is still 2/3 that the car is behind a door you did not select, so you are more likely to win a car if you switch to the closed door you did not select. Still not sure about this problem? You can play this game repeatedly and see the probability of winning car when you stay with your original door (1/3) or switch to the unopened door you did not select (2/3). A computerized version of this game appeared in *The New York Times* online interactive feature. Try it at http://www.nytimes.com/2008/04/08/science/08monty.html

What is a Problem?

Even now there are few schools that encourage the young or old to think out questions for themselves. And yet, life is a continuous problem for the living, and first of all we should be equipped to think, if possible.

—Clarence Darrow (1932, p. 25)

Everyone has problems, so it would seem that it would be an easy word to define. We all know a problem when we see one, but how would you define the general term "problem?" Psychologists think of a **problem** as a gap or barrier between where you are and where you want to be. You have a problem if you cannot think of a way of getting around the gap or barrier so that you can reach the place you want to be. This definition of a problem is graphically represented in Figure 9.1. As you will see later in this chapter, the way a problem is represented can influence how or whether you can solve it. Be sure that you understand the way the word "problem" is visually defined in Figure 9.1.

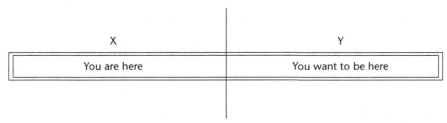

There is a gap or barrier separating you from where you want to be. This is a problem.

Figure 9.1 A visual representation of a "problem." To solve the problem, you need to find a way to get over the gap or around the barrier that is keeping you from the place (or state) where you want to be.

Decision making, problem solving, and creativity are related concepts, with considerable overlap. As described in the last chapter, decision making usually refers to those "problems" where you have multiple options from which to select a solution—the task is selecting the best option (or one that is good enough). In problem solving, you need to generate the options because no (good) options are readily available. When thinking creatively, the options you generate are novel and also provide a good solution. The boundaries between these terms are fuzzy and may be best thought of as a continuum with considerable overlap rather than distinct categories.

Problem solving is a "hot" topic. Perhaps its current popularity is caused by the overwhelming number of new types of problems that we are faced with—ones that did not exist a generation ago, such as an overwhelming number of types of technology that often do not work as intended (this is overwhelming for me), cyber bullying, the digital divide (the poor have less access to information than the middle class), global warming (few of us believed it was a real problem a generation ago), accidents at nuclear power plants—and problems that have been with us a long time but still need solutions, such as poverty, war, prejudice, hunger, loneliness, and many more. Because so much of what we really care about are problems, some schools are altering their curriculum to make it problem-based. The idea behind **problem-based learning** is that students would learn better if they were engaged in real-life problem solving. A veterinary school that uses problem-based learning, for example, might start all students on their first day of class with a visit to a horse with a swollen stomach. Students would be given some facts relevant (or irrelevant) to the horse's condition and then told to solve the problem—make a diagnosis and suggest a treatment. Students would need to scramble to the library and other places where they could find relevant information, check their hypotheses with the actual state of the horse (did he stop eating; does he appear to be in pain), and return to class with their diagnosis and treatment plans. The class and professor would discuss the various solutions, and in this way, the students would learn about the disease and how to treat it. These sorts of learning assignments are engaging, but the problems have to be selected systematically, so that the students learn all of the topics they will need to know by graduation. The jury is still out on the effectiveness of problem-based learning (Hung, 2011). Some argue that the memory load is too high for students who lack the background to solve difficult problems (Kirschner, Sweller, & Clark, 2006). To be successful, students enrolled in a problem-based curriculum need a knowledgeable tutor who can help them when they get stuck on a problem and assess their knowledge as they move through the program to ensure that they are making adequate progress toward the knowledge and skills they will need.

Anatomy of a Problem

> Finding the right answer is important, of course. But more important is developing the ability to see that problems have multiple solutions, that getting from X to Y demands basic skills and mental agility, imagination, persistence, patience.
>
> —Mary Hatwood Futrell, President, NEA (cited in Heiman & Slomianko, 1986, p. 18)

Consider this more mundane problem that differs in several important ways from the pick-the-door-that-hides-a-car problem presented at the start of this chapter or the horse with a swollen stomach: Keith has to catch a 9:00 A.M. plane for Philadelphia, and he is already behind schedule. The quickest route to the airport is the freeway, except when the traffic is heavy.

The traffic is almost always heavy with commuters during the morning rush hour. There is a back road route that might be a good one, if the road along the river is not flooded. The road is frequently closed because of flooding after heavy rains. As you can probably guess, it rained last night. The surface street route is the longest. If Keith chooses this route, he may miss his plane. Of course, if he spends too much time pondering this problem, he will surely miss his plane. Which route should he take?

To understand any complex phenomenon, like problem solving, we need a model or theoretical framework that we can use to study and understand how people solve all sorts of problems. A model is an "as, if" statement. This means that we will examine the phenomenon that we want to know about "as if" it were something else. Theoretical models of this sort are useful for organizing what we know about thinking and for suggesting new types of research and ways to improve the process we are trying to understand.

In their classic book, Newell and Simon (1972) conceptualized all problems as being composed of the same basic parts or structures. Their idea is that problems can be understood by reducing them to their anatomical parts. According to this view, the anatomy of a problem can be thought of as having a starting or initial state (Keith's home) and a final or goal state (the airport). All of the possible **solution paths** from the **initial state** to the **goal state** comprise the **problem space**. In solving a problem, people search through the problem space to find the best path from the initial state to the goal; that is, they consider all of the alternatives that would lead to the goal and select the best one. Or, if they cannot initially find any way to get from the start to the goal state, they generate possible solution paths.

In addition to an initial state, a goal state, and the paths connecting them, there are **givens:** information and rules that place constraints on the problem. The givens include the knowledge needed to reach the goal. This information can be explicitly stated or implicitly assumed. Two implicit givens in the problem presented earlier were the knowledge that Keith would drive a car to the airport and that he would either take the freeway route, back-road route, or surface-street route. This anatomy or framework for conceptualizing problems has proven useful in understanding the process of problem solving. The anatomy of the airport problem is schematically shown in Figure 9.2. We return to the airport problem later in the chapter as different problem-solving strategies are considered.

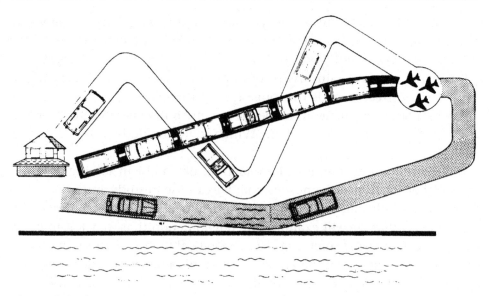

Figure 9.2 The anatomy of the airport problem. Givens: Keith will drive to the airport. He will take one of these routes. He must take the fastest route.

Problems differ in many ways, including difficulty and where in the problem space the gap occurs. In the airport problem, the difficulty lies in choosing the path (route) that would get Keith to the goal in the shortest time.

Consider Rubik's cube as a difficult problem. The goal for a Rubik's cube is to align each small colored square so that each of the six sides of the cube will be a uniform color. This is a prohibitive problem because there are millions of combinations of possible moves (paths to the goal). The "trick" is to determine which combination of moves will lead to the goal. In this sort of problem, the difficulty lies in reducing the number of possible paths so that only potentially correct ones will be chosen. Newell and Simon (1972) calculated that the average 40-move chess game has 10^{120} paths. This number is so large that it is almost impossible for most of us to imagine! Perhaps this is why we view great chess masters with such awe. They have the knowledge to avoid blind paths (bad moves) that will not lead to the goal (winning) and to select the best combination of moves.

Situation Awareness

Most real-life problems occur in a context, where a single occurrence or sequence of events creates a problem, sometimes called a **situation** to denote that it is different from the sort of problem you might be assigned in a math or physics class that does not occur naturally. Contemporary theories of problem solving consider how people gather and use information to handle a situation and implement actions to solve the problems they raise. Consider this situation posed by Wiig (2003). Suppose you are a customer service manager, and an important customer returns a high-technology piece of equipment because it is not working correctly. You need to make sense out of this situation—being sure that your understanding of what is happening matches reality. You recognize that there is a problem with the technology and then have to decide what to do about it. A guiding principle in your decision is that your company is committed to being a leader in your industry, which means that you offer high-quality products and service. You can think of this guiding principle as the "givens" in this problem—it is the rule under which the problem is solved. In Wiig's example, you decide that the technical problems are serious, and it follows that your company needs to redesign the product. This is shown graphically in Figure 9.3.

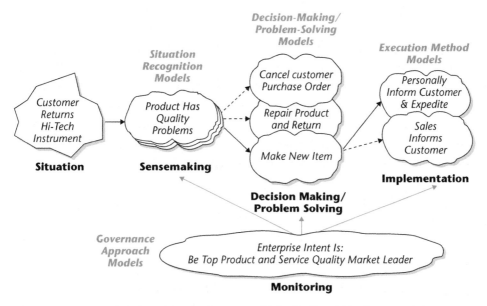

Figure 9.3 A model of problem solving in which the "problem" occurs in a context where the problem-solver needs to recognize a "situation" that needs action and bases that action on a series of steps in which she makes sense out of the situation, decides what action to take based on guiding principles, and then implements the action. Figure from Wiig, K. M. (2003). *Journal of Knowledge Management*, Vol. 7, No. 5 (2003), pp. 6–24, Knowledge Research Institute. www.krii.com.

Stages in Problem Solving

> The aim of heuristics is to study the methods and rules of discovery and invention . . . . Heuristic, as an adjective, means 'serving to discover.' "
>
> —George Polya (1945, pp. 112–113)

In 1926, Graham Wallas examined anecdotal accounts of creative scientists and concluded that problem solving progresses in a series of stages. Although there is disagreement among psychologists as to whether all problem solving is done in qualitatively different stages, a brief review of the hypothesized stages may prove useful to problem-solvers.

The first stage is **preparation** or **familiarization**. This includes the time spent in understanding the nature of the problem, the desired goal, and the givens. This is a crucial part in problem solving because a correct solution cannot be generated without an adequate understanding of the problem. This roughly corresponds to recognizing the situation and sense-making in the Situation Awareness Model. The second stage is the **production stage**. During this stage, the problem-solver produces the solution paths that define the problem space. This phase corresponds to decision making/ problem solving and implementation in the Situation Awareness Model. **Judgment** or **evaluation** is the third stage. During this stage, individuals evaluate the solution paths in order to select the best one. This is similar to monitoring in the Situation Awareness Model. The fourth stage is a strange one that may or may not occur, depending on the problem. Sometimes when we cannot find a solution path, we stop working on the problem, at least for a short while. The period when we are not actively considering the problem is called the **incubation stage**. There are many reports from famous scientists that a solution came to them during the incubation phase—seemingly "out of the blue." Because of the fascination incubation holds for most people, it deserves separate consideration.

Incubation

Have you ever had the experience of working unsuccessfully on a problem, then having the solution come to you sometime later when you were not consciously thinking about it? If so, then you have experienced incubation effects first-hand. The term "incubation" suggests a mother hen sitting on great ideas that are about to hatch.

Incubation is a poorly understood phenomenon. If your employer found you sitting with your feet propped on your desk, gazing out the window, he probably would not be pleased to learn that you were "incubating" on company time. A familiar experience is having a correct answer come to you immediately after turning in an exam or paper. This is most likely the result of incubation. It is a good idea to work well ahead of deadlines to allow ample time for incubation effects to occur. We do not know how people are able to produce solutions during "time-outs." The sudden realization that you have found a solution is called **insight**. It is the AHA! experience when a problem is suddenly solved. There is no evidence that people continue to work on the problem at an unconscious level, although some people have suggested that this is how incubation occurs. Most likely, the time-out period serves to dissipate fatigue and allow individuals to get out of sets or ruts in their thinking processes so that they can view the problem from a different perspective.

Herbert A. Simon (1977), the Nobel Prize-winning psychologist, has attempted to explain incubation as due, in part, to selective forgetting. He suggested that when we are working on a problem, we rely on a relatively small number of concepts held in a limited capacity short-term or working memory. (See the chapter on memory for a detailed discussion of this concept.) When we are not working on a problem, the information held in short-term memory is quickly forgotten. If this information was not productive for discovering a solution, then having forgotten it will be beneficial to finding a good solution. A review of the research literature found that people really do benefit from taking time out when solving problems (Sio & Ormerod, 2009). It is a good idea to put aside a problem that you are having difficulty solving and return to it at a later time. This is especially good advice during an exam when you can skip a difficult problem and move on to solve other ones that are easier. At least you will be sure of getting credit for the easier problems, but watch your time limits carefully so that you can correctly finish as many problems as possible in the allotted time. (Of course, it is also a good idea to work on the problems worth the most points first to maximize your exam score.)

Luann by Greg Evans. Used with permission by King Features.

Persistence

> I have a bias, which leads me to believe that no problem of human relations is ever insolvable.
>
> —Ralph Bunche (quoted in Beilensen & Jackson, 1992, p. 31)

Although persistence does not usually appear as a stage in problem solving, it is probably the most important variable in determining success. An individual who persists at a problem is much more likely to solve it than an individual who gives up. Persistence is close to Levine's (1994) idea of "intimate engagement" (p. 3), the willingness to work on a problem in an involved and concentrated way. For example, suppose that you are given a problem to solve in mathematics. It should be obvious that if you give up as soon as you find that the solution is not immediately apparent, you will not perform as well in solving the problem as someone who continues to work on it. Although, if you are thinking that a short time-out to allow for incubation might work, you are already getting the idea that you increase the probability of solving difficult problems by applying the concepts presented in this chapter.

Grit, which is defined as "perseverance and passion for long-term goals" (Duckworth, Peterson, Matthews, & Kelly, 2007) is critical for success in many fields. Gritty people stay on course despite the inevitable failures, disappointments, and boredom. It is a trait found in high-achieving individuals, ranging from world-class athletes, spelling bee champions, investment bankers, and successful students. In a series of studies, Duckworth and her colleagues found that grit is an important predictor of success—at least as important as intelligence. We all face problems of various sorts, ranging from the personal to global. Success at any difficult task will require hard work and persistence, even in the face of set-backs.

Heller, Saltzstein, and Caspe (1992) compared the way experienced physicians go about solving the problem of making an accurate diagnosis with the way novice physicians make a diagnosis. When you visit a physician, you are there because you have a problem. You need to find the cause for your symptoms, so that the symptoms and the underlying cause can be treated. Novice physicians terminated their search for a cause as soon as they found a plausible alternative. By contrast, the senior physicians persisted in their search through the problem space even after they found a possible cause. Similar results were found when students who were successful in solving problems in a genetics class were compared to unsuccessful students. The most salient difference between the successful and unsuccessful problem-solvers was the tendency to consider more options; that is, the good problem-solvers persisted longer than the poor problem-solvers when searching for solutions and continued to work on the problem after a plausible solution was found.

The same results were found in studies of mathematical problem solving. When college students are given mathematical problems to solve, most will try to recall a solution for a similar problem (retrieval from memory of a familiar solution) instead of trying to reason from their knowledge of mathematics (Lithner, 2000). Those who continue to work on the problem when they cannot readily recall a solution are more successful than those students who "give up." This is an important point: in order to become a good problem-solver, you must be willing to work at the problem and to search the problem space for solution paths, even when none are obvious or a plausible one has been found.

Well-Defined and Ill-Defined Problems

> Here is Edward Bear, coming downstairs. Now, bump, bump, bump, on the back of his head, behind Christopher Robin. It is, as far as he knows, the only way of coming downstairs, but sometimes he feels that there really is another way, if only he could stop bumping for a moment and think of it.
>
> —A. A. Milne (*Winnie-the-Pooh*, 1926, p. 3)

Problems come in all shapes and sizes. Consider the following two problems:

1. The parallelogram problem (after Wertheimer, 1959).

Some time back in fifth or sixth grade, you learned that in order to find the area of a rectangle, you should multiply the height by the length. Now you are given the following parallelogram that is 4" long and 2" high. What is its area?

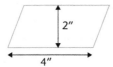

2. Write a poem expressing the joy you feel when spring flowers bloom.

Do these problems seem qualitatively different to you? The parallelogram problem has a single correct answer. Have you figured it out? Wertheimer (1959) suggested that the correct answer lies in perceptual reorganization, or seeing the problem in a new way. The new way consists of seeing the parallelogram in terms of a rectangle and two triangles. Thus, the parallelogram becomes:

Once the problem is restructured this way, it is only a short leap to figure out that the area of the parallelogram can be found with the same formula for the area of a rectangle because the two triangles can be fit together so that a new rectangular figure is formed with a 4″ length and a 2″ height. In the present example, the area of the parallelogram is 2″ x 4″ = 8 square inches. There is no other correct answer. The goal (correct answer) is **well defined**, as is the path to the goal.

Writing a poem is a different sort of problem. The goal (a beautiful poem) is ill defined, as there are many forms a poem can take. There are countless ways to write a poem. The greatest difficulty in this case lies in evaluating the quality of the end product. The goal is uncertain in **ill-defined** problems, thus part of the difficulty lies in determining whether the problem has been solved.

Most of the problems that confront people outside of school are ill defined. The problem-solver must decide how to define the goal and then evaluate how well the goal has been attained. By contrast, many of the problems that students are asked to solve in school are well defined, that is, there is a single correct answer. Other examples of ill-defined problems are: creating a way to increase sales for a business; finding more effective ways to study; writing a clear, easy-to-read textbook; saving money for college tuition; building a better mousetrap; deescalating the nuclear arms race, getting a date with the attractive newcomer at your school, and improving the environment. In ill-defined problems, the goal may be vague or incomplete, which makes the generation of solution paths difficult and their evaluation even more difficult.

One of the best ways to approach ill-defined problems is to make the goal explicit. It is usually possible to state the goal in several different ways for ill-defined problems. For example, the problem of increasing sales can be re-identified as the problem of increasing profits because the real goal is to find ways to make more money. When stated in this form, the problem changes from its initial conceptualization. Solution paths can now include ways to cut losses, reduce inventories, or collect bad debts. The best way to approach ill-defined problems is to specify multiple goals in objective terms so that a variety of solution paths can be considered. This sort of exercise will suggest additional solutions and can improve the way you search for solutions.

Sometimes the distinction between well-defined and ill-defined problems blurs. Consider again the problem of getting Keith to the airport on time. If the problem is selecting among the three routes to the airport, it is well defined, but if other solution paths and goals are possible—e.g., fly to the airport, take a different plane from a nearer airport, or take the subway—then the problem becomes somewhat more difficult to define. Even when a problem seems to be well-defined, it is useful to consider whether other goal states would solve the problem, and, if so, what sorts of solution paths are possible with different goals.

Problem Planning and Representation

> In the mathematics and science courses I took in college, I was enormously irritated by the hundreds of hours that I wasted staring at problems without any good idea about what approach to try next in attempting to solve them. I thought at the time that there was no educational value in those "blank" minutes and I see no value in them today.
> —Wickelgren (1974, p. ix)

Recent research in problem solving has focused on the importance of devising a plan for finding and selecting solutions. Planning is a higher-order thinking skill that is used to direct and regulate behavior. A plan provides a structure that problem-solvers can use in a step-by step manner to help them reach the desired goal.

Multiple Statements of the Goal

Stating the goal in many different ways, which results in multiple goal states, even when the problems appears to be well defined, is an example of a planful approach to problem solving. The generation of multiple goal states will increase the size of the problem space and provide more opportunities for finding a good solution. This sort of plan is **transcontextual**, which means that it can be used in any context with any sort of problem. Here is an example of this approach:

Various opinion polls have identified "fear of crime" as an important concern of many Americans. Not too surprisingly, politicians have made crime a major part of their campaign pledges. Fear of crime is an important and ill-defined problem. Suppose we turn this problem into a clearly articulated goal.

> **Goal #1:** *Reduce crime.* Given this goal, what are some possible solutions or paths of action that will move our society from its present start state of "fear of crime" toward the goal of reducing crime? Here are two possible solutions that (might) move us toward the goal of reducing crime:
>
> Make capital punishment a national law.
>
> Incarcerate criminals for life if they are convicted of three major crimes.

Now, let's restate the goal in other ways and see how each restatement of the goal suggests different solutions. One approach for restating the goal state is to view the problem from different perspectives. What is a goal state for those citizens who are potential victims of crime?

> **Goal #2:** *Make life safer for honest citizens.* This sort of goal shifts solutions from the criminals to the potential victims of crime. Some possible solutions that come to mind for attaining this goal:
>
> Provide everyone with a home security system.
>
> Teach everyone self-defense.
>
> Organize anti-crime groups in every neighborhood.
>
> Buy all honest citizens large dogs.

> **Goal #3:** *Reduce the number of criminals.* Given this goal, solutions now focus on numbers rather than methods and on the criminals instead of the honest people in the community. For example,
>
> Send criminals to Siberia.
>
> Return to gallows and public floggings to send a strong anti-crime message to would-be criminals.

Begin community programs that act as a deterrent to a life of crime (e.g., improve education and sports programs).

Goal #4: *Change people's perceptions so that they no longer fear crime.* This sort of goal will not affect the actual crime rate; rather, it will change how people think about crime. Some possible solutions for this goal:

Give everyone drugs that reduce anxiety (so they no longer fear crime).

Provide information that shows that the crime rate is really very low (this could be true or false; either would satisfy this goal, although lying is obviously unethical).

Goal #5: *Reduce violent crimes.* This goal also shifts how we think about the problem because it concerns the degree of violence instead of the number of crimes, number of criminals, or how people feel about crime. Some possible solutions:

Make it illegal to own a gun.

Legalize drug use.

Another way to generate goal states is to view the problem from the perspective of the criminals. What would it take to get them NOT to engage in crime? It soon becomes clear that crime is not a homogeneous category, and different sorts of actions are needed for different sorts of crimes. Suppose that you are a car-jacker. What would prevent you from hijacking cars? Would having a job make a difference? What about installing car locator systems in every car. Would that make you less likely to high-jack cars? What if you abused your spouse? What would work to stop spousal abuse?

Of course, some of these possible solutions are ludicrous, such as sending criminals to Siberia or giving everyone anti-anxiety drugs, and others are unethical. The idea behind this example is that new perspectives on a difficult problem emerge when we are forced to state an ill-defined goal in several ways. It is likely that several solutions can be used together so that fear of crime is alleviated. Try this sort of exercise with other difficult problems. You may be surprised to find that you can think of different categories of solutions by specifying qualitatively different sorts of goals and by viewing the problem from different perspectives. Restating the goal in multiple ways and considering different perspectives are two examples of using a plan to solve problems.

Although plans for solving problems can vary in complexity, most will consist of a series of basic steps that are similar across all of the models: (a) Recognition that a problem exists; this is an important stage that often is the mark of creativity, a topic that is addressed in the next chapter. Consider any major change, such as the change from horse and buggy to motorized vehicles. For most of the pre-automotive world, horses worked very well, and the proposition that they could be replaced by a box on wheels that constantly broke down and needed fuel to run was ludicrous. Few people saw any problem with travel by horse and therefore did not see a problem that needed to be solved.; (b) Construction of a representation of the problem that includes the initial and goal states; (c) Generation and evaluation of possible solutions; (d) Selection of a possible solution; and (e) Execution of the possible solution to determine if it solves the problem.

Unfortunately, some or all of the steps will have to be repeated if the goal is not attained. Problem solving is not a simple or linear process. It often requires changes in the representation of the problem or redefinition of the goal as well as generation of numerous possible solutions and reevaluation of the possible solutions. There are many models of problem solving that involve a series of steps and iterative processes. The eight-step model proposed by Basadur and Basadur (2011) may be useful for anyone who is thinking about how to "attack" a problem. These authors suggest a four-stage approach, with two steps in each phase. These are 1) generation—identifying a problem and finding facts that are relevant; 2) conceptualization—defining the problem and finding ideas that are relevant; 3) optimization—evaluating and selecting possible solutions and planning how to implement a solution; and 4) implementation—accepting a solution and putting it into action. These phases and steps are shown in Figure 9. 4.

Representation of the Problem Space

> There is little doubt that diagrammatic representations considerably help humans solve certain classes of problems.
>
> —Patrick Oliver (2001, p. 63)

The best way to solve a problem is to devise the best representation. In an extensive set of studies of the way scientists think about difficult problems, Dunbar (1998) found that when scientists represented a problem, they naturally included those features of the problem that they thought would be important in solving the problem, with systematic differences between the representations reflecting different beliefs about the nature of the

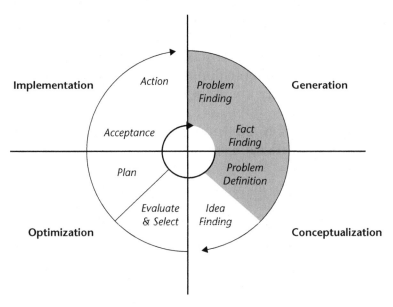

Figure 9.4 A model of problem solving proposed by Basadur and Basadur (2011). Basadur, M., & Basadur, T. (2011). Where are the generators? *Psychology of Aesthetics, Creativity, and The Arts*, 5(1), 29–42. doi:10.1037/a0017757.

problem. Consider, for example, an economics problem like a high rate of unemployment. Members of different political parties will represent the same problem in different ways because they have different beliefs about the cause of the problem. The same sort of representational differences were found in studies of the way scientists solve problems in their academic discipline. According to Dunbar, the molecular biologists who recently identified a gene for some types of breast cancer were successful in their quest for this elusive gene because they used a different representation for this genetics problem than the unsuccessful scientists.

Mayer (2002) found that good visual representations can help readers comprehend difficult text. Readers who have already read the chapter on memory will recognize this finding as an example of the principle that visual and verbal information work together to enhance memory. One principle of good thinking that appears in almost every chapter of this book is to use multiple representational systems—that is, adding diagrams to printed text and using verbal descriptors with spatial information.

In discussing the way good representations are constructed, Newell (1983) said that "Memory must be tickled," a phrase that I have often used because I believe that it is a critical consideration in how we think. Every time you think, your knowledge about the problem must be accessed and utilized. Every problem-solver must be able to make inferences from problem statements to build an adequate problem representation—one in which missing and conflicting information is made obvious and critical relationships are easy to grasp. Try this example:

> Draw a representation and write an algebraic formula that corresponds to the following statement:
>
> There are six times as many students as professors at this university.
>
> If you are like many college students, you drew a diagram like this one:

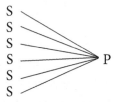

This translates into 6S = P.

If I gave you the number of students, you could use this formula to find that number of professors and vice versa. Can you see why the formula derived from this representation is wrong? The formula states that there are more professors than there are students, rather than the reverse! The reason that so many students have difficulty with this problem and others like it lies in the way in which the words are translated into a diagram. The juxtaposition of the words "six times the number of students" seems to automatically suggest that the number of students should be multiplied by six. Mayer found a significant improvement in the mathematical problem-solving skills of college students after only three hours of training on how to devise correct representations (Lewis & Mayer, 1987). It is difficult to overstate the importance of a good representation when solving problems.

The section below contains suggestions for devising good representations and demonstrates the intimate relationship between the representation and the solution to the problem. Good representations share certain characteristics. They take advantage of spatial locations to group information in a visual format; they also act as a check on how well you understand the problem. Let's try some examples of ways to represent problems.

Write It Down

All problems are initially represented in your head. It is a good idea to get the paths and goals on paper or into some other concrete form. This tactic will reduce the memory load and allow you to view the problem visually. The simplest example of the aid provided by a pencil and paper is a straightforward multiplication problem. Solve the following problem without writing anything:

$$\begin{array}{r} 976 \\ \times\ \underline{893} \end{array}$$

Of course, you would consider this a ridiculous request because it is a simple problem with paper and pencil and a difficult one to perform in your head because of the demands on working memory. Whenever there are several facts or different options to keep track of, it is a good idea to use paper and pencil.

Draw a Graph or Diagram

> A bear, starting at point P, walked one mile due south. Then he changed direction and walked one mile due east. Then he turned again to the left and walked one mile due north, and arrived exactly at the point P he started from. What was the color of the bear?
>
> —Polya, 1957, p. 234

Does this problem seem strange or even impossible to you? If you draw a simple "map" of the bear's route, it will be a pie-shaped wedge. Where on earth is this possible? Think about a globe. Did you just say "Why, of course, point P must be the North Pole" to yourself? Once you realize that you are at the North Pole, this problem becomes easy to solve. The bear must be white, because only polar bears live at the North Pole.

Consider the following problem:

> A venerable old monk leaves the monastery at exactly 6:00 A.M. to climb a winding mountain trail to the solitude of the mountain peak. He arrives at exactly 4:00 P.M. After spending the night in sleep and prayer, he leaves the mountain peak at exactly 6:00 A.M. and arrives at the monastery at exactly 4:00 P.M. There are no constraints on the speed at which he walks. In fact, he stops several times along the way to rest. Is there some point on the mountain trail that he passes at exactly the same time each day?

Stop and think about this problem for a moment. Does it seem like a difficult one? There are two ways to consider this problem that will make the answer seem simple, but before you go on, decide how you would go about solving this problem, and then solve it. As you can probably guess, a good representation of the central elements of the problem will be an important determinant of the solution.

One solution is to draw a graph of the monk's ascent and descent. The graph can take any shape since you know nothing about his hourly progress. The graphs of the ascent and descent should appear as in Figure 9.5.

Now, superimpose the two graphs and see if there must be some point where the graphs intersect. If there is, then there is some time when the monk passed the same point at the same time on each day. This is shown in Figure 9.6.

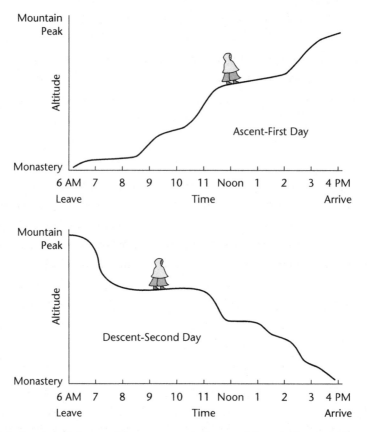

Figure 9.5 Graphs of the monk's ascent and descent. The graphs can take any shape because the monk can rest as often as he wishes when he climbs the hill and when he descends.

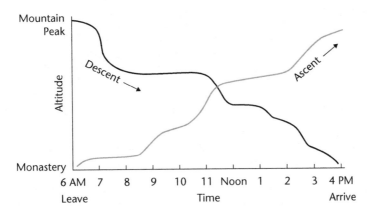

Figure 9.6 By superimposing the ascent and descent graphs, it is easy to see that there must be some place at which the graphs intersect. Thus, there must be a place on the mountain trail that the monk crosses at the same time each day.

Drawing a graph provides a clear picture of the results. Actually, an easier way of solving this problem involves changing the representation and re-stating the facts in the problem in an equivalent but different form. As-sume two people traverse the same mountain path at the same time on the same morning. If one starts at the monastery and the other starts at the mountain peak, both leaving at 6:00 AM and both arriving at their oppo-site destinations at 4:00 PM, it is obvious they must meet somewhere along the path no matter how often each chooses to rest and reflect. Thus, with a change in representation, a difficult problem can become trivial.

I used to teach a laboratory course in experimental psychology. In that course, college students were required to conduct experiments, gather data, and interpret their data in meaningful ways. Although the students were taught the statistical methods needed for data analysis, I found that when they graphed their results they obtained a much better understanding of the phenomenon they investigated. They were able to use their experimen-tal results to formulate sound conclusions because they understood the nature of their findings. The students found that a simple graph was a more valuable tool for comprehension than the elaborate statistical procedures that they were required to use.

Graphs and other kinds of diagrams are especially useful comprehension strategies in mathematical and scientific problem solving. For example, a common problem in undergraduate statistics courses requires finding the area between two points under a certain kind of curve called a "normal" or "bell-shaped" curve. This problem can be difficult or confusing for students, but it becomes easy if they draw the curve and shade in the area they want to find. In fact, I do not give my statistics students the algebraic rules for finding the appropriate area. Students find it easier to figure it out for themselves from the diagrams they draw.

Let's try another example in which graphs or diagrams will simplify the search for a solution path. To save money and their sanity, Melvin, Brock, Marc, and Claire decide to form a babysitting cooperative. They agree to baby sit for each other's children with the understanding that when one of them stays with another's children, the recipient will repay the sitter with an equal number of babysitting hours. They decide to tally babysitting hours at the end of the month. During the month, Melvin sat with Brock's children 9 hours, Marc sat with Melvin's children 3 hours, and Claire stayed with Melvin's children 6 hours. Marc baby sat 9 hours with Claire's children, and Brock baby sat 5 hours with Claire's children. Which of these people has 12 hours of baby- sitting time due to him or her?

A good diagram of the relationship between these four people is clearly needed. The relevant givens will involve the four people and the number of hours owed to each. Let's start with the first sentence, "Melvin sat with Brock's children 9 hours." Thus, Brock owes Melvin 9 hours of babysitting at the end of the month. The operation being used is the transformation of number of hours spent babysitting into number of hours owed to each sitter. A simple diagram of this relationship is:

The next sentence translates into "Melvin owes Marc 3 hours, and Melvin owes Claire 6 hours."

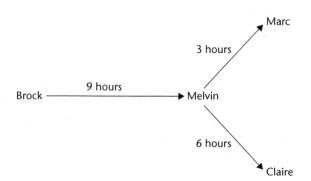

Then, changing the third sentence so that it reflects what is owed, Claire owes Marc 9 hours, and Claire owes Brock 5 hours.

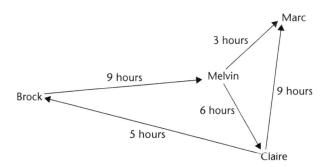

It is easy to see from this diagram that only Marc is owed 12 hours of babysitting, 3 hours from Melvin and 9 hours from Clair. A good diagram of the hours owed is essential in finding the solution to this problem.

There are several other ways of representing the information in the babysitting co-op problem that will display all of the essential relationships and thus also give the correct answer. When a colleague (Dr. Susan Nummedal, emeritus faculty at California State University, Long Beach) posed this problem to her students, she found that they devised a variety of representations to solve the problem. One student used a simple bar graph to keep track of the number of hours sat by each participant. This representation is shown in Figure 9.7.

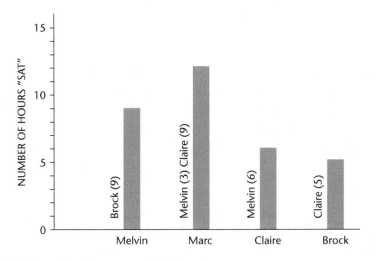

Figure 9.7 Alternative form representation.

Other students used a variety of table formats. One listed the number of hours "gave" as a positive number and "received" as a negative number because it was owed. Another student split the information into "sitter" and "sat for" categories, filled in a table of information summing across the columns for the total number of "sat for" hours for each participant, and summed down the rows for the total number of "sitter" hours for each participant. These representations are offered in tables 9.1 and 9.2, respectively.

As the babysitting co-op problem demonstrates, there are often many ways of representing a given problem. As you work through the problems in this chapter, try a variety of representations. A good representation will present all of the relevant information in a way that it can be readily understood and assimilated. Good representations provide the necessary solution paths to the goal.

Try a Hierarchical Tree

Hierarchical trees are branching diagrams. They are most frequently used to assess mathematically the probability or likelihood of uncertain

Table 9.1

	Gave	Received	Total Due
Melvin	+9	-3, -6	0
Marc	+3, +9		12
Claire	+6	-9, -15	-8
Brock	+5	-9	-4

Table 9.2

		Sitter				Total Number of Hours Sat For
		Melvin	Marc	Claire	Brock	
Sat For	Melvin		3	6		9
	Marc				0	
	Claire		9		5	14
	Brock	9				9
Total Number of Hours Sat		9	12	6	5	

outcomes. (See the chapter on reasoning for the use of tree diagrams in solving "if, then" problems and the chapter on probability for the use of decision trees in calculating probabilities.) Hierarchical trees or tree diagrams can be useful aids in decision making and problem solving. In this context, they are called decision trees. If the problem you are working on is fairly complex, with each possible solution path requiring subsequent additional paths, a hierarchical tree or tree diagram should be considered.

Here is a classic problem that has a long history in the psychological literature on problem solving. Although the problem is a medical one, no specialized knowledge is needed to solve it:

> Suppose you are a doctor faced with a patient who has a malignant tumor in his stomach. It is impossible to operate on the patient, but unless the tumor is destroyed the patient will die. There is a kind of ray that can be used to destroy the tumor. If the rays reach the tumor all at once at a sufficiently high intensity, the tumor will be destroyed. Unfortunately, at this intensity the healthy tissue that the rays pass through on the way to the tumor will also be destroyed. At lower intensities the rays are harmless to healthy tissue, but they will not affect the tumor either. What type of procedure might be used to destroy the tumor with the rays, and at the same time avoid destroying the healthy tissue? (Duncker, 1945, pp. 307–308)

Research has shown that this is a difficult problem to solve (and modern medical advances since 1945 make new solutions possible). Although a variety of solutions were attempted, the best solution is to use several weak rays, each coming from different places outside the body focused so that they would meet and summate at the tumor site. In this manner, the healthy tissue will not be hurt by the weak rays, and the tumor will receive a high level of radiation. This solution was formulated from a broader category of solutions that included having each ray grow stronger as it reached the tumor.

One subject's search for solution paths is shown in Figure 9.8 in a hierarchical tree diagram. Note that the goal is explicitly stated at the top of the tree. General broad strategies are listed one level below the goal, with more specific ways of satisfying each strategy on lower levels.

Another example of using trees to solve problems is the familiar use of family trees. Estate lawyers, who often face a tangled web of family

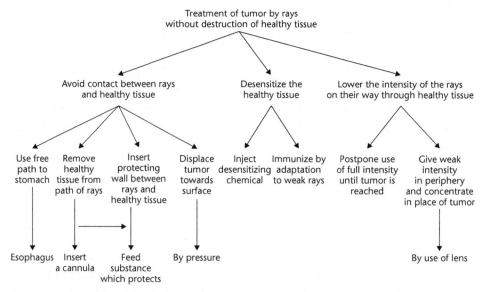

Figure 9.8 A hierarchical tree diagram of one subject's attempted solutions to Duncker's x-ray problem. (After Duncker, 1945).

relationships, need to be able to determine the relations between family members in order to handle wills and estate taxes. Multiple spouses, cohabitation, step-children, half-siblings, and out-of-wedlock births can make the difficult matter of inheritance a legal nightmare. A carefully drawn family tree that places each member on the appropriate generational branch is an invaluable aid in solving tangled inheritance claims.

Make a Matrix

A **matrix** is a rectangular array of facts or numbers. It is really just a fancy word for a chart. When the givens in a problem can be broken down into categories, a matrix may be a good method of representation. Consider the problem posed by Whimbey and Lochhead (1982):

> Three men—Fred, Ed, and Ted—are married to Joan, Sally, and Vickie, but not necessarily in that order. Joan, who is Ed's sister, lives in Detroit. Fred dislikes animals. Ed weighs more than the man who is married to Vickie. The man married to Sally breeds Siamese cats as a hobby. Fred commutes over 200 hours a year from his home in Ann Arbor to his job in Detroit. Match up the men with the women they married. (p. 67)

What are the categories of information given in this problem? The givens concern husbands and wives. Set up a three-by-three matrix and fill in as much of it as you can with the information given above:

	Joan	Sally	Vickie
Fred			
Ed			
Ted			

Because Joan is Ed's sister, she cannot be his wife, so fill in a "NO" in the Joan–Ed cell of the matrix. Skip the next two statements for the time being and go on to the statement that Ed weighs more than the man married to Vickie; therefore, Ed is not married to Vickie. Ed must be married to Sally. So far, the matrix appears as below:

	Joan	Sally	Vickie
Fred		NO	
Ed	NO	YES	NO
Ted		NO	

Peruse the problem for more clues. Have you found the important one? Fred lives in Ann Arbor and Joan lives in Detroit; therefore, we would conclude that they are probably not married. Because Fred is not married to Joan or Sally, he must be married to Vickie. Who is left for Ted? Joan must be married to Ted.

The completed matrix:

	Joan	Sally	Vickie
Fred	NO	NO	YES
Ed	NO	YES	NO
Ted	YES	NO	NO

Admittedly, this is an artificial problem, not much like the ones we encounter in real life, but problems just like this appear on the Law School Aptitude Test (LSAT), which is used for admissions for most law schools in the United States and many other countries around the world. A little practice with matrix problems before taking the test will help you achieve a career in law (assuming that is why you would be taking the LSAT). To do well on the logic problems found on the LSAT and other tests used for university admissions, you need to recognize the type of problem—if you can quickly see that a problem calls for a matrix set-up, you could solve the problems much more quickly than if you spent time deciding on which representation to use.

Even if these problems seem artificial, there are many times when a matrix representation can help in everyday life. For example, there is considerable controversy over the issue of vitamin C as a deterrent for the common cold. How would you decide if vitamin C prevents colds? Most probably, you would give vitamin C to some people and not others and count the number of colds in each group. Suppose you found the following results: 10 people who took vitamin C did not catch a cold, 4 people who took vitamin C caught a cold, 8 people who did not take vitamin C did not catch a cold, and 6 people who did not take vitamin C caught a cold. What would you conclude?

Because we have categories of information (took or did not take vitamin C and caught or did not catch a cold), a matrix displaying the appropriate values will help us to understand the givens.

Vitamin C				
	Took Vitamin C	**Didn't Take Vitamin C**		
Caught a cold	4	6	Total number who caught a cold: 10	Of those who caught a cold, % who took vitamin C: 40%
				Of those who caught a cold, % who didn't take vitamin C: 60%
Didn't catch a cold	10	8	Total number who didn't catch a cold: 18	Of those who didn't catch a cold, % who took vitamin C: 55.5% (10/18)
				Of those who didn't catch a cold, % who didn't take vitamin C: 44.4% (8/18)
	Total number who took vitamin C: 14	Total number who didn't take vitamin C: 14	Total number in the study: 28	

By examining every cell of the matrix, you can determine if vitamin C prevented colds. To see if vitamin C worked, you need to consider how many of those who caught a cold had taken vitamin C. The answer is 4 out of 10, or 40%. You also need to consider how many of those who did not catch a cold had taken vitamin C. The answer is 10 out of 18, or 55.5%. Few would be willing to conclude from these data that vitamin C helped to prevent colds from these data. (Research concepts are discussed more fully in the chapter "Thinking as Hypothesis Testing" the chapter on probability. Statistical tests are used to decide if these numbers are significantly different.) By representing the information in a matrix, the results can be more easily determined. This is essentially the same problem that was discussed in the likelihood and uncertainty chapter, in which you were asked to decide if a positive outcome on a cancer screening test actually meant you had cancer. Given the overlap between the topics, you would expect that techniques that are useful in one context would also be useful in related contexts.

Manipulate Models

It is often a good idea to make a concrete representation for abstract problems. I am sure that you have seen an architect's model for a planned complex like a shopping center, office building, or college campus. The miniature buildings and walkways are not made because architects love doll-sized buildings. Although they are often made to communicate architectural plans to others who are not skilled at reading blueprints, the miniature models also help the architect solve problems. With the movable parts, she or he can move the buildings to find the best way to place them before construction begins.

Let's try a problem where making a model will help in finding a solution. There are two groups of beings on a mythical planet in a far away galaxy: they are Hobbits and Orcs. One day, three Hobbits got lost while exploring the homeland of the Orcs. The Hobbits could get home safely if they could cross the river that separates their two homelands. The Orcs agreed to help the Hobbits cross the river, but the only boat they had could hold only two beings at a time, and the Hobbits could not let themselves ever be outnumbered by the Orcs, or the Orcs would eat them.

Your problem is to figure out a sequence of moves that will carry all three hobbits to the other side of the river and return all three Orcs on their own side. The constraints are that only two beings can fit in the boat at one time, and if at any time the Orcs on one shore outnumber the Hobbits, you will have to start over.

This would be an impossible problem to solve without some external form of representation. Use some small objects to represent the Hobbits and Orcs and move them across an imaginary river. Three large paper clips for the hobbits and three small paper clips for the Orcs will work well. You will have to imagine that you are transporting them in a boat. Be sure to write down all of your moves. Plan to take as long as 10 to 15 minutes to solve this problem. As you work toward the solution, be aware of how you are thinking about the moves. Do not go on until you have worked through the problem.

The complete sequence of moves needed to move the Hobbits is shown in Figure 9.9. One of the greatest difficulties with this problem is the need to move all three Orcs across the river, a situation that is not desired, in order to move the Hobbits without allowing them to become outnumbered. Problems of this sort have come to be known as **detour problems** because the path to the goal is not a direct linear one. Intermediate steps are required that seem directly opposite to the goal—in this case, moving all three Orcs to the opposite side of the river when the desired goal is to have all of them on the side from which they originated. It is important to recognize that the route to a goal will often involve detours.

As a more realistic example, consider Leon's goal to become very wealthy. One solution path to the goal may involve going deeply into debt in order to finance his education. While going deeply into debt is seemingly antagonistic to becoming wealthy, it may be a necessary detour. Be sure to consider solution paths that involve detours when faced with difficult problems.

Select the Best Representation

It is a good idea to utilize an external form of representation (e.g., paper and pencil, a model) whenever there are more than a few givens that need to be manipulated. The immediate or working memory span can quickly become overloaded. If you have already read the chapter on decision making, you will recognize the importance of writing down alternatives and considerations so that you can reduce the load on working memory and allow the problem-solver to generate more alternative solutions. Experimental results or almost any other pattern of numbers should always be graphed. If your problem is mathematical or spatial, a diagram is likely to be helpful. Diagrams can help to disentangle any situation in which the givens have many complex interrelationships. Diagrams can make important relationships explicit, a fact that can often lead directly to the goal. Hierarchical trees are a natural form of representation when the material

PROBLEM STATE   MOVES ACROSS RIVER

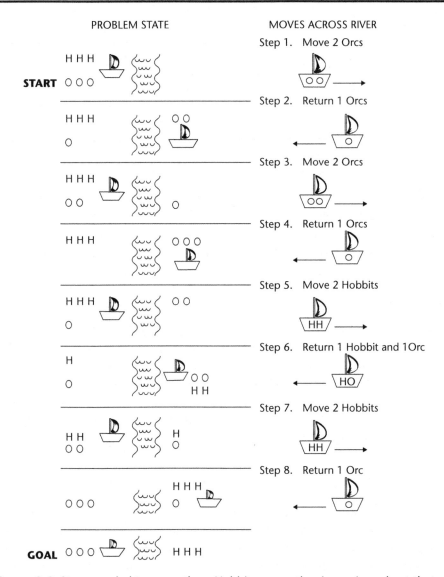

Step 1.   Move 2 Orcs

Step 2.   Return 1 Orcs

Step 3.   Move 2 Orcs

Step 4.   Return 1 Orcs

Step 5.   Move 2 Hobbits

Step 6.   Return 1 Hobbit and 1 Orc

Step 7.   Move 2 Hobbits

Step 8.   Return 1 Orc

Figure 9.9 Steps needed to move three Hobbits across the river using a boat that will hold only two beings without allowing the Orcs to ever outnumber the Hobbits.

itself forms a hierarchically arranged structure. Matrices are likely to be useful when the givens can be grouped into categories for meaningful comparisons. "Mock-ups" or miniature models can aid in problem solving when movement and placement of the givens determine the solution. Often, the way a problem is represented can mean the difference between a solution or nonsolution. If you find that one form of representation is not fruitful, try a different one.

Problem-Solving Strategies

> Solving problems can be regarded as the most characteristically human activity.
>
> —George Polya, p. ix (1981)

It does no good to tell someone who is faced with a problem that he should plan a solution, if he has no idea how to plan. The steps look deceptively simple—generate and evaluate possible solutions. But what if you cannot think of any solutions? There are several strategies that can be used in a systematic manner to help you generate solutions. Although no single strategy can guarantee perfect solutions every time, learning how to use several different strategies can give you direction and confidence when presented with a new problem.

Schoenfeld (1985) found that many mathematicians and scientists claimed to use specific strategies and rules when solving problems in their academic disciplines. Many of the scientists and mathematicians believed that their students would solve problems better if they learned some basic skills for attacking problems. In addition, several researchers have found that instruction in general problem-solving skills can improve problem-solving ability (e.g., Lithner, 2000). You can think of the following strategies or problem-solving aids as ways to plan a solution.

Means–Ends Analysis

Most often, progress toward the goal is not made along a single well-paved road. When the goal is not immediately attainable, we often need to take detours or break the problem down into smaller problems, called **subproblems**, each with its own goal, called a **subgoal**. Like all of the strategies for solving problems, selecting and utilizing subgoals requires planning. The procedure by which people select subgoals and use them to progress toward the goal is called **means–ends analysis**. This is a general, often powerful method for problem solving. The problem is first broken down into subgoals. Operations that will reduce the distance between the problem-solver's current state and the subgoals are then used. In this manner, the problem-solver will move closer and closer to the goal. Work through the following examples in order to clarify this concept.

The first step in means-ends analysis is to enumerate appropriate subgoals and to select the most promising one. Suppose that during a game of chess you decide that a good subgoal is to put the opposing king in check. The goal, of course, is to win the game, but it will be necessary to work toward subgoals to attain the goal. Putting the opposing king in check is the immediate "end" towards which you are working. You now need to select the "means" for obtaining that end, hence the term "means-ends analysis." In order to achieve your subgoal, determine the current state position of your pieces. Then, identify any difference between where your pieces are and where you want them to be. Operations would be selected that would reduce this difference and place the opposing king in check. Suppose no single move can achieve this subgoal. The means-ends analysis procedure would recycle, this time selecting a smaller subgoal, perhaps moving another piece out of the way. The constant recycling of these two processes—setting subgoals and reducing distances—will allow you to make progress toward the goal.

A favorite problem of psychologists that can be used to demonstrate means-ends analysis is the Tower of Hanoi problem. The name of this puzzle is derived from an interesting legend. Suppose that there are three pegs and 64 disks, each one a different size, stacked on one of the pegs in size order. (It may help to think of the disks as 64 different size doughnuts that can stack one on top of each other on the pegs.) The task is to transfer all of the disks from the first peg to the third peg using the middle peg as an intermediary. The rules for moving disks include moving only one disk at a time and never placing a disk on top of a smaller one. The legend around this task is that there are monks in a monastery near Hanoi who are working on this puzzle, and when they complete it the world will come to an end. Even if this legend were true, you would have little cause for worry because if they were to make perfect moves at the rate of one per second, it would take close to a trillion years to complete this task (Raphael, 1976).

Since you probably do not want to spend quite that much time solving the Tower of Hanoi, you can try a simplified version of it using only three disks. You can easily work this problem using any three coins of different sizes (a quarter, penny, and dime will work well) and three small sheets of paper. Stack the coins with the smallest on top and largest on the bottom on one sheet of paper. The task is to move the coins from the first piece of paper to the third so that they will be in the same size order. You may move only one coin at a time. All three pieces of paper may be used in solving the problem. Write down all of the moves you make in solving this problem. The initial and goal states are shown in Figure 9.10.

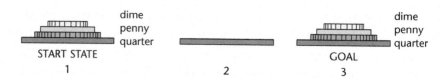

Figure 9.10 Start state and goal for the Tower of Hanoi problem. Use the strategy of means–ends analysis to solve this problem.

In a means-end analysis of the Tower of Hanoi problem, one obvious sub-goal is to get the quarter on the third piece of paper. This cannot be done immediately because the dime and penny are on it; therefore, a second subgoal needs to be considered. A second subgoal is to end up with the penny on the quarter. This can be accomplished when the penny is on the second paper and the quarter is on the third paper. This subgoal cannot yet be pursued because the dime must be moved first. In this manner, subgoals or ends are considered along with the means to accomplish them. A complete solution with all of the moves is shown in Figure 9.11. If you try the problem with four or five coins instead of three, you will find that it gets much more complicated, although the strategy remains the same. A quick search on the Internet will show several sites that have computerized versions of the Tower of Hanoi problem for those of you who want to try it with many more disks than shown in Figure 9.11.

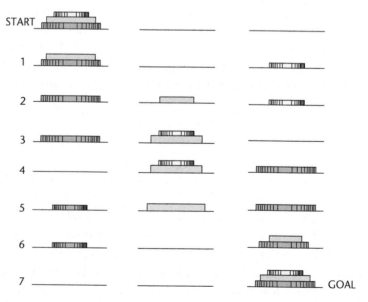

Figure 9.11 Solution to the Tower of Hanoi problem. Notice how subgoals are planned and obtained in reaching the goal.

Working Backwards

Means–Ends analysis is a **forward-looking strategy**, which means that all of the planning is done by considering operations that move you closer to subgoals and, ultimately, the final goal. Sometimes it is a better strategy to plan operations by **working backwards** from the goal to your present or initial state. The simplest example of this can be found in the paper and pencil mazes that many children love to solve.

Some of these mazes have several possible paths leading away from the start box and only one correct path ending in the goal box. Even young children realize that they can solve the maze more quickly if they work the maze backward, beginning from the goal and drawing their path to the start box. An example of this type of maze is shown in Figure 9.12.

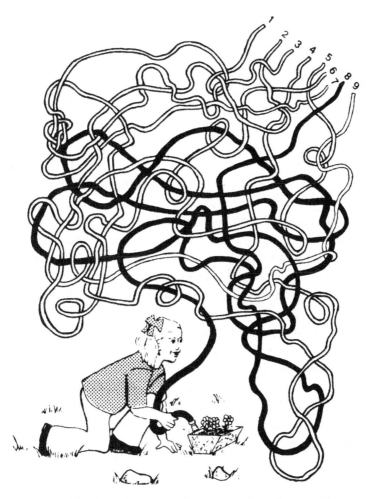

Figure 9.12 Working backwards is a good strategy when there are fewer paths from the goal than from the start.

Working backward is a good strategy to use whenever there are fewer paths leading from the goal than there are leading from the start. Of course, mazes are not the only situation when working backward is a good strategy. Recall the problem presented in Chapter 1 about water lilies that double in lake every twenty-four hours. From the time the first water lily appears until the lake is completely covered takes 48 days. On what day is it half covered?"

The only way to solve this problem is to work backwards. Do you remember how to solve this problem? Can you solve it with this hint? If the lake is covered on the 48th day and the area covered by the lilies doubles every day, how much of the lake is covered on the 47th day? The answer is half. Thus, by working backward, the problem is easy to solve. A forward-looking strategy with this problem will insure insanity.

It is often a good idea to combine forward and backward strategies. If you are faced with the task of solving proofs in geometry and trigonometry, a combination of forward and backward strategies may often prove most useful. You can start from the goal, transforming expressions on each line, and then alternate operations between the start state and the goal until the solution path meets somewhere between the two.

Generalization and Specialization

When confronted with a problem, it is sometimes helpful to consider it as an example of a larger class of problems (generalization) or to consider it as a special case (specialization). The form of problem representation that is most compatible with the generalization and specialization strategy is the tree diagram. Most goals can be classified as both a subset of a larger category and as a heading for a smaller one. Let's work an example to clarify what this means. As a furniture designer, you are given the problem of designing a chair that will be especially well suited for reading. How would you go about solving this problem?

As you probably realized, this is an ill-defined problem. The difficulty is largely centered on evaluating which of several possible chairs will best satisfy the goal. Use a tree diagram to classify chairs in general, and "chairs for reading" in particular. Although there are many possible diagrams, one example is presented in Figure 9.13.

I hope that you worked through this problem and drew your own tree diagram. As you can see in Figure 9.13 thinking about "chairs for reading" as

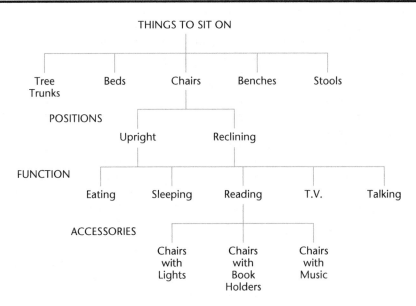

Figure 9.13 Possible tree diagram for the problem of designing a chair for reading.

a subset of the category "chairs" can help you to incorporate other features of chairs in your design while custom tailoring the chair with some of the possibilities that are unique to "chairs for reading." Thus, the process of generalization and/or specialization can help you to consider your problem from both broad and narrow perspectives.

Random Search and Trial-and-Error

Recall that the anatomy of a problem consists of a start or initial state, a goal, and solution paths leading from the start state to the goal. One strategy for searching between possible solution paths is random search. While this probably seems like a nonstrategy or "un-strategy," in some cases, it will work quite well. When there are very few possible solution paths, random search will lead to the goal in a short time. A truly random search would mean that there is no systematic order in which the possible paths are explored and no memory for paths already tried. A systematic trial-and-error search through the problem space (containing the paths, goal, and start state) is preferable. Trial-and-error search is best applied to well-defined problems with few possible solution paths. Simple, short anagrams are good candidates for these search methods. Unscramble the following letter to form an English word:

THA

Because there are only six possible orders for these three letters (THA; TAH; HTA; HAT; ATH; AHT), trying each one until a solution is found is fairly straightforward and simple strategy. If you used a truly random search, you would not keep track of which letter orderings you used and would repeat some until the correct order was found. Systematic trial-and-error is almost always superior to random search, although only slightly better when there are very few possibilities.

Both trial-and-error and random search are poor strategies when the number of possible paths increases, because of the sheer number of possible combinations. Often, in larger problems, it is helpful to eliminate some of the paths and then search within a smaller subset with a trial-and-error strategy.

Rules

Some kinds of problems, like series problems, depend on rules. Once the underlying principles are established, the problem is solved. Most problems in mathematics and the physical sciences follow rules. *A good way to discover rules is to look for patterns in the givens or subgoals.* Problems requiring rule-discovery are often used on tests of intelligence.

Complete the following pattern:

ABBACCCADDDDA————

This is a fairly simple series problem. The next six letters are EEEEEA. Certain patterns are common in problems of this sort. To detect them, count the number of repeating symbols, look across the series for repetitions at long intervals, try simple additions and subtractions, etc. This is not a trivial problem. The decoding of enemy war messages during World War II was a major factor contributing to our victory. The United States and British governments employed many professional decoders whose job was to find rules that could be used to decipher German and Japanese military messages.

Suppose that there is intelligent life in outer space, and that they are also wondering about us. How would they let us know that they exist? Some scientists, science fiction authors, and members of the general public believe that they would make their presence known by sending messages. No one believes that these messages would be in English, or Chinese, or

Samoan, or any other Earth language. They would send messages in their own native tongue or native whatever if they do not have tongues. How would we on Earth recognize such messages? The United States military has decided that if we are being sent messages from outer space, the one distinguishing characteristic of these messages would be a rule-governed "grammar" or patterned repetition. As strange as this may seem, the military does monitor outer space for anything that seems like a patterned communication. So far, they have not received any, and we can continue to believe, for the time being at least, that we are the most intelligent beings in space (or that the more intelligent beings do not want us to know they are out there, or that they cannot reach us, or they do not want to reach us.)

Hints

Hints are additional information that is given after an individual has begun to work on a problem. Often the hint provides additional information that is important to your solution. Sometimes a hint will require that you change the way you have been approaching the problem or limit the number of possible solutions. A common example of the use of hints is the "hot-cold" game played by children. An object is hidden in a room. The child who is "it" wanders around the room while the other children yell "hotter" if she is moving closer to the hidden object and "colder" if she is moving away from the hidden object. In this problem, the child who is "it" should take one small step at a time continuing in the same direction when the hint is "hotter" and trying a slight change in direction when the hint is "colder." Research on the way people use hints has shown that general hints like "think of new ways of using objects" do not facilitate the problem solution. The more specific the hint, the greater the benefit derived from it.

One of psychology's favorite problems is the two-string problem. Imagine walking into a room with two strings hanging from the ceiling. The strings are too far apart for you to reach both at the same time, yet your task is to do exactly that. This situation is depicted in Figure 9.14.

The best solution to the two-string problem involves setting one string in a swinging motion, usually by tying a heavy object to the end of one string to serve as a weight, so that the problem-solver can reach the string as it swings toward him. When researchers provided hints for the problem-solver by pretending to accidentally bump against one string to get it swinging, most of the problem-solvers hit upon this solution, but few were consciously aware that they utilized this hint (Maier, 1931).

Figure 9.14 The two-string problem. How could you reach both strings at the same time? (After Maier, 1931).

Good problem-solvers will seek out hints. Gathering additional information can be thought of as hint-seeking behavior. It is almost always a good strategy to get all of the information that you can about your problem. The additional givens will help you to restructure the problem space and provide direction so that solution paths may be found more easily.

Split-Half Method

The split-half method is an excellent search strategy when there is no priori reason for selecting from a sequentially organized set of possible solution paths. Suppose, for example, that there is a stoppage in the plumbing system that prevents water from coming out of your kitchen faucet. The stoppage is somewhere between the place where your pipes connect with the other pipes on your street and your kitchen faucet. How would you search for the pipe stoppage while making as few holes as possible in the pipe?

In this example, the solution (the place where the pipe is stopped) lies somewhere along a linear route. The best way to search in this problem is the split-half method. Because this problem requires that you break the pipe each place you search, you want to search as efficiently as possible.

Begin halfway between the street connection and your kitchen sink. If you find that water can still run freely at this point, you know that the stoppage is between this point and your sink. If this happens, look again half-way between this point and your kitchen sink. If the water is still running freely at this point, then you will know that the stoppage is closer still to the sink and you will look again midway between that point and your sink.

Suppose that on your first attempt you find that the water is not running at this point. Then the stoppage must be between the street and this mid-point. Your next search would be midway between the current search point and the street connection. In this manner, you would continue searching until the stoppage is found. This is a good method anytime you have a problem that is structurally similar to this one, such as trying to locate a break in the electrical wiring in your home or auto.

You can use the split-half method to play a party game called "Guess Your Age." (I made this game up.) Your friends can pretend to be any age. You can guess the age of anyone between 0 and 100 with no more than 7 guesses. How would you do it? Begin with the age that is midway between 0 and 100, which, of course, is 50. The player would have to respond by telling you if the age she is thinking of is older or younger than 50. Thus, she would respond with "younger" or "older." Suppose that she responds, "younger." What age should you guess next? You would pick the age mid-way between 0 and 50, which is 25. Suppose she now responds, "older." Your third guess should be halfway between 25 and 50. Because we are only concerned with whole numbers, your next guess would be 38. If she now responds younger, you would guess 32, as this number is midway between 25 and 38. If the next response is older, you would guess 35 (midway be-tween 32 and 38). If the response is younger, you would guess 33. At this point you know that she is pretending to be either 33 or 34. Thus, any age can be guessed with at most seven guesses. Try this method out with some friends. It will be good practice in using the split-half strategy. Consider this strategy whenever there are several possible equally likely solutions aligned along a single dimension.

Brainstorming

> The best way to have good ideas is to have lots of ideas.
> —Linus Pauling (cited in Goertzel & Goertzel, 1995, p. 274)

Brainstorming is fun. It was originally proposed by Osborn (1963) as a method for group problem solving, but it is also useful for individuals working alone. Brainstorming is useful in generating additional solution paths and thus should be considered whenever the difficulty involves finding solution paths. The goal of brainstorming is to produce a large number of possible solutions. Problem-solvers are encouraged to think up wild, unusual, imaginative ideas and to write them all down, no matter how silly they seem. The underlying principle is that the greater the quantity of ideas, the greater the likelihood that at least one of them will be good. To foster creative use of imagination, rules include no criticism or ridicule, even when the ideas may appear ridiculous. Judgments about the worth of the ideas are deferred until a later evaluation phase. Sometimes parts of the various ideas are combined or refined to improve upon them.

Brainstorming can be done in large or small groups or alone. After the brainstorming session, the list of possible solutions can be perused to find ones that will solve the problem in light of the problem constraints, which often include financial and time limitations and/or ethical considerations. Brainstorming was used effectively by a food manufacturer faced with the problem of finding a better way to bag potato chips. The problem-solvers (corporate executives) were asked to think up the best packaging solution they had ever seen. Someone said that bagging wet leaves was the best packaging solution he had ever seen. If you attempt to bag dry leaves, they crumble and don't fit into trash bags well, but if you hose them down before bagging them you can use fewer bags and fill them more easily with less empty space in each bag. Following this lead, they tried wetting potato chips and then putting them into bags. The result was disastrous—the potato chips dried into tasteless crumbs. But this idea ultimately led to the popular potato chip that comes stacked in a can. The identical chips are formed from a liquid potato mixture that is cooked into chip-shaped molds. In this manner, a wild and not-too-good solution (wetting potato chips) was parlayed into a highly successful product. It's true—the original potato chip problem remains to be solved, but the executives were quite happy with the new potato chip product.

Recent research supports a two-stage method of brainstorming (Boddy, 2012). In the first stage, people work individually and in silence, which often produces more ideas than when working in groups (Heslin, 2009; Paulus, 2000), followed by the open generation of ideas by a group and then their evaluation. In general, research supports the idea that these two stages of brainstorming—alone and then in a group—can be a productive way to generate good ideas that solve problems.

Contradiction

The best solution to many problems often involves contradictory properties. For example, consider the problem of the perfect pizza box—one that keeps the pizza hot, but does not allow steam to collect inside the box so that the crust does not get wet and soggy. These are contradictory properties—keep the pizza covered so it stays hot *and* do not let the steam condense and turn the crust soggy. The next time you send out for a pizza, examine the box. Most pizza boxes represent a blend of these two properties—the lid is closed to keep it hot, but it also has small vents to allow some of the steam to escape. The result is a compromise solution. The pizza gets cold sooner because the vents let cold air in, and the pizza gets only a little soggy because the amount of condensed moisture is limited.

One suggestion for solving any problem that involves contradictions is to never compromise; instead, devise a solution that satisfies all of the desirable properties of a good solution. Sure, but how? In the pizza box problem, Valdman and Tsourikov (see Patentstorm #7678036 issued 2010) designed a box with "dimples" (raised dots) on the bottom so that the moisture would condense below the crust and not on it while trapping hot air below the pizza to serve as additional insulation. Valdman and Tsourikov have designed a computer-assisted program that suggests ways to satisfy contradictions in any problem without compromising. They culled the files of the United States Patent Office and discovered over 200 general principles that can be used alone or in combination to solve a wide range of problems. The program begins by asking for a clear definition of the type of problem that is being solved. It is looking for general principles (e.g., the need for insulation and eliminating condensation, without regard to pizza). Solutions are suggested from its computerized bank of solutions based on other problems that involve similar sorts of contradictions. They call their algorithm (steps used to solve a problem) the Theory of Inventive Problem Solving. Although their advertisements for this commercially-available software program make fantastic claims of success, additional studies by unbiased researchers are needed before we can evaluate its efficacy. Using their basic ideas, we can all imagine an optimal solution to any problem and then finds ways to satisfy seemingly contradictory properties of the optimal solution.

A set of problem-solving guidelines designed especially for technical problems is based on the idea that contradictions can help us find good solutions for problems that have multiple possible solutions (Moehrle, 2005,

2010). For example, suppose you are designing a desk. One important property is that it have lots of surface space for your stuff, but, on the contrary (the contradiction part), a large area takes up lots of space and can make it heavy. Once you start thinking in terms of contradictions, you might come up with a desk that is perforated (to make it lighter) and has extensions that can be removed so it does not have to take up as much space at times when you need less.

Analogies and Metaphors

> We can scarcely imagine a problem absolutely new, unlike and unrelated to any formerly solved problem; but if such a problem could exist, it would be insoluble. In fact, when solving a problem, we should always profit from previously solved problems, using their result or their method, or the experience acquired in solving them.
>
> —George Polya (1945, p. 92)

Gick and Holyoak (1980, p. 306) asked, "Where do new ideas come from?" Many scientists and mathematicians respond that their ideas or solutions to problems come from recognizing analogies and metaphors drawn from different academic disciplines. In fact, it seems that the most common form of inference is made by noting similarities (analogies and metaphors) between two or more situations. Like hints, the analogy must be recognized as relevant to the problem being considered and then modified for the particular situation.

Consider the following problem:

> A small country fell under the iron rule of a dictator. The dictator ruled the country from a strong fortress. The fortress was situated in the middle of the country, surrounded by farms and villages. Many roads radiated outward from the fortress like spokes on a wheel. A great general arose who raised a large army at the border and vowed to capture the fortress and free the country of the dictator. The general knew that if his entire army could attack the fortress at once it could be captured. His troops were poised at the head of one of the roads leading to the fortress, ready to attack. However, a spy brought the general a disturbing report. The ruthless dictator had planted mines on each of the roads. The mines were set so that small bodies of men could pass over them safely, since the dictator needed to be able to move troops and workers to and from the fortress. However, any large force would detonate the mines. Not only would this blow up the road and render it impassable,

but the dictator would then destroy many villages in retaliation. A full-scale direct attack on the fortress therefore appeared impossible. (Gick & Holyoak, 1980, p. 351)

To help you solve this problem, I will also give you a hint. The solution is analogous to one discussed earlier in this chapter, although the context is entirely different. Stop for a few minutes and attempt to work on this problem. Think about the problems presented earlier. It should help if you draw a diagram.

The solution to this problem is analogous to the one used in the inoperable stomach tumor problem. In that problem (Duncker, 1945), the best solution involved sending weak rays through the body simultaneously from several different points so that they would converge on the tumor as depicted below.

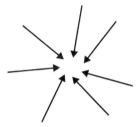

Similarly, the army could be divided into small groups that would attack the fortress from all sides. Did you recognize that these problems were essentially similar in form and could be solved with the same solution? In a study of the use of diagrams as an aid in analogical problem solving, Pedone, Hummel, and Holyoak (2001) found that by animating the diagram so that the arrows moved in to a central point, college students were more likely to use the display as a retrieval cue that helped in solving the x-ray and fortress problems. It seems that these diagrams work best when problem-solvers have their attention drawn to the structure of the problem so that they can recognize that these two types of problems have similar structures, even though they have very different surface characteristics (content).

Gordon (1961), originator of a group called "Synectics," presented guidelines for the use of analogies in solving problems. The term "Synectics" was taken from a Greek term that means joining together different and apparently unrelated elements. Gordon suggests that we consider four different types of analogies when faced with a problem:

Personal Analogy. If you want to understand a complex phenomenon, think of yourself as a participant in the phenomenon. For example, if you want to understand the molecular structure of a compound, think of yourself as a molecule. How would you behave? What other molecules would you want to attach yourself to? Get away from reliance on scientific notations and actually pretend to be a molecule bouncing in a compound. You may see relationships from this perspective that you were blind to when acting as a scientist.

The use of personal analogies is especially well-suited for solving a wide range of conflict problems. If each side of a conflict can imagine how the problem appears to the other side, including acceptable goals, new solutions can become apparent. Both sides can identify common interests and use them to invent options that they both find acceptable.

Direct Analogy. Compare the problems you are working on with several problems in other domains. According to Gordon, this method was used by Alexander Graham Bell: "It struck me that the bones of the human ear were very massive indeed, as compared with the delicate thin membrane that operated them, and the thought occurred that if a membrane so delicate could move bones relatively so massive, why should not a thicker and stouter piece of membrane move my piece of steel. And the telephone was conceived" (Gordon, 1961, p. 41).

A particularly fertile area for analogies is biology, where many solutions to biological problems have been evolving since the first life form appeared on Earth. When a Synectics group was faced with the problem of devising a bottle closure that could be used with glue or nail polish, the analogy they used was the biological closure of the anus (rectum). Apparently, this solution worked quite well. (You can think about this the next time you use a bottle of LePage's mucilage, or maybe you would prefer not to.)

Symbolic Activity. This solution strategy utilizes visual imagery. Its goal is to get away from the constraints of words or mathematical symbols. Students who utilized imagery to visualize the tumor problem and the fortress problem were most likely to notice spontaneously that the two problems were analogous. If you work on generating a clear image of a problem, you may "see" a solution that had been overlooked.

Fantasy Analogy. In your wildest dreams, what would you want of a solution? An example of this is to imagine two small insects that would automatically zip your jacket or a silk worm that would spin silk rapidly to keep you warm when the temperature drops. These are fantasy analogies. Like brainstorming, a fantasy analogy can result in wild, impractical solutions that can later be modified to practical, workable ones.

Although it is clear that analogies are important aids in problem solving, it is rare for most people to notice a potential analogy spontaneously. If you are able to diagram the underlying relationships, as in the problem above, or to state the general rules, as in the contradictions problem, you are more likely to notice structural relationships and find useful analogies. Recent research suggests that when people are told to think about the way a novel problem is like a similar problem they encountered before, people may be more likely to be successful in finding analogous solutions (De Acedo Lizarraga, Baquedano, & Closas, 2011).

Consult an Expert

> If at first you don't succeed, try, try, again. Then quit. No use being a damned fool about it.
>
> —W. C. Fields (quoted in Shapiro, 2011)

Often in life, we do not have to solve problems alone. Sometimes the best way to solve a problem is to let experts do it for us, or at least help us with solving the problem. People seek accountants for help with their tax problems, attorneys for their legal problems, and physicians for their health problems. We elect officials to handle the problems of running our country and rely on military experts to wage wars. These people became experts in their field by obtaining the appropriate knowledge in their subject area and through repeated applications of this knowledge to real-world problems. Consulting an expert is often an excellent solution strategy. Their greater experience and knowledge will allow them to solve many problems in their area of expertise much more efficiently than a novice. If you decide to consult an expert, the problem becomes: (a) how to know somebody who is an expert, and (b) how to select which "expert" to use. Once you have passed these hurdles, your problems still are not over. You need to be sure that the expert has all of the facts and has considered all of the relevant alternatives. Listen carefully to the expert's analysis of the risks and alternatives, but make the decision yourself. An expert is a problem-solving aid, not the solution. For some guidelines in recognizing an appropriate expert, consult Carlson (1995) and review the section on authorities in the chapter on reasoning.

Crowdsourcing

If calling one expert is a good idea, what about a lot of them? This is the idea behind **crowdsourcing**, which is posing a job or a problem to a group of people, usually by posting it to the internet. The idea is that there are a lot of talented people with diverse backgrounds and different motivations who will work on a problem. Internet sites are quickly evolving where companies post problems and interested problem-solvers go at it. There are many business models, but for the most part, companies pay for good solutions. Innocenter is one such site. (Many similar sites are being developed; see for example, IdeaConnection). For example, Colgate-Palmolive had an ornery problem that eluded their in-house scientists (Howe, 2006). They needed to inject fluoride powder into toothpaste tubes without dispersing the surrounding air. This problem was quickly solved by someone with a master's degree in particle physics who loved to tinker with problems like this one. The solution: "Impart an electric charge to the powder while grounding the tube. The positively charged fluoride particles would be attracted to the tube without any significant dispersion" (Howe, 2006, p. 2). I do not know what this means, but it sounds good, and apparently the folks at Colgate-Palmolive agreed because they paid the problem-solver $25,000. The advantage of crowdsourcing is that it attracts people with a broad range of information, experience, and knowledge.

In crowdsourcing, individual participants work alone. But in real life, problem solving is often done in groups. A recent study sheds some light on what makes a group "intelligent." Psychologists wanted to understand the factors that make some groups more likely to solve problems than others (Wooley, Chabris, Pentland, Hashmi, & Malone, 2010). It seems that groups have a **collective intelligence**, which depends much less on the average intelligence of the members of the group or even the intelligence of the smartest member of the group than it does on how they relate to each other. Social sensitivity emerged as the most important factor for group problem solving, which included being sensitive to other people's moods and taking turns in allowing all members of the group to speak. The authors suggest that we might have better outcomes if we gave groups tools that help them collaborate (such as electronic white boards or wikis) or just explained the importance of these group skills. It is too early to say if these suggestions will work to make groups better at solving problems, but it is an interesting idea that might be worth trying if you are working on an important problem in a group setting.

Select the Best Strategy

Twelve different strategies have been presented as aids in problem solving. When confronted with a problem, how do you know which to use? It is important to keep in mind that these strategies are not mutually exclusive. It will often be best to use them in combinations. The best strategy or strategies depends on the nature of the problem. After all, if you are taking an exam, you could be expelled if you consult the paper of an "expert" student sitting next to you.

Along with each strategy, I presented some guidelines for its appropriate use. In general, a few higher-level "strategies for selecting strategies" include:

1. If the problem is ill defined, restate the goal or the problem in several different ways.

2. When there are very few possible solutions, a trial-and-error approach will work well.

3. If a problem is complex, try simplification, Means–Ends analysis, and generalization and specialization.

4. When there are fewer paths leading away from the goal than there are from the start state, work backwards.

5. If you can gather additional information, do it. Look for and utilize hints, and consult experts with specialized knowledge, or try a diverse group of problem-solvers if it is a problem suitable for crowdsourcing.

6. If there is an ordered array of equally likely alternatives, try the split-half method and seek rules.

7. If the problem is a lack of possible solution paths, brainstorm with others to generate alternative solution paths, but start with a silent phase in which you generate solutions alone.

8. Problems in design and engineering are good candidates for devising solutions that seem, at first, to require contradictions in their solution. Contradictions can help with personal problems as well.

9. Using analogies and metaphors and consulting an expert are widely applicable to all sorts of problems, but be prepared to use visualization and to deliberately seek analogies in order to recall an analogous solution.

10. Remember that these are only guidelines to solving problems. The best way to be an expert problem-solver is to practice solving lots of problems.

Problem-Solving Problems

> Clinging to the past is the problem. Enhancing change is the answer.
> —Gloria Steinem (1994)

There are many possible reasons why people find some problems difficult, perhaps even impossible to solve. Sometimes we are stuck in "thinking ruts" and cannot seem to think our way of them. Two of these "ruts" are functional fixedness and mental set.

Functional Fixedness and Mental Set

Recall the two-string problem presented earlier in this chapter. The task was to grasp simultaneously two strings that hung from the ceiling. The correct solution involved setting one string into motion, perhaps by tying a heavy object like a pair of pliers to its end to serve as a weight. One reason why this was such a difficult problem is functional fixedness. Subjects were fixated or "stuck" on the usual function of a pair of pliers and have difficulty thinking of them as having a different function.

Another example of **functional fixedness** was presented in the Introduction (Chapter 1). In a classic problem, subjects were asked to attach a candle to the wall so that it could be burned, using only a box of thumbtacks and some matches. Subjects had difficulty thinking of the box as a candle-holder since they saw it in terms of its usual function—a container for thumbtacks. But, when they were given the same materials with each of the items labeled, including a separate label for the box, the problem was quickly solved by most of the participants (Glucksberg & Weisberg, 1966). Although these are "old" problems in psychology, the underlying principles keep getting reinvented. In a recent study of functional fixedness, McCaffrey (2012) found that during problem solving, individuals frequently notice some new or obscure feature of the problem that can be used to find a solution. He recommends that when we get stuck on a problem, we try the **generic-parts technique**, which requires problems solvers to repeatedly ask two questions: 1) Can this be decomposed further? 2) Does this description imply a use? As you continue to decompose (take apart) the parts of a problem, each gets smaller, and with each smaller part, the problem-solver is required to think beyond the common function of the object. So, for example, when presented with a candle, you would break it into a wick and wax. The wick is made up of string and string can be used to tie things. In this way, a candle can be seen as an instrument for tying things, which is far removed from its usual function of being burned to provide light.

Mental set refers to the problem-solver's state of mind. It is a general term for the inability to think of a new solution or new type of solution for familiar problems. I think of functional fixedness and mental state as "ruts in one's thinking." They are predispositions to think and respond in certain ways. To demonstrate how powerful some sets can be, work on the nine-dot problem in Figure 9.15. Stop now and work on this problem.

The difficulty posed by the nine-dot problem comes from a perceptual set imposed by the square arrangement. Most people attempt to solve the problem by staying within the imaginary boundary formed by the outer dots. If you extend your lines beyond this imaginary boundary, you will find that the problem is easy to solve. In addition, most people attempt solutions in which the line goes through the center of each dot. One solution to the nine-dot problem is shown in Figure 9.16.

There are several other solutions to the nine-dot problem. Each of them involves breaking-set in some way. Two solutions (Adams, 1979, pp. 25–26) are presented in Figure 9.17. A few other more exotic solutions, including one submitted by a 10-year-old girl, which consists of one very fat line

Figure 9.15 The nine-dot problem. Using no more than four straight lines and without lifting your pencil from the paper, draw a line through all nine dots.

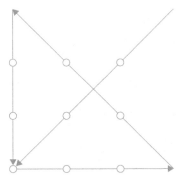

Figure 9.16 One possible solution to the nine-dot problem. Note that the solution involves breaking "set." Most people assume that the lines must form a square and that each line must pass through the center of each dot.

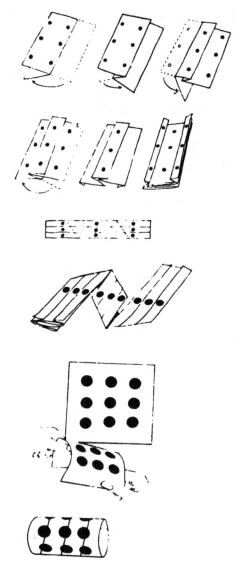

Figure 9.17 Other possible solutions to the nine-dot problem. Copyright © 2001 James L. Adams. Reprinted by permission of Basic Books, a member of the Perseus Books Group.

drawn through all nine dots can be found in Adams' (1979) gem of a book, *Conceptual Blockbusting*. The set of staying within the rectangular area is pervasive and difficult to break.

Misleading and Irrelevant Information

My father used to love this riddle:

> Suppose you are a bus driver. On the first stop you pick up 6 men and 2 women. At the second stop 2 men leave and 1 woman boards the bus.

At the third stop 1 man leaves and 2 women enter the bus. At the fourth stop 3 men get on and 3 women get off. At the fifth stop 2 men get off, 3 men get on, 1 woman gets off, and 2 women get on. What is the bus driver's name?

Could you answer this question without rereading the problem? The bus driver's name is, of course, your name because the riddle began, "Suppose you are a bus driver." All of the information about the rest of the passengers was irrelevant. Often information that is irrelevant to the problem serves to mislead problem-solvers down dead-end paths. Real-life problems often involve deciding what information is relevant. To avoid being misled by information, be clear about the goal state. Simplification will sometimes help in separating the relevant from the irrelevant givens.

Let's try another example:

If you have black socks and brown socks in your drawer mixed in the ratio of 4 to 5, how many socks will you have to take out to make sure of having a pair of the same color?" (Fixx, 1978).

Think about this problem. What is relevant? What is irrelevant? The answer is three socks because any two must match if there are only brown and black socks. The information about the ratio of socks is irrelevant and misleading. Imagine yourself actually picking socks from a drawer and this problem will be easier to solve.

A common attribute of ill-defined problems is that they potentially involve a huge amount of information. Consider the very real-world problems in international relations, such as "How can we influence our own government so that it reduces air pollution?" or "How can we provide food for the countless numbers of people who go hungry in our own country and the rest of the world?" (I am assuming that these are common problems for many countries around the world.) The "problem," with broad problems such as these, requires the selection of information that could lead to the desired goal. The difficulty with problems like these is not the absence of paths to the goal, but in too many possible paths. Which path is most likely to be the best? How can we choose from among the better options? There are no simple answers for these questions, which is why we continue to have environmental threats and hunger.

World View Constraints

Often, we fail to solve problems because of the world-view constraints placed on us by our social class, nationality, or political views. Consider the following problem:

> A ping pong ball 1″ in diameter falls into a 3″ length of pipe that is 1 1/8″ in diameter. The pipe is firmly affixed to the concrete pavement. It is extremely important to remove the ball. You and some friends are faced with this task. All you have is some fine wire and your collective abilities to solve this problem. What do you do?

Most people approach this task by attempting to bend fine wire into tweezers to pluck it up. A better solution is to urinate into the pipe so that the ball will float to the top. This probably never occurred to you because it is not an acceptable thought for most people in our society. Although this has never been verified, it would probably be an easier task for people in other societies where urination is not considered as private an act as it is in our society.

I have taught critical thinking courses in many countries around the world. Although there are universals in critical thinking, it is also true that our thinking occurs in a culture, and culture influences the kinds of problems we recognize and often the sorts of solutions we generate. It is difficult to imagine the effect that culture has on the way we think without an extended experience in a culture other than the one you know best. It is for this reason that I tout the educational benefits of extended foreign travel. It can change your own world view and help you to appreciate the extent to which the problems we identify and the solutions we generate are influenced by cultural factors.

Chapter Summary

- All problems can be conceptualized as being composed of "anatomical" parts that include a start state, a goal state, and paths leading from the start to the goal. This entire structure is called the problem space. You have a problem when there is a gap or barrier between where you are (start state) and where you want to be (goal state).

- Situation awareness refers to problems that occur in real-life contexts. A situation triggers the recognition that there is a problem that needs to be solved.

- It is common to divide the problem-solving process into four stages: preparation or familiarization, production, judgment or evaluation, and incubation. Incubation is an optional stage that does not always occur, but there is good evidence that people can sometimes solve difficult problems during a "time-out." Grit, which is persistence despite failures, fatigue, and boredom, is a critical trait of good problem-solvers.

- Problems can be classified along a continuum ranging from well-defined to ill-defined. Well-defined problems have explicit paths and goals, and often a single correct answer. Ill-defined problems are subject to multiple interpretations and judgments about the goal state. Most of the problems encountered in life are ill-defined.

- Solution strategies need to be planned. A plan for solving a problem will include the construction of a representation and the generation and evaluation of possible solutions.

- An invaluable aid in solving problems is to devise an external form of representation. The best representation to choose will depend on the type of problem.

- Twelve different strategies for generating and evaluating solutions were presented. Often several will be used together in solving a problem. General guidelines were offered for the appropriate use of each.

- There are four common sources of difficulty that problem-solvers encounter. Functional fixedness refers to the failure to utilize items in unusual ways. Mental set, which is closely related to functional fixedness, refers to the predisposition to respond to any situation in a fixed way. Misleading and irrelevant information can "derail one's trail of thought" and can lead you down blind paths. The constraints imposed upon us by our society cause us to view problems from our own narrow frames of reference.

The skills for planning how to solve and solving problems that were presented in this chapter are applicable to almost any problem. After reading this chapter, you should be:

- planning and monitoring a strategy for finding a solution
- identifying any problem as either well-defined or ill-defined and adjusting your solution plan according to the type of problem

- using graphs, diagrams, hierarchical trees, matrices, and models as solution aids

- devising a quality representation of a problem

- selecting the problem-solving strategies that are appropriate for the problem

- using all of the following strategies: mean–ends analysis, working backwards, generalization and specialization, random search and trial-and-error, rules, hints, the split-half method, brainstorming, contradiction, analogies and metaphors, and consulting an expert and crowdsourcing (when appropriate)

- demonstrating an awareness of functional fixedness and using the generic-parts technique as an attempt to avoid it

- distinguishing between relevant and irrelevant information

- understanding how world views can constrain the problem-solving process.

- Recognizing the critical role of persistence.

Terms to Know

You should be able to define or describe the following terms or concepts. If you find that you are having difficulty with any term, be sure to reread the section in which it is discussed.

A Problem. Problems are defined as states where there is a gap or barrier between where the problem-solver is and where she or he wants to be.

Problem-based learning. A curriculum in which students are presented with problems that are similar to ones they would encounter in their discipline instead of the more standard classroom practice of learning concepts first, usually followed by applications of the concepts.

Anatomy of a Problem. Newell and Simon (1972) have conceptualized all problems as consisting of parts or components—an initial state, a goal state, and solution paths that link the initial state to the goal state.

Initial State. The starting or beginning place in a problem. A problem is solved when the problem-solver can find "paths" from the initial state to the goal.

Goal State. The desired end state in a problem. When a problem-solver finds "paths" to the goal, the problem is solved.

Solution Paths. Methods or means for solving problems. Routes that lead from the initial state to the goal state in a problem.

Problem Space. All possible paths from the initial state to the goal state in a problem.

Givens. Information or rules that place constraints on the problem.

Situations. In a situation-awareness framework for problem solving, a situation is the event or sequence of events that trigger the recognition that there is a problem. Situations occur in real-life contexts.

Preparation of Familiarization Stage. The first stage in problem solving, which includes the time spent in understanding the nature of the problem, the desired goal, and the givens.

Production Stage. The second stage in problem solving. During this state, the problem-solver produces the solution paths that define the problem space.

Judgment or Evaluation Stage. The third stage in problem solving during which time the problem-solver evaluates the solution paths in order to select the best one.

Incubation. A period in problem solving when the problem-solver is not actively working on the problem. Sometimes people report that a solution comes to them during this "time out" period.

Grit. The persistence to work on a problem despite disappointments, boredom, and failures.

Insight. Sudden knowledge of a solution to a problem. Also known as the Aha! experience.

Well-Defined Problems. Problems with a well defined correct answer, often a single correct answer.

Ill-Defined Problems. Problems with many possible correct answers. The difficulty with these problems lies in evaluating possible solutions to decide which one is best. Often the goal in these problems is vague or incomplete.

Transcontextual. A problem-solving strategy that is useful in many contexts with a wide variety of problems. An example of a transcontextual strategy is to state the goal four different ways whenever a problem is encountered.

Hierarchical Trees. Branching diagrams that serve as a representational aid in solving problems. Instances of categories provide the "nodes" of the trees.

Matrix. A rectangular array of numbers or facts that is used as a means of representing problems that contain categories of information.

Detour Problems. Problems in which the path to the goal is not a direct linear one. Intermediate steps are required that seem directly opposite to the goal.

Subproblems. When difficulty is encountered in solving a problem, it can be broken down into several smaller problems or "subproblems."

Subgoal. When difficulty is encountered in solving a problem, it can be broken down into several smaller problems called "subproblems." Each subproblem has its own goal, called a "subgoal."

Means–End Analysis. A general problem-solving strategy in which operations are used to reduce the distance between the problem-solver's current state and the nearest possible subgoal or goal.

Working Backwards. A problem-solving strategy in which operations are planned that move from the goal to the present or initial state. This method is usually contrasted with the forward-looking strategy.

Forward-Looking Strategy. A problem-solving strategy in which all of the planning is done by considering operations that move the problem-solver closer to subgoals and the goal. This method is usually contrasted with working backwards from the goal.

Generalization. A problem-solving strategy in which the problem is considered as an example of a larger class of problems.

Specialization. A problem-solving strategy in which the problem is considered as a special case drawn from a larger set of problems.

Random Search. A problem-solving strategy in which all possible solution paths from the initial state to the goal are considered in an unsystematic (random) manner. This method is usually contrasted with trial-and-error search.

Trial-and-Error. A problem-solving strategy in which all solution paths from the initial state to the goal are searched systematically. This method is usually contrasted with random search.

Rules. The principles that underlie some problems. For example, solutions to problems that require a prediction of the next element in a series depend on the discovery of their rules.

Hints. Additional information that is given after an individual has begun to work on a problem.

Split-Half Method. A problem-solving strategy that is useful when there is no a priori reason for selecting from a sequentially organized set of possible solution paths. The method consists of continually selecting a point that is halfway between the present state and the goal as a systematic means for "guessing" at the solution.

Brainstorming. A group or individual method for generating solution paths for problems. Problem-solvers are encouraged to think up wild, imaginative solutions and to defer judgment on these solutions until a later time when they may be modified or combined. Current research suggests that individuals should brainstorm individually before engaging in the group process. The goal is to produce a large number of possible solutions.

Contradiction. A problem-solving strategy in which opposite desirable qualities are considered at the same time, such as the need to have a large work surface and to keep overall size small.

Analogies. Problem-solving strategies in which similarities are noted between two or more situations, while simultaneously discerning that there are also differences; for example, by noting similarities between two different problems, the problem-solver may discover that similar solutions are applicable.

Personal Analogy. A problem-solving strategy suggested by Gordon (1961) in which you think of yourself as a participant in the phenomenon that you want to understand.

Direct Analogy. A problem-solving strategy suggested by Gordon (1961) in which you note similarities between your problem and related problems in other domains.

Symbolic Activity. The deliberate use of visual imagery or other symbolic representation as a problem-solving aid.

Fantasy Analogy. A problem-solving strategy suggested by Gordon (1961) in which problem-solvers utilize their imagination to conceptualize ideal solutions.

Crowdsourcing. Problems are posted to a public site and people are invited to attempt a solution.

Collective Intelligence. The overall intelligence of a group—often, groups excel at problem solving when the members are sensitive to the needs and abilities of other group members.

Functional Fixedness. A type of mental set in which individuals only consider the usual use (function) of objects.

Generic-parts technique. A way of overcoming functional fixedness by decomposing each component of a problem into smaller parts.

Mental Set. Predispositions to think and respond in a certain way.

World View Constraints. Limitations on the way we approach problems placed on us by our social class, nationality, or political views.

CHAPTER 10

CREATIVE THINKING

Contents

> The history of civilization is essentially the record of man's [and woman's] creative ability.
>
> —Alex Faickney Osborn (1963, p. ix)

You have probably seen water dripping from an air conditioning unit on a hot day or wiped up the water stain left on a table from a cold drink, but you probably never thought how the processes involved in condensation could be used to provide water in areas of the world that are facing drought. Creative thinkers have devised ways of extracting water from the humidity in the air—the process involves cooling the air so that the water can be collected. This is apparently an old idea that is now feasible with modern technology. Several companies are working hard to "make water from air," a process with immense ramifications—there are billions of people in the world who do not have access to clean drinking water. Like most other examples of creative thinking, it seems like such a simple idea to extrapolate from something we have all seen, but the leap to move beyond the nuisance of a wet glass stain to providing water for arid regions of the world is a prototypical example of creative thinking.

Defining Creativity

If we are to make real strides in boosting the creativity of scientists, mathematicians, artists, and all upon whom civilization depends, we must arrive at a far more detailed understanding of the creative process, its antecedents, and its inhibitors. The study of creativity must be seen as a basic necessity.

—Beth A. Hennessey and Teresa M. Amabile (2010, p. 570)

Creativity is a difficult word to define. We say that someone "is creative" when she has produced an outcome or a product that is both unusual and appropriate (or meaningful or useful or particularly good). Thus, creativity is defined by two aspects of its consequence (novelty and quality) and not the process that led to the consequence (Runco & Jaeger, 2012).

Both the unusualness and appropriateness criteria require judgments: How unusual is the idea and how well does it meet some objective? Because both of these criteria vary along quantitative dimensions, creativity exists in degrees. This means that any action or thought can be more or less creative. Creativity is not a single trait that people either have or do not have. Creative thinking involves cognitive processes that occur in a context. These processes involve novelty in one or more of the processes that lead to creative outcomes—ways of identifying that a problem exists, defining a problem, generating and evaluating possible solutions, and judging how uniquely and how well the problem is solved.

Suppose that you are invited to supper at your friend Hazel's house. You know that she is an adventuresome cook and, therefore, you look forward to the meal with relish. The main dish is an original concoction of hot dogs and fruit salad in a cold mustard sauce. (This part is a true story. I was once served this at a friend's house.) The coup de grace is a dessert that she made on her new ice cream maker—liver and broccoli flavored ice cream. Although these are unusual dishes, few people would willingly eat them. Most of us would not judge these culinary delights as creative because they do not satisfy the criterion that the idea or product be good or useful.

It is easy to see why creativity has been an elusive topic. Someone or some group must judge an act or idea as unusual and good or useful before it can be labeled creative, and there will often be disagreement on the way these attributes are judged. Judgments of creativity also change over time so that a "zany" idea at one time in history (e.g., the earth revolves around the sun and not the reverse) may come to be viewed as "monumental" at some time later.

Prince (1970, p. i) offered a somewhat poetic definition of creativity, which, I believe, is itself creative. Consider his definition:

> CREATIVITY: an arbitrary harmony, an expected astonishment, a habitual revelation, a familiar surprise, a generous selfishness, an unexpected certainty, a formidable stubbornness, a vital triviality, a disciplined freedom, an intoxicating steadiness, a repeated initiation, a difficult delight, a predictable gamble, an ephemeral solidity, a unifying difference, a demanding satisfier, a miraculous expectation, an accustomed amazement.

Gardner (1989) added an additional requirement to the definition of creativity. He wanted creativity to include the idea that the creative individual *regularly* solves problems or fashions products that are creative. This additional requirement would remove "luck" from the creative process because luck or random actions cannot explain regular results. However we choose to define creativity, we need it, and we all possess it to some extent. Our everyday lives are more pleasurable because of our creative actions; the arts depend on it for their existence; science and mathematics could not progress without it. Every time we express a complex thought or fill a blank piece of paper with our words, we are creating; when we do it particularly well in an unusual way, then we are creative.

Lateral and Vertical Thinking

> Vertical thinking is concerned with digging the same hole deeper. Lateral thinking is concerned with digging the hole somewhere else.
> —Edward De Bono (1977, p. 195)

The distinction between lateral and vertical thinking was first made by De Bono (1968, p. 11). It is best illustrated with a short story that is probably an old fable that has been told for many generations:

Many years ago, when a person who owed money could be thrown into jail, a merchant in London had the misfortune to owe a huge sum to a money-lender. The money-lender, who was old and ugly, fancied the merchant's beautiful teenage daughter. He proposed a bargain. He said he would cancel the merchant's debt if he could have the girl instead.

Both the merchant and his daughter were horrified at the proposal. So the cunning money-lender proposed that they let Providence decide the matter. He told them that he would put a black pebble and a white pebble into an empty money-bag and then the girl would have to pick out one of the pebbles. If she chose the black pebble she would become his wife and her father's debt would be cancelled. If she chose the white pebble she would stay with her father and the debt would still be cancelled. But if she refused to pick out a pebble her father would be thrown into jail and she would starve.

Reluctantly the merchant agreed. They were standing on a pebble-strewn path in the merchant's garden as they talked and the money-lender stooped down to pick up the two pebbles. As he picked up the pebbles, the girl, sharp-eyed with fright, noticed that he picked up two black pebbles and put them into the money-bag. He then asked the girl to pick out the pebble that was to decide her fate and that of her father.

What would you do if you had been the girl? If you think about this problem in a careful, logical, straightforward way, you are using **vertical thinking**, a type of thinking that will not be much help in this situation. Typical "vertical thinking" answers are: let the girl sacrifice herself or expose him for the crook he is. Consider DeBono's suggested solution: The girl should fumble when she draws the pebble from the bag, dropping it onto the pebble-strewn path. She should then tell the villain that they can determine the color of the pebble she took by seeing the color of the one left in the bag. Because the remaining pebble must be black, the money-lender will be forced to admit that she had chosen the white pebble or expose himself as a crook.

Virtually everyone agrees that this is both a good and unusual answer to the girl's dilemma. **Lateral thinking** is a way of thinking "around" a problem, amplifying the problem space, i.e., increasing the number of possible alternatives. "Lateral thinking generates the ideas and vertical thinking develops them" (De Bono, 1968, p. 6). Lateral thinking, then, is sometimes used as a synonym for creative thinking or idea discovery, while vertical thinking is the refinement and improvement of existing ideas.

The world's most famous fictional detective, Sherlock Holmes, often exhibited lateral thinking. One of my favorite examples was Holmes' response to an idea by his faithful assistant, the good Dr. Watson. Watson pointed out that a certain dog would not be at all helpful in solving a mystery because the dog had done nothing on the night of the murder. Sherlock cleverly noted that the dog was extremely important in solving the mystery precisely because he had done nothing on the night of the murder, because dogs would be expected to bark or become excited at the sight of strangers or of violent struggles.

Creative Genius or Pedestrian Process?

> The human mind treats a new idea the way the body treats a strange protein; it rejects it.
>
> —B. Medawar (quoted in Byrne, 1988, p. 16)

Are creative individuals qualitatively different from the rest of us, or do we all have (to some extent) what it takes to create something great?

Increasingly, psychologists have come to believe that there is "nothing special" about creative giants like Einstein, Madame Curie, and Mozart and that the creative process can be understood as an extension of common everyday thinking processes. Weisberg (1993) championed the everyday view of creativity in his analysis of the antecedents of creative thinking. For example, he presented a brief biography of Alexander Calder (1898–1976), a popular artist who is best known for his brightly colored mobiles. Calder invented the mobile as an art form. As a child, Calder used wire to make jewelry for his sister. His parents were artists who made certain that he had art lessons and was surrounded with both sculpture (his father's profession) and drawings (his mother's profession). He visited the studios of Piet Mondrian, an abstract artist who used strong, primary colors and abstract designs in his work. It is easy to see how these life experiences led to an art form in which brightly colored abstract patterns were strung together and hung in space. The creative act was the assimilation of these diverse forms and influences—one that, at least in hindsight, could have been predicted from Calder's life experiences.

The view that even great creative products can be produced by almost anyone with at least slightly above-average intelligence and expertise in a discipline, is gaining in popularity. There are no cognitive abilities that separate creative and noncreative people. According to this view, most of us have "what it takes" to be highly creative. From a cognitive perspective, creative thinking uses thought processes that are quite ordinary. We can all come up with "novel products of value" (Weisberg's, 1993, p. 4). All we need to do is learn how—and there's the rub!

Sensitivity, Synergy, and Serendipity

> Inspirational thunderbolts do not appear out of the blue. They are grounded in solid knowledge. Creative people are generally very knowledgeable about a given discipline. Coming up with a grand idea without ever having been closely involved with an area of study is not impossible, but it is very improbable.
>
> —Ulrich Kraft (2007)

Creativity has been described as the three Ss: sensitivity, synergy, and serendipity (Parnes, Noller, & Biondi, 1977). **Sensitivity** is the use of our senses, our "windows to the world" that we use to touch, smell, taste, and see. It has been suggested that highly creative people may experience the physical world with greater intensity than the rest of us, although I do not know of any data to support this possibility. It does seem that creative thinking involves the "noticing" or remembering of some critical aspect of the environment or a problem that the rest of us overlooked. One of the benchmarks of a creative person is the ability to find problems and not just solutions to them. Look at Figure 10.1. This is called "Boring's Wife-and-Mother-In-Law." Can you guess why? Look closely. Can you see both an old woman and a young woman in the picture?

Count the prongs on Figure 10.2. Do they disappear as you count them? This is an impossible figure—impossible because it cannot ever exist, except in the artist's mind. In creating each of these figures, the artists displayed a sensitivity to details that is both unusual and appropriate. Perhaps these are examples of heightened sensitivity to visual stimuli.

Sensitivity is the problem-finding part of creativity. Consider, for example, the problem of children unspooling toilet paper from the roll. I am guessing that many readers did not know that this was a problem, but people

Figure 10.1 Boring's Wife-and-Mother-in-Law. Can you see both an old woman and a young woman in this picture?

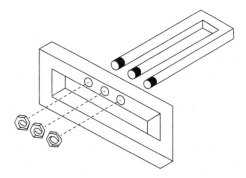

Figure 10.2 An impossible figure. Try to count the prongs.

who live with small children do, and most of them shrug and mutter that the children will outgrow their love for this activity. But, for Tamara Monosoff, the unspooling of toilet paper by children was a problem in need of a solution. She invented a device (loosely based on the design for a rod that is used to curl hair) to solve this problem. Her investment of $50,000 to get the device manufactured and to market paid off handsomely when she sold the rights to this product (and others) for over $100,000. She started the web site Mom Invented (http://www.mominventors.com/) and now has over 20,000 followers who share advice for creative products.

There is nothing like the Invention Convention to see creative problem solving at its best—and sometimes at its funniest. Hundreds of inventors from around the world compete every year at this annual convention in the hope that their creative invention will make them rich. The first stage of problem solving is recognizing that a problem exists, and every product at the convention is designed to solve a problem that the inventor has identified (often, however, the problem is like the unfurling of toilet paper—one that most of us never recognized as problematic). Identifying problems is not as easy as you might think.

What have modern-day inventors come up with? The variety of products displayed at the Invention Convention includes an electronic wristband that can send a secret signal from a baseball coach to team members to communicate the next play without allowing the opposing team to figure out what the signal means. Another invention was a large stick with a flat disk on the end that was designed to be placed over an overflowing trash can and pressed down. Another creative invention is a toe stub protector that fits around the leg of any piece of furniture on which you are likely to stub your toe. There is also a large device that fits over the ear to prevent tiny hearing aids from falling out. (Hearing aids are designed to be tiny so they will be inconspicuous; the large device designed to keep them from falling out does exactly the reverse.) And another is a terry slip cover that goes over the back of toilets makes them softer and more comfortable, like a couch. These are only a few of the products developed by modern inventors, all of whom are looking for investment capital so their product can pull in the big bucks from prospective investors. In past years, products have included bedroom slippers with headlights (to avoid the stubbed toe problem), dual-headed toothbrushes that brush both sides of your teeth at the same time, and people-shaped crackers to feed to your dog and other pets. If any readers get inspired from this chapter and invent a product that actually makes money or solves an important problem, remember me on your way to the bank. I would love to hear about it.

Synergy is the bringing together of seemingly disparate parts into a useful and functioning whole. It is close to Koestler's (1964) notion of **bisociative thinking** in which two previously unconnected "frames of reference" are amalgamated. If you can take ideas from different domains and bring them together so that they work successfully in a new context, you have demonstrated synergy. Examples of synergy can be found in the brief biography of Calder, which was presented earlier, who brought together his experiences with wire objects, bright colors, and abstract drawing to create his wildly popular mobiles, and in the description of devices that make water from the condensation of air. The creativity lies in finding bridges between two different domains of knowledge.

According to von Oech (1983), Johannes Gutenberg conceived of the printing press by combining two previously unconnected ideas—the wine press and the coin punch. The purpose of the coin punch was to leave an impression on a small area such as a coin. By contrast, the wine press applied pressure over a large area in order to squeeze the juice out of grapes. One day Gutenberg put the coin punch under the wine press and found that he could get images on paper. This simple, but original, combination resulted in the printing press and literally changed the world by making books widely available.

Gordon (1961) suggested that one way to promote creativity is to bring people from diverse fields together to find problems and to create solutions, the two mainstreams of the creative process. The idea behind this recommendation is that in order to bring together diverse ideas, you need to have a broad range of experiences and knowledge. One argument for a liberal arts education is that it provides the breadth of knowledge needed to view the world from different perspectives and to permit the combination of ideas across domains of knowledge. In a thoughtful review, Mannix and Neale (2005) found that when individuals are exposed to minority opinions in diverse groups, they "think in a divergent way, and are more likely to detect novel solutions or come to new decisions" (p. 47), but the effect depends on the way in which groups are diverse (with the best outcomes when group members differ in education or personality) and whether or not the group process is carefully controlled (with best outcomes from groups that honor the opinions of all participants and do not push for conformity). Thus, recent research suggests that the idea that diverse groups will be more creative than homogeneous groups is supported, but only under certain conditions.

Serendipity is an unexpected discovery that is unplanned. Biographies of great scientists often contain accounts of serendipitous events, some of which seem preposterous. I have often felt that focusing on serendipity did the scientist a great injustice. A new miracle drug may have been the result of an accidental spill, but it was the prepared scientist who could appreciate the results of the accident that created the drug. The scientist was able to select the relevant information from the accident so that it could be used in a novel way instead of simply labeling it a mistake and forgetting about it. Although serendipity may have contributed to a creative act, the persistence, motivation, and hard work on the part of the creator allowed the serendipitous event to occur. Serendipity may play a role in great scientific discoveries, but such fortuitous "accidents" seem most likely to occur in the laboratory at 2 A.M.

Several websites have emerged to foster the exchange of novel ideas with the goal of increasing creative products and solutions. *Kaneko: Open Space for Your Mind* (thekaneko.org), for example, lists a variety of such innovations, including an umbrella with lights so that you can be seen on a rainy night and a box that can be used by toddlers when they are painting or doing other messy activities so that the mess can be folded up when they finish. Creative individuals in several parts of the world (including rural areas of the Philippines and India) solved the problem of dark housing with the use of soda bottles filled with water (Global Envision, 2011). Electricity is expensive and often unavailable to many poor people around the world. Soda bottles filled with water (and a bit of bleach) are installed through a hole in tin roofs to let in daylight. This innovation, which has been attributed to Alfredo Moser from Brazil, is bringing sustainable lighting to interior places that have been dark for many decades. This remarkably simple and cheap solution is literally lighting the lives of millions of people around the world.

Jokes, puns, and witticisms could also be considered as a form of creative expression. A joke brings together two ideas that are not usually combined: Did you hear the one about the two former schoolmates who meet unexpectedly for the first time in 25 years? As they caught up on the details of their lives, one asked the other if he had any children. Sorrowfully he replied, "Yes, one living and one married." The listener was expecting the phrase "one living and one dead" and the surprise juxtaposition of "living and married" is the humorous element in this joke. Laughter is often the response to original ideas also. The surprising combination of elements (synergy) makes for good jokes and creative ideas.

Creativity as Investment Theory: Buy Low; Sell High

> Even companies that pride themselves on their encouragement of wacky, creative thinkers-outside-the-box require them to be wacky and creative in the right sort of way—and to think outside the appropriate box.
>
> —Peter Martin (2001, July 17, p. 10)

Suppose you were to decide right now to "do something creative." Where and how would you begin? Would you search popular and scholarly media to identify emerging trends, such as the development of smaller computers, more powerful drugs, or faster means of transportation and apply your knowledge and skills in one of these areas? If so, then you would be exhibiting a not-very-creative approach to deciding which ideas or products to pursue. Sternberg and Lubart (1996) maintain that creative people make unusual decisions about the topics and products in which they are willing to invest their own time and effort; those of us who are not recognized as creative may have made errors in selecting a topic that is not worth pursuing. Creative people work on topics that are unpopular at the time; they make creative contributions to the field, and then move on to another unpopular topic. In this way, creativity is like the classic mantra of finance, "buy low; sell high." In other words, creative people invest in unpopular topics (topics where there is low interest) and move on to another unpopular topic when the first one gains in popularity (leave the area when interest is high). The definition of creativity requires "something unusual," so creative people, by definition, buck the crowd instead of following it.

The investment theory of creativity addresses an important question in the world of ideas—what is worth thinking about? In the chapter on problem solving, the problem finding (or identifying) is similar to the idea of deciding how to invest cognitive resources. Finding the right problem to solve (or a problem worth solving) is at least as important as deriving a successful solution. Problem solving and creativity are closely related topics. Creative problem-solvers (and finders) will have knowledge about the topic, sufficient intellectual ability (i.e., intelligence), an encouraging environment, an appropriately flexible thinking style, a personality that is open to new ideas, and the motivation to persist at a task.

Creativity as a System

> A scientific theory or other product is creative only if the innovation gains the acceptance of a field of experts and so transforms the culture.
> —Jeanne Nakamura and Mihaly Csikszentmihalyi
> (2001, p. 337)

Creativity will involve more than just knowledge about a field or the willingness to propose a novel idea. There are many different ways of examining this strange creature we call "creativity." Some psychologists have adopted a systems approach to creativity, which means that they believe it is the confluence of many different types of variables that make creativity more or less probable. Of course, the creative individual is central to the process, but she or he works in a domain of knowledge (e.g., art, physics, decorating, teaching, horse breeding, and any other domain you can think of). The contributions of an individual to a domain are judged by the people in that field—the art critics, funding agencies for physics research, editors of decorating magazines, etc. The people in the field act as the gatekeepers for a domain—they decide what is and is not valued. Docents in art museums often tell stories of artists who died penniless because their unusual style was not recognized as genius until after their death. Of course, they never mention those dead, penniless artists whose art is still not recognized as having value—and may never be. The role of the gatekeepers to a domain is critical in understanding creativity because these influential people can spur creativity or stifle it, depending on their own views of what is novel and appropriate for their domain. In a fascinating case study of these influences, Nakamura and Csikszentmihalyi (2001) recounted an interview with Linus Pauling, a scientist who won a Nobel Prize for his work in the fields of organic chemistry and nuclear disarmament, and ignoble scorn for his work on the role of Vitamin C in preventing colds. This fascinating account emphasizes the importance of variables that are beyond the control of a creative individual.

Creativity as a Group Process

> None of us is as smart as all of us.
>
> —Japanese proverb

Sawyer (2007) talks about group genius—the creativity that results when people from diverse backgrounds come together. As described earlier, the role of group diversity on creativity depends on many variables, including the type of diversity and how the group operates (Mannix & Neale, 2005). Sawyer describes creativity as a continuous process of small and constant change. Successful companies are always changing—they are open to creativity. Recall from the chapter on decision making that, under some circumstances, groups can make better decisions, but this outcome depends on making sure that the group understands that the process of deciding as a group can lead to overconfidence and to the tendency to require unanimity (Hastie, 2006). Group members need to be able to voice their dissent and to come up with new ideas instead of making the group rush to unanimity. This conclusion is supported by research by Svensson, Norlander, and Archer (2002), who found that groups tend to produce more creative responses than participants working alone. Most creative work is done in organizations with two or more people working together (Thompson & Choi, 2006). Hargadon and Bechky (2006) listed four patterns of behavior that can move teams beyond individual creativity: 1) seeking help, 2) giving help, 3) reframing a situation, and 4) reinforcing responses. If you want to enhance group creativity, is it important to structure the group interactions so that members are free to ask for and give help, and they are encouraged to reframe the situation and reinforce each other's responses. Recall from the chapter on problem solving that reframing a problem is a critical step in finding solutions.

Creativity as a Cognitive Process

> The man with a new idea is a Crank until the idea succeeds.
> —Mark Twain (1897; aka Samuel L. Clemens)

If the creative act is "nothing special," then we should be able to understand it and predict when it will occur using a common cognitive framework. Several different psychologists have suggested that creativity is as "simple" as problem solving, except that the problem or the solutions are novel and appropriate. According to this view, creative thinking is a multistage process that consists of identifying a problem, deciding what is important about the problem, and arriving at a novel way of solving it. "Creativity" brings together many topics that have been addressed in earlier chapters; yet, it is also more elusive and mysterious because, by definition, we cannot tell anyone how to create the "unusual." What makes the processes of identifying problems, searching for solutions, selecting the most promising ones, and conveying the outcome creative?

Stretching and Rejecting Paradigms

A **paradigm** is an example that is used as a pattern. In psychology, it usually refers to an experimental set-up. In this context, it is used to mean "a usual way of thinking or responding." Consider this example: Suppose that you are a manufacturer of golf clubs. Like all manufacturers, you want to sell more golf clubs. Paradigmatic thinking about this problem might lead you to increase your advertising budget so that advertisements for your golf clubs reach more people (McFadzean, 2000). If you stretch the paradigm, you might start to think that instead of reaching more people with your advertisements, you want to target buyers of golf clubs, so you would plan your advertising to reach fewer people, but a more select group. If you reject the paradigm, you change the nature of the problem that is being solved. Callaway Golf, a U.S. manufacturer of golf clubs did exactly that (Kim & Mauborgne, 1999) with their creative idea—"Big Bertha Golf Clubs." What, you don't know about Big Bertha? Instead of making golf clubs that would compete with other well-known brands of golf clubs, they made new golf clubs aimed at a new golf-playing audience—people who do not play golf.

The creative people at Calloway thought about all of the people at country clubs who play tennis instead of golf because these tennis players find the idea of using a tiny club to hit a tiny ball too daunting a task. After all, the head of a tennis racket is much larger than the head of golf club, so it should be easier to hit a tennis ball with the large head of a tennis racket than a tiny golf ball with a small head of a golf club (other things being equal, which of course, they are not). Callaway saw a business opportunity that no one had seen. A golf club with a large head makes playing golf less difficult and more fun for people who do not play golf. Thus, they combined the larger head of the tennis racket with the shaft of a golf club to create Big Bertha—a profitable move that expanded the market for golf clubs. This creative act involved rejecting the business-as-usual paradigm.

The Problem of Problem Definition

All of our great inventors were problem finders. They recognized problems that the rest of the world never saw. For example, why did people need electric lights when gas worked well, or why should we even want to travel in a metal box propelled with a new-fangled engine when horses were more reliable (at that time)? We all studied the great inventors of the past, people like Benjamin Franklin, George Washington Carver, and Thomas Edison. Present-day inventors also find problems. What can we learn from these and other creative successes?

Selecting Relevant Information

Virtually every creative act involves a novel way of defining a problem and selecting information that is relevant to reaching the goal. We usually think of creativity in the arts and sciences, but it can and should exist in a host of everyday settings that range from planning your finances so that your money lasts until the end of the month to getting your teacher to accept a late paper.

Consider a couple seeking marriage counseling. The wife complains that her husband spends too much time at work, and if he really loved her, he would spend more time at home. The husband complains that he has a great deal of pressure at the office and that he has to work long hours to "get ahead." If his wife loved him more, she would understand. There are multiple possible ways to define their problem. They could pose the problem as: "Should we get a divorce?" But, other possible problem definitions include: (a) How can we find ways to spend more time together? (b) How can we assure each other that we are still in love? (c) How can the husband "get ahead" while spending less time at work? (d) How can they learn to adjust to the present situation? (e) Is "getting ahead" an important goal? (f) What can the wife do so that she does not feel lonely and resentful when her husband is at work?

If you consider the problem for a few more minutes, you can come up with many other problem definitions. The nature of the solution will change every time the problem is redefined. The selection of relevant information to help you reach a goal is related to your knowledge of the problem space (topic). In this example, you would need to know more about the couple to help them find a good solution. Suppose that you know that the wife is an aspiring artist. You could suggest that she pursue her art interests so that she would feel less lonely and deserted. Alternatively, if you know about the availability of other jobs for the husband, you could suggest that he change jobs. In fact, some therapists who have adopted this technique report that they can help families overcome destructive conflicts by teaching them how to discover creative solutions to their interpersonal problems.

Lateral thinking or "thinking around a problem" is really just another term for "redefining the problem." In the story about the clever girl who knew she was being offered two black pebbles, she did not conceptualize the problem as "What should I do when I pick the black pebble?" Instead, she redefined the problem as "How can I avoid the appearance that I picked up the black pebble?" It is not so much "thinking around the problem" as it is redefining the problem so that it can be solved in a favorable way. This point was also made in the previous chapter on problem solving. By focusing on the fact that the pebbles on the path were black and white, and therefore, she could drop one without it being identified, the heroine of this short story was able to generate a novel solution.

Generation, Exploration, and Evaluation

> Creativity is a puzzle, a paradox, some say a mystery.
> —Margaret A. Boden (1990, p. vii)

If creative thinking is just a variant of everyday problem solving, then there should be general principles that can be applied across domains of knowledge. Are the creative dancer, scientist, teacher, and writer all using the same sorts of processes in their creation, despite the fact that they are using different modes of expression with very different problems? Although there are obvious differences, they all have to generate possible solutions to their problem and explore the "problem space," a term that was defined in the problem-solving chapter as all of the possible goals and ways of getting from the start point to the goal. Finke, Ward, and Smith (1992) have posited a two-phase model that they call **geneplore**, named for the repeated cycles of generation and exploration that are part of every problem-solving process. Creative individuals need to be involved and committed so that they continue the processes long enough to allow a creative solution to emerge. Evaluation is also a creative act because the problem-solver must be able to recognize when a good solution has been obtained. Effective evaluation is needed to terminate the process or the problem-solver can be caught in unending loops of exploration and generation. Notice that a problem-solving view of creativity also entails all of the other stages of cognition. A successful exploration of the problem space requires that the problem-solver be able to notice and remember critical aspects of the problem. Thus, as in all thinking, "memory must be tickled." Although it is clear that memory is an important component of both creative and non-creative problem solving, the utilization of memory must differ in some way between these two processes. When thinking creatively, the memory task is more than retrieval of a known fact; it involves a broader search, with fewer constraints on the type and breadth of information retrieved. In fact, one detrimental effect of expertise is finding that the ability to retrieve a well-known solution or response may hinder creativity. Thus, experts who can retrieve solutions to problems as readily as we might retrieve an arithmetic fact are less likely to consider additional possible solutions than the novice who needs to think through a solution. This model of creative thinking offers two possibilities for those who are interested in enhancing creative thinking: a) conduct broad searches of memory, or in other words, do not stop thinking about a problem as soon as a solution has been found; and b) practice synthesizing information that has been retrieved (i.e., remembered or "thought of") so that information can be combined in novel ways.

Advertising Age, which as you probably guessed is a magazine for the advertising industry, picked this example as their "Creativity pick of the day" (April 23, 2012). A creative Mexican company is encouraging dog owners to swap their dog poop for free Wi-Fi. This is how it works: People deposit bags of dog waste in a special box in a public park. The weight is calculated and the company provides free minutes of Wi-Fi in the park based on the weight collected. With this incentive, the park is poop-free and everyone gets free Wi-Fi. It is a creative way to create a climate in which people clean up after their dog. The creativity is the choice of a reward for creating a clean park—Wi-Fi for the community in exchange for dog poop. It is the sort of creative idea that makes most of us ask, "Why didn't I think of that?"

Insight and Incubation

> Professional insight is sometimes marvelous and sometimes flawed.
> —Daniel Kahneman and Gary Klein (2009, p. 515)

Not surprisingly, both the terms "insight" and "incubation" were discussed in the chapter on problem solving and appear again in discussions of creativity, which is sometimes thought of as solving problems in a creative way. Insight was described as the sudden awareness of a solution;

incubation was described as period of time when an individual is not actively working on a problem that is followed by a successful solution. These two stages in the problem-solving process are often associated with creative solutions. Although these are both "hidden" processes that are seemingly mysterious, it is possible to examine them within the framework of a general cognitive model.

Klein (2011) argued that although programs designed to teach critical thinking have "a great deal of value" (p. 210), they need to provide more training in insight. Klein has done much of his work with the Intelligence Community, which in this case means the U.S. military. Not surprisingly, the military has increased its critical thinking training over the last decade in recognition of the fact that both war and peace are far more complicated than in earlier times. Researchers who want to help people develop better intuitions have focused on the cues that experts use when solving problems. Recall from earlier discussions that System 1 thinking is so fast and effortless that it is assumed to reflect sudden insight or rapid intuition. It differs from System 2, which is slower and more deliberate. Recall also that experts who develop accurate intuitions practiced for many years in their field of expertise and received rapid and useful feedback so that they could improve their intuitions. Some intuitions are highly flawed, even when the "expert" is highly confident. Kahneman and Klein (2009) agree that the best way to develop insight (or intuition) is to work in a regular and predictable environment. So, if you were hoping for a quick and easy way to develop the insight needed for creative thinking, you will do best if you are trying to develop expertise in fields like chess or medicine, which can provide the types of feedback needed for expert insight. We are far from knowing how to train for insight.

I hope that you can recall from the chapter on memory the idea that the information people store in memory is connected in web-like networks. For example, your information about flowers is connected such that what you know about roses is (metaphorically) stored close to your information about petunias, azaleas, and other flowers. If you know a great deal about flowers, then you have an extensive and highly interconnected network of information. If you grew up in the tropics, then your knowledge of flowers is probably very different from that of someone who grew up in Antarctica because you probably would have very different information about flowers. The interconnectedness of knowledge is important here. According to a network model of memory, all of your knowledge about flowers is also connected to your knowledge of water and sun, which in turn are connected to many different types of information. Theoretically, if you start at any point in this giant interconnected web, you could trace your way to any other place in the web. A hypothetical schematic of a section of someone's knowledge network is shown in Figure 10.3.

When a new idea suddenly comes to someone, it means that he has successfully traveled his personal knowledge network from one place to another—the new idea representing the connection between two previously unconnected nodes. Think about someone you love. What sorts of ideas and images come to mind? Does the image of a rose seem appropriate? If so, it may be because I brought your knowledge of roses to mind in the last paragraph and the path from your love to that of roses was "activated." Does the phrase, "My love is like a red, red rose" have any meaning for you? Does the sudden association of your love and roses seem insightful?

Psychologists call the "thinking about" or the "reminding" process **spread of activation** to denote the idea that the activity that was begun when I

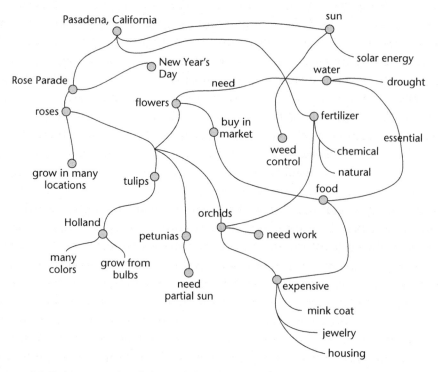

Figure 10.3 An example of the way information in memory is interconnected in a giant web-like knowledge structure. Creativity involves "noticing" or making unusual connections.

told you to think about a loved one spread to your knowledge of roses. People with large knowledge nets will have more places for the activation to spread, and the best way to have a large knowledge net is to have a large number of interconnected knowledge structures. There is no substitute for knowledge about a topic; just as there is no substitute for the ability to use the information stored in memory in thoughtful ways. If you want to be more creative in the sciences, for example, you would need to acquire knowledge about the field so that relevant information will be available for solving problems about science. We use our knowledge nets for new ideas, and skimpy nets yield few ideas. It is the ability to use the information stored in memory that allows us to create by going beyond what we have learned.

Let's consider what else is happening when you solve a problem. Suppose that you are reading a murder mystery in which the prime suspect is the hero, and hence, unlikely to be the murderer. You are focusing on another character who, you believe, "did it." Dutifully, you generate possible solutions and explore the problem space, but to no avail. You cannot connect your prime suspect to the murder scene, so you "forget" about the problem and resume other activities. In other words, you create a period of incubation. Then, when you return to the book, you "see" that it was not your prime suspect, but some other character. Using the jargon of the problem-solving literature, you were fixated on one solution type (finding a way to link your suspect to the crime) and the incubation period allowed you to "forget" this type of solution so that other more profitable paths could be pursued—sort of a release from fixation.

Good problem-solvers know how to search through a large problem space so as to make it an efficient process. When there is a large number of possible paths to a goal, good problem-solvers use heuristics, or search plans, to "prune the search tree" (Boden, 1990, p. 78). If you have an extensive knowledge net concerning some topic, then you have more potential paths or links between concepts and more retrieval cues that can help you remember and select relevant information when it is needed.

Analogical Thinking

> Analogy is inevitable in human thought.
> —Robert Oppenheimer (1956, p. 129)

Analogies underlie much of our everyday thinking, our artistic expressions, and scientific achievements. Sternberg (1977, p. 353) noted,

Reasoning by analogy is pervasive in everyday experience. We reason analogically whenever we make a decision about something new in our experience by drawing a parallel to something old. When we buy a new goldfish because we liked our old one, or when we listen to a friend's advice because it was correct once before, we are reasoning analogically.

Thinking involves the ability to note resemblances or correspondence between two objects while simultaneously discerning that there are also differences. When you use analogies, you observe that two entities are similar with respect to some property and dissimilar with respect to others. Analogies are discussed in several chapters in this book because they are pervasive in human thought.

One of the most famous creative uses of analogy is seen in the story of Archimedes, a famous Greek mathematician, physicist, and inventor (287–212 BC). According to a standard version of the tale, he was given the task of determining if the crown of King Hiero II was pure gold—the only kind of crown worthy of a king. But, Archimedes did not know how to solve this problem because of the irregular shape of the crown. One day, while lowering himself into a bathtub full of water, the tub overflowed. The answer was immediately obvious. Like his body, a solid gold crown would display a volume of water identical to that displaced by a bar of gold that was equal in weight to that of the crown. Because gold is denser than silver, an object (like a crown) would displace less water than another object of the same weight that had been mixed with silver. The story goes on to say that in his excitement, he ran naked through the street yelling, "Eureka, I have found it!" He found that Hiero's crown displaced more water than an equal weight of gold, thus showing that the crown had been alloyed with silver (or some other metal less dense than gold). He had a true creative insight mediated by the analogy of his body displacing his bathtub water and the knowledge that a gold crown would displace a predetermined volume of water. (In some versions of the story, the crown was pure gold and the king was very happy, so do not take the story literally.)

Although the use of analogies from distant domains is a common theme in discussions of creativity, in fact, the spontaneous noting of similarities in very different contexts is not a common occurrence. As discussed in the chapter on problem solving, analogical transfer is more likely to occur when we learn to think about the structure of a problem (e.g., displace water as a form of measurement) instead of the surface or domain features (how is a gold crown like taking a bath). Perhaps it is because it is unusual that it figures prominently in our belief about creativity—which requires an unusual outcome or process.

Analogies are also important in "selling" creative ideas. Business thrives on new ideas, but all new ideas involve unknowns, and risk is an inherent part of unknowns. When describing a new business venture, the proposers need to reduce the stakeholders' uncertainty and convince them that the proposed new venture is likely to pay off (Cornelissen & Clarke, 2010). One way to communicate that the new venture is not as risky as it may seem at first is to use an analogy in which a large profit was made when a similar idea was turned into a business venture. Consider this example: A new business venture involved creating a security system that would be used when interacting on the Internet. This new idea was described as "You know, you have kind of an electronic wallet and have all your IDs on one thing, and it would become your passport around the net" (Santos & Eisenhardt, 2009, quoted in Cornelissen & Clareke, 2010, p. 547). This analogy explained the basics of the new business plans in language that investors could understand, and with these concrete examples, it seemed less risky than some abstruse idea.

Making the Familiar Strange

Although the usual function of analogies is to make the unfamiliar familiar, Gordon (1961, 1976), the founder of a creative technique known as Synectics, suggested that we reverse the process for creative results. Gordon (1976) suggested that we use analogies and metaphors by trying "strange new contexts in which to view a familiar problem" (p. 251). For example, consider a naive student examining a fish's heart for the first time. Because the student knows nothing about anatomy, the context is strange, yet the flow of blood through the heart may remind him of a filter system for a local swimming pool. The student's analogy is a creative contribution to his understanding of anatomy.

Gordon suggested four specific types of analogies to use when attempting to solve a problem creatively. They are personal analogy, direct analogy, symbolic analogy, and fantasy analogy. Each is described in the chapter on the development of problem-solving skills. Analogies can also be used creatively to find problems. For example, executives at Bradford Associates (Westport, Connecticut) spent an afternoon sipping martinis and brainstorming about possible new products that would be marketable. As they were enjoying their own liquid refreshments, they decided that the time had come "for a six-pack that a dog could ask for by name." They are now marketing a chicken-flavored soft-drink for dogs known as "Arf'n'Arf." Here is a clear example of the use of analogies to find problems (the need for a doggie soft drink). Similarly, a popular dog product is now being developed for people. Many dogs enjoy munching on bone shaped biscuits that help to keep their teeth and gums healthy. A similar biscuit that will help humans to keep their gums and teeth healthy is now available on some market shelves.

Bionics is a special type of analogy. It relies on analogies from nature that can be adapted to human problems. For example, special properties of the eyes of beetles have suggested a new type of ground speed indicator for airplanes, and the principles of adhesion used by cockleburs served as the prototype for Velcro-type closures. Bionics is also involves the idea that the broad impact of solutions be considered because (borrowing another analogy from nature) small changes in our ecological system can result in disastrous consequences to other life forms in the food chain. Consider modern surgery to unclog clogged arteries. A thin tube is threaded into the artery. When the clog is reached, a small "balloon" is inflated in the artery to open the clogged area. This is the same technique that has been used by plumbers to open clogged pipes. Thus, cardiac surgeons are saving lives with a common problem-solving technique that was designed for plumbing. Many creative acts involve adapting solutions from one field for use in an unrelated field.

Remote Associations Test

There is a test of creativity that rests on the notion that creative people can form connections between seemingly very different topics. Mednick and Mednick (1967) created a test to tap this dimension of creativity. It is called the Remote Associations Test (RAT). Test takers are given three words and are asked to come up with a fourth word that relates to all three. As an example, think of what word relates to the following:

RIVER   NOTE   BLOOD

Can you come up with the relational word? (The answer is bank—river bank, bank note, blood bank.) Try some other remote associations similar to the ones on the RAT:

1.	BOARD	DUCK	DOLLAR
2.	FILE	HEAD	TOE
3.	BOILED	LID	FLOWER
4.	BALL	MALARIA	BUTTER
5.	CLASS	STAGE	SOCCER

(The answers are at the end of the chapter.)

Do creative people come up with remote associations when they think creatively? It seems that some do, but there is very little direct evidence that tests like the RAT can predict creativity in natural contexts.

Encouraging Creativity

One of the objections I hear to setting forth creativity as a goal for higher education is, "We can't all be Einsteins." This is undeniable; it is also irrelevant.

—Patricia Hutchings (1986, p. 14)

There has been considerable debate over the question of whether it is possible to make people more creative by providing them with special experiences that are designed to enhance creativity. There is a sizable body of research literature that shows that it is possible. This notion is not really a surprising conclusion given that creative thinking shares many features with everyday sorts of problem solving, and the evidence reviewed in the first chapter and several places throughout this book showed that improved thinking is a possible outcome of education. What are the many variables that are important in determining when and how much creativity can be enhanced?

The Person, the Problem, the Process

Discovery consists of looking at the same thing as everyone else and thinking something different.

—Albert Szent-Gjorgyi (Nobel Prize Winner in Medicine; quoted in von Oech, 1983, p. 7)

It is clear that creativity is not something that exists in an all-or-none fashion. People are more or less creative, just as they are more or less athletic or good-looking or prejudiced. The question of whether there is some inborn or inherited trait that is associated with high creativity has been difficult to answer. Most of the research has centered on the relationship between creativity and intelligence. Are intelligent people the most creative people?

In general, people with above-average scores on intelligence tests tend to be creative, while those with low IQ scores tend not to be; but the relationship is not a perfect one. The smartest people are not always the most creative. There is a certain minimum intelligence that is needed to be creative, but beyond the minimal level, IQ doesn't seem to matter much. Even if you are not a particularly intelligent person, you may have great creative potential. In addition, we all have differential abilities. A person with a broad knowledge net about football strategies and skill in running and throwing is more likely to be a creative football player than an individual who has little knowledge of the field and is clumsy with a football, but the second individual may be more creative in an unrelated domain of knowledge, such as poetry or ballet. People can be "habitually creative" in areas they know very well, such as expert chefs who routinely substitute a new ingredient in well-known recipes or can intentionally make a creative leap such as changing the way food is prepared, perhaps by frying soda that has been frozen or combining flavors in a novel (but generally good) way (Glaveanu, 2012).

Personality Factors

> Multiple studies have found that the primary determinant of new product failure is an absence of innovativeness.
> —Rajesh Sethi, Daniel Smith, and C. Whan Park (2001, p. 73)

Most creative ideas are initially met with failure and ridicule. Imagine trying to tell a doubting public that you were making a machine that would allow people to fly like birds, or a device that would light homes at night without burning a candle, or that illnesses are caused by organisms that are so tiny we cannot see them. Mueller, Melwani, and Goncalo (2012) recognize the strong bias that most people have against creative ideas. They tell about Robert Goddard, the father of modern rocket propulsion, who endured repeated ridicule from other scientists who laughed at his "ludicrous and impossible" dreams. Creative people need to be able to withstand the scorn of their peers.

There are certain personality factors that are consonant with creativity. Because creativity (as we have defined it) requires an unusual or novel act, the creative individual must not be swayed by a need for conformity nor be resistant to change. In order to persist in doing or thinking the unusual, the creative person will also need to have enough self-confidence so as not to be dissuaded from a pursuit when others denigrate or deride it. There also needs to be a love or joy for pursuits that are cognitively complex. Perhaps there is some validity to the notion of the "eccentric" artist or scholar. If you read the first chapter of this book, you will recognize that these are dispositions of critical thinkers—not surprisingly, I return to some of the same themes that were presented in the first chapter as I near the end of this book.

The creative person must be self-motivated so that he or she will persist at a task. Sometimes, school experiences tend to favor the noncreative students, as many traditional assignments do not call for creative responses. Creative people may have to create their own rewards for their actions and find satisfaction in the creative process itself. The ability and willingness to take risks and to tolerate ambiguity is also needed for creative act.

Persistence, Conscientiousness, and Curiosity

A "hungry mind" is a core determinant of individual differences in academic achievement.

—Sophie von Stumm, Benedikt Hell,
and Tomas Chamorro-Premuzic (2011, p. 574)

Although intelligence is a factor in creativity, two personality factors are at least as important. In order to succeed at any difficult task, people need to persist even when they repeatedly fail. The history of creative inventions is the story of persistence even after repeated failures. Conscientiousness, which is the use of care when doing something, is a related personality trait. It is unlikely that sloppy work will lead to creative outcomes. There is a very large body of research literature showing that being conscientious is associated with better academic and occupational performance (O'Connor & Paunonen, 2007; Poropat, 2009). It now seems that intellectual curiosity is the third leg of a stool that supports creative thinking and academic performance (von Stumm, Hell, & Chamorrow-Premuzic, 2011).

The idea that curiosity is a critical trait for creativity is not new. Dewey (1910, quoted in von Stumm et al., 2011, p. 582) recognized this:

In a few people, intellectual curiosity is so insatiable that nothing will discourage it, but in most its edge is easily dulled and blunted. . . . Some lose it in indifference or carelessness; others in a frivolous flippancy; many escape these evils only to become incased in a hard dogmatism which is equally fatal to the spirit of wonder.

We need to teach children and learn for ourselves that failure is an important part of life and that every great success was built upon previous failures. Creative people are able to "slow down" and take the time to review and rethink their usual way of doing things and resist quick closure on problems (Larson, 2001). In the first chapter of this book, I made the case for the importance of a critical thinking attitude. The same themes are repeated in this chapter on enhancing creativity. The only seeming contradiction comes from recent research on creativity in teams. Team cohesion seems to be detrimental to creativity (Sethi, Smith, & Park, 2001). If team members are quick to agree with each other (high cohesion), then unusual solutions or conclusions will never emerge from a team because usual and common outcomes will be generated most often. We need teams that foster and encourage dissent (in a positive way). Group leaders who insist on consensus are inadvertently stifling creativity. If everyone in a group agrees, then it is likely that only one person is doing the thinking. Of course, it can be uncomfortable to "go against the crowd," yet creative people are able to be a lone dissenter. In order to be an effective dissenter, creative people often persuade group members to consider seriously his or her unusual perspective. In real-life settings, social skills are vital for successful ideas.

In a classic study of creative people (Barron, 1958), writers, artists, musicians, and mathematicians were given a battery of tests to determine if they had any personality traits in common. In general, these highly creative individuals were nonconforming, unconventional, and generally less concerned with "making a good impression." One contemporary American hero is the recently deceased Richard Feynman. Feynman was the Nobel Prize-winning physicist who became famous in the nonscientific world when he investigated the tragic explosion of the Challenger. He demonstrated that "O" rings, rubber circular gaskets used on the Challenger, get brittle when they get cold. His simple test consisted of dunking an "O" ring in ice water and showing that it could crack when cold. The attitude of risk-taking and nonconformity is exemplified by the title of an autobiographical book about his life entitled *What Do You Care What Other People Think?* (1989). Of course, this does not mean that if you become nonconforming and unconventional, you will then become highly creative, but it suggests that a more open-minded and less self-conscious approach to life's problems can pay off. Feynman also demonstrated a natural curiosity and immense breadth of knowledge. His interests were not limited to physics and extended to many domains, including the arts and music.

I had the great honor meeting this remarkable man. I recall with great clarity a time when I sat next to him at an informal dinner party. He remarked to my daughter, who was young at that time, that growing old was a peculiar thing. When he was my daughter's age, he could never get enough dessert, and now that he is old and can have all the dessert he wishes, he no longer wants it! At the time, I thought that this was an odd discussion between a child and an older man; now I think it was just part of the eccentricity that marked his genius.

Creativity as a Goal

> We want creative citizens, who can take responsibilities and who are able to solve problems that do not yet exist today.
> —Olli-Pekka Heinonen (Finland's Minister of Education, quoted in Shavinina, 2001, p. 292)

The easiest way to enhance creativity is to value it. In an experimental study of the effect of telling college students that creativity is valued, Shalley (1991) found that college students produced more creative products (had creativity goals) than students who had been told that they were being judged on the number of products they produced (had productivity goals) or told nothing about expectations for creativity or number produced. The underlying idea behind this research was that most people pay more attention and exert more effort toward being creative if they believe that creativity is permitted or valued. It seems that people will be more creative when they are told to be creative. This is probably not a surprising result to the college students who are reading this. After all, how often are students encouraged or even permitted to be creative in school? Most often, the learning goal in school is to be able to repeat back something that was learned in class or to be able to apply a skill in an appropriate setting. Apparently, we can be more creative if we are expected to be creative.

Types of Motivation

> People will be most creative when they feel motivated primarily by the interest, enjoyment, satisfaction, and challenge of the work itself—not by external pressures.
> —Beth A. Hennessey and Teresa M. Amabile (1988, p. 11)

Creative thinking, likes all activities, takes place in a social context—a fact that is often overlooked in the cognitive literature. Amabile (2001) has studied the environmental/social factors that can encourage or discourage creativity. Like other researchers in the field of creativity, she concluded that much of what happens in school and work settings is not conducive to the development of creativity. She found that creative individuals often view their work as a labor of love. They work long hours because they are impelled by their curiosity and their own desire to achieve a goal. Hard work is a repeated theme among those who study the creative process. This sort of motivation is called **intrinsic motivation** because it comes from within the individual. By contrast, much of the motivation provided at school and work is **extrinsic motivation**, which is motivation that comes from others, such as promises of a good grade or money. According to Amabile, the best way to promote creativity is to arrange the environment so as to maximize intrinsic motivation. Six conditions that tend to kill intrinsic motivation are (a) constant evaluation, (b) surveillance, (c) reward, (d) competition, (e) restricted choice (e.g., limited choice of materials to use), and (f) an extrinsic orientation towards work.

The general finding that intrinsic motivation, that is doing something for sheer enjoyment and interest, is superior to extrinsic motivation in encouraging creativity has held up over decades of work (Hennessey & Amabile, 2010), but there are conditions when extrinsic motivation (e.g., promise of a reward) can also be effective. When rewards confirm the idea that someone is competent and creative, they can facilitate creativity. Extrinsic rewards tend to dampen creativity when these rewards make people feel as though they are being controlled by the situation—when self determination is being undermined. But, when rewards convey the idea that creativity is valued and encouraged, they can lead to more creative outcomes (Deci & Ryan, 2008; Dewett & Gruys, 2007).

Many decades of research have shown that blanket statements like "external rewards hinder creativity" have to be modified because, at least sometimes, external rewards can stimulate creative responses. For example, in Nakamura and Csikszentmihalyi's (2001) case study of the life of Linus Pauling, it is clear that Pauling changed the focus of his work to organic chemistry because he was given grant money for research in organic chemistry. He then went on to make highly creative advances in this new field of study, so the extrinsic motivation provided by the grants did not seem to diminish his creative genius; instead, the grants refocused his creativity in a new domain. In a study of the effects of extrinsic rewards on creativity, researchers found that there are many other variables that influence creativity and, under some conditions, external rewards, like providing money for creative outcomes, can enhance creativity, especially when the individual maintains control of the situation. The effect of intrinsic rewards on creativity remains a contested area of research—we need to understand much better the conditions under which external rewards help or hinder creativity.

Most school and work environments tend to be heavily weighted towards the negative end of these six factors; teachers and supervisors watch while students and employees work, competition is either overt or covert, but almost always present, and the workers receive grades or payment for their efforts. It is impossible to avoid extrinsic motivators completely as there will always be deadlines, competition, and restrictions. Despite these realities, it is possible to design school and work environments to foster creativity by reducing the focus on extrinsic motivators and emphasizing the intrinsic rewards of the creative process. Environmental factors like these are only part of the creativity equation—creativity needs more than a conducive environment to flourish. In addition to changes in the environment, creativity training also needs a skills component. No one can become a creative scientist or great author or talented artist without the factual knowledge and technical skills that are relevant to their chosen field. There is no substitute for knowledge.

There is at least one conclusion on which everyone can agree: a quality education (both inside and outside of school) will give you the basis for remote associations or divergent thoughts or novel ideas. Creative people need a head filled with thoughts and facts in order to create with them. The inferences from Amabile's work are clear: Cultivate a love of learning; reward your own creative efforts; take the college courses that will fill your mind with new thoughts (and not just the easiest courses offered). Creative endeavors result from hard, intellectual work that is self-motivated and self monitored. Do not be afraid to engage in it.

Strategies for Creative Thinking

The nation that neglects creative thought today will assuredly have its nose ground into the dust of tomorrow.
—Fred Hoyle (1915–2001, astronomer and physicist)

Creativity has never been given the attention it deserved in standard educational settings. Over a half century ago, Lowenfeld (1962) called creativity "education's stepchild," a fact that remains true today. There seems to be no place in the traditional school curriculum for creativity training. There have been many programs developed with the specific goal of training people to be creative in order to fill this gap, probably because leaders in the corporate and manufacturing worlds know that they must produce new and better products than the competition, or they find will find themselves working for the competition.

Basic Principles

> Real world problems can only be solved through the study of differing viewpoints. It is not enough to tolerate differing viewpoints, you must examine them deeply enough to understand why they differ from yours.
> —Maggie Shiffrar (May 17, 2012 Commencement Address,
> Rutgers Graduate School)

Although there are considerable differences between creativity training programs, they all share some basic common principles:

- Teach students to think of different ways to accomplish an objective and then how to select the best one.

- Provide plenty of examples and exercises to model and practice creative skills.

- Teach students how to ask relevant questions and how to discover when a problem exists.

- Evaluate the quality of an idea by its consequences.

- Reward original and relevant ideas, but be certain to keep the reward secondary to the enjoyment of the creative process. Let students know that their ideas are valuable and that they remain in control of their work.

- Provide unstructured situations. Teach them the value of persistence when they fail.

- Provide students with a tangible plan for finding solutions. This means that they should be trained in ways that will help them to make relevant information that they have stored in memory accessible and to find ways to bridge areas of knowledge. Plans include recognizing puzzling facts, seeking information, generating possible solutions, changing perspectives, and restating the goal.

- Restrain from labeling or categorizing problems or solutions too quickly in the problem-solving process because labeling tends to encourage fixation—the opposite sort of set that is needed for flexible thinking.

- Create the expectation that creative outcomes result from hard work, persistence, a broad knowledge base, and the willingness to continue thinking after a satisfactory solution or answer has been found.

- Encourage risk-taking and nonconformity, along with a repertoire of responses that are needed for teamwork.

You may be thinking that there is no such thing as "strategies for creative thinking" because creativity involves breaking rules, not following them— a sort of a free activity. But, most creative actions take place within a framework of rules. Even the most beautiful sonnet contains 14 lines of specified meter and rhyme, all great ballets are performed with the principles and techniques of dance, and all scientific discoveries are made by experts who are knowledgeable in their field. In order to depart from a framework or to bend the usual rules, the creative individual must have some knowledge of convention as well as some guidelines for unconventional thinking.

There are some popular educational programs that claim to increase creativity, but unless there are solid data to back up these claims, you are not thinking critically if you accept the claims at face value. Mall book stores have rows of books that lure readers who want to be more creative to "try on different hats" and to stimulate different ways of thinking by "thinking outside of the box"— quick claims that offer little in the way of empirically validated findings (De Bono, 1985, 1992). Critical thinkers look for evidence to support claims— especially when the claim is that thinking can be improved.

Quantity Breeds Quality

Since 1990, 30% of [Glaxo Wellcome's] revenues has come from new products . . . Glaxo Wellcome aims to increase research and development productivity threefold to produce 20 new compounds from exploratory research each year, leading to the launch of three significant new products annually.
—Sue Godfrey (Executive Director, Glaxo Wellcome, 1998, p. 14)

The notion that if you have lots of ideas, some of them will be good is the major thrust of **brainstorming**. Brainstorming was discussed in the chapter on the development of problem-solving skills as a way to find solution paths that solve problems. It is a creative way to generate solution paths and is often used in creative problem solving. As explained in the last chapter, brainstorming is a way of producing a list of ideas that can subsequently be evaluated. Research supports the finding that people usually generate more ideas when they brainstorm alone than when in groups. Most brainstorming is now done in two stages—alone, then followed by group activities. The only rule of brainstorming is that all judgment be deferred until some later time so that no one hesitates to offer unusual or off-beat ideas.

The quantitative advantages of brainstorming are without question. But do more ideas necessarily imply better ones? Often, the best ideas result from the combination (synergy) and alteration of the ideas listed. The atmosphere of deferred judgment is clearly consistent with the discussion on environment presented earlier in the chapter. It encourages risk-taking and unconventionality, both of which are prerequisites to creative thinking. At the very least, brainstorming is fun. It is a recommended strategy for enhancing creative thought because it incorporates several of the principles for creative thinking, but the evidence that brainstorming produces more high-quality ideas than other techniques is still limited.

Creative Ideas Checklist

Another method for producing creative ideas is to present people with a checklist of diverse categories or adjectives or questions that could conceivably apply to the question or problem at hand. These lists are called **creative ideas checklists**. By forcing people to change the type of answer that they are considering, flexibility in thinking is encouraged. Doolittle (1995) found that the use of many different types of solutions is more important in creative problem solving than just having many different solutions that all involve the same category of response. In order to understand this distinction, consider a problem that involves moving A to B. There may be many different ways to move A (car, boat, roller skates), but a flexible list would include other categories of responses, such as having them meet in the middle, or moving B, or moving both to point C, or solving the problem without moving either A or B.

In one study of the use of lists to stimulate creative ideas, Davis and Roweton (1968) gave students the following list, which was labeled "Aids in Thinking of Physical Changes":

A. Add or Subtract Something

B. Change Color

C. Change the Materials

D. Change by Rearranging the Parts

E. Change Shape

F. Change Size

G. Change Design or Style

Students who were given this list were told to, "List as many physical changes as you can for a thumbtack." Davis and Roweton reported that the group that had received the checklist produced a greater number of ideas and more creative ideas than a control group that had not been given the checklist. A cookie manufacturer began making "reverse" chocolate chip cookies—chocolate cookies with white chocolate chips. They became an overnight financial and taste success. You should recognize this simply as "d" in the above list—a change by rearranging the parts. This simple creative act has paid well for its innovator.

Perhaps the most famous checklist is a generalized one that can be applied in a variety of situations. Whiting (1958, p. 62) attributes this list to Osborn. Suppose you wanted to design a new type of refrigerator or computer display. These prompts should provide direction for beginning the creative process.

Put to Other Uses? New ways to use as is? Other uses if modified?

Adapt? What else is like this? What other idea does this suggest? Does past offer parallel? What could I copy? Whom could I emulate?

Modify? New twist? Change meaning, color, motion, odor, form, shape? Other changes?

Magnify? What to add? More time? Greater frequency? Stronger? Larger? Thicker? Extra value? Plus ingredient? Duplicate? Multiply? Exaggerate?

Minify? What to substitute? Smaller? Condensed? Miniature? Lower? Shorter? Lighter? Omit? Streamline? Split up? Understate?

Substitute? Who else instead? What else instead? Other ingredient? Other material? Other process? Other power? Other place? Other approach? Other tone of voice?

Rearrange? Interchange components? Other pattern? Other layout? Other sequence? Transpose cause and effect? Change pace? Change schedule?

Reverse? Transpose positive and negative? How about opponents? Turn it backward? Turn it upside down? Reverse roles? Change shoes? Turn tables? Turn other cheek?

Combine? How about a blend, an alloy, an assortment, an ensemble? Combine units? Combine purposes? Combine appeals? Combine ideas?

In a twist on the idea of lists that stimulate creative thinking, McGuire (1997) listed several techniques for finding creative hypotheses that are worth pursuing. The research literature in psychology and other sciences is huge, but much of it involves problems that are trivial (at least in the opinions of some people). How can researchers find and recognize those research problems that are potentially important? The list of strategies for answering this question includes: (a) **counterexamples** or thinking about ways the opposite would be true (e.g., instead of thinking that bad parents cause neurosis, suppose bad parenting causes good mental health); (b) **reverse causal direction** (e.g., instead of hypothesizing that coffee causes headaches, maybe having headaches leads people to drink coffee); (c) **push an example to an extreme** (e.g., if children's use of grammar shows that they learn general grammatical rules, what would perfect grammar in children suggest?); (d) **extrapolate from similar problems** (e.g., older adults can improve their memory for names with mnemonics, so perhaps they could improve their memory for locations with mnemonics); (e) **shift attention to the opposite end of a problem** (e.g., instead of thinking about the cost of a new technology, think about its benefits); and (f) **pay attention to outliers or unusual responses** (what is it about Person X that led her to respond differently from the other participants?). McGuire's list is considerably longer than the sample items presented here, but these examples should demonstrate the main idea of manipulating how one thinks to discover hypotheses that are potentially important enough to warrant empirical investigation. He notes that he has only informal data on the effectiveness of these strategies and calls for more research on the important problem of finding out which techniques can enhance creativity.

Although the purpose of creative ideas checklists is to create novel ideas, it is also possible that they could have an inhibiting effect. If you only considered the possibilities on a small checklist, you could miss other ideas by narrowing your search to ones that are suggested by the list. These lists cannot be used as algorithms that would always lead to a creative response, but they may be helpful as heuristics to help get a stalled thinking process moving again.

We have all had the experience at one time or another of being "stuck," when ideas do not seem to flow. If you go through these checklists, pondering each item, you are bound to get your thoughts flowing again. Using the cognitive framework introduced earlier, they all provide probes for searching knowledge networks so that different sorts of information can become available for use.

Attribute Listing

> More innovation is the key weapon for UK companies to outperform world competitors.
>
> —Peter McHardy and Teresa Allan (2000, p. 496)

In **attribute listing**, every characteristic or quality of the item or situation is listed and then examined for possible modification or recombination. Let's try an example.

Suppose you want to make something really different for dinner tonight. In fact, you want to make a food that no one else in the world has ever tasted before. How would you go about doing this? First, you could list many different foods:

eggs
hot dogs
Baked Alaska
stewed tomatoes
steak tartare
chocolate pudding
etc.

Alongside each food, you would list several of its attributes, such as shape, consistency, color, texture, odor, temperature, etc. You would then randomly pair attributes to come up with a new food. You might think of the "soft and shimmery" attribute of Jell-o and the cold, hard attribute of ice cream and combine the two so that you'd freeze the Jell-o or whip the ice cream. Attribute listing is a good procedure for fashion design. You could list every part of a dress, for example, and every attribute of that part. A partial example is:

Dress Part	Attribute
collars	pointed, rounded, none, Nehru
sleeves	raglan, short, rolled, long
waist	cinched, gathered, dropped, loose
skirt	full, straight, ruffled, pointed

A talented dress designer could combine possible dress attributes, coming up with thousands of unique designs (e.g., a dress with a Nehru collar, short sleeves, gathered waist, and ruffled skirt.) This unique combination shows why I should stay out of fashion design—while the resulting dress would be unusual, it would probably not pass the evaluative test for creativity—appropriate or good.

Crovitz's Relational Algorithm

Those of you who have already read the chapter on the development of decision-making skills know that an algorithm is a step-by-step guide that leads to a solution. Crovitz's (1970) **Relational Algorithm** is a solution guide that relies on changing the relations between items. Crovitz lists 42 "relational words" (p. 100). They are:

about	at	for	of	round	to
across√	because	from	off	still	under √
after	before	if	on	so	up√
against√	between√	in√	opposite	then	when
among	but	near√	or	though	where √
and	by	not	out	through	while
as	down√	now	over	till	with

When you are in need of a creative solution, you have only to try different ways of "relating" the elements. Crovitz uses Duncker's classic x-ray problem as an example. Although this problem was described in the chapter on the development of problem-solving skills, I will present it again briefly. The problem is to get rid of an inoperable stomach tumor with x-rays without harming the healthy tissues. However, when the radiation is intense enough to destroy the tumor, it will also harm the healthy tissue surrounding it. The best solution involves using several weak rays through different parts of the body so that they will summate on the tumor. Crovitz (1970,

p. 102) demonstrated how the relational algorithm can be used to find a solution to this and other problems. The procedure is fairly simple. Form a sentence with each relational word using it as it might relate to the tumor. For example:

- Take the rays **through** the esophagus.
- Take the sensitivity **from** the tissues.
- Take tissue **off** the tumor.
- Take strong rays **after** weak rays.
- Take a shield **on** stomach walls.
- Take the tumor **across** the stomach.
- Take a cannula **through** the stomach wall.
- Take the power **from** the rays.
- Take the tumor **to** the exterior.

Crovitz claimed that this method works well because it forces the individual to consider new relationships between the parts of the problem.

Plus, Minus, Interesting

Plus, Minus, Interesting (PMI) is a plan for beginning the problem-solving process that was suggested by de Bono (1976). When you are searching for a solution to an intractable problem, one way to begin is to list all of the "givens" in a problem and all possible solutions (even ones that are unrealistic) and to consider for each what is positive about it, what is negative about it, and what makes it interesting. The idea behind this process is that a careful and methodic consideration of various components of different solutions and other aspects of the problem will help the problem-solver to find new solutions by highlighting positive aspects and eliminating negative ones. The use of the "interesting" category will help the problem-solver to consider what makes a solution interesting and thereby lead to the consideration of additional alternatives. It is a plan for seeking information that may be relevant to a solution, and like all of the other strategies, it provides a guide for exploring knowledge nets.

Activating Inert Knowledge

All of the strategies for creative thinking are designed to increase the "flow of ideas." Psychologists call this improving "**ideational fluency**." The problem-solver is given a plan for generating ideas. She is told the kind of information she should consider (givens and possible solutions) and how to evaluate them. Earlier in this book, I talked about the importance of tickling memory. This is particularly important when you seem to have "run out of ideas." There are several simple plans that can be employed when this happens. For example, in a study described by Perkins (1985), children were instructed to list words that they might use when writing a composition about a selected topic. The children were given a few minutes to complete this prewriting task. The researchers reported that after only a few hours of training with this method, the children were writing longer and better passages. Let's consider the simple elegance behind this procedure. By listing topic-relevant words, the students were required to think about their knowledge of the topic *before* they began to write. They made their knowledge about the topic more available for use in their composition. It forced them to plan their response.

There is some evidence that people can learn to be more creative by practicing creative tasks such as writing slogans, nicknames, and identifying similarities and differences between objects (Benedek, Finke, & Neubauer, 2006). The researchers concluded that ideational fluency can be increased with training, and they argue for the use of computer-based training programs to enhance creativity. It is clear that we can all be more creative when creativity is valued and encouraged.

Writing is one of the most creative tasks that we can be asked to do. Students and even prolific authors often complain about "writer's block." The simple method of first generating words related to a topic is applicable at all levels and should help to eliminate writer's block because it is a way of activating one's knowledge of the topic so that it can be used. I have used it in several college classes that I teach with good results.

Browsing

In our society, we have great institutions that function as repositories for ideas. They are called libraries. Of course, the Internet offers a seemingly limitless amount of information that could stimulate new ideas. Pick up newspapers and magazines, case histories and biographies, scholarly journals, joke books, and even children's literature. Use a broad range of sources. You cannot make "remote associations" or borrow ideas from other fields if your own knowledge is confined to a narrow discipline. This technique is easier than ever because there are many quality resources available online, so we can "browse" in our jammies late at night, but be careful—there is also a great deal of worthless and even harmful junk on the Internet. Be sure that you can tell the difference between scholarly and applied research, and unsubstantiated "hot air" that is blowing around on the Internet.

Use qualitative and quantitative information. Census reports can suggest new problems because they succinctly state what people are doing, where they are doing it, what they are eating, how they are living, and how they are dying. Learn something new every day. If you pick up a journal at random and read one new article a day, you will be surprised at how the newly acquired information crops up in everyday contexts. You can also browse with quality television shows like Point of View, 60 minutes, and National Geographic. They contain a wealth of fascinating information on almost any topic of interest. Do not forget to go to museums, art galleries, theater, and the opera. If you feel that you cannot afford these outings, remember that many have a "free day" once a month and offer reduced rates for students, the elderly, and groups.

Visual Thinking

> When Mozart was asked where he got his ideas he said, "Whence and how they come I know not; nor can I force them."
> —(quoted in P. E. Vernon, 1970, p. 53)

Creative thinking often calls for images. The musician must first "hear" the sounds before she places the notes on paper, the poet must hear the rhyme before it is written, the painter must see the forms before his first brush stroke, and the chef must "taste" the combination of ingredients before the new recipe is created. It does seem that there are certain creative acts for which words are inadequate. Most people report that, at least some of the time, they think in images. An **image** is a picture-like representation in the mind. (See the chapter on the development of memory skills for a discussion of imagery.)

Gonzalez, Campos, and Perez (1997) examined the relationship between imagery and creativity. They gave high school students tests of imagery and spatial ability and the Torrence Test of Creative Thinking. They found positive relationships between imagery and creativity, which were stronger for the students with high IQs than for students who score within the average range on intelligence tests. Other researchers have suggested a relationship between creativity and imagery. The rationale behind this proposed relationship is that good imagers should be able to "see" problems in ways that should help them to generate solutions that are different from their peers who are low in the ability to create images. A suggested method for solving problems is to draw a diagram, thus transforming a verbal problem into a visual one. Adams (1979) calls visual thinking an "alternative thinking language." It is an alternative to verbal-based thought. Adams suggests that we each take a drawing course to improve our ability to see and, in turn, to think creatively. He claims that we can improve our visual thinking with practice, but like many similar claims, the evidence is not presented in a form that can be scrutinized.

Imagine the following (Adams, 1979, p. 91):

A pot of water coming to a boil and boiling over;

Your Boeing 747 being towed from the terminal, taxiing to the runway, waiting for a couple of other planes, and then taking off;

Your running cow changing slowly into a galloping racehorse;

An old person you know well changing back into a teenager;

A speeding car colliding with a giant feather pillow.

Putting it all Together

Several different strategies or methods to produce creative thoughts have been presented. It would be naive to believe that if you can recite each of these methods, you will automatically have creative thoughts. They are merely guidelines for hard work, and some of us will have to work harder than others.

It is clear that creative thinking is a skill that can be cultivated. The strategies presented in this chapter are the plans for developing that skill. You may be wondering, "Where do I begin?" You begin with a problem or a need. For some, creative ideas will immediately seem to flow; for others, it will be more like pulling teeth. If you find yourself "out of fresh new ideas," try the techniques listed above. Visualize the situation, use analogies and metaphors, consider relations, list attributes, mull checklists, and brainstorm. The creative process within you should ignite with some help from these strategies.

Chapter Summary

- Creativity involves the dual notion of unusual or unique and good or useful. Because both of these attributes always involve judgment, people may not agree on which actions or outcomes deserve to be labeled "creative."

- DeBono has made a distinction between vertical thinking and lateral thinking. Vertical thinking is logical and straightforward, while lateral thinking is a creative way to think "around" a problem.

- An increasingly popular view in psychology is that creative individuals are not qualitatively different from the rest of us. We all have the ability to be creative.

- Virtually all creative acts will involve novel ways of defining a problem, selecting relevant information, and judging the quality of the solution.

- Creativity has been described as a blend of sensitivity, synergy, and serendipity. It is as if a fortuitous event brings together remote ideas in a person who is sensitive to their combination.

- Creativity can be understood as a cognitive process that involves using the information stored in memory to go beyond what is learned from experience. Cognitive psychologists describe the process as a spread of activation through a knowledge network with repeated cycles of generation and exploration.

- Although it is true that, in general, intelligent people are, broadly speaking, more creative than less intelligent people, it seems that a minimal level of intelligence is all that is needed for creative expression.

- Groups tend to be more creative than individuals working alone, but only when the group process fosters creativity by structuring group interactions so that members are supportive of each other but also able to dissent.

- Insight, which has been described throughout this book as characteristic of System 1 thinking, is an important component to creative thinking. To develop insight, you will need to work on predictable projects and develop expertise. There is no quick and easy route to insight.

- Analogies are often part of the creative process in which solutions are adapted from different domains of knowledge.

- Creative people tend to be self-motivated, persistent, tolerant of ambiguity, self-confident, and willing to take risks.

- Intrinsic motivation seems to be one of the best predictors of creative behavior. In order to encourage the production of creative outputs, the environment should be designed to support intrinsic motivation. Extrinsic motivation can encourage creativity, but it works only when it conveys the idea that the person is creative and self-determination is not undermined.

- Several strategies to foster creative thinking were presented. Brainstorming is based on the supposition that if you have many ideas some of them will be good. Each item on a checklist of creative ideas can be applied to a problem to see if a creative spark is struck. Crovitz's relational algorithm relies on changing the relations between the parts of a problem to arrive at a solution. The Plus, Minus, Interesting strategy encourages novel solutions by requiring the problem-solver to evaluate various aspects of the problem. Analogies and metaphors tune us in to similarities and differences that can be valuable in creating novel solutions. Visual thinking seems to be involved in many sorts of creative endeavors—especially the arts and sciences. The easiest way to foster creativity is to value it.

- All of the strategies to enhance creativity involve searching an individual's knowledge net so that remote ideas can be associated, analogies can be applied across domains of knowledge, and information that is stored in memory can become available.

The following creative thinking skills were developed in this chapter. Review each skill and be sure that you understand how to use each one.

- defining a problem in multiple ways
- brainstorming to increase the number of ideas produced (first alone, then in a group)
- working with people from different backgrounds in order to increase the probability of bisociative thinking
- considering the physical changes listed in the creative ideas checklist
- arranging the environment to maximize intrinsic motivation or use extrinsic motivation in ways that convey positive messages about creativity
- encouraging an attitude of risk-taking

- evaluating possible solutions using the suggestions for altering a product
- listing and combining attributes to devise a novel product
- forming sentences about the problem using relational words
- evaluating solutions and other aspects of the problem along the dimensions of plus, minus, interesting
- listing terms that are related to the problem before you attempt a solution
- gathering additional information
- using analogies to make the unfamiliar known and distorting analogies to make the familiar unknown
- visualizing the problem
- using hypothesis-generating suggestions, such as considering counterexamples, opposites, anomalous data, and the others
- discouraging group cohesiveness so unusual thoughts can be considered.

Terms to Know

You should be able to define or describe the following terms and concepts. If you find that you are having difficulty with any term, be sure to reread the section in which it is discussed.

Creativity. The act of producing something that is original and useful.
Lateral Thinking. Thinking "around" a problem. Used to generate new ideas. Sometimes used as a synonym for creative thinking. Compare with vertical thinking.
Vertical Thinking. Thinking that is logical and straightforward. Used in the refinement and development of ideas. Compare with lateral thinking.
Sensitivity. Responsiveness to the information we perceive through our senses, which includes "noticing" stimuli that may be critical to a creative solution.
Synergy. The bringing together of seemingly disparate parts into a useful and functioning whole. Creative thinking often seems to involve such combinations.
Bisociative Thinking. Bringing together two previously unassociated ideas or "frames of reference."
Serendipity. A happy, unexpected discovery.
Paradigm. An example that is used as a pattern.
Geneplore. Term coined by Finke, Ward, and Smith (1992) to denote the cycles of generation and exploration that are part of the creative process.

Metaphor. An analogy or comparison that notes similarities between two things that are basically dissimilar.

Insight. Sudden awareness of a solution.

Incubation. A period of time when not working on a solution that is followed by a successful solution.

Spread of Activation. When information is recalled, related information in memory becomes partially activated and more available for recall.

Ideational Fluency. A flow of ideas. Strategies to enhance creativity are designed to enhance the way ideas are generated.

Intrinsic Motivation. Inherent desire to engage in a task for its own sake and without regard for reward or punishment.

Extrinsic Motivation. Engaging in a task in order to receive reward or to avoid punishment.

Brainstorming. A group or individual method for generating solution paths for problems. Problem-solvers are encouraged to think up wild, imaginative solutions and to defer judgment on these solutions until a later time when they may be modified or combined. The goal is to produce a large number of possible solutions. Best when first done alone, followed by group process.

Creative Ideas Checklists. Lists that suggest ways to generate creative ideas by varying a problem's components and relationships between the components.

Attribute Listing. A method of generating creative solutions in which every characteristic or quality of the item or situation is listed and then examined for possible modification or recombination.

Relational Algorithm. A method for generating creative ideas that relies on changing the relations between items using relational words such as "on," "between," "under," and "through."

Plus, Minus, Interesting. De Bono's (1976) plan for searching for a solution by noting positive, negative, and other interesting aspects of the solutions being considered.

Ideational Fluency. The process of generating many ideas in order to solve problems.

Bionics. The use of analogies from nature that can be adapted to human problems.

Image. A picture-like representation in the mind.

Answers to remote associations presented earlier in the chapter: 1. Bill 2. Nail 3. Pot 4. Fly 5. Coach

CHAPTER 11

THE LAST WORD

Contents

Thinking is like loving and dying:
Each must do it for him (her) self.

—Anonymous

Congratulations! Because of your expertise in critical thinking, you landed a high-level management position with one of the world's largest international chocolate companies. Sadly, you received news that child labor is being used to produce cocoa. Consumers have no idea how complex it is to get cocoa to market. Your company has 40,000 separate suppliers in Africa. An international work force is dependent on the success of your company to pay their bills, and consumers seem to care more about getting high-quality chocolate than the use of forced child labor. Changes in your production methods will drive up the price of your product, which will probably reduce sales and consequently profits, but it is hard to estimate how sales will vary as a function of price because your company has never had a single large price increase. The ethics are clear—you will not continue to use child labor. But your ethics cloud when you learn that many of these children are supporting their families, who might starve without their income. The problem is real-world messy. It involves many of the skills presented throughout this book. How do you tackle a problem of this size and severity? (Case adapted from Chatterjee & Elias, 2007)

This scenario is a case study that is used in business schools, but it is based on an investigative series of child labor in the production of cocoa that was authored by Sumana Chatterjee (2008). She described her experiences: "My job was to spark the thinking process" (para 2). This sort of messy real-world problem is exactly the sort that requires critical thinking. Apply what you have learned in this book to this problem and the many others that you will face as a responsible adult in the 21st century. You need to frame the problem in multiple ways and then determine which thinking skills will help you get to a desired goal.

As you worked your way through this book, you learned how to use a wide variety of critical thinking skills; now all you have to do to become a better thinker is use them appropriately. Each chapter dealt primarily with one category of critical thinking skills—using likelihoods to reduce uncertainty, analyzing and making arguments, solving problems with a variety of hints and prompts, and reasoning with quantifiers, to name just a few. The separation of critical thinking skills into categories was necessary so that the skills could be learned and practiced in manageable units. Unfortunately, critical thinking does not break into neat and separate categories, and mixed sorts of skills are needed in most situations. Memory must always be accessed, the type of representation and the words we use influence how we think, evidence always needs to be considered, thinking must be logical, and so on. As you go through life, you will need to use all of the skills that you practiced and improved in each of the chapters. But, most importantly, you need to adopt the attitudes and dispositions of a critical thinker. You need to find problems that others have missed, support conclusions with good evidence, and work persistently on a host of problems.

It may be useful to think about critical thinking skills as a tool box filled with many skills. The trick, if there is one, is to select the right skill for the right task. A framework for thinking is proposed to guide that process.

Framework for Thinking

Thinking . . . is continuous, a series of informed improvisations more like those of a jazz musician than the playing of a classical musician performing a set piece of music from a score.
—Richard M. Restak (1988, p. 233)

Unfortunately, there is no simple "how to" formula that can be used in every situation that calls for critical thought. You already know about the importance of planning as one of the attitudes or predispositions for critical thinking, but knowing that it is important to plan is of little value if you do not know how to plan. Consider the following advice about wilderness survival that appeared in a phone directory:

Wilderness Survival

Things you must NOT do:

- Wear brand new boots.
- Leave an open fire unattended.
- Panic. If you meet trouble, stop and think.

I am sure that the first two recommendations are excellent, but I am less confident about the value of telling someone to think without any instructions about how to go about it. Presented below is a general, all-purpose framework or guide that can be used to direct the thinking process. It is not a sure-fire guarantee to good thinking (there are none), but it is a way of getting started and ensuring that the executive processes needed in thinking—planning, monitoring, and evaluating—are being used in a reflective manner. You can probably guess why these are called executive processes. They function like the "boss" in a busy office by directing the flow of work and deciding where to put the available resources. The framework is a series of questions, some of which may be repeated several times during the thinking process, which are general enough to be useful in a wide variety of applications, including reasoning from premises, analyzing arguments, testing hypotheses, solving problems, estimating probabilities, making decisions, and thinking creatively.

Although the framework will remain the same for all thinking tasks, the actual skills used will vary with the nature of the task. The proposed framework is an adaptation of the problem-solving procedures originally proposed by the brilliant mathematician and scholar George Polya in 1945. Polya's model was presented in the chapter on problem solving.

As you progressed through the chapters in this book, you gained experience in applying this framework in different contexts and different knowledge domains. The thinking skills you acquired as you worked through this book will transfer to other contexts if you acquire the habit of *using* the framework. It is an easy-to-use guide that, through repeated practice, should become automatic. The following questions guide the thought process:

What is the Goal?

Critical thinking was defined as the use of those cognitive skills or strategies that increase the probability of a desirable outcome. This term is used to describe thinking that is purposeful, reasoned, and goal directed. The first step in improving thinking is to be clear about the goal or goals. What is it that you want to do? Real life problems are messy. Sometimes there are multiple goals, and sometimes you will return to this question several times, as your understanding of the goal will often change after you have worked for a while. A clearly articulated goal will provide direction to the thinking process and allow you to make better decisions about the skills you need to use. In the course of thinking about real world problems, you may need to change direction and redefine the problem and the desired outcome several times, but it is still important to have an outcome in mind to provide some focus. After all, if you do not know where you are going, you can never be sure whether you have arrived. In the problem in the opening scenario, an initial goal might have been to produce high-quality cocoa at a reasonable price without using child labor. But after learning more about the situation, the goals might shift to include the idea that you also need to help the families of the children from starving when you terminate the children's jobs. Complex real-world problems have a large variety of possible goals. The skills needed to reach these goals might include deciding between a set of possible alternative solutions, generating a novel solution, synthesizing information, evaluating the validity of evidence, determining the probable cause of some events, considering the credibility of an information source, and quantifying uncertainty.

Are you making a decision about whether to have a heart transplant or what flavor ice cream to select from the corner store? Impulsive thinking about ice cream flavors is not a bad thing and does not require critical thinking; life and death decisions do. Not everything we do in life requires critical thought, but many of life's important decisions do. The way you identify the goal should help you plan the time and effort required by the situation.

What is Known?

This is the starting point for directed thinking. Although this may seem fairly straightforward now, when you actually use this framework on real problems, you will find that you may have to return to the "knowns" several times as you interpret and reinterpret the situation. Some information will be known with certainty; other information may be only probably true or partially known. This step will also include recognizing gaps in what is known and the need for further information gathering. For example, you would want to know if the children are really being exploited or whether they work perhaps two hours a day making a good wage and spend another five hours in a quality school. (Sounds like wishful thinking, but you would need to know about the work conditions in your manufacturing plants before you can derive a solution to the problem of child labor.) There will be much data gathering and, along with it, considerations about whether the information is credible.

Which Thinking Skill or Skills will Get You to Your Goal?

Once you have some idea of where you are (the knowns or givens) and where you are going (the goal or purpose), you are better able to plan goal-directed thinking processes. Knowing how to get from where you are to where you want to be is the power of critical thinking. Just as there are many different possible goals, there are many different strategies for attaining them. Let's consider the "thinking is like a map" analogy that was presented in the first chapter because it can help to clarify some abstract concepts by making them more concrete. Suppose you are about to go on a trip to visit two old friends. One has become a Buddhist monk and lives high on a mountaintop in the Himalayas. The other has become a surfing champion and is living on the beautiful island of Hawaii. You would have to use a different method of travel to reach each destination; one involves scaling a mountain, the other deciding between a plane or boat (assuming that you are not presently on the mountaintop or in Hawaii). Similarly, you will have to use different thinking skills with different types of thought processes.

This step will involve generating and selecting the appropriate strategy to reach the goal. How can you be sure that no child labor was used to produce the products you purchase from all of your suppliers? There will need to be independent verification from trusted sources. Can you find adult family members who can learn how to produce cocoa after the children are removed from the manufacturing plants? Maybe you can set up an on-site school so the children who are now working can easily get an education that prepares them for their adult life.

Have You Reached Your Goal?

A concern with accuracy is probably the best predictor of success. Does your solution make sense? Did you find a way to eliminate all child labor from your own plant and that of your suppliers, while keeping production costs low enough to sell your chocolate at a reasonable price and while being sure that the children's families can succeed?

A Desirable Outcome

The definition of critical thinking that was used throughout this book involved the conscious use of critical thinking skills to achieve a desirable outcome. Does the idea of a "desirable outcome" seem more appropriate now that you have read this book? Schneider (2007, p. 269) provided a thoughtful analysis of what is meant by a desirable outcome:

> Some of the decisions you and I will make will be bad bets because we lacked important information and failed to use that at our disposal. But a person who wanted to win at the game of life would certainly want to act of the basis of the most accurate beliefs he could muster. Thus, the ultimate answer to the question of why beliefs matter is that those whose belief machines lead them astray will lose more of life's bets. Misery may love company, but it positively adores a corrupt belief machine.

Does the working definition of critical thinking seem like it captured the multiple dimensions of complexity that are inherent in critical thinking? Can you and will you use some of the thinking skills in your own life—to make decisions, read about and plan research, understand the structure of a written passage, think creatively, remember more effectively, and more? Are you more likely to have a desirable outcome because of something that you learned? Have you adopted at least some of the attitudes of a critical thinker?

Can Critical Thinking Save the World?

> The greatest threat to the world is ideological fanaticism, By ideological fanaticism I mean the unshakeable conviction that one's belief system and that of other in-group members is always right and righteous and that others' belief systems are always wrong and wrong-headed.
>
> —Scott Lilienfeld (2007, para. 3)

Lilienfeld (2007) asked if psychology can save the world. I am changing his question by substituting "critical thinking" for "psychology" because I believe that it is closer in meaning to what he meant. Can people learn to think better, and in doing so, resist some of the greatest horrors of the last century—Hitler's Nazism, Mao Tse Tsung's Cultural Revolution, and Pol Pot's Khmer Rouge? The answer to this question would require a grand experiment—teaching the skills of critical thinking and then seeing if we have a better world.

Even if we can never have a definitive answer to this question, there are many people around the world who believe that critical thinking can be "an effective (partial) antidote against ideological fanaticism" (Lilienfeld, 2007, para. 5). As I write this final chapter, much of world is outraged over the shooting of a young girl by the Taliban in Pakistan. Her crime? She spoke out in support of education for girls. Taseer (2012, para. 11) called her attackers "merchants of hatred," who fear education because an educated citizenry would resist the hate that is being taught instead. He eloquently explained that "Terrorism bears within it the seeds of its own destruction. What schools with a good syllabus can offer is the timeless and universal appeal of critical thinking. This is what the Taliban are most afraid of. Critical thinking has the power to defuse terrorism; it is an internal liberation that jihadism simply cannot offer."

Happily, there are some data to support the idea that we might avoid or reduce the severity of ideological fanaticism. The Holocaust was "unprecedented in its cruelty"; yet even in the nightmare that was World War II, there were incredible acts of heroism and altruism (Oliner, 1992). Rescuers risked their own lives and that of their family members to save Jews and members of other persecuted groups from a certain death. How did they differ from "bystanders" who did nothing but watch the raging carnage taking place around them? This is a complex question; Oliner, who compared rescuers to bystanders on numerous dimensions, found that the rescuers encouraged independent thinking in their own children and seem to have learned this disposition from their parents. Similarly, a recent study showed teens who were adept at making arguments when discussing contentious topics with their parents (e.g., grades, drugs) were more independent thinkers that other teens and were also better able to resist drug use (Allen, Chango, Szwedo, Schad, & Marston, 2012). It just may be that instruction in critical thinking can save the world, at least in some small part.

Going Forward

Ideas are far more powerful than guns. We don't let our people have guns. Why should we let them have ideas?

—Joseph Stalin (1879–1933)

As you look back on your journey through this book, I hope that you will recall that there is a large body of research literature showing that thinking skills and dispositions can improve with specific instruction designed to enhance critical thinking (e.g., Abrami et al., 2008). When critical thinking skills are learned and applied appropriately, people can become better thinkers. And perhaps, most hopefully, the ability to think critically just might help us achieve a better world. As you face the decisions and problems of living, I hope that you can use the knowledge gained from this book to achieve a meaningful life. You are what and how you think. Be sure to act on your thoughts and to use them to advance yourself and to improve even a small corner of the world. Think well and with great wisdom. The future depends on it.

"You've taught me how to think."

Woman to large creature: "You've taught me how to think." (Issue Publication Date: 09/12/1988, Edward Koren / *The New Yorker* Collection / www.CartoonBank.com.)

LIST OF CRITICAL THINKING SKILLS

Chapter 1

Thinking: An Introduction

Skill	Description	Examples of Use
A. Recognizing the difference between System 1 and System 2 thinking.	System 1 thinking is fast and automatic; System 2 is slower and more effortful. System 1 is informed by System 2.	If you are deciding whether to trust someone, your first and fast response reflects System 1; a slower more thoughtful response based on what you know about the person reflects System 2. System 1 is more likely to be accurate when an expert has worked in a field with regular feedback so that judgments can become self-correcting.
B. Developing the disposition of a critical thinker (CT).	CTs are willing to plan, be flexible, be persistent, are willing to correct errors, be mindful, and are able to achieve consensus when necessary.	A politician with the disposition of a CT gathers and considers information to make decisions that are in the best interest of the citizens, admits when wrong, and is able to persuade others that the chosen decision is best.

Chapter 2

Thinking Starts Here: Memory as the Mediator of Cognitive Processes

Skill	Description	Examples of Use
A. Monitoring your attention.	When reading, listening, or viewing information that you need to know be aware of, how well you are paying attention.	If you are reading a book, it is easy to move your eyes across the words without getting any meaning. Stop at the end of each section and write a sentence or two about what you have read as a way to monitor your attention.
B. Developing an awareness of the influence of stereotypes and other beliefs on what we remember.	Our beliefs about groups of people influence what we attend to and what we remember about them.	If, for example, you believe that overweight people are lazy, be especially vigilant for ways this belief is determining what you pay attention to and what you remember about an overweight friend.
C. Making abstract information meaningful as an aid to comprehension and recalling.	Concrete information that you are able to visualize is easier to recall than abstract concepts that are not easily visualized.	Abstract concepts such as some principles in physics or government are difficult to comprehend and recall. Relate them to something that is already known and meaningful.
D. Using advance organizers to anticipate new information and to prepare for reading information that provides a guide	Information that provides a guide for learning can be helpful when viewed before learning.	Most books have a table of contents that you should read carefully before reading the text because the organizing structure will make learning and remembering easier.

Skill	Description	Examples of Use
for learning can be helpful when viewed before learning.		
E. Organizing information so that it can be recalled more easily.	Random lists of items are more difficult to recall than information that is organized into categories.	Organize information in ways that are meaningful to you. For example, when learning human anatomy, organize parts according to their role in the body, proximity to each other, or some other categorization.
F. Overlearning because you know that it will increase the probability and accuracy of recall.	Memory traces are strengthened when you review newly learned materials several times after the initial learning.	Review any topic you recently learned as a way of ensuring long-term retention.
G. Recognizing that although you may be very confident that you are recalling an event accurately, there is a high probability that your memory is not as accurate as it feels.	People are often highly confident about memories that are inaccurate.	By understanding that you may be confident in your memory for some event and that this memory may be inaccurate, you can avoid many errors based on using that memory (e.g., wrongfully convicting someone based on eye witness testimony).
H. Generating retrieval cues at both acquisition and retrieval.	Isolated information is more difficult to recall than information that has many connections in memory.	When learning something, link the new information to something that you already know. Look for connections so that the newly learned information will be easier to recall.

(Continued)

Skill	Description	Examples of Use
I. Practicing recall for information that you are intentionally trying to learn.	This is called the "testing effect." By repeatedly recalling information, it gets easier to recall in the future.	When you finish learning a new skill, such as how to use new software, try new examples of how it might be used and continue to use the software spaced over many days and weeks until it is well-learned.
J. Monitoring how well you are learning.	While you are learning something new, make judgments about how well you are learning.	Be sure that you can summarize newly learned information and estimate how well you are learning. If the learning is not going well, exert more effort in the learning process.
K. Using external memory aids.	An external aid is a written list or calendar reminder, among others.	If you need to do something at some point in the future, use an alarm system on you smart phone or write it down where you will see it when it needs to be done.
L. Applying cognitive interview techniques.	A cognitive interview is a series of techniques that can help people recall events, these techniques include being complete, changing the order of recall, and changing perspective.	When trying to remember where you left your phone, consider the order of events forward and backward when you last used it and try to "see" these events from different viewpoints.
M. Developing an awareness of biases in memory so that you can consider the	People tend to recall information that that supports a favored conclusion and to recall events that	Deliberately seek and attend to information that disconfirms a belief and learn to discount (not ignore) vivid, personal, and familiar events. Remember that "quiet" disasters such as

Skill	Description	Examples of Use
way your own beliefs, attitudes, and background knowledge could be influencing what and how you remember.	are vivid, personal, and familiar.	deaths from driving are more frequent than ones that involve a group of people at one time, such as a plane crash, yet many more people fear plane crashes.
N. Employing keywords and images, rhymes, places, and first letters as internal memory aids.	Mnemonics are memory aids that individuals use to help them recall information.	To remember a list of points you need to list in response to an essay question, use the first letters to make a word or sentence or visualize them at different locations along a route.

Chapter 3

The Relationship between Thought and Language

Skill	Description	Examples of Use
A. Recognizing and defending against the inappropriate use of emotional language, labeling, name calling, ambiguity, vagueness, and arguments by etymology.	This is an assortment of common misleading verbal techniques based on language usage in which a bias for or against a position is created with the connotative meaning of the words used to describe and define the concepts.	CT recognizes the use of biased language in numerous contexts, such as the following examples: (a) accidental killing of us troops referred to as "friendly fire"; (b) use of labels such as "pro-choice" and "pro-life" to create favorable impressions; (c) reports of research that "suggests" a finding instead of stating the results; (d) use of the term "disinformation" instead of "lies"; (e) calling an opponent a "pinko"; (f) using obscure terminology as a way

(*Continued*)

Skill	Description	Examples of Use
		of inhibiting comprehension; (g) arguing that homosexuality must be sick because the word "gay" originally meant lewd and lascivious.
B. Developing the ability to detect misuse of definitions, reification, euphemism, and bureaucratese.	These techniques mislead by using arbitrary definitions, treating a construct as though it physically exits, substituting a more "polite" term for the one that is intended, and using stilted language.	In a discussion of whether alcoholism is a disease, CT knows that the answer depends on the way the term "disease" is defined. A hypothetical construct is defined and then treated as though it were objectively real, such as the use of terms like "self-defeating personality" to attribute blame to women who are battered. Euphemism is substituting "bathroom tissue" for "toilet paper" (which can also be thought of as a euphemism); "Witnesseth" in legal documents is bureaucratese.
C. Thinking about the reason for a communication, the background knowledge of the listener, and the context when deciding what and how to communicate.	Six rules: tell listener what they want to know, don't say what they already know, vary style according to listener characteristics, be truthful, use a simple style, use context to clarify meaning.	If telling a child about your job as a programmer, explain in simple language how you write the information that makes computers do tasks and show a simple example.

Skill	Description	Examples of Use
D. Understanding the use of framing with leading questions and negation.	A framed question or negation creates an expectation for the type of response.	CT recognizes the bias in questions like "which of the presidential candidates is worse?" (implication that both are bad) and "don't you agree that the company plan is sure to work?" (bias toward a positive response).
E. Using analogies appropriately, which includes examining the nature of the similarity and its relationship to the conclusion.	Analogies are effective persuasive techniques—good analogies are based on underlying relationships that are validly transferable between the analogy and base domain.	In response to a suggestion that welfare recipients serve on welfare boards, a board member replied that this was like suggesting that the mentally retarded serve on the boards for their mental institutions. CT asks if the analogy between the mentally retarded (who cannot act intelligently) and welfare recipients is valid.
F. Deliberately giving a variety of examples when thinking about members of a category so that you are not thinking about category members in terms of a prototype (e.g., thinking about many ways to be successful, not just the most common examples like making a high salary).	People tend to think about examples from a category in terms of the most typical member—for example, a robin or sparrow for a bird.	By deliberately giving atypical answers, you might respond with penguin or emu when asked about a bird.

(*Continued*)

Skill	Description	Examples of Use
G. Recognizing the emotional components of some words and the way word choices can affect how you think and feel.	Words have cognitive and emotive meanings.	Mother's Cookies have an appealing name even if you know they are baked by a large international corporation and not a lone sweet mother who cares about you.
H. Recognizing when an anchor may be biasing your judgments about a quantity or cost and deliberately trying other values that could be alternative anchors.	An anchor is a beginning number that influences your judgments.	You are more likely to give more money to a charity when the request for a donation starts at $1,000 rather than if it starts at $5.
I. Employing questioning and explaining as a skill for text comprehension.	The ability to state a main idea and identify supplementary ideas are essential for comprehension.	An extended presentation is made in which the speaker includes a main idea, supplemental information, and irrelevant information. CTs can summarize meaningfully what has been said.
J. Practicing at retrieval of information so that remembering becomes more accurate and easier with spaced practice.	One of the best ways to learn something is to practice remembering it.	In order to remember these skills, answer questions spaced over time about each skill and then check the accuracy of your answer.

Skill	Description	Examples of Use
K. Selecting and using graphic organizers (linear arrays, hierarchies, networks, matrices, flow charts).	Converting information from verbal to graphic formats is one measure of comprehension that can be useful in applying the information provided.	Information about a spatial topic, such as the plan for a new community, is presented in prose. CTs can convert the information to a spatial representation. Alternatively, CTs can chart relationship information when it is presented in prose (e.g., matrices, hierarchies).

Chapter 4

Reasoning: Drawing Deductively Valid Conclusions

Skill	Description	Examples of Use
A. Discriminating between deductive and inductive reasoning.	Recognizing the differences between reasoning from a rule to an individual (deductive) and from individual observations to formulate rules (inductive).	Inferring attitudes from behaviors (inductive) and predicting behavior from someone's stated attitudes (deductive).
B. Identifying premises and conclusions.	Being able to recognize what is being advocated and the reasons for it.	Reading a ballot issue and knowing the positions that are supported and why they are being supported.
C. Using quantifiers in reasoning.	Understanding the use of terms like "every," "some," and "not".	Knowing that "doctors recommend" means "some doctors recommend".

(Continued)

Skill	Description	Examples of Use
D. Using circle diagrams to check category membership.	Combining class membership categories to determine what can be concluded with circles that represent category relationships.	Some high school students studied Latin. All students who studied Latin went to college. Can we conclude that some high school students went to college? Solve this with circle diagrams by combining all combinations of representations of the premises.
E. Solving categorical syllogisms with verbal rules.	There are 7 rules that can used to determine if the conclusion from a categorical syllogism is valid.	All students need math. Harry is not a student. Is it valid that Harry does not need math? Check for a middle term (one not in the conclusion) and whether it is distributed in a premise. Check for negation in the conclusion and premises and whether the conclusion is particular. By going though each rule, you can determine if a conclusion is valid.
F. Understanding the difference between truth and validity.	Knowing that a conclusion can be valid, but false.	It may be valid to believe that welfare spending should be increased given a set of premises, but the premises and the conclusion may be wrong.
G. Recognizing when syllogisms are being used to change attitudes.	A particular attitude is being advocated when premises are followed with evaluative statements that support a belief.	For example, "juveniles commit many crimes. They need alternatives to crime. So, fund activities for juveniles.

Skill	Description	Examples of Use
H. Using linear diagrams to solve linear syllogisms.	Being able to arrange objects along a dimension.	Kalin arrived before Joe or Roberto, but after Alex. Who arrived first?
I. Watching for marked adjectives.	Mark adjectives bias evaluations.	"How dumb is he?" is not a neutral question.
J. Using the principles of linear orderings as an aid to clear communication.	It is easier to understand linear orderings when the first term in the second premise is the second term in the first premise and when all statements are positive.	Running burns more calories than walking, and walking burns more calories than sitting.
K. Reasoning with "if, then" statements.	"If, then" statements express contingency relationships.	If Heather wants to graduate, she will study. The "if" part is the antecedent; the "then" part is the consequence.
L. Avoiding the fallacies of confirming the consequent and denying the antecedent.	Denying the antecedent is saying that the "if" part did not occur; affirming the consequent is saying that the consequent occurred.	Look at the example above. Saying that Heather does not want to graduate does not mean that she will not study. Saying that she will study does not mean that she wants to graduate.
M. Examining reasoning in everyday contexts for missing quantifiers.	Often statements will not include terms like "all," "some" or "no."	Saying that children who are abused will have difficulty in personal relationships does not mean "all" children who are abused although that may be what people want to hear.

Chapter 5

Analyzing Arguments

Skill	Description	Examples of Use
A. Identifying arguments.	An argument is an attempt to persuade a listener or reader with at least one reason and one conclusion.	We must increase social security benefits because they have not kept pace with inflation. But, some elderly are rich and don't need an increase.
B. Diagramming the structure of an argument.	In an argument, conclusions are supported by reasons. There are also counterarguments, assumptions, and limiting conditions.	Cheating is okay because everyone does it, and teachers expect students to cheat becomes:
C. Evaluating premises for their acceptability.	Premises are acceptable if we can reasonably believe they are true.	The reason "everyone does it" is not acceptable. The reason "teachers expect students to cheat" is not acceptable.
D. Judging the credibility of an information source and knowing the difference between expertise in factual matters and in value matters.	Judgments of credibility and bias are central to determining the quality of information. Credible sources have expertise, first-hand knowledge, and no basis for gain.	The executives of a car company tout the safety features of their new model car. A veterinarian argues for the use of animals in research.

Skill	Description	Examples of Use
E. Determining the consistency, relevance to the conclusion, and adequacy in the way premises support a conclusion.	Premises need to relate to the conclusion and they need to be consistent with each other.	Cotton candy is a healthy snack because it is all natural and high in nutrients. In this argument, the premise that sugar, the only ingredient in cotton candy, is all natural may be true, but it does not make it a healthy snack. It is not high in nutrients, so this argument is unacceptable.
F. Remembering to consider missing components by assuming a different perspective.	The most persuasive information may be omitted, either deliberately or accidentally.	"Candidate Dogooder is great because he is kind to his dog." Is other information omitted, like he is a convicted rapist?
G. Assessing the overall strength of an argument.	Good arguments have strong support. There may be counterarguments, but even when they are considered, overall strength can be good.	The political parties cannot get along even though some members of each party are willing to compromise. The failure to pass good laws is evidence that they cannot get along. This is a fairly strong argument because the evidence (premise) is strong and even though it is weakened some by the counterargument, it is still strong.
H. Recognizing, labeling, and explaining what is wrong with each of the 21 fallacies that was presented.	There are many common fallacies—deliberately weak arguments, claims that x is true because there is no disconfirming evidence, association arguments.	We cannot ban semi-automatic weapons because all guns will be banned once we start. The health plan is bad because the conservatives support it. Ghosts must exist because no one can prove that they don't.

(Continued)

Skill	Description	Examples of Use
I. Recognizing differences among opinion, reasoned judgment, and fact.	Opinion is an unsupported preference; reasoned judgment is a conclusion based on reasons for believing it; facts have verifiable truth values.	CTs can recognize the differences between: "unions are needed for the protection of workers, and that's a fact." "Sugar-os is a good cereal because it contains fiber." and "Sugar-os are a good cereal because I love the way sugar-os taste."
J. Understanding how visual arguments can be effective.	Images can present conclusions and premises.	An image of a sexy teen admired by many is making the argument that it is good for teens to appear sexy.
K. Judging your own arguments for their strength.	Arguments should be structured so that the reasons support what is being advocated.	When writing an essay against the death penalty, the writer can identify her own reasons and counterarguments and show their relative strength.

Chapter 6

Thinking as Hypothesis Testing

Skill	Description	Examples of Use
A. Recognizing the need for and using operational definitions.	An operational definition is an explicit set of procedures that specify how to recognize and measure a construct.	An advocate for a group claims that unreported spousal abuse is increasing at an alarming rate. CTs will ask how spousal abuse has been defined and measured.
B. Understanding the need to isolate and control variables	In determining cause, a single variable is manipulated, and	A commercial states that cholesterol levels were reduced when a group began exercising and using

Skill	Description	Examples of Use
in order to make strong causal claims.	the results attributed to that variable are compared to comparable control groups in which the variable was not manipulated.	margarine. It concludes that margarine use reduces cholesterol. CTs note the confounding of exercise and margarine use and do not attribute the drop in cholesterol to margarine.
C. Checking for adequate sample size and unbiased sampling when a generalization is made.	Valid generalizations from samples can only be made when the sample size is adequately large (relative to the variability) and the sample is representative of the population.	As part of a conversation, a young adult states that she knows that old people like to watch wrestling because her grandmother did. CTs recognize that this sample is too small and biased for generalizations about all old people.
D. Being able to describe the relationship between any two variables as positive, negative, or unrelated.	Two variables are positively related when increases in one occur concomitantly with increases in the other, negatively when increases in one occur concomitantly with decreases in the other, and are unrelated when changes in one variable are independent of changes in the other.	A newspaper article states that over the last 10 years, marijuana use has steadily increased and scholastic achievement test scores have decreased. CTs can describe this as a negative relationship, but understand that the decline in marijuana probably did not cause the rise in test scores.

(*Continued*)

Skill	Description	Examples of Use
E. Understanding the limits of correlational reasoning.	Although a significant correlation between two variables can suggest that changes in one variable causes change in the other variable, this is weak evidence for determining cause.	A social scientist shows that there has been steady increase in the number of single parent families and in the number of crimes committed by juveniles over the last 15 years. She concludes that single-parent families are responsible for the increase in juvenile crime. CTs note that these data are correlational and cannot be used to determine cause.
F. Seeking converging validity to increase your confidence in a decision.	The use of multiple types of measures that support the same conclusion is convergent validity.	To decide if a program really does improve learning, gather data from multiple users and use different types of data, such as school grades and standardized tests.
G. Checking for and understanding the need for control groups.	A control group is used for comparison to understand if an intervention "worked." We are limited in what we can conclude without a control group.	When viewing test scores, you may see that on average, 7th graders at your local school improved over the last three years. Without a control group, you cannot understand what this means. By comparing the scores with everyone in the state, you may find that all scores were raised because the test was made much easier.
H. Being aware of the bias in most estimates of variability.	Most data are variable, and people tend to underestimate variability.	A CT knows the even though he can name many outstanding graduates from a snooty college, many students from that college did not have outstanding careers after graduation. Students are variable.

(Continued)

Skill	Description	Examples of Use
I. Considering the relative "badness" of different sorts of errors.	Some errors are worse than others, and because there is always uncertainty in hypothesis testing, the relative "badness" of an error needs to be considered.	Under U.S. law, it is worse to wrongly convict someone of a crime than it is to let a guilty person go free, so we require evidence that is "beyond a reasonable doubt" when deciding on a guilty verdict.
J. Determining how self-fulfilling prophecies could be responsible for experimental results or every day observations.	When we believe that a certain outcome is likely, we often act in ways that make it more likely.	If you believe that soup cures a cold, you are more likely to judge cold symptoms as improved after having soup, even if there is no effect.
K. Knowing when causal claims can and can't be made.	To decide if x caused y to occur, x must occur before y and you must be able to rule out other confounding variables that might have caused y.	If children who attended preschool are better readers, you cannot know if going to preschool caused the improvement or some other variable, such as richer kids attend preschool. This is why we need random assignment to groups to determine cause.

Chapter 7

Likelihood and Uncertainty: Understanding Probabilities

Skill	Description	Examples of Use
A. Computing expected values in situations with known probabilities.	An expected value is what is most likely to happen in the long run—over many trials.	The expected value of any probabilistic event can be computed by multiplying the probability of each outcome with its value.
B. Recognizing when regression to the mean is operating and adjusting predictions to take this phenomenon into account.	An extreme score on some measure is most likely followed by a score that is closer to the mean.	It is a common phenomenon that a star "rookie" who excels in his or her first season performs closer to average in the second season. CT recognizes that this is an example of regression to the mean.
C. Using the "and" rule to avoid conjunction errors.	The co-occurrence of two or more independent events is less likely than the occurrence of either one alone.	Physicians describe the typical heart attack victim as male and over 55. CT realizes that the typical heart attack victim is more likely to be either male or over 55 than both male and over 55.
D. Using the "or" rule to calculate cumulative probabilities.	The probability of either of several (or more) probabilistic results is the sum of the probability of each event.	If the chance of rain is 0.5 for Saturday and for Sunday, the probability of rain on exactly one of these days is 0.5 (rain Saturday is 0.5; not rain Saturday is 0.5. Each of these "branches" is connected to rain on Sunday which is 0.5 and not rain on Sunday, which is 0.5; thus rain on both days = 0.25; rain Saturday only 0.25; rain Sunday only 0.25; rain neither day 0.25).

Skill	Description	Examples of Use
E. Recognizing and avoiding gambler's fallacy.	Gambler's fallacy is the belief that is a probabilistic event that has not occurred in recent trials it is more likely to occur.	When flipping a fair coin, someone who believes in this fallacy will predict that a head is more likely to occur if the previous four flips were tails.
F. Utilizing base rates when making predictions.	The initial or a priori proportion of some group in the population is a valid guide for predicting likelihoods.	A speaker meets a "quiet man who is good with numbers." The speaker concludes that this man is more likely an accountant than a farmer. CT knows that the number of accountants in the population is small relative to farmers and predicts farmer as the more likely occupation.
G. Using tree diagrams as a decision making aid in probabilistic situations.	A tree diagram represents every possible outcome in a series of outcomes (e.g., birth of boys or girls) with probability values along each branch.	A tree diagram for the problem about rain on one day in the weekend is:
H. Adjusting risk assessments to account for the cumulative nature of probabilistic events.	The likelihood of two events occurring is always less than the less likely event.	If the probability of becoming a professional basketball player is 0.01 and the probability of living in NY is 0.02, then the probability of becoming a professional basketball player and living in NY is less than 0.01.

(*Continued*)

Skill	Description	Examples of Use
I. Understanding the differences between mean and median.	The median is the middle number in a series arranged in ascending (or descending order); the mean is the sum of all numbers divided by the number of numbers added together.	If three friends earned $8, $20, and $500 an hour, the median is $20, the mean is $176 an hour—big difference.
J. Avoiding overconfidence in uncertain situations.	By definition, there is uncertainty in probabilistic events, but most people are more confident in their decisions than the probabilities allow.	The stock market is probabilistic with many random variations, yet some people invest too much money on a particular stock because they have overestimated the probability that the stock will continue to rise.
K. Understanding the limits of extrapolation.	Extrapolation is using trends in data to make estimations of future events—a process that is meaningful only if it is not extended too far in time and other factors can be assumed to remain constant.	The population council concludes that, based on current birth rates, there will be no resources to feed the multitudes by the year 2050. CTs know that the extrapolation is based on the assumption that there will be no changes in contraception, fertility practices, or food resources.
L. Using probability judgments to improve decision making.	Most future events are uncertain. It is often possible to estimate the probability of outcomes, which can lead to better decisions.	If the probability of rain in your region is 68% in a particular month, it would not be a good idea to plan an outside wedding if the idea of rain on your wedding is highly aversive.

(*Continued*)

Skill	Description	Examples of Use
M. Considering indicators like historical data, risks associated with different parts of a decision, and analogies when dealing with unknown risks.	New risks can be considered by using historical data, calculating the probability of component parts, and using analogies.	A chemical warfare plant is planned for your community. CTs can think about risks by looking at other similar plants, estimating component risks, and using analogies from other chemical plants.

Chapter 8

Decision Making: It is a Matter of Choice

Skill	Description	Examples of Use
A. Listing alternatives and considering the pros and cons of each.	Coming up with several possible ways to satisfy the goals of the decision.	Two alternatives are 1) provide incentives to keep health care costs down; 2) add basic medical information to high school curricula.
B. Reframing the decision so as to consider different types of alternatives.	The deliberate use of different ways of phrasing a decision that needs to be made.	Changing the wording in a decision such as "how can we provide low cost health care to everyone?" To "how can we reduce the cost of quality health care?"
C. Recognizing the need to seek disconfirming evidence and deliberately seeking disconfirming evidence.	There is a pervasive bias to seek information that confirms what we believe to be true.	Make a conscious effort to find information that would not support the decision to have children when you are inclined to have children.

(*Continued*)

Skill	Description	Examples of Use
D. Understanding the way that information that is readily recalled or information that appears representative of a random process can influence how decisions are made.	Information that is readily recalled seems more familiar and more frequent than information that is difficult to recall.	We tend to overestimate the threat of events that are easy to recall, such as a cruise boat sinking instead of events that really are more frequent, such as diabetes.
E. Considering how overly optimistic assessments bias the selection of alternatives.	People tend to believe that outcomes that they want to happen are more likely to occur than those they do not want to happen.	People who buy lottery tickets wildly overestimate their chance of winning a large amount of money.
F. Recognizing arguments that are based on entrapment and considering why the costs have been high.	Entrapment occurs when a course of action requires additional investments beyond those already made.	Shana decides to stick with her boyfriend who treats her badly because she has already invested several years in the relationship.
G. Being mindful of the way liking can affect the evaluation of alternatives.	When we like someone, we tend to evaluate information from that person as more accurate than from someone we dislike.	If a friendly physician recommends an operation, we need to be as likely to get a second opinion as when the recommendation comes from an unfriendly physician.
H. Evaluating positive assessments of alternatives that	Reciprocity is a powerful variable. We are likely to "repay" someone	We are more likely to buy a product when we receive a sample than if we do not receive a sample.

Skill	Description	Examples of Use
are based on reciprocity or familiarity.	even when the "gift" we receive is worthless and unwanted.	
I. Seeking information to reduce uncertainty when making risky decisions.	Decisions involve future events, and there is always uncertainty in the future. We can often reduce the uncertainty with more data gathering.	If you want to know about employment opportunities for someone with a computer science degree, you would review various employment predictions, including the ones from the department of labor.
J. Preparing a decision-making worksheet for important decisions.	It is a procedure for listing alternatives and important considerations and then calculating a decision.	In deciding what to do about a revolution, the leaders could list possible actions, analyze and weigh them, and then calculate a decision.
K. Understanding the distinction between the quality of a decision and its outcome.	Given the uncertainty of the future, sometimes a good decision will have a poor outcome and a poor decision will have a good outcome.	You might win by betting all of your money on a horse race, but it is still a poor decision.
L. Understanding the way emotional states like reactance and anger can affect the way we evaluate alternatives and behaving in ways that minimize their effects.	Reactance is wanting to do something we are not permitted to do, even if we would not want to do it if we were permitted.	By forbidding teen lovers to see each other, they may increase their resolve to be together just because it is not permitted.

(Continued)

Skill	Description	Examples of Use
M. Recognizing that hindsight analysis of a decision is usually biased and of limited value. Hindsight analysis is the reevaluation of a decision after its consequences are known.	Hindsight analysis is the reevaluationof a decision after its consequences are known.	After a parolee kills someone, many people want to fire the parole board. CT knows that the decision to parole the convict may have been reasonable at the time it was made.

Chapter 9

Development of Problem-Solving Skills

Skill	Description	Examples of Use
A. Planning and monitoring a strategy for finding a solution.	When solving a problem, a CT will be clear about stating the goal and the ways of getting from the start state to the goal.	If you want to save money for a new car, you need to know how much money you will need (cost of car, insurance, title, etc.) and make a plan for saving money in installations to reach your goal.
B. Identifying any problem as either well-defined or ill-defined and adjusting your solution plan according to the type of problem.	Most real-life problems are ill-defined; that is, there are many possible goals and ways to achieve them.	Several ways of increasing sales are described. CTs redefine the problem to include other ways to increase profits (e.g., cut inventory).

Skill	Description	Examples of Use
C. Using graphs, diagrams, hierarchical trees, matrices, and models as solution aids.	It is useful to use a visual representation to solve many problems.	Draw the information given in math and word problems as an aid to solving them.
D. Devising a quality representation of a problem.	Visual representations of problems can assist with comprehension and serve as a problem-solving aid.	A problem is described verbally. The task for the CT is to depict the information in a graphic display in order to solve it.
E. Selecting the problem-solving strategies that are appropriate for the problem.	There are many different strategies that can help solve problems. CTs know how to select from among them.	A problem involving categories of information is approached with a matrix, which is well suited for this sort of problem.
F. Using all of the following strategies: mean-ends analysis; working backwards; simplification; generalization and specialization; random search and trial-and-error; rules; hints; split-half method; brainstorming; contradiction; analogies and	Several strategies for solving problems were presented in the book. CTs know when each is the appropriate tool for solving a problem.	When designing a desk with a large surface area that takes up only a small amount of space, use the method of contradiction—you may end up with a desk that expands and folds for storage.

(*Continued*)

Skill	Description	Examples of Use
metaphors; consulting an expert; and crowdsourcing (when appropriate).		
G. Demonstrating an awareness of functional fixedness so as to avoid it.	Functional fixedness is the inability to see how something can be used in a way that is different from its usual function.	When you use a shoe as a hammer or a stapler to fix a hem, you are demonstrating that you can "break out of" functional fixedness.
H. Distinguishing between relevant and irrelevant information.	In real life, we often have information available that is not relevant to solving a problem.	Focusing on climate-related information can help us solve the problem of climate change without being side-tracked with irrelevant information that paints political parties in good or bad ways—political digressions unrelated to climate change.
I. Understanding how world views can constrain the problem-solving process.	We all operate in a culture and we often cannot "see" solutions that are not culturally acceptable.	In some cultures, people often barter for goods when money is short, but few people in cultures where this is not customary think about the possibility of bartering.
J. Recognizing the critical role of persistence.	One of the best predictors of success when solving problems is persisting until a good solution is found.	When encountering a difficult problem, a CT doesn't quit when a solution is not immediately obvious, but keeps working on it.

Chapter 10

Creative Thinking

Skill	Description	Examples of Use
A. Defining a problem in multiple ways.	Phrase the problem in several different ways to come up with different types of solutions.	Instead of asking "How can I get a new job?" Ask "What do I really want from a job?" Or "How can I have more money?"
B. Brainstorming to increase the number of ideas produced.	Without censoring or evaluation, list as many solutions to the problems as possible.	In finding ways to save money, list every money savings idea you can. Best if done alone first and then in a group.
C. Working with people from different backgrounds in order to increase the probability of bisociative thinking.	People from various backgrounds will approach novel problems in different ways.	Form a diverse team to solve difficult problems, such as how to improve the lives of poor people around the world.
D. Considering the physical changes listed in the creative ideas checklist.	Generate and use lists of ways that a solution can vary.	If designing a new toy, list ways that toys can vary—size, color, etc.
E. Arranging the environment to maximize intrinsic motivation.	Intrinsic motivation is often related to creative thinking. It is the desire to work on a problem because the process is enjoyable.	Avoid setting time limits on solutions (to the extent possible) and paying for creative outcomes.

(Continued)

Skill	Description	Examples of Use
F. Encouraging an attitude of risk taking.	Creative thinking is unusual by definition. We need to encourage people to take some risks and break away from traditions.	Do not punish poor outcomes or failures to solve novel problems because these responses will discourage risk taking.
G. Evaluating possible solutions using suggestions for altering products.	Think how you can combine, reverse, or substitute to create a novel product.	When thinking about new ways to cook, combine ingredients that usually do not go together and substitute honey or apple sauce for sugar.
H. Listing and combining attributes to devise a novel product.	Create a matrix of relevant attributes and then combine cells.	List the parts of a dress and the ways each can differ, then create combinations.
I. Forming sentences about the problem using relational words.	Think about through, off, after, from, and to when considering new ways to get something done.	When planning a route with a mountain in the way, think about driving around it, over it, even through it, if that is possible.
J. Evaluating solutions and other aspects of the problem along the dimensions of plus, minus, and interesting.	List the positive, negative, and interesting aspects of various solutions.	Use these three columns to evaluate solutions to the problem of world hunger.
K. Listing terms that are related to the problem before you attempt a solution.	Before attempting a solution, write down all terms that come to mind when you think about the problem.	When thinking about ways to improve the possibilities for peace in the Middle East, list all the relevant terms that come to mind in a 10-minute interval.

Skill	Description	Examples of Use
L. Gathering additional information.	Keep the problem in mind as you.	Go about idea-enhancing activities. Read, watch quality programs, write, etc. as you think about a problem,
M. Using analogies to make the unfamiliar known and distorting analogies to make the familiar unknown.	Apply solutions and ideas across different domains of knowledge.	Use knowledge about the ways animals keep cool to design a way to keep food cool.
N. Visualizing the problem.	Image yourself as part of the problem and try to "see" it from other perspectives.	View the problem of teen violence from the perspective of the teens, police, victims, parents, etc.
O. Using the hypothesis generating suggestions such as counter-examples, opposites, anomalous data, and the others.	Thinking about ways the opposite could be true (clothing could be warm and light), extrapolating from similar problems, and paying attention to outliers can help CTs be more creative.	Think why one person responded very differently from the other people—could it be a difference in how the question was understood? How can something be both hot and cold at the same time?
P. Discouraging group cohesiveness so unusual thoughts can be considered	When groups require that all decisions be unanimous, they lose the input from unusual thinkers.	Encourage people to come up with different sorts of solutions and to value disagreement.

Chapter 11

The Last Word

Skill	Description	Examples of Use
A. When deciding which skill to use, think about the thinking skills framework.	The thinking skills framework is four questions: What is the goal? What is known? Which skills will get you to your goal? Have your reached your goal?	If you want to be healthy and happy, your goal is to make good health, career, and personal decisions. The knowns are information about your strengths and weaknesses. Will you exercise regularly? Eat well? Study to achieve a career goal? Engage in meaningful relationships? These sorts of long-term goals will need to be reevaluated throughout your life span.

BIBLIOGRAPHY

Abrami, P.C., Bernard, R.M., Borokhovski, E., Wade, A., Surkes, M.A., Tamim, R., & Zhang, D. (2008). Instructional interventions affecting critical thinking skills and dispositions: A stage 1 meta-analysis. *Review Of Educational Research, 78*, 1102–1134. doi:10.3102/0034654308326084

Ackerman, J.M., Nocera, C.C., & Bargh, J.A. (2010). Incidental haptic sensations influence social judgments and decision. *Science, 328*(5986), 1712–1715. doi:10.1126/science.1189993

Adams, J.L. (1979). *Conceptual blockbusing: A guide to better ideas.* New York: Norton.

Advertising Age. (2012, 23 April). Mexican campaign encourages you to swap dog poop for free wi-fi. Retrieved from http://adage.com/article/creativity-pick-of-the-day/mexican-campaign-encourages-swap-dog-poop-wi-fi/234324/

Allen, J.P., Chango, J., Szwedo, D., Schad, M., & Marston, E. (2012). Predictors of susceptibility to peer influence regarding substance use in adolescence. *Child Development, 83*, 337–350. doi: 10.1111/j.1467-8624.2011.01682.x

Allport, G.W. (1954). *The nature of prejudice.* Cambridge, MA: Addison-Wesley.

Amabile, T.M. (1996). *Creativity in context: Update to the social psychology of creativity.* Boulder, CO: Westview.

Amabile, T.M. (1997). Motivating creativity in organizations: On doing what you love and loving what you do. *California Management Review, 40*, 39–58.

Amabile, T.M. (2001). Beyond talent: John Irving and the passionate craft of creativity. *American Psychologist, 56*, 333–336.

American Cancer Society. (2012). Learn about cancer. Retrieved from http://www.cancer.org/Cancer/CancerCauses/TobaccoCancer/QuestionsaboutSmokingTobaccoandHealth/questions-about-smoking-tobacco-and-health-cancer-and-health

American Management Association. (2010). *AMA 2010 Critical skills survey.* Executive Summary. Retrieved from http://www.p21.org/documents/Critical%20Skills%20Survey%20Executive%20Summary.pdf

American Psychiatric Association. (1994). *Diagnostic and statistical manual of mental disorders.* Washington, DC: Author.

American Psychiatric Association. (2012, 20 January). DSM-5 proposed criteria for autism spectrum disorder designed to provide more accurate diagnosis and treatment. Retrieved from http://www.psych.org/MainMenu/Newsroom/

NewsReleases/2012-News-Releases/DSM-5-Proposed-Criteria-for-Autism-Spectrum-Disorder-Designed.aspx?FT=.pdf

American Psychiatric Association. (2013). *Diagnostic and Statistical Manual*, Fifth Edition: DSM-5 Author, Washington, DC. ISBN-10: 0890425558

Anderson, B. F. (1980). *The complete thinker: A handbook of techniques for creative and critical problem solving*. Englewood Cliffs, NJ: Prentice-Hall.

Anderson, D. M., & Rees, D. I. (2011, November). Medical marijuana laws, traffic fatalities, and alcohol consumption. Institute for the Study of Labor, Discussion Paper No. 6112. Retrieved from http://ftp.iza.org/dp6112.pdf

Anderson, J. R., Bothell, D., Byrne, M. D., Douglass, S., Lebiere, C., & Qin, Y. (2004). An integrated theory of the mind. *Psychological Review, 111*(4), 1036–1060. doi:10.1037/0033-295X.111.4.1036

Andersson, H., & Bergman, L. R. (2011). The role of task persistence in young adolescence for successful educational and occupational attainment in middle adulthood. Developmental Psychology, 47(4), 950–960. doi:10.1037/a0023786

Animal Farm Defense. (2009, 12 October). Legal defense based on the Orwellian notion that "some are more equal than others." *The New York Times*. Retrieved from http://schott.blogs.nytimes.com/2009/10/12/animal-farm-defense/

Appleton-Knapp, S. L., Bjork, R. A., & Wickens, T. D. (2005). Examining the spacing effect in advertising: Encoding variability, retrieval processes, and their interaction. *Journal of Consumer Research, 32*(2), 266–276. doi:10.1086/432236

Ariely, D. (2003). Dan Ariely. Retrieved from http://momentum.media.mit.edu/ariely-long.html

Ariely, D. (2009). *Predicably irrational: The hidden forces that shape our decisions*. Revised and expanded ed. New York, NY: HarperCollins.

Aristotle. (1954). Rhys Roberts (Trans.), *Rhetoric III* 1410b, 1st Modern Library ed. New York: Modern Library (exact wording varies by translation).

Arkes, H. R. (1996). The psychology of waste. *Journal of Behavior and Decision Making, 9*, 213–224.

Arkes, H. R., & Gaissmaier, W. (2012). Psychological research and the prostate-cancer screening controversy. *Psychological Science, 23*(6), 547–552. doi: 10.1177/0956797612437428

Arkes, H. R., & Hammond, K. R. (1986). Law. In H. R. Arkes & K. R. Hammond (Eds.), *Judgement and decision making: An interdisciplinary reader* (pp. 211–212). Cambridge, MA: Cambridge University Press.

Arum, R., & Roksa, J. (2011). *Academically adrift*. Chicago, IL: University of Chicago Press.

Asimov, I. (1989, 31 March). Combatting US scientific illiteracy. *Los Angeles Times*, p. 8.

Association of American Colleges & Universities. (2010). *Raising the bar: Employers' views on college learning in the wake of the economic downturn*. Retrieved from http://www.aacu.org/leap

Atkinson, R. C. (1975). Mnemotechnics in second-language learning. *American Psychologist, 30*(8), 821–828.

Ayton, P., Onkal, D, & McReynolds, L. (2011). Effects of ignorance and information on judgments and decisions. *Judgment and Decision Making, 6*, 381–391.

Bahrick, H. P., & Hall, L. K. (1991). Lifetime maintenance of high school mathematics content. *Journal of Experimental Psychology: General, 120*(1), 20–33.

Ball, L.J., Phillips, P., Wade, C.N., & Quayle, J.D. (2006). Effects of belief and logic on syllogistic reasoning: Eye-movement evidence for selective processing models. *Experimental Psychology, 53,* 77–86. doi:10.1027/1618-3169.53.1.77

Balota, D.A., Pilotti, M., & Cortese, M.J. (2001). Subjective frequency estimates for 2,938 monosyllabic words. *Memory & Cognition, 29,* 639–647. doi:10.3758/BF03200465

Bargh, J.A. (2007). *Social psychology and the unconscious: The automaticity of higher mental processes.* New York, NY: Psychology Press.

Bargh, J. (2008, 23 October). *Research by Williams and Bargh featured in The New York Times.* Retrieved from http://www.yale.edu/acmelab/news.html

Bargh, J.A., & Williams, L.E. (2006). The automaticity of social life. *Current Directions in Psychological Science, 15,* 1–4.

Barkun, M. (2006). A culture of conspiracy: Apocalyptic visions in contemporary America. Berkley and Los Angeles, CA: University of California Press.

Baron, J. (1990). Harmful heuristics and the improvement of thinking. In D. Kuhn (Ed.), *Developmental perspectives on teaching and learning thinking skills* (pp. 28–47). New York: Basel, Karger.

Baron, J. (1993). Why teach thinking?—An essay. *Applied Psychology: An International Review, 42,* 191–214.

Baron, J. (1994). Nonconsequentialist decisions. *Behavioral and Brain Sciences, 17,* 1–42.

Baron, J. (1995). My side bias in thinking about abortion. *Thinking and Reasoning, 1,* 221–225.

Baron, J. (1997). Biases in the quantitative measurement of values for public decision. *Psychological Bulletin, 122,* 72–88.

Baron, J., & Brown, R.V. (1991). *Teaching decision making to adolescents.* Hillsdale, NJ: Lawrence Erlbaum Associates.

Barron, F. (1958). The psychology of imagination. *Scientific American, 199,* 151–166.

Bartlett, J. (1980). Familiar quotations: A collection of passages, phrases, and proverbs traced to their sources in ancient and modern literature. 15th and 125th anniversary eds. Boston: Little Brown.

Basadur, M., & Basadur, T. (2011). Where are the generators? *Psychology of Aesthetics, Creativity, and the Arts, 5*(1), 29–42. doi:10.1037/a0017757

Bearman, C.R., Ball, L.J., & Ormerod, T.C. (2007). The structure and function of spontaneous analogising in domain-based problem solving. *Thinking & Reasoning, 13*(3), 273–294. doi:10.1080/13546780600989686

Bednall, T.C., & Kehoe, E.J., (2011). Effects of self-regulatory instructional aids on self-directed study. *Instructional Science, 39,* 295–226. doi:10.1007/s11251-009-9125-6

Begley, S. (2010, 5 August). The limits of reason: Why evolution may favor irrationality. *Newsweek Magazine.* Retrieved from http://www.thedailybeast.com/newsweek/2010/08/05/the-limits-of-reason.html

Beilensen, J., & Jackson, H. (Eds.). (1992). *Voices of struggle, voices of pride.* White Plains, NY: Peter Pauper Press, Inc.

Bell, C. (2012, October). Critical evaluation of information sources. Retrieved from http://library.uoregon.edu/guides/findarticles/credibility.html

Benedek, M., Fink, A., & Neubauer, A.C. (2006). Enhancement of ideational fluency by means of computer-based training. *Creativity Research Journal, 18*(3), 317–328. doi:10.1207/s15326934crj1803_7

Berger, D. (1995). Errors in judgments and decisions: Understanding our cognitive fallibilities. In P. Foster (Ed.), *Critical thinking: Views and values in college teaching* (pp. 48–68). Riverside, CA: La Sierra University Press.

Bernstein, D.M., Erdfelder, E., Meltzoff, A.N., Peria, W., & Loftus, G.R. (2011). Hindsight bias from 3 to 95 years of age. *Journal of Experimental Psychology: Learning, Memory, and Cognition, 37*(2), 378–391. doi:10.1037/a0021971

Beshears, J., Choi, J.J., Laibson, D., & Madrian, B.C. (2006, January). The importance of default options for retirement savings outcomes: Evidence from the United States. *NBER Working Paper Series.* Retrieved from http://www.nber.org/papers/w12009.pdf?new_window=1

Binning, K.R., Sherman, D.K., Cohen, G.L., & Heitland, K. (2010). Seeing the other side: Reducing political partisanship via self-affirmation in the 2008 presidential election. *Analyses of Social Issues and Public Policy, 10,* 276–292. doi:10.1111/j.1530-2415.2010.01210.x

Bishop, F.L., Jacobson, E.E., Shaw, J.R., & Kaptchuk, T.J. (2012). Scientific tools, fake treatments, or triggers for psychological healing: How clinical trial participants conceptualize placebos. *Social Science & Medicine, 74*(5), 767–774. doi:10.1016/j.socscimed.2011.11.020

Blalock, G., Kadiyali, V., & Simon, D.H. (2005, 5 December). Driving fatalities after 9/11: A hidden cost of terrorism. Retrieved from http://dyson.cornell.edu/faculty_sites/gb78/wp/fatalities_120505.pdf

Bluedorn, H. (2008). Red herring. Fallacy Detective. Retrieved from http://www.fallacydetective.com/news/read/red-herring

Bloom, P. (2012). Reason. In J. Brockman (Ed.), What is your favorite deep, elegant or beautiful explanation? New York, NY: HarperCollins.

Boddy, C. (2012). The Nominal Group Technique: An aid to brainstorming ideas in research, *Qualitative Market Research: An International Journal, 15*(1), 6–18. doi:10.1108/13522751211191964

Boden, M.A. (1990). *The creative mind: Myths & mechanisms.* New York: Basic Books.

Bonnefon, J., Dubois, D., Fargier, H., & Leblois, S. (2008). Qualitative heuristics for balancing the pros and cons. *Theory and Decision, 65*(1), 71–95. doi:10.1007/s11238-007-9050-6

Bonnefon, J., Eid, M., Vautier, S., & Jmel, S. (2008). A mixed Rasch model of dual-process conditional reasoning. *The Quarterly Journal of Experimental Psychology, 61,* 809–824. doi:10.1080/17470210701434573

Bonnefon, J., Feeney, A., & De Neys, W. (2011). The risk of polite misunderstandings. *Current Directions in Psychological Science, 20*(5), 321–324. doi:10.1177/0963721411418472

Bornstein, B.H., & Greene, E. (2011). Jury decision making: Implications for and from psychology. *Current Directions in Psychological Science, 20,* 63–67. doi:10.1177/0963721410397282

Bower, G.H. (1970). Organizational factors in memory. *Cognitive Psychology, 1,* 18–46.

Bower, G.H., & Clark, M.C. (1969). Narrative stories as mediators for serial learning. *Psychonomic Science, 14,* 181–182.

Bower, G.H., Lazarus, R., LeDoux, J.E., Panksepp, J., Davidson, R.J., & Ekman, P. (1994). What is the relation between emotion and memory? In P. Ekman & R.J.

Davidson (Eds.), The nature of emotion: Fundamental questions (pp. 301–318). New York, NY: Oxford University Press.

Bradbury, R. (1950). *Fahrenheit 451*. New York: Simon & Schuster.

Braine, M.D. (1978). On the relation between the natural logic of reasoning and standard logic. *Psychological Review, 85*(1), 1–21.

Bransford, D. (1979). *Human cognition: Learning, understanding and remembering*. Belmont, CA: Wadsworth.

Bransford, J.D., Arbitman-Smith, R., Stein, B.S., & Vye, N.J. (1985). Improving thinking and learning skills: An analysis of three approaches. In J.W. Segal & S.F. Chipman (Eds.), *Thinking and learning skills: Volume 1. Relating instruction to research* (pp. 133–206). Hillsdale, NJ: Lawrence Erlbaum Associates.

Bransford, J.D., & Johnson, M.K. (1972). Contextual prerequisites for understanding: Some investigations of comprehension and recall. *Journal of Verbal Learning & Verbal Behavior, Vol. 11*(6), 717–726.

Brennan, J. (1993, May). Why polls can be poles apart. *The Los Angeles Times*, p. A5.

Brim, O.G. Jr. (1966). High and low self-estimates of intelligence. In O.G. Brim, R.S. Crutchfield & W.H. Holtzman (Eds.), *Intelligence: perspectives 1965*. New York: Harcourt, Brace & World.

Broda-Bahm, K. (2010, 1 February). Stop searching for the perfect analogy (but don't surrender a communication lifesaver). *Persuasive Litigator*. Retrieved from http://www.persuasivelitigator.com/2010/02/stop-searching-for-the-perfect-analogy-but-dont-surrender-a-communication-lifesaver.html

Brown, A.L., & Campione, J.C. (1990). Communities of learning and thinking or a context by any other name. In D. Kuhn (Ed.), *Developmental perspectives of teaching and learning thinking skills. Contributions to human development* (Vol. 21, pp. 108–126). Basel, Switzerland: Karger.

Bruer, J.T. (1993). *Schools for thought: A science of learning in the classroom*. Cambridge, MA: MIT Press.

Bucciarelli, M., & Johnson-Laird, P.N. (1999). Strategies in syllogistic rasoning. *Cognitive Science, 23*, 247–306.

Bugliosi, V. (1978). *Till death do us part*. New York: Bantam Books.

Buonomano, D. (2011). *Brain bugs: How the brain's flaws shape our lives*. New York, NY: W.W. Norton.

Burton, R. (2009, 12 March). PBS's latest infomercial, *Salon*. Retrieved from http://www.salon.com/2009/03/12/mark_hyman/

Butler, H.A. (2012). Halpern Critical Thinking Assessment predicts real-world outcomes of critical thinking. *Applied Cognitive Psychology*. doi:10.1002/acp.2851

Butler, H., & Halpern, D.F. (2012). Educating psychological literate students: The importance of critical thinking. In S. McCarthy, V. Karandashev & L. Dickson (Eds.), *Teaching Psychology around the World Vol 3*. Cambridge, U.K.: Cambridge Scholars Publishing.

Butler, H.A., & Halpern, D.F. (2011). Critical Thinking. *Oxford Bibliographies Online*. New York, NY: Oxford University Press. Available from OBO website: http://aboutobo.com/

Byrne, R. (1988). *One thousand nine hundred eleven best things anybody ever said*. New York: Fawcett.

Campbell, J., & Mayer, R.E. (2009). Questioning as an instructional method: Does it affect learning from lectures? *Applied Cognitive Psychology, 23*(6), 747–759. doi:10.1002/acp.1513

Carey, J., Foltz, K., & Allan, R.A. (1983, 7 February). The mind of the human machine. *Newsweek.*

Carkhuff, R.R. (1973). *The art of problem solving.* Amherst, MA: Human Resource Development Press.

Carlson, E. (1995). Evaluating the credibility of sources: A missing link in the teaching of critical thinking. In D.F. Halpern & S.G. Nummedal (Eds.), Psychologists teach critical thinking (Special issue). *Teaching of Psychology, 22*, 39–41.

Carney, R.N., & Levin, J.R. (2011). Delayed mnemonic benefits for a combined pegword-keyword strategy, time after time, rhyme after rhyme. *Applied Cognitive Psychology, 25*(2), 204–211. doi:10.1002/acp.1663

Carpenter, S.K., Cepeda, N.J., Rohrer, D., Kang, S.K., & Pashler, H. (2012). Using spacing to enhance diverse forms of learning: Review of recent research and implications for instruction. *Educational Psychology Review, 24*, 369–378. doi:10.1007/s10648-012-9205-z

Carroll, D.W. (1986). *Psychology of language.* Belmont, CA: Brooks/Cole.

Carroll, L. (1871). *Through the looking glass.* London: Oxford University Press

Catapano, P. (2011, 25 March). War of semantics. *The New York Times.* Retrieved from http://opinionator.blogs.nytimes.com/category/the-thread/page/4/?scp=7&sq=timothyfish&st=cse

Ceci, S.J., & Ruiz, A.I. (1993). Inserting context into our thinking about thinking: Implications for a theory of everyday intelligent behavior. In M. Rabinowitz (Ed.), *Cognitive science foundations of instruction.* Hillsdale, NJ: Lawrence Erlbaum Associates.

Chance, P. (1986). *Thinking in the classroom: A survey of programs.* New York: Teachers College Press.

Chang, J. (1993). *Wild swans: Three daughters of China.* New York: HarperCollins.

Chapman, L.J., & Chapman, J.P. (1959). Atmosphere effect re-examined. *Journal of Experimental Psychology, 58*, 220–226.

Chatterjee, S. (2008). Student profile: Case study. *Yale School of Management.* Retrieved from http://mba.yale.edu/news_events/CMS/Articles/6332.shtml

Chatterjee, S., & Elias, J. (2007, 27 November). Yale Case 07–039 (revised August 14, 2008). *Yale School of Management.* Retrieved from http://mba.yale.edu/MBA/curriculum/pdf/cadburycase.pdf

Chen, I. (2011, 6 September). How accurate are memories of 9/11? *Scientific American,* Retrieved from www.scientificamerican.com/article.cfm?id=911-memory-accuracy

Cheng, P.W., & Holyoak, K.J. (1985). Pragmatic reasoning schemas. *Cognitive Psychology, 17*(4), 391–416.

Ciladini, R.B. (1993). *Influence: Science and practice* (3rd ed.). Glenview, IL: Scott Foresman.

Cialdini, R.B., Trost, M.R., & Newsom, J.T. (1995). Preference for consistency: The development of a valid measure and the discovery of surprising behavioral implications. *Journal of Personality and Social Psychology, 69*, 318–328. doi:10.1037/0022-3514.69.2.318

Clemens, S. L. (1897). *Following the equator*. Hartford: The American Publishing Co.

Clinton's message to USA's students: Learn to earn. (1994, February). *USA Today International Edition*, p. 6A.

Cohen, G. L., Garcia, J., Apfel, N., & Master, A. (2006). Reducing the racial achievement gap: A social-psychological intervention. *Science, 313*, 1307–1310.

Cole, K. C. (1995, June). Finding the truth is a slippery thing. *Los Angeles Times*, p. B2.

Cole, K. C. (2001, June). Leaders; Poor math skills add up to bad public policy. *Los Angeles Times*, p. 8.

Connor-Greene, P. A. (2000). Assessing and promoting student learning: Blurring the line between teaching and testing. *Teaching of Psychology, 27*, 84–88.

Conway, M. A., Cohen, G., & Stanhope, N. (1991). On the very long-term retention of knowledge acquired through formal education: Twelve years of cognitive psychology. *Journal of Experimental Psychology: General, 120*(4), 395–409.

Cornelissen, J. P., & Clarke, J. S. (2010). Imagining and rationalizing opportunities: Inductive reasoning and the creation and justification of new ventures. *Academy of Management Review, 35*, 539–557.

Cowan, N. (2005). *Working memory capacity*. New York, NY US: Psychology Press. doi:10.4324/9780203342398

Cox, D., & Cox, A. D. (2001). Communicating the consequences of early detection: The role of evidence and framing. *Journal of Marketing, 65*, 91–103.

Crenshaw, D. (2008*). The myth of multitasking: How 'doing it all' gets nothing done*. San Francisco, CA: Jossey-Bass.

Crovitz, H. F. (1970*). Galton's walk: Methods for the analysis of thinking, intelligence and creativity*. New York: Harper & Row.

Cukier, K. (2010, 25 February). Data, data everywhere. *The Economist*. Retrieved from http://www.economist.com/node/15557443

Cybernation International (2002, January). *The People's Cybernation*. Retrieved from http://www.cyber-nation.com/victory/quotes/thoughtsandthinking.html

daCosta DiBonaventura, M., & Chapman, G. B. (2008). Do decision biases predict bad decisions? Omission bias, naturalness bias, and influenza vaccination. *Medical Decision Making, 28*(4), 532–539. doi:10.1177/0272989X07312723

Dahlstrom, W. (1993). Tests: Small samples, large consequences. *American Psychologist, 48*, 393–399. doi:10.1037/0003-066X.48.4.393

Damer, T. E. (1987). *Attacking faulty reasoning* (2nd ed.). Belmont, CA: Wadsworth.

d'Angelo, E. (1971). *The teaching of critical thinking*. Amsterdam: Gruner.

Dansereau, D. F. (1995). Derived structural schemas and the transfer of knowledge. In A. McKeough, J. Lupart & A. Marini (Eds.), *Teaching for transfer: Fostering generalization in learning* (pp. 93–121). Mahwah, NJ: Erlbaum.

Danziger, S., Levay, J., & Avnaim-Pesso, L. (2011). Extraneous factors in judicial decisions. *Proceedings of the National Academies of Science, 108*, 6889–6892. doi:10.1073/pnas.1018033108

Darrow, C. (1932). *The story of my life*. New York: Charles Scribner's Sons.

Davis, G. A., & Roweton, W. (1968). Using idea checklists with college students: Overcoming resistence. *Journal of Psychology, 70*, 221–226.

Dawes, R. M. (1994). *House of cards*. New York, NY: Free press.

Day, R. S., Rodin, G. C., & Stoltzfus, E. R. (1990). *Alternative representations for medication instructions: Effects on young and old adults.* Paper presented at the 3rd Cognitive Aging Conference, Atlanta.

De Acedo Lizarraga, M., De Acedo Baquedano, M., & Closas, A. (2011). Development and validation of a questionnaire to assess analogy and creativity in open problem-solving. *Studia Psychologica, 53*(3), 235–252.

De Bono, E. (1968). *New think: The use of lateral thinking in the generation of new ideas.* New York: Basic Books.

De Bono, E. (1976). *Teaching thinking.* London: Temple Smith.

De Bono, E. (1977). Information processing and new ideas—lateral and vertical thinking. In R. B. Noller, S. J.. Parnes &. A. M. Biondi (Eds.), *Guide to creative action: Revised edition of creative behavior guidebook.* New York: Scribner's.

De Bono, E. (1985). *Six thinking hats.* Boston: Little-Brown.

De Bono, E. (1992). *Serious thinking: Using the power of lateral thinking to create new ideas.* New York: HarperCollins.

De Mello, A.. (n.d.). *Brainy Quote.* Retrieved from http://www.brainyquote.com/quotes/quotes/a/anthonydem133824.html

Deci, E. L., & Ryan, R. M. (2008). Facilitating optimal motivation and psychological well-being across life's domains. *Canadian Psychology/Psychologie Canadienne, 49*(1), 14–23. doi:10.1037/0708-5591.49.1.14

Decyk, B. N. (1994). Using examples to teach concepts. In D. F. Halpern (Ed.), *Changing college classrooms: New teaching and learning strategies for an increasingly complex world* (pp. 39–63). San Francisco: Jossey-Bass.

Dees, S. M., & Dansereau, D. F. (2000). *TCU guide maps: A resource for counselors.* Fort Worth, TX: Texas Christian University, Institute of Behavioral Research.

de Groot, A. D. (1946). *Het denken van de schaker [The thought of the chess player].* Amsterdam: North-Holland.

de Groot, A. D. (1965). *Thought and choice in chess.* The Hague, The Netherlands: Mouton.

Dennis, J. P., & Wal, J. S. V. (2010). The Cognitive Flexibility Inventory: Instrument development and estimates of reliability and validity. *Cognitive Therapy Research, 34,* 241–253. doi:10.1007/s10608-009-9276-4

Deutscher, G. (2010, 26 August). Does your language shape how you think? *The New York Times.* Retrieved from http://www.westcovinabackpain.com/?gclid=CPnJ3M-84KMCFQVcagodrlbr7Q

Dewett, T., & Gruys, M. L. (2007). Advancing the case for creativity through graduate business education. *Thinking Skills and Creativity, 2*(2), 85–95. doi:10.1016/j.tsc.2007.04.001

Dewey, J. (1933). *How we think: A restatement of the relation of reflective thinking to the educative process.* Boston: Heath.

DiSalvo, D. (2011, 3 January). Power balance scam shows again that the pseudoscience song remains the same. *Psychology Today.* Retrieved from http://www.psychologytoday.com/blog/neuronarrative/201101/power-balance-scam-shows-again-the-pseudoscience-song-remains-the-same

Djulbegovic, M., Beyth, R. J., Neuberger, M. M., Stoffs, T. L., Vieweg, J., Djulbegovic, B., & Dahm, P. (2010). Screening for prostate cancer: systematic review and meta-analysis of randomised controlled trials. *British Medical Journal, 341,* 4543. doi: 10.1136/bmj.c4543

Doolittle, J.H. (1995). Using riddles and interactive computer games to teach problem solving. In D.F. Halpern & S.G. Nummedal (Eds.), Psychologists teach critical thinking (Special issue). *Teaching of Psychology, 22*, 33–36.

Dreman, D. (1979). *Contrarian investment strategy: The psychology of the stock market success.* New York: Random House.

Driver, R., Newton, P., & Osborne, J. (2000). Establishing the norms of scientific argumentation in classrooms. *Science Education, 84*, 287–312.

Drosnin, M. (1997). *The Bible code.* New York: Simon & Schuster.

Drysdale, W. (1887). *Proverbs from Plymouth pulpit.* New York: D. Appleton and Company.

Duckworth, A.L., Peterson, C., Matthews, M.D., & Kelly, D.R. (2007). Grit: Perseverance and passion for long-term goals. *Journal of Personality and Social Psychology, 92*, 1087–1101. doi:0.1037/0022-3514.92.6.1087

Dunbar, K. (1998). Problem solving. In W. Bechtel (Eds.), *A companion to cognitive science* (pp. 289–298). London: Blackwell.

Dunbar, K. (2001). The analogical paradox: Why analogy is so easy in naturalistic settings yet so difficult in the psychological laboratory. In D. Gentner & K. Holyoak (Eds.), *The analogical mind: Perspectives from cognitive science* (pp. 313–334). Cambridge, MA: The MIT Press.

Duncan, G.J., Dowsett, C.J., Claessens, A., Magnuson, K., Huston, A.C., Klebanov, P., . . . Japel, C. (2007). School readiness and later achievement. *Developmental Psychology, 43*, 1428–1446. doi:10.1037/0012-1649.43.6.1428

Duncker, K. (1945). On problem solving. *Psychological Monographs,* (Whole No. 270).

Dunning, B. (2011, 27 December). Approaching a subject skeptically. Retrieved from http://skeptoid.com/episodes/4290

Ekman, P. (1992). *Telling lies: Clues to deceit in the marketplace, politics and marriage.* New York: Norton.

Emery, G. (2001, 3 July) Failed psychic predictions for 1998: Psychic report card dubious once again. Retrieved from http://wysiwyg//17/www.csicop.org/article/psychic-predictions/1998.html

Erdelyi, M. (2010). The ups and downs of memory. *American Psychologist, 65*(7), 623–633. doi:10.1037/a0020440

Evans, J.T., & Elqayam, S. (2011). Towards a descriptivist psychology of reasoning and decision making. *Behavioral and Brain Sciences, 34*(5), 275–290. doi:10.1017/S0140525X11001440

Facione, P. (1991). *Teaching and college-level critical thinking skills.* Paper Presented at the 11th Annual International Conference on Critical Thinking and Educational Reform, Sonoma, CA.

Facione, P.A., Facione, N.C., & Giancarlo, C.A. (2000). The disposition toward critical thinking: Its character, measurement, and relationship to critical thinking skill. *Informal Logic, 20*(1), 61–84.

Factcheck.org. (2012, 8 August). Is Romney to blame for cancer death? Retrieved from http://factcheck.org/2012/08/is-romney-to-blame-for-cancer-death/

Ferguson, G. (1981). Architecture. In N.L. Smith (Ed.), *Metaphors for evaluation: Sources of new methods.* Beverly Hills, CA: Sage.

Festinger, L. (1964). *Conflict, decision and dissonance.* Palo Alto, CA: Stanford University Press.

Feynman, R. (1989). *What do you care what other people think?* New York: Bantam.

Finke, R. A., Ward, T. B., & Smith, S. M. (1992). *Creative cognition: Theory, research, and applications.* Cambridge, MA: Bradford.

Fischer, G. W., & Johnson, E. J. (1986). Behavioral decision theory and political decision making. In R. R. Lau & D. O. Sears (Eds.), *The 19th Annual Carnegie Symposium on Cognition: Political Cognition* (pp. 55–65). Hillsdale, NJ: Lawrence Erlbaum Associates.

Fischer, S. C., & Spiker, V. A. (2000). *A framework for critical thinking research and training.* (Report Prepared for the U.S. Army Research Institute.).

Fischhoff, B. (1993). Controversies over risk: Psychological perspective on competence. *Psychological Science Agenda, 6,* 8–9.

Fisher, R. P. (1995). Interviewing victims and witnesses of crime. *Psychology, Public Policy, & Law, 1*(4), 732–764.

Fisher, R., Ury, W., & Patton, B. (2011). *Getting to yes: Negotiating agreement without giving in.* (Revised ed.). New York, NY: Penguin Books.

Fixx, J. F. (1978). *Solve it.* New York, NY: Doublday.

Flannelly, L. T., & Flannelly, K. J. (2000). Reducing people's judgment bias about their level of knowledge. *Psychological Record, 50,* 587–600.

Fong, G. T., Krantz, D. H., & Nisbett, R. E. (1986). The effects of statistical training on thinking about everyday problems. *Cognitive Psychologist, 18*(3), 253–292.

Fox, C. R. (2006). The availability heuristic in the classroom: How soliciting more criticism can boost your course ratings. *Judgment and Decision Making, 1,* 86–90.

Frammolino, R. (1993, December). Most college GEDs fail simple tests, study finds. *The Los Angeles Times,* pp. A41, A43.

Frederick, S. (2005). Cognitive reflection and cecision making. *Journal of Economic Perspectives, 19,* 25–42.

Freud, S. (1930). *Civilization and its discontents.* Newark, DE: The Hogarth Pres.

Galinsky, A. D., Maddux, W. W., Gilin, D., & White, J. B. (2008). Why it pays to get inside the head of your opponent: The differential effects of perspective taking and empathy in negotiations. *Psychological Science, 19*(4), 378–384. doi:10.1111/j.1467-9280.2008.02096.x

Gardner, H. (1985). *The mind's new science: A history of the cognitive revolution.* New York: Basic Books.

Gardner, H. (1989). *To open minds.* New York: Basic Books.

Gawrilow, C., Gollwitzer, P. M., & Oettingen, G. (2011). If-then plans benefit executive functions in children with ADHD. *Journal of Social and Clinical Psychology, 30*(6), 616–646. doi:10.1521/jscp.2011.30.6.616

Geiselman, R. E., & Fisher, R. P. (1985, December). Interviewing victims and witnesses of crime. *Research in Brief, National Institute of Justice,* 1–4.

Gerbner, G., Grass, L., Morgan, M., & Signorielli, N. (1980). *Violence profile No. 11: Trends in network television drama and viewer conceptions of social reality.* Philadelphia: Annenberg School of Communication.

Gervais, S., & Odean, T. (2001). Learning to be overconfident. *The Review of Financial Studies, 14,* 1–27.

Gick, M. L., & Holyoak, K. J. (1980). Analogical problem solving. *Cognitive Psychology, 12,* 306–355.

Gifford-Jones, W. (1977). *What every woman should know about hysterectomy.* New York: Funk & Wagnalls.

Gigerenzer, G. (2003, 31 March). Smart heuristics. Retrieved from http://www.edge. org/3rd_culture/gigerenzer03/gigerenzer_print.html#video

Gigerenzer, G. (2007). *Gut feelings: The intelligence of the unconscious.* New York, NY: Penguin Books.

Gigerenzer, G. (2008). Why heuristics work. *Perspectives on Psychological Science, 3,* 20–29. doi:10.1111/j.1745-6916.2008.00058.x

Gigerenzer, G., Gaissmaier, W., Kurz-Milcke, E., Schwartz, L.M., & Woloshin, S. (2007). Helping doctors and patients make sense of health statistics. *Psychological Science in the Public Interest, 8,* 53–96. doi:10.1111/j.1539-6053.2008.00033.x

Gigerenzer, G., & Goldstein, D.C. (1996). Reasoning the fast and frugal way: Models of bounded rationality. *Psychological Review, 103,* 650–669.

Gigerenzer, G. & Goldstein, D.G. (2011). The recognition heuristic: A decade of research. *Judgment and Decision Making, 6,* 100–121.

Gigerenzer, G., & Hoffrage, U. (1995). How to improve Bayesian reasoning without instruction. *Psychological Review, 102,* 684–704.

Gigerenzer, G., Hoffrage, U., & Goldstein, D.G. (2008). Postscript: Fast and frugal heuristics. *Psychological Review, 115,* 238–239. doi:10.1037/0033-295X.115.1.238

Gigerenzer, G., Todd, P.M., & the ABC Research Group. (2000). *Simple heuristics that make us smart.* New York: Oxford University Press.

Gilovich, T. (1991). *How we know what isn't so: The fallibility of human reason in everyday life.* New York: Macmillan.

Gladwell, M. (2005). *Blink.* New York, NY: Little Brown & Company.

Glaveanu, V. (2012). Habitual creativity: Revising habit, reconceptualizing creativity. *Review of General Psychology, 16*(1), 78–92. doi:10.1037/a0026611

Global Envision. (2011, 18 August). Used soda bottle light up the world, for free. Retrieved from http://www.globalenvision.org/2011/08/18/used-soda-bottles-light-world-free

Glucksberg, S., & Weisberg, R.W. (1966). Verbal behavior and problem solving: Some effects of labeling in a functional fixedness problem. *Journal of Experimental Psychology, 71*(5), 659–664.

Godfrey, S. (1998). Are you creative? *Journal Of Knowledge Management, 2,* 14–16. doi:10.1108/EUM0000000004604

Goertzel, T., & Goertzel, B. (1995). *Linus Pauling: A life in science and politics.* New York: Basic Books.

Goldberg, J. (2011, 27 December). What? Now I'm the bad guy? *Los Angeles Times,* p. A11.

Goldstein, D.G., & Gigerenzer, G. (2002). Models of ecological rationality: The recognition heuristic. *Psychological Review, 109,* 75–90. doi:10.1037//0033-295X.109.1.75

Goldstein, E.R. (2011, 9 November). *The anatomy of influence.* The Chronicle of Higher Education, The chronicle review. Retrieved from http://chronicle.com/article/The-Anatomy-of-Influence/129688/

Gonzalez, M.A., Campos, A., & Perez, M.J. (1997). Mental imagery and creative thinking. *Journal of Psychology, 131,* 357–364.

Goodwin, G.P., & Johnson-Laird, P.N. (2010). Conceptual illusions. *Cognition, 114*(2), 253–265. doi:10.1016/j.cognition.2009.09.014

Gordon, W.J.J. (1961). *Synectics.* New York: Harper & Row.

Gordon, W. J. J. (1976). Metaphor and invention. In A. Rothenberg & C. R. Hausman (Eds.), *The creativity question*. Durham, NC: University Press.

Gottfredson, L. S. (1997a). Intelligence and social policy. *Intelligence, 24,* 1–320.

Gottfredson, L. S. (1997b). Mainstream science on intelligence: An editorial with 52 signatories, history, and bibliography. *Intelligence, 24,* 13–23.

Gould, S. J. (1985) The median isn't the message. *Discover Magazine.* Retrieved from http://www.ratbags.com/rsoles/comment/gouldmedian.htm

Griggs, B. (2009). Could moon landings have been faked? Some still think so. CNN. Com/technology. Retrieved from http://articles.cnn.com/2009-07-17/tech/moon.landing.hoax_1_moon-landing-apollo-astronauts-bill-kaysing?_s=PM:TECH

Griskevicius, V., Tybur, J. M., Ackerman, J. M., Delton, A. W., Robertson, T. E., & White, A. E. (2012). The financial consequences of too many men: Sex ratio effects on saving, borrowing, and spending. *Journal of Personality and Social Psychology, 102*(1), 69–80. doi:10.1037/a0024761

Groopman, J. (2007). *How doctors think.* New York, NY: Houghton Mifflin Company.

Guerra-Ramos, M. T. (2011). Analogies as tools for meaning making in elementary science education: How do they work in classroom settings? *Eurasia Journal of Mathematics, Science, and Technology Education, 7,* 29–39.

Gunther, M. (1977). *The luck factor.* New York: Macmillan.

Haier, R. J., Karama, S., Leyba, L., & Jung, R. E. (2009). MRI assessment of cortical thickness and functional activity changes in adolescent girls following three months of practice on a visual-spatial task. *BioMed Central Research Notes, 2,* 174. doi:10.1186/1756-0500-2-174

Halpern, D. F. (1998). Teaching critical thinking for transfer across domains: Dispositions, skills, structure training, and metacognitive monitoring. *American Psychologist, 53,* 449–455.

Halpern, D. F., & Blackman, S. (1985). Magazines vs. physicians. The influence of information source on intentions to use oral contraceptives. *Women and Health, 10,* 9–23.

Halpern, D. F., Blackman, S., & Salzman B. (1989). Using statistical risk information to assess oral contraceptive safety. *Applied Cognitive Psychology, 3,* 251–260.

Halpern, D. F., Hansen, C., & Riefer, D. (1990). Analogies as an aid to understanding and memory. *Journal of Educational Psychology, 82*(2), 298–305.

Halpern, D. F., & Irwin, F. W. (1973). Selection of hypotheses as affected by their preference values. *Journal of Experimental Psychology, 101,* 105–108.

Halpern, D. F., Millis, K., Graesser. A., Butler, H., Forsyth, C., & Cai, Z. (2012). Operation ARA: A computerized learning game that teaches critical thinking and scientific reasoning. *Thinking Skills and Creativity, 7,* 93–100.

Halpern, D. F., & Wai, J. (2007). The world of competitive Scrabble: Novice and expert differences in visuospatial and verbal abilities. *Journal of Experimental Psychology: Applied, 13,* 79–94. doi:10.1037/1076-898X.13.2.79

Hannay, T. (2012). The controlled experiment. In J. Brockman (Ed.), *What is your favorite deep, elegant explanation?* New York, NY: HarperCollins.

Hargadon, A. B., & Bechky, B. A. (2006). When collections of creatives become creative collectives: A field study of problem solving at work. *Organizational Science, 17,* 484–500.

Harman, G. (1986). *Change in view: Principles of reasoning.* Cambridge, MA: MIT Press.

Harris, S. B. (1993). The resurrection myth in religion, science, and science fiction. *Skeptic, 2,* 50–59.

Hasher, L., & Zacks, R. T. (1984). Automatic processing of fundamental information: The case of frequency of occurrence. *American Psychologist, 39*(12), 1372–1388.

Haskins, G. R. (2006, 15 August). A practical guide to critical thinking. Retrieved from http://skepdic.com/essays/Haskins.html

Hastie, R. (2006). Making groups wiser. Retrieved from http://www.apa.org/about/gr/science/advocacy/2006/hastie.pdf

Heiman, M., & Slomianko, J. (1986). *Critical thinking skills.* Washington, DC: National Education Association.

Heit, E. (2000). Properties of inductive reasoning. *Psychonomic Bulletin & Review, 7*(4), 569–592.

Heller, R., Saltzstein, H. D., & Caspe, W. (1992). Heuristics in medical and non-medical decision-making. *The Quarterly Journal of Experimental Psychology: A: Human Experimental Psychology,44A,* 211–235.

Helsdingen, A. S., van den Bosch, K., van Gog, T., & van Merrienboer, J. J. G. (2010). The effects of critical thinking instruction on training complex decision making. *Human Factors, 54,* 537–545. doi:10.1177/0018720810377069

Henle, M. (1962). On the relation between logic and thinking. *Psychological Review, 69,* 366–378.

Hennessey, B. A., & Amabile, T. M. (1988). The conditions of creativity. In R. J. Sternberg (Ed.), *The nature of creativity: Contemporary psychological perspectives* (pp. 11–38). Cambridge, MA: Cambridge University Press.

Hennessey, B. A., & Amabile, T. M. (2010). Creativity. *Annual Review of Psychology, 61,* 569–598.

Herbers, J. (1982, 14 February). Polls find conflict in views on aid and public welfare. *New York Times,* p. 19.

Herrnstein, R. J., Nickerson, R. S., de Sanchez, M., & Swets, J. A. (1986). Teaching thinking skills. *American Psychologist, 41,* 1279–1289.

Heslin, P. A. (2009). Better than brainstorming? Potential contextual boundary conditions to brainwriting for idea generation in organizations. Journal of Occupational and Organizational Psychology, *82*(1), 129–145.

Hill, K. (2012, 8 March). Understanding coincidence. *James Randi Educational Foundation.* Retrieved from http://www.randi.org/site/index.php/swift-blog/1646-understanding-coincidence.html

Hoerger, M., Quirk, S. W., Lucas, R. E., & Carr, T. H. (2010). Cognitive determinants of affective forecasting errors. *Judgment and Decision Making, 5*(5), 365–373.

Holland, J. H., Holyoak, K. J., Nisbett, R. E., & Thagard, P. R. (1993). Deductive reasoning. In A. I. Goldman (Ed.), *Readings in philosophy and cognitive science* (pp. 23–41). Cambridge, MA: The MIT Press.

Holley, C. D., Dansereau, D. F., McDonald, B. A., Garland, J. D., & Collins, K. W. (1979). Evaluation of a hierarchical mapping technique as an aid to prose processing. *Contemporary Educational Psychology, 4*(3), 227–237.

Holliday, R. E., Humphries, J. E., Milne, R., Memon, A., Houlder, L., Lyons, A., & Bull, R. (2012). Reducing misinformation effects in older adults with cognitive interview mnemonics. *Psychology of Aging, 27*(4), 1191–1203. doi:10.1037/a0022031

Holt, J. (1964). *How children fail*. New York: Dell.

Holt, J. (1989). *Learning all the time*. New York, NY: Addison Wesley

Holt, J. (2011, 25 November). Two brains running. *New York Times*. Retrieved from http://www.nytimes.com/2011/11/27/books/review/thinking-fast-and-slow-by-daniel-kahneman-book-review.html?_r=1&src=me&ref=books

Horwitz, T. (2008, 17 June). Leader of the pack. *The New York Times*. Retrieved from http://www.nytimes.com/2008/06/17/opinion/17horwitz.html?_r=0

Howe, J. (2006, June). The rise of outsourcing. *Wired Magazine*. Retrieved from http://www.wired.com/wired/archive/14.06/crowds.html?pg=3&topic=crowds&topic_set =

Huff, D. (1954). *How to lie with statistics*. New York: W. W. Norton & company.

Hung, W. (2011). Theory to reality: A few issues in implementing problem-based learning. *Educational Technology Research and Development, 59*(4), 529–552. doi:10.1007/s11423-011-9198-1

Hunt, M. (1982). *The universe within: A new science explores the human mind*. New York: Simon & Schuster.

Hutchings, P. (1986). Some late night thoughts on teaching creativity. *American Association for Higher Education, 39*, 9–14.

Hyman, R. (1977). Cold reading: How to convince strangers that you know all about them. *The Skeptical Inquirer*. Retrieved from http://www.skepdic.com/Hyman_cold_reading.htm

Hyman, R. (2001, 20 January). Australian skeptics guide to "Cold Reading." Retrieved from http://www.skeptics.com.au/journal/coldread.htm

Innocence Project. (n.d.). Understand the causes. Retrieved from http://www.innocenceproject.org/understand/Eyewitness-Misidentification.php

Izawa, C. (1993). Efficient learning: The total time, exposure duration, frequency, and programming of the study phase. In C. Izawa (Ed.), *Cognitive psychology applied* (pp. 15–42). Hillsdale, NJ: Lawrence Erlbaum Associates.

Jacoby, L. L., Kelley, C. M., & Dywan, J. (1989). Memory attributions. In H. L. I. Roedinger & F. I. M. Craik (Eds.), *Varieties of memory and consciousness: Essays in honour of Endel Tulving* (pp. 391–422, xx, 445). Hillsdale, NJ: Lawrence Erlbaum Associates.

James Randi Educational Foundation. (2013). One million dollar paranormal challenge. Retrieved from http://www.randi.org/research/index.html

James, W. (1890). *The principles of psychology*. New York: Holt.

Janis, I. L. (1972). *Victims of groupthink: A psychological study of foreign-policy decisions and fiascoes*. Boston, MA: Houghton Mifflin.

Janis, I. L., & Mann, L. (1977). *Decision making: A psychological analysis of conflict, choice, and commitment*. New York: The Free Press.

Jepson, C., Krantz, D. H., & Nisbett, R. E. (1993). Inductive reasoning: Competence or skill? R. E. Nisbett *Rules for reasoning* (pp. 70–89). Hillsdale, NJ: Lawrence Erlbaum.

Johnson, E. J., & Goldstein, D. (2003, 21 November). Do defaults save lives? *Science, 302*, 1138–1139. doi: 10.1126/science.1091721

Johnson, S. (1759). Idler 044 [The use of memory considered]. Retrieved from www.readbookonline.net/readonline/29909

Johnson, W. (1946). *People in quandries: The semantics of personal judgement*. New York: Harper & Row Publishers.

Johnson-Laird. P. N. (2011). The realities of reason. *APS Observer*. Retrieved from http://www.psychologicalscience.org/index.php/publications/observer/2012/february-11-2012-observer-publications/the-realities-of-reason.html

Johnson-Laird, P. N., Legrenzi, P., & Legrenzi, M. S. (1972). Reasoning and a sense of reality. *British Journal of Psychology, 63*(3), 395–400.

Johnson-Laird, P. N., & Wason, P. C. (1970). A theoretical analysis of insight into a reasoning task. *Cognitive Psychology, 1*(2), 134–148.

Johnson-Laird, P. N., & Wason, P. C. (1977). *Thinking: Readings in cognitive science*. Cambridge, England: Cambridge University Press.

Jonas, E., Schulz-Hardt, S., Frey, D., & Thelen, N. (2001). Confirmation bias in sequential information search after preliminary decisions: An expansion of dissonance theoretical research on selective exposure to information. *Journal of Personality and Social Psychology, 80*(4), 557–571. doi:10.10371/0022-3514.80.4.557

Jones, E. A., Dougherty, B. C., Fantaske, P., & Hoffman, S. (1995). *Identifying college graduates' essential skills in reading and problem-solving: Perspectives of faculty, employers and policymakers. (Contract No. R117G10037/CDFA84.117G.)*. University Park: U.S. Department of Education/OERI.

Jones, E. A., Hoffman, S., Moore, L. M., Ratcliff, G., Tibbetts, S., & Click, B. A. (1995). *National assessment of college student learning: Identifying college graduates' essential skills in writing, speech and listening, and critical thinking*. (NCES 95–001). Washington, DC: U.S. Government Printing Office.

Kahane, H. (1980). *Logic and contemporary rhetoric: The use of reason in everyday life* (2nd ed.). Belmont, CA: Wadsworth.

Kahane, H. (1992). *Logic and contemporary rhetoric: The use of reason in everday life* (6th ed.). Belmont, CA: Wadsworth.

Kahneman, D. (2011). *Thinking: Fast and slow*. New York, NY: Farrar, Strauss and Giroux.

Kahneman, D., & Klein, G. (2009). Conditions for intuitive expertise: A failure to disagree. *American Psychologist, 64*(6), 515–526. doi:10.1037/a0016755

Kahneman, D., & Tversky, A. (1973). On the psychology of prediction. *Psychological Review, 80*, 237–251.

Kahneman, D., & Tversky, A. (1979). Prospect theory: An analysis of decision under risk. *Econometrica, 47*, 263–291.

Karpicke, J. D., & Roediger, H. L. (2007). Repeated retrieval during learning is the key to long-term retention. *Journal of Memory and Language, 57*, 151–162. doi:10.1016/j.jml.2006.09.004

Kaufman, J. (2008, 30 June). Need press? Repeat: 'green,' 'sex,' 'cancer,' 'secret,' 'fat.' Sideways. *The New York Times*. Retrieved from http://www.nytimes.com/2008/06/30/business/media/30toxic.html?_r=1&th=&adxnnl=1&oref=slogin&emc=th&adxnnlx=1214846607-pduGrZGmVTAFC8NATtbJkg

Kellogg, R. T. (1990). Effectiveness of prewriting strategies as a function of task demands. *American Journal of Psychology, 103*(3), 327–342.

Keren, G., & Teigen, K. H. (2001). Why is p=.90 better than p=.70? Preference for definitive predictions by lay consumers of probability judgements. *Psychonomic Bulletin & Review, 8*, 191–202.

Kim, W. C., & Mauborgne, R. (1999). Strategy, knowledge, innovation and the knowledge economy. *Sloan Management Review, 40*, 41–54.

King, A. (1989). Effects of self-questioning training on college students' comprehension of lectures. *Contemporary Educational Psychology, 14*(4), 366–381.

King, A. (1992). Facilitating elaborative learning through guided student-generated questioning. *Educational Psychologist, 27*(1), 111–126.

King, A. (1994). Inquiry as a tool to critical thinking. In D. F. Halpern (Ed.), *Changing college classrooms: New teaching and learning strategies in an increasingly complex world* (pp. 13–38). San Francisco: Jossey-Bass.

King, A., Staffieri, A., & Adelgais, A. (1998). Mutual peer tutoring: Effects of structuring tutorial interaction to scaffold peer learning. *Journal of Educational Psychology, 90*, 134–152. doi:10.1037/0022-0663.90.1.134

Kingsolver, B. (1990). Animal dreams. New York, NY: HarperCollins.

Kirschner, P. A., Sweller, J., & Clark, R. (2006). Why minimal guidance during instruction does not work: An analysis of the failure of constructivist, discovery, problem-based, experiential, and inquiry-based teaching. *Educational Psychologist, 41*(2), 75–86.

Klahr, D., & Simon, H. A. (2001). What have psychologists (and others) discovered about the process of scientific discovery? *Current Directions in Psychological Science, 10*, 75–79.

Klauer, K. C., & Meiser, T. (2000). A source-monitoring analysis of illusory correlations. *Personality & Social Psychology Bulletin, 26*, 1074–1093.

Klein, G. (2011). Critical thoughts about critical thinking. Theoretical issues in ergonomics. *Science, 12*, 210–224. doi:10.1080/1464536X.2011.564458

Klein, G. A., Calderwood, R., & Clinton-Cirocco, A. (1986). Rapid decision making on the fireground. In *Proceedings of the Human Factors and Ergonomics Society 30th Annual Meeting,* (Vol. 1, pp. 576–580). Norwood, NJ: Ablex.

Kluger, J. (2006, 26 November). Why we worry about the things we shouldn't . . . and ignore the things we should. *Time.* Retrieved from http://www.time.com/time/magazine/printout/0,8816,1562978,00.html

Kneer, J., Glock, S., & Rieger, D. (2012). Fast and not furious? Reduction of cognitive dissonance in smokers. *Social Psychology, 43*(2), 81–91. doi:10.1027/1864-9335/a000086

Knight, K., & Dansereau, D. F. (1992). Tools for drug and alcohol education: Using decision worksheets in personal problem solving. *Journal of Drug Education, 22*(3), 261–271.

Koestler, A. (1964). *The act of creation.* London: Hutchinson.

Konnikova, M. (2011, 18 October). Lessons from Sherlock Holmes: The importance of perspective-taking. *Scientific American.* Retrieved from http://blogs.scientificamerican.com/guest-blog/2011/10/18/lessons-from-sherlock-holmes-the-importance-of-perspective-taking/?WT_mc_id=SA_CAT_MB_20111019

Koriat, A., Lichtenstein, S. F., & Fischhoff, B. (1980). Reasons for confidence. *Journal of Experimental Psychology: Human Learning and Memory, 6*, 107–118.

Kosonen, P., & Winne, P. H. (1995). Effects of teaching statistical laws on reasoning about everyday problems. *Journal of Educational Psychology, 87*, 33–46.

Kraft, U. (2007). Unleashing creativity. In F. E. Bloom (Ed.), *Best of the brain from Scientific American* (pp. 9–19). Washington, DC: Dana Press.

Kruglanski, A. W. (1992). On methods of good judgment and good methods of judgment. *Political Psychology, 13*, 455–475.

Krulwich, T. (2009, 9 December). There's a fly in my urinal. NPR. Retrieved from http://www.npr.org/templates/story/story.php?storyId=121310977

Kuhn, D. (1993). Connecting scientific and informal reasoning. *Merrill-Palmer Quarterly, 39*, 74–103.

Kuhn, D. (2001). How do people know? *Psychological Science, 12*(1), 1–8.

Kylesten, B., & Nählinder, S. (2011). The effect of decision-making training: Results from a command-and-control training facility. *Cognition, Technology & Work, 13*(2), 93–101. doi:10.1007/s10111-010-0157-0

Laing, G. (2010). An empirical test of mnemonic devices to improve learning in elementary accounting. *Journal Of Education For Business, 85*, 349–358. doi:10.1080/08832321003604946

La Place, P.S. (1951). *A philosophical essay on probabilities* (exact wording varies by translation) New York: Dover Publications, Inc.

La Rochefoucauld. (1959). The maxims of La Rouchefoucauld. Louis Kronenberger (Trans.). New York: Random House.

Langer, E.J. (1989). *Mindfulness.* Reading, MA: Addison-Wesley Pub. Co.

Langer, E.J. (2000). Mindful learning. *Current Directions in Psychological Science, 9*, 220–223.

Larrick, R.P., Morgan, J.N., & Nisbett, R.E. (1990). Teaching the use of cost-benefit reasoning in everyday life. *Psychological Science, 1*, 362–370.

Larson, C.F. (2001). Management for the new millennium—the challenge of change. *Research Technology Management, 6*, 10–12.

Lee, C. (2011, 4 January). Behavioral understanding to aid investment advice. *American Banker, 176*, 10.

Leedy, P.D. (1981). How to read research and understand it. New York, NY: Macmillan.

Lehman, D.R., Lempert, R.O., & Nisbett, R.E. (1988). The effects of graduate training on reasoning: Formal discipline and thinking about everyday-life events. *American Psychologist, 43*(6), 431–442.

Leive, C. (1994). Miss America. *Glamour*, pp. 234–237, 275–281.

Lenski, S.D. (2001). Intertextual connections during discussions about literature. *Reading Psychology, 22*, 313–335.

Lepore, E. (2010, 7 November). Speech and harm. *The New York Times.* Retrieved from http://opinionator.blogs.nytimes.com/2010/11/07/speech-and-harm/

Levi, D.S. (1991). *Critical thinking and logic.* Salem, WI: Sheffield.

Levine, M. (1994). *Effective problem solving.* Englewood Cliffs, NJ: Prentice-Hall.

Lewandowsky, S., Stritzke, W.K., Oberauer, K., & Morales, M. (2005). Memory for fact, fiction, and misinformation. *Psychological Science, 16*(3), 190–195. doi:10.1111/j.0956-7976.2005.00802.x

Lewandowsky, S., Stritzke, W.K., Oberauer, K., & Morales, M. (2009). Misinformation and the 'war on terror': When memory turns fiction into fact. In W.K. Stritzke, S. Lewandowsky, D. Denemark, J. Clare, F. Morgan, W.K. Stritzke, … F. Morgan (Eds.), *Terrorism and torture: An interdisciplinary perspective* (pp. 179–203). New York, NY: Cambridge University Press. doi:10.1017/CBO9780511581199.010

Lewis, A.B., & Mayer, R.E. (1987). Students' misconceptions of relational statements in arithmetic word problems. *Journal of Educational Psychology, 79*, 363–371.

Lichtenstein, S., Slovic, P., Fischhoff, B., Layman, M., & Combs, B. (1978). Judged frequency of lethal events. *Journal of Experimental Psychology: Human Learning & Memory, 4*(6), 551–578.

Lilienfeld, S. (2007, 26 September). Can psychology change the world? *The British Psychological Society, Research Digest.* Retrieved from http://bps-research-digest. blogspot.com/2007/09/can-psychology-save-world.html

Lilienfeld, S. O., Ammirati, R., & Landfeld, K. (2009). Giving debiasing away: Can psychological research on correcting cognitive errors promote human welfare? *Perspectives on Psychological Science, 4,* 390–398. doi:10.1111/j.1745-6924.2009. 01144.x

Lilienfeld, S. O., Wood, J. M., & Garb, H. N. (2000). The scientific status of projective techniques. *Psychological Science in the Public Interest, 1,* 27–66.

Lilienfeld, S. O. (2010, 15 December). Fudge factor: A look at a Harvard science fraud case. *Scientific American.* Retrieved from http://www.scientificamerican .com/article.cfm?id=fudge-factor

Lionni, L. (2005) *Fish is fish.* New York, NY: Alfred A. Knoph, Inc.

Lithner, J. (2000). Mathematical reasoning and familiar procedures. *International Journal of Mathematical Education in Science & Technology, 31,* 83–96.

Loftus, E. F. (1993). The reality of repressed memories. *American Psychologist, 48*(5), 518–537.

Loftus, G. R., & Loftus, E. F. (1982). *Essence of statistics.* Monteray, CA: Brooks/Cole.

Lorayne, H. (1975). *Remembering people.* New York: Stein & Day.

Lorayne, H., & Lucas, J. (1974). *The memory book.* New York: Stein & Day (Also published in paperback by Ballantine Books, 1975).

Love, J. (2010, 28 October). Woodward urges government transparency. *The Chronicle.* Retrieved from http://dukechronicle.com/article/woodward-urges-government-transparency

Lovett, M. C., & Schunn, C. D. (1999). Task representations, strategy variability, and base-rate neglect. *Journal of Experimental Psychology: General, 128*(2), 107–130.

Lowenfeld, V. (1962). Creativity: Education's stepchild. In S. J. Parnes & H. F. Harding (Eds.), *A source book from creative thinking.* New York: Scribner's.

Lyons, L. (2005, 1 November). Paranormal beliefs come (super)naturally to some. *Gallup.* Retrieved from http://www.gallup.com/poll/19558/paranormal-beliefs-come-supernaturally-some.aspx

Macmillan Publishers. (1989). *Macmillan dictionary of quotations.* New York: Author.

Maier, N. R. F. (1931) Reasoning in humans: 11. The solution of a problem and its appearance in consciousness. *Journal of Comparative and Physiological Psychology, 12,* 181–194.

Mankato MN Visitor's Bureau (n.d.). Retrieved from http://city-mankato.us.

Mann, L. (1972). Use of a "balance sheet" procedure to improve the quality of personal decision making: A field experiment with college applicants. *Journal of Vocational Behavior, 2,* 291–300.

Mannix, E., & Neale, M. A. (2005). What differences make a difference? The promise and reality of diverse teams in organizations. *Psychological Science in the Public Interest, 6*(2), 31–55. doi:10.1111/j.1529-1006.2005.00022.x

Marin, L., & Halpern, D. F. (2011). Pedagogy for developing critical thinking in adolescents: Explicit instruction produces greatest gains. *Thinking Skills and Creativity, 6,* 1–13. doi:10.1016/j.tsc.2010.08.002

Markovits, H., & Lortie-Forgues, H. (2011). Conditional reasoning with false premises facilitates the transition between familiar and abstract reasoning. *Child Development, 82,* 646–660. doi:10.1111/j.1467-8624.2010.01526.x

Martin, P. (2001, July). Life after the myth. *Financial Times,* p. 10.

Massey, C., Simmons, J. P., & Armor, D. A. (2011). Hope over experience: Desirability and the persistence of optimism. *Psychological Science, 22,* 274–281. doi:10.1177/0956797610396223

Mayer, R. E. (1987). *Educational psychology: A cognitive approach.* Boston: Little, Brown.

Mayer, R. E. (2002). Cognitive theory and the design of multimedia instruction: An example of the two-way street between cognition and instruction. In D. F. Halpern & M. G. Hakel (Eds.), *From theory to practice: Applying the science of learning to the university and beyond. New directions for teaching and learning.* San Francisco: Jossey-Bass.

McCabe, D. P., Roediger, H., & Karpicke, J. D. (2011). Automatic processing influences free recall: Converging evidence from the process dissociation procedure and remember-know judgments. *Memory & Cognition, 39,* 389–402. doi:10.3758/s13421-010-0040-5

McCabe, D. P., & Soderstrom, N. C. (2011). Recollection-based prospective metamemory judgments are more accurate than those based on confidence: Judgments of remembering and knowing (JORKs). *Journal of Experimental Psychologyv General, 140*(4), 605–621. doi:10.1037/a0024014

McCaffrey, T. (2012). Innovation relies on the obscure: A key to overcoming the classic problem on functional fixedness. *Psychological Science, 23,* 215–218. doi:10.1177/0956797611429580

McFadzean, E. (2000). Techniques to enhance creative thinking. *Team Performance Management, 6,* 62–72.

McGuire, W. J. (1981). The probabilogical model of cognitive structure and attitude change. In R. E. Petty, T. M. Ostrom & T. C. Brock (Eds.), *Cognitive responses in persuasion* (pp. 392–406). Hillsdale, NJ: Lawrence Erlbaum Associates.

McGuire, W. J. (1997). Creative hypothesis generating in psychology: Some useful heuristics. *Annual Reviews of Psychology, 48,* 1–30.

McHardy, P., & Allan, T. (2000). Closing the gap between what industry needs and what HE provides. *Education and Training, 42,* 496–508.

McKay, B., Bar-Natan, D., & Kalai, G. (1999). Solving the Bible code puzzle. *Statistical Science, 14,* 150.

McKeachie, W. J. (1992). Update: Teaching thinking. In D. J. Stroup & R. Allen (Eds.), *Critical thinking: A collection of readings.* Dubuque, IA: Brown.

McKee, M., & Stuckler, D. (2010). How cognitive biases affect our interpretation of political messages. *British Medical Journal, 340,* 2276, doi:10.1136/bmj.c2276

Mednick, S. A., & Mednick, M. T. (1967). *Remote associates test: Examiners manual.* Boston: Houghton Mifflin.

Merron, K., Fisher, D., & Torbet, W. R. (1987). Meaning making and management action. *Groups & Organizational Studies, 12,* 274–286.

Miller, J. E. Jr. (1972). *Words, self, reality: The rhetoric of imagination.* New York: Dodd, Mead.

Milne, A. A. (1926). *Winnie the Pooh.* New York: Dutton.

Minson, J. A., & Mueller, J. S. (2012). The cost of collaboration: Why joint decision making exacerbates rejection of outside information. *Psychological Science, 23*(3), 219–224. doi:10.1177/0956797611429132

Mitroff, D., & Stephenson, R. (2007). The television tug-of-war: A brief history of children's television programming in the United States. In J. Bryant (Ed.), The children's television community (pp. 3–34). Mahwah, NJ: Lawrence Erlbaum Associates Publishers.

Moehrle, M. G. (2005). What is TRIZ? From conceptual basics to a framework for research. *Creativity and Innovation Management, 14*(1), 3–13. doi:10.1111/j.1476-8691.2005.00320.x

Moehrle, M. G. (2010). MorphoTRIZ—Solving technical problems with a demand for multi-smart solutions. *Creativity and Innovation Management, 19*(4), 373–384. doi:10.1111/j.1467-8691.2010.00582.x

Molnar, A., Boninger, F., & Fogarty, J. (2011, November). The educational cost of schoolhouse commercialism. National Education Research Policy. Retrieved from http://nepc.colorado.edu/files/CommTrends-2011.pdf

Moons, W. G., Mackle, D. M., & Garcia-Marques, T. (2009). The impact of repetition-induced familiarity on agreement with weak and strong arguments. *Journal of Personality and Social Psychology, 96,* 32–44. doi:10.1037/a0013461

Moseley, D., Baumfield, V., Elliott, J., Gregson, M., Higgins, S., Miller, J., & Newton, D. P. (2005). *Frameworks for thinking: A handbook for teaching and learning.* Cambridge, MA: Cambridge University Press.

Moss, J. (1950). *How to win at poker.* Garden City, NY: Garden City Books.

Mountjoym D. (2001, 19 October). Assembly California Legislature. Assemblyman Fifty-ninth district. Republican whip.

Mueller, J. S., Melwani, S., & Goncalo, J. A. (2012). The bias against creativity: Why people desire but reject creative ideas. *Psychological Science, 23,* 13–17.

Munby, H. (1982). *Science in the schools.* Toronto: University of Toronto.

Munson, R. (1976). The elements of reasoning. Boston, MA: Wadsworth.

Mussweiler, T., & Strack, F. (2000). The use of category and exemplar knowledge in the solution of anchoring tasks. *Journal of Personality & Social Psychology, 78*(6), 1038–1052.

Mwamwenda, T. S. (1999). Undergraduate and graduate students' combinatorial reasoning and formal operations. *Journal of Genetic Psychology, 160*(4), 503–506. doi:10.1080/00221329909595563

Myers, D. (2010). Intuition's powers and perils. *Psychological Inquiry, 21,* 371–377. doi:10.1080/1047840X.2010.524469

Mynatt, C. R., Doherty, M. E., & Tweney, R. D. (1977). Confirmation bias in a simulated research environment: An experimental study of scientific inference. *Quarterly Journal of Experimental Psychology, 29*(1), 85–95.

Mynatt, C. R., Doherty, M. E., & Tweney, R. D. (1978). Consequences of confirmation and disconfirmation in a simulated research environment. *Quarterly Journal of Experimental Psychology, 30*(3), 395–406.

Nakamura, J., & Csikszentmihalyi, M. (2001). Catalytic creativity: The case of Linus Pauling. *American Psychologist, 56,* 337–341.

Nelson, D., & Vu, K. L. (2010). Effectiveness of image-based mnemonic techniques for enhancing the memorability and security of user-generated passwords. *Computers in Human Behavior, 26*(4), 705–715. doi:10.1016/j.chb.2010.01.007

Nelson, G. P. (1998 April). You don't have to be a rocket scientist to think like one. *Star Tribune,* p. A14.

Nelson, T. O., & Narens, L. (1990). Metamemory: A theoretical framework and new findings. *The Psychology of Learning and Motivation, 26,* 125–141.

Nesbit, J. C., & Adesope, O. O. (2006). Learning with concept and knowledge aaps: A meta-analysis. *Review Of Educational Research, 76,* 413–448.

Newell, A. (1983). The heuristic of George Polya and its relation to artificial intelligence. In M. G. R. Groner & W. F. Bischof (Eds.), *Methods of heuristics* (pp. 195–243). Hillsdale, NJ: Lawrence Erlbaum Associates.

Newell, A., & Simon, H. A. (1972). *Human problem solving.* Englewood Cliffs, NJ: Prentice-Hall.

Newsweek (2009, 24 September). The angry evolutionist: More people believe in angels than in evolution—and Richard Dawkins isn't going to take it anymore. Retrieved from http://magazine-directory.com/Newsweek.htm

Nickerson, R. S. (1986). Reflections on reasoning. Hillsdale, NJ: Lawrence Erlbaum Associates.

Nickerson, R. S. (1998). Confirmation bias: A ubiquitous phenomenon in many guises. *Review of General Psychology, 2*(2), 175–220.

Nickerson, R. S., & Adams, M. J. (1979). Long-term memory for a common object. *Cognitive Psychology, 11,* 287–307. doi:10.1016/0010-0285(79)90013-6

Nisbett, R. E. (1993). *Rules for reasoning.* Hillsdale, NJ: Lawrence Erlbaum.

Nisbett, R. E., Aronson, J., Blair, C., Dickens, W., Flynn, J., Halpern, D. F., & Turkheimer, E. (2012*).* Intelligence: New findings and theoretical developments. *American Psychologist, 67,* 130–159. doi:10.1037/a0026699

Norman, D. A. (1976). *Memory and attention: An introduction to human information processing.* New York: Wiley.

Norman, D. A. (1988). *The psychology of everyday things.* New York: Basic Books.

Norman, G. R., & Eva, K. W. (2010). Diagnostic error and clinical reasoning. *Medical Education, 44*(1), 94–100. doi:10.1111/j.1365-2923.2009.03507.x

O'Brien, B. (2009). Prime suspect: An examination of factors that aggravate and counteract confirmation bias in criminal investigations. *Psychology, Public Policy, and Law, 15*(4), 315–334. doi:10.1037/a0017881

Oberauer, K., & Lewandowsky, S. (2011). Modeling working memory: A computational implementation of the Time-Based Resource-Sharing theory. *Psychonomic Bulletin & Review, 18*(1), 10–45. doi:10.3758/s13423-010-0020-6

O'Connor, M. C., & Paunonen, S. V. (2007). Big five personality predictors of post-secondary academic performance. *Personality and Individual Differences, 43,* 971–990.

Oliner, S. P. (1992). *Altruistic personality: Rescuers of Jews in Nazi Europe.* New York, NY: Simon & Schuster.

Oliver, P. (2001). Diagrammatic reasoning: An artificial intelligence perspective. *Artificial Intelligence Review, 15,* 63–78.

Oppenheimer, J. R. (1956). Analogy in science. *American Psychologist, 11,* 127–135.

O'Reilly, B. (2006, 31 January). The O'Reilly factor. Retrieved from http://www.billoreilly.com/show?action=viewTVShowByDate&date=20060131

Orwell, G. (1949). *1984*. New York: Harcourt, Brace.

Osborn, A.F. (1963). *Applied imagination: Principals and procedures of creative problem solving*. New York: Scriber's.

Oskamp, S. (1965). Overconfidence in case-study judgments. *Journal of Consulting Psychology, 29*, 261–265. doi:10.1037/h0022125

Ozubko, J.D., & Fugelsang, J. (2011). Remembering makes evidence compelling: Retrieval from memory can give rise to the illusion of truth. *Journal of Experimental Psychology: Learning, Memory and Cognition, 37*, 270–276.

Parducci, A. (1968). The relativism of absolute judgments. *Scientific American, 219*(6), 84–90.

Parnes, S.J., Noller, R.B., & Biondi, A.M. (1977). *Guide to creative action: Revised edition of creative behavior guidebook*. New York: Scribner's.

Partnership for 21st Century Skills. (2004). Overview. Retrieved from http://p21. org/index.php?option=com_content&task=view&id=260&Itemid=120

Pascal, B. (1670). Pensees. Retrieved from http://oreganstate.edu/instruct/phl302/ texts/pascal.pensees-contents.html

Patentstorm. (2010, 16 March). Ripple bottom pizza box and its associated method of construction. Retrieved from http://www.patentstorm.us/patents/7678036/ description.html

Paulos, J.A. (1994). Commentary: Counting on dyscalculia. *Discovery*, 30–36.

Paulos, J.A. (2001). *Innumeracy: Mathematical Illiteracy and its Consequences*. New York, NY: Hill and Wang.

Paulos, J.A. (2009, 10 December). Mammogram math. *The New York Times*. Retrieved from http://www.nytimes.com/2009/12/13/magazine/13Fob-wwln-t. html

Paulus, P.B. (2000). Groups, teams, and creativity: The creative potential of idea-generating groups. Applied Psychology: An International Review, *49*(2), 237–263.

Pearson Assessment. (2008). Wechsler Adult Intelligence Scale, 4th ed. Retrieved from http://www.pearsonassessments.com/HAIWEB/Cultures/en-us/Product detail.htm?Pid=015-8980-808

Peck, J. (1986). Not killing is a crime? In B. Lown & E. Chazov (Eds.), *Peace: A dream unfolding* (p. 146). Ontario, Canada: Sommerville House Books Ltd.

Pedone, R., Hummel, J.E., & Holyoak, K.J. (2001). The use of diagrams in analogical problem solving. *Memory & Cognition, 29*, 214–221.

Pellegrino, J.W., & Goldman, S. (1984). Inductive reasoning ability. In R.J. Sternberg (Ed.), *Human abilities: An information processing approach*. San Francisco, CA: Freeman.

Pence, G.E. (2001, January). Setting a common, careful policy for bioethics. *The Chronicle of Higher Education*, p. 20.

Perkins, D.N. (1985). Postprimary education has little impact on informal reasoning. *Journal of Educational Psychology, 77*, 562–571.

Phan, H.P. (2010). Critical thinking as a self-regulatory process component in teaching and learning. *Psicothema, 22*, 284–292.

Phelps, E.A., & Sharot, T. (2008). How (and why) emotion enhances the subjective sense of recollection. *Current Directions in Psychological Science, 17*(2), 147–152. doi:10.1111/j.1467-8721.2008.00565.x

Pickrell, A. (2010, 23 June). Chick shack: Ted Strickland for governor. Retrieved from http://www.tedstrickland.com/page/m/4c81f9de/408b78fb/2c910abd/4e11c8bb/4269597075/VEsH/

Pitt, J., & Leavenworth, R. (1968). *Logic for argument*. New York: Random House.

Pogrow, S. (1992). A validated approach to thinking development for at-risk populations. In C. Collins & J. Mangieri (Eds.), *Teaching thinking: An Agenda for the Twenty-First Century* (pp. 87–101). Hillsdale, NJ: Lawrence Erlbaum Associates.

Polya, G. (1945). How to solve it: A new aspect of mathematical method. Princeton, NJ: Princeton University Press.

Polya, G. (1957). How to solve it: A new aspect of mathematical method. Garden City, NY: Doubleday.

Polya, G. (1981). *Mathematical discovery* (Combined ed.). New York: John Wiley & Sons.

Poropat, A. (2009). A meta-analysis of the five-factor model of personality and academic performance. *Psychological Bulletin, 135*, 322–338.

Power Balance. (2010). *Energy balance and systemic harmony are the keys*. Retrieved from http://www.balanceband.com/technology/

Pratkanis, A. R., & Aronson, E. (1992). *Age of propaganda: The everyday use and abuse of persuasion*. New York: W. H. Freeman.

Prince, G. M. (1970). *The practice of creativity*. New York: Harper.

Puvathingal, B. J., & Hantula, D. A. (2012). Revisiting the psychology of intelligence analysis: From rational actors to adaptive thinkers. *American Psychologist, 67*(3), 199–210. doi:10.1037/a0026640

Quattrone, G. A., & Jones, E. E. (1980). The perception of variability within in-groups and out-groups: Implications for the law of small numbers. *Journal of Personality and Social Psychology, 38*, 141–152. doi:10.1037/0022-3514.38.1.141

RAND Corporation. (1992). Health care and the uninsured: Who will pay? *RAND Research Review, XVI*, 6–8.

Raphael, B. (1976). *The thinking computer*. New York, NY: W. H. Freeman.

Rassin, E., Eerland, A., & Kuijpers, I. (2010). Let's find the evidence: An analogue study of confirmation bias in criminal investigations. *Journal of Investigative Psychology and Offender Profiling, 7*, 231–246. doi:10.1002/jip.126

Regier, T., & Kay, P. (2009). Language, thought, and color: Whorf was half right. *Trends in Cognitive Sciences, 13*(10), 439–446. doi:10.1016/j.tics.2009.07.001

Renshon, S. A. (1992). The psychology of good judgment: A preliminary model with some applications to the Gulf War. *Political Psychology, 13*, 477–495.

Resnick, L. B. (1985). Cognition and instruction: Recent theories of human competence. In B. L. Hammonds (Ed.) *Psychology and learning* (pp. 123-186). Washington, DC: American Psychological Association.

Restak, R. M. (1988). *The mind*. New York: Bantam Books.

Riggio, H. R., & Halpern, D. F. (2006). Understanding human thought: Educating students as critical thinkers. In W. Buskist & S. F. Davis (Eds.), *Handbook of the teaching of psychology* (pp.78–84). Malden, MA: Blackwell Publishing.

Rips, L. J. (1988). Deduction. In R. J. Sternberg & E. E. Smith (Eds.), *The psychology of human thought* (pp. 116–152). New York: Cambridge University Press.

Roediger, H., Agarwal, P. K., McDaniel, M. A., & McDermott, K. B. (2011). Test-enhanced learning in the classroom: Long-term improvements from quizzing. *Journal of Experimental Psychology, Applied, 17*, 382–395. doi:10.1037/a0026252

Roediger, H.L.I., & Bergman, E.T. (1998). The controversy over recovered memories. *Psychology, Public Policy, & Law, 4*(4), 1091–1109.

Roediger, H.L., & Karpicke, J.D. (2006). The power of testing memory: Basic research and implications for educational practice. Perspectives on Psychological Science, 1, 181–210.

Roediger, H.L., & McDermott, K.B. (1995). Creating false memories: Remembering words not presented in lists. *Journal of Experimental Psychology: Learning, Memory, and Cognition, 21*, 803–814. doi:10.1037/0278-7393.21.4.803

Rogerson, M.D., Gottlieb, M.C., Handelsman, M.M., Knapp, S., & Younggren, J. (2011). Nonrational processes in ethical decision making. *American Psychologist, 66*(7), 614–623. doi:10.1037/a0025215

Rohrer, D., Taylor, K., & Sholar, B. (2010). Tests enhance the transfer of learning. *Journal of Experimental Psychology: Learning, Memory, and Cognition, 36*, 233–239. doi:10.1037/a0017678

Rokeach, M. (1960). The open and closed mind: Investigations into the nature of belief systems and personality systems. New York: Basic Books.

Rosch, E. (1977). Human categorization. In N. Warren (Ed.), *Studies in cross-cultural psychology* (Vol. 1). New York: Academic Press.

Rosenthal, R., & Fode, K.L. (1963). Psychology of the scientist: V. Three experiments in experimenter bias. *Psychological Reports, 12*, 491–511. doi:10.2466/pr0.1963.12.2.491

Rothenberg, A. (1979). The emerging goddess: The creative process in art, science, and other fields. Chicago, IL: University of Chicago Press.

Rothy, V. (2009). Anacrinism and its others: Sexuality, race, temporality. New York, NY: SUNY Press.

Rubinstein, M.F., & Pfeiffer, K.R. (1980). *Concepts in problem solving.* Englewood Cliffs, NJ: Prentice-Hall.

Runco, M.A., & Jaeger, G.J. (2012). The standard definition of creativity. *Creativity Research Journal, 24*, 92–96. doi:10.1080/10400419.2012.650092

Saletan, W. (2004, 8 February). You can make it with Plato. *Slate Magazine.* Retrieved from http://www.slate.com/articles/news_and_politics/ballot_box/2004/02/youcan_make_it_with_plato.html

Sanfrey, A.G., Rilling, J.K., Aronson, J.A., Nystrom, L.E., & Cohen, J.D. (2003). The neural basis of economic decision-making in the Ultimatum Game. *Science, 300*, 1755–1758.

Santorum, R. (2011, 24 December). Quotation of the day. *New York Times.* Retrieved from http://query.nytimes.com/gst/fullpage.html?res=9A07E1DB123DF937A1 5751C1A9679D8B63&ref=quotationoftheday

Sapir, E. (1960). *Culture, language and personality.* Berkeley: University of California Press.

Saville, G. (n.d.) Brainy Quotes. Retrieved from http::/www.brainyquote.com/quotes/quotes/g/georgesavi381348.html

Sawyer, K. (2007). *Group genius: The creative power of collaboration.* New York, NY: Basic Books.

Schacter, D.L., Guerin, S.A., & St. Jacques, P.L. (2011). Memory distortion: An adaptive perspective. *Trends in Cognitive Sciences, 15*, 467–474. doi:10.1016/j.tics.2011.08.004

Schauble, L., & Glaser, R. (1990). Scientific thinking in children and adults. In D. Kuhn (Series Ed., Vol. Ed.), *Contributions to human development: Vol. 21.*

Developmental perspectives on teaching and learning thinking skills (pp. 9–27). New York: Basel, Karger.

Schmidt, H.G., Peeck, V.H., Paas, F., & Van Breukelen, G.J.P. (2000). Remembering the street names of one's childhood neighbourhood: A study of very long-term retention. *Memory, 8*(1), 37–49.

Schneider, D.J. (2007). The belief machine. In R.J. Sternberg, H.L. Roediger, III & D.F. Halpern (Eds.), *Critical thinking in psychology* (pp. 251–270). Cambridge, UK: Cambridge University Press.

Schoenfeld, A.H. (1985). Mathematical problem solving. Orlando, FL: Academic Press.

Scholl, B.J., Simons, D.J., & Levin, D.T. (2004). "Change blindness" blindness: An implicit measure of metacognitive error (pp. 145–163). In D.T. Levin (Ed.), *Thinking and seeing: Visual metacognition in adults and children.* Cambridge, MA: MIT Press.

Schulman, B.J. (2007, 1 April). Beware the politician who won't flip-flop. *Los Angeles Times.* Retrieved from http://articles.latimes.com/2007/apr/01/opinion/op-schulman1

Schwartz, B., Ben-Haim, Y., & Dacso, C. (2011). What makes a good decision? Robust satisficing as a normative standard of rational decision making. *Journal for the Theory of Social Behaviour, 41*(2), 209–227. doi:10.1111/j.1468-5914.2010.00450.x

Schwarz, N. (2007). Evaluating surveys and questionnaires. In R.J. Sternberg, H.L. Roediger, III and D.F. Halpern. (Eds.), *Critical thinking in psychology.* (pp. 54–74). New York, NY: Cambridge University Press.

Science in the Public Interest. (2000). Bar exams: Energy bars flunk. *Nutrition Action Healthletter, 27,* 10–12.

Scriven, M. (1976). *Reasoning.* New York: McGraw-Hill.

Seamon, J.G., Williams, P.C., Crowley, M.J., Kim, I.J., Langer, S.A., Orner, P.J., & Wishengrad, D.L. (1995). The mere exposure effect is based on implicit memory: Effects of stimulus type, encoding conditions, and number of exposures on recognition and affect judgments. *Journal of Experimental Psychology: Learning, Memory, & Cognition, 21,* 711–721.

Sears, A., & Parsons, J. (1991). Towards critical thinking as an ethic. *Theory and Research in Social Education, 19*(1), 45–68.

Seech, Z. (1993). *Open minds and everyday reasoning.* Belmont, CA: Wadsworth.

Seligman, M. (1991). *Learned optimism.* New York: Knopf.

Sethi, R., Smith, D.C., & Park, C.W. (2001). Cross-functional product development teams, creativity, and the innovativeness of new consumer products. *Journal of Marketing Research, 38,* 73–85.

Shaklee, H. (1987). *Estimating cumulative risk: Flood and contraceptive failure.* Twenty-Eighth Annual Meeting of the Psychonomic Society, Seattle, WA.

Shalley, C.E. (1991). Effects of productivity goals, creativity goals, and personal discretion on individual creativity. *Journal of Applied Psychology, 7*(2), 179–185.

Shapiro, F. (2011, 27 January). Quotes uncovered: If at first ... Retrieved from http://www.freakonomics.com/2011/01/27/quotes-uncovered-if-at-first/

Shaver, K.G. (1981). *Principles of social psychology.* Cambridge, MA: Winthrop.

Shavinina, L.V. (2001). A new wave of innovations in psychology: High intellectual and creative education multimedia technologies. *Review of General Psychology, 5,* 291–315.

Shear, M. D. (2011, 22 November). Democrats cry foul over new Romney ad. *The New York Times*. Retrieved from http://www.nytimes.com/2011/11/23/us/politics/romney-ad-slams-obama-on-economy.html

Shepard, R. (1990). *Mind sights: Original visual illusions, ambiguities, and other anomalies*. New York, NY: W. H. Freeman.

Shermer, M. (1997). *Why people believe weird things: Pseudoscience, superstition, and other confusions of our time*. New York: W. H. Freeman.

Shermer, M. (2003, June). I knew you would say that. Retrieved from http://www.michaelshermer.com/2003/06/i-knew-you-would-say-that/

Shermer, M. (2008, 25 July). How anecdotal evidence can undermine scientific results. *Scientific American*. Retrieved from http://www.scientificamerican.com/article.cfm?id=how-anecdotal-evidence-can-undermine-scientific-results

Shermer, M. (2008, September). Folk numeracy & middle land. *Scientific American*. Retrieved from http://www.avaxhome.ws/magazines/science/sciamerican_092008.html

Shermer, M. (2009, July). I want to believe. *Scientific American*. Retrieved from http://www.michaelshermer.com/2009/07/i-want-to-believe/

Shermer, M., Benjamin, A., & Randi, J. (2011, 8 November). Anecdotes do not make a science: The skeptics reply. Retrieved from http://www.skeptic.com/eskeptic/11-08-10/

Shiffrar, M. (2012, 17 May). Commencement Address, Rutgers Graduate School—Newark, School of Public Affairs & Administration. Retrieved from http://www.newark.rutgers.edu/commencement-2012-shiffrarspeech

Shubik, M. (1971). The dollar auction game: A paradox in noncooperative behavior and escalation. *Journal of Conflict Resolution, 15*, 109–111.

Shuman, D. W., & Champagne, A. (1998). Removing the people from the legal process: The rhetoric and research on judicial selection and juries. *Psychology, Public Policy, & Law, 3*(2–3), 242–258.

Siegal, E. (1991, May). Persuasion and decision-making. *APS Observer*, p. 8.

Silver, N. (2011, 27 October). Herman Cain and the hubris of experts. *The New York Times FiveThirtyEight*. Retrieved from http://fivethirtyeight.blogs.nytimes.com/2011/10/27/herman-cain-and-the-hubris-of-experts/

Simon, H. A. (1956). Rational choice and the structure of the environment. *Psychological Review, 63*, 129–138.

Simon, H. A. (1977). The psychology of scientific problem solving. In H. A. Simon (Ed.), *Models of discovery*. Dordrecht, Netherlands: D. Reidel.

Simon, H. A. (1978). Rational decision-making in business organizations. *Nobel Memorial Lecture*. Retrieved from http://www.nobelprize.org/nobel_prizes/economics/laureates/1978/simon-lecture.pdf

Simons D. J., & Chabris, C. F. (2011). What People Believe about How Memory Works: A Representative Survey of the U.S. Population. *PLOS ONE 6*(8), e22757. doi:10.1371/journal.pone.0022757 Retrieved from http://www.plosone.org/article/info:doi%2F10.1371%2Fjournal.pone.0022757

Simons, D. J., & Levin, D. T. (1998). Failure to detect changes to people during a real-world interaction. *Psychonomic Bulletin and Review, 5*(4), 644–649.

Simonson, I., Nowlis, S. M., & Simonson, Y. (1993). The effect of irrelevant preference arguments on consumer choice. *Journal of Consumer Psychology, 2*, 287–306.

Singer, B., & Benassi, V. A. (1981). Occult beliefs. *American Scientist, 69*, 49–55.

Singmann, H., & Klauer, K. C. (2011). Deductive and inductive conditional inferences: Two modes of reasoning. *Thinking & Reasoning, 17*, 247–281. doi:10.108 0/13546783.2011.572718

Sio, U., & Ormerod, T. C. (2009). Does incubation enhance problem solving? A meta-analytic review. *Psychological Bulletin, 135*(1), 94–120. doi:10.1037/ a0014212

Skippar, B. (2012, 9 May). No pot plant here, neighbor. *Douglas Dispatch.* Letter to the Editor.

Smith, L. (1992, June). Rick's place revisited. *The Los Angeles Times*, p. A1.

Smith. R. V, (1998). *Graduate research: A guide for students in the sciences.* Seattle, WA: University of Washington Press.

Snell, L., Peterson, B., Albert, J. & Grinstead, C. (2001, 20 May). Three sisters give birth on the same day. *Chance Magazine*, 23–25. Retrieved from http://www. dartmouth.edu/~chance/chance_news/recent_news/chance_news_10.05.html

Snyder, M., & Uranowitz, S. W. (1978). Reconstructing the past: Some cognitive consequences of person perception. *Journal of Personality & Social Psychology, 36*(9), 941–950.

Sparks, J. R., & Rapp, D. N. (2011). Readers' reliance on source credibility in the service of comprehension. *Journal of Experimental Psychology: Learning, Memory, and Cognition, 37*, 230–247. doi:10.1037/a0021331

Stahl, N. N., & Stahl, R. J. (1991). We can agree after all! Consensus on critical thinking using the delphi technique. *Roeper Review, 14*(2), 79–88.

Stanovich, K. (2009). *What intelligence tests miss: The psychology of rational thought.* New Haven, CT: Yale University Press.

Stanovich, K. E. (1999). *Studies of individual differences in reasoning.* Mahwah, NJ: Lawrence Erlbaum Associates, Inc.

Stanovich, K. E., & West, R. F. (1997). Reasoning independently of prior belief and individual differences in actively open-minded thinking. *Journal of Educational Psychology, 89*(2), 342–357.

Stanovich, K. E., & West, R. F. (2008). On the failure of cognitive ability to predict myside and one-sided thinking biases. *Thinking & Reasoning, 14*(2), 129–167. doi:10.1080/13546780701679764

Steinem, G. (1994). *Moving beyond words.* New York: Simon & Schuster.

Sternberg, R. J. (1977). Component processes in analogical reasoning. *Psychological Review, 84*, 353–373.

Sternberg, R. J. (1982). Who's intelligent? *Psychology Today, 16*, 30–33, 35–39.

Sternberg, R. J. (2011). Understanding reasoning: Let's describe what we really think about. *Behavioral and Brain Sciences, 34*, 269–270. doi:10.1017/ S0140525X11000148

Sternberg, R. J., & Lubart, T. I. (1996). Investing in creativity. *American Psychologist, 51*, 677–688.

Sternberg, R. J., Roediger, H. L., III., & Halpern, D. F. (Eds.). (2007). *Critical thinking in psychology.* New York, NY: Cambridge University Press.

Stewart, J. K. (1985). From the director. *National Institute of Justice: Research in brief.* Washington, DC: US Department of Justice.

Stupple, E. N., Ball, L. J., Evans, J. T., & Kamal-Smith, E. (2011). When logic and belief collide: Individual differences in reasoning times support a selective processing model. *Journal of Cognitive Psychology, 23*(8), 931–941. doi:10.1080/204 45911.2011.589381

Svensson, N., Norlander, T., & Archer, T. (2002). Effects of individual performance versus group performance with and without de Bono techniques for enhancing creativity. *Korean Journal of Thinking & Problem Solving, 12*, 15–34.

Taplin, J. E., & Staudenmayer, H. (1973). Interpretation of abstract conditional sentences in deductive reasoning. *Journal of Verbal Learning & Verbal Behavior, 12*(5), 530–542.

Taseer, S. (2012, 22 October). The girl who changed Pakistan: Malala Yousafzai. *Newsweek Magazine.* Retrieved from http://www.thedailybeast.com/newsweek/2012/10/21/the-girl-who-changed-pakistan-malala-yousafzai.html

Tate, M. A., & Alexander, J. (1996). Teaching critical evaluation skills for World Wide Web resources. *Computers in Libraries, 16*, 49–52.

Tavris, C., & Aronson, E. (2007). *Mistakes were made (but not by me).* Orlando, FL: Harcourt.

Tetlock, P. E. (1994). The psychology of futurology and the future of psychology. *Psychological Science, 5*, 1–4.

Texas Library Association. (2002, 29 January). Knowledge is power. Retrieved from http://www.txla.org/groups/godort/kip-award.html

Thaler, R. H., & Sunstein, C. R. (2008). *Nudge: Improving decisions about health, wealth, and happiness.* New York, NY: Penguin Books.

Thaler, R. H., & Sunstein, C. R. (2011, 11 October). Here's how Washington State's nudge for state park donations works via its web site. Retrieved from http://nudge.org/

The Gallup Organization. (2001, 3 July). Americans' belief in psychic and paranormal phenomena is up over the last decade. Retrieved from http://www.gallup.com/poll/releases/pr010608.asp

The Quoteaholic. (2002, 15 January). Galileo. Retrieved from http://www.quoteaholic.com

The Review. (1920). Science and pseudoscience review in mental health. Retrieved from http://www.pseudoscience.org/definitions-pseudo.html

Thinking Skills Review Group. (2004, October). *Thinking skills approaches to effective teaching and learning: What is the evidence for impact on learners?* London, England: The EPPI-Centre, University of London.

Thompson, L., & Choi, H. S. (2006). *Creativity and innovation in organizational teams.* Mahwah, NJ: Erlbaum

Timnick, L. (1989). McMartin defense urges jury to end years of 'vile allegations.' Retrieved from http://articles.latimes.com/1989-10-18/local/me-376_1_peggy-mcmartin-buckey

Toulmin, S., Rieke, R., & Janik, A. (1979). *An introduction of reasoning.* New York: Macmillan.

Tulving, E. (2002). Episodic memory and common sense: How far apart? In A. Baddeley, J. P. Aggleton & M. A. Conway (Eds.), *Episodic memory: New directions in research* (pp. 269–287). New York, NY US: Oxford University Press.

Tversky, A. (1972). Elimination by aspects: A theory of choice. *Psychological Review, 79*, 281–299.

Tversky, A., & Kahneman, D. (1974). Judgment under uncertainty: Heuristics and biases. *Science, 185*, 1124–1131.

Tversky, A., & Kahneman, D. (1981). The framing of decisions and the psychology of choice. *Science, 211*, 453–458.

Tversky, A., & Kahneman, D. (1983). Extensional versus intuitive reasoning: The conjunction fallacy in probability judgment. *Psychological Review, 90*, 293–315.

Tversky, B. (1973). Encoding processes in recognition and recall. *Cognitive Psychology, 5*, 275–287.

Tzeng, J. (2010). Designs of concept maps and their impacts on readers' performance in memory and reasoning while reading. *Journal of Research in Reading, 33*(2), 128–147. doi:10.1111/j.1467-9817.2009.01404.x

U.S. Preventive Services Task Force. (2009). Cancer screening and treatment in women: Recent findings. Retrieved from http://www.ahrq.gov/research/cancer wom.htm#breast

U.S. Preventive Services Task Force. (2011). Screening for prostate cancer. Retrieved from http://www.uspreventiveservicestaskforce.org/uspstf/uspsprca.htm

van Gelder, T. (2001). How to improve critical thinking using educational technology. Retrieved from http://www.ascilite.org.au/conferences/melbourne01/pdf/papers/vangeldert.pdf

van Haneghan, J., Barron, L., Young, M., Williams, S., Vye, N., & Bransford, J. (1992). The "jasper" series: An experiment with new ways to enhance mathematical thinking. In D. F. Halpern (Ed.), *Enhancing Thinking Skills in the Sciences and Mathematics* (pp. 15–38, ix, 155). Hillsdale, NJ: Lawrence Erlbaum Associates.

Vaughan, J.L. (1984). Concept structuring: The technique and empirical evidence. In C.D. Holley & D.F. Dansereau (Eds.), *Spatial learning strategies: Techniques, applications, and related issues.* (pp. 127–147). New York, NY: Academic Press.

Vernon, P. (1970). *Creativity: Selected readings.* Harmondsworth, England: Penguin.

von Oech, R. (1983). *A whack on the side of the head.* New York: Warner Books.

von Stumm, S., Hell, B., & Chamorro-Premuzic, T. (2011). The hungry mind: Intellectual curiosity is the third pillar of academic performance. *Perspectives on Psychological Science, 6*, 574–588. doi:10.1177/1745691611421204

Vygotsky, L.S. (1978). *Mind in society.* Cambridge, MA: Harvard University Press.

Wales, C.E., & Nardi, A. (1984). *Successful decision-making.* Morgantown, WV: Center for Guided Design.

Walsh, J. (1981). A plenipotentiary for human intelligence. *Science, 214*, 640–641.

Wandersman, A.H., & Hallman, W.K. (1993). Are people acting irrationally? Understanding public concerns about environmental threats. *American Psychologist, 48*, 681–686.

Wang, P. (1994). *How to retire with twice as much money.* CNN Money, 77–84. Retrieved from http://money.cnn.com/magazines/moneymag/moneymag_archive/1994/10/01/89184/index.htm

Wansink, B. (2012). Nutrition education and behavioral economics. *Journal of Nutrition Education and Behavior, 44.* doi:10.1016/j.jneb.2012.04.003

Wargo, E. (2012, January). The inner workings of decision making. *APS Observer, 25,* 12–18.

Wason, P. C. (1960). On the failure to eliminate hypotheses in a conceptual task. *Quarterly Journal of Experimental Psychology, 12,* 129–140.

Wason, P. C. (1968). On the failure to eliminate hypotheses: A second look. In P. C. Wason & P. N. Johnson-Laird (Eds.), *Thinking and reasoning.* Baltimore: Penguin.

Weinberger, J., & Westen, D. (2008). RATS, we should have used Clinton: Subliminal priming in political campaigns. *Political Psychology, 29,* 631–651. doi:10.1111/j.1467-9221.2008.00658.x

Weisberg, R. W. (1993). *Creativity: Beyond the myth of genius.* New York, New York: W. H. Freeman.

Wertheimer, M. (1959). *Productive thinking.* New York: Harper.

What's the Harm (http://whatstheharm.net),

Whimbey, A., & Lochhead, J. (1982). Problem solving and comprehension. New York, NY: Taylor & Francis.

Whiting, C. S. (1958). *Creative thinking.* New York: Reinhold.

Whorf, B. (1956). *Language, thought, and reality.* Cambridge, MA: MIT Press.

Wickelgren, W. (1974). *How to solve problems.* San Francisco: Freeman.

Wiedemann, A. U., Lippke, S., Reuter, T., Ziegelmann, J. P., & Schwarzer, R. (2011). How planning facilitates behaviour change: Additive and interactive effects of a randomized controlled trial. *European Journal of Social Psychology, 41,* 42–51. doi:10.1002/ejsp.724

Wiig, K. M. (2003). A knowledge model for situation-handling. *Knowledge Research Institute, Inc.* Retrieved from http://www.krii.com

Wilcox, E. (undated). Help jurors remember your witness. *The trial lawyer's library.* Retrieved from http://www.trialtheater.com/wordpress/trial-skills/direct-examination/become-a-courtroom-paparazzi/

Wilgis, M., & McConnell, J. (2008). Concept mapping: An educational strategy to improve graduate nurses' critical thinking skills during a hospital orientation program. *The Journal of Continuing Education in Nursing, 39,* 119–126.

Williams, L., & Bargh, J. (2008). Experiencing physical warmth promotes interpersonal warmth. *Science, 24,* 606–607. doi:10.1126/science.1162548

Wilson, N., & Smetana, L. (2011). Questioning as thinking: A metacognitive framework to improve comprehension of expository text. *Literacy, 45*(2), 84–90. doi:10.1111/j.1741-4369.2011.00584.x

Wilson, R., & Crouch, E. A. C. (1987). Risk assessment and comparisons: An introduction. *Science, 286,* 267–270.

Winerman, L. (2012, March). Tracking the scent of information. Monitor on psychology (pp. 44–47), Washington, DC: American Psychological Association.

Wolff, P., & Gentner, D. (2011). Structure-mapping in metaphor comprehension. *Cognitive Science: A Multidisciplinary Journal, 35,* 1456–1488.

Wood, J. M., Nezworski, M., Lilienfeld, S. O., & Garbm, H. N. (2008). The Rorschach inkblot test, fortune tellers, and cold reading. In S. O. Lilienfeld, J. Ruscio & S. Lynn (Eds.), *Navigating the mindfield: A user's guide to distinguishing science from pseudoscience in mental health* (pp. 145–157). Amherst, NY: Prometheus Books.

Wooley, A. W., Chabris, C. F., Pentland, A., Hashimi, N., & Malone, T. W. (2010, 29 October). Evidence for a collective intelligence factor in the performance of human groups. *Science, 30,* 686–688. doi:10.1126/science.1190483

Worthen, J. B., & Hunt, R. (2011). *Mnemonology: Mnemonics for the 21st century.* New York, NY US: Psychology Press.

Zimbardo, P. G., & Leippe, M. R. (1991). *The psychology of attitude change and social influence.* New York: McGraw-Hill.

Zweig, J. (2008, 6 May). Buffer advice: Buy smart ... an low. *CNNMoney.* Retrieved from http://money.cnn.com/2008/05/05/news/companies/buffet.pm.wrap/index.htm?section=money_latest

INDEX

Note: Italic *f* and *t* refer to figures and table respectively.

CPSIA information can be obtained at www.ICGtesting.com
Printed in the USA
BVOW10s0918061215

429472BV00004B/11/P